The Fibre Channel Consultant Series

Fibre Channel: A Comprehensive Introduction

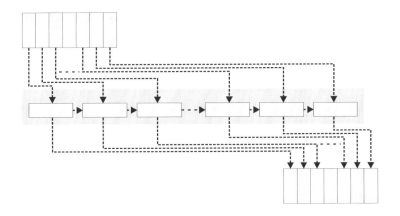

Robert W. Kembel

Be sure to check out the other books in the Fibre Channel Consultant series:

Fibre Channel A Comprehensive Introduction	ISBN 978-0-931836-10-7
Fibre Channel Switched Fabric	ISBN 978-0-931836-11-4
Fibre Channel over Ethernet (FCoE)	ISBN 978-0-931836-12-1
Fibre Channel Arbitrated Loop	ISBN 978-0-931836-13-8

ISBN 978-0-931836-10-7

Published by:

Northwest Learning Associates, Inc.
12 Water Street
Hingham, MA 02043
781-626-4746, Fax: 781-626-4751
email: info@nlabooks.com
Visit our web site at www.NLAbooks.com

Printed in the United States of America

20 19 18 17 16 15 14 13 12 11 10 9 8 7 6 5 4

Contents

Section II. FC-1: Encoding and Decoding, Ordered Sets, Link Initialization

Section V. Session Management

Section VI. Fibre Channel Services

Section VII. Fibre Channel Topologies

Section VIII. FC-4: Protocol Mappings

Section IX. Reference Information

List of Figures

List of Tables

Foreword

I was very flattered when invited to write the Foreword for the first edition of this book. It seemed to me most appropriate to use that invitation to honor the people who had made key contributions to the development of Fibre Channel, and especially those whose work had not been widely recognized due to changes in corporate policy and/or job assignments. To do that took quite a long Foreword, and my thanks go to the publishers for including it unabridged.

I am extremely flattered to again be asked to write the Foreword, this time for the second edition. However what I want to write this time is quite different (and briefer) than before, and the change is, I believe, representative of the changes that have occurred in the "wider world" since the first edition was published.

The first, and most significant change, is that Fibre Channel has become an industry in its own right. The major Fibre Channel products are no longer standards, but real products. Several companies whose primary business is Fibre Channel were founded by long-time standards committee participants. Major players in the storage and input/output markets have made strategic commitments to Fibre Channel. The portfolio of products grows larger and more diverse each month including not only disk and tape storage devices and their controllers, but also infrastructure products such as switches, hubs, long-distance extenders, multi-channel test equipment, performance measurement products, simulators, and ever more sophisticated management software. There are new controllers supporting multiple protocols—not only SCSI but also Internet Protocol (IP) and the Virtual Interface Architecture (VI). And finally there are companies whose sole business is testing and characterization of Fibre Channel products.

The second change is that the Fibre Channel *community*, as exemplified by the newly united Fibre Channel Industry Association (FCIA), has become focused on delivering complete working solutions rather than a usable technology. In addition to standards meetings working on new versions of the technologies, there are now sessions to define interoperability levels and test definitions, and testing centers and plugfests to ensure that problems are identified and fixed before products are placed in the hands of users.

The third, and most exciting change, is that work begun with Fibre Channel has given rise to a new concept of how systems are structured and able to evolve as requirements and data quantities change. This concept is a Storage Area Network (SAN) and, while the name was undoubtedly inspired by the connectivity provided by Fibre Channel, the concept has been extended to be much more than just another interface definition. The SAN concept involves the fundamental separation of storage and processing resources, and a beginning of the provision and management of storage as a separate *service*. The inspiration for the concept is the fast growth in data storage requirements due to continuing internet penetration, that has caused spending on storage to outstrip that on the processing systems themselves.

A SAN consists of not just the storage but also an interconnection infrastructure, access controls, management facilities, data protection (RAID), data migration (backup, restore), support for online maintenance, etc. As such a SAN represents a whole new way of provisioning and managing storage, and access to the data contained by that storage, and the concept has found a very receptive audience in the CTOs and MIS Managers struggling with the protection and utilization of an ever-increasing volume of data.

While the roots of the SAN concept are found in the mainframe systems of the last 20 years, with multi-path connectivity to storage resources and the ability to spread storage operations over those multiple paths, the SAN has significant differences. A SAN is heterogeneous with its constituents purchased from multiple vendors and integrated for the first time at the customer site. A SAN also has to be based on open industry standards, use commodity components, and take advantage of the latest in interconnection technologies to maximize connectivity and operating distances. Finally a SAN must take advantage of available processing power and developments in graphical user interfaces to simply management and support.

It is no accident that many people who are now prominent in the Fibre Channel community have significant experience with those mainframe peripheral configurations. Bob Kembel, the author of this book, played a key role in the development of some of the mainframe configurations, and continues to be involved in the education of developers and support personnel in relation to those configurations. Bob has been active in the Fibre Channel Technical Committee since the early 1990s, and served as editor of the *Fibre Channel - Private Loop Direct Attach (FC-PLDA) Technical Report*. He is uniquely qualified to present the details of how Fibre Channel operates, and to place the concepts on which FC is based in a historical perspective.

This book is also a product of many training seminars Bob has given at companies throughout the world, to many different types of students. The contents are representative of teaching methods that have proven to be successful. In reading through the book the first thing that struck me was the wealth of original material it contains. This is no simple repetition of the standards documents. Time and again I found tables and figures that are significantly clearer than the text in the standards. For readers making the transition from older peripheral interfaces based on multi-drop bus structures, I specifically recommend *"Fibre Channel Fabric"* on page 513, that introduces you to the switched fabric in a clear and comprehensive manner.

Since the first edition was published, I resigned as Chair of the Fibre Channel Technical Committee, and have withdrawn from the day-to-day standardization activities. I have a different, and wider, point of view than when I wrote the previous Foreword. I would like to recommend this book to you, not as a reference to a set of industry standards, but as a guide to a set of functions that are most important to the FC products of today and tomorrow. I can tell you with certainty that the current SAN implementations implement only a fraction of the functionality defined in the standards. I believe that as more and more of the functions are realized in products, the power and elegance of the basic architecture that was put in place in Fibre Channel in the early 1990s will become ever more important, and that the additional functionality will provide key differentiation in the marketplace. Please look at this book not as a guide to the standards of the past, but as an introduction to the features of the SANs of the future.

Roger Cummings

Technical Director, Office of the CTO
Symantec Corporation
November 1999

Preface

Welcome to the third edition of the Fibre Channel Consultant: A Comprehensive Introduction!

When I set out to write this book, I approached my mentor for advice about how to proceed. His advise was - don't. He pointed out that once you start down the path of trying to explain how Fibre Channel works in detail there is no easy stopping point. As I watched the book grow from 300 pages to 400 pages and then past 600 pages, I gained a new appreciation for what he was trying to tell me. The current set of Fibre Channel standards, technical reports, and technical proposals and presentations easily exceeds 1,500 pages of material incorporated in numerous standards and related documents. What neither of us foresaw was the amount of continuing development to expand and enrich this revolutionary technology.

I think the sheer bulk of material associated with Fibre Channel and the fact it is described in multiple standards emphasizes the need for this kind of book. In the years I have been involved in Fibre Channel, first as an implementer and then as a consultant and document technical editor, I have encountered many developers who are simply overwhelmed by the quantity of information available. It is to these people that this book is primarily addressed.

I must confess that I have no magical formula for taking this very comprehensive and flexible thing called Fibre Channel and reducing it to a simple and understandable form. There are other good books on the market aimed at the casual reader who only wants a basic understanding of the concepts and mechanisms associated with Fibre Channel. However, what I have tried to do is sort through the mountain of standards material available and present the most relevant parts in sufficient detail so you can use this book as a reference source. To that end, the text frequently plunges into the depths of describing the function of various bits and fields that the serious reader will have to endure.

One of my goals in writing this book was to bring together in one place information that is currently contained in multiple standards documents. While this book does not replace the associated standards, it may relieve the need for you to open every standard you own in the course of trying to find the answer to a question or understand how some function works. The standards committee recognized the difficulties associated with multiple documents and recently initiated a project consolidating the three principal framing and signaling protocol standards into a single document (FC-FS). This document forms the basis for this edition of the book.

In an attempt to make the concepts clearer, I have used a liberal dose of illustrations, tables, and Fibre Channel traces to accompany the text. Hopefully, you will find these helpful.

Finally, I want to point out that this book is only one in the Fibre Channel Consultant series. For more information on Fibre Channel Arbitrated Loop or Switched Fabric operation I would encourage you to read these companion books.

Robert W. Kembel

Acknowledgments

The history of this book begins with my participation in the American National Standards Institute Committee for Fibre Channel, and the growth of a career in writing, course development, and teaching that has been so personally and professionally rewarding for me. Four men always come to mind when I reflect upon my present career path, and each of them deserves special mention. First is Gary Stephens, founder of FSI Consulting, who continues to be a model, guide, and mentor for me. Gary's style of innovative thinking shows me options and directions that intrigue and inspire me. Next is Horst Truestedt, technical editor of the ANSI Fibre Channel Arbitrated Loop standard. His wisdom and particular vision in the Fibre Channel community continues to be a source of strength and integrity for me. Third is Roger Cummings, past Chairman of the ANSI T11 Committee, who offers a unique blend of patience, insight, and direction that has been a stable factor in my own professional development. Fourth is David Deming of Solution Technology whose personal persuasion and enthusiastic support led me to write this book. Each of these men is a special friend and colleague, and I am grateful for their presence in my life.

As I pause to consider the people whose time and talent have contributed directly to this book and to me personally in writing it, I realize once again what a collaborative effort this has been. I want to thank Jan Dedek, President of Ancot Corporation, who loaned me the test equipment that has been instrumental in analyzing the Fibre Channel link and observing many of the patterns I have described or illustrated throughout this book. Fellow instructors contributed many good ideas and critically important suggestions: Gary Stephens, Horst Truestedt, Gary Warden, and Dennis Moore. A team of five editors undertook the arduous task of reading complex information and ensuring that the text is clear, correct, and consistent. These editors were Jim McVeigh, Bonnie Marson, Ellen Hull, Lynne Brown, and Michelle Boyer. No book is complete without its cover and this book's cover artist was Dave Fischer. To each of these very special people, thank you!

Years ago I married an author who was deeply involved in the publishing and marketing of her books. At the time I thought that sounded glamorous. Julie was a teacher of adults, developing and presenting her materials, and always looking for ways to improve her presentation skills. In the years of our marriage I have taken on many of the same tasks. In this way we share our very different professional worlds. I thank her for her collaboration, and for the continual support, encouragement, and listening ear that has enabled me to complete this book

There are many men and women who will never know how much they have contributed to my knowledge and in this way, to the book. They are the collective students who have listened to me lecture on the subject of Fibre Channel. They have asked thought-provoking questions. They have challenged things I have said. They have inspired me to explore, synthesize, illustrate, and demonstrate. They are the real incentive and the potential reward for writing a book of this kind. To all of them and to the many other important people I have not specifically named, I offer a sincere thank you.

1. Introduction

Fibre Channel burst onto the data storage scene sweeping away old notions about the nature of storage attachment and input/output (I/O) interfaces. It was the first widely adopted open standard interface that merged traditional I/O performance and reliability with the connectivity and distance capabilities of networks. This powerful fusion of storage and networking technologies has given rise to a whole new industry concept - the Storage Area Network.

While not the first storage interface to embody networking technologies, Fibre Channel brought unprecedented levels of performance, scalability, flexibility, and industry support. At a time when other open I/O interfaces provided 20 megabytes per second (e.g., SCSI, the Small Computer System Interface or ESCON, the Enterprise Connection Architecture), Fibre Channel provided 100 megabytes per second. While other interfaces operated in half-duplex mode, limiting data movement to a single direction at a time, Fibre Channel provided full-duplex capability. When other interfaces supported only a few devices spanning a distance of meters, Fibre Channel allowed thousands of devices to be connected over distances of kilometers.

From its inception, Fibre Channel has been a trendsetting interface in the industry. Not only has Fibre Channel led the way in terms of performance, connectivity and distance for I/O attachment, it been a catalyst for advances in other interfaces as well. Would the SCSI bus have ever gone beyond 20 MB/s without competition from 100 MB/s Fibre Channel? Would gigabit Ethernet have happened had it not been for gigabit Fibre Channel? Would the industry even be considering storage attachment via networks without the pioneering efforts associated with Fibre Channel? While we will never know the answers to these questions, it is clear that Fibre Channel has played a central role in the evolution of storage interfaces.

1.1 Storage Attachment Architectures

While many different interfaces have been used to attach storage devices, they can all be reduced to one of three fundamental architectures.

1.1.1 Direct Attach Storage (DAS)

Historically, most storage devices such as disk and tape drives have been attached directly to a single system using either proprietary interfaces, or standardized interfaces such as the Small Computer System Interface (SCSI) or Integrated Device Electronics (IDE) interface. These interfaces enable a limited number of devices to be attached over short distances. An example of two systems with Direct Attached Storage (DAS) is shown in Figure 1 on page 2.

The I/O interface in the system is provided by a hardware function variously referred to as a Host Bus Adapter (HBA), controller, or I/O Channel depending on the interface and environment. The interface in the storage device is usually referred to as simply either the controller, the port, or just the interface.

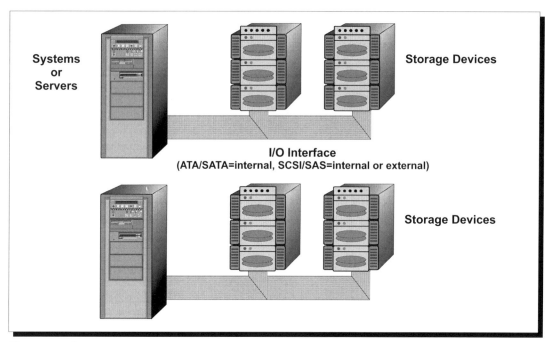

Figure 1. Direct Attach Storage (DAS)

While Direct Attach Storage provides a cost-effective solution for individual systems or servers, it is limited in the number of devices that can be attached. The SCSI bus has a limitation of 16 attachments per bus over a maximum distance of 12 meters. The IDE interface is even more limited as it allows only two devices per bus and a maximum distance of about 0.5 meter.

For larger configurations, device and distance limitations can become serious drawbacks. As larger configurations require more devices, more interfaces are needed resulting in more host bus adapters in the systems, more complex cabling, and ultimately a more expensive solution.

Data and Storage Isolation. Direct Attach storage (DAS) often results in isolated islands of data and storage resources. Each system manages its own data storage. The file system component of the operating system determines the organization of data on storage devices, allocating space for the files along with data about the files called metadata (e.g., directory structures). File systems map files to logical blocks or sectors on the storage device. By accessing the appropriate logical blocks or sectors, the file system can access the desired files. Because different operating systems usually use different file systems, the organization of data on the storage devices is often unique to that particular operating system.

Due to limitations of the physical interfaces and the use of different file systems, data and storage resources on one system are usually not available to other systems. In order to make data and storage resources available to multiple systems, many installations have turned to the use of Network Attached Storage (NAS).

1.1.2 Network Attached Storage (NAS)

With the advent of low-cost networking technology, individual systems could be connected using a Local Area Network (LAN). This allowed information to be transferred from one system to another. In addition to transferring information between systems, resources such as printers and data storage devices could also be shared. This led to the evolution of the client-server computing model where individual users access print and file servers via the LAN. An example of several clients having access to the same file server is shown in Figure 2.

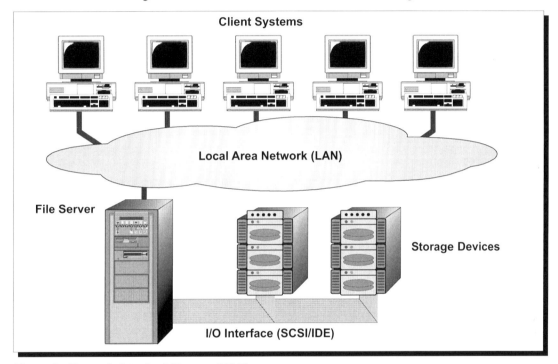

Figure 2. Network Attached Storage (NAS)

With the adoption of networks came a whole new set of components and terminology such as network interface cards (NICs), bridges, routers, and switches. As networks evolved, many different physical interfaces and transports were developed. Signals could be sent via coaxial cables, shielded twisted pair (STP), unshielded twisted pair (UTP), or optical fiber. The network itself might be based on Ethernet, Token Ring, FDDI, or a number of different technologies. Even protocols transported across the networks may be different and use NetBEUI (NetBIOS Extended User Interface), IPX/SPX, Appletalk, or any number of other protocols. However, far and away the most popular combination has become the Ethernet physical interface and the Transmission Control Protocol/Internet Protocol (TCP/IP).

Network file systems overcome file system dependencies created by the different operating systems in client workstations. For Unix systems, the Network File System (NFS) is widely used. For Windows systems, the Common Internet File System (CIFS) is normally used. Most modern operating systems provide support for either the NFS or CIFS file system protocols and allow files located remotely on the file server to be accessed as if they were local files.

Note that the file server still has its own operating system and file system for accessing the attached storage devices. However, the nature of the server's file system is hidden from the clients because all client accesses are done via NFS or CIFS requests that refer to the files themselves, not the logical blocks or sectors on the server's storage devices.

Network attached storage may be provided either by file servers (that are normally general purpose computers running a standard operating system) or specialized devices referred to as Network Attached Storage (NAS) devices. NAS devices are tightly integrated servers and storage optimized for the sole purpose of file serving. By eliminating functions and services not needed to support this specialized function, NAS devices may provide a more efficient and cost effective solution than is possible by using general-purpose components.

While network attached storage (provided by file servers or NAS devices) enables multiple clients to access storage devices and data, the speed of access is limited by the speed of the network. At a time when the SCSI bus has reached 80 MB/s, 160 or even 320 MB/s and the IDE bus provides 66 MB/s to 133 MB/s, most network connections are limited to 100 megabits per second (Mbps) - a difference of nearly two orders of magnitude. In addition, overhead introduced by the file system protocols and network processing further impacts performance. For these reasons, most systems still continue to store critical data on directly attached storage devices.

1.1.3 Storage Area Networks (SAN)

When Fibre Channel development began, it was realized that if traditional I/O interface characteristics could be combined with network-like characteristics a breakthrough in data storage could be achieved. Accomplishing this would not be a simple task. For any new interface to replace existing I/O interfaces, it must overcome a significant number of hurdles. It should:

- Support multiple current (and future) storage and networking protocols such as SCSI, ESCON, and TCP/IP to preserve existing investments in skills, software, and hardware wherever possible
- Provide speeds equal to or greater than existing I/O interfaces
- Provide efficient, high-performance transfers with low-latency communications
- Greatly extend distances (greater than 50 km.) to enable access to remote sites, systems, and storage devices for remote mirroring, disaster recovery, and data archiving
- Dramatically increase connectivity, allowing potentially thousands of systems and storage devices to be interconnected
- Reliably deliver information with very low error rates (less than one error per 10^{12} bits)
- Provide scalability across a wide range of cost and performance environments, not only for today's products but products that may be developed in the future
- Use serial transmission to simplify the physical interface cables and connectors
- Be an open, industry-supported standard to encourage the widest possible adoption

In fulfilling these objectives (and more), Fibre Channel successfully pioneered the concept of open system Storage Area Networks, or SANs. As with traditional I/O interfaces, Storage Area Networks are used to attach storage devices to systems or servers and provide access using traditional logical block or sector-level access. However, unlike traditional I/O interfaces, SAN attachment provides characteristics more commonly associated with networks rather than I/O interfaces such as increased connectivity and distances.

Storage Area Networks are sometimes referred to as the network behind the servers as shown in Figure 3. However, limiting the SAN to a server environment is inaccurate. The SAN can include not only servers, but mainframe systems, workstations, and even individual client systems. The storage devices can include disk arrays, disk drives, tape drives, automated tape libraries and other types of I/O devices.

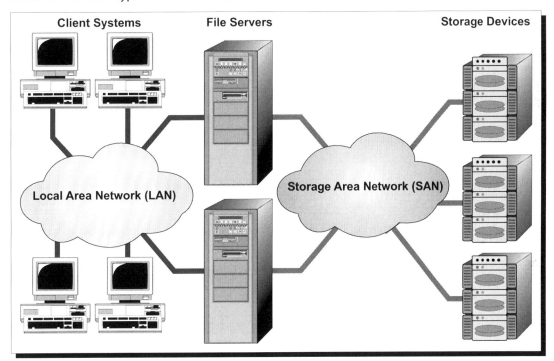

Figure 3. Storage Area Network (SAN)

SAN technology enables storage devices and data to be accessed from many sources. No longer are storage devices and data isolated behind individual servers. Now the data and storage space provided by devices can be shared by many systems. Because a SAN provides performance comparable to traditional I/O interfaces access is as fast as if the devices were directly attached. Storage devices can be viewed as a pool of storage resources rather than isolated islands of data and storage providing more efficient utilization and management of storage resources.

1.2 The Fibre Channel Network

A Fibre Channel network consists of two or more devices connected by an interconnection scheme called a topology. Because Fibre Channel networks are usually used for storage applications, the devices typically are servers, workstations, personal computers, mainframe computers, supercomputers, disk array controllers, and peripheral devices such as disk and tape drives or subsystems. Figure 4 shows a Fibre Channel network with several attached devices.

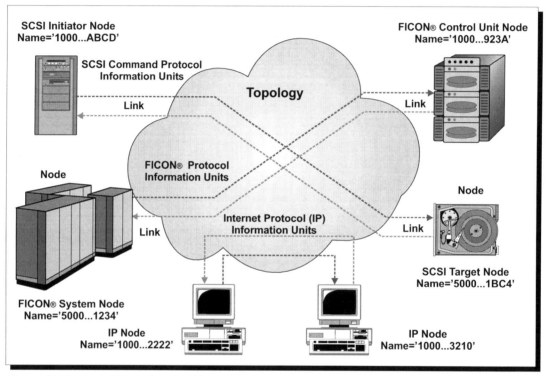

Figure 4. Example Fibre Channel Network

1.2.1 Fibre Channel Node

Sources and destinations of information in a Fibre Channel network are called nodes. In the example shown by Figure 4, the server, mainframe system, workstations, storage array, and disk drive are all nodes in the network.

Each node in a Fibre Channel network has a unique Node_Name. The Node_Name is a 64-bit identifier assigned to that specific node (it could be thought of as somewhat analogous to a serial number). Node_Names distinguish one node from another within the network and are normally assigned such that no two nodes ever have the same Node_Name resulting in a worldwide Node_Name (WWNN) for every node. The Node_Name may be used for network management purposes or when identification of the node is required.

Information intended for other nodes originates in one or more application-level processes that communicate with other nodes. An application process could be a device driver in a system, the controller function in a disk array, the firmware in a peripheral device, a network application such as a file transfer, or other similar processes.

Each node must support at least one communication protocol. A protocol is a set of procedures and information used to perform operations with other nodes. The Small Computer System Interface (SCSI-3) command set is an example of a command protocol and the Internet Protocol (IP) is an example of a packet protocol. A node may support a single protocol or it may support multiple protocols to facilitate different types of communication with other nodes.

Each protocol consists of one or more protocol Information Units. An Information Unit contains information required by that protocol. The number of Information Units, their content (e.g., command, data, status, packet, control), and the rules regarding their usage are defined by the associated protocol. When Fibre Channel is used to transport a particular protocol, a protocol mapping document defines the structure and content of the Information Units.

1.2.2 Fibre Channel Node Port (Nx_Port)

Each node has one or more node ports (N_Port, NL_Port, or generically just Nx_Port). The node port is a hardware function that allows the node to send or receive information via the Fibre Channel interface. Node ports may be integrated into the node or packaged as a pluggable card. Many peripheral devices such as disk or tape drives have integrated ports while most systems use pluggable ports for flexibility. Depending on the protocol being used, node ports may be referred to as Host Bus Adapters (HBAs) or Network Interface Cards (NICs).

A node may have a single node port or it may have multiple node ports. When a node has multiple node ports, those ports may connect to the same interconnection topology or to different topologies. Multiple node ports can be used to provide greater bandwidth and redundancy. An illustration of a Fibre Channel node port is shown in Figure 5 on page 8.

Each node port has a Port_Name. The Port_Name is a unique 64-bit identifier assigned to the port at the time of manufacture or installation. Port_Names are usually assigned so that no two ports ever have the same name. This results in a unique Worldwide Port_Name (WWPN) for each port. The Port_Name is used to identify the port in a Fibre Channel network and may be used for management purposes or when port identification is required.

Each node port also has a unique 24-bit address identifier called the N_Port ID (the node port may also have additional addresses referred to as alias addresses). Because the N_Port ID is 24-bits, the maximum size of a Fibre Channel network is 2^{24} ports (slightly over 16 million ports). The address identifier may be used by the topology to route information from the sending node port to the receiving node port and is used by the receiving node port to verify that information it received was delivered to the correct port. Address identifiers are assigned during initialization of the node port and topology. If the configuration changes, or the node port is moved to a different location in the topology, the node port's address identifier may change. Because of this, the Port_Name should be used when the identity of a port needs to be determined or verified.

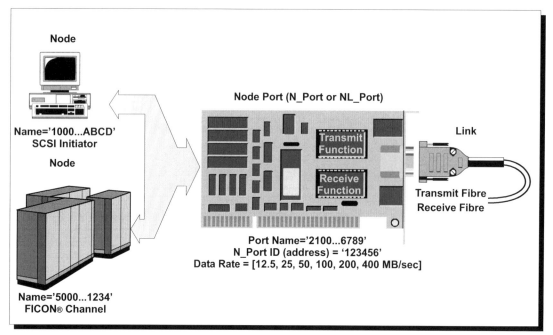

Node

Name='1000...ABCD'
SCSI Initiator

Node

Name='5000...1234'
FICON® Channel

Node Port (N_Port or NL_Port)

Transmit Function

Receive Function

Link

Transmit Fibre
Receive Fibre

Port Name='2100...6789'
N_Port ID (address) = '123456'
Data Rate = [12.5, 25, 50, 100, 200, 400 MB/sec]

Figure 5. Fibre Channel Structure: Node Port

Each topology places specific functional requirements on the node port. This is necessary to accommodate the characteristics of that particular topology. When this occurs, the port is further identified to indicate which topology, or topologies, the port supports. For example, Fibre Channel provides a loop topology called arbitrated loop that requires ports to implement a set of loop-specific protocols. A node port capable of supporting this topology is referred to as an NL_Port (the 'L' indicates an arbitrated loop-capable port). Unless this distinction is required for clarity, the term Nx_Port may be used as a generic term for either type of node port.

Each port has separate transmit and receive functions. This allows the port to send and receive information simultaneously and provides full-duplex capabilities.

Unlike traditional I/O interfaces such as SCSI and IDE, Fibre Channel uses serial data transmission. When using serial transmission, information is sent serially, one bit at a time. This avoids skew problems associated with parallel bus-type interfaces and allows greatly extended distances with simpler cables and connectors.

The port's transmit function contains an encoder that transforms the data to be sent into a format suitable for serial transmission. This is necessary because normal binary data does not have the appropriate characteristics such as embedded clock information and frequency distribution. After encoding, the information is serialized and transmitted one bit at a time.

The port's receive function receives the serial data, recovers the clock from the data stream, deserializes the received data, and decodes the deserialized information.

1.3 Fibre Channel Addresses

Fibre Channel uses a single-level 24-bit address space providing a total of 16,777,216 addresses (although not all addresses are usable). Each node port acquires an address during initialization of the node port and its attached topology. If the configuration changes between one initialization and the next, a node port may acquire a different address during the subsequent initialization.

The Fibre Channel standards specify usage of the 24-bit address space as shown in Table 1 on page 9. Several addresses at the high-end of the address range (referred to as well-known addresses) are assigned specific functions by the standards. Functions associated with the well-known addresses are discussed in *Fibre Channel Services* on page 479.

Address	Description
x'00 00 00'	Node Port is unidentified (used before an address is acquired)
x'00 00 01' - x'00 00 EF'	Reserved in the Switched Fabric topology - selected addresses used by NL_Ports on a private arbitrated loop, N_Ports in Point-to-Point
x'00 00 F0' - x'00 FF FF'	Reserved in Fabric topology, N_Ports in Point-to-Point
x'10 00 00 - x'EF FF FF'	Available for Node Ports in a Switched Fabric Topology
x'F0 00 00' - x'F0 FA FF'	Reserved
x'FF FB 00' - x'FF FB FF'	Multicast Group Addresses (256)
x'FF FC 00'	Reserved
x'FF FC 01' - x'FF FC EF'	Fabric Domain Controllers (239 maximum - usually one per switch)
x'FF FC F0' - x'FF FE FF'	Reserved
x'FF FF F0'	N_Port Controller (used with Virtual Fabrics)
x'FF FF F1' - x'FF FF F3'	Reserved for future services
x'FF FF F4'	Event Server
x'FF FF F5'	Multicast Server (used for Class-6 Reliable Multicast)
x'FF FF F6'	Clock Synchronization Server
x'FF FF F7'	Obsolete (was Key Distribution Server)
x'FF FF F8'	Obsolete (was Alias Server)
x'FF FF F9'	Obsolete (was Quality of Service Facilitator - QoSF)
x'FF FF FA'	Management Server (Configuration Server, Zone Server, Unzoned Name Server, Security Policy Server)
x'FF FF FB'	Time Server
x'FF FF FC'	Directory Server (Name Server)
x'FF FF FD'	Fabric Controller
x'FF FF FE'	Fabric Login
x'FF FF FF'	Broadcast

Table 1. Fibre Channel Addresses

1.3.1 Multicast Group Addresses

During normal Fibre Channel operations, an address is associated with a single node port. However, the standard allows the same address to be associated with a group of ports, such as a multicast group.

Multicast groups allow a port to send frames to the address associated with the multicast group. The fabric switching function recognizes the address as a multicast group address and sends a copy of the frame to every member of the multicast group.

When a multicast operation provides acknowledgment of delivery, it is called "reliable". If the multicast operation does not provide delivery confirmation, it is called "unreliable".

1.4 Physical Interface - The Fibre Channel Link

A Fibre Channel port connects to the topology via a link. The link is a cable or other connection that carries the port's transmit and receive signals. The link may consist of two optical fibers or electrical transmission lines such as shielded twisted pair, twinaxial cable, or Category 5e and above unshielded twisted pair.

The original Fibre Channel standards were developed around a signaling rate of 1.0625 gigabits per second (Gbps) resulting in a uni-directional bandwidth of 100 megabytes per second (or 200 MB/s full-duplex). As technology capabilities have advanced, faster speeds have been added to the standards to provide greater bandwidth and throughput capabilities.

A second signaling method, based on work done for 10 gigabit Ethernet, was developed and standardized in 2003. To differentiate between the two signaling methods, the original signaling method was referred to as "Base2" and the new signaling method, "Base10".

In 2006, work on a third signaling method was developed. This method allows the use of low-cost Ethernet cabling (category 5 enhanced and above) and is referred to as "BaseT".

The Fibre Channel Industry Association maintains a roadmap to provide direction for the future development of the standards and is shown in Figure 6 on page 11.

Link-level protocols are used to control the link. They are used to reset and initialize the link, and signal that the link or port is not operational. The link-level protocols on an arbitrated loop topology also implement the arbitration and loop circuit management functions.

1.4.1 Fiber Optic Links

Optical fiber is capable of sending information over much greater distances than is possible using electrical transmission lines. The Fibre Channel standards support several types of optical fiber, providing maximum distances that can span in excess of 50 km. (30 miles) between a transmitter and receiver. This distance can be extended even further by using repeaters or proprietary links. One vendor has demonstrated an extender capable of operating over a distance of 120 km. (72 miles) without intermediate repeaters or amplifiers.

Optical data transmission is accomplished by using electrical signals to control an optical emitter such as a LASER diode. The resultant optical pulses are injected into a fiber optic cable. Within the fiber optic cable, light pulses are carried via a glass strand approximately the diam-

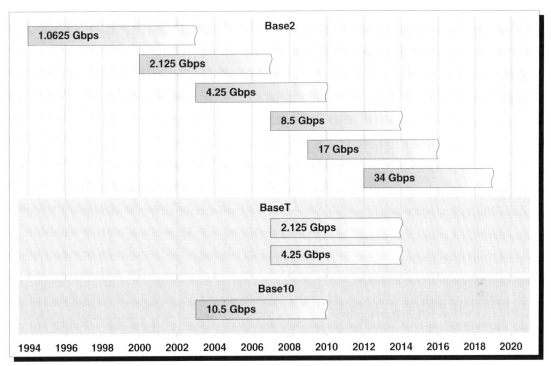

Figure 6. Fibre Channel Roadmap

eter of a human hair. At the receiving end of the optical fiber, the optical pulses are converted back into electrical signals by use of a photo detector.

While it is possible to send signals in both directions simultaneously through a single optical fiber, it is generally simpler and more cost effective (at least for computer interfaces) to use two separate fibers, one carrying information in each direction. Using two fibers also makes it easier to convert between optical and electrical media because it is much more difficult to send electrical signals in both directions simultaneously through the same transmission line.

1.4.2 Electrical Links

Many applications do not require the distance capability or noise immunity provided by optical fiber. Where the distance between devices permits, electrical interfaces can be used to provide a significant cost savings when compared to optical fiber.

Having multiple media options provides flexibility and allows Fibre Channel to be used in a wide range of environments. Electrical interfaces provide a cost-effective solution for peripheral devices such as disk drives; optical interfaces provide a solution for longer distance interconnects between systems or from systems to disk controllers. In many applications, distances are measured in inches and optical fiber simply does not make economic sense.

1.5 Fibre Channel Topologies

Node ports are interconnected by an interface topology. Unlike traditional I/O interfaces, Fibre Channel provides a rich set of interconnection schemes, or topologies. Of the four basic interconnection options (point-to-point, multi-drop bus, ring, and switched), Fibre Channel supports all but the bus (by comparison, the SCSI physical interface has one topology: the bus). This provides flexibility and enables the use of Fibre Channel in a wide range of environments.

Figure 7 shows the four different topologies. Of these, Fibre Channel supports all but the multi-drop bus topology (optical links don't lend themselves to multidrop configurations).

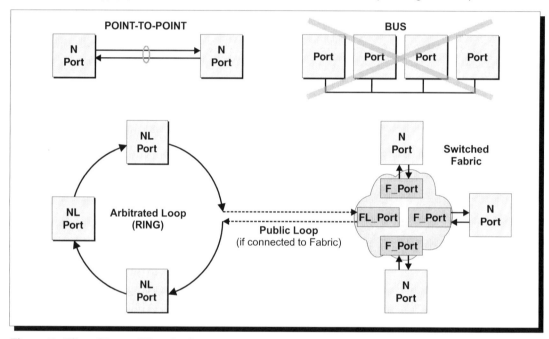

Figure 7. Fibre Channel Topologies

The topology determines the number devices that can be connected, how information is routed among the devices, the total bandwidth available to the devices, and delivery latencies. The topology also determines whether the transmission medium is dedicated to a port or shared with other ports and, if it is shared, the protocol used for sharing the medium.

1.5.1 Point-to-Point

Point-to-point is the simplest Fibre Channel topology, allowing two N_Ports to be connected by a link. While this may appear to be a trivial configuration, the characteristics of a point-to-point connection are attractive for certain applications. A point-to-point connection provides the ports with guaranteed bandwidth, guaranteed latency, and in-order frame delivery.

While only two ports can be connected by a point-to-point link, a node could have multiple node ports and point-to-point links providing connections to other nodes.

No switching takes place in a point-to-point topology, frames can only go to the port at the other end of the link. When a node has multiple ports and point-to-point links, the node makes any necessary routing decisions through its choice of which N_Port to use.

1.5.2 Arbitrated Loop

Arbitrated loop provides an intermediate-sized topology based on a loop topology. Because of to the way addressing is done, a maximum of one fabric port (FL_Port) and 126 node ports (NL_Ports) are able to participate in loop operations. If a loop contains only NL_Ports, it is called a private loop. If it connects to an FL_Port on a switch, it is called a public loop.

As with other shared medium topologies, the arbitrated loop requires a medium access control protocol. Like the SCSI bus, arbitrated loop uses an arbitration protocol for managing access to the loop. When a port needs to access the loop, it must first arbitrate for access to the loop.

Once a port wins arbitration, it opens a loop circuit with another port. This creates a dynamic point-to-point circuit between the two ports allowing frame transmission to begin. As long as the loop circuit is open, the two ports have sole use of the loop — all other ports are acting as repeaters and retransmitting information between the ports in the loop circuit.

Because only one circuit can be open at a time, only two loop ports can communicate at a time. Because of this characteristic, the loop is sometimes referred to as a blocking topology (a characteristic shared by bus-based topologies as well). That is, a loop circuit between one pair of ports blocks frame transmission by other ports.

When the two ports complete their frame transmission, the loop circuit is closed and the loop is then available for other ports to use (after winning arbitration).

Due to the shared nature of the arbitrated loop, it is best suited for configurations with devices that don't require the full bandwidth of the loop for extended periods of time. Fibre Channel disk drives and small system configurations are typical loop applications. When a configuration outgrows the capabilities of the loop, larger configurations can be created by attaching one or more loops to a Fibre Channel switched fabric, creating a hybrid fabric-attached loop topology.

1.5.3 Switched Fabric

A Fibre Channel switched fabric (or simply fabric) is based on a switched network consisting of one or more Fibre Channel switches. Because the internal configuration of the fabric is not specified by the standards, it is commonly shown simply as a switching cloud. Unlike the other topologies, the fabric supports the full 24-bit Fibre Channel address space and enables very large and complex configurations to be created.

Unlike point-to-point and arbitrated loop, the switched fabric configuration supports multiple concurrent communications. Because of this, even a simple fabric can provide very high aggregate bandwidth capabilities. For example, a 16-port Fibre Channel switch operating at 200 MB/s per port is capable of providing 3,200 MB/s of aggregate bandwidth.

Simple Fibre Channel fabrics may consist of just a single Fibre Channel switch and attached devices. Typical Fibre Channel switches provide from eight to 256 ports each. More complex fabrics can be created by connecting multiple Fibre Channel switches. In this manner, configurations consisting of hundreds of switches and thousands of ports are possible.

When a multi-switch fabric is used, the switches may be located at the same physical location or separated from each other. Switches could be distributed to various locations within a computing center, in different buildings throughout a computing campus, or even nationwide.

When switches in a fabric are distributed across different sites, the connections between those switches may use standard Fibre Channel links (such as the very-long link specification supporting distances in excess of 50 km.), or other wide-area network connections such as corporate intranets or Dense Wavelength Division Multiplexing (DWDM) facilities.

Fibre Channel routers are special devices that route frames between fabrics (switches forward frames within a single fabric). Because each fabric has its own independent address space, a router may need to perform address translation by modifying the addresses in Fibre Channel frames, or even insert or delete header information.

1.6 Session Management - Login Services

Before operations, other than some link services, can take place with another port, a port must establish a login session with the other port. Sessions are established and managed using Fibre Channel Extended Link Services. Figure 8 on page 15 shows Node_Port 1 establishing login sessions with Node_Ports 2 and 3. This allows Node_Port 1 to perform application-level operations with these Node_Ports, but not with Node_Port 4 (unless a login session is established with Node_Port 4).

During the login, the two ports exchange information about their frame transmission and reception capabilities (called service parameters), their Fibre Channel port names, and the name of the node containing each port. This information identifies the entities and determines the use of various features and options during subsequent communications between the ports.

Once a login session is established, one or more operations may take place between the ports. Prior to the login, operations associated with upper-level protocols, such as SCSI commands, are not allowed because the parameters necessary to conduct those operations have not been established. Following a successful login, upper-level operations are allowed for as long as the login session exists. If a port wants to perform operations with multiple ports, a separate login session with each is necessary.

Fibre Channel has three different levels of login:

- *Fabric Login (FLOGI)* is used by a node port (N_Port or NL_Port) to establish a session with the fabric. Fabric login is required before the fabric will accept frames from the port.

- *N_Port Login (PLOGI)* is used by one node port (N_Port or NL_Port) to establish a session with another node port. If a port wants to end the login session between the ports, it can perform a Logout (LOGO).

- *Process Login (PRLI)* is used by an upper-level process (e.g., SCSI) in one node port to establish a session with the corresponding upper-level process in another node port. Be-

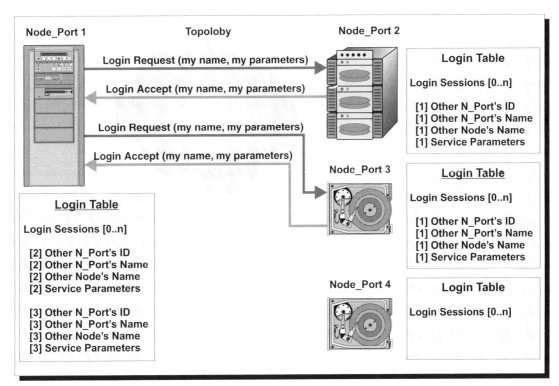

Figure 8. Fibre Channel Login Session

cause node ports may support multiple upper-level protocols or processes simultaneously, N_Port Login does not necessarily imply establishment of a session between the
upper-level processes at the two ports.

If a port decides to end the current session, it initiates a logout. Logout concludes the session,
terminates any work in progress associated with that session, and resets the service parameters associated with the other port. If subsequent communications with the other port are desired, a new login session must be established.

Fibre Channel provides explicit mechanisms to perform the login and logout actions described
above. It also allows for the login and logout actions to be implicit. If the two ports already
know the identity and service parameters of each other, they may simply assume a login session is established without actually performing the login process. Explicit login and logout are
normally used in heterogeneous environments, while some closed environments may use implicit login if the characteristics of the other ports are known or predefined.

1.7 Upper-Level Protocols (ULP)

Nodes must have a procedure for communicating with other nodes. That procedure is called a protocol and defines what one node says to another node. The protocol may be based on commands (e.g., SCSI or FICON command protocols) or packets (e.g., Internet Protocol, IP).

Each protocol consists of protocol-specific Information Units, such as commands, data, status, sense information, or other protocol-defined information. The structure, number, and usage of Information Units associated with each protocol is defined by that protocol.

In Fibre Channel, these command and packet protocols are referred to as upper-level protocols (or ULPs) to distinguish them from protocols used to manage the physical interface. The interface protocols are sometimes referred to as lower-level protocols (or LLPs).

Some Fibre Channel nodes support multiple application processes that use different protocols. A system may use the Small Computer System Interface (SCSI-3) command protocol to access storage devices and the Internet Protocol (IP) to communicate with other systems. A disk controller may recognize the SCSI command protocol for open system clients and FICON command protocol for mainframe clients. In the past, different storage protocols were transported using different physical interfaces. With Fibre Channel, the same port and physical interface can be used for both.

Because of the multi-protocol nature of Fibre Channel, when an Information Unit is transported, it is necessary to identify the protocol type associated with that Information Unit. This allows the receiving node to determine which protocol is associated with that particular Information Unit and process it appropriately.

In addition to application-level protocols, Fibre Channel defines two internal protocols called Link Services. Link Services are used for managing the Fibre Channel environment and provide facilities for managing sessions with other ports, retrieving Fibre Channel related error information, performing error recovery actions, and other similar services. Because every node must support the Link Services protocols in addition to its application-level protocols, every Fibre Channel node is inherently multi-protocol.

1.8 Fibre Channel Structure

Fibre Channel is based on a structured architecture providing specifications from the physical interface through the mapping and transport of multiple upper-level protocols. Because the structure of Fibre Channel differs from the OSI reference model (see *OSI Reference Model* on page 591), the divisions in Fibre Channel are usually referred to as Fibre Channel levels rather than layers. The levels are labeled Fibre Channel level-0 (FC-0) through Fibre Channel level-4 (FC-4) and are shown in Figure 9 on page 17.

Each level defines a specific set of Fibre Channel functions. By structuring the architecture in this manner, behavior at one level is largely insulated from the other levels providing a modular and expandable architecture. This allows enhancements to one part of the architecture with minimal impact on the others and allows activities at the different levels to proceed in parallel.

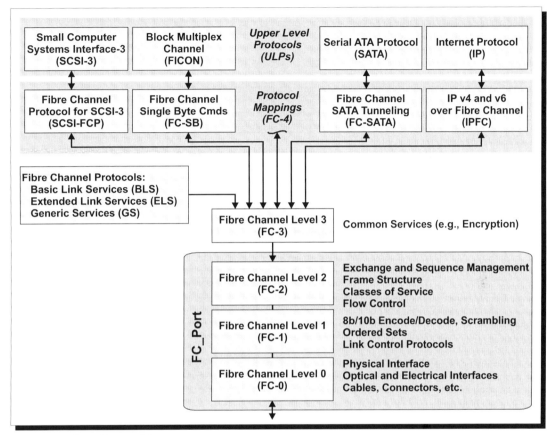

Figure 9. Fibre Channel Structure

While these architectural levels serve to define the behavior and functions at each level, they do not represent physical or programming interfaces between the various levels (those interfaces are dependent upon the specific implementation).

1.9 FC-4: Protocol Mappings

Before a protocol can be transported using Fibre Channel, it is necessary to specify how that protocol will operate in a Fibre Channel environment, a process referred to as protocol mapping. A protocol mapping specifies the content and structure of the information sent from one node to another by that protocol. These protocol-specific structures are called protocol Information Units, or just Information Units. For command-type protocols, the Information Units normally consist of command information, data transfer controls, data, and status or command completion information. For packet-type protocols, the Information Units are usually just the logical packets. The number of Information Units, their structure and usage are specified by each protocol mapping.

When an operation is performed using a given protocol, the protocol-specific process (driver) in one node exchanges (sends and receives) protocol-specific Information Units with its counterpart process (driver) in the other node.

While the processes in the nodes understand the structure and content of the Information Units, the Fibre Channel port does not. The port simply delivers the Information Units without regard to their structure, content or function.

1.10 FC-3: Common Services

FC-3 provides a placeholder for possible future functions. These functions are referred to as common services and were envisioned as functions that span multiple ports or multiple protocols. The FC-3 level could also be used to transform or modify a protocol Information Unit prior to delivery by the FC-2 level. This transformation could include data compression, data encryption, code set translation or other similar functions. It could also include functions that transform an Information Unit into multiple Information Units (e.g., disk mirroring).

1.11 Fibre Channel Transport (FC-2)

Fibre Channel's FC-2 provides facilities to identify and manage operations between node ports and services to deliver Information Units.

1.11.1 Operation Management - The Exchange

Fibre Channel provides a mechanism called the *Exchange* to identify and manage an operation between two ports. All operations are performed by exchanging one or more Information Units (IUs) between the ports. Normally, each Exchange represents a operation using a specific protocol and all of the Information Units within that Exchange are associated with that protocol type. While the standards allow multiple protocols within the same Exchange, it would be unusual for this to actually occur.

The port that originates an Exchange is referred to as the *Exchange originator* and the other port the *Exchange responder*. The Exchange originator assigns a 16-bit identifier to the Exchange called the Originator Exchange_ID (OX_ID). Both the originator and responder place this identifier in every frame of the Exchange. The Exchange responder may also assign a 16-bit identifier called the Responder Exchange_ID (RX_ID). If the responder assigns an RX_ID, both the originator and responder place this identifier in subsequent frames of the Exchange.

In Figure 10 on page 19, Node 1 originates several SCSI-FCP Exchanges with Node 2. In the first Exchange (XCHG_a), Node 1 sends a Test Unit Ready Command IU to Node 2. Node 2 processes the command in the IU and sends back a SCSI Status IU completing the operation.

In XCHG_b, Node 1 sends an Inquiry Command IU to Node 2. Node 2 processes the command in the IU, sends back a Data IU containing the inquiry data and finally sends a SCSI Status IU to complete the operation.

Whenever an Information Unit is processed, the Exchange_IDs (OX_ID and RX_ID) identify which Exchange the Information Unit belongs to and enables each port to associate the Information Unit with the correct Exchange.

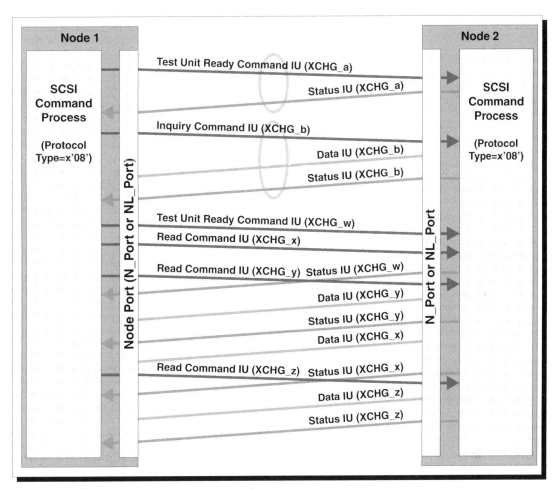

Figure 10. Fibre Channel Exchange Examples

If a port has multiple Exchanges open, it may multiplex between them in order to better utilize the link as shown by Exchanges w, x, y and z in Figure 10. To facilitate Exchange multiplexing, each port must maintain information about the current state of each open Exchange. Maintaining this state information uses resources within the port and, as a result, the number of Exchanges that a port can support depends on the design the port.

Because Fibre Channel is a full-duplex interface, Information Units for one Exchange may be transmitted in one direction while Information Units for a different Exchange are being transmitted in the opposite direction. This full-duplex behavior is true even for half-duplex protocols, such as the SCSI-3 command protocol as can be seen in Figure 10 on page 19

1.11.2 Information Unit Delivery - The Sequence

Each Information Unit is delivered using a Sequence of one or more frames. If the Information Unit fits entirely within one frame, a single-frame Sequence is used to deliver the Information Unit. When an Information Unit is too large to fit in one frame, a multi-frame Sequence is used to deliver the Information Unit.

When a multi-frame Sequence is used, the sending port segments the Information Unit and sends it as a Sequence of frames, using as many frames as necessary. The receiving port re-assembles the frames in the Sequence and delivers the reassembled Information Unit to the higher-level process. The segmentation and reassembly of Information Units is performed by the Fibre Channel ports and is transparent to the higher-level processes within the node.

Figure 11 shows the delivery of several Information Units by using Sequences of frames.

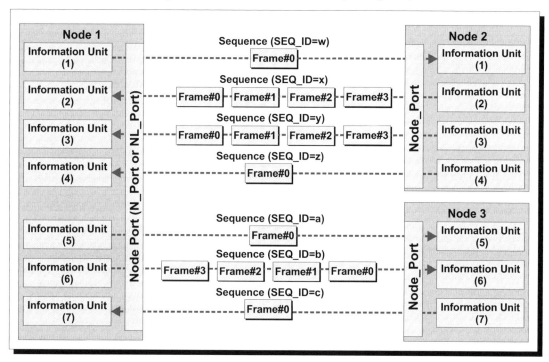

Figure 11. Fibre Channel Sequence

Because every Information Unit is associated with an Exchange, the Sequence used to deliver that Information Unit is also associated with that Exchange.

More than one Sequence may be open at a time. Because Fibre Channel is a full-duplex architecture, a port may be sending a Sequence for one Exchange while receiving a Sequence for a different Exchange. This allows a Fibre Channel port to take advantage of the full-duplex interface, even when using half-duplex upper-level protocols such as SCSI-3.

The port may multiplex between different Sequences. It may begin a Sequence for one Exchange and switch to a different Sequence for another Exchange. Multiplexing between different Sequences may allow the port to better utilize the link and optimize performance.

Each Sequence is identified with a Sequence Identifier (SEQ_ID) so that frames can be associated with the correct Sequence. This allows a receiving port to reassemble the frames in each Sequence, even if frames for different Sequences arrive intermixed.

A port may finish sending a Sequence and begin another Sequence before delivery confirmation is received for the first Sequence (a condition referred to as streamed Sequences). When Sequences are streamed in this manner, the receiving port may receive frames of the two Sequences interleaved, or even receive the entire second Sequence first. A port may also receive frames from different ports interleaved with one another. When this occurs, the port must correctly de-multiplex the frames in order to process each Sequence and reassemble the associated Information Units.

1.11.3 Data Delivery - The Frame

The node port packages each Information Units into a Sequence of frames that are sent to the destination port. Frames are the smallest unit of granularity in the transfer of Information Units between ports. The format of a Fibre Channel frame is a shown in Figure 12 on page 21.

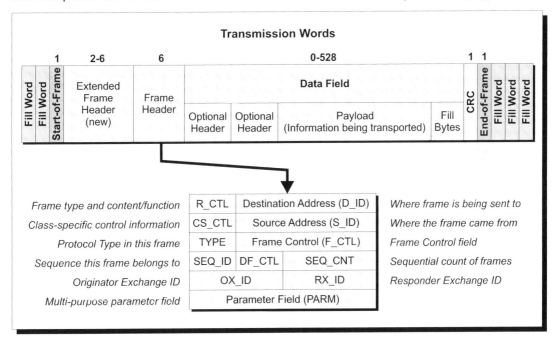

Figure 12. Fibre Channel Frame

Start of Frame (SOF). Frames consist of transmission words containing four transmission characters each. The first word of every frame is a start-of-Frame (SOF) delimiter. The Start-of-Frame delimiter is a unique set of four transmission characters that identify the start of the frame and provide information about the characteristics of that frame.

Frame Header. After the Start-of-Frame delimiter is either the standard frame header or one or more extended frame headers. Extended frame headers are used to provide additional information, such as fabric identification when routing frames between fabrics or tagging frames to identify the virtual fabric to which they belong.

The standard frame header consists of six words of frame-related control information identifying the frame type and content or function of the frame, the destination and source addresses, the protocol type contained in the frame, the operational context (Exchange_IDs, Sequence_ID, and Sequence Count), along with several control fields.

Frame Data Field. The frame data field contains the information being sent to the other port. The maximum size of the frame data field is limited to 2,112 bytes (528 words) in order to limit the size of buffers needed to hold frames as they are being processed. The data field is always a multiple of four bytes. If the Information Unit is not a multiple of four, up to three fill bytes may be added in the last word of the data field.

The data field may contain one or more optional headers. Optional headers provide standardized extensions to the frame header for information that is not needed by all protocols and applications. By putting this information in optional headers, the size of the frame header is minimized while still allowing for additional header information when necessary. When optional headers are present, the amount of space available for the payload is reduced because both share the data field of the frame.

Frame Payload. The frame payload contains the protocol Information Unit (or a portion thereof) being transported by this frame. This is where information such as commands, data, and status are placed.

Frame CRC. The frame CRC is a 32-bit cyclic redundancy check word that is used to verify that the frame contents were received correctly.

End of Frame (EOF). The End-of-Frame (EOF) delimiter is a unique set of four transmission characters that identify the end of the frame.

Following a frame the port sends fill words (e.g., IDLE), or other transmission words, until the start of the next frame. This provides the receiving port at the other end of the link with a continuous signal for clock reference and an indication that the link is operational.

1.12 FC-1: Encode/Decode, Scrambling and Link Control

Information sent on a Fibre Channel link consists of transmission words containing four transmission characters each. There are three categories of transmission words: data words, Ordered Sets and invalid transmission words.

Data words occur within frames, between the Start-of-Frame (SOF) delimiter and End-of-Frame (EOF) delimiter. *Ordered Sets* delimit frame boundaries and occur outside of frames. The Start-of-Frame and End-of-Frame delimiters are Ordered Sets. Ordered Sets derive their name from the fact that they consist of a set of four characters with a special order. All Ordered Sets contain at least one special character that is outside of the normal data space.

8b/10b Encoding/Decoding. A serial interface such as Fibre Channel does not provide a separate clock to indicate when individual bits are valid. Therefore, it is necessary to encode clocking information within the data stream. The encoding scheme used by Fibre Channel encodes eight-bit data bytes into ten-bit transmission characters and is called the "8b/10b" encoding scheme (see *8b/10b Encoding and Decoding* on page 95).

Encoding gives the transmitted data several desirable characteristics:

- Clock information is encoded into the data stream so the receiver can recover a clock from the incoming data.

- There is a balance between the number of one bits and zero bits transmitted on the link. This simplifies receiver design and makes threshold detection more robust.

- Encoding provides several special characters in the ten-bit code space that are distinct from the characters used to send data.

While encoding eight-bit data bytes into ten-bit transmission characters may seem inefficient, the encoded data stream has superior transmission characteristics providing reliable transmission with low error rates. Because of its robustness, 8b/10b encoding has been used by multiple high-performance serial interfaces including the PCI Express, Gigabit Ethernet optical links, Infiniband, Serial Attached SCSI (SAS), Serial ATA (SATA), and others.

Frame Scrambling. To reduce the probability of long strings of repeating characters during frame transmission, the frame contents may be scrambled prior to encoding and unscrambled after decoding at the receiver (see *Frame Scrambling* on page 229). Whether the frame contents are scrambled depends on the specification for the physical link. Scrambling is not used a 4 Gbits and below, but may be used on faster links.

Link-Level Protocols. Finally, the FC-1 level defines link-level protocols and link control facilities. Link-level protocols are used to reset or initialize the link or indicate that the link or port has failed or manage the arbitrated loop protocols. These protocols are implemented by a *Port State Machine (PSM)* in the point-to-point and fabric topologies and by a *Loop Port State Machine (LPSM)* in the arbitrated loop topology.

1.13 FC-0: Physical Interface

Fibre Channel's FC-0 level specifies physical interface characteristics such as data rates defined by the standard, optical and electrical variants that can be used at each data rate, connectors associated with each media type, maximum distance capabilities of each media type, and other characteristics such as wavelengths of light and signal levels.

Optical fiber provides intermediate and extended-distance links that are immune to electrical interference common with electrical cables. Single-mode optical fiber in conjunction with long wavelength lasers support extended distances (in excess of 50 km. without repeaters). Multi-mode optical fiber and low-cost shortwave lasers provide an economical optical interface for intermediate distances (500 meters at 1.0625 Gbits/sec.).

Electrical interfaces provide a cost-effective Fibre Channel interconnection scheme where distances are limited and electrical characteristics and interference are controlled. However, distances achievable with electrical interfaces are limited to approximately 30 meters at 1.0625 Gbits/sec., 15 meters at 2.125 Gbits/sec. and 7.5 meters at 4.250 Gbits/sec.

Many Fibre Channel installations use pluggable media interfaces to provide flexibility in the choice of cabling. Some links may use optical fiber to provide extended distances and noise immunity while other links in the same system may use electrical cabling for low-cost connectivity. Physical interface characteristics and pluggable media interface devices are discussed in *FC-0 Concepts* on page 39.

1.14 Access Control

When storage devices are directly attached to a single system or server, limiting access to the device and associated data is usually not a consideration. The presence of a physical connection is all that is required to be able to access the data.

However, Fibre Channel provides the ability to interconnect many systems and storage devices in complex configurations. Because of this, access controls may be provided to limit access to storage devices and data.

1.14.1 Point-to-Point Topology

In the point-to-point topology, no special access controls are needed. The system has access to the device by virtue of the physical connection. Even in this configuration, access controls may be provided by the system to prevent unauthorized users from access storage devices or data, but this is not affected by the physical interface used between the system and devices.

Access control may be implemented by requiring a user to login with a user ID and password before allowing access to selected data. This prevents unauthorized other users from accessing data. Access control lists defined by a system administrator specify which users have access to which storage devices and data.

1.14.2 Arbitrated Loop Topology

In the arbitrated loop topology, multiple systems and storage devices may be present on the same loop. When this occurs, it may be desirable to provide additional access controls beyond those provided by the operating system. This is necessary for several reasons.

Many operating systems discover attached devices when the operating system is initialized. When a device is discovered, the operating system may attempt to use that device. If multiple systems are present on the same arbitrated loop, they may attempt to use the same device. Unfortunately, not all operating systems can successfully share access to devices, even if they can physically access the device.

Many operating systems are designed for a single-user, single-system environment. In this environment, the operating system assumes it has total ownership of all devices it discovers. In these environments, the operating system may not provide device-sharing and file-locking mechanisms to prevent multiple systems from accessing the same file at the same time. As a result, if multiple systems are present and attempt to access the same device or file, data corruption may result.

The access problem may become even more severe when different operating systems are present. In this case, the file systems in the operating systems organize information differently on the storage devices. If one operating system modifies the data structure on a device, the device may become unusable to the other operating system.

Enforcement of access controls in an arbitrated loop falls upon the devices themselves because there is no centralized point of control. Fibre Channel initiators may employ access control lists to define which targets in the loop should be accessed. Fibre Channel targets may also implement access control lists to define initiators to which access should be granted. As with other access control list mechanisms, the lists are maintained by a system administrator.

1.14.3 Switched Fabric Topology

In the switched fabric topology, access control can be provided by the fabric itself. The fabric may be partitioned into multiple zones (similar to VLANs in a local-area network) to limit which devices have access to each other. Devices within a zone can access other members of that zone, but not devices outside the zone. Figure 13 on page 26 shows a fabric with three zones.

Multiple zones can be defined within the same fabric. This allows multiple systems and storage devices to be attached to the same fabric while still providing needed access controls. Membership in a zone may be defined based on Fibre Channel addresses, Fibre Channel names (Node_Names or Port_Names), protocols supported, or some combination of these.

Devices may belong to more than one zone. This gives them access to other devices in all the zones it belongs to. For example, a tape subsystem may belong to multiple zones so systems or servers in each zone could use the tape subsystem to backup their data. However, just because the tape subsystem belongs to multiple zones does not give other members of those zones the same access privileges.

The fabric switching function may enforce zoning by restricting frame forwarding based on zone definitions. If a device attempts to send a frame to a destination outside of its zone, the fabric does not forward the frame. This type of zoning is referred to as hard zoning.

Zoning may also be enforced by other entities such as the Name Server. The Name Server is a service that maintains a database of information about node ports in the fabric. When a device wants to locate other devices, it can query the Name Server to retrieve the desired information (e.g., "send me a list of all devices that support the SCSI Fibre Channel protocol"). When Name Server zoning is in effect, the Name Server filters the information returned to only include information about other members of the same zone or zones as the requestor. Because this method only limits information, not physical access, it is referred to as soft zoning.

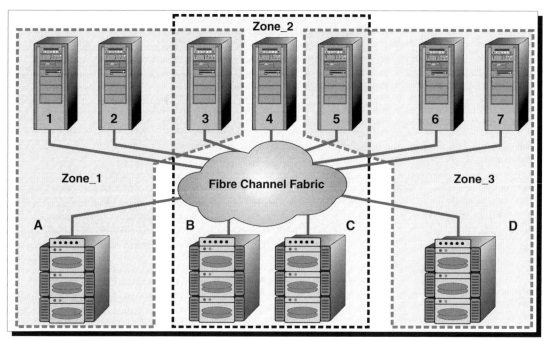

Figure 13. Fibre Channel Zoning

1.15 Nx_Port Initialization

Multiple actions are required in order to bring a Fibre Channel link to an operational condition. These steps are summarized in Figure 14 on page 27. While the actual steps may vary depending upon the configuration and environment, the example shown is typical of a SCSI Fibre Channel environment.

Link initialization begins when a node port is powered on, enabled or the cable is connected. Multi-speed ports typically begin by perform speed negotiation to determine their highest mutually-supported speed (the speed may also be manually configured by an administrator).

Following this, the port may perform mode determination to determine whether it is connected in an Arbitrated Loop topology. If so, it performs loop initialization, otherwise it performs non-loop initialization. The mode may also be manually configured by an administrator.

The node port then performs Fabric login, using the FLOGI Extended Link Service (ELS) to establish a session with the Fabric. If the Fabric login is successful, the Fabric assigns the node port an address and provides access to the Fabric.

Depending upon the environment, the node port and fabric port may optionally perform authentication (following a successful N_Port login, the two node ports may also perform authentication). Authentication and the authentication protocols are described in *Fibre Channel Security* on page 447.

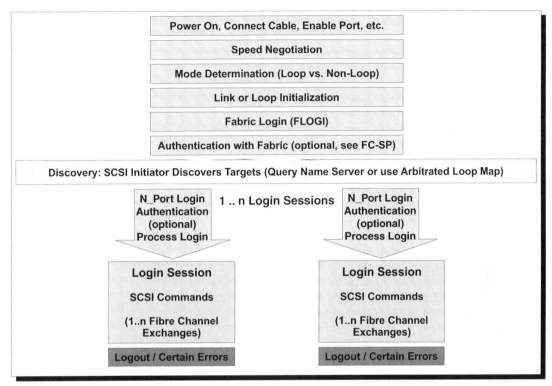

Figure 14. Fibre Channel Initialization

Normally, a SCSI initiator performs a discovery procedure to find its target devices. In a Fabric environment, this is done by querying the Name Server, a function provided by Fibre Channel switches. In an Arbitrated Loop environment (not connected to a Fabric), the initiator may use the loop map built during loop initialization.

Upon completion of the discovery process, a SCSI initiator performs N_Port Login (PLOGI ELS), an optional authentication and Process login (PRLI ELS) to establish a login session with each of the targets and enable SCSI command processing. If a login session ends, either as a result of Logout or certain errors, SCSI commands are not permitted until a login session is reestablished.

1.16 Chapter Summary

Direct Attach Storage (DAS)

- Historically, I/O devices have been attached directly to a single system using the:
  - Small Computer System Interface (SCSI) bus
  - Integrated Device Electronics (IDE) bus
- Results in limited connectivity (number of devices)
- Results in limited distance capabilities
- Data and storage resources are 'isolated' to a single system
  - Limits sharing of data and storage resources
- File system differences further limit data and storage resources

Network Attached Storage (NAS)

- Advent of Local Area Networks (LANs) facilitated data sharing
- Introduced new concepts, components and terminology:
  - Network interface cards (NICs), bridges, routers, switches, shielded twisted pair, unshielded twisted pair, optical fiber,
  - Ethernet, Token Ring, FDDI, NetBEUI, IPX/SPX, Appletalk, Internet Protocol
- Introduced network file systems such as NFS and CIFS to facilitate file sharing
- Access occurs at LAN speeds, not I/O speeds
  - 10 or 100 Mbits/sec vs. 80-100 MB/s

Storage Area Network (SAN)

- Apply networking technologies to traditional I/O device attachment
  - Keep the best of both approaches
- From I/O interfaces:
  - High-performance
  - Existing command protocols (SCSI/ESCON)
  - Extremely reliable transfers
- From networking world:
  - Support more connectivity (devices)
  - Support longer distances (kilometers)
  - Use serial data transmission

Fibre Channel

- Designed to fulfill the needs of SANs
- High performance - 100/200/400 MB/s
  - 1,275 MB/s in limited deployment
- Supports extended distances by using optical fiber - in excess of 50 km. without repeaters
- Supports multiple protocols - SCSI, ESCON, TCP/IP using the same hardware
- Provide reliable data transmission
  - Bit-error rate less than 10^{-12}
- Provide scalability across a wide range of environments - disk drive to supercomputer
- Encourages industry support through open standards

The Fibre Channel Network

- A Fibre Channel network consists of two or more nodes and an interconnect topology
- Uses serial data transmission
  - 1 Gb, 2Gb, 4 Gb today
  - 8.5 Gb and 10 Gb in the near future
- Supports both optical fiber and electrical cables
  - In excess of 50 kilometers using optical fiber
  - About 30 meters with electrical cables (1 Gb)
- Can transport multiple protocols concurrently
  - SCSI protocol for open system storage
  - FICON protocol for mainframe systems
  - TCP/IP for networking

Fibre Channel Node

- Node contains one or more processes that communicate with other nodes
  - Communication uses one or more defined command or packet protocols
  - Each protocol consists of Information Units (e.g., command, data, status, etc.)
  - Each protocol type must be identified
- Node must support Fibre Channel protocols
  - Basic and Extended Link Services
- Each node is identified with a Node_Name
  - 64-bit worldwide unique identifier (WWNN)

Node Port (N_Port/NL_Port)

- Each node contains one or more node ports
  - Provides Fibre Channel interface to topology
  - Operates at one or more data rates
  - Has a 24-bit address identifier
- Transmit function: packages the data in frames, encodes data, and serializes the encoded data
- Receive function: deserializes the received data, decodes data and processes the frames
- Each port is identified with a Port_Name
  - 64-bit worldwide unique identifier (WWPN)
- Different topologies place different requirements on the node port
  - Arbitrated loop requires additional functions - port with this function is called an NL_Port

Serial Data Transmission

- Information is sent serially, one bit at a time
  - Eliminates the skew problem inherent in parallel data transmission
  - Simplifies the cabling and connectors
  - Information can be switched or routed easily
  - Switching one line instead of multiple lines
- Serial transmission requires very high clock speeds to achieve a high data rate
  - 1x Fibre Channel (100 MB/s) is 1 Gbps
  - 2x Fibre Channel (200 MB/s) is 2 Gbps
  - 4x Fibre Channel (400 MB/s) is 4 Gbps
  - 8x Fibre Channel (850 MB/s) is 8.5 Gbps

Multiple Media Options

- Fibre Channel supports multiple media options
- Optical fiber provides:
  - Long distance capability - in excess of 50 km.
  - Immunity to induced electromagnetic signals
  - No emitted radio frequency signals (RFI)
- Electrical cables provide:
  - Low-cost alternative for short distance
  - up to 30 meters (at 1 Gbps)
  - about 10-15 meters at 2 Gbps
  - about 5-10 meters at 4 Gbps
  - Best solution for disk arrays, peripheral attach, processor clustering?

Fibre Channel Levels

- Fibre Channel uses a layered architecture
  - Most current interface architectures follow this approach
  - Provides "modularization" of functions
- Fibre Channel levels:
  - FC-0: Physical Interface
  - FC-1: Encoding and link-level protocols
  - FC-2: Framing and data transport
  - FC-3: Data transformation (e.g., encryption)
  - FC-4: Protocol mapping
  - ULP: Upper-Level Protocol being transported (e.g., SCSI command protocol, IP, FICON, etc.)

Session Management: Login

- Prior to performing application-level operations, a session must be established
  - Done by performing a login
  - Uses FC Extended Link Services protocol
- Ports exchange names and service parameters
  - Port_Name and Node_Name
  - Service Parameters = capability information
- Session may be ended by
  - Logout
  - Certain error conditions
- A port can have login sessions with multiple other ports at the same time

Operation Management: Exchange

- Used to identify and track an operation
  - Operation consists of the exchange of one or more protocol Information Units
  - Protocol Information Units are defined by each specific protocol
- Multiple Exchanges may occur within a single login session
- Exchange_IDs identify each Exchange
  - Originator of Exchange assigns an Originator Exchange_ID (OX_ID)
  - Responder of Exchange may assign Responder Exchange_ID (RX_ID)

Information Units

- Each protocol has protocol-specific information to transport such as:
  - Logical Unit Numbers, device addresses
  - Commands and command attributes
  - Data
  - Status and perhaps, sense data
  - Packet or datagrams (TCP/IP for example)
- Information units are defined by the FC-4 protocol mapping
- Use of the Information Units is also defined by the FC-4 protocol mapping

Information Unit Delivery: Sequence

- Each Information Unit (IU) is delivered by a Sequence of frames
  - A Sequence is always contained within an Exchange
  - An Exchange may have multiple Sequences
- Each Sequence is delivered with a specific set of delivery characteristics
  - Called the class of service
  - Defines characteristics such as confirmation of delivery, reservation of bandwidth, guarantees of latency, etc.

Data Delivery: Frame

- Data is transferred frames
  - Frames are limited to a maximum of 2,112 bytes of data
  - Total maximum size including the header and frame overhead is 2,148 bytes
- Information larger than a single frame is transferred using a multi-frame Sequence
  - Information is segmented into frames by the sender and reassembled by the receiver
- The node port manages the frame transmission and reception
  - Handles the segmentation and reassembly of Sequences
  - Provides flow control to pace the rate of frame transmission

Addressing and Topologies

- Fibre Channel supports a 24-bit address space
  - Provides over 16 million addresses
  - Address is used for forwarding frames
- Fibre Channel supports multiple topologies
- Point-to-point
  - 2 ports on a dedicated link
- Arbitrated loop
  - Up to 127 ports on a shared loop
- Switched fabric
  - Up to 2^{24} ports in a switched interconnect
  - Multiple concurrent communications for high aggregate throughput

Access Control (Zoning)

- It may be desirable to limit access to devices in Fibre Channel networks
  - Limit access to sensitive data
  - Prevent problems due to operating systems that do not implement sharing mechanisms
  - Prevent problems due to different file systems
- Access controls may be provided by
  - Access control lists (ACLs) in the devices
  - Zoning within the topology
  - Restricting information made available to the port from the Name Server

Node Port Initialization

- Multiple actions are required before a node port is operational:
  - Speed Negotiation allows ports to determine their highest mutually-supported speed
  - Mode determination enables a port to determine Arbitrated Loop vs. non-loop mode
  - Link, or Arbitrated Loop, initialization brings the link to an operational state
  - Fabric Login enables a port to access the Fabric and acquire a Fabric address
  - SCSI Initiators discover their target devices by Querying the Name Server or using the arbitrated loop map
  - SCSI Initiators perform N_Port Login and Process Login with each target
  - SCSI Commands are now enabled

2. Fibre Channel Standards

Due to the scope of the Fibre Channel standards, it is neither practical nor desirable to specify the entire Fibre Channel structure and functions in a single document. Rather, there is a family of Fibre Channel standards, each defining a specific aspect of the overall architecture.

Early Fibre Channel standards were developed under the auspices of the American National Standards Institute (ANSI). Due to a restructuring in the national standards organizations, later standards have been developed by the National Committee for Information Technology Standards (NCITS). In addition to the official ANSI and NCITS approved standards, there are several technical reports and non-NCITS developed supporting documents.

The mapping of the SCSI protocol to Fibre Channel was standardized by the NCITS SCSI committee, not the Fibre Channel committee.

The mapping of the Internet Protocol (IP) to Fibre Channel and the definition of Management Information Bases (MIBs) has been done by the Internet Engineering Task Force (IETF). This is the standards body responsible for internet-related standards.

The structure of the principal Fibre Channel standards is shown in Figure 15 on page 32. A current list of approved and draft standards can be found on the web at www.T11.org and www.INCITS.org.

2.1 Fibre Channel Physical and Signaling Standards

The foundation of the Fibre Channel architecture is the *Fibre Channel Physical and Signaling Interface (FC-PH)* standard that was approved as a standard in October, 1994. Since adoption of this standard, two supplementary standards have been approved that enhance the functionality beyond the original standard. These two standards are the *Fibre Channel Physical and Signaling Interface-2 (FC-PH2)* and *Fibre Channel Physical and Signaling Interface-3 (FC-PH3)*. These are supplementary documents and must be used in conjunction with the original standard for a complete definition.

The physical and signaling standards define the FC-0, FC-1, and FC-2 levels mentioned previously. These three levels define the functions and behavior of a Fibre Channel Nx_Port when communicating with another Nx_Port in a point-to-point topology, or with an F_Port in a fabric environment. They do not define the loop-specific behavior of an NL_Port or FL_Port used on an arbitrated loop.

Fibre Channel Physical and Signaling Interface-2 (FC-PH-2). When the original FC-PH standard was approved, several proposed items were excluded to prevent delay in adoption of the standard. The plan was that these functions would be incorporated through incremental enhancements to the base standard or in separate standards.

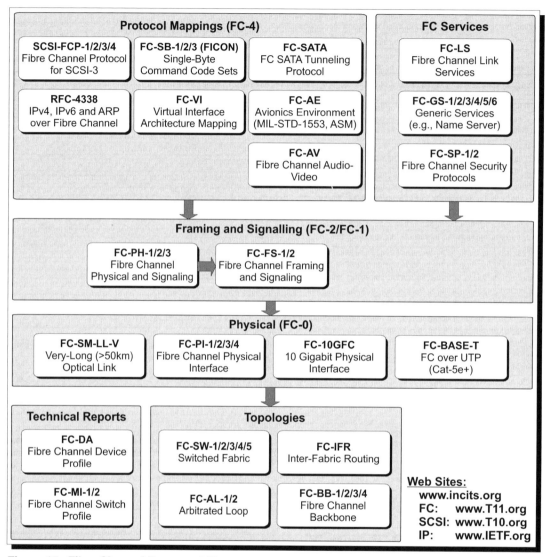

Figure 15. Fibre Channel Document Structure

The first enhancement to the base standard was the *"Fibre Channel Physical and Signaling Interface-2 (FC-PH-2)"* approved in early 1997. This standard added several enhancements to the original standard such as the definition of two new data rates, 200 and 400 megabytes per second (over optical fiber only), new media variants and new Extended Link Services

Fibre Channel Physical and Signaling-3 (FC-PH-3). The third enhancement to the base standard was the *"Fibre Channel - Physical and Signaling Interface-3 (FC-PH-3)"* that was approved in 1998. This document added many enhancements to the original standard. Among the enhancements and additions were new media variants, including enhanced electrical cables and specifications, priority and preemption of an existing Class-1 connection, Class-6 that provides a reliable multicast capability and several more additional Extended Link Services

Fibre Channel Framing and Signaling (FC-FS). Because of difficulties associated with FC-PH and its two supplementary standards (FC-PH-2 and FC-PH-3) the committee launched a project to merge these three documents into a single new document called *Fibre Channel Framing and Signaling (FC-FS)*. At the same time, the FC-0 physical interface definition was moved to a separate standard called *Fibre Channel Physical Interface (FC-PI)*.

Merging the three FC-PH documents helped in understanding the complete framing and signaling standard and removed sometimes inconsistent or redundant information. In addition to merging the three existing FC-PH standards, FC-FS also consolidated definitions of Extended Link Services that had been scattered among others standards-related documents, including technical reports. The consolidation greatly simplified understanding the approved link services and standardized those that were previously only described in technical reports.

Fibre Channel Physical Interface (FC-PI). The Fibre Channel Physical Interface standard contained the FC-0 specifications that were separated from FC-FS. By separating the physical interface specifications from the protocol levels, the standardization process was simplified and expedited.

The technical content of Fibre Channel Physical Interface (FC-PI) is significantly different from that of the Fibre Channel Framing and Signaling (FC-FS). As a result, different experts tend to work on the FC-0 versus the FC-1 and FC-2 levels. By separating these levels, progress on each is expedited due to the more focused nature of the committee members.

Very Long Optical Link Specification (SM-LL-V). This standard defines a very long distance optical link capable of operating at distances in excess of 50 km. (30 miles). Unlike the earlier long-distance link specifications that specified a maximum distance and allocated a loss budget, the very long distance standard specifies signal criteria and allows the link to be as long as desired, provided signals meet the specified criteria. These links require considerable attention to the overall loss budget to ensure an adequate signal level at the receiver. By using a higher-powered laser transmitter, it should be possible to provide adequate signal levels at distances in excess of 100 km. (60 miles).

Several products have been announced that support very long distance links, frequently on the order of 100 km., or even greater. These distances facilitate remote data mirroring, backup, and disaster-recovery sites.

10 Gigabit Fibre Channel (10GFC). The 10 gigabit Fibre Channel physical interface standard was approved in 2003. This standard specifies a physical interface that provides approximately 1,250 megabytes per second of bandwidth. The primary application of 10GFC to date has been for inter-switch links (ISLs).

Due to the higher signaling rates used, and to maintain commonality with other physical interfaces operating at approximately the same rate, a 64b/66b encoding scheme is used. While this results in less encoding overhead, it is different than the one used by the 1, 2, 4 and 8 Gbit links and raises an interesting question of compatibility with the lower-speed links.

In addition to a single optical link operating at 10.5 gigabits per second, the standard also defined a 4-lane serial/parallel interface operating at 3.1875 gigabits per lane using conventional 8b/10b encoding over either copper or optical cabling.

Fibre Channel Base-T (FC-BaseT). This project (scheduled for completion in late 2006 or early 2007) specifies a physical variant based on category 5e or above unshielded twisted pair (UTP) cabling used for Ethernet links. Because of the limited bandwidth provided by UTP cabling, this physical variant uses a unique modulation scheme that is different than the other electrical variants in Fibre Channel.

2.2 Fibre Channel Services Standards

Fibre Channel standards have defined three categories of services: Basic and Extended Link Services, Generic Services and Security Protocols.

Basic and Extended Link Services (FC-LS). The Fibre Channel Link Services standard defines the various basic and extended link service commands (see *Basic Link Services* on page 307 and *Extended Link Services* on page 317).

Fibre Channel Generic Services (FC-GS). Fibre Channel defines several service functions that are available to node port clients and are collectively called generic services. Examples of commonly available services are the Name Server and Management Server. The FC-GS series of standards defines the functions and commands provided by each service and the protocol used to access those services.

- FC-GS: Fibre Channel Generic Services was the initial generic services standard approved in 1996 (since withdrawn).

- FC-GS-2: The Fibre Channel Generic Services-2 standard was approved in 1999 and provided a second-generation generic services. It clarified several areas of inconsistency, or ambiguity present in FC-GS, and added the Name Server function and a Key Distribution Server (since withdrawn).

- FC-GS-3: The Fibre Channel Generic Services-3 standard, approved in 2001, was the third generation of the generic services. This standard extended the development of the generic services and specified additional services to provide a set of management functions.

- FC-GS-4: The Fibre Channel Generic Services-4 standard was approved in 2004 and continues to extend and enhance the functionality of the generic services.

- FC-GS-5: The Fibre Channel Generic Services-5 standard is scheduled for approved in 2006 and continues to extend and enhance the functionality of the generic services.

- FC-GS-6: The T11 standards committee approved the Fibre Channel Generic Services-5, sixth generation generic services project in 2006. The content and functions of this document will be determined as this standard is developed during 2006 and 2007.

Fibre Channel Security Protocols (FC-SP). The Fibre Channel Security Protocols standard specifies authentication protocols, security policies and policy objects and an enhancement to zoning called SP-zoning (see *Fibre Channel Security* on page 447).

2.3 FC-4 Protocol Mapping Standards

Multiple existing upper-level protocols, as well as some new protocols, have been mapped to Fibre Channel.

Protocol mappings can be done by any group, either as a standards project or as a proprietary activity. While the following list is not a complete list of all protocol mappings, it identifies the primary mappings in use, or mappings of that are of special interest.

Fibre Channel Protocol for SCSI-3 (SCSI-FCP). The SCSI protocol mapping was done by the SCSI standards committee (INCITS T10) as part of the SCSI standards activity and defines how various SCSI protocol objects (such as the Command Descriptor Block (CDB), Logical Unit Number (LUN), data, status, and sense information) are structured and transported via the Fibre Channel interface.

- SCSI-FCP: The initial mapping of the SCSI command protocol to Fibre Channel was provided by the SCSI FCP standard approved in 1996. This provided basic SCSI functionality and was primarily oriented towards support of SCSI block type devices such as disk drives or disk subsystems.

- SCSI FCP-2: This update to the standard was approved in 2003 and is a second generation protocol mapping defining how the SCSI-3 command protocol operates across the Fibre Channel interface. FCP-2 added several enhancements and functional improvements, such as enhanced error recovery for tape devices, to the original SCSI FCP standard and obsoleted unused functions.

- SCSI FCP-3: The FCP-3 standard was approved in 2006 and incorporated additional functions, such as support for bidirectional commands and Simple_Q task priority.

- SCSI FCP-4: The T10 committee approved a fourth generation mapping project in 2006. The content of this project will be determined throughout 2006 and into 2007.

Fibre Channel Single-Byte Command Code Sets (FC-SB). The Fibre Channel Single-Byte Command Code Sets protocol mappings specify how the ESCON command protocol is transported via Fibre Channel.

- FC-SB: The initial mapping of the ESCON protocol to Fibre Channel was approved in 1996 and provided what was essentially a one-to-one mapping of ESCON frames to Fibre Channel frames. Because of the low performance of the native ESCON frame protocol, this mapping did not provide adequate performance on longer links and was never implemented.

- FC-SB-2: The Fibre Channel Single-Byte Command Code Sets (FC-SB-2) protocol mapping represented an entirely new mapping of the ESCON command protocol for transport via Fibre Channel (referred to by IBM as the Fibre Connection architecture, or FICON). This standard, approved in 2001, specified a more efficient mapping than that provided by the original FC-SB standard (which has since been withdrawn).

- FC-SB-3: This standard, approved in 2003, extended the functionality provided by FC-SB-2 and streamlined several of the operations to improve efficiency, particularly on extended distance links.

Fibre Channel Avionics Environment (FC-AE). The Fibre Channel Avionics Environment project defines usage of Fibre Channel to transport information between avionics subsystems. As a part of this work, protocol mappings for the MIL-STD-1553, ASM and FC-RDMA protocols were performed.

Fibre Channel Audio-Video (FC-AV). Fibre Channel Audio Video is a project to define how high-definition and broadcast-quality audio and video information may carried via Fibre Channel. The focus of this work has been towards studio and broadcast television applications.

2.4 Topology-Related Standards

While the FC-PH and FC-FS documents describe the behavior of a node port when communicating in a point-to-point or fabric environment, they do not describe how other Fibre Channel topologies behave. That is done by the standards described in the following sections.

Fibre Channel Switched Fabric (FC-SW). The Fibre Channel Switched Fabric series of standards specifies switch behavior and inter-switch communications.

- FS-SW: The initial Fibre Channel Switch Fabric (FC-SW) standard was approved in 1998. It provided a basic definition of fabric behavior and communications between different switches required to coordinate operations and manage address assignment. This version did not define a routing protocol or flow control mechanisms and was insufficient to support heterogeneous fabrics and has since been withdrawn.

- FS-SW-2: The Fibre Channel Switch Fabric-2 (FC-SW-2) standard was approved in 2001 and specified inter-switch link (ISL) behavior, Switch Internal Link Services, and the Fabric Shortest Path First (FSPF) routing protocol. The FC-SW-2 standard enabled switches from different manufacturers to interoperate in a multi-switch fabric.

- FS-SW-3: The Fibre Channel Switch Fabric-3 (FC-SW-3) standard was approved in 2004 and provided additional definition of interswitch behavior and communication.

- FS-SW-4: The Fibre Channel Switch Fabric-4 (FC-SW-4) standard was expected to be approved in late 2006. This version added support for virtual fabrics and continued to further the definition of interswitch behavior and communication.

- FS-SW-5: At the time of writing, the committee had approved a fifth generation of the FC-SW standards. The exact nature of the content of this version will be determined throughout 2006 and 2007.

Fibre Channel Arbitrated Loop (FC-AL). The Fibre Channel Arbitrated Loop standard (FC-AL) was approved in 1996 and defined an entirely new Fibre Channel topology based upon a loop, or ring, topology. This topology was developed to provide a low-cost, shared bandwidth interconnect suitable for connecting a modest number of devices. Because of its low cost connectivity, the arbitrated loop has seen widespread adoption, particularly for attaching Fibre Channel disk drives.

FC-AL-2 is a second-generation standard approved in 1999 that provided several corrections necessary to address functional anomalies discovered during implementation of the original standard and added new functions to improve the performance and operation of the loop while preserving backward compatibility with existing FC-AL devices.

Fibre Channel Inter-Fabric Routing (FC-IFR). The Fibre Channel Inter-Fabric Routing project was started in 2005 to provide a standard specifying how frames can be routed from one Fabric to another (and potentially travelling through intermediate Fabrics).

Fibre Channel Backbone (FC-BB). The Fibre Channel series of standards define how bridge devices can enable Fibre Channel entities to communicate through intermediate, non-Fibre Channel networks such as an IP network or a Synchronous Optical Network (SONET).

2.5 Technical Reports

Technical reports provide auxiliary information in support of the standards. Technical reports tend to fall into one of two categories; supporting technical information or implementation profiles. Technical reports normally do not define any new standards behavior, however, in some cases new behaviors are documented in technical reports prior to being incorporated into the standards.

Examples of technical reports that provide supporting technical information are the "Fibre Channel Methodology of Jitter and Signal Quality Specification (FC-MJSQ)" and the "Fibre Channel Signal Modeling (FC-SM)" technical reports.

Examples of technical reports classed as implementation profiles are the "Fibre Channel Methodology for Interconnects (FC-MI)" and "Fibre Channel Device Attach (FC-DA)" technical reports. Both of these technical reports contain lists of options or features from the standards that have a possible interoperability impact. Associated with each option or feature is a recommended behavior.

The purpose of profile documents such as these it to foster interoperability by ensuring products are implementing to a common set of the options and features provided by the standards. FC-MI is directed to switch implementations and FC-DA to device implementations.

2.6 Chapter Summary

Fibre Channel Standards

- Fibre Channel is not a single standard, but a family of standards
  - The core is the Fibre Channel Framing and Signaling standard (FC-FS)
  - Protocol mappings (FC-4s) are covered by separate standards, one per protocol
  - Topologies, except for point-to-point, are covered in separate standards
  - Link Services have their own standard
  - Generic Services (e.g., Name Server) are covered in a separate standard
- Technical reports supplement the standards and provide guidance to implementers

Fibre Channel Framing and Signaling

- Initially, FC-PH defined Fibre Channel transport
  - Defined the node port and its interactions
  - Included FC-0, FC-1, and FC-2
  - Two supplemental standards were adopted: FC-PH2 (1997) and FC-PH3 (1998)
- These three standards have been replaced
  - Fibre Channel Physical Interface (**FC-PI**) specifies FC-0
  - Fibre Channel Framing and Signaling (**FC-FS**) specifies FC-1 and FC-2
  - Fibre Channel Link Services (**FC-LS**) defines the link services

Protocol Mappings

- Multiple upper-level protocols have been mapped to Fibre Channel
- Each protocol mapping has its own standard
  - SCSI-3 Fibre Channel Protocol (**SCSI-FCP**) maps the SCSI-3 command set
  - **FC-SB-3** maps the ESCON protocol (FICON)
  - **RFC-4338** maps IPv4, IPv6 and ARP over Fibre Channel (IPFC)
  - **FC-SATA** defines SATA tunneling via Fibre Channel
  - **FC-VI** maps the Virtual Interface Architecture
  - **FC-AE** maps the avionics environment

Fibre Channel Topologies

- Point-to-point is defined in FC-PH/FC-FS
- Arbitrated Loop has its standards
  - 1st generation, FC-AL, approved in 1996
  - 2nd generation, **FC-AL-2**, approved in 1999
- Switched Fabric has its standards (FC-SW)
  - Specifies fabric behavior and inter-switch communication
  - Latest version (2006) is **FC-SW-4**
- Inter-Fabric Routing (**FC-IFR**) started in 2005
  - Defines routing between separate Fabrics
- Fibre Channel Backbone (**FC-BB**) specifies sending FC frames through non-FC network

Fibre Channel Generic Services

- Defines Fibre Channel service functions and command for each
  - Name Server, Management Server, Time Server
- Defines the protocol used to communicate with these servers:
  - Fibre Channel Common Transport (FC-CT)
- Multiple generations of FC-GS-x standards
  - FC-GS and FC-GS-2: now withdrawn
  - FC-GS-3: approved in 2001
  - FC-GS-4: approved in 2004
  - FC-GS-5: in final approval (2006)

Technical Reports

- Technical reports supplement the standards
- May specify agreed upon usage of options:
  - Fibre Channel Device Attach (FC-DA) for devices
  - Fibre Channel Methodology for Interconnects (FC-MI) for switches
  - Fibre Channel Avionics Environment (FC-AE)
- May provide technical guidance:
  - Methodology of Jitter and Signal Quality Specification (FC-MJSQ)
  - Fibre Channel Signal Modeling (FC-SM)

3. FC-0 Concepts

Fibre Channel's level 0 (FC-0) defines a wide variety of physical interface options that include both optical fiber and copper transmission lines. Figure 16 illustrates the relationship of FC-0 to the other levels of the standard.

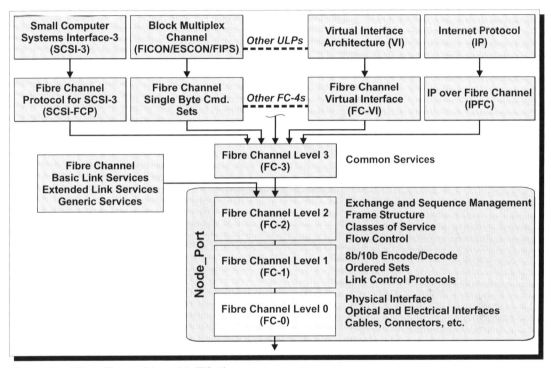

Figure 16. Fibre Channel Level 0 (FC-0)

The capabilities provided by each physical variant reflect the transmission characteristics of the medium itself. The different options offer a wide range of cost, performance, distance, and noise immunity characteristics. By providing different physical interface options, Fibre Channel allows a given implementation to select the most appropriate variant for that particular application. A graph comparing several of the more common Fibre Channel optical physical links is shown in Table 17 on page 40.

An example illustrating the advantage of different Fibre Channel physical variants in a campus environment is shown in Figure 18. In this example, three different physical variants are used. Single-mode optical fiber is used between buildings (or sites) because of its long-distance data transmission capabilities. Within each building, lower cost multimode optical fiber is used be-

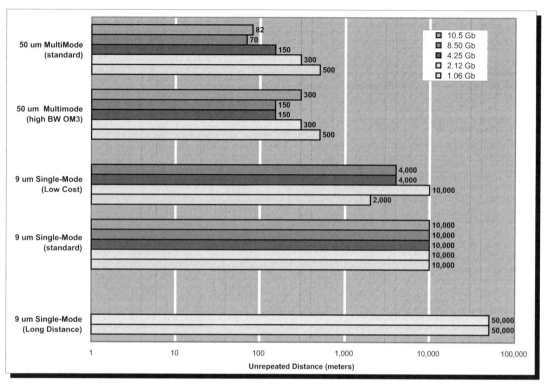

Figure 17. Common Fibre Channel Optical Links

tween the wiring closets located on different floors. Finally, low-cost copper cabling connects the Fibre Channel devices to the wiring closets.

3.0.1 Physical Variant Identification

To provide a simple identification of different physical variants defined by the standard, a nomenclature scheme was developed to identify the speed, media type, transmitter, and distance attributes of that particular variant. Figure 19 on page 41 illustrates this notational scheme.

A particular physical variant is identified by specifying one option from each of the four groups of characteristics.

3.1 Media Conversion

Many approaches have been developed to facilitate converting from one physical medium type to another. These approaches can be used by a Fibre Channel port or interconnection device such as a Fibre Channel switch, repeater, or arbitrated loop hub.

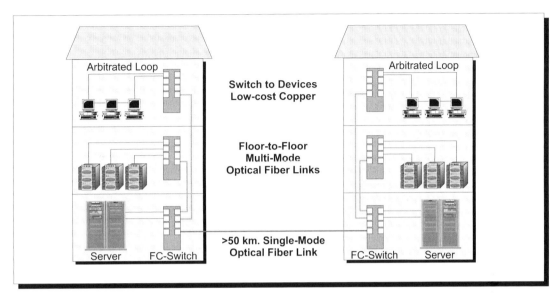

Figure 18. Fibre Channel Campus Wiring

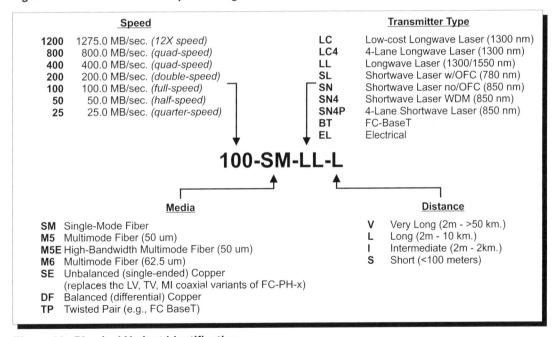

Speed

1200	1275.0 MB/sec. *(12X speed)*
800	800.0 MB/sec. *(quad-speed)*
400	400.0 MB/sec. *(quad-speed)*
200	200.0 MB/sec. *(double-speed)*
100	100.0 MB/sec. *(full-speed)*
50	50.0 MB/sec. *(half-speed)*
25	25.0 MB/sec. *(quarter-speed)*

Transmitter Type

LC	Low-cost Longwave Laser (1300 nm)
LC4	4-Lane Longwave Laser (1300 nm)
LL	Longwave Laser (1300/1550 nm)
SL	Shortwave Laser w/OFC (780 nm)
SN	Shortwave Laser no/OFC (850 nm)
SN4	Shortwave Laser WDM (850 nm)
SN4P	4-Lane Shortwave Laser (850 nm)
BT	FC-BaseT
EL	Electrical

100-SM-LL-L

Media

SM	Single-Mode Fiber
M5	Multimode Fiber (50 um)
M5E	High-Bandwidth Multimode Fiber (50 um)
M6	Multimode Fiber (62.5 um)
SE	Unbalanced (single-ended) Copper (replaces the LV, TV, MI coaxial variants of FC-PH-x)
DF	Balanced (differential) Copper
TP	Twisted Pair (e.g., FC BaseT)

Distance

V	Very Long (2m - >50 km.)
L	Long (2m - 10 km.)
I	Intermediate (2m - 2km.)
S	Short (<100 meters)

Figure 19. Physical Variant Identification

3.1.1 Gigabit Interface Connector (GBIC)

The *Gigabit Interface Connector* (GBIC) is a small hot-swappable serial-to-serial connector module that can be used to provide a pluggable media interface for Fibre Channel devices. The GBIC is inserted through an access slot and guided into an internal connector. An illustration of a Fibre Channel adapter card with a GBIC is shown in Figure 20 on page 42.

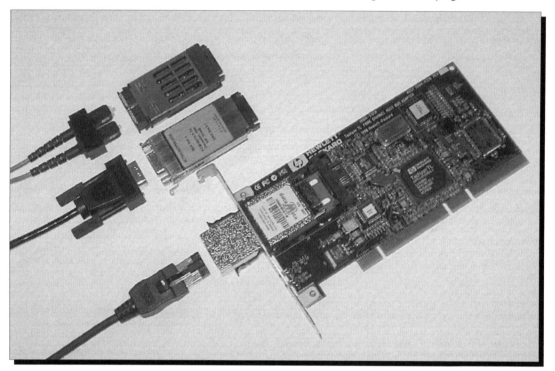

Figure 20. Gigabit Interface Connector (GBIC)

Because the GBIC is hot-swappable and accessible from outside of the enclosure, it provides an extremely flexible media interface approach. GBIC modules support the full range of Fibre Channel media options, including DB-9 and Style-2 (HSSDC) electrical connectors as well as both multimode and single-mode optical fiber.

The GBIC form factor and internal interface are standardized and GBICs are available from multiple suppliers. Because of the similarities of the Fibre Channel and gigabit ethernet optical interfaces some GBICs may be designed to operate with either interface.

In addition to the Fibre Channel signal interfaces, the GBIC may provide a separate serial interface that allows the host device to retrieve management information from the GBIC. This information may include the manufacturer, media type, serial number, and current status of the GBIC. Management information facilitates configuration mapping and asset management within the configuration.

Fibre Channel test equipment can also take advantage of the GBIC to provide media flexibility. By simply by changing the GBIC the test equipment can be configured to operate with any of the Fibre Channel physical interface options.

Products designed to use the GBIC must provide the necessary mounting hardware, electrical connector and supporting management interface, if used. These items add cost to the base product in addition to the cost of the GBIC itself. Because of this, many low-cost designs forego the use of flexible media interfaces to keep the cost of the product to a minimum.

3.1.2 Small Form Factor Pluggable (SFP)

The need for greater port density and smaller connectors led to the development of the small form factor pluggable (SFP) module. The SFP provides the media flexibility associated with the GBIC, but in a package approximately one-half the size of the GBIC. An illustration of three SFP modules (two electrical and one optical) is shown in Figure 21.

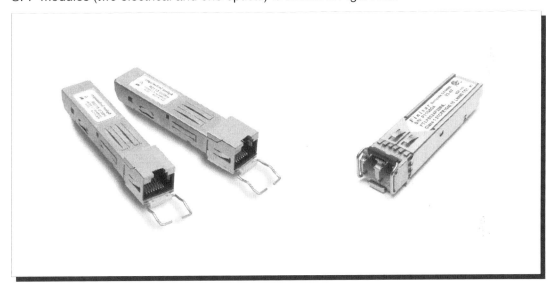

Figure 21. Small Form Factor Pluggable (SFP) Module

Because the SC optical connector is too large for this size package, the smaller LC optical connector is used.

3.1.3 Media Interface Adapter (MIA)

The media interface adapter is an external hot-swappable module that can be used to provide media conversion outside the box. The MIA plugs into the electrical interface connector on a Fibre Channel device and provides an electrical-to-optical conversion. This allows devices with electrical interfaces to be attached to optical fibers. An illustration of a Media Interface Adapter is shown in Figure 22 on page 44.

Figure 22. Media Interface Adapter (MIA)

The MIA requires electrical power and the associated device must supply power to the corresponding pins on the electrical connector. These necessary pins were defined in the FC-PH3 version of the standard.

Because the MIA is mounted external to the enclosure, it does not add cost or complexity of the host device. This allows low-cost devices to use an electrical interface and still provide media flexibility by use of the external MIA.

Unlike the GBIC, the MIA does not provide an interface to allow the host device to retrieve management information from the MIA. This may limit the amount of management information that is available in configurations using the MIA.

Both the GBIC and MIA are in the signal path and affect the quality of the Fibre Channel signals. In a properly designed system the effect is minimal. In a poorly designed or marginal system the addition of a GBIC or MIA may result in an increase in transmission errors.

3.1.4 Gigabit Link Module (GLM)

The Gigabit Link Module (GLM) was the first pluggable media interface design used by Fibre Channel devices. The GLM is a small daughter card that provides both the parallel-to-serial conversion and media interface. Like GBICs, the GLM is available in both electrical and optical interface versions. However, unlike the GBIC, the GLM is not hot swappable and requires that power is removed from the host device before the GLM is changed. An illustration of a Fibre Channel adapter card using a GLM is shown in Figure 23 on page 45.

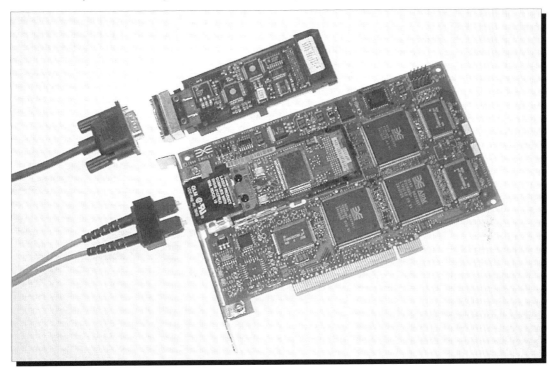

Figure 23. Gigabit Link Module (GLM)

The GLM interface and form factor are standardized and GLMs are available from multiple vendors. The interface to the host device is consists of two 20-bit data interfaces. Each 20-bit interface transfers two transmission characters per clock cycle. In addition, the interface contains clock and control lines for the transmit and receive data.

The GLM performs parallel-to-serial conversion and contains the bit-level transmit and receive bit clocks. The GLM develops the transmit bit clock by multiplying a supplied 53.625 megahertz oscillator by twenty to provide the 1,062.5 megahertz bit-rate clock. The receive clock is derived by a phase-locked loop (PLL) contained in the GLM. The phase-locked loop synchronizes to the incoming data stream at 1,062.5 megahertz and is used to deserialize the data. The PLL frequency is divided by twenty to provide a character rate clock to the host device.

The GLM is not hot swappable and requires opening the host-device enclosure to replace or change the GLM. Because of this, the majority of new designs are based on the GBIC rather than the GLM.

3.2 General FC-0 Characteristics

All links consist of two fibers. One fiber is used for transmitting information, the other fiber for receiving information. In order for two ports to communicate, it is necessary for the transmitter output of one port to connect to the receiver input of the other. To accomplish this connection, all link cables contain a crossover between the two signals. An example of the connection between two link control facilities is shown in Figure 24 on page 46. In this example, the link control facilities could be associated with a pair of node ports, or a node port and a fabric port.

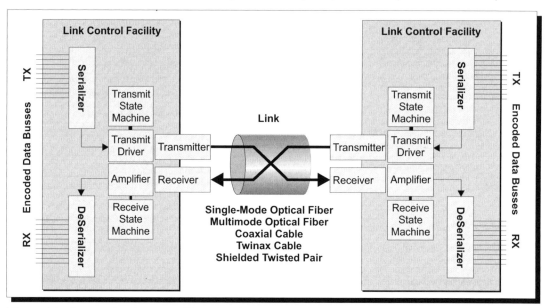

Figure 24. Connection Between Two Link Control Facilities

All physical links consist of a single point-to-point connection. A single transmitter is always connected to the same receiver (optical switches are not supported). There are no Fibre Channel topologies or configurations containing multi-drop or multi-tap connections. Creating multi-drop configurations in optical transmission is difficult and multi-drop connections in an electrical interface introduce problems associated with unpredictable loading and transmission line characteristics. Limiting the connection to a single point-to-point configuration helps ensure signal integrity and allows any needed signal termination to be built into the port.

When an entity, such as a fabric or repeater, receives and retransmits the serial data stream the transmitted data stream is retimed before transmission to prevent jitter accumulation. Because of the potential differences in the bit rate of the received data and retransmitted data due to clock tolerances, an elasticity buffer is required to compensate for the data rate tolerances. All data rates have a clock tolerance of +/- 100 ppm.

When a phase discontinuity occurs, a receiver must be capable of recovering from a phase discontinuity and reacquire synchronization within 2,500 bit times (2.5 μs at 1062.5 Mbaud).

All links must provide bit-error rate (BER) less than or equal to 10^{-12}. While not clearly stated in the original FC-PH standard, this error rate applies end-to-end and includes all intermediate fabric elements or repeaters. Furthermore, the error rate must take into account worst case conditions that may occur, such as end-of-life aging conditions, power supply tolerances, etc.

While a bit-error rate of 10^{-12} may seem like an extremely low error rate, it corresponds to one error every 16.6 minutes at 1,062.5 megabits per second (8.3 minutes at 2,125 megabits per second). Some applications require a more stringent bit-error rate, such as 10^{-15}. This results in approximately one error every 11 days, a more acceptable behavior for critical applications.

The FC-0 level does not detect invalid bit patterns, 8b/10b encoding errors, or running disparity errors. However, as some conditions may cause a degradation of receiver sensitivity or Loss-of-Synchronization, the transmitted bit stream must meet the following requirements (that are never violated in the normal transmission of valid 8b/10b encoded data streams):

- The maximum code balance in any 10 bits shall be in the range of 40% to 60%. 8b/10b encoded characters that are not of neutral disparity are inherently either 40% (four one bits and six zero bits), or 60% (six one bits and four zero bits).

- The maximum run length of consecutive bits is 12 bits of the same polarity within any group of 20 bits. For example, the pattern "0011111010" has a run length of five.

- Between the 20-bits groups cited above, the transmitted data stream shall have a contiguous set of at least 300 bits with a balance between 49.5% and 50.5%. Within this group, the maximum run length shall not exceed five.

3.3 Signal Quality, Jitter, and the Eye Diagram

To ensure interoperability between different implementations, it is necessary to specify the signal characteristics of a Fibre Channel transmitter in both the time and amplitude domains. Figure 25 on page 48 illustrates a signal showing idealized characteristics.

When a transmitter has been transmitting a zero bit and is requested to send a one bit, some time is necessary for the signal to make the transition from the zero level to the one level. This time is called the *rise time* of the signal. Similarly, when the transmitter has been transmitting a one bit and is instructed to send a zero bit some time is required to make that transition as well. This time is called the *fall time* of the signal. Due to the different data rates available, Fibre Channel specifies the rise and fall times as a percentage of the normalized bit time.

When a transmitter is requested to send a one bit, the amplitude of the resulting bit may be either greater or less than the nominal amplitude value due to component variations. Similarly, when a transmitter is requested to transmit a zero bit, the amplitude may be greater than, or less than, the nominal amplitude. It is possible for the one value to exceed the nominal amplitude, a condition called overshoot, or the zero value to extend below the nominal amplitude, a condition called undershoot. Fibre Channel defines the amplitude characteristics as a percentage of the normalized amplitude, including specifications for the overshoot and undershoot.

When a transmitter transmits a one bit or zero bit, variations in the transmitter result in the individual pulses exhibiting differences from one pulse to the next. These differences are due to the internal switching characteristics of the transmitter and are inherent in all designs. When

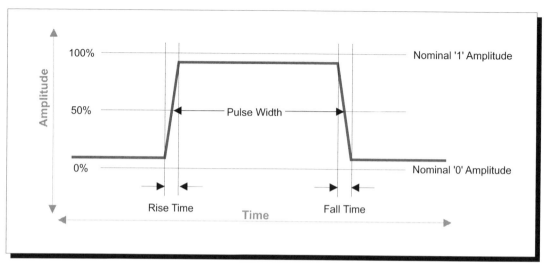

Figure 25. Idealized Signal Characteristics

these variations result in differences in the time domain, the result is called jitter. These variations also occur in the amplitude of the transmitted pulse causing amplitude variations that affect the actual signal level of the different pulses. The transmitter, cable, connectors, and the receiver associated with a link all contribute to both the time and amplitude variations.

Time displacement, or jitter, is especially significant in that excessive jitter narrows the window available for reliably sampling a received pulse. An example of a pulse with jitter is shown in Figure 26. In this example, the time window available when the signal may be reliably sampled has been reduced by the amount of the jitter contained in the signal.

When the signals for multiple one and zero bits with both amplitude and time jitter are overlaid an "eye diagram" results with the eye representing the amplitude and time bounds for reliable sampling. If an attempt is made to sample the signal outside of the opening, errors may result. In the example shown in Figure 26, the amount of acceptable amplitude variation is indicated as +/-Y, where Y is expressed as a percentage of the nominal bit amplitude. The amount of acceptable time variation is from when the nominal bit time begins or ends to the 50% point on the eye opening, indicated as X_1 and the amount of time variation until the signal is at an acceptable level, indicated as X_2. The values specified for nominal bit times, amplitudes, X, and Y values are discussed later in conjunction with the different transmitter types.

3.4 Bit-Error Rate Thresholding

Bit-error rate thresholding is a technique that establishes a measurement interval (referred to as the error window) for counting transmission errors. If the number of errors during an error window exceeds a predetermined threshold, a Registered Link-Incident Report (see *Registered Link-Incident Report (RLIR)* on page 374) may be generated.

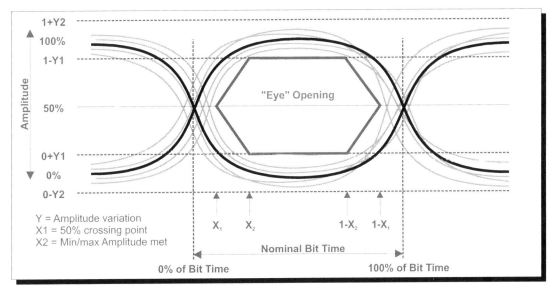

Figure 26. Eye Diagram

Bit-errors may be manifested as invalid transmission words, disparity errors, CRC errors, Primitive Sequence protocol errors, or temporary Loss-of-Synchronization. For the purposes of bit-error rate thresholding, only invalid transmission words are counted.

During an error window, transmission errors may occur singly or in bursts. To prevent erroneous counts resulting from error bursts, errors occurring within a specified period (referred to as the error interval) are treated as a single error as shown in Figure 27.

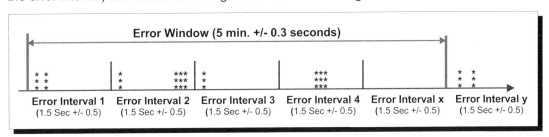

Figure 27. Bit-Error Rate Measurement Intervals

Bit-error counting begins when the Port State Machine (PSM) enters the Active (AC) state. If the bit-error rate threshold is exceeded (15 errors per error window by default), counting restarts after a vendor-specific time. At least 15 subsequent errors must occur before the next bit-error rate threshold is detected. Error counting may restart when the error window ends.

Defaults values for the bit-error rate threshold measurement are shown in Figure 27. These values may be changeable using the Set Bit-Error Reporting Parameters (SBRP) Extended Link Service request.

3.5 Chapter Summary

FC-0: Physical Interface

- FC-0 defines the physical interface options available for Fibre Channel
  - Data rates
  - Media options - optical or electrical
  - Cables and connectors
  - Distance for each data rate and media combination
- Having multiple media options allows for configuration flexibility
  - Optical media for long distance
  - Copper for lower cost over short distances

Link Control Facility

- Fibre Channel refers to the transmitter and receiver functions as the link control facility
- Transmitter
  - Transmit state machine
  - Serializer
  - Optical or electrical driver
- Receiver
  - Optical or electrical receiver
  - Deserializer
  - Receive state machine

Physical Variants

- Each of the physical variants is identified using four groups of characters
  - 1st group is the link data rate (25, 50, 100, 200, 400)
  - 2nd group is the media type (optical or copper)
  - 3rd group is the transmitter and receiver type (Laser, LED, electrical)
  - 4th group is the distance (long, intermediate, short)
- Both ends of the link must have compatible physical variants in order to communicate

Signal Characteristics

- Some amount of time is required for a signal to change states
  - Called the rise time or fall time
- When a signal changes states, it may not provide exactly the same amplitude every time
- These characteristics lead to jitter in the time and amplitude of a signal
- Jitter is a significant factor in determining the maximum data rate
- Jitter is inherent in the electronic, optical, and physical components

The "Eye" Diagram

- An eye diagram is used to specify signal requirements
  - Specifies the acceptable amount of jitter in the time domain
  - Specifies the amount of amplitude variation
- When a series of multiple ones and zeros are observed, an eye diagram results
  - Shows the amount of jitter for the series of bits
  - Shows the amount of amplitude variation
- An example of the eye diagram is shown in Figure 26 on page 49

Bit-Error Rate Reporting

- A port may measure transmission errors over time
  - The measurement interval is referred to as the "error window"
- Transmission errors may occur in bursts
  - Error events within an "error interval" are treated as a single error
  - This prevents error bursts from resulting in multiple errors being recorded
- If a pre-determined threshold is exceeded, a Registered Link-Incident Report may be sent
- The measurement parameters may use defaults or be managed using the Set Bit-Error Reporting Parameters (SBRP) ELS

4. Fiber Optic Links

As its name implies, Fibre Channel supports the use of optical fiber for data transmission. Information is transmitted by sending pulses of light through an optical fiber. In Fibre Channel applications, a "1" bit is sent by turning the light on, a "0" bit by turning the light off. The data rate of an optical link is determined by how fast the light can be turned on and off and how well the optical fiber is able to carry the pulses of light. The distance capability of the fiber is determined by how much light is injected into the fiber, how much degradation the pulses suffer in transmission (how much light is lost in transmission and to what extent pulse distortion occurs), and the detection capabilities of the receiver.

There are two common transmitters used for fiber-optic communications systems, lasers and light emitting diodes (LEDs). Lasers are used in high-speed applications, and for long-distance links due to their faster switching speed and superior optical qualities. LEDs may be used in lower-speed, low-cost applications (LEDs are too slow for Fibre Channel links).

The optical fiber consists of a core, the cladding and a protective jacket. The core carries the light from the transmitter to the receiver. While the core may be made of any light-transmissive material, optical fibers for Fibre Channel use a glass core because of the superior transmission capabilities of glass. The optical fiber consists of a single strand of glass with a core diameter that is between 9 micrometers (μm) and 62.5 μm depending upon the type of optical fiber.

Surrounding the core is the cladding. The cladding confines the light to the core and prevents the light from escaping. The cladding accomplishes this by taking advantage of an optical phenomenon that occurs when light travels through mediums with different transmission characteristics. When light encounters such a boundary, at some angle of incidence, the light is reflected at the boundary. The optical characteristics of the core and cladding differ just enough to keep the light confined in the core, a process called *total internal reflection*.

At the far end of the fiber, the light is received by a photodiode that converts the optical energy to an electrical signal. This signal is amplified and passed through a threshold detector that determines if the light represents a "1" level or a "0" level. From this point on, the processing of the signal is the same, whether the link is optical or copper. An illustration of the basic components of a fiber optical communications link is shown in Figure 28 on page 52.

Optical fiber provides several distinct advantages over copper transmission lines that make it a very attractive medium for many applications. Among the advantages are:

- Greater distance capability than is possible with copper at the same data rate
- Insensitive to induced electromagnetic interference (EMI)
- No emitted electromagnetic radiation (RFI)
- No electrical connection between the two ports
- Not susceptible to crosstalk
- Compact and lightweight cables and connectors

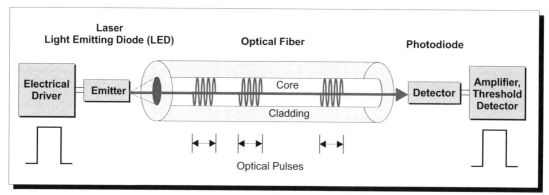

Figure 28. Fiber Optic Data Transmission

On the other hand, optical links do have some drawbacks. Some of the disadvantages are:

- Optical links tend to be more expensive than copper links over short distances
- Optical connections don't lend themselves to backplane printed circuit wiring
- Optical connections may be affected by dirt and other contamination

Optical fibers provide a very high-performance transmission medium that has been refined and proven over many years. Fibre Channel is not the first application of fiber optics to computer interfaces, and has generally specified the data rates and distances in a rather conservative manner, making fiber optic variants suitable for a wide range of commercial applications.

4.1 Fibre Channel Optical Variants

the Fibre Channel standards specie numerous optical variants based on both single-mode and multimode optical fibers. The purpose in specifying multiple options is to provide flexibility when making cost versus performance trade-offs for different applications. A table of the different optical variants, grouped by signaling rate, is shown in Table 2 on page 53.

To ensure interoperability between different transmitters and receivers and realization of the required bit-error rate, it is necessary to specify the characteristics of the optical link. The primary attributes requiring specification are the data rate, the characteristics of the transmitter, interconnecting fiber including connectors, and the receiver. Because each media may have different characteristics requiring specification, the following sections are organized according to the media type.

4.2 Optical Fiber

Optical fiber can be categorized as either single-mode fiber or multimode fiber based upon the manner in which the light propagates through the fiber. An example of the propagation of light through the two different types of fiber is shown in Figure 29 on page 54.

Speed (MBs)	Media Type	Transmitter	Distance Max.	Min.	Variant ID
1200 MBs (10.5 Gb)	9 μm SM Fiber	1300 nm. LW Laser	10,000m	2.0m	1200-SM-LL-L
	50 μm MM Fiber (OM3)	850 nm. SW Laser	300m	0.5m	1200-M5E-SN-I
	50 μm MM Fiber	850 nm. SW Laser	82m	0.5m	1200-M5-SN-I
	62.5 μm MM Fiber	850 nm. SW Laser	33m	0.5m	1200-M6-SN-I
1200 MBs (4-Lane CWDM) (4x3.18 Gb)	9 μm SM Fiber	1300 nm. LW Laser	10,000m	2.0m	1200-SM-LC4-L
	50 μm OM3 Fiber	850 nm. SW Laser	550m	2.0m	1200-M5E-SN4-I
	50 μm MM Fiber	1300 nm. LW Laser	290m	2.0m	1200-M5-LC4-L
	50 μm MM Fiber	850 nm. SW Laser	290m	2.0m	1200-M5-SN4-I
	62.5 μm MM Fiber	1300 nm. LW Laser	290m	2.0m	1200-M6-LC4-L
	62.5 μm MM Fiber	850 nm. SW Laser	118m	2.0m	1200-M6-SN4-I
1200 MBs (4-Lane Parallel)	50 μm MM Fiber (OM3)	850 nm. SW Laser	300m	0.5m	1200-M5E-SN4P-I
	50 μm MM Fiber	850 nm. SW Laser	150m	0.5m	1200-M5-SN4P-I
	62.5 μm 4-Lane MM Fiber	850 nm. SW Laser	75m	0.5m	1200-M6-SN4P-I
800 MBs (8.500 Gb)	9 μm SM Fiber	1300 nm. LW Laser	10,000m	2.0m	800-SM-LC-L
	9 μm SM Fiber	1300 nm. LW Laser	4,000m	2.0m	800-SM-LC-M
	50 μm MM Fiber (OM3)	850 nm. SW Laser	150m	0.5m	800-M5-SN-I
	50 μm MM Fiber	850 nm. SW Laser	70m	0.5m	800-M5-SN-I
	62.5 μm MM Fiber	850 nm. SW Laser	35m	0.5m	800-M6-SN-I
400 MBs (4.250 Gb)	9 μm SM Fiber	1300 nm. LW Laser	10,000m	2.0m	400-SM-LC-L
	9 μm SM Fiber	1300 nm. LW Laser	4,000m	2.0m	400-SM-LC-M
	50 μm MM Fiber (OM3)	850 nm. SW Laser	150m	0.5m	400-M5-SN-I
	50 μm MM Fiber	850 nm. SW Laser	150m	0.5m	400-M5-SN-I
	62.5 μm MM Fiber	850 nm. SW Laser	70m	0.5m	400-M6-SN-I
200 MBs (2.125 Gb)	9 μm SM Fiber	1550 nm. LW Laser	> 50,000m	2.0m	200-SM-LL-V
	9 μm SM Fiber	1300 nm. LW Laser	10,000m	2.0m	200-SM-LC-L
	50 μm MM Fiber (OM3)	850 nm. SW Laser	300m	0.5m	200-M5-SN-I
	50 μm MM Fiber	850 nm. SW Laser	300m	0.5m	200-M5-SN-I
	62.5 μm MM Fiber	850 nm. SW Laser	150m	0.5m	200-M6-SN-I
100 MBs (1.0625 Gb)	9 μm SM Fiber	1550 nm. LW Laser	> 50,000m	2.0m	100-SM-LL-V
	9 μm SM Fiber	1300 nm. LW Laser	10,000m	2.0m	100-SM-LC-L
	9 μm SM Fiber	1300 nm. LW Laser	2,000m	2.0m	100-SM-LL-I
	50 μm OM3 MM Fiber	850 nm. SW Laser	500m	0.5m	100-M5-SN-I
	50 μm MM Fiber	850 nm. SW Laser	500m	0.5m	100-M5-SN-I
	50 μm MM Fiber	850 nm. SW Laser	500m	2.0m	100-M5-SL-I
	62.5 μm MM Fiber	850 nm. SW Laser	300m	0.5m	100-M6-SN-I
	62.5 μm MM Fiber	850 nm. SW Laser	175m	2.0m	100-M6-SL-I

Table 2. Summary of Optical Variants

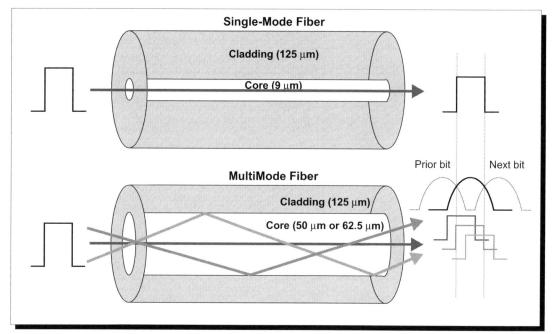

Figure 29. Single-Mode and Multimode Propagation

Due to performance and cost differences between the two types of optical fiber, single-mode fiber is usually used for longer distance links (kilometers), while multimode fiber offers a lower cost alternative for intermediate distances (tens to hundreds of meters).

4.2.1 Single-Mode Optical Links

In single-mode fiber, all of the light propagates along the same path in the fiber. This is accomplished by reducing the diameter of the core to such a degree that all the light is constrained to follow the same path (think of it as a very narrow one-lane street that is 9 μm, or millionths of a meter wide).

Fibre Channel links based on single-mode optical fiber use a long wavelength laser operating in the infrared portion of the spectrum at 1300 nanometers (nm.) or 1550 nm. as the light source (these wavelengths are not visible to the human eye). Because of the superior characteristics of single-mode optical fiber and use of a laser light source, these links provide the highest performance (data rate versus distance) of the Fibre Channel links.

4.2.2 50 Micrometer Multimode Optical Links

Multimode optical fiber provides a lower-cost optical alternative to single-mode fiber for applications where the distance capabilities of single-mode fiber are not required. The cost differential results from the lower manufacturing cost associated with the multimode fiber and optical components.

In multimode fiber, the core diameter is much larger (50 μm or 62.5 μm typically) resulting in multiple propagation modes, or paths, that the light can follow. Because of the multiple propagation paths, some of the light may take one path, while other light that makes up our pulse may take other paths (think of the light as rays, or particles). This results in a phenomena called *modal dispersion*. Modal dispersion results in spreading of the pulse and ultimately limits the distance and data rate that can be achieved with multimode fiber.

Fibre Channel links based on 50 μm multimode optical fiber use a short wavelength laser operating at 850 nanometers (nm.) as the light source (this is in the red region and visible to the human eye). The low-cost shortwave laser is based on laser diodes developed for use in compact disc (CD) players and benefits from the production volumes associated with that market.

At higher data rates, the distance capability of the 50 μm multimode fiber is limited by the modal dispersion of the fiber. Because the effect of the dispersion is cumulative with distance, the longer the distance, the greater the accumulated dispersion. As the pulse widths are reduced due to higher data rates, less dispersion is tolerable and the distance must be reduced. Because of this, there are no long distance links associated with multimode optical fibers.

An improved version of 50 μm multimode optical fiber, called OM-3 or high-bandwidth fiber, provides improved distance capabilities at higher data rates. Most new installations will install OM-3 fiber to take advantage of the improved performance.

4.2.3 62.5 Micrometer Multimode Optical Links

The 62.5 μm multimode fiber variants were included to accommodate installations that had this type of optical fiber already installed. Due to the increased modal dispersion, and corresponding distance reduction associated with 62.5 μm multimode fiber, 50 μm multimode fiber is preferred for new installations operating at data rates in excess of 25 MB/s.

Fibre Channel links based on 62.5 μm multimode fiber use a short wavelength laser operating at 850 nanometers (nm.) as the light source.

At higher data rates, the distance capability of the 62.5 μm multimode fiber becomes is by the loss of optical power due to the mismatch of transmitter and receiver components and the optical fiber (transmitters and receivers are designed for 50 μm fibers) combined with the increased modal dispersion of the fiber. Due to the modal dispersion characteristics of this fiber, there are no long distance links.

4.3 Key Optical Specifications

There are several key specifications for optical links. This section provides a brief discussion of some of the more important characteristics. The reader should consult the latest standards for detailed specifications for each of the optical variants.

4.3.1 Wavelength and Spectral Purity

The output generated by laser diodes is subject to manufacturing variations, and it is necessary to specify a range of wavelengths to accommodate normal variations. This is specified by the *spectral center* entry the optical link specifications. In addition to the center wavelength of the laser, the standards also specify the optical purity of the signal. While lasers are excellent sources of light, they are not perfect and do emit a narrow range of wavelengths. The acceptable range is specified by the RMS Spectral Width.

4.3.2 Transmitter Optical Specifications

Applications using lasers need to consider the potential for damage to the eye should a user look into the transmitter, or end of a cable connected to an operating laser. To ensure no eye damage can occur, all single-mode links limit the optical power to a level below the accepted safety threshold. Such devices are categorized as Class 1 laser devices in accordance with IEC 825 that specifies laser safety requirements. Note that this use of the term "Class 1" is not related to Fibre Channel's Class-1 service.

The optical power is specified by the *launched power*. This parameter has both a maximum value (necessary to ensure compliance with safety requirements) and minimum value (necessary to ensure distance capabilities) specified. Intermediate distance variants have a relaxed minimum power specification because less optical energy is lost due to attenuation in the link.

When the laser is turned off to send a "0" bit, it may still continue to emit some amount of optical energy. The ratio of the average optical energy in a "1" bit to that of a "0" bit over a random pattern of bits is specified by the *Extinction Ratio* parameter.

The relative intensity noise, RIN_{12}, specifies the amount of laser noise relative to the average optical power.

4.3.3 Eye Opening and Jitter

The final two characteristics specified for the transmitter are the eye opening (see *Signal Quality, Jitter, and the Eye Diagram* on page 47) and the amount of deterministic jitter.

4.3.4 Receiver Sensitivity

The receiver requires a minimum amount of signal to reliably detect the signal and meet the required bit-error rate. The minimum receiver sensitivity specification defines the weakest signal that a receiver must be capable of receiving while still meeting the bit-error rate requirement. The maximum receiver sensitivity specification defines how strong a signal a receiver must be capable of handling without overloading and causing unacceptable errors.

4.3.5 Return Loss of Receiver

This parameter specifies the amount of the received optical energy that the receiver may reflect back into the fiber.

4.3.6 Cable Plant Losses

Some amount of the optical energy is lost in the cable plant (optical fiber and connectors due to dispersion and reflections).

4.3.7 Loss Budget

The difference between the transmitter minimum output and the receiver sensitivity minus the dispersion and reflection related penalties is the loss budget. This represents the amount of power that can be lost in the cable plant and still meet acceptable levels.

The loss budget accounts for signal loss through the optical fiber itself, as well as any associated splices. In addition, each connector between the transmitter and receiver also introduces a small amount of loss due to the imperfect mating of the two halves of the connector.

4.4 Optical Connectors

Fibre Channel initially adopted the industry standard SC optical connector for both single-mode and multimode optical links. The SC connector was already a standardized connector with multiple suppliers and Fibre Channel only specified those areas where the Fibre Channel requirements differed from the existing standard.

Figure 30 on page 57 provides a drawing of the SC connector. Because Fibre Channel links consist of two fibers, most applications use a duplex version of the SC plug and receptacle.

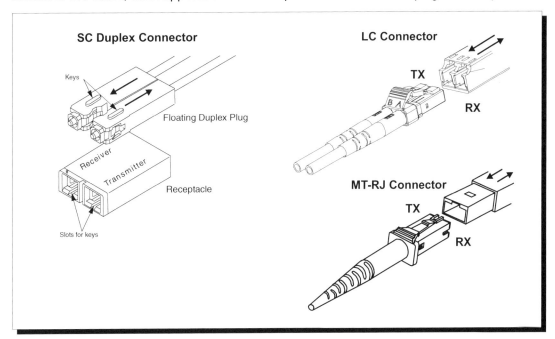

Figure 30. Optical Cable Connector

Since the original standard was adopted the industry has developed smaller form factor connectors. Rather than attempt to standardize a single small form factor optical connector, the Fibre Channel Physical Interface (FC-PI) standard instead specified connector requirements.

This leaves the ultimate choice of connector up to the manufacturer. Small form factor connectors referenced by the standard include the LC, MT-RJ, and SG connectors.

4.5 Troubleshooting Optical Links

While optical links are generally robust and reliable, failures do occur. In general failures will manifest themselves in one of two ways; an increased number of temporary errors (an excessive bit-error rate), or a catastrophic link failure.

4.5.1 Strategies for Catastrophic Failures

In the case of a failed transmitter, broken fiber, or failed receiver, no optical energy is transmitted or received, depending upon the failure. The problem is to determine which component has failed, and in the case of the fiber, where that failure is.

The obvious approach of seeing if any light is being transmitted or received won't work because the light is not visible to the human eye, and in the case of OFC components, the OFC circuit will shut down the laser transmitter anyway.

Optical Power Meter. To allow measurement of the amount of optical energy, an optical power meter is used. These typically consist of a fiber connector, calibrated detector, and the electronics necessary to process the signal and display the power level. Optical power meters are calibrated for use at one, or more, specific wavelengths (due to the response characteristics of the detector) and must be matched to the actual link under test. Power meters are a standard optical test item that are available from multiple sources priced from a few hundred dollars and up. Use of an optical power meter will determine if a signal is being sent by the transmitter and received at the receiver end of the fiber.

Optical Test Source. A companion to the optical power meter is the calibrated optical test source. The test source provides an optical signal at a specified wavelength and power level. As was the case with the power meter, the optical test source has to be matched to the fiber under test.

The optical power meter allows the technician to determine if the transmitter is sending a signal and whether that signal is being received at the far end of the fiber. But what can be done when the signal is entering the fiber, but not coming out at the other end? In many cases, it may be possible to substitute a known-good fiber, or use a spare fiber in place of the failed link. However, in some cases of long-distance links made up of several individual segments, this may not be a practical approach.

Optical Time Domain Reflectometer. When it is necessary to locate the point of failure within an optical link, an optical time domain reflectometer may be used. This sophisticated piece of test equipment that transmits an optical pulse down the fiber under test and monitors for reflected signals. By determining the time from the original pulse to any reflections, and knowing the speed through the fiber, the distance to the source of reflection can be determined.

Any discontinuity in the optical path results in the generation of reflections. These reflections travel back up the fiber in the direction opposite to information flow. The amplitude of the reflection is an indication of the degree of the discontinuity. Connectors and mechanical splices introduce minor discontinuities; a broken fiber is a major discontinuity.

4.5.2 Excessive Bit-Error Rates

In addition to the catastrophic problems caused by transmitter or receiver failures or a broken fiber, it is also possible to have links that are generating an excessive number of errors, or excessive bit-error rates (greater than one error per 10^{12} bits.

The sources of high bit-error rates are marginal transmitters, receivers, or links.

The transmitter must meet all the parameters specified for the associated media type. This includes the data rate, amplitude, wavelength, etc. Operation outside of the allowable values for any of these may cause high error rates. All of these parameters may be affected by temperature, power supply fluctuations, and component aging; all of them could conceivably be at their worst case values simultaneously. Laser diodes and LEDs, in particular, are both susceptible to aging with a resultant reduction in the amount of optical power generated.

Likewise, the receiver must be capable of reliable operation within the parameters specified for receivers including reliable operation at minimum signal levels and data rate extremes. The phase locked loop used in receivers is particularly sensitive to induced noise, such as might occur on the power leads to the phase locked loop.

In addition, the fiber optic link itself may contribute to errors. Link induced errors are usually the result in excessive loss between the transmitter and receiver. This loss can be caused by an improper installation, use of the wrong fiber during installation, interconnection of fibers of different types (for example, 50 µm and 62.5 µm multimode fiber), or a myriad of conditions that lead to excessive loss or reflections.

Fortunately, the optical test source and optical power meter can determine if the signal loss within the link falls within the acceptable loss budget. Probably one of the most common reasons for too much loss is contamination of the ends of the fibers or mating surfaces in the transmitter or receiver.

Cleaning Kit. Considering that the diameter of the fiber carrying the light is roughly equivalent to that of a human hair, it is evident that one particle of dust, or oil from a fingerprint may block or diffuse a significant amount of the available energy. For this reason, most fiber optic field support services have developed a cleaning kit and procedure for cleaning the ends of the cable and transmitter or receiver.

4.6 Chapter Summary

Fiber Optic Links

- Signals are sent through an optical fiber using pulses of light
  - The light is turned on for a "1"
  - The light is turned off for a "0"
- The distance capability is determined by
  - The amount of light injected into the fiber
  - Signal loss and pulse distortion in the fiber
  - The sensitivity of the receiver
- The long wavelength light (1300 nm./1550 nm.) used in Fibre Channel is infrared
  - Not visible to the human eye

Optical Fiber

- Optical fiber consists of:
  - A glass core that carries the light and is 9, 50, or 62.5 micrometers in diameter
  - The cladding, a layer of glass surrounding the core and keeps the light from escaping
  - A protective jacket that protects the fiber and provides strength
- There are two common types of optical fiber categorized by how light propagates through the fiber
  - Single-mode fiber
  - Multimode fiber

Optical Transmitters

- There are two common sources of light used
  - Lasers
  - LED
- Lasers are used for
  - High-speed links due to their faster switching rates
  - Long-distance links because of their higher light output
- LEDs are used for low-cost links over intermediate distances
  - They will not switch fast enough to go beyond about 25 MBs

Single-Mode Fiber

- Single-mode optical fiber is used for long distance links (in excess of 50 km.)
- The core diameter is very small, 9 micrometers
  - This results in a single propagation mode (path) through the fiber
  - All the light follows the same path
- Due to the manufacturing process and tolerances, this a more expensive fiber
- Lasers are always used as the transmitter
  - LEDs are not focused enough to inject sufficient optical power into a single-mode fiber

Multimode Fiber

- Multimode fiber is used for intermediate distance
- The core diameter is larger than single-mode, typically 50 or 62.5 micrometers
  - As a result, the light has multiple propagation modes (paths) through the fiber
  - The light may follow many different paths
- Due to the relaxed tolerances, this is a less expensive fiber
- Lasers or LEDs may be used as the transmitter
  - Lasers for high data rates and long distances
  - LEDs for lower data rates and intermediate distances

Modal Dispersion

- Multimode fiber allows the pulse to disperse over distance
  - Due to different parts of the light taking different paths through the fiber
  - Some paths are longer than other paths causing some of the light to arrive later
- This causes dispersion of the pulse
  - The leading and trailing edges are spread out
  - The pulse amplitude is reduced
- This effect limits the distance and data rate achievable with multimode fiber

Optical Connectors

■ The initial optical connector was the industry-standard SC connector
■ Usually a duplex configuration is used due to the two fibers
  • Transmit fiber
  • Receive fiber
■ The optical fibers crossover in the cable
■ The connector is keyed to prevent incorrect insertion

Small Form Factor Connectors

■ Recently, smaller form factor optical connectors have been developed
  • LC (seems to be the current leader)
  • MT-RJ
  • SG
■ Enables higher density switches, hubs, and ports
■ Current standards do not specify a single optical connector
  • Connector requirements are specified
  • Industry adoption will determine actual usage

5. Electrical Links

During early development of Fibre Channel, interest was focused on the use of optical interfaces due to their superior distance, data rate, and electrical noise immunity. Fibre Channel was viewed primarily as a system interface where the number of interfaces would be relatively small and span intermediate distances. As technology progressed, it became apparent that Fibre Channel could also be used as a device interface. In this type of application, the cost per connection was critical, while distance capabilities were secondary. A prime example of this type of application is a disk-storage subsystem that provides high data rates through the interconnection of a large number of individual disk drives, all relatively close together.

To accommodate the need for high-speed interfaces over short distances, Fibre Channel standards defined electrical links based on several different transmission line types. None of the electrical transmission lines can match the distance capabilities of optical fiber without the need for intermediate repeaters, but for many short distance applications, electrical connections may provide the most cost-effective solutions.

There are three types of electrical interfaces distinguished by the transmission line and modulation method; unbalanced transmission lines using coaxial cable and single-ended drivers and receivers, balanced transmission lines using twinaxial cable or shielded twisted pair and differential drivers and receivers and FC-BaseT links using unshielded twisted pair.

5.1 Single-Ended Links

Coaxial cable consists of a center conductor that carries the signal, an insulating layer, and an outer shield. The shield confines the electrical signals to the cable and provides a ground return path for the electrical circuit. Coaxial cable is an unbalanced transmission line that is driven with a single-ended electrical driver. A one bit corresponds to the state where the center conductor is positive (above a certain threshold) with respect to the shield. An example of an unbalanced transmission line is shown in Figure 31. While single-ended links are defined in the standard, they are not commonly used in products.

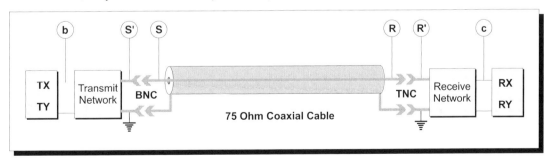

Figure 31. *Single-Ended, Unbalanced Link*

5.2 Differential Links

Electrical signals can be sent using balanced transmission lines. In this type of transmission line, two wires carry the signal in each direction as shown in Figure 32. The majority of electrical links in Fibre Channel products use differential signaling. In general, balanced transmission lines can be either shielded or unshielded depending upon the application. In Fibre Channel, all balanced transmission lines are shielded to prevent excessive signal radiation.

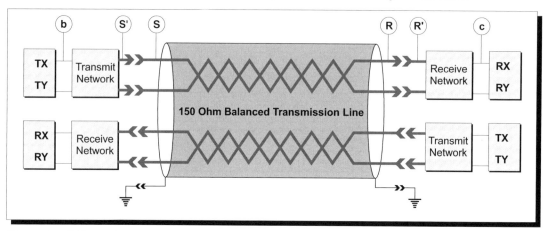

Figure 32. Differential, Balanced Link

Differential signaling uses two drivers and two receivers, one for each of the conductors in the pair. Whenever one of the conductors is driven to the positive signal level, the other is driven to the negative signal level. When transmitting a bit of the opposite polarity, the levels are reversed. To identify the two conductors, one is labeled "+" and the other "-". When the "+" conductor is positive with respect to the "-" conductor, the transmission line is carrying a one bit. When the "-" conductor is positive with respect to the "+" conductor, the transmission line is carrying a zero bit. This is shown in Figure 33 on page 65 (this example shows a 600 mv. peak-to-peak signal swing, the standards specify a minimum voltage swing of 300 mv. and a maximum of either 800 or 1000 mv. depending upon the signaling rate).

Differential signaling provides several advantages when compared to single-ended signaling:

- Improved noise immunity: Noise that is coupled into both signal lines is cancelled out at the receiver. The behavior is referred to as common-mode rejection.

- Lower signal radiation: Less signal is radiated from the cable because energy radiated from one conductor is cancelled out by that radiated from the other conductor.

- Low voltage signaling: The signal swing is normally smaller than when using single-ended links because the voltage swings on the two conductors are additive at the receiver.

- Less power and heat dissipation: The smaller voltage swing translates into less power consumption and head dissipation.

- Higher signaling rates: Lower voltage swings make higher signaling rates possible.

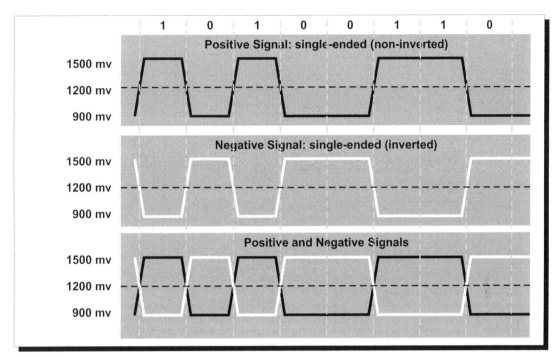

Figure 33. Differential Signaling Example

5.2.1 Signal Coupling and Equalization

Electrical links use capacitive coupling to couple the signal into, and out of, the link. There is no DC connection between the actual transmitter and receiver. An example of transmit and receive networks for use with balanced transmission lines is shown in Figure 34. While this example includes an equalizer, this may or may not be necessary depending upon the length, and characteristics, of the transmission line. Equalization is discussed in more detail in *Receiver Equalization* on page 68.

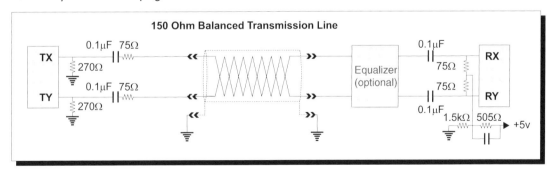

Figure 34. Differential Transmit and Receive Networks

Due to the wide variations in cable performance, maximum electrical cable distances are not specified by the standard. Rather, transmit and receive signal criteria and cable characteristics determine the maximum distance. The maximum distance for 1.0625 Gbps differential links is approximately 30 meters, falling to about 15 meters for 2.125 Gbps links and 7.5 meters for 4.25 Gbps links.

5.2.2 Cable and Connector Losses

Figure 35 shows a measured signal waveform at the end of a 1 meter electrical cable. This example shows a good eye opening that does not violate the mask and provides the receiver with a wide margin for sampling the received bit stream.

Compare the signal in Figure 35 to the one shown in Figure 36. This is the same signal at the end of a 10 meter electrical cable. As can be seen from this example, there is significant closure of the eye opening due to the loss introduced by the cable and connectors. Because of the signal degradation caused by the cable and connectors, the received signal shown in Figure 36 violates the eye mask and may result in an excessive bit error rate.

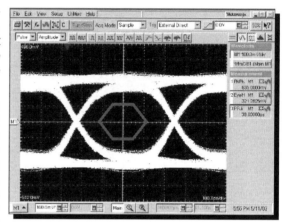

Figure 35. Eye Diagram (1 Meter Cable)

Failure to meet the required bit error rate may result in an excessive number of transmission errors and operational failures or degraded performance.

Electrical cables (and printed circuit board wiring) and connectors cause signal loss between the transmitter and receiver. The amount of signal loss is determined by the characteristics of the cables and connectors used. When the cable and connector loss is known, along with the transmitter output and required receiver input, the maximum allowable cable length can be determined.

There are two primary methods for countering signal loss and degradation caused by an electrical cable plant.

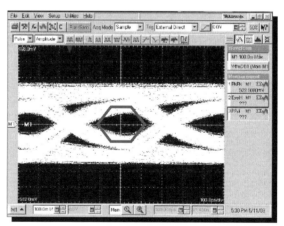

Figure 36. Eye Diagram (10 Meter Cable)

- Transmitter de-emphasis changes the transmitted signal waveform to counter the expected interconnect loss.
- Receiver equalization changes the interpretation of the received signal realizing it has been altered by the interconnect.

Chapter 5. Electrical Links

5.2.3 Transmitter De-Emphasis

When a signal is transmitted via an electrical cable, energy is stored by the cable capacitance. When a series of consecutive bits of the same polarity are transmitted, the stored charge accumulates and interferes with the next bit of the opposite polarity (the next bit must discharge the energy stored by the cable capacitance). This reduces the amplitude of the first bit following a transition as shown by the lower set of waveforms in Figure 37 (the gray band in this figure represents the receiver threshold). Note how the amplitude of the final zero bit may not be sufficient for reliable detection at the receiver.

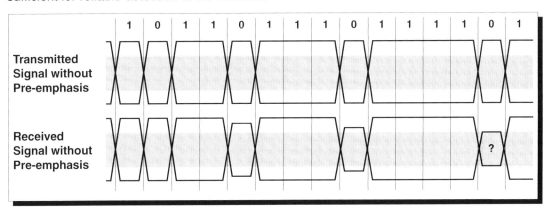

Figure 37. Transmit Signal Without De-Emphasis

Transmitter de-emphasis compensates for this effect by transmitting the first bit after a transition at full amplitude and reducing the amplitude of subsequent bits to reduce the stored charge in the cable as shown in the top set of waveforms in Figure 38. The lower set of waveforms show the resulting signal with transmitter de-emphasis and intersymbol interference. All of the bits are now above the receiver threshold, even the final zero bit after the four one bits.

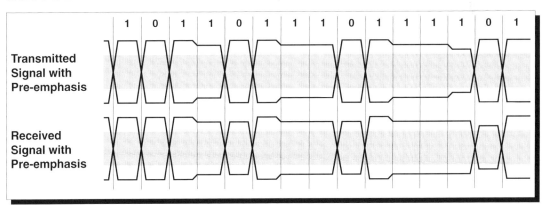

Figure 38. Transmit Signal With De-Emphasis

Figure 39 shows a measured signal waveform at the end of a 1 meter electrical cable when transmitter de-emphasis is used (this is the same cable plant as shown in Figure 35 on page 66). In the figure, you can clearly see how the first bit following a transition has a higher amplitude than subsequent bits.

The amount of de-emphasis required depends on the characteristics of the electrical link. Implementations supporting de-emphasis may provide just a single-level of de-emphasis or multiple levels as was shown in Figure 38 on page 67. Implementations that supporting electrical links may provide a fixed amount of de-emphasis, or allow the behavior to be varied depending on the link's characteristics.

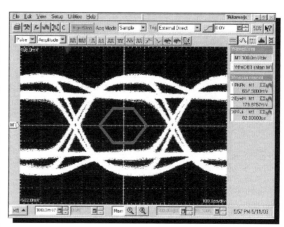

Figure 39. De-emphasis (1 Meter Cable)

Figure 40 shows the same signal at the end of a 10 meter electrical cable as was shown earlier but now with transmitter de-emphasis. Compare the eye opening in this figure to the one shown in Figure 36 on page 66. The increased opening of the eye is due to the de-emphasis applied to the transmitted signal.

5.2.4 Receiver Equalization

Receiver equalization is another strategy to improve signal quality. Receiver equalization can be used in conjunction with transmitter de-emphasis or by itself.

Receiver equalization amplifies higher frequency signal components in order to offset the high-frequency attenuation of the cable.

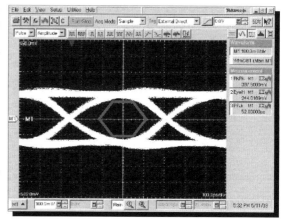

Figure 40. De-emphasis (10 Meter Cable)

With receiver equalization, the receiver amplifies (boosts) input frequencies near the signaling rate while attenuating higher and lower frequencies. This results in increased amplitude when a bit transition occurs. As with transmitter de-emphasis, the goal is to compensate for the cable attenuation associated with bit transitions. Equalization can potentially recover signals when no eye is apparent at the receiver. An example of receiver equalization is shown in Figure 41 on page 69.

One advantage of receiver equalization is that it can automatically adapt to the cabling environment. On the other hand, it may also amplify noise, and because equalization is applied after the signal is received, it may not be possible to observe the resulting received signal.

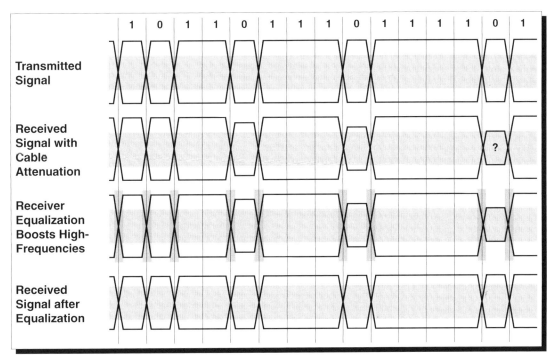

Figure 41. Receiver Equalization

5.3 FC BaseT

To provide an even lower-cost electrical link, the standards committee developed an electrical variant based on the popular Ethernet category 5e (enhanced) or better unshielded twisted pair. This variant is referred to as FC BaseT and uses the link configuration shown in Figure 42. The hybrids shown in the figure couple the signal into, and out of, the cable and isolate the transmit signal from the incoming receive signal.

Because of the relatively low bandwidth provided by each signal pair in the cable, bidirectional signaling is used on each signal pair in the cable (the same wires are used for both transmitting and receiving). In addition, a more sophisticated modulation method, called Pulse Amplitude Modulation (PAM-8), is used. Both of these techniques were pioneered by the development of 1 Gbps Ethernet (1000BASE-T) and have been proven in the field.

36-bit words (eight data bits and the D/K indication) are transcoded into a 33-bit word consisting of one control bit (D/K indication) and 32-data bits. The 33-bit word is then converted into three PAM-8 symbols. Each PAM-8 symbol corresponds to 2.75 information bits. Doing a bit of math, (2.75 bits per symbol) x (3 symbols per word) x (4 wire pairs) = 33 bit word.

The technical details of the PAM-8 encoding and modulation are beyond the scope of this book and the reader should consult the Fibre Channel FC-BaseT standard for detailed information and descriptions.

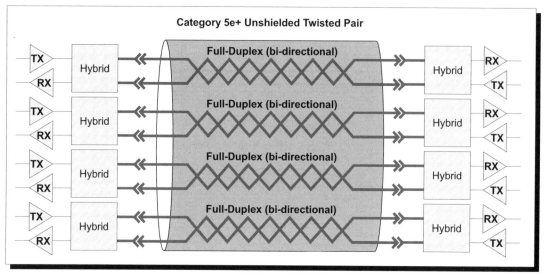

Figure 42. FC BaseT Electrical Link

The expected distances for the different types of Ethernet cabling are listed in Table 3.

Signaling Rate	Cat 5e	Cat 6	Cat 6a
1 Gbps	100 m.	100 m.	100 m.
2 Gbps	60 m.	70 m.	100 m.
4 Gbps	30 m. (expected)	40 m.	100 m.

Table 3. FC BaseT Distances

5.4 Electrical Connectors

Multiple electrical connectors have been specified by the standards to accommodate the different transmission line types and various cost and performance objectives. Electrical connectors are shown in Figure 43 on page 71.

5.4.1 Single-Ended Electrical Connectors

Single-ended transmission lines use coaxial cable and matching connectors. Two different styles of coaxial connectors have been approved. The first is the familiar BNC connector and its threaded equivalent, the TNC connector. The BNC connector is used on the transmit end of the cable, the TNC on the receive end. To provide a full duplex link, two cables are required.

The second style of coaxial cable connector is the industry standard 50Ω SMA. When this style of connector is used, both ends of the cable are terminated with a male connector. Because this arrangement does not provide polarization of the transmit and receive signals, any incorrect connection must not result in damage to any component in the system.

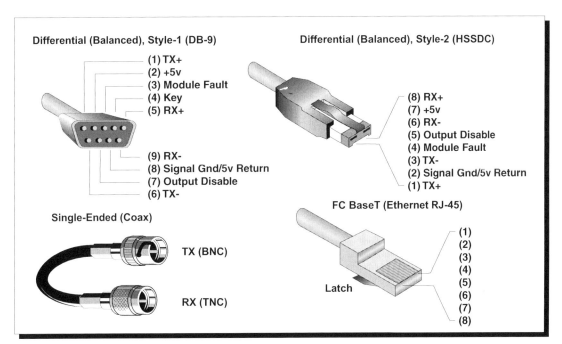

Differential (Balanced), Style-1 (DB-9)

(1) TX+
(2) +5v
(3) Module Fault
(4) Key
(5) RX+

(9) RX-
(8) Signal Gnd/5v Return
(7) Output Disable
(6) TX-

Single-Ended (Coax)

TX (BNC)

RX (TNC)

Differential (Balanced), Style-2 (HSSDC)

(8) RX+
(7) +5v
(6) RX-
(5) Output Disable
(4) Module Fault
(3) TX-
(2) Signal Gnd/5v Return
(1) TX+

FC BaseT (Ethernet RJ-45)

(1)
(2)
(3)
(4)
(5)
(6)
(7)
(8)

Latch

Figure 43. Connectors for Electrical Interfaces

5.4.2 Differential Electrical Connectors

Differential transmission line, either shielded twisted pair or twinax (twinaxial) cables contain four active conductors and a shield. Between the two ends of the cable, a crossover occurs so that the transmit pair at one end of the cable is connected to the receive pair at the other end.

The initial connector specified for use with balanced transmission lines was the industry standard DB-9 connector conforming to IEC 807-3. This connector is referred to as the style-1 connector. Pins 1 and 6 are used for the transmit pair and pins 5 and 9 for the receive pair. The connector shell is connected to the cable shield.

To provide a higher-density connector options, FC-PH-3 added a second connector, referred to as the Style-2 connector in the standards. This connector is based on the AMP High-Speed Serial Data Connector (HSSDC) design.

5.4.3 FC BaseT Connector

FC BaseT links use the standard RJ-45 Ethernet connector and category 5e, 6 or 6a cables.

5.4.4 Fibre Channel SCA-2 Disk Drive Connector

Fibre Channel disk drives use an integrated 40-position SCA-2 connector. The connector contains all of the drive's signal and power connections in a single connector. This connector is designed for hot swap applications and provides guide pins with early ground mating for ESD discharge. A photograph of a Fibre Channel disk drive and the SCA-2 connector is shown in Figure 44 on page 72.

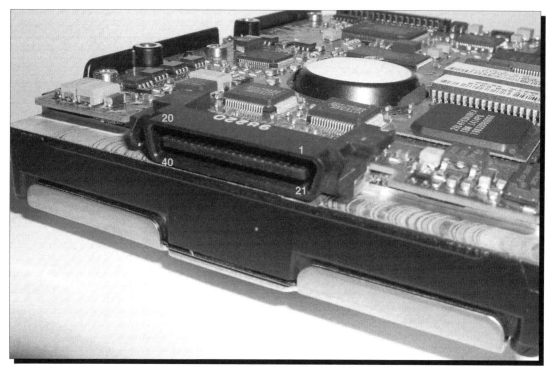

Figure 44. SCA-2 40-Pin Disk Connector

In addition to the power, ground and Fibre Channel signal lines, the connector contains several control signals. Table 4 on page 73 lists the SCA-2 connector pinout.

ENBL Bypass CH1 and CH2. These signals enable to drive to control an external port bypass circuit (PBC). These signals are used on an arbitrated loop to bypass a non-functional drive.

Power Control. When this optional signal is asserted by a backplane and supported by the drive, 5v and 12v power is supplied to the drive circuitry. When negated, power is removed from the drive circuitry.

Ready LED. The Ready LED signal is used to indicate the state of the device.

1. If the drive is not mated, the signal is not asserted and the LED is off.

2. If the drive is mated, but not spinning, the signal is asserted when a SCSI command or Task Management Function is received by the drive. The LED is mostly off but presents and indication when a command is received.

Pin	Signal Name	Pin	Signal Name
1	-EN Bypass Port A	21	12v Charge
2	12v	22	Ground
3	12v	23	Ground
4	12v	24	+Port A_In
5	-Parallel ESI	25	-Port A_In
6	-Drive Present (connected to drive's ground)	26	Ground
7	Ready LED out (bidirectional signal)	27	+Port B_In
8	Power_Control	28	-Port B_In
9	Start_1 / Mated	29	Ground
10	Start_2 / Mated	30	+Port A_Out
11	-EN Bypass Port B	31	-Port A_Out
12	SEL_6 / -EFW	32	Ground
13	SEL_5 / -P_ESI_5	33	+Port B_Out
14	SEL_4 / -P_ESI_4	34	-Port B_Out
15	SEL_3 / -P_ESI_3	35	Ground
16	Fault LED Out (bidirectional signal)	36	SEL_2 / -P_ESI_2
17	DEV_CTRL_CODE_2	37	SEL_1 / -P_ESI_1
18	DEV_CTRL_CODE_1	38	SEL_0 / -P_ESI_0
19	5v	39	DEV_CTRL_CODE_0
20	5v	40	5v Charge

Table 4. FC Disk 40-Pin SCA-2 Connector Pinout

3. If the drive is mated and in the process of spinning up, the signal is asserted so that the LED alternates between on and off at a 0.5 second rate.

4. If the drive is mated and ready, the signal is asserted continuously, except when a SCSI command or Task Management Function is received. The LED is mostly on but presents and indication when a command is received.

Start / Mated Controls. The motor Start / Mated signals control the drive motor spin-up behavior as described in Table 5 on page 74. A backplane may optionally assert case 1 shown in the table to signal the drive to prepare for removal.

Parallel ESI. The Parallel ESI is an optional input specifying how the drive should interpret the SEL_ID inputs. When this signal is asserted, the SEL_ID inputs are interpreted as enclosure status information. When this signal is not asserted, or not supported, the SEL_ID inputs are interpreted as the Hard Address to be requested during loop initialization.

Drive_CTRL_CODE. These inputs provide encoded values used to control the drive and signal the link rate. Following completion of power-on reset and a 250 msec. delay, the

Case	Start_2/Mated	Start_1/Mated	Behavior
1	OPEN	OPEN	Drive is not mated - no spin-up will occur.
2	OPEN	GROUND	Drive is mated. After a 250 msec. delay, the drive will spin up after a SCSI START command is received.
3	GROUND	OPEN	Drive is mated. After a 250 msec. delay, the drive will spin up after a delay of 12 x the modulo(8) value of the SEL)ID.
4	GROUND	GROUND	Drive is mated. After a 250 msec. delay, the drive will spin up after completion of it reset and POST functions.

Table 5. Start/ Mated Signal Behavior

drive samples these inputs to determine the link rate. Subsequently, it samples these inputs at least once a second to detect a changed link rate of power failure warning.

Value	Behavior
7	1.0625 Gbit operation
6	2.125 Gbit operation
5	4.250 Gbit operation
4	8.500 Gbit operation
3:1	Reserved
0	Power Failure Warning

Table 6. Start/ Mated Signal Behavior

5.5 RFI and EMI Considerations

Due to the high frequencies associated with Fibre Channel links, attention must be given to the potential for radio frequency interference (RFI) resulting from signal leakage of Fibre Channel cables, connectors, and associated logic. Various regulatory agencies have set strict standards on the amount of energy emitted at specified frequencies. The data rate of a Fibre Channel link is rich in radio frequency components. The signal contains strong harmonic components, especially the odd-order harmonics. Balanced transmission lines offer superior performance in regards to radiated energy because the signals in the two lines tend to cancel one another and it is not surprising balanced transmission lines predominate.

All electrical cables specified for use in Fibre Channel are shielded to limit the amount of radiated energy. In most cases, a single level of shielding is not sufficient to adequately contain the leakage below acceptable levels and most external cables are double shielded. Another potential source of radio frequency signal leakage is the connectors associated with the cables. Grounding of the cable shield is accomplished by the shell of the connector. The DB-9 connector was not originally designed for use at these frequencies and the shell may not provide complete grounding around its circumference. In addition, the relatively large plastic center insulator (that holds the contacts) results in another potential source of leakage.

5.6 Chapter Summary

Electrical Links

- Optical fiber got much of the early attention in Fibre Channel
- However, there is significant use of electrical links
  - Electrical links are lower cost than optical
  - Electrical links are easier to use in many applications, such as disk arrays
- The distance achievable with Electrical links is less than optical
- Users need to trade off the cost savings versus the distance limitations

Electrical Links

- There are three kinds of electrical links
- Single-ended links
  - Use standard coaxial cable
  - Single-ended drivers and receivers
  - Single-ended links are not generally used due to RFI problems
- Differential links
  - Uses balanced transmission lines
  - Shielded twisted pair, twinax cable (a coaxial cable with two center conductors)
  - Differential drivers and receivers
- FC-BaseT links

FC BaseT

- FC-BaseT completed in late 2006
- Uses existing Ethernet cables and connectors
  - Provides a low-cost cabling infrastructure
  - Familiar to network installers
  - Users can install cables and connectors
- FC BaseT uses a different modulation scheme
  - 8-Level Pulse Amplitude Modulation (PAM-8)
  - Each PAM-8 symbol = 2.75 bits
  - Each word consists of 12 symbols
- Symbols are sent via four bidirectional signal pairs in the cable
- Technology is based on Ethernet 1000BASE-T

Cable and Connector Losses

- Cables and connectors cause signal loss and distortion
  - Cables attenuate high-frequencies
  - Cable and connector losses reduces signal levels
  - Cable capacitance causes inter-symbol interference
  - Can result in an excessive error rate
- Two main approaches to countering cable loss and distortion
  - Transmitter de-emphasis
  - Equalization

Transmitter De-Emphasis

- Modify the transmit signal waveform to compensate for cable distortion
  - Cable capacitance stores charge as bits are sent
  - More consecutive bits of the same polarity, the greater the stored charge
  - Next bit of opposite polarity must overcome this stored charge
- Send first bit after a transition at full amplitude
  - Send subsequent bits at a lower amplitude
  - Reduces the amount of stored energy a bit must overcome

Equalization

- Electrical cable plant causes high-frequency signal loss
- Equalization compensates by either:
  - Introducing a corresponding amount of low-frequency attenuation (done in the cable), or
  - Boosting the high-frequency components of the signal (done in the receiver)
- Improves the eye opening for marginal signal conditions

Coupling

- Electrical links can be either capacitor or transformer coupled
- Capacitive coupling:
  - Is lower cost and provides higher signal levels
  - Although, may limited to inside an enclosure
- Transformer coupling:
  - Provides better noise immunity
  - May be used outside the enclosure

Electrical Connectors

- Different style connectors are used for single-ended and differential interfaces
- Single-ended uses coaxial connectors:
  - BNC and TNC
  - SMA connector
- Differential connections use:
  - DB-9 (most common at 1 Gbps)
  - High-speed serial data connector (HSSDC)
  - SCA-2 connector for disk drives
- FC BaseT
  - Standard RJ-45 Ethernet connector

RFI and EMI

- Electrical interfaces create radio frequency interference (RFI)
- Regulatory agencies (FCC) limit the amount of RF that a product can emit
- Designers need to be sensitive to RFI issues due to the high-frequency components associated with Fibre Channel's data rates
  - Fundamental frequency is 531 MHz (for a 1.0625 Gbps link)
- Also, electrical transmission lines are susceptible to induced interference (EMI)
- Careful attention to layout and shielding is necessary

6. Speed Negotiation

With the arrival of 200-megabyte (2.125 gigabit) Fibre Channel ports, the standards committee formed a study group to address backward speed compatibility with 100-megabyte (1.0625 gigabit) ports. As with other Fibre Channel capabilities, the goal was to define a procedure allowing multi-speed ports to automatically negotiate the highest mutually supported speed, as well as enabling a multi-speed port to correctly detect and operate with a single-speed port.

As work progressed, several objectives were defined for the speed negotiation process. One was that the process should allow a firmware-driven implementation to arrive at the highest mutually supported speed within a reasonable amount of time (two to three seconds). Because speed negotiation only occurs when a link becomes active, negotiation time is not a factor in link performance (although it does contribute to the port initialization time).

While it was originally hoped to find a process that would work on a Fibre Channel arbitrated loop, all the proposed schemes resulted in an unacceptable time for all ports to converge to a common speed. Consequently, speed negotiation is limited to a single direct link between two Fibre Channel ports as shown in Figure 45 (see *Arbitrated Loop Considerations* on page 88 for a discussion of how this scheme may be used, with limitations, in a loop topology).

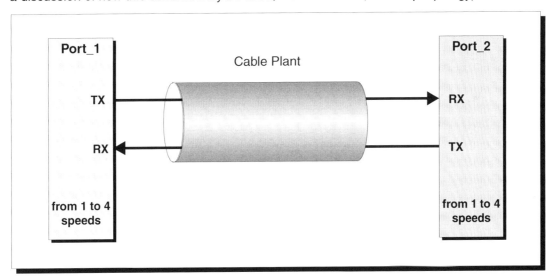

Figure 45. Speed Negotiation Configuration

The two ports involved in the speed negotiation can by any legal combination of N_Ports, NL_Ports, F_Ports, FL_Ports, E_Ports, B_Ports, or hub ports. In order to successfully complete the speed negotiation procedure, there must be at least one common speed that permits functional operation between the two ports. Functionality at the final speed is required of the ports, serializers/deserializers (SERDES), transceivers, physical media devices (GBICs, MIAs, etc.), cables, connectors, converters, and any other components in the path.

One of the original goals was to define a process that would allow the ports to successfully negotiate the highest mutually supported speed from up to 10 different speeds. Again, as work progressed, it became clear that the time required to examine this many speeds resulted in an unacceptable convergence time. Consequently, the maximum number of speeds supported by the negotiation process was reduced to four. This is not to imply that both ports must support four speeds, or even more than one speed. It simply means that the algorithm only allows for examining up to four speeds at each port. In fact, the four speeds examined do not even have to be the same four speeds at the two ports.

It was initially proposed that all ports be required to support a common speed that could be used to perform speed negotiation prior to adopting a higher speed between the ports (e.g., 1.0625 gigabits per second). This was rejected because it would require all future Fibre Channel ports to support that common speed, even if it would never be used in the operational environment. This proposed requirement became particularly objectionable in the case of 10-gigabit ports. Consequently, the suggestion to require a common speed was dropped.

The next round of proposals suggested using firmware to generate low-frequency signals (or "tones") to convey speed information between the two ports. However, it soon became clear that tone-based signaling would not work due to the bandpass filters in the receive circuitry of Fibre Channel ports (bandpass filters remove extraneous noise outside the frequency spectrum of the Fibre Channel signaling). Consequently, the speed negotiation process had to rely on the ability of a port to successfully acquire transmission word synchronization in order to detect that a given speed is supported.

Using transmission word synchronization as the criteria for determining speed raises the further question: How long should synchronization be required to decide that a link is functional at a given speed? Waiting long enough to verify the bit-error rate (1×10^{-12} bits) would take over 16 minutes on a 1.0625 gigabit link (and this would only provide one sample). Consequently, the criteria for successful operation during the speed negotiation process is error-free transmission word synchronization for a minimum of 1,000 consecutive transmission words. This criteria is significantly less stringent than the bit-error rate specification for a Fibre Channel link, but is considered sufficient for the speed negotiation process.

To avoid excessive negotiations, it was decided that once two ports had successfully negotiated a speed, they would not attempt negotiation again unless a link failure was detected or the ports were directed to repeat the speed negotiation by higher-level processes. It is possible for the speed negotiation process to complete and the ports begin operation at a given speed, then later determined that the link is not capable of meeting the bit-error rate requirements at that speed. It is also possible that conditions could improve such that higher-speed operation may become possible. In either case, any decision to adopt a lower speed or attempt to negotiate a higher speed is left up to higher-level processes.

The speed negotiation algorithm that was finally agreed upon is described in this chapter and is in the process of being standardized in the Fibre Channel Framing and Signaling (FC-FS) document (reference 30 in the Bibliography on page 640).

6.1 Speed Negotiation Procedures

The speed negotiation process involves four major elements: a signal detection procedure, a Negotiate Master procedure, a Negotiate Follow procedure, and an optional Slow Wait procedure. Each of these procedures is described in the following sections.

6.1.1 Receive and Transmit Speed Stepping

The signal detection and speed negotiation procedures both rely on acquisition of synchronization with the incoming received signal.

Because a port has no way of knowing the speed of the incoming receive signal, it simply steps through all of its supported receive speeds. Each speed is sampled long enough to acquire synchronization with the received signal if the speeds match. In order to allow the sampling to be controlled by firmware, the sample time is allowed to vary from 2 to 30 msec. (this time is referred to as the receive cycle time, or t_rxcycl).

A port also has no way of knowing if the other port is capable of receiving at any specific speed. If the port transmits at a speed the other port is not capable of receiving, the other port will not be able to acquire synchronization at that speed. To enable the other port to acquire synchronization, a port steps through all of its transmit speeds. To ensure the receiving port has sufficient time to acquire synchronization, each transmit speed step (referred to as the transmit cycle time, or t_txcycl) must be long enough for the receiver to complete up to four full receive samples (the number of speeds supported by this algorithm). To ensure that time for four complete samples is provided at each speed, the transmit cycle time is set to 154 msec. which is slightly greater than five receive sample times (this is because the transmit speed could change during the first receive sample, before receive synchronization is acquired).

6.1.2 Wait for Signal

Before speed negotiation can begin, each port must determine it is receiving a valid signal. Some implementations provide an indication called Loss-of-Signal (LOS) to indicate that no signal is present. However, other implementations do not provide this indication and it is necessary to detect the presence of a valid signal by attempting to acquire synchronization.

To detect if a valid signal is present, the port steps its receiver through each supported speeds (beginning with its highest speed) to determine if it can acquire synchronization at any speed. Each speed is sampled from 2 to 30 msec. (receive cycle time, or t_rxcycl, as mentioned earlier) to determine if synchronization can be acquired. While performing this receive sampling, the port also steps its transmitter through each of its transmit speeds (also beginning with the highest speed). Each transmit speed is sent for 154 msec. (transmit cycle time, or t_txcycl). This provides a signal for the attached port at the other end of the link to attempt to acquire synchronization as it steps through its receive speeds. By maintaining each transmit speed for t_txcycl, enough time is allowed for the receiver at the other end of the link to complete four full receive speed samples. Figure 46 on page 80 is a flowchart of the Wait for Signal procedure.

Consider the case shown in Figure 47 on page 81. In this example, assume Port_1 is capable of operating at speeds 8, 4, 2, and 1 and Port_2 is capable of operating at speeds 2 and 1, but not speeds 4 or 3. Port_1 begins transmitting at its highest rate, speed 8, Port_2 begins trans-

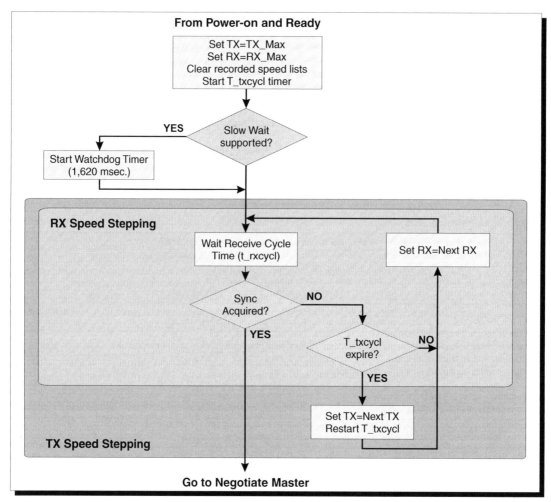

From Power-on and Ready

Set TX=TX_Max
Set RX=RX_Max
Clear recorded speed lists
Start T_txcycl timer

Slow Wait
supported?

YES

Start Watchdog Timer
(1,620 msec.)

RX Speed Stepping

Wait Receive Cycle
Time (t_rxcycl)

Set RX=Next RX

Sync
Acquired?

NO

YES

T_txcycl
expire?

NO

YES

Set TX=Next TX
Restart T_txcycl

TX Speed Stepping

Go to Negotiate Master

Figure 46. Wait for Signal Flowchart

mitting at its highest rate, speed 2. Port_1 attempts to acquire synchronization at its highest receive speed (speed 8) but is not successful.

After the receive cycle time (t_rxcycl), Port_1 tries its next highest speed (speed 4) but is still not able to acquire synchronization. It then tries its next highest speed (speed 2), but by now Port_2 has shifted to a lower transmit speed (speed 1). Finally, Port_1 tries its final receive speed (speed 1) and acquires synchronization. Port_1 knows there is a valid signal present from Port_2 (although it has not yet determined the highest mutually supported speed).

Port_2 also attempts to acquire synchronization at its highest supported speed (speed 2) but is not successful because Port_1 is transmitting at speed 8. It then tries its next highest sup-

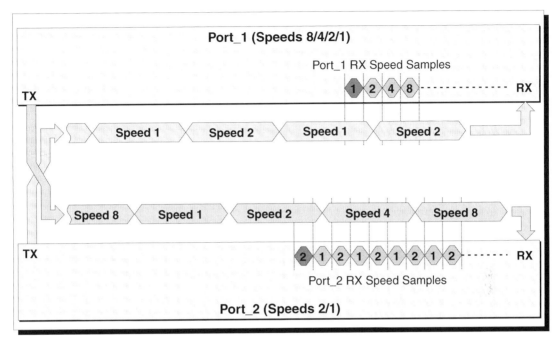

Figure 47. Receive Sampling in the Wait for Signal Procedure

ported speed (speed 1) but this is not successful either. From Port_2's perspective, no valid signal has yet been detected. Port_2 continues to step through its receive speeds and eventually detects a valid signal at speed 2. At this point, both ports have detected valid signal and the process continues as described in *Negotiate Master* on page 82.

What happens if the other port is not connected or powered on? There is no signal present at the receive input and the port is unable to acquire synchronization at any speed. The port simply stays in the signal-detection process stepping through its transmit and receive speeds until a valid signal is detected.

Continually stepping through the transmit and receive speeds while attempting to detect a valid signal creates a potential problem. The speed negotiation procedure was designed so it could be implemented in firmware. When this is done, the processor is executing the procedure by controlling the hardware and timing the various events. This processing could have an adverse effect on the processor's ability to service other tasks.

For example, a disk drive might have two Fibre Channel ports. One port is connected and functional, while the other port is disconnected. The disconnected port stays in Wait for Signal until it detects a valid signal. The time spent in Wait for Signal on the disconnected port could affect performance on the functional port. To lessen the burden on the processor, the speed negotiation procedure provides an option called Slow Wait. The details of this option are described in *Negotiation Slow Wait (Optional)* on page 86.

6.1.3 Speed Negotiation Watchdog Timer

Due to errors or marginal link conditions, there may be times when portions of the speed negotiation process fail to complete. To prevent hung conditions, a watchdog timer is implemented during the Negotiate Master and Negotiate Follow processes.

During the Negotiate Master and Negotiate Follow processes, it is expected that synchronization will be detected periodically because the ports are stepping through supported receive speeds. The watchdog timer is restarted when synchronization is detected. If synchronization is not detected for an extended period, the watchdog timer expires and causes the negotiation process to restart.

The time allocated for the watchdog timer is 1,620 msec. (t_wddly) which is sufficient for the negotiation process to make two complete passes though up to four speeds.

6.1.4 Negotiate Master

Once a port successfully acquires synchronization as described in *Wait for Signal* on page 79 (or Loss-of-Signal is inactive), it begins the actual speed negotiation by entering the Negotiate Master process. During the Negotiate Master process, one of the ports is selected to step through its transmit speeds while attempting to find the highest mutually supported speed. The other port enters the Negotiate Follow process and attempts to track (follow) the speeds transmitted by the master port. A flowchart of the Negotiate Master procedure is shown in Figure 48 on page 83.

Finding a method to select the negotiation master is an interesting challenge. Upon entry to the process, neither port has any knowledge of the capabilities of the other port. All that is known is that a signal is present at each port. Furthermore, the two ports may enter the Negotiate Master process at any time, asynchronous to one another. The first port to detect signal could be at any step in the Negotiate Master process when the second port detects signal and begins the process.

Step Through Receive Speeds. When a port begins the Negotiate Master process it sets both its transmit and receive speeds to its highest supported speed, delays from 2 to 30 msec. (t_rxcycl), and tests if receive synchronization was acquired. If synchronization was not acquired at the highest speed, the port steps to its next-lower receive speed, delays from 2 to 30 msec. (t_rxcycl), and attempts to acquire synchronization at that speed. If synchronization was not acquired, the port steps to its next-lower receive speed, delays from 2 to 30 msec. (t_rxcycl), and attempts to acquire synchronization at that speed. This process continues until 154 msec. (t_txcycl) have elapsed (enough time to perform four full receive samples).

The action taken depends on the receive speed at which synchronization was acquired.

- If synchronization was acquired at the port's highest supported speed, the port goes to *Negotiate Follow* on page 85.

- If synchronization was acquired at a lower receive speed than the current transmit speed, the port adds this speed to a list of known receive speeds (note that the port may already have detected one receive speed in *Wait for Signal* on page 79).

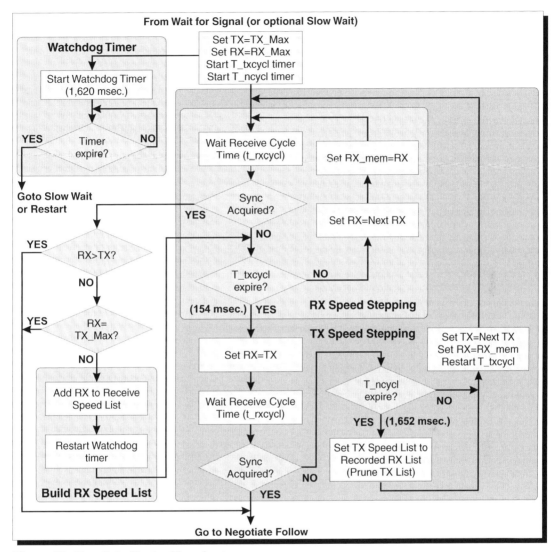

Figure 48. Negotiate Master Flowchart

In the example shown in Figure 49 on page 84, Port_1 detects signal by acquiring synchronization at speed 1 and starts the Negotiate Master procedure. Port_1 adds speed 1 to its list of detected speeds and resumes speed stepping with both its transmitter and receiver set to its maximum speed. While stepping through its receive speeds, Port_1 will also detect speed 2 and add that to its receive list. Port_2 acquires synchronization at speed 2 and starts the Negotiate Master procedure. While in the Negotiate Master procedure, it acquires synchronization at speed 2 (its maximum speed) and goes to the Negotiate Follow procedure.

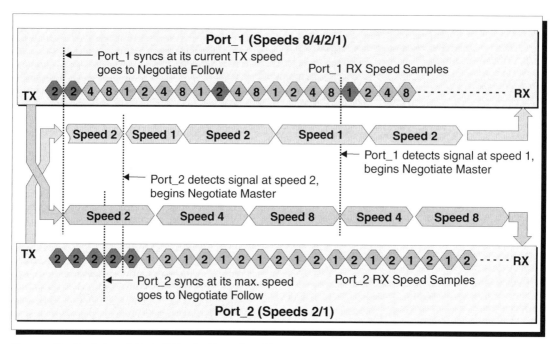

Figure 49. Port_1 and Port_2 Begin Negotiate Master

Step Through Transmit Speeds. If the 154 msec. (t_txcycl) timer expires and the port is still in the Negotiate Master process, it sets its receive speed to its current transmit speed, delays from 2 to 30 msec. (t_rxcycl), and tests for receive synchronization one last time. If synchronization is not acquired, the port continues the Negotiate Master process by setting both its transmit and receive speeds to its next-lower speed and repeating the process of stepping through all of its receive speeds (beginning with the current transmit speed).

• If synchronization is acquired at the current transmit speed, the port goes to Negotiate Follow (see *Negotiate Follow* on page 85). This is the case for Port_1 in Figure 49 when it acquires synchronization at speed 2.

• If synchronization is acquired at a lower receive speed than the current transmit speed, the port adds this speed to its list of known receive speeds detected by the port. Note that the port may already have detected one receive speed during the Wait for Signal process (see *Wait for Signal* on page 79) and one or more receive speeds while transmitting at a higher speed.

Because the port is now transmitting at a speed lower than its highest supported speed, there is one additional possibility. This is, the port may acquire synchronization at a higher speed than the one at which it is currently transmitting.

• If a port acquires synchronization at a higher speed than the port is currently transmitting, it goes to Negotiate Follow (see *Negotiate Follow* on page 85).

A port in the Negotiate Master process continues to step through its transmit speeds at a 154 msec. (t_txcycl) rate per speed, sampling up to four receive speeds (at a 2 to 30 msec. rate) during each transmit cycle, until it detects a condition causing it to go to the Negotiate Follow process or 1,652 msec. (t_ncycl) have elapsed (enough time to make two complete passes through up to four transmit frequencies. During the Negotiate Master process, the port is building a list of receive speeds at which is has acquired receive synchronization.

If the 1,652 msec. (t_ncycl) timer expires, the port begins stepping its transmitter through the speeds in its accumulated receive list. These are speeds at which the port had previously acquired synchronization and represent potential final speeds that might result from the negotiation process. As before, the port transmits at each speed in the receive list for 154 msec. (t_txcycl) and samples at each of its receive speeds after a 2 to 30 msec. (t_rxcycl) delay at each receive speed. As before, the port takes the same actions if synchronization is acquired.

The exit from the Negotiate Master process for the second port is when synchronization is acquired at its highest speed (or the highest speed in its receive speed list, if it is working from the receive speed list) or when synchronization is acquired at the current transmit speed.

While this process may not be intuitive, it may help to think about the relationship of the transmit speeds at the two ports when the second port begins the Negotiate Master process. The first port to enter the Negotiate Master process begins stepping through its transmit speeds. When the second port enters the Negotiate Master process it begins stepping through its transmit speeds, beginning with its highest speed. Therefore, a decision can be made based on the relationship of the two transmit speeds.

- If the other port is transmitting at a higher supported speed, this port goes to Negotiate Follow and attempts to track the transmit speed of the other port.

- If the other port is transmitting at a lower supported speed, it goes to Negotiate Follow and attempts to track the transmit speed of this port.

- If both ports are transmitting at the same speed, this must be the highest mutually supported speed and they both go to the Negotiate Follow procedure. The current speed must be the highest mutually supported speed because each port begins transmitting at its highest speed and steps down to slower speeds. It isn't possible for both of them to be at a lower speed without one of the previous conditions occurring.

- If receive synchronization can't be achieved at a given speed, that speed is not supported by one of the ports.

6.1.5 Negotiate Follow

In the Negotiate Follow process, the port attempts to establish a stable link by following the speed being transmitted by the other port (that may still be in the Negotiate Master process and stepping through its transmit speeds). A flowchart of the Negotiate Follow procedure is shown in Figure 50 on page 86.

Upon entry to Negotiate Follow, a port sets its transmitter speed to its current receive speed. After a delay (t_rxcycl), it checks if receive synchronization has been acquired. If so, the port confirms that synchronization is maintained for a minimum of 217 msec. This time is referred

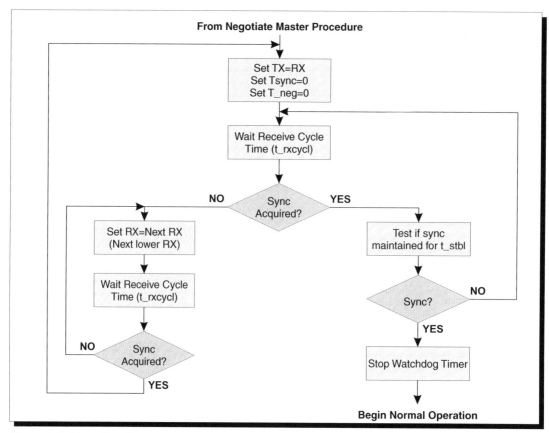

Figure 50. Negotiate Follow Flowchart

to as the speed stability time (or t_stbl) and indicates that the other port is no longer stepping through its transmit speeds (transmit speed stepping occurs once every 154 msec., so maintaining synchronization for t_stbl can only occur if the other port is not changing its transmit speed). If synchronization is maintained for t_stbl, the port begins normal operation.

If synchronization was not acquired at the current receive speed, or did not last for the speed stability time (t_stbl), the port switches to its next lower receive speed and tests if synchronization was acquired. If synchronization was acquired, the port sets its transmit speed to its current receive speed and tests for speed stability at that rate.

If the port is unable to achieve a stable environment before the watchdog timer expires, the port returns to the Wait for Signal process as described in *Wait for Signal* on page 79.

6.1.6 Negotiation Slow Wait (Optional)

The optional Slow Wait procedure reduces the amount of processor overhead that may be associated with the Wait for Signal procedure or following expiration of the watchdog timer.

While use of the Slow Wait procedure can reduce processor overhead by up to 80%, it can also delay detection of valid signal by up to 5 seconds. A flowchart of the Slow Wait procedure is shown in Figure 51.

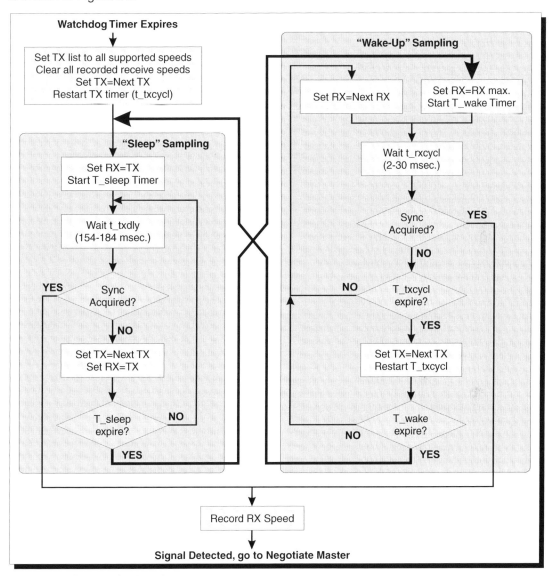

Figure 51. Slow Wait Flowchart

In the Slow Wait process, receive speed sampling occurs at the transmit cycle rate (154 msec., or t_txcycl) rather than the normal receive cycle rate (2 to 30 msec., or t_rxcycl). During

---

this reduced rate sampling, both the transmit and receive speeds are stepped at the same time. This reduces the rate of receive speed sampling and thereby, the amount of processing required by the procedure.

If synchronization is acquired during the slow sampling process, the port records the speed in its receive speed list and begins Negotiate Master (see *Negotiate Master* on page 82). If 5 seconds (t_sleep) elapses and synchronization is not acquired during the slow sampling process, the port briefly "wakes up" and resumes normal receive sampling at a 2 to 30 msec. rate. This is to prevent the possibility that the two ports may both be in the Slow Wait procedure and stepping their transmit and receive speeds in such a way that neither is able to successfully acquire synchronization at the slow receive speed sampling rate.

If synchronization is not acquired during this "wake-up" period of normal receive sampling (900 msec., or t_wake), the port returns to the slow sampling rate for another 5 seconds.

6.2 Arbitrated Loop Considerations

While the speed negotiation procedure does not support configurations other than one port directly connected to another port, arbitrated loops may be supported with some restrictions.

When the configuration consists of an arbitrated loop hub, each hub port must be capable of performing the speed negotiation procedure with the attached port (which could be an NL_Port, FL_Port, or another hub port). Alternatively, all the hub ports may operate at the same fixed speed.

If the configuration consists of one or more loop segments containing multiple loop ports (for example, a disk enclosure or JBOD), the loop segment must present the external appearance of a single speed-negotiating port or a single fixed-speed port.

6.3 Chapter Summary

Speed Negotiation

■ Fibre Channel supports multiple link rates
- 100 MB/sec. (1.0625 Gbps)
- 200 MB/sec. (2.125 Gbps)
- 400 MB/sec. (4.250 Gbps)
- 850 MB/sec. (8.500 Gbps)
- 1,200 MB/sec. (10.2 Gbps)

■ Mixed-speed environments will become more common in the future
- 100/200/400 MB/sec. (1/2/4 Gbps) environments are here today

■ Speed negotiation allows multi-speed devices to communicate

Speed Negotiation Objectives

■ Allow multi-speed ports to automatically determine their highest mutually supported speed

■ Support a maximum of four different speeds
- Not required to be the same four speeds at each port

■ Complete negotiation process in < 2 seconds

■ Provide backward compatibility with existing ports

■ Must be implementable in software/firmware

■ Cannot require all ports to support a specified speed

■ Limited support for arbitrated loop ports

Signal Criteria

■ Speed negotiation is based on the acquisition of synchronization at negotiated speed

■ Process does not guarantee that the bit-error rate is met at the negotiated speed
- Criteria used is 1,000 consecutive transmission words without error
- Bit-error rate specification is 10^{-12}
- It requires over 16 minutes to transmit 10^{12} bits at 1.0625 Gbaud

■ May complete negotiation and later determine the link fails to meet bit-error rate requirements

Signal Detection

■ First part of the procedure is to determine if a signal is present
- May be hardware indication (Loss-of-Signal)
- May be detected by receiver synchronization

■ Each port steps through its transmit speeds
- Provides signal for other port to sync to

■ Each port steps through its receive speeds
- Attempts to acquire synchronization to detect signal
- If synchronization is acquired for 1000 words without error, valid signal is present

■ When signal is detected, the port enters the Negotiate Master process

Negotiate Master

■ Once signal is detected by both ports, a negotiation master is selected
- Selection is based on the relationship of the ports' transmit speeds
- The ports enter this process asynchronously

■ Upon entry to Negotiate Master, each port begins transmitting at its maximum speed
- Begins stepping through its receive speeds

■ Port goes to Negotiate Follow if:
- Synchronization is acquired at port's maximum speed
- Synchronization is acquired at a speed higher than the current transmit speed

Negotiate Master

■ While in Negotiate Master, the port builds a list of detected receive speeds

■ If port stays in Negotiate Master too long, it prunes its transmit speed list
- Only uses its list of detected receive speeds
- These are speeds known to be supported by the other port

■ Starts stepping through the pruned transmit speed list

■ Eventually, this port will go to Negotiate Follow also

Negotiate Follow

- In Negotiate Follow the port attempts to follow the received speed
  - Sets its transmitter to the received speed
- Tests for speed stabilization
  - If the received speed does not change for a stabilization period, speed negotiation is done.
  - If the received speed changes, the port follows the received speed and tests for stabilization at that speed

Slow Wait

- Speed negotiation may affect other processes in the device
  - Speed negotiation procedure can be implemented in the software or firmware
- Slow Wait reduces processing overhead by approximately 80%
  - At the expense of a potentially longer convergence time (as long as 5 seconds)
- Slow Wait is entered if the watchdog timer expires
  - No synchronization was achieved at any speed during a 1,620 msec. window
  - No signal is present or there is no common speed

Slow Wait Procedure

- While in Slow Wait, the port steps its transmitter and receiver together at a slow rate (154 msec.)
  - Reduces processing overhead
  - If sync is acquired, the port goes to Negotiate Master
- Once every 5 seconds, port wakes up and performs the full negotiation process
  - Eliminates the possibility that the ports may be stepping in lockstep and neither acquires sync
  - However, a port may take up to 5 seconds to detect sync while in Slow Wait

7. FC-1 Concepts

Fibre Channel's FC-1 level defines how data is encoded prior to transmission and decoded upon reception, how special transmission words are identified and used to delimit the start and end of frames, and perform link-level protocols such as initialization and resets. Figure 52 illustrates the relationship of FC-1 to the other Fibre Channel levels.

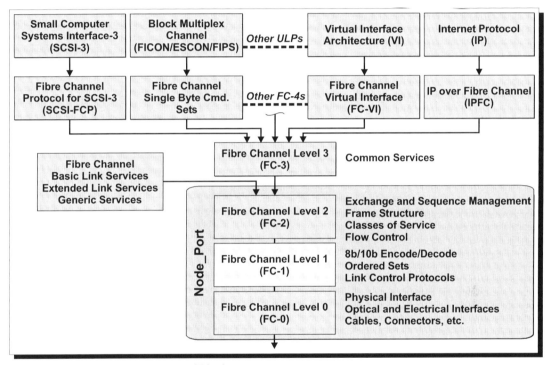

Figure 52. Fibre Channel Level 1 (FC-1)

7.1 8b/10 Encoding and Decoding

In order to reliably transfer data over a high-speed serial link, the data is encoded prior to transmission and decoded upon reception. Encoding tailors the frequency characteristics of the data and ensures that sufficient clock information is present in the serial data stream to allow the receiver to synchronize to the embedded clock information and successfully recover the data at the required error rate.

The encoding scheme also provides a balance between the number of one bits and zero bits transmitted, a condition referred to as DC balance. DC balance provides several benefits, including the following:

- Limiting the amount of DC offset that accumulates at the receiver and facilitates setting the level detect thresholds.
- Removing the need for DC restoration circuits that are difficult to design at the frequencies associated with Fibre Channel transmission.
- Insuring that the duty cycle of lasers used in optical transmission is maintained at 50% for optimal performance and power dissipation.

The 8b/10b encoding scheme provides 10-bit characters conforming to the coding rules that are not required for representing data characters (there are more available code points in the 10-bit space than the corresponding 8-bit data space). These 10-bit special characters are available to identify control or management functions.

The 8b/10b encoding/decoding scheme is described in *8b/10b Encoding and Decoding* on page 95.

7.2 Ordered Sets

Fibre Channel is a word-oriented architecture, treating a group of four characters as a word.

To provide control functions, Fibre Channel defines a special category of transmission words called Ordered Sets. An Ordered Set is a transmission word (a set of four characters) that begins with one of the special characters provided by the 8b/10b encoding scheme, and is followed by three data characters. Ordered Sets are used to identify the start and end of frames and provide other control and signaling functions at the transmission word level.

More information regarding Ordered Sets, their definition, and use can be found in *Ordered Sets* on page 111.

7.3 Link-Level Protocols

Ordered Sets are used to implement link-level protocols that are used when frame-level functions are not possible. These protocols are used to initialize the link, perform link resets, and recover from hang conditions caused by failed ports or operations.

More information about link-level protocols and their use can be found in *Port State Machine and Link Control Facility* on page 125.

7.4 Chapter Summary

FC-1 Functions

- FC-1 provides three primary functions
- Encoding and decoding the transmitted data stream
  - All information transmitted on a Fibre Channel link is encoded
- Providing unique transmission words for signaling and control functions
  - Identifying the Start-of-Frame and End-of-Frame, for example
- Implementing low-level link protocols
  - Resetting the link
  - Signaling that a port is offline or not operational

8b/10b Encoding

- All information transmitted on a Fibre Channel link is encoded
  - The sender encodes 8-bit bytes into 10-bit transmission characters
  - The receiver decodes the 10-bit transmission characters back to 8-bit bytes
- Encoding is used to:
  - Provide sufficient clocking information for data recovery (clock information is encoded into the data stream)
  - Provide a 50% duty cycle (on-off) with no DC component (easier for receivers)
  - Provide special characters outside the 8-bit code space

Ordered Sets

- Fibre Channel defines several transmission words for control functions called Ordered Sets
- Ordered Sets are a set of 4 characters with a defined order
- All Ordered Sets begin with a special 10-bit character that is outside the 8-bit data space
- Ordered Sets are used for:
  - Start-of-Frame delimiters
  - End-of-Frame delimiters
  - Flow control signaling (a receiver is ready for another frame)
  - Controlling the link
  - Other low-level control and signaling functions

Link-Level Protocols

- Fibre Channel defines link-level protocols using Ordered Sets
- Used for low-level link initialization and control functions
- The link-level protocols are:
  - Link or Arbitrated Loop Reset
  - Link or Arbitrated Loop Initialization
  - Link or Arbitrated Loop Failure

8. 8b/10b Encoding and Decoding

Fibre Channel's FC-1 level defines the method used to encode data prior to transmission and subsequently decode the data upon reception.

The particular scheme used encodes 8-bit data bytes into 10-bit transmission characters to improve the transmission characteristics of the serial data stream. This scheme is called "8b/10b" encoding, referring to the number of data bits input to the encoder and the number of bits output from the encoder.

To facilitate the processing of information at the transfer rates associated with Fibre Channel, data fields and structures are aligned on word boundaries when possible. Normally, a word consists of four 8-bit bytes, or a total of 32 bits (plus parity, when used). However, when each of the 8-bit bytes is encoded prior to transmission, the resulting transmission word consists of 40 bits representing the four 10-bit transmission characters. Figure 53 below illustrates the numbering of bits and bytes within the 32-bit word.

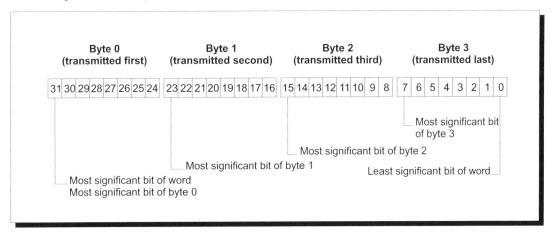

Figure 53. Bit, Byte, and Word Structure

One of the attributes of the 8b/10b encoding scheme is that it defines several unique special characters. These special characters are selected from the 10-bit transmission characters that meet all the coding rules but are not required for the representation of 8-bit data bytes (there are 1024 10-bit patterns, not all of which are necessary to represent 8-bit data).

Fibre Channel uses one of these characters to identify the beginning of special transmission words used for control and signaling functions. These special transmission words are called Ordered Sets.

8.1 Why Encode the Data?

All information transmitted via a Fibre Channel serial link is encoded into 10-bit transmission characters prior to transmission and decoded back into 8-bit bytes following reception. Encoding the data improves the transmission characteristics of the serial bit stream and facilitates successful recovery of the data at the receiver. The 8b/10b encoding scheme provides the following characteristics:

- Provides sufficient transition density to facilitate reliable creation of a receive clock by use of a phase locked loop and limits the number of consecutive ones or zeros to a maximum of five, regardless of the original 8-bit data stream.
- Maintains a balance between the number of ones and zeros transmitted, thereby ensuring that the received signal is free of any DC component.
- Provides unique special characters that exist outside of the normal 8-bit data space.
- Provides methods for the detection of most, but not all, transmission errors.
- Provides constant bit, byte, and word data rates, simplifying the clocking of information prior to encoding and after decoding.
- Is simple to implement on a byte-wide basis.

8.2 Running Disparity

The encoding process transforms 8-bit input characters into 10-bit transmission characters having the desired attributes. Not all possible 10-bit patterns are used. To prevent excessive DC components and run length problems, only characters containing six ones and four zero, five ones and five zeros, or six zeros and four ones are allowed. Any other weighting of bits is an invalid character.

Characters with five ones and five zeros are inherently free of any DC component. However those characters consisting of six ones and four zeros, or six zeros and four ones contain a DC component equal to 2 bits in the positive direction (ones) or 2 bits in the negative direction (zeros). This difference in the number of bits is referred to as the disparity of the character. Characters with more one bits than zero bits have positive disparity, while characters with more zero bits than one bits have negative disparity. Characters with an equal number of one and zero bits are referred to as a neutral disparity because their effect on the balance of ones and zeros is neutral.

To prevent an ever increasing DC component (or disparity), all characters with an unequal number of ones and zeros have two different encodings. One encoding contains six ones and four zeros, the other six zeros and four ones.

When the encoder creates a character with more ones than zeros, it remembers this by setting a variable called the Current Running Disparity (CRD) to positive. When the encoder creates a character with more zeros than ones, it sets the Current Running Disparity to negative. The

Current Running Disparity is fed back to the encoder to select the appropriate encoding of the next character to balance the number of one and zero bits transmitted. As a series of non-neutral characters are processed, the disparity alternates between positive disparity (six ones and four zeros) and negative disparity (six zeros and four ones) maintaining a balance between the number of one bits and zero bits transmitted.

Neutral disparity characters (with five ones and five zeros) have no effect on the Current Running Disparity as they do not affect the relationship between the relative number of one bits and zero bits transmitted. However, to meet other constraints on the data stream (such as run length restrictions), many of the neutral disparity characters also have two different encodings that are controlled by the Current Running Disparity variable.

8.3 Data Characters and Special Characters

The 8b/10b encoding scheme translates all 256 data characters (x'00' through x'FF') into 10-bit transmission characters. Each of the 256 data characters is encoded into either one or two 10-bit patterns as discussed previously.

After assignment of 8-bit data characters to 10-bit transmission characters, there are still several valid 10-bit patterns available that meet all the coding rules for valid characters. These 10-bit patterns are defined as special characters in the coding scheme. It should be noted that the special characters are outside of the 8-bit code space associated with the 256 data values.

The encoder is capable of encoding both data and special characters, and it needs to be informed whether the 8-bit value being supplied on the input represents a data character or one of the special characters. This is accomplished by providing a control input called the D/K input with "D" indicating a data character and "K" indicating a special character.

Only a limited number of 8-bit values encode to valid special characters when the D/K input is in the "K" condition. Therefore, the values that are valid as inputs when encoding special characters (K codes) are limited.

8.4 8b/10b Bit and Byte Notation

The 8b/10b encoding scheme and Fibre Channel's FC-1 level both employ a special notation for identifying both encoded and unencoded data bits. In this notation, the normal bit numbering associated with unencoded data bits is replaced with a letter notation using the upper case letters *HGFEDCBA* to identify each of the eight bits. This notational convention is an artifact of the original notation used in the 8b/10b patent and subsequent publication.

The use of a letter notation is also extended to the encoded 10-bit transmission character where individual bits are represented using the lower case letters *abcdeifghj*. Figure 54 on page 98 illustrates the relationship between the normal numbering of bits and bytes within the 32-bit word and the letter notation used by the 8b/10b scheme. It should be noted that there is no implied correspondence or relationship between the upper and lower case letters as they are separated by the encoding process.

Characters also have a notational convention that is used by the 8b/10b encoding scheme and Fibre Channel's FC-1 level. In this notational convention, which is of the form D/Kxx.y, the first character is either a D or K, indicating whether the 8b/10b character is a data character (D) or a special character (K). The *xx* portion of the notation is the decimal value of the five least-significant bits. The *xx* portion is followed by a period, then finally, the *y* portion that is the decimal value of the 3 most significant bits.

This notational convention derives from the fact that in the encoder process the five least significant bits first in a 5b/6b encoder, then the three most significant bits in a 3b/4b encoder. When the encoding process is described, the five least significant bits are discussed first, then the three most significant bits. An illustration of both the bit and byte notation is shown in Figure 54.

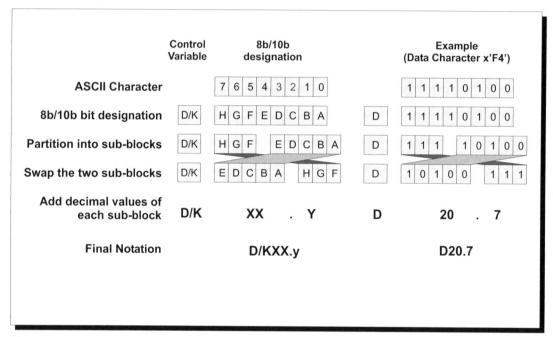

Figure 54. 8b/10b Notation

8.5 Encoding/Decoding

The actual encoding and decoding processes can be implemented by means of a table lookup or algorithmically. The description presented here follows the approach described by the inventors when the scheme was first published.

The 8b/10b encoding process can be broken into two distinct operations. In the first step, the least significant five bits of the original byte are encoded into 6 bits by a 5b/6b encoder. In a second step, the remaining three most significant bits of the original byte are encoded into four bits in a 3b/4b encoder. Splitting the encoding process into two steps simplifies the logic needed to implement the encoder.

The encoder needs to know whether the input represents a data character or special character to properly encode the input data. That information is provided by the D/K input signal. The encoder also need to know the state of the Current Running Disparity to generate the correct output disparity and maintain the DC balance. Figure 55 provides a simplified diagram of the encoder function.

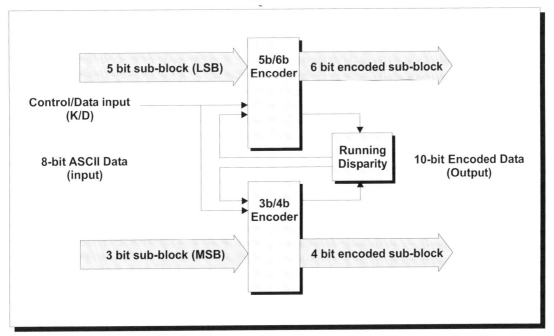

Figure 55. Encoder Block Diagram

8.5.1 5b/6b Subblock Encoding

In the first step of the encoding process, the encoder examines the sub-block consisting of input bits *EDCBA* (ASCII bits 43210), performs the 5b/6b encoding, generates output bits *abcdei* and updates the Current Running Disparity based on the disparity of the generated output bits. During this encoding process, the Current Running Disparity used reflects the disparity at the end of encoding the prior character.

There are 32 possible input data values to the 5b/6b encoder that are represented using decimal notation as D00 through D31. There are only five valid special character input values to the 5b/6b encoder that are represented as K23, K27, K28, K29, and K30. All special characters, with the exception of K28, produce the same 6-bit results as do the equivalent data characters. K28 is also the only six bit sub-block ending with four consecutive ones or zeros (depending upon the Current Running Disparity).

Examination of the two output columns of the 5b/6b encoder table (Table 7 on page 101) reveals a number of interesting characteristics of the encoding process.

- All six-bit sub-blocks consist of either three one bits and three zero bits, four one bits and two zero bits, or four zero bits and two one bits.

- When there are two different six bit output values for a character, the two values are the complement of one another.

- When possible, bits *ABCDE* are mapped one-for-one to bits *abcde* (note that the order of the bits changes in the encoding process and tables) with the *i* bit used to manage the disparity of the sub-block. This simplifies the design of the encoder by minimizing the number of bits that have to be processed.

8.5.2 3b/4b Subblock Encoding

In the second step of the encoding process, the encoder examines the sub-block consisting of input bits *HGF* (ASCII bits 765), performs the 3b/4b encoding, generates output bits *fghj*, and updates the Current Running Disparity based on the disparity of the generated output bits. During this encoding process, the Current Running Disparity used by the encoder is the disparity at the end of the 5b/6b encoding of the current character.

There are eight possible input data values to the 3b/4b encoder that are represented using decimal notation as D/Kxx.0 through D/Kxx.7, where D/K indicates whether a data character or special character is being encoded and the 'xx' portion represents the five least significant bits (*EDCBA* or ASCII bits 43210) that were processed by the 5b/6b encoder.

When a special character of the form K28.y is being encoded, y may be any value from 0 through 7. For the remaining special characters (K23.7, K27.7, K29.7, and K30.7), the only allowable y value is 7. This results in a total of twelve special characters.

When there are two different outputs defined for the same input bits to manage the disparity, those outputs are the frequently the complement of one another (note that Dxx.7 has some special case conditions). Encoding tables showing both the 5b/6b sub-block encoding and 3b/4b sub-block encoding are provided in Table 7 on page 101.

8.5.3 8b/10b Data Byte Encoding

By combining both the 5b/6b and 3b/4b steps of the encoding process a complete 8b/10b encoding table can be produced showing the encoding of the full set of 256 data characters. For reference, the complete data character encoding is provided in Table 8 on page 102.

5b/6b Sub-block Encoding Table

Input		Output	
Data Input	43210 EDCBA	CRD - abcdei	CRD + abcdei
D00.y	00000	100111	011000
D01.y	00001	011101	100010
D02.y	00010	101101	010010
D03.y	00011	110001	
D04.y	00100	110101	001010
D05.y	00101	101001	
D06.y	00110	011001	
D07.y	00111	111000	000111
D08.y	01000	111001	000110
D09.y	01001	100101	
D10.y	01010	010101	
D11.y	01011	110100	
D12.y	01100	001101	
D13.y	01101	101100	
D14.y	01110	011100	
D15.y	01111	010111	101000
D16.y	10000	011011	100100
D17.y	10001	100011	
D18.y	10010	010011	
D19.y	10011	110010	
D20.y	10100	001011	
D21.y	10101	101010	
D22.y	10110	011010	
D/K23.y	10111	111010	000101
D24.y	11000	110011	001100
D25.y	11001	100110	
D26.y	11010	010110	
D/K27.y	11011	110110	001001
D28.y	11100	001110	
K28.y	11100	001111	110000
D/K29.y	11101	101110	010001
D/K30.y	11110	011110	100001
D31.y	11111	101011	010100

3b/4b Sub-block Encoding Table

Input		Output[1]	
Data Input	765 HGF	CRD - fghj	CRD + fghj
D/Kxx.0	000	1011	0100
Dxx.1	001	1001	
Kxx.1	001	0110	1001
Dxx.2	010	0101	
Kxx.2	010	1010	0101
D/Kxx.3	011	1100	0011
D/Kxx.4	100	1101	0010
Dxx.5	101	1010	
Kxx.5	101	0101	1010
Dxx.6	110	0110	
Kxx.6	110	1001	0110
Dxx.7	111	1110/0111[2]	0001/1000[2]
Kxx.7	111	0111	1000

1. The Current Running Disparity used by the 3b/4b encoder is the Current Running Disparity at the end of the 5b/6b encoding, not the Current Running Disparity at the beginning of the character being encoded.

2. The alternate encoding (0111) is used for D17.7, D18.7, and D20.7 when the CRD is (-) to prevent five consecutive one bits. The alternate encoding (1000) is used for D11.7, D13.7, and D14.7 when the CRD is (+) to prevent five consecutive zero bits.

Table 7. 5b/6b and 3b/4b Sub-block Encoding Tables

Complete 8b/10b Data Character Encoding Table

Input			Output			
Data Byte		765	43210	CRD -		CRD +	
Hex	Name	HGF	EDCBA	abcdei	fghj	abcdei	fghj
00	D00.0	000	00000	100111	0100	011000	1011
01	D01.0	000	00001	011101	0100	100010	1011
02	D02.0	000	00010	101101	0100	010010	1011
03	D03.0	000	00011	110001	1011	110001	0100
04	D04.0	000	00100	110101	0100	001010	1011
05	D05.0	000	00101	101001	1011	101001	0100
06	D06.0	000	00110	011001	1011	011001	0100
07	D07.0	000	00111	111000	1011	000111	0100
08	D08.0	000	01000	111001	0100	000110	1011
09	D09.0	000	01001	100101	1011	100101	0100
0A	D10.0	000	01010	010101	1011	010101	0100
0B	D11.0	000	01011	110100	1011	110100	0100
0C	D12.0	000	01100	001101	1011	001101	0100
0D	D13.0	000	01101	101100	1011	101100	0100
0E	D14.0	000	01110	011100	1011	011100	0100
0F	D15.0	000	01111	010111	0100	101000	1011
10	D16.0	000	10000	011011	0100	100100	1011
11	D17.0	000	10001	100011	1011	100011	0100
12	D18.0	000	10010	010011	1011	010011	0100
13	D19.0	000	10011	110010	1011	110010	0100
14	D20.0	000	10100	001011	1011	001011	0100
15	D21.0	000	10101	101010	1011	101010	0100
16	D22.0	000	10110	011010	1011	011010	0100
17	D23.0	000	10111	111010	0100	000101	1011
18	D24.0	000	11000	110011	0100	001100	1011
19	D25.0	000	11001	100110	1011	100110	0100
1A	D26.0	000	11010	010110	1011	010110	0100
1B	D27.0	000	11011	110110	0100	001001	1011
1C	D28.0	000	11100	001110	1011	001110	0100
1D	D29.0	000	11101	101110	0100	010001	1011
1E	D30.0	000	11110	011110	0100	100001	1011
1F	D31.0	000	11111	101011	0100	010100	1011

Input			Output			
Data Byte		765	43210	CRD -		CRD +	
Hex	Name	HGF	EDCBA	abcdei	fghj	abcdei	fghj
20	D00.1	001	00000	100111	1001	011000	1001
21	D01.1	001	00001	011101	1001	100010	1001
22	D02.1	001	00010	101101	1001	010010	1001
23	D03.1	001	00011	110001	1001	110001	1001
24	D04.1	001	00100	110101	1001	001010	1001
25	D05.1	001	00101	101001	1001	101001	1001
26	D06.1	001	00110	011001	1001	011001	1001
27	D07.1	001	00111	111000	1001	000111	1001
28	D08.1	001	01000	111001	1001	000110	1001
29	D09.1	001	01001	100101	1001	100101	1001
2A	D10.1	001	01010	010101	1001	010101	1001
2B	D11.1	001	01011	110100	1001	110100	1001
2C	D12.1	001	01100	001101	1001	001101	1001
2D	D13.1	001	01101	101100	1001	101100	1001
2E	D14.1	001	01110	011100	1001	011100	1001
2F	D15.1	001	01111	010111	1001	101000	1001
30	D16.1	001	10000	011011	1001	100100	1001
31	D17.1	001	10001	100011	1001	100011	1001
32	D18.1	001	10010	010011	1001	010011	1001
33	D19.1	001	10011	110010	1001	110010	1001
34	D20.1	001	10100	001011	1001	001011	1001
35	D21.1	001	10101	101010	1001	101010	1001
36	D22.1	001	10110	011010	1001	011010	1001
37	D23.1	001	10111	111010	1001	000101	1001
38	D24.1	001	11000	110011	1001	001100	1001
39	D25.1	001	11001	100110	1001	100110	1001
3A	D26.1	001	11010	010110	1001	010110	1001
3B	D27.1	001	11011	110110	1001	001001	1001
3C	D28.1	001	11100	001110	1001	001110	1001
3D	D29.1	001	11101	101110	1001	010001	1001
3E	D30.1	001	11110	011110	1001	100001	1001
3F	D31.1	001	11111	101011	1001	010100	1001

Table 8. 8b/10b Data Character Encoding (Part 1 of 4)

Complete 8b/10b Data Character Encoding Table

Input				Output				Input				Output			
Data Byte		765	43210	CRD -		CRD +		Data Byte		765	43210	CRD -		CRD +	
Hex	Name	HGF	EDCBA	abcdei	fghj	abcdei	fghj	Hex	Name	HGF	EDCBA	abcdei	fghj	abcdei	fghj
40	D00.2	010	00000	100111	0101	011000	0101	60	D00.3	011	00000	100111	0011	011000	1100
41	D01.2	010	00001	011101	0101	100010	0101	61	D01.3	011	00001	011101	0011	100010	1100
42	D02.2	010	00010	101101	0101	010010	0101	62	D02.3	011	00010	101101	0011	010010	1100
43	D03.2	010	00011	110001	0101	110001	0101	63	D03.3	011	00011	110001	1100	110001	0011
44	D04.2	010	00100	110101	0101	001010	0101	64	D04.3	011	00100	110101	0011	001010	1100
45	D05.2	010	00101	101001	0101	101001	0101	65	D05.3	011	00101	101001	1100	101001	0011
46	D06.2	010	00110	011001	0101	011001	0101	66	D06.3	011	00110	011001	1100	011001	0011
47	D07.2	010	00111	111000	0101	000111	0101	67	D07.3	011	00111	111000	1100	000111	0011
48	D08.2	010	01000	111001	0101	000110	0101	68	D08.3	011	01000	111001	0011	000110	1100
49	D09.2	010	01001	100101	0101	100101	0101	69	D09.3	011	01001	100101	1100	100101	0011
4A	D10.2	010	01010	010101	0101	010101	0101	6A	D10.3	011	01010	010101	1100	010101	0011
4B	D11.2	010	01011	110100	0101	110100	0101	6B	D11.3	011	01011	110100	1100	110100	0011
4C	D12.2	010	01100	001101	0101	001101	0101	6C	D12.3	011	01100	001101	1100	001101	0011
4D	D13.2	010	01101	101100	0101	101100	0101	6D	D13.3	011	01101	101100	1100	101100	0011
4E	D14.2	010	01110	011100	0101	011100	0101	6E	D14.3	011	01110	011100	1100	011100	0011
4F	D15.2	010	01111	010111	0101	101000	0101	6F	D15.3	011	01111	010111	0011	101000	1100
50	D16.2	010	10000	011011	0101	100100	0101	70	D16.3	011	10000	011011	0011	100100	1100
51	D17.2	010	10001	100011	0101	100011	0101	71	D17.3	011	10001	100011	1100	100011	0011
52	D18.2	010	10010	010011	0101	010011	0101	72	D18.3	011	10010	010011	1100	010011	0011
53	D19.2	010	10011	110010	0101	110010	0101	73	D19.3	011	10011	110010	1100	110010	0011
54	D20.2	010	10100	001011	0101	001011	0101	74	D20.3	011	10100	001011	1100	001011	0011
55	D21.2	010	10101	101010	0101	101010	0101	75	D21.3	011	10101	101010	1100	101010	0011
56	D22.2	010	10110	011010	0101	011010	0101	76	D22.3	011	10110	011010	1100	011010	0011
57	D23.2	010	10111	111010	0101	000101	0101	77	D23.3	011	10111	111010	0011	000101	1100
58	D24.2	010	11000	110011	0101	001100	0101	78	D24.3	011	11000	110011	0011	001100	1100
59	D25.2	010	11001	100110	0101	100110	0101	79	D25.3	011	11001	100110	1100	100110	0011
5A	D26.2	010	11010	010110	0101	010110	0101	7A	D26.3	011	11010	010110	1100	010110	0011
5B	D27.2	010	11011	110110	0101	001001	0101	7B	D27.3	011	11011	110110	0011	001001	1100
5C	D28.2	010	11100	001110	0101	001110	0101	7C	D28.3	011	11100	001110	1100	001110	0011
5D	D29.2	010	11101	101110	0101	010001	0101	7D	D29.3	011	11101	101110	0011	010001	1100
5E	D30.2	010	11110	011110	0101	100001	0101	7E	D30.3	011	11110	011110	0011	100001	1100
5F	D31.2	010	11111	101011	0101	010100	0101	7F	D31.3	011	11111	101011	0011	010100	1100

Table 8. 8b/10b Data Character Encoding (Part 2 of 4)

Complete 8b/10b Data Character Encoding Table

Input Data Byte Hex	Name	765 HGF	43210 EDCBA	CRD- abcdei	fghj	CRD+ abcdei	fghj	Input Data Byte Hex	Name	765 HGF	43210 EDCBA	CRD- abcdei	fghj	CRD+ abcdei	fghj
80	D00.4	100	00000	100111	0010	011000	1101	A0	D00.5	101	00000	100111	1010	011000	1010
81	D01.4	100	00001	011101	0010	100010	1101	A1	D01.5	101	00001	011101	1010	100010	1010
82	D02.4	100	00010	101101	0010	010010	1101	A2	D02.5	101	00010	101101	1010	010010	1010
83	D03.4	100	00011	110001	1101	110001	0010	A3	D03.5	101	00011	110001	1010	110001	1010
84	D04.4	100	00100	110101	0010	001010	1101	A4	D04.5	101	00100	110101	1010	001010	1010
85	D05.4	100	00101	101001	1101	101001	0010	A5	D05.5	101	00101	101001	1010	101001	1010
86	D06.4	100	00110	011001	1101	011001	0010	A6	D06.5	101	00110	011001	1010	011001	1010
87	D07.4	100	00111	111000	1101	000111	0010	A7	D07.5	101	00111	111000	1010	000111	1010
88	D08.4	100	01000	111001	0010	000110	1101	A8	D08.5	101	01000	111001	1010	000110	1010
89	D09.4	100	01001	100101	1101	100101	0010	A9	D09.5	101	01001	100101	1010	100101	1010
8A	D10.4	100	01010	010101	1101	010101	0010	AA	D10.5	101	01010	010101	1010	010101	1010
8B	D11.4	100	01011	110100	1101	110100	0010	AB	D11.5	101	01011	110100	1010	110100	1010
8C	D12.4	100	01100	001101	1101	001101	0010	AC	D12.5	101	01100	001101	1010	001101	1010
8D	D13.4	100	01101	101100	1101	101100	0010	AD	D13.5	101	01101	101100	1010	101100	1010
8E	D14.4	100	01110	011100	1101	011100	0010	AE	D14.5	101	01110	011100	1010	011100	1010
8F	D15.4	100	01111	010111	0010	101000	1101	AF	D15.5	101	01111	010111	1010	101000	1010
90	D16.4	100	10000	011011	0010	100100	1101	B0	D16.5	101	10000	011011	1010	100100	1010
91	D17.4	100	10001	100011	1101	100011	0010	B1	D17.5	101	10001	100011	1010	100011	1010
92	D18.4	100	10010	010011	1101	010011	0010	B2	D18.5	101	10010	010011	1010	010011	1010
93	D19.4	100	10011	110010	1101	110010	0010	B3	D19.5	101	10011	110010	1010	110010	1010
94	D20.4	100	10100	001011	1101	001011	0010	B4	D20.5	101	10100	001011	1010	001011	1010
95	D21.4	100	10101	101010	1101	101010	0010	B5	D21.5	101	10101	101010	1010	101010	1010
96	D22.4	100	10110	011010	1101	011010	0010	B6	D22.5	101	10110	011010	1010	011010	1010
97	D23.4	100	10111	111010	0010	000101	1101	B7	D23.5	101	10111	111010	1010	000101	1010
98	D24.4	100	11000	110011	0010	001100	1101	B8	D24.5	101	11000	110011	1010	001100	1010
99	D25.4	100	11001	100110	1101	100110	0010	B9	D25.5	101	11001	100110	1010	100110	1010
9A	D26.4	100	11010	010110	1101	010110	0010	BA	D26.5	101	11010	010110	1010	010110	1010
9B	D27.4	100	11011	110110	0010	001001	1101	BB	D27.5	101	11011	110110	1010	001001	1010
9C	D28.4	100	11100	001110	1101	001110	0010	BC	D28.5	101	11100	001110	1010	001110	1010
9D	D29.4	100	11101	101110	0010	010001	1101	BD	D29.5	101	11101	101110	1010	010001	1010
9E	D30.4	100	11110	011110	0010	100001	1101	BE	D30.5	101	11110	011110	1010	100001	1010
9F	D31.4	100	11111	101011	0010	010100	1101	BF	D31.5	101	11111	101011	1010	010100	1010

Table 8. 8b/10b Data Character Encoding (Part 3 of 4)

Complete 8b/10b Data Character Encoding Table

Data Byte Hex	Name	765 HGF	43210 EDCBA	CRD − abcdei	fghj	CRD + abcdei	fghj
C0	D00.6	110	00000	100111	0110	011000	0110
C1	D01.6	110	00001	011101	0110	100010	0110
C2	D02.6	110	00010	101101	0110	010010	0110
C3	D03.6	110	00011	110001	0110	110001	0110
C4	D04.6	110	00100	110101	0110	001010	0110
C5	D05.6	110	00101	101001	0110	101001	0110
C6	D06.6	110	00110	011001	0110	011001	0110
C7	D07.6	110	00111	111000	0110	000111	0110
C8	D08.6	110	01000	111001	0110	000110	0110
C9	D09.6	110	01001	100101	0110	100101	0110
CA	D10.6	110	01010	010101	0110	010101	0110
CB	D11.6	110	01011	110100	0110	110100	0110
CC	D12.6	110	01100	001101	0110	001101	0110
CD	D13.6	110	01101	101100	0110	101100	0110
CE	D14.6	110	01110	011100	0110	011100	0110
CF	D15.6	110	01111	010111	0110	101000	0110
D0	D16.6	110	10000	011011	0110	100100	0110
D1	D17.6	110	10001	100011	0110	100011	0110
D2	D18.6	110	10010	010011	0110	010011	0110
D3	D19.6	110	10011	110010	0110	110010	0110
D4	D20.6	110	10100	001011	0110	001011	0110
D5	D21.6	110	10101	101010	0110	101010	0110
D6	D22.6	110	10110	011010	0110	011010	0110
D7	D23.6	110	10111	111010	0110	000101	0110
D8	D24.6	110	11000	110011	0110	001100	0110
D9	D25.6	110	11001	100110	0110	100110	0110
DA	D26.6	110	11010	010110	0110	010110	0110
DB	D27.6	110	11011	110110	0110	001001	0110
DC	D28.6	110	11100	001110	0110	001110	0110
DD	D29.6	110	11101	101110	0110	010001	0110
DE	D30.6	110	11110	011110	0110	100001	0110
DF	D31.6	110	11111	101011	0110	010100	0110
E0	D00.7	111	00000	100111	0001	011000	1110
E1	D01.7	111	00001	011101	0001	100010	1110
E2	D02.7	111	00010	101101	0001	010010	1110
E3	D03.7	111	00011	110001	1110	110001	0001
E4	D04.7	111	00100	110101	0001	001010	1110
E5	D05.7	111	00101	101001	1110	101001	0001
E6	D06.7	111	00110	011001	1110	011001	0001
E7	D07.7	111	00111	111000	1110	000111	0001
E8	D08.7	111	01000	111001	0001	000110	1110
E9	D09.7	111	01001	100101	1110	100101	0001
EA	D10.7	111	01010	010101	1110	010101	0001
EB	D11.7	111	01011	110100	1110	110100	1000
EC	D12.7	111	01100	001101	1110	001101	0001
ED	D13.7	111	01101	101100	1110	101100	1000
EE	D14.7	111	01110	011100	1110	011100	1000
EF	D15.7	111	01111	010111	0001	101000	1110
F0	D16.7	111	10000	011011	0001	100100	1110
F1	D17.7	111	10001	100011	0111	100011	0001
F2	D18.7	111	10010	010011	0111	010011	0001
F3	D19.7	111	10011	110010	1110	110010	0001
F4	D20.7	111	10100	001011	0111	001011	0001
F5	D21.7	111	10101	101010	1110	101010	0001
F6	D22.7	111	10110	011010	1110	011010	0001
F7	D23.7	111	10111	111010	0001	000101	1110
F8	D24.7	111	11000	110011	0001	001100	1110
F9	D25.7	111	11001	100110	1110	100110	0001
FA	D26.7	111	11010	010110	1110	010110	0001
FB	D27.7	111	11011	110110	0001	001001	1110
FC	D28.7	111	11100	001110	1110	001110	0001
FD	D29.7	111	11101	101110	0001	010001	1110
FE	D30.7	111	11110	011110	0001	100001	1110
FF	D31.7	111	11111	101011	0001	010100	1110

Table 8. 8b/10b Data Character Encoding (Part 4 of 4)

8.5.4 8b/10b Special Character Encoding

Of the 12 special characters defined by the 8b/10b encoding scheme, only the K28.5 character is used by Fibre Channel. Furthermore, use of the K28.5 special character is limited to the first character of a transmission word known as an Ordered Set (the remaining three characters of the word must be valid data characters). The definition and usage of these special transmission words are discussed later in *Ordered Sets* on page 111.

When the 5b/6b and 3b/4b encodings for the valid special characters are combined, a complete table of all the encoded special characters can be formed as shown in Table 9. The underlined entries in the table are a unique pattern known as the comma pattern that is explained in the next section.

Special Character Encoding Table				
Input	**Output**			
Special Character Name	**CRD -**		**CRD +**	
	abcdei	**fghj**	**abcdei**	**fghj**
K28.0	001111	0100	110000	1011
K28.1	<u>001111</u>	<u>1</u>001	<u>110000</u>	<u>0</u>110
K28.2	001111	0101	110000	1010
K28.3	001111	0011	110000	1100
K28.4	001111	0010	110000	1101
K28.5	<u>001111</u>	<u>1</u>010	<u>110000</u>	<u>0</u>101
K28.6	001111	0110	110000	1001
K28.7	<u>001111</u>	<u>1</u>000	<u>110000</u>	<u>0</u>111
K23.7	111010	1000	000101	0111
K27.7	110110	1000	001001	0111
K29.7	101110	1000	010001	0111
K30.7	011110	1000	100001	0111

Table 9. 8b/10b Special Character Encoding

8.5.5 Comma Pattern

Three special characters contain a unique seven-bit pattern called the comma pattern that consists of two bits of one polarity followed by five bits of the opposite polarity. This pattern only occurs as the first seven bits of the K28.1, K28.5, and K28.7 special characters and is underlined in Table 9. The comma pattern does not occur within any of the data characters, nor within the data bits between any two adjacent data characters (it is possible to obtain a false comma pattern between the last five bits of the K28.7 and selected data or special characters, but use of the K28.7 is not allowed in Fibre Channel except for diagnostic purposes). The 8b/10b encoding scheme takes advantage of the uniqueness of the comma pattern to identify the character alignment within the serial data stream.

After the FC-0 clock recovery phase locked loop has achieved bit synchronization, the incoming data bits are shifted through the deserializer shift register. A circuit, called the comma detect circuit, monitors the low-order bits of this shift register. When a comma pattern is detected, character alignment is known and received bits can be gated to the 8b/10b decoder function.

Following successful detection of the comma pattern, the receiver simply counts the number of bit times to determine when the next character begins. Every ten bit times represents a new character and every 40 bit times a new transmission word.

8.6 Bit and Byte Transmission Order

The bytes within a transmission word are transmitted in order from most significant to least significant (byte 0 to byte 3). In an Ordered Set, the K28.5 character is transmitted first, followed by the three remaining data characters. The order of byte transmission reflects the order in which FC-2 requires the received data for most efficient processing.

Within a transmission character, the encoded bits are transmitted in *abcdeifghj* order. The order of bit and byte transmission are both shown in Figure 56 on page 107.

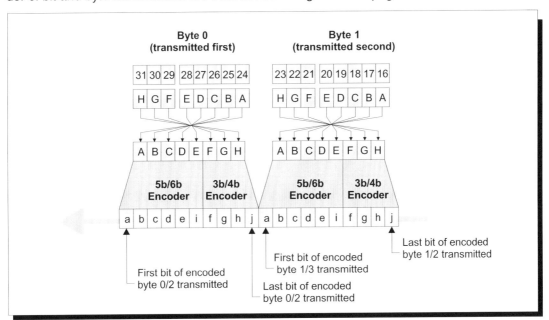

Figure 56. Bit and Byte Transmission Order

8.7 Error Detection

The 8b/10b coding scheme provides multiple mechanisms to detect transmission errors. They can be broadly categorized as invalid transmission characters or disparity errors.

8.7.1 Code Violation Errors

A received character must consist of a valid six-bit sub-block and valid four-bit sub-block. Characters failing to meet this requirement are considered invalid transmission characters as a result of violating the coding requirements. The following list summarizes the error conditions:

- If any six-bit sub-block is received that contains more than four one bits or four zero bits, it is in error (the valid combinations are four ones and two zeros, three ones and three zeros, and four zeros and two ones).
- If any four-bit sub-block is received that contains more than three one bits or three zero bits, it is in error.
- If the combination of the six-bit sub-block and four-bit sub-block contains more than six one bits or six zero bits, it is in error.
- If more than five consecutive one or zero bits occur, the character is in error.

8.7.2 Disparity Errors

The second category of errors are based on the fact that the disparity of the received sub-block must be appropriate, even if the sub-block would otherwise be valid. The encoding rules ensure that the disparity will alternate between successive non-neutral disparity characters (neutral disparity characters have no effect during the encoding process and are ignored during the checking process). This behavior can be used to determine if an error has occurred that affects the disparity of the received data stream. The basic checking rules are:

- If the Current Running Disparity of the receive fibre is positive and a positive disparity character is received, too many one bits have been received.
- If the Current Running Disparity of the receive fibre is negative and a negative disparity character is received, too many zero bits have been received.
- If a neutral disparity character is received, the Current Running Disparity is unchanged.

8.7.3 Error Detection

The error detection capabilities of the 8b/10b scheme do not ensure that all transmission errors will be detected, or that the point of detection necessarily reflects the character in error.

Errors associated with undefined or invalid six-bit or four-bit sub-blocks are generally detected immediately and identify the sub-block in error. Some transmission errors, such as the corruption of a one bit to a zero and concurrent corruption of a zero bit to a one bit may not be detected if they occur within the same sub-block. In this case, one valid sub-block may be converted into another, incorrect sub-block, without being detected by the coding scheme.

Some disparity errors may not be detected until a subsequent character is processed. An example of the delayed detection is shown in Figure 57 on page 109. In this example, a single-bit error causes a neutral disparity character to be altered into a valid, positive disparity character. Because the resultant character is a valid character, the decoder processes the character without detecting the fact that an error occurred. Following processing of the erroneous character one or more neutral disparity characters are received, and processed correctly. The actual detection of the error is delayed until the next non-neutral disparity character is received.

	RD	Character	RD	Character	RD	Character	RD	Character
Binary Notation		00110101		01001010		10110111		10110111
Hex Notation		x'35'		x'4A'		x'B7'		x'B7'
8b/10b Notation		D21.1		D10.2		D23.5		D23.5
Encoded 10-bit Character	-	101010 1001	-	010101 0101	-	111010 1010	+	000101 1010
Received Bit Stream	-	101010 1011	+	010101 0101	+	111010 1010	+	000101 1010
8b/10b Notation		D21.0		D10.2		D23.5		D23.5
Hex Notation		x'15'		x'4A'		x'B7'		x'B7'

Transmission Error occurs here ⎯⎯⎯⎯⎯⎯⎯⎯⎯⎯

Disparity Error is detected here ⎯⎯⎯⎯⎯⎯⎯⎯

Figure 57. Delayed Error Detection Due to Neutral Disparity Characters

The characteristics of the coding scheme detect substantially more than half of all error patterns providing improved characteristics when compared to simple parity schemes as commonly used on parallel data bus interfaces. However, most serial transmission environments, including Fibre Channel, use a cyclic redundancy check (CRC) to provide an additional level of checking on the data frames used to transport information.

8.8 8b/10b Summary

The 8b/10b encoding scheme provides significant benefits facilitating serial data transmission at rates approaching the technology limits. While it may seem that converting eight bits to ten bits wastes 20% of the potential capabilities of the technology, a more accurate assessment is that the characteristics of the encoding scheme allow reliable transmission of data closer to the limits of the technology.

The amount of logic necessary to implement the both encoding and decoding functions is relatively small, on the order of 400 gates resulting in a compact and efficient design.

8.9 Chapter Summary

Bits, Bytes, and Words

- Fibre Channel is a word-oriented architecture
  - A word consists of four bytes, or 32 bits
  - After encoding, a transmission word consists of four 10-bit transmission characters, or 40 bits
- All fields are not necessarily word-sized, but word boundaries are maintained
- This alignment facilitates processing information at high data rates

Why Encode the Data?

- Encoding the data facilitates high-speed transmission on a serial link. It provides:
  - A sufficient number of transitions to enable reliable clock recovery
  - A balance between the number of 1's and 0's sent (DC Balance)
  - Unique special characters outside the 8-bit code space
  - Detection of most (but not all) transmission errors
  - Constant bit, byte, and word rate to simplify the transmit and receive logic

Special Characters

- Normal 8-bit data characters are encoded into 10-bit transmission characters
- Not all valid 10-bit characters are required to represent all the data characters
  - The remaining valid 10-bit transmission characters are used as special characters
  - There are only 12 special characters
- 8b/10b distinguishes between the two types of characters
  - Data characters are identified with a "D"
  - Special characters are identified with a "K"

8b/10b Notation

- The 8b/10b encoding scheme uses its own notation derived from the encoding process
- Characters are identified as either data or special characters (D/K)
- 8-bit bytes are split into two sub-blocks
  - The low-order 5 bits (xx) are processed first
  - Then the high-order 3 bits (y) are processed
  - The value of each sub-block is expressed in decimal
  - The two sub-blocks are separated by a period
- The resulting format is D/Kxx.y

Running Disparity

- As each character is encoded, the encoder examines the number of one and zero bits
- The relationship is referred to as the disparity
  - If there are more ones than zeros, the disparity is positive (six 1's and four 0's)
  - If there are more zeros than ones, the disparity is negative (six 0's and four 1's)
  - If there are the same number, the disparity is neutral (five 1's and five 0's)
- The current running disparity is remembered and controls the encoding of the next character
  - The encoder produces one of two 10-bit outputs based on the running disparity

Encoding and Decoding

- At the transmitter, 8-bit bytes are split into the 5-bit and 3-bit sub-blocks
  - The 5-bit sub-block is encoded into 6 bits
  - The 3-bit sub-block is encoded into 4 bits
  - The result is a 10-bit character
- At each step, the running disparity is updated and used to control encoding of the next sub-block
  - Running disparity is used to maintain DC balance
  - Selects the correct encoded value to balance the number of ones and zeros

9. Ordered Sets

Fibre Channel uses several transmission words to perform control and signaling functions. All of these words consist of an ordered set of four transmission characters, the first of which is the K28.5 special character. The remaining three characters of the word are data characters (Dxx.y), that are used to define the meaning or function of the Ordered Set.

There are three types of Ordered Sets. They are:

- Frame delimiters, that identify the start and end of frames.
- Primitive Signals, that are normally used to indicate events or actions.
- Primitive Sequences, that are used to indicate states or conditions and are normally transmitted continuously until something causes the current state to change.

9.1 Transmission Word Categories

Figure 58 illustrates the relationship of the different kinds of transmission words and identifies the three different types of Ordered Sets.

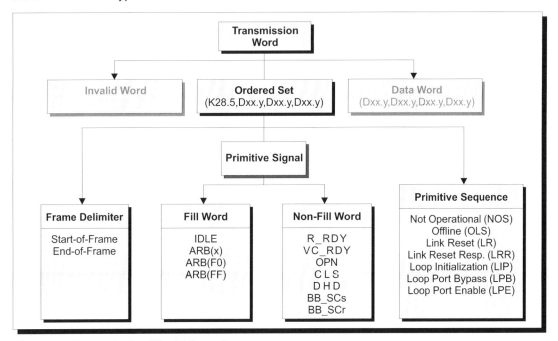

Figure 58. Transmission Word Hierarchy

Data words only have meaning within the content of a Fibre Channel frame. That is, they only have meaning when encountered between a Start-of-Frame delimiter (SOF) and an End-of-Frame (EOF) delimiter. Within the content of a frame, there are only data words.

Ordered Sets occur outside of the frame content. They either identify the start of a frame, the end of a frame, or occur between the end of one frame and the start of the next. There are no Ordered Sets within a frame, and in fact, should one occur, the frame is abnormally terminated

9.2 Frame Delimiters

Frame delimiters are used to delimit, or identify, the start and end of frames. Both the Start-of-Frame and End-of-Frame groups contain multiple Ordered Sets to provide additional control or information about the frame.

9.2.1 Start-of-Frame (SOF)

The Start-of-Frame delimiter identifies the start of a frame and prepares a receiver for frame reception. In addition to identifying the beginning of a frame, the Start-of-Frame delimiter provides other indications regarding the frame. Table 10 lists the Start-of-Frame delimiters.

Frame Delimiter	Abbr.	CRD	Ordered Set		
SOF Connect Class-1	SOFc1	Neg	K28.5	D21.5	D23.0	D23.0
SOF Initiate Class-1	SOFi1	Neg	K28.5	D21.5	D23.2	D23.2
SOF Normal Class-1	SOFn1	Neg	K28.5	D21.5	D23.1	D23.1
SOF Initiate Class-2	SOFi2	Neg	K28.5	D21.5	D21.2	D21.2
SOF Normal Class-2	SOFn2	Neg	K28.5	D21.5	D21.1	D21.1
SOF Initiate Class-3	SOFi3	Neg	K28.5	D21.5	D22.2	D22.2
SOF Normal Class-3	SOFn3	Neg	K28.5	D21.5	D22.1	D22.1
Obsolete (was SOF Activate Class-4)	SOFc4	Neg	K28.5	D21.5	D25.0	D25.0
Obsolete (was SOF Initiate Class-4)	SOFi4	Neg	K28.5	D21.5	D25.2	D25.2
Obsolete (was SOF Normal Class-4)	SOFn4	Neg	K28.5	D21.5	D25.1	D25.1
SOF Fabric	SOFf	Neg	K28.5	D21.5	D24.2	D24.2
SOF Initiate Loop (same as SOFi3)	SOFiL	Neg	K28.5	D21.5	D22.2	D22.2

Table 10. Start-of-Frame Delimiters

Start-of-Frame Connect Class-1 (SOFc1). The Start-of-Frame Connect Class-1 is used
   to request a Class-1 connection (see *Class-1* on page 273). When a fabric is present,
   the SOFc1 requests the fabric to establish a dedicated connection between the source
   and destination ports contained in the frame header. Once a port has sent a SOFc1, it
   must wait for an acknowledgment confirming that the connection has been established
   before sending further frames. SOFc1 implicitly identifies the first frame of a Sequence
   because Class-1 connections can only be established, and terminated, on Sequence
   boundaries.

Start-of-Frame Initiate (SOFi1, SOFi2, SOFi3). The Start-of-Frame Initiate delimiter is used to identify the first frame of a Sequence. One might assume that the SEQ_CNT field of the frame header equal to x'0000' would serve this same function, but there are conditions where the first frame of a Sequence may not begin with a SEQ_CNT value of x'0000'. Consequently, this delimiter provides a positive identification of the first frame of a Sequence that is independent of the SEQ_CNT field.

The first frame of a Class-1 connection uses the SOFc1, that implicitly identifies the initiation of a Sequence. The first frame of subsequent Sequences during that Class-1 connection use the SOFi1 delimiter.

The first frame of all Class 2 and Class 3 Sequences use the SOFi2 and SOFi3 delimiters, respectively. Because these classes of service are connectionless, they do not have a connect form of the Start-of-Frame delimiter.

Start-of-Frame Normal (SOFn1, SOFn2, SOFn3). The Start-of-Frame normal delimiter is used on frames other than the first frame of a Sequence. The class of service indicated in the SOFnx must match the class of service of the first frame of the Sequence (i.e., the class of service cannot change within a Sequence).

Start-of-Frame Fabric (SOFf). The Start-of-Frame fabric delimiter is used on Class-F frames. Class-F is used within the fabric for switch-to-switch communications.

9.2.2 End-of-Frame (EOF)

The End-of-Frame delimiter signals the end of the frame and deconditions the frame reception logic. Table 11 on page 114 lists the End-of-Frame delimiters.

The current running disparity (CRD) is forced negative by transmission of the EOF delimiter, and remains negative after each Ordered Set until transmission of the next SOF delimiter. Because the running disparity of the information within the frame is variable, two different EOF delimiters are used depending upon the running disparity of the frame's content.

- If the current running disparity following transmission of the CRC is negative, the EOF delimiter preceded by 'Neg.' in the CRD column of Table 11 on page 114 is used.

- If the current running disparity following transmission of the CRC is positive, the EOF delimiter preceded by 'Pos.' in the CRD column of Table 11 on page 114 is used.

Forcing the running disparity negative at the end of a frame ensures that the transmission link is always in a known state. All frame switching or routing occurs between the end of one frame and the start of a subsequent frame and occurs on a transmission word boundary. Therefore, when the switching or routing occurs, the running disparity is preserved, even though the receiver may now be receiving information from a different source.

End-of-Frame Terminate (EOFt). The EOFt delimiter indicates this is the last frame of the associated Sequence. In Class-1, Class-2 and Class-F the EOFt delimiter is used on the last acknowledgment frame of the Sequence. In Class-3, the EOFt is used on the last data frame of the Sequence (there are no acknowledgment frames in Class-3)

Frame Delimiter	Abbr.	CRD	Ordered Set			
EOF Normal	EOFn	Neg	K28.5	D21.4	D21.6	D21.6
		Pos	K28.5	D21.5	D21.6	D21.6
EOF Terminate	EOFt	Neg	K28.5	D21.4	D21.3	D21.3
		Pos	K28.5	D21.5	D21.3	D21.3
EOF Disconnect Terminate (Class-1) Obsolete (was EOF Deactivate Terminate Class-4)	EOFdt	Neg	K28.5	D21.4	D21.4	D21.4
		Pos	K28.5	D21.5	D21.4	D21.4
EOF Abort	EOFa	Neg	K28.5	D21.4	D21.7	D21.7
		Pos	K28.5	D21.5	D21.7	D21.7
EOF Normal Invalid	EOFni	Neg	K28.5	D10.4	D21.6	D21.6
		Pos	K28.5	D10.5	D21.6	D21.6
EOF Disconnect Terminate Invalid (Class-1) Obsolete (was EOF Deactivate Terminate Invalid Class-4)	EOFdti	Neg	K28.5	D10.4	D21.4	D21.4
		Pos	K28.5	D10.5	D21.4	D21.4
Obsolete (was EOF Remove Terminate Class-4)	EOFrt	Neg	K28.5	D21.4	D25.4	D25.4
		Pos	K28.5	D21.5	D25.4	D25.4
Obsolete (was EOF Remove Terminate Invalid Class-4)	EOFrti	Neg	K28.5	D10.4	D25.4	D25.4
		Pos	K28.5	D10.5	D25.4	D25.4

Table 11. End-of-Frame Delimiters

End-of-Frame Normal (EOFn). End-of-Frame normal indicates that this is not the last frame of the Sequence.

End-of-Frame Disconnect/Deactivate-Terminate (EOFdt). The End-of-Frame disconnect/deactivate delimiter indicates that a Class-1 connection is ending. Because Class-1 connections always occur on Sequence boundaries, the EOFdt delimiter also indicates the end of a Sequence.

End-of-Frame Abort (EOFa). If, for some reason, the sender of a frame is unable to complete that frame normally, it can end the frame by using the EOFa indicating that frame transmission was aborted. A port receiving a frame terminated with an EOFa takes no action as a result of that frame and ignores (discards) it.

End-of-Frame Disconnect/Deactivate-Terminate Invalid (EOFdti). End-of-Frame disconnect/deactivate terminate invalid (EOFdti) is used to replace the EOF disconnect/deactivate-terminate (EOFdt) when an error is detected by the topology forwarding the frame between the sending and receiving node ports. The EOFdti delimiter only applies to Class-1 service.

End-of-Frame Normal Invalid (EOFni). End-of-Frame normal invalid (EOFni) is used to replace both the EOF normal and EOF terminate delimiters when an error is detected by the topology forwarding the frame between the sending and receiving node ports.

9.3 Primitive Signals

Primitive Signals indicate events at the sending port. The original Fibre Channel Physical and Signaling (FC-PH) standard only defined two Primitive Signals. Subsequent enhancements to the standard (FC-PH2 and FC-PH3) as well as the arbitrated loop standard have added several additional Primitive Signals. Table 12 lists Primitive Signals defined by the Fibre Channel (FC-PH1/2/3, FC-FS) and arbitrated loop (FC-AL2) standards.

Primitive Signal	Abbr.	Ordered Set				Document
Arbitrate	ARB(x)	K28.5	D20.4	AL_PA	AL_PA	FC-AL
Arbitrate (Fairness and Initialization Signal)	ARB(F0)	K28.5	D20.4	D16.7	D16.7	FC-AL
Arbitrate (Alternative to IDLE)	ARB(FF)	K28.5	D20.4	D31.7	D31.7	FC-AL2
Buffer-to-Buffer State Change - SOF	BB_SCs	K28.5	D21.4	D22.4	D22.4	FC-FS
Buffer-to-Buffer State Change - R_RDY	BB_SCr	K28.5	D21.4	D22.6	D22.6	FC-FS
Clock Synchronization X	SYNx	K28.5	D31.3	CS_X	CS_X'	FC-PH3
Clock Synchronization Y	SYNy	K28.5	D31.5	CS_Y	CS_Y'	FC-PH3
Clock Synchronization Z	SYNz	K28.5	D31.6	CS_Z	CS_Z'	FC-PH3
Close	CLS	K28.5	D05.4	D21.5	D21.5	FC-AL
Dynamic Half-Duplex	DHD	K28.5	D10.4	D21.5	D21.5	FC-AL2
Idle	IDLE	K28.5	D21.4	D21.5	D21.5	FC-PH
Mark	MRK(tx)	K28.5	D31.2	MK_TP	AL_PS	FC-AL
Open Full-Duplex (Point-to-point)	OPN(yx)	K28.5	D17.4	AL_PD	AL_PS	FC-AL
Open Half-Duplex (Point-to-point)	OPN(yy)	K28.5	D17.4	AL_PD	AL_PD	FC-AL
Open Broadcast Replicate	OPN(fr)	K28.5	D17.4	D31.7	D31.7	FC-AL
Open Selective Replicate	OPN(yr)	K28.5	D17.4	AL_PD	D31.7	FC-AL
Receiver Ready	R_RDY	K28.5	D21.4	D10.2	D10.2	FC-PH
Virtual Circuit Ready	VC_RDY	K28.5	D21.7	VC_ID	VC_ID	FC-PH2

Table 12. Primitive Signals

9.3.1 Fill Words

Fill words are transmitted on a link when a port is operational and has no other specific information to send. In a Fibre Channel environment, the transmitter portion of a port that is functional is always sending transmission words to maintain synchronization with the receiver at the other end of the link. In the absence of frames or other required Primitive Signals or Sequences, fill words are transmitted.

The only fill word defined by the original FC-PH standard was the IDLE used in point-to-point and fabric topologies. With the development of the arbitrated loop standard, the various forms of the ARB Primitive Signal were also added to the fill word category.

While the interconnect topology defines which fill word is to be transmitted at any point in time, some requirements are independent of the topology.

1. Other Primitive Signals, such as R_RDY, OPN, CLS, etc. must be preceded and followed by a minimum of two fill words at the originating port.

2. After transmission of a frame, the sending port must transmit at least six words before starting transmission of the next frame. These transmission words may contain non-fill words provided that each non-fill word meets rule 1 above.

9.3.2 Fill Words and Clock Elasticity

Fill words may be inserted or deleted by entities, such as repeaters, that exist between the source and destination of a frame. Insertion and deletion allows those entities to compensate for clock differences due to the tolerances allowed by the standards. However, when deletion occurs, the receiver shall be guaranteed to receive a minimum of two transmission words between the end of one frame and the start of the next.

Elasticity Buffer. When receiving, a receiver synchronizes to the incoming data stream using a circuit called a phase-locked loop (PLL). The phase-locked loop provides a recovered clock that is used to clock received words into a small elasticity buffer. The receiver clocks words out of the buffer using a local oscillator that provides an internal clock as shown in Figure 59.

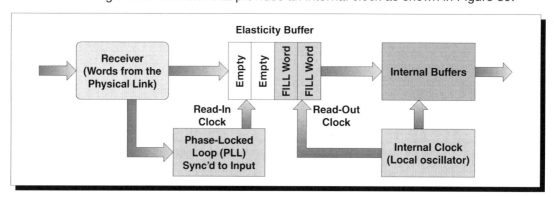

Figure 59. Clock Recovery and Elasticity Buffer

Although the clock provided by the PLL is nominally operating at the specified rate, it may differ slightly from the internal clock rate due to oscillator frequency tolerances. Because of the tolerances of the oscillators, the rate at which words are clocked into the buffer by the phase-locked loop (based on the transmit oscillator sending words to this port) and the rate at which words are clocked out of the buffer using the internal clock may differ.

If the PLL is synchronized at a rate higher than the internal clock (due to clock tolerances), the buffer will fill because words are being clocked into the buffer faster than they are being clocked out. If the buffer overflows, a word is lost and an error may occur. To avoid this problem, the receiver may delete a fill word to prevent overflow of the buffer as shown in Figure 60 on page 117.

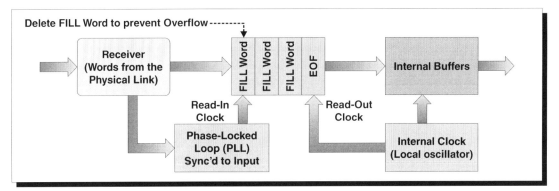

Figure 60. Fill Word Deletion From Elasticity Buffer

If the PLL is synchronized at a rate lower than the internal clock (due to clock tolerances), the buffer will empty because words are being clocked into the buffer at a slower rate than they are being clocked out. If buffer underflow occurs, the receiver doesn't have a word to clock into its internal buffers when it is needed. To avoid buffer underflow, a receiver may insert fill words into the elasticity buffer between frames if necessary as shown in Figure 61.

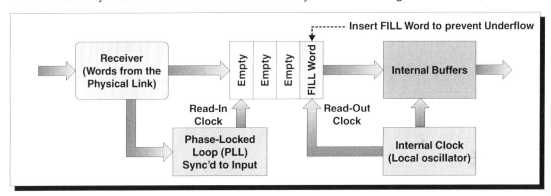

Figure 61. Fill Word Insertion Into Elasticity Buffer

The requirements for fill word transmission ensure that the slowest allowable receiver will be able to keep up with the fastest allowable transmitter.

9.3.3 Flow Control Ordered Sets

Two Ordered Sets are used to control frame transmission on a link, Receiver Ready (R_RDY) and Virtual Circuit Ready (VC_RDY). In addition, two Ordered Sets (BB_SCr and BB_SCs) may be used to provide a buffer-to-buffer credit recovery mechanism.

Receiver Ready (R_RDY). During frame transmission, R_RDY indicates that the receiver has freed a receive buffer and is ready to receive another frame (see *Buffer-to-Buffer Flow Control (BB_Credit)* on page 263).

R_RDY is used for the first frame of a Class-1 connection (the frame with the SOFc1 delimiter, and all Class-2 (SOFi2, SOFn2) and Class-3 (SOFi3, SOFn3) frames. It is not used for subsequent Class-1 frames.

When the alternate buffer-to-buffer credit management model is used, R_RDY is also used to dynamically signal the availability of receive buffers when a loop circuit is opened. This use of R_RDY provides a credit granting service similar to that provided during login, but on a dynamic basis. Arbitrated loop operations use both methods to communicate buffer-to-buffer credit.

Virtual Circuit Ready (VC_RDY). VC_RDY originally provided a link-level flow control mechanism for Class-4 virtual circuits (now obsolete). VC_RDY may optionally be used to provide flow control on the interswitch links between switches.

Buffer-to-Buffer State Change - R_RDY (BB_SCr). BB_SCr is used by the buffer-to-buffer credit recovery mechanism (see *Buffer-to-Buffer Credit Recovery* on page 265). When supported, BB_SCr is transmitted every BB_SC_N R_RDYs to enable the attached port to determine if any R_RDYs have been lost.

Buffer-to-Buffer State Change - SOF (BB_SCs). BB_SCs is used by the buffer-to-buffer credit recovery mechanism (see *Buffer-to-Buffer Credit Recovery* on page 265). When supported, BB_SCs is transmitted every BB_SC_N Start-of-Frame delimiters (SOFc1, SOFi2, SOFn2, SOFi3 or SOFn3) to enable the attached port to determine if frames have been lost.

9.3.4 Clock Synchronization (SYNx, SYNy, SYNz)

The use of these Ordered Sets for point-to-point and switched fabric configurations is defined by FC-PH3. No usage of these Ordered Sets is defined for arbitrated loop environments.

9.4 Arbitrated Loop Specific Primitive Signals

The arbitrated loop standard (FC-AL) added several Ordered Sets to manage the loop protocols necessary for arbitration and opening and closing of loop circuits. Many of the loop-specific Ordered Sets contain one or two, one-byte addresses used to identify a port, or ports, on the loop. This one-byte address is called the arbitrated loop physical address, or AL_PA and corresponds to the least significant byte of the 24-bit address identifier assigned to the port.

9.4.1 Arbitration Ordered Sets

The arbitration Ordered Sets are used to indicate that a loop port requires access to the loop and to manage the access fairness mechanism. All arbitration Ordered Sets are categorized as fill words and subject to fill word substitution or clock elasticity deletion and insertion.

ARB(x). This Ordered Set is used by a port in the arbitrating state to indicate that it is arbitrating for access to the loop. A port in the arbitrating state substitutes its ARB(x) for every IDLE and lower priority ARB received. The (x) value indicates that the third and fourth byte of the Ordered Set are set to the arbitrated loop physical address (AL_PA) assigned to that loop port.

ARB(F0). ARB(F0) is used during loop initialization and by the access fairness protocol. During loop initialization, ARB(F0) signals loop ports that an initialization master has been selected and the LISM phase of initialization is complete.

During access fairness processing this Ordered Set is transmitted by the current arbitration winner to determine if any loop ports are arbitrating. If any port is arbitrating, that port will substitute its own ARB(x) for the received ARB(F0). If no other port is arbitrating, the ARB(F0) will propagate around the loop and be received by the current arbitration winner. This indicates that the access fairness window has ended.

ARB(FF). The ARB(FF) Ordered Set can be used as an alternative to the IDLE Ordered Set once a minimum of six IDLEs have been sent. The bit pattern associated with the ARB(FF) minimizes radio frequency interference (RFI) on a loop with no activity.

While originally intended for Arbitrated Loop environments, ARB(FF) may also used on 4 Gbit and faster non-loop links to minimize emitted radio frequency interference (RFI).

9.4.2 Arbitrated Loop Open Primitive Signals

After a loop port wins arbitration, it opens a loop circuit with another port in the loop. The OPN Primitive Signals provide the capability to open different types of loop circuits.

Open Point-to-Point (OPNyx, OPNyy). The OPNy Ordered Set is used by the open originator to establish a point-to-point like circuit with another loop port. It has two forms, the OPN(yx), that indicates that the open originator is capable of operating full-duplex and the OPN(yy), that indicates that the open originator is specifying that the loop circuit shall operate in half-duplex mode only. In half-duplex mode, the open originator assumes the role of sending device data frames, while the open recipient assumes the role of receiving device data frames.

Open Replicate (OPNyr, OPNfr). The OPNr is used to set replicate mode in one or more loop ports. The OPN(yr) sets replicate mode in the specified port, while OPN(fr) sets replicate mode in all ports in the loop. When replicate mode is set, a port examines received frames to determine if it recognizes the Destination_ID and also replicates the received frame on its transmit output. This mode facilitates multicast and broadcast operations in an arbitrated loop topology.

9.4.3 Arbitrated Loop Circuit Closing Primitive Signals

There are two Primitive Signals associated with the closing of a loop circuit; DHD and CLS.

Dynamic Half-Duplex (DHD). DHD was added by FC-AL2 to indicate that the port sending the DHD has no more device data frames to send. Once a port sends the DHD, it is not permitted to send any additional device data frames, though it can send R_RDYs and link control frames (ACKs, BSYs, and RJTs), if appropriate for the class of service.

Close Ordered Set (CLS). The CLS Ordered Set is sent by a loop port to begin the process of closing the current loop circuit. No address is associated with the CLS and it is recognized by any port that is in an appropriate state.

9.5 Primitive Sequences

Primitive Sequences implement link-level protocols used for link initialization, resets, and failure signaling. All Primitive Sequences require a minimum of three consecutive occurrences of the same Ordered Set before the Primitive Sequence is recognized as valid and action taken. Table 13 on page 120 lists Primitive Sequences defined by the Fibre Channel standards.

Primitive Sequence	Abbreviation	Ordered Set				Document
Link_Reset	LR	K28.5	D09.2	D31.5	D09.2	FC-PH
Link_Reset_Response	LRR	K28.5	D21.1	D31.5	D09.2	FC-PH
Loop Initialization:	LIP					
Loop failure, no valid AL_PA	LIP(F8,F7)	K28.5	D21.0	D24.7	D23.7	FC-AL
Loop failure, valid AL_PA	LIP(F8,AL_PS)	K28.5	D21.0	D24.7	AL_PS	FC-AL
No loop failure, no valid AL_PA	LIP(F7,F7)	K28.5	D21.0	D23.7	D23.7	FC-AL
No loop failure, valid AL_PA	LIP(F7,AL_PS)	K28.5	D21.0	D23.7	AL_PS	FC-AL
Selective reset AL_PD	LIP(AL_PD,AL_PS)	K28.5	D21.0	AL_PD	AL_PS	FC-AL
Reset all	LIP(fx)	K28.5	D21.0	D31.7	AL_PS	FC-AL2
Loop Port Bypass	LPB					
Selected port	LPB(yx)	K28.5	D09.0	AL_PD	AL_PS	FC-AL
All ports	LPB(fx)	K28.5	D09.0	D31.7	AL_PS	FC-AL2
Loop Port Enable:	LPE					
Selected port	LPE(yx)	K28.5	D05.0	AL_PD	AL_PS	FC-AL
All ports	LPE(fx)	K28.5	D05.0	D31.7	AL_PS	FC-AL
Not_Operational	NOS	K28.5	D21.2	D31.5	D05.2	FC-PH
Offline	OLS	K28.5	D21.1	D10.4	D21.2	FC-PH

Table 13. Primitive Sequences

9.5.1 FC-PH Defined Primitive Sequences

FC-PH defines four Primitive Sequences (NOS, OLS, LR, and LRR) that are used during link initialization and error recovery in point-to-point and switched fabric environments. These Primitive Sequences are not used during arbitrated loop operations.

Not Operational (NOS). The Not Operational Primitive Sequence is transmitted by a port in a point-to-point or fabric environment to indicate that the transmitting port has detected a link failure or is in an Offline condition, waiting for the OLS Primitive Sequence to be received. The link failure protocol is described in *Link Failure Protocol and Link Failure States* on page 138.

Offline (OLS). The Offline Primitive Sequence is transmitted by a port to indicate one of the following conditions:

- The port is beginning the link initialization protocol.

- The port has received and recognized the NOS Primitive Sequence.

- The port is entering the Offline state.

The link initialization and Offline procedures are described in *Link Initialization, Offline Procedures, and Offline State* on page 135.

Link Reset (LR). The Link Reset Primitive Sequence is used to initiate a link reset. The Link Reset protocol is described in detail in *Link Reset Protocol and Link Recovery States* on page 133.

Link Reset Response (LRR). Link Reset Response is transmitted by a port to indicate that it has recognized a LR Primitive Sequence and performed the appropriate link reset actions as described in detail in *Link Reset Protocol and Link Recovery States* on page 133.

9.5.2 Arbitrated Loop Initialization Primitive Sequences

The arbitrated loop topology uses a different initialization protocol than used by the point-to-point and fabric topologies. Rather than using the NOS, OLS, LR, and LRR Primitive Sequences, the arbitrated loop uses the Loop Initialization Primitive Sequence (LIP).

Five forms of the LIP Primitive Sequence allow the initializing loop port to indicate the reason for the loop initialization, the AL_PA of the initializing loop port (if it has one), and, in the case of the Reset LIP, the loop port(s) to be reset.

Initialization LIP(F7,F7). This LIP indicates that the loop port in the initializing state is requesting loop initialization but does not currently have a valid AL_PA. This could result from a device being powered on, hot plugged into the loop, or when a nonparticipating loop port without an AL_PA is attempting to become participating and needs to acquire an AL_PA to do so.

Initialization LIP(F7,AL_PS). The LIP(F7,AL_PS) indicates that the loop port identified by the AL_PS value is requesting loop initialization. This LIP may be used if the loop port detects a performance degradation, arbitration wait timeout, or for another unspecified reason.

Loop Failure LIP(F8,F7). This form of the LIP indicates that the loop port in the initializing state is requesting loop initialization due to a loop failure. The loop port does not currently have a valid AL_PA and uses x'F7' instead. This LIP could occur if a nonparticipating loop port without an AL_PA detects a loop failure, or a loop port in the process of acquiring an AL_PA detects a loop failure.

Loop Failure LIP(F8,AL_PS). LIP(F8,AL_PS) indicates that the loop port identified by the AL_PS value has detected a loop failure. This LIP may occur when a loop interconnection has failed, a loop port has failed, a loop port has been powered off or removed from the loop when no bypass circuit is present, or if the bypass circuit itself fails.

Reset LIP(AL_PD,AL_PS). Reset LIP performs a vendor-specific reset at the loop port specified by the AL_PD value (FC-AL2 allows x'FF' to be used as a destination indicating all ports). All loop ports other than the one identified by the AL_PD value treat this as a normal LIP and do not perform a reset. The AL_PS value identifies the loop port originating the request.

The extent of the Selective Reset LIP is defined by each upper-level protocol or application depending upon the information associated with that environment. The FC-AL standard simply says that the designated loop port perform a vendor specific reset. The selective reset LIP may be useful during error recovery to reset a port that is in a questionable or hung state.

9.5.3 Arbitrated Loop Port Bypass Primitive Sequences

The loop port bypass Primitive Sequences are used to set and reset the LP_Bypass variable in the Loop Port State Machine (LPSM). When this variable is set, the LPSM retransmits received transmission words and does not attempt to arbitrate or participate in loop circuits. Some implementations may use the state of this variable to control an optional port bypass circuit to electrically bypass the loop port.

Selective Loop Port Bypass LPB(yx), LPB(fx). When recognized, this Primitive Sequence causes the designated port (yx) or all ports (fx) to set the LP_Bypass variable and optionally activate a control line to an external port bypass circuit, if present.

Loop Port Enable LPE(yx), LPE(fx). When recognized, this Primitive Sequence causes the designated port(yx) or all ports(fx) to reset the LP_Bypass variable and optionally deactivate a control line to an external port bypass circuit, if present.

9.6 Processing of Unrecognized Ordered Sets

Unrecognized, but otherwise valid, Ordered Sets are treated as IDLEs or fill words by the port and no explicit action is taken upon their receipt. This allows future functions to define new Ordered Sets without causing errors in existing designs because they would simply be ignored.

9.7 Chapter Summary

Transmission Words

- All transmission words belong to one of three categories
  - Ordered Sets begin with a special character
  - Data words begin with an encoded data character
  - Invalid word = 8b/10b code or disparity error
- There are three categories of Ordered Sets:
  - Frame delimiters
  - Primitive Signals
  - Primitive Sequences
- All Ordered Sets begin with the K28.5 special character
  - Note: This changes with 10 Gbit FC

Frame Delimiters

- Start-of-Frame identifies the beginning of a frame, and:
  - The delivery characteristics associated with that frame (class of service)
  - If a connection should be made
  - If the frame is initiating a new Sequence
- End-of-Frame identifies the ending of a frame, and:
  - If a connection should be removed
  - If the frame is terminating a Sequence
  - If an error condition was detected or the frame is invalid

Primitive Signals

- Used to signal events
  - Meaningful on a single occurrence
- FC-PH defined only two Primitive Signals
  - IDLE
  - R_RDY
- FC-AL added several more
  - To arbitrate, open, and close loop circuits
- FC-PH2 and FC-PH3 also added new Primitive Signals
  - Clock synchronization and virtual circuit flow control

Fill Words - IDLE

- When a port has no other information to send, it sends fill words
  - IDLE was the only fill word defined by FC-PH
  - Arbitrated loop added additional fill words
  - ARB(FF) can also be used in non-loop environments
- Fill words are 40-bit transmission words, like any other Ordered Set
- A port originating frames must send at least six transmission words between frames
  - Six fill words, or five fill words and an R_RDY
- Fill words provide time for a receiving port to react to received words

Clock Elasticity

- A second use for fill words is to allow repeater functions to insert or delete words
- Allows them to compensate for clock tolerances between the receive data and transmitted data
  - If the receive data is arriving faster than the repeater's transmit clock, a fill word will be discarded periodically
  - If the receive data is arriving slower than the repeater's transmit clock, a fill word will be inserted periodically
- Originally, only the fabric performed fill word insertion or deletion
  - Also used by arbitrated loop ports

Receiver Ready (R_RDY)

- R_RDY is a link-level flow control signal
- Indicates that the receiver has freed a receive buffer and is ready for another frame
- Controls the flow between
  - Two N_Ports in a point-to-point topology
  - An N_Port and an F_Port in a fabric topology
  - Two ports on an arbitrated loop (NL or FL ports)
- R_RDY is not used by all classes of service
  - Class-1 once a connection is established

Virtual Circuit Ready (VC_RDY)

- Virtual circuit ready (VC_RDY) originally for Class-4 VC_ID flow control
  - VC_ID field identified the virtual circuit
  - Class-4 is now obsolete
- May now be used as an optional flow control signal on inter-switch links (ISLs)

Loop Primitive Signals

- Arbitrated loop added several new Primitive Signals to manage the loop
  - ARB(x) indicates that port(x) is arbitrating for access to the loop
  - ARB(F0) is used by the access fairness protocol
  - OPN is used to open a loop circuit
  - DHD is used to convert a full-duplex loop circuit into a half-duplex circuit
  - CLS is used to close a loop circuit

Primitive Sequences

- Used to perform link-level protocols
- Requires three consecutive occurrences of the same Ordered Set before action is taken
- FC-PH defined four Primitive Sequences:
  - Not Operational Sequence (NOS)
  - Offline Sequence (OLS)
  - Link Reset (LR)
  - Link Reset Response (LRR)
- Arbitrated loop added several more to manage the loop

Loop Primitive Sequences

- Used to perform loop initialization and manage the loop
- Multiple forms of the loop initialization (LIP) Primitive Sequence
  - Identify the reason for the initialization
  - And the port that began the loop initialization
  - Also allows a port to reset other ports in the loop
- Loop port bypass allows a port to be electrically bypassed or enabled
  - Used to control an optional bypass circuit
  - Used to allow the loop to continue operating if a port fails
  - Used for management purposes

10. Port State Machine and Link Control Facility

The Port State Machine (PSM) and link control facility in a Fibre Channel port control the link level operation of the port. The Link Control Facility (LCF) controls the basic transmitter and receiver operations of the port while the Port State Machine controls the link-level protocols.

10.1 Transmitter Operation

In a serial transmission scheme, the data being transmitted is converted to a serial bit stream by a parallel-to-serial converter (sometimes called a serializer). Because transmitted information has been encoded in the 8b/10b encoder prior to serialization, each transmission character consists of 10 bits. Upon reception, the serial data stream is converted to parallel 10-bit characters and then decoded. An illustration of the serializing and deserializing process is shown in Figure 62.

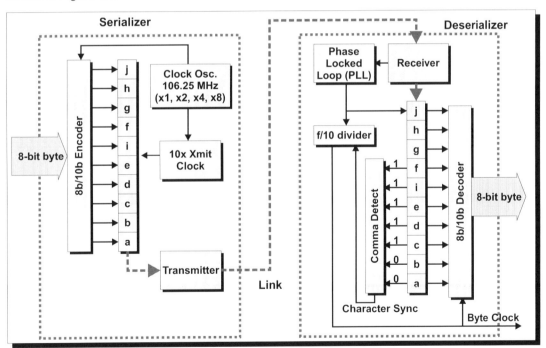

Figure 62. Serializing the Data Stream

When data is transmitted at Fibre Channel's full-speed rate of 1,062.5 megabits per second, characters are clocked into the shift register at a rate of 106.25 megabytes per second (every 10 bits equals one character). This requires a character clock rate of 106.25 MHz. To reduce the character clock rate, some implementations process the encoded data two characters at a time reducing the clock rate by 50% to 53.125 MHz. Both 10-bit (one character) and 20-bit (two character) interfaces have been used in actual implementations. Figure 62 on page 125 illustrates an example with the optional 10-bit interface.

When serializing the data, the transmit clock shifts data out of the serializer shift register at the transmit bit rate. This clock rate is ten times the character clock rate. At Fibre Channel's full-speed data rate, this corresponds to 1,062.5 MHz. Because it is not practical to generate this frequency directly from a crystal oscillator, a phase locked loop frequency multiplier is used. This frequency multiplier provides a transmit clock either ten times the character clock rate (on a 10-bit interface), or twenty times the halfword clock rate (on a 20-bit interface).

The transmitter is in one of four possible states depending upon whether it is enabled or in a failure mode.

10.1.1 Not-Enabled State

A transmitter may enter the Not-Enabled state as a result of error conditions detected by the link control facility or as a result of internally generated signals. For example, the port is in the process of initializing and is not yet enabled for transmission.

10.1.2 Working State

A transmitter enters the Working state when it becomes enabled. This could be as a result of the port enabling the transmitter at the end of port initialization.

While in the Working state, the transmitter is processing transmission characters and serializing those characters into the serial data stream. In order for a request to send a character to be valid, it must be a request for either one of the following:

- Transmission of an Ordered Set properly aligned on a transmitter word boundary
- Transmission of a data word properly aligned on a transmitter word boundary

The following conditions are invalid requests and are not allowed (there is no requirement to check for these invalid requests, they are simply not allowed to occur):

- Lack of a transmission character available upon completion of the current character
- Requests not consistent with the current transmission word and character boundaries
- Requests for Ordered Set transmission on a non-word boundary

10.1.3 Open-Fiber State (Obsolete)

The Open-Fiber state is entered when the link control facility determines that a laser safety condition exists. Normally, this state is entered when the receiver detects a loss-of-signal indicating that the optical cable associated with the link may have been unplugged (and the user may be looking into the cable to see if the light is on).

Once the transmitter is in the Open-Fiber state, it remains in this state until the laser safety condition is removed. Any requests from the link control facility to enter the Not-Enabled or Working states shall be ignored until the laser safety condition is corrected.

The Open-Fiber state is not required by all laser variants, as some wavelengths and power levels are inherently safe.

10.1.4 Failure State

If a failure is detected in the transmitter, it enters the Failure state. Normally, this state indicates that the physical interface transmitter (laser or other driver) has failed. The standard does not require that a transmitter monitor the transmit signal to provide this function. It was included for those implementations desiring to provide an indication of transmit signal degradation such as might occur due to laser aging.

10.2 Receiver Operation

When the receiver is enabled and detects a signal, it attempts to synchronize its internal phase locked loop clock to the received data stream. The phase locked loop consists of a voltage controlled oscillator (VCO) and a phase comparator. The phase comparator compares transitions in the received data stream to transitions of the voltage controlled oscillator. When a transition occurs in the received data stream the phase comparator generates a correction signal to the VCO to adjust the frequency and phase of the VCO. When the phase locked loop has synchronized the VCO to the incoming data stream the data is deserialized and converted back to parallel form. The receiver is in one of three possible states depending upon whether it is enabled and synchronization achieved.

10.2.1 Reset State

A receiver is in the reset state when a reset condition exists, or the receiver is disabled. In this state the receiver is not operational, received data is ignored, and no attempt is made to acquire synchronization to the incoming data.

10.2.2 Synchronization-Acquired State

Because the encoded data stream does not contain all the necessary clocking information, the receiver must provide a means of supplying the missing clock information. This is generally accomplished by using a phase locked loop circuit that synchronizes to the transitions in the received data stream and provides a receive clock. An example of the receive portion of a typical serial link is shown in Figure 62 on page 125. Like the transmit function, the deserialized data can be processed either 10 bits (one character) or 20 bits (two characters) at a time.

There are three distinct aspects to the synchronization process: bit synchronization, character synchronization, and transmission word synchronization.

Bit Synchronization. When a receiver is first powered on, or the link becomes operational and the receiver begins detecting an input signal, the receive phase locked loop is not synchronized to the incoming data stream. Before transmission characters can be successfully processed, the receive phase locked loop must synchronize to the exact frequency of the transmit clock sending the serial data stream. Once the phase locked loop is synchronized to the transmit clock and the receiver can detect bits within the minimum acceptable bit-error rate (BER), it has obtained bit synchronization.

Character and Word Synchronization. Once bit synchronization has been achieved, bits can be successfully detected and sampled, but the receiver still needs to determine the character boundaries before characters can be processed. Until character synchronization is achieved, the receiver stays in the Loss-of-Synchronization state.

The receiver identifies character boundaries by searching for the 7-bit comma pattern contained in the first seven bits of the K28.5 character. All valid transmission words transmitted while attempting to initialize the link, or an arbitrated loop, are Ordered Sets as described in *Ordered Sets* on page 111 and begin with a K28.5 character. Once the comma pattern is detected, the receiver simply counts bits to determine the beginning of the next transmission character (10 bits) or transmission word (40 bits).

After the receiver has detected three consecutive Ordered Sets beginning with a comma pattern without any intervening 8b/10b errors or invalid transmission words, it enters the Synchronization-Acquired state and is ready to begin processing received data.

10.2.3 Loss-of-Synchronization State

The receiver enters a Loss-of-Synchronization state when any of the following occurs:

- Detection of a Loss-of-Synchronization condition
- Power on
- Exit from the Reset state
- Detection of a loss-of-signal

Loss-of-Synchronization Procedure. To prevent loss-of-synchronization on transient errors, loss-of-synchronization is not detected until the following procedure is completed.

While in the Synchronization-Acquired state, the receiver checks each received transmission word to determine whether that word is valid. The transmitter will not exit the Synchronization-Acquired state until it has detected at least four invalid transmission words. An invalid transmission word is one that meets any of the following error conditions:

- A Code Violation error occurs when an invalid 8b/10b character or running disparity error is detected within the word.
- An invalid Special Code alignment error occurs when a valid Special Character (Kxx.y) is detected in the second, third, or fourth position of a transmission word.
- An invalid running disparity error occurs when a defined Ordered Set is received with improper beginning running disparity (e.g., SOF is received with positive running disparity).

There are five states associated with the Loss-of-Synchronization procedure indicating the number of invalid transmission words that have been detected without two intervening valid transmission words. The Loss-of-Synchronization procedure is shown in Figure 63.

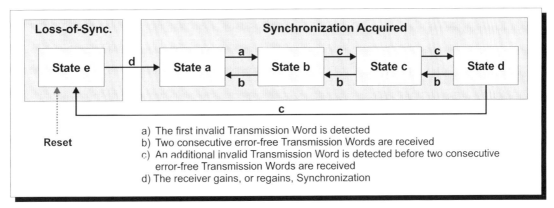

Figure 63. Loss-of-Synchronization Flow

10.3 Loopback Mode

Loopback mode is required between the port's transmitter and receiver. This mode allows the transmit data to be looped back to the receiver for diagnostic purposes. In order for loopback testing to occur, the link control facility must be explicitly placed in loopback mode. The means to enable loopback mode is implementation dependent and not defined by the standard.

When loopback mode is active, the transmit data is passed directly to the receiver and overrides a signal that may be detected by the receiver from the link. This operation may take place in either the parallel or serial portion of the design.

A receiver may be placed in loopback mode whenever it is not in the Reset state. When the receiver is placed in loopback mode, a temporary loss-of-synchronization may occur due to the possible shift in the transmit bit and character alignment. Should this occur, no attempt should be made to use the looped back receive data until synchronization is reacquired.

A transmitter may be placed in loopback mode whenever it is not in the Failure state. When the transmitter is in the Working state and placed in loopback mode, the activity on the attached fiber is unpredictable (data bits may or may not be transmitted on the fiber). When the transmitter is in the Open-Fiber state, setting loopback mode does not change the Open-Fiber behavior because doing so could present a safety hazard.

10.4 Port State Machine (PSM)

An N_Port or F_Port may be in one of four primary operational states, and associated substates, as controlled by conditions within the port, received Primitive Sequences, and the IDLE Primitive Signal. A diagram of the Port State Machine is shown in Figure 64 on page 130.

The four primary states of the Port State Machine and their associated substates are:

- The Active state (AC)
- The Link Recovery state, consisting of the following three substates: LR Transmit substate (LR1), LR Receive substate (LR2), and LRR Receive substate (LR3).

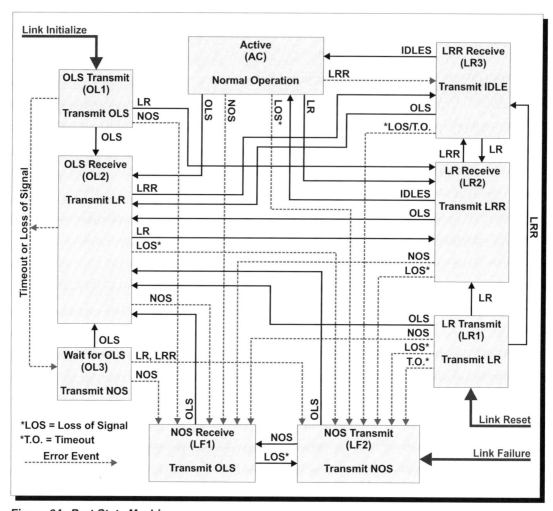

Figure 64. Port State Machine

- The Offline state, consisting of the following three substates: OLS Transmit substate (OL1), OLS Receive substate (OL2), and Wait for OLS substate (OL3).

- The Link Failure state, consisting of the following two substates: NOS Receive substate (LF1) and NOS Transmit substate (LF2).

A state transition table for the Port State Machine (PSM) is shown Table 14 on page 131.

10.5 Active (AC) State

A port enters the Active (AC) state upon completion of the link reset protocol. In the Active (AC) state, the port is able to transmit and receive frames and Primitive Signals such as IDLE

Port State Machine States			
Current State	**Input**	**Condition/Action**	**Next State**
Active (AC) Transmit normal FC-PH signals	LR		LR Receive (LR2)
	LRR	Increment the Primitive Sequence Protocol Error count in the LESB	LRR Receive (LR3)
	NOS	Increment the Link Failure count in the LESB	NOS Receive (LF1)
	OLS		OLS Receive (OL2)
	IDLE	Remain in Active state (normal operation)	
	R_RDY	Increment Buffer-to-Buffer Credit (normal operation)	
	Timeout	There is no limit to the time a port may remain in this state	
	Loss-of-signal	Increment the Loss-of-signal count in the LESB	NOS Transmit (LF2)
	Loss of Sync	If Loss-of-Sync > R_T_TOV, Increment the Loss-of-synchronization count in the LESB	NOS Transmit (LF2)
LR Transmit (LR1) Transmit LR	LR		LR Receive (LR2)
	LRR		LRR Receive (LR3)
	NOS	Increment the Link Failure count in the LESB	NOS Receive (LF1)
	OLS		OLS Receive (OL2)
	IDLE	Ignored	
	R_RDY	Ignored (Buffer-to-Buffer credit is reset by LR)	
	Timeout	If in this state longer than R_T_TOV, increment the Link Failure count in the LESB and exit	NOS Transmit (LF2)
	Loss-of-signal	Increment the Loss-of-signal count in the LESB	NOS Transmit (LF2)
	Loss-of-Sync	Not checked in this state (Timeout occurs)	
LR Receive (LR2) Transmit LRR	LR	Ignored	
	LRR		LRR Receive (LR3)
	NOS	Increment the Link Failure count in the LESB	NOS Receive (LF1)
	OLS		OLS Receive (OL2)
	IDLE		Active (AC)
	R_T_TOV Timeout	If in this state longer than R_T_TOV, increment the Link Failure count in the LESB and exit	NOS Transmit (LF2)
	Loss-of-signal	Increment the Loss-of-signal count in the LESB	NOS Transmit (LF2)
	Loss-of-Sync	Not checked in this state (R_T_TOV Timeout occurs first)	
LRR Receive (LR3) Transmit IDLE	LR		LR Receive (LR2)
	LRR	Ignored	
	NOS	Increment the Link Failure count in the LESB	NOS Receive (LF1)
	OLS		OLS Receive (OL2)
	IDLE		Active (AC)
	Timeout	If in this state longer than R_T_TOV, increment the Link Failure count in the LESB and exit	NOS Transmit (LF2)
	Loss-of-signal	Increment the Loss-of-signal count in the LESB	NOS Transmit (LF2)
	Loss-of-Sync	Not checked in this state (R_T_TOV Timeout occurs first)	

Table 14. Port State Machine Transition Table (Part 1 of 3)

Port State Machine States			
Current State	**Input**	**Condition/Action**	**Next State**
OLS Transmit (OL1)	LR	During link initialization only	LR Receive (LR2)
	LRR	Ignored	
	NOS	During link initialization only, increment the Link Failure count in the LESB	NOS Receive (LF1)
Transmit OLS for a minimum of 5 msec. then examine inputs	OLS	During link initialization only	OLS Receive (OL2)
	IDLE	Ignored	
	Timeout	If during link initialization only, no Primitive Sequence or event occurs causing an exit from this state, exit to OL3	Wait for OLS (OL3)
	Loss-of-signal	Ignored	
	Loss of Sync	Ignored	
OLS Receive (OL2)	LR		LR Receive (LR2)
	LRR		LRR Receive (LR3)
	NOS	Increment the Link Failure count in the LESB	NOS Receive (LF1)
	OLS	Ignored	
	IDLE	Ignored	
Transmit LR	Timeout	Increment the Primitive Sequence Protocol Error count in the LESB	Wait for OLS (OL3)
	Loss-of-signal	This is not counted as an error in the LESB	Wait for OLS (OL3)
	Loss of Sync	Loss-of-Sync > R_T_TOV is not counted as an error in the LESB	Wait for OLS (OL3)
Wait for OLS (OL3)	LR	Increment the Primitive Sequence Protocol Error count in the LESB	NOS Transmit (LF2)
	LRR	Increment the Primitive Sequence Protocol Error count in the LESB	NOS Transmit (LF2)
	NOS		NOS Receive (LF1)
	OLS		OLS Receive (OL2)
Transmit NOS	IDLE	Ignored	
	Timeout	There is no limit to the time a port may remain in this state	
	Loss-of-signal	Ignored	
	Loss of Sync	Ignored	
NOS Receive (LF1)	LR		LR Receive (LR2)
	LRR	Ignored	
	NOS	Ignored	
	OLS		OLS Receive (OL2)
	IDLE	Ignored	
Transmit OLS	Timeout	If NOS is no longer recognized and the port remains in this state for R_T_TOV, increment the Link Failure count in the LESB and exit	NOS Transmit (LF2)
	Loss-of-signal	Increment the Loss-of-signal count in the LESB	NOS Transmit (LF2)
	Loss of Sync	If Loss-of-Sync > R_T_TOV, increment the Loss-of-synchronization count in the LESB	NOS Transmit (LF2)

Table 14. Port State Machine Transition Table (Part 2 of 3)

Port State Machine States			
Current State	Input	Condition/Action	Next State
NOS Transmit (LF2) Transmit NOS	LR	Ignored	
	LRR	Ignored	
	NOS		NOS Receive (LF1)
	OLS		OLS Receive (OL2)
	IDLE	Ignored	
	Timeout	There is no limit to the time a port may remain in this state	
	Loss-of-signal	Ignored	
	Loss of Sync	Ignored	

Table 14. Port State Machine Transition Table (Part 3 of 3)

and R_RDY. When a port in the Active (AC) state recognizes a Primitive Sequence, it exits the Active state and enters a new state based on the Primitive Sequence received.

Certain conditions encountered within the port may cause the port to exit the Active (AC) state and perform one of the following Primitive Sequence protocols:

- Link Reset (*Link Reset Protocol and Link Recovery States* on page 133)
- Link Initialization or Online to Offline transition (*Link Initialization, Offline Procedures, and Offline State* on page 135)
- Link Failure (*Link Failure Protocol and Link Failure States* on page 138)

10.6 Link Reset Protocol and Link Recovery States

The link reset protocol is performed as a result of a link timeout, Class-1 connection error, or completion of link initialization. The Link Reset protocol is shown in Figure 65 on page 134.

The link reset procedure initiates when a port enters the LR Transmit (LR1) substate, begins transmitting the LR Primitive Sequence, and performs the link reset actions. When the port at the other end of the link recognizes LR, it enters the LR Receive (LR2) substate, begins transmitting the LRR Primitive Sequence, and performs the link reset actions.

When a port in the LR Transmit (LR1) substate recognizes LRR, it enters the LRR Receive (LR3) substate and begins transmitting IDLE. When a port in the LR Receive (LR2) substate recognizes IDLE, it enters the Active (AC) state and also begins transmitting IDLEs. These IDLEs cause the port in the LRR Receive (LR3) state to enter the Active (AC) state, completing the link reset action.

10.6.1 LR Transmit Substate (LR1)

A port enters the LR Transmit substate to begin the link reset procedure. This may be as a result of a link timeout, an uncertain or ambiguous Class-1 connection state, or completion of the link initialization protocol. While in the LR1 state, the port transmits the LR Primitive Sequence.

A port in the LR Transmit substate discards all received Class-1 frames. The standard does not specify the action taken with regard to frames in other classes of service that may be received, or are currently being held in receive buffers.

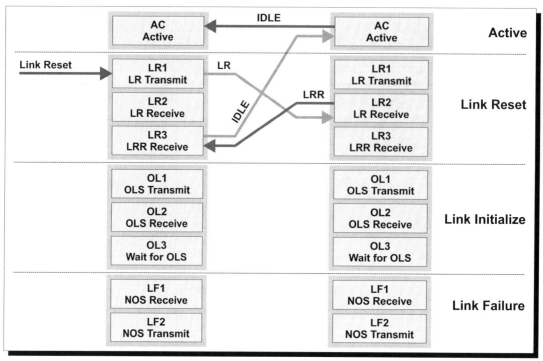

Figure 65. Link Reset Protocol

If a port stays in the LR transmit substate (LR1) longer than R_T_TOV or detects a Loss-of-Signal, it logs a link failure in the Link Error Status Block (LESB), goes to the NOS Transmit state (LF2), and begins transmitting the NOS Primitive Sequence.

10.6.2 LR Receive Substate (LR2)

A port enters the LR Receive substate when it receives and recognizes the LR Primitive Sequence and is not in the Wait for OLS (OL3) or NOS Transmit (LF2) substates. While the port is in this state, it transmits the LRR Primitive Sequence.

The Fibre Channel standard does not specify what effect receiving LR has on a frame currently being transmitted, or queued for transmission. Class-1 frames will be discarded by the other port, so the action taken for them is irrelevant. Frames in other classes of service may or may not be processed by a port currently transmitting LR so the results may be ambiguous.

If a port stays in the LR Receive substate (LR2) longer than R_T_TOV or detects a Loss-of-Signal, it logs a link failure in the Link Error Status Block (LESB), goes to the NOS Transmit state (LF2), and begins transmitting the NOS Primitive Sequence.

10.6.3 LRR Receive Substate (LR3)

A port enters the LRR Receive substate when it receives and recognizes the LRR Primitive Sequence while it is in the Active (AC), LR Transmit (LR1), LR Receive (LR2), or OLS Receive (OL2) states. While the port is in this state, it transmits the IDLE Ordered Set.

The standard does not specify what effect receiving LR has on a frame currently being transmitted, or queued for transmission should LRR be received while in the Active (AC) state.

If a port stays in the LRR receive substate (LR3) longer than R_T_TOV or detects a Loss-of-Signal, it logs a link failure in the Link Error Status Block (LESB), goes to the NOS Transmit state (LF2), and begins transmitting the NOS Primitive Sequence.

10.6.4 Class-1 Connection Recovery

When the link reset protocol is used to abnormally terminate a Class-1 connection, the process is referred to as connection recovery. Connection recovery results in the following actions:

- Any established or pending Class-1 connection is removed. If the Class-1 connection is through a fabric, the link reset protocol is initiated by the fabric on the other link participating in the Class-1 connection.

- All Class-1 Sequences that are active or open in the port when LR is sent or received are abnormally terminated.

- Any Class-1 frames received by the port transmitting LR are discarded (a port receiving LR or LRR cannot also be receiving frames).

- A port that receives and recognizes the link reset may process or discard any Class-2 or Class-3 frames currently held in its receive buffers.

- A fabric port transmitting LR may process or discard any Class-1 connect, Class-2, or Class-3 frames currently in its receive buffers that are associated with the N_Port connected to the link.

- End-to-end credit values associated with the two ports involved in a Class-1 connection are reset to their login values. Any Class-2 end-to-end credit is not affected.

- Buffer-to-buffer credit values for the two ports connected to the link being reset are restored to their login values.

10.7 Link Initialization, Offline Procedures, and Offline State

A port enters the Offline state to perform link initialization after a port has been powered on, internally reset, or has been Offline. A port also enters the Offline state prior to powering off or performing internal diagnostics that might affect the link. The Link Initialization protocol is shown in Figure 66 on page 136.

If a node port transmits the OLS Primitive Sequence while a Class-1 connection is pending or active, the locally attached fabric port enters the OLS Receive (OL2) substate, removes the Class-1 connection, and notifies the remote fabric port attached to the other node port in the

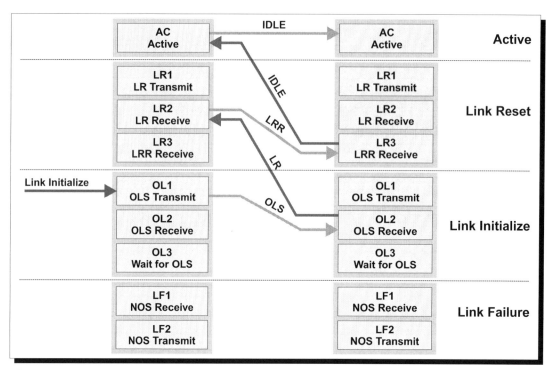

Figure 66. Link Initialization Protocol

Class-1 connection to initiate the link reset protocol. This ensures that a port entering the Offline state during a Class-1 connection causes connection recovery the remote node port.

If no Class-1 connection is pending or active, the locally attached fabric port enters the OLS Receive (OL2) substate but does not initiate a link reset with any other fabric port.

OLS is not propagated through the fabric in either case.

10.7.1 Link Initialization Protocol

The point-to-point and fabric topologies share a common link initialization procedure using the NOS, OLS, LR, and LRR Primitive Sequences and the IDLE Primitive Signal. The arbitrated loop topology uses a different initialization process.

The link initialization protocol is used to initialize a point-to-point link (two connected N_Ports), a fabric attached link (one N_Port and one F_Port), or inter-switch link (two connected E_Ports on one E_Port and one B_Port). Either port connected to the link may begin the link initialization procedure.

To begin the link initialization procedure, the port enters the OLS Transmit substate (OL1) and transmits the OLS Primitive Sequence for a minimum of 5 msec. After the minimum OLS transmission period has elapsed, the port proceeds as indicated for the OLS Transmit sub-state.

- If LR is received, the port continues the link initialization by entering the LR Receive sub-state (LR2) and performing the Link Reset protocol.
- If no signal is present when the required OLS transmission period completes, Loss-of-Synchronization occurs for greater than R_T_TOV, or no other event causes the port to leave the OL1 state, the port goes to the Wait for OLS substate (OL3) and waits to receive OLS from the attached port.

10.7.2 Online to Offline Protocol

When the port is in the Active (AC) state, it is Online. While online, the port may transmit and receive frames, Primitive Signals, and Primitive Sequences.

To change from the Online state to the Offline state, the port performs the Online to Offline procedure. To perform this procedure, the port enters the OLS Transmit (OL1) substate, transmits the OLS Primitive Sequence for a minimum of 5 msec. and is then Offline.

While Offline, the port does not respond to received frames, Primitive Signals, or Primitive Sequences. The port may power off, perform diagnostic procedures, transmit any signal except Primitive Sequences that would cause the other port to leave the OLS Receive substate (OL2) or Wait for OLS substate (OL3), turn off its transmitter or take any other actions, without causing errors at the other port.

10.7.3 OLS Transmit Substate (OL1)

Upon entry to the OLS Transmit substate, the port transmits the OLS Primitive Sequence for a minimum of 5 msec. Following transmission of the OLS Primitive Sequence, the port will be in one of two possible conditions:

- The port is in the Offline state (see *Online to Offline Protocol* on page 137) and not subject to state transitions, or
- The port is performing the link initialization procedure (see *Link Initialization Protocol* on page 136) and is enabled for state transitions.

10.7.4 OLS Receive Substate (OL2)

A port enters the OLS Receive substate when it receives and recognizes the OLS Primitive Sequence. In this state, the port transmits the LR Primitive Sequence (initiating a link reset).

10.7.5 Wait for OLS Substate (OL3)

A port enters the Wait for OLS substate when it detects a Loss-of-Synchronization for greater than R_T_TOV or Loss-of-Signal while in the OLS Receive (OL2) substate. This could occur if the other port enter the OLS Transmit substate (OL1) to transition to the Offline condition.

A port also enters the Wait for OLS substate if it started link initialization in the OLS Transmit substate (OL1), transmitted the OLS Primitive Sequence for a minimum of 5 msec. and did not receive a response from the other port that caused this port to enter a different state.

10.8 Link Failure Protocol and Link Failure States

The link failure protocol indicates a Loss-of-Signal or Loss-of-Synchronization lasting longer than the R_T_TOV value was detected while not in the Offline state. The link failure protocol is also used after a link reset protocol timeout error (e.g., waiting for LRR or IDLE while performing the link reset). The Link Failure protocol is shown in Figure 67.

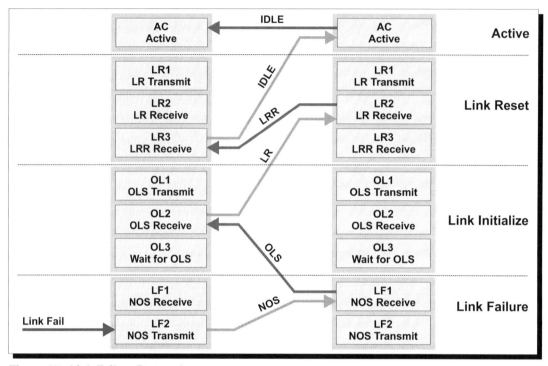

Figure 67. Link Failure Protocol

A port initiating the link failure protocol enters the NOS Transmit (LF2) substate and transmits the NOS Primitive Sequence to provide notification to the port at the other end of the link of the failure, if possible. While in the NOS Transmit state, and when the receiver is in operation, the port processes and responds to received Primitive Sequences.

If an N_Port transmits NOS while a Class-1 is pending or active, the locally attached F_Port enters the NOS Receive (LF1) substate, removes the Class-1 connection, and notifies the F_Port attached to the other N_Port in the Class-1 connection to initiate the link reset protocol. This ensures that a link failure during a Class-1 connection is indicated to the remote N_Port.

If no Class-1 connection is pending or active, the locally attached F_Port enters the NOS Receive (LF1) substate but does not initiate a link reset with any other F_Port.

NOS is not propagated through the fabric in either case.

10.8.1 NOS Transmit Substate (LF2)

A port enters the NOS Transmit substate when it detects a link failure. While in this state, the port transmits the NOS Primitive Sequence. The behavior of a port in the NOS Transmit substate is defined in the *Port State Machine (PSM)* on page 129.

10.8.2 NOS Receive Substate (LF1)

A port enters the NOS Receive substate when it receives and recognizes the NOS Primitive Sequence. While in this state, the port transmits the OLS Primitive Sequence. The behavior of a port in the NOS Receive substate is defined in *Port State Machine (PSM)* on page 129.

10.9 Chapter Summary

Link Control Facility

- Controls the port's transmit and receive functions
- Transmitter states:
  - Not enabled
  - Working
  - Open fiber
  - Failure
- Receiver states:
  - Reset
  - Synchronization acquired
  - Loss-of-Synchronization

Port State Machine (PSM)

- Port State Machine controls link-level protocols
  - Link Failure protocol
  - Link Initialization protocol
  - Link Reset protocol
- Uses Primitive Sequences
  - Not Operational Sequence (NOS)
  - Offline Sequence (OLS)
  - Link Reset (LR) and Link Reset Response (LRR) Sequences
- PSM applies to non-loop environments only
  - Arbitrated loop uses the Loop Port State Machine (LPSM)

Link Failure Protocol

- When a port detects a link failure it initiates the link failure protocol
  - Loss-of-Signal
  - Loss-of-Synchronization for greater than R_T_TOV
  - Primitive Sequence protocol errors
- Enters state LF2 and transmits NOS
  - Other port enters state LF1 and transmits OLS to begin the link initialization protocol

Link Initialization Protocol

- When a port begins link initialization, it goes to state OL1 and transmits OLS for > 5 msec.
  - Other port goes to state OL2 and transmits LR to begin the link reset protocol
  - If the other port is not operational, the port times out and goes to state OL3 and waits for OLS from the other port
- Online to Offline procedure
  - A port may enter the offline condition
  - Preparing to power-off or perform diagnostics
  - Port goes to state OL1, transmits OLS and ignores received transmission words

Link Reset Protocol

- When a port needs to reset the link, it goes to state LR1 and transmits LR
  - Causes the other port to go to LR2 and transmits LRR
  - 1st port recognizes LRR, goes to state LR3 and transmits IDLE
  - 2nd port recognizes IDLE, goes to the Active (AC) state and transmits IDLE
  - 1st port recognizes IDLE and goes to the Active (AC) state also
  - Once a port is in the Active (AC) state, frame transmission is allowed
- Link Reset ends Class-1 connections
- Link Reset restores buffer-to-buffer credit values

Link Error Status Block

- Port state machine maintains error counters in the Link Error Status Block (LESB)
  - Link Failure counter
  - Loss-of-Synchronization counter
  - Loss-of-Signal counter
  - Primitive Sequence Protocol Error counter
- Other LESB counters maintained outside the port state machine
  - Invalid Transmission Word counter
  - Invalid CRC Error counter

11. 10-Gigabit Fibre Channel

One of the more exciting developments in Fibre Channel technology is the development of links capable of operating at 10 gigabits per second. 10-gigabit links provide the bandwidth needed for backbone, or core, switches in Fibre Channel networks as well as supporting the needs of high-performance systems and devices. 10-Gigabit Fibre Channel (10GFC) provides twelve times the bandwidth of first generation 100 MB/s links. This provides a link bandwidth of 1,275 MB/s, or 1.275 Gbps (1,200 MB/s deliverable after overhead is deducted).

In making the leap to 10-Gigabit Fibre Channel, the goal was to provide dramatically higher bandwidth while minimizing the impact on the existing Fibre Channel architecture. Because of this, there is no change to existing protocol mappings (such as the SCSI-FCP protocol mapping), frame structure, or frame usage. Figure 68 shows how 10GFC fits into the Fibre Channel structure. As this figure shows, changes to support 10-Gigabit Fibre Channel are largely confined to the FC-0 and FC-1 levels.

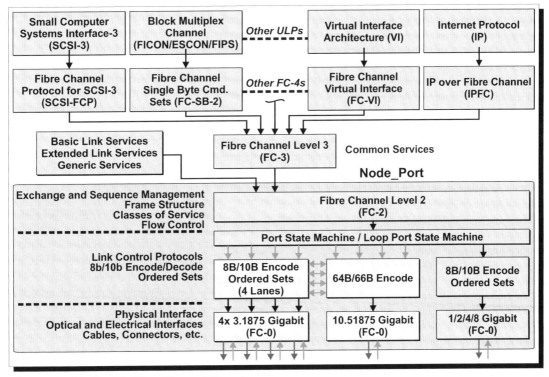

Figure 68. 10-Gigabit Fibre Channel Structure

To support the higher signaling rates used by 10-Gigabit Fibre Channel, two new external physical interfaces (and their variants) have been specified.

The first new physical interface uses four serial links operating at 3.1875 Gbps each. The four serial links can use four separate multimode optical fibers (1200-Mx-SN4PL-S) or a single multimode optical fiber using wavelength division multiplexing (1200-Mx-SN4-S). Distances on the order of 100 meters are supported using standard 50 um. optical fiber and 150 meters using high-bandwidth 50 um. multimode optical fiber (2000 MHz*km). Because each link is similar to existing Fibre Channel links, this variant may become the first that is widely deployed.

The second physical interface uses a traditional approach based on a single serial link operating at 10.51875 gigabits per second. Using single-mode optical fiber with a long-wavelength laser transmitter (1310 nm.), distances of 10 km. are attainable. Unlike existing Fibre Channel physical interfaces, the 10.51875 gigabit variant uses a new 64B/66B coding scheme (see *64B/66B Encode/Decode* on page 152). Because this variant requires considerable new technology and higher signaling rates, deployment may trail the four link variant described above.

While Fibre Channel pioneered the development of affordable gigabit technologies, development of 10-gigabit technology is occurring in tandem within multiple standards bodies. The primary work is being done within IEEE to develop a 10-gigabit Ethernet standard. The Fibre Channel committee is leveraging as much of that work as possible. The goal is to develop one set of physical-layer components usable by both interfaces. This seems reasonable given that the 10-Gigabit Fibre Channel signaling rate is only 2% faster than the 10-gigabit Ethernet rate.

11.1 10-Gigabit Media Independent Interface (XGMII)

The XGMII is an optional interface that provides a 10.2-gigabit (1.275 gigabyte) per second parallel interface between the FC-1 Port State Machine (PSM) or Loop Port State Machine (LPSM) and lower-level functions. This interface uses signal levels compatible with common CMOS and ASIC processes and is intended as an internal interface, or for chip-to-chip interfaces with distances limited to approximately 7 cm.

XGMII provides two independent 32-bit-wide data paths to support full-duplex operation, one for transmit data and one for receive data. All transmit transfers are synchronous to a single transmit clock and all receive transfers are synchronous to a single receive clock.

To minimize the XGMII clock frequency, data is clocked on both the rising and falling edges of the clocks. Both transmit and receive clocks operate at a frequency of 159.375 MHz providing an XGMII transfer rate of 1,275 MB/s (eight times 159.375).

The four XGMII bytes are referred to as *lanes*. Lane 0 corresponds to byte 0 (bits 31-24), lane 1 corresponds to byte 1 (bits 23-16), etc.

11.1.1 XGMII Ordered Sets

In addition to the eight data bits, there is one control bit associated with each XGMII lane. If the control bit is zero, the lane contains a data byte. If the control bit is one, the lane contains a control character. The control bit provides a mechanism to transfer special characters across XGMII. Special characters are used by Ordered Sets such as Start-of-Frame and End-of-Frame. Figure 69 on page 143 shows an SOFi3 Ordered Set being transferred across XGMII.

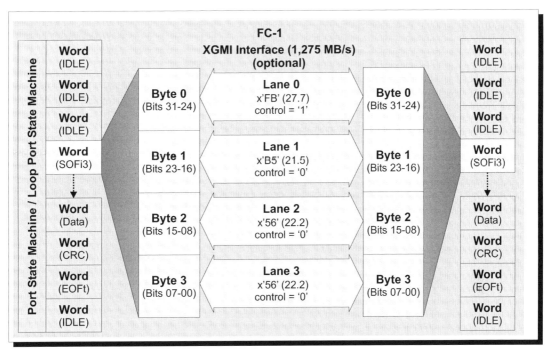

Figure 69. Ten Gigabit Media Independent Interface (XGMII)

Character representations for the special characters are shown in Table 15. With the exception of IDLE, hex values associated with control characters correspond directly to the hex values associated with 8B/10B special characters (e.g., x'FB' = 27.7).

Abbreviation	Description	Control	Hex Value	D/Kxx.y Value
	Normal data characters	0	x'00' to x'FF'	D00.0 to D31.7
S	Start-of-Frame (only valid in lane 0)	1	x'FB'	K27.7
T	Terminate (only valid in lane 3)	1	x'FD'	K29.7
P	Primitive Signal (only valid in lane 0)	1	x'5C'	K28.2
Q	Primitive Sequence (only valid in lane 0)	1	x'9C'	K28.4
E	Error (valid in all lanes)	1	x'FE'	K30.7
I	IDLE (valid in all lanes)	1	x'07'	none

Table 15. XGMII Data and Control Characters

11.2 10-Gigabit Attachment Unit Interface (XAUI)

The 10-Gigabit Attachment Unit Interface (XAUI) provides a means to extend XGMII distances and allow 10-gigabit physical media devices to be located farther from the protocol chip. Each byte-wide XGMII lane is converted into a serial link as shown in Figure 70 on page 144.

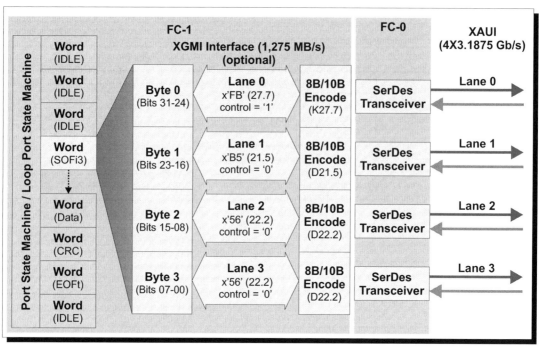

Figure 70. XGMII + XAUI Interface

Data on each serial lane is encoded using the same 8B/10B coding scheme used on standard Fibre Channel links. This provides all the benefits of the 8B/10B coding scheme including special characters, embedded clock, and DC balance.

Each lane operates at 3.1875 gigabaud (3X the base Fibre Channel link rate of 1.0625 gigabaud) resulting in a total XAUI bandwidth of 12.750 gigabits per second. This provides the required 1,275 MB/s bandwidth (1,200 MB/s deliverable) while still using a link speed that can be implemented with available CMOS technology.

The XAUI signaling may be used as an inter-chip interface, or between devices over limited distances. When used between devices, the signals may be carried via four separate optical fibers at distances of 300-500 meters, via four separate electrical transmission lines at distances of a few meters, or via a single optical fiber using wavelength division multiplexing.

Wavelength division multiplexing (WDM) is a technique allowing multiple data streams to be transferred via the same optical fiber. When WDM is used, separate lasers operating at different wavelengths are used for each data stream. The outputs of the lasers are combined and sent via a single optical fiber. Depending on the separation of the wavelengths used, this technique is referred to as either Coarse Wavelength Division Multiplexing (CWDM) or Dense Wavelength Division Multiplexing (DWDM). An illustration of the coarse wavelength division multiplexing used by XAUI is shown in Figure 71 on page 145.

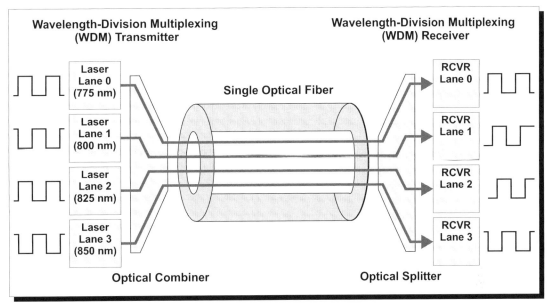

Figure 71. Wavelength Division Multiplexing (WDM)

When signals arrive at the receiving end of the fiber, a wavelength splitter separates the data streams based on the wavelengths. Each wavelength is directed to a separate receiver where the clock and data are recovered, deserialized, and finally decoded for processing.

11.2.1 XAUI Ordered Sets

Ordered Sets sent via XAUI are different from the Ordered Sets used on standard Fibre Channel links. The first difference is that Ordered Sets (as with all transmission words) are striped across the four lanes. Instead of the Ordered Set appearing as a series of transmission characters on the same fiber, it now appears as a column of characters across the four lanes.

To provide commonality between 10-Gigabit Ethernet and the XGMII, the characters that make up the Ordered Sets are different from with existing Fibre Channel links. On existing Fibre Channel links, K28.5 is the only special character used. In 10-Gigabit Fibre Channel, other special characters are used in addition to K28.5. While special characters only appear in byte 0 of a transmission word on existing Fibre Channel links, special characters are present in all character positions on XAUI links.

XAUI Frame Delimiters. Table 16 on page 146 lists Start-of-Frame and End-of-Frame delimiters used on XAUI by 10-Gigabit Fibre Channel. Except for the first character (K27.7 replaces K28.5), Start-of-Frame Ordered Sets are identical to those defined by existing Fibre Channel (FC-PH1/2/3, FC-FS) standards.

Note that bytes 1, 2 and 3 of the XAUI End-of-Frame Ordered Set correspond to bytes 2, 3, and 4 of the FC-PH/FC-FS Ordered Sets and byte 4 is the K29.7 character.

Frame Delimiter	Abbr.	Ordered Set			
SOF Connect Class-1	SOFc1	K27.7	D21.5	D23.0	D23.0
SOF Initiate Class-1	SOFi1	K27.7	D21.5	D23.2	D23.2
SOF Normal Class-1	SOFn1	K27.7	D21.5	D23.1	D23.1
SOF Initiate Class-2	SOFi2	K27.7	D21.5	D21.2	D21.2
SOF Normal Class-2	SOFn2	K27.7	D21.5	D21.1	D21.1
SOF Initiate Class-3 / SOF Initiate Loop	SOFi3 / SOFiL	K27.7	D21.5	D22.2	D22.2
SOF Normal Class-3	SOFn3	K27.7	D21.5	D22.1	D22.1
Obsolete (was SOF Activate Class-4)	SOFc4	K27.7	D21.5	D25.0	D25.0
Obsolete (was SOF Initiate Class-4)	SOFi4	K27.7	D21.5	D25.2	D25.2
Obsolete (was SOF Normal Class-4)	SOFn4	K27.7	D21.5	D25.1	D25.1
SOF Fabric	SOFf	K27.7	D21.5	D24.2	D24.2
EOF Normal	EOFn	D21.4	D21.6	D21.6	K29.7
EOF Terminate	EOFt	D21.4	D21.3	D21.3	K29.7
EOF Disconnect Terminate (Class-1) Obsolete (was EOF Deactivate Terminate Class-4)	EOFdt	D21.4	D21.4	D21.4	K29.7
EOF Abort	EOFa	D21.4	D21.7	D21.7	K29.7
EOF Normal Invalid	EOFni	D10.4	D21.6	D21.6	K29.7
EOF Disconnect Terminate Invalid (Class-1) Obsolete (was EOF Deactivate Terminate Invalid Class-4)	EOFdti	D10.4	D21.4	D21.4	K29.7
Obsolete (was EOF Remove Terminate Class-4)	EOFrt	D21.4	D25.4	D25.4	K29.7
Obsolete (was EOF Remove Terminate Invalid Class-4)	EOFrti	D10.4	D25.4	D25.4	K29.7

Table 16. XAUI Frame Delimiters

XAUI Primitive Signals. Table 17 lists Primitive Signals used across XAUI by 10-Gigabit Fibre Channel. With the exception of the first character (K28.2 replaces K28.5), the Ordered Sets are identical to those defined by the Fibre Channel (FC-PH1/2/3, FC-FS) and arbitrated loop (FC-AL2) standards. (Note that while XAUI supports the arbitrated loop Primitive Signals and Primitive Sequences, it does not support the arbitrated loop protocols).

Primitive Signal	Abbr.	Ordered Set			
Arbitrate	ARB(x)	K28.2	D20.4	AL_PA	AL_PA
Arbitrate (Fairness and Initialization Signal)	ARB(F0)	K28.2	D20.4	D16.7	D16.7
Arbitrate (Alternative to IDLE)	ARB(FF)	K28.2	D20.4	D31.7	D31.7
Buffer-to-Buffer State Change - SOF	BB_SCs	K28.2	D21.4	D22.4	D22.4
Buffer-to-Buffer State Change - R_RDY	BB_SCr	K28.2	D21.4	D22.6	D22.6
Clock Synchronization X	SYNx	K28.2	D31.3	CS_X	CS_X'
Clock Synchronization Y	SYNy	K28.2	D31.5	CS_Y	CS_Y'
Clock Synchronization Z	SYNz	K28.2	D31.6	CS_Z	CS_Z'

Table 17. XAUI Primitive Signals (Part 1 of 2)

Chapter 11. 10-Gigabit Fibre Channel

Close	CLS	K28.2	D05.4	D21.5	D21.5
Dynamic Half-Duplex	DHD	K28.2	D10.4	D21.5	D21.5
Align - Lane deskew via code group alignment	A	K28.3	K28.3	K28.3	K28.3
Sync - Synchronization and End-of-Frame pad	K	K28.5	K28.5	K28.5	K28.5
Skip - Clock elasticity compensation	R	K28.0	K28.0	K28.0	K28.0
Mark	MRK(tx)	K28.2	D31.2	MK_TP	AL_PS
Link Signaling	LSS	K28.2	LSD_ID	LSF_ID	LSM / LS_OH
Open Full-Duplex (Point-to-point)	OPN(yx)	K28.2	D17.4	AL_PD	AL_PS
Open Half-Duplex (Point-to-point)	OPN(yy)	K28.2	D17.4	AL_PD	AL_PD
Open Broadcast Replicate	OPN(fr)	K28.2	D17.4	D31.7	D31.7
Open Selective Replicate	OPN(yr)	K28.2	D17.4	AL_PD	D31.7
Receiver Ready	R_RDY	K28.2	D21.4	D10.2	D10.2
Virtual Circuit Ready	VC_RDY	K28.2	D21.7	VC_ID	VC_ID

Table 17. XAUI Primitive Signals (Part 2 of 2)

XAUI Primitive Sequences. Table 18 lists Primitive Sequences used across XAUI by 10-Gigabit Fibre Channel. With the exception of the first character (K28.4 replaces K28.5), the Ordered Sets are identical to those defined by the Fibre Channel (FC-PH1/2/3, FC-FS) and arbitrated loop (FC-AL2) standards.

Primitive Sequence	Abbreviation	Ordered Set			
Link_Reset	LR	K28.4	D09.2	D31.5	D09.2
Link_Reset_Response	LRR	K28.4	D21.1	D31.5	D09.2
Local Fault (Link Status)	LF	K28.4	D00.0	D00.0	D01.0
Loop Initialization:	LIP				
Loop failure, no valid AL_PA	LIP(F8,F7)	K28.4	D21.0	D24.7	D23.7
Loop failure, valid AL_PA	LIP(F8,AL_PS)	K28.4	D21.0	D24.7	AL_PS
No loop failure, no valid AL_PA	LIP(F7,F7)	K28.4	D21.0	D23.7	D23.7
No loop failure, valid AL_PA	LIP(F7,AL_PS)	K28.4	D21.0	D23.7	AL_PS
Selective reset AL_PD	LIP(AL_PD,AL_PS)	K28.4	D21.0	AL_PD	AL_PS
Reset all	LIP(fx)	K28.4	D21.0	D31.7	AL_PS
Loop Port Bypass (selected port)	LPB(yx)	K28.4	D09.0	AL_PD	AL_PS
Loop Port Bypass (all ports)	LPB(fx)	K28.4	D09.0	D31.7	AL_PS
Loop Port Enable (selected port)	LPE(yx)	K28.4	D05.0	AL_PD	AL_PS
Loop Port Enable (all ports)	LPE(fx)	K28.4	D05.0	D31.7	AL_PS
Not_Operational	NOS	K28.4	D21.2	D31.5	D05.2
Offline	OLS	K28.4	D21.1	D10.4	D21.2
Remote Fault (Link Status)	RF	K28.4	D00.0	D00.0	D02.0

Table 18. XAUI Primitive Sequences

11.2.2 XAUI Inter-Lane Skew

Due to variations in the physical components and transmission medium used on each XAUI lane, skew can occur between the lanes. While a column of four characters is sent aligned, characters on one lane may arrive at the receiver at a different time than characters on another lane. Figure 72 illustrates inter-lane skew.

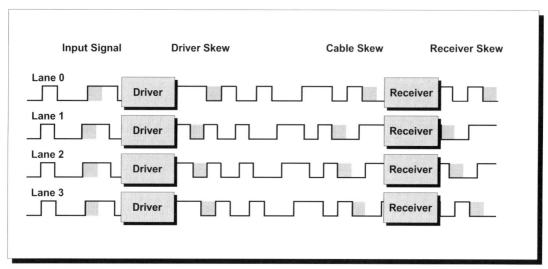

Figure 72. XAUI Inter-Lane Skew

Because of inter-lane skew, it is necessary to deskew received characters and align the columns. To facilitate column alignment, XAUI uses a special Align [A] Ordered Set consisting of an align character (K28.3) in each lane. During Idle intervals, the XAUI sender inserts Align [A] Ordered Sets periodically to enable the XAUI receiver to align the columns of received data. To prevent possible recurring misalignment, the interval between Align Ordered Sets is varied between 16 and 31 character times using a random number generator. Randomizing the interval between Aligns distributes the electromagnetic spectrum and reduces electromagnetic interference (EMI).

Deskewing at the XAUI receiver requires a deskew buffer for each lane. As characters are received, they are stored in the deskew buffer for that lane. During idle intervals, the transmitter sends an Align Ordered Set (a column of K28.3 characters) at random intervals ranging between 16 and 31 columns. When the receiver detects an align character in each lane, it can align readout of the deskew buffers in order to extract the complete column.

Figure 73 on page 149 shows use of align characters and deskew buffers to align the received data stream.

11.2.3 XAUI Sync and Clock Compensation

During Idle intervals, the transmitter sends either the Align [A], Sync [K], or Skip [R] Ordered Set.

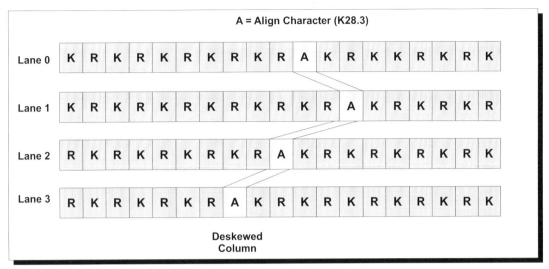

Figure 73. XAUI Deskew Column Alignment

The Sync [K] Ordered Set consists of a column of K28.5 characters. K28.5 contains the comma pattern ('0011111' or '1100000') used for character alignment by the deserializer.

XAUI may be extended by the use of repeaters or other entities. This can result in configurations with multiple clock boundaries (the XAUI received data is clocked by the sender's oscillator, retransmitted XAUI data is clocked using a local oscillator). To compensate for the tolerances of the two clocks, it may be necessary to insert or delete columns — a process referred to as clock elasticity.

The Skip [R] Ordered Set provides for clock elasticity. Any Skip [R] Ordered Set may be deleted for clock elasticity. A Skip [R] Ordered Set may be inserted anywhere in the Idle stream with the exception of the first column following an End-of-Frame.

The idle stream consisting of Align [A], Sync [K], and Skip [R] is randomized to reduce electromagnetic interference. Randomization produces an idle stream with no discrete frequency spectrum. An illustration of the idle stream randomizer is shown in Figure 74 on page 150.

11.2.4 Primitive Signal Transmission

When XGMII is used, a Primitive Signal code replaces one of the IDLE columns. When XAUI detects a Primitive Signal, it is transmitted in place of the next Align [A], Sync [K], or Skip [R] Ordered Set scheduled for transmission. If a Primitive Signal is transmitted when Align [A] was scheduled for transmission, the Align is sent immediately following the Primitive Signal.

All Primitive Signals are preceded or followed by a minimum of two IDLEs ([A], [K], or [R]) at the transmitter. Due to possible deletion of Skip [R] Ordered Sets, a receiver may only see one column between frames.

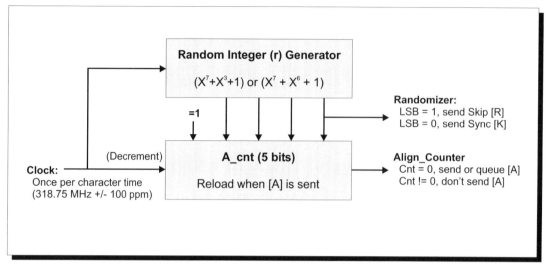

Figure 74. XAUI Idle Stream Randomizer

When XAUI receives a Primitive Signal, it is transferred via XGMII as shown by Figure 75 on page 151. This figure shows insertion of two R_RDYs following transmission of a frame.

11.2.5 Primitive Sequence Transmission

When XGMII is used, Primitive Sequences are sent by repeating the Primitive Sequence code for the duration of the Primitive Sequence.

XAUI sends Primitive Sequences by transmitting the Primitive Sequence Ordered Set once after each Align [A] Ordered Set. As long as XAUI is presented with a Primitive Sequence, it will continue to send the Primitive Sequence Ordered Set once following each Align [A] Ordered Set. This ensures that Align [A], Sync [K], and Skip [R] Ordered Sets are still present on XAUI during Primitive Sequence transmission. Figure 76 on page 152 shows the beginning of an OLS Primitive Sequence during the Idle stream after transmission of a frame.

The XAUI receiver samples the word following each Align [A] Ordered Set. If the word is a Primitive Sequence, it transmits the received Primitive Sequence on the XGMII receive data bus.

If the Primitive Sequence changes at the transmitting XGMII, XAUI simply changes the Ordered Set transmitted after the next Align [A] Ordered Set. Figure 77 on page 153 shows the transmitted Primitive Sequence changing from OLS to LRR.

If the word following an Align [A] Ordered Set is not a Primitive Sequence, XAUI emits the received word on the XGMII receive data bus. This ends Primitive Sequence reception on XGMII. Figure 78 on page 154 shows the end of an LRR Primitive Sequence.

	FRAME			IDLES			R_RDY	IDLES			R_RDY	IDLES												
XGMII Transmit																								
XGMII Lane 0	d	dc	dt	I	I	I	K+28.2	I	I	I	K+28.2	I	I	I	I	I	I	I	I	I	I	I	I	I
XGMII Lane 1	d	dc	dt	I	I	I	D+21.4	I	I	I	D+21.4	I	I	I	I	I	I	I	I	I	I	I	I	I
XGMII Lane 2	d	dc	dt	I	I	I	D+10.2	I	I	I	D+10.2	I	I	I	I	I	I	I	I	I	I	I	I	I
XGMII Lane 3	d	dc	T	I	I	I	D+10.2	I	I	I	D+10.2	I	I	I	I	I	I	I	I	I	I	I	I	I
XAUI																								
XAUI Lane 0	[d]	[dc]	[dt]	[A]	[R]	[K]	K28.2	[K]	[R]	[K]	K28.2	[K]	[K]	[R]	[K]	[R]	[R]	[K]	[K]	[R]	[K]	[R]		
XAUI Lane 1	[d]	[dc]	[dt]	[A]	[R]	[K]	D21.4	[K]	[R]	[K]	D21.4	[K]	[K]	[R]	[K]	[R]	[R]	[K]	[K]	[R]	[K]	[R]		
XAUI Lane 2	[d]	[dc]	[dt]	[A]	[R]	[K]	D10.2	[K]	[R]	[K]	D10.2	[K]	[K]	[R]	[K]	[R]	[R]	[K]	[K]	[R]	[K]	[R]		
XAUI Lane 3	[d]	[dc]	[T]	[A]	[R]	[K]	D10.2	[K]	[R]	[K]	D10.2	[K]	[K]	[R]	[K]	[R]	[R]	[K]	[K]	[R]	[K]	[R]		
XGMII Receive																								
XGMII Lane 0	d	dc	dt	I	I	I	K+28.2	I	I	I	K+28.2	I	I	I	I	I	I	I	I	I	I	I	I	I
XGMII Lane 1	d	dc	dt	I	I	I	D+21.4	I	I	I	D+21.4	I	I	I	I	I	I	I	I	I	I	I	I	I
XGMII Lane 2	d	dc	dt	I	I	I	D+10.2	I	I	I	D+10.2	I	I	I	I	I	I	I	I	I	I	I	I	I
XGMII Lane 3	d	dc	T	I	I	I	D+10.2	I	I	I	D+10.2	I	I	I	I	I	I	I	I	I	I	I	I	I

Figure 75. XAUI Primitive Signal Transmission

11.2.6 XAUI Ordered Set Transmission Rules

Align [A] is transmitted when the Align counter (A_cnt) reaches zero unless a frame or Primitive Signal is being transmitted. If A_cnt reaches zero during frame or Primitive Signal transmission, the count remains at zero and Align [A] is transmitted as the first Ordered Set after the End-of-Frame or the Primitive Signal.

If A_cnt is non-zero following transmission of End-of-Frame or a Primitive Signal, Sync [K] is transmitted.

11.2.7 XAUI Frame Transmission

When a frame is transmitted via XAUI, Idle stream transmission is interrupted and the words that make up the frame are transmitted across the four lanes (byte 0 is sent in lane 0, byte 1 in lane 1, etc.). An illustration of frame transmission via XAUI is shown in Figure 79 on page 155.

XGMII Transmit

FRAME   IDLES

XGMII Lane 0	d	dc	dt	I	I	I	---	I	O	O	O	O	O	O	O	O	O	O	O	O	O	O	O
XGMII Lane 1	d	dc	dt	I	I	I	---	I	L	L	L	L	L	L	L	L	L	L	L	L	L	L	L
XGMII Lane 2	d	dc	dt	I	I	I	---	I	S	S	S	S	S	S	S	S	S	S	S	S	S	S	S
XGMII Lane 3	d	dc	T	I	I	I	---	I															

XAUI Lane 0	[d]	[dc]	[dt]	[A]	[R]	[K]	---	[K]	[R]	[K]	[R]	[K]	[K]	[R]	[K]	[A]	[O]	[K]	[K]	[R]	[K]	[R]	[R]
XAUI Lane 1	[d]	[dc]	[dt]	[A]	[R]	[K]	---	[K]	[R]	[K]	[R]	[K]	[K]	[R]	[K]	[A]	[L]	[K]	[K]	[R]	[K]	[R]	[R]
XAUI Lane 2	[d]	[dc]	[dt]	[A]	[R]	[K]	---	[K]	[R]	[K]	[R]	[K]	[K]	[R]	[K]	[A]	[S]	[K]	[K]	[R]	[K]	[R]	[R]
XAUI Lane 3	[d]	[dc]	[T]	[A]	[R]	[K]	---	[K]	[R]	[K]	[R]	[K]	[K]	[R]	[K]	[A]		[K]	[K]	[R]	[K]	[R]	[R]

XGMII Receive   ◄—— **OLS Receive**

XGMII Lane 0	d	dc	dt	I	I	I	---	I	I	I	I	I	I	I	I	I	O	O	O	O	O	O	O
XGMII Lane 1	d	dc	dt	I	I	I	---	I	I	I	I	I	I	I	I	I	L	L	L	L	L	L	L
XGMII Lane 2	d	dc	dt	I	I	I	---	I	I	I	I	I	I	I	I	I	S	S	S	S	S	S	S
XGMII Lane 3	d	dc	T	I	I	I	---	I	I	I	I	I	I	I	I	I							

Figure 76. XAUI Primitive Sequence Transmission Begin

11.2.8 Interframe Gap

The originator is required to insert a minimum of 6 words (columns) between an End-of-Frame and the next Start-of-Frame. If IDLEs are removed for clock elasticity, the receiver may receive as few as one column between frames. This is a change from FC-AL-2 and FC-PH/FC-FS that require a minimum of 2 Primitive Signals between frames at the receiver.

11.3 64B/66B Encode/Decode

Unlike existing Fibre Channel links, 10-Gigabit Fibre Channel links based on a single fiber do not use the familiar 8B/10B coding scheme. Rather, a 64B/66B scheme is used to reduce the coding overhead. Whereas the 8B/10B scheme has a 25% overhead (2 additional bits per byte), this scheme has only a 3.125% coding overhead (2 additional bits per 64-bit block).

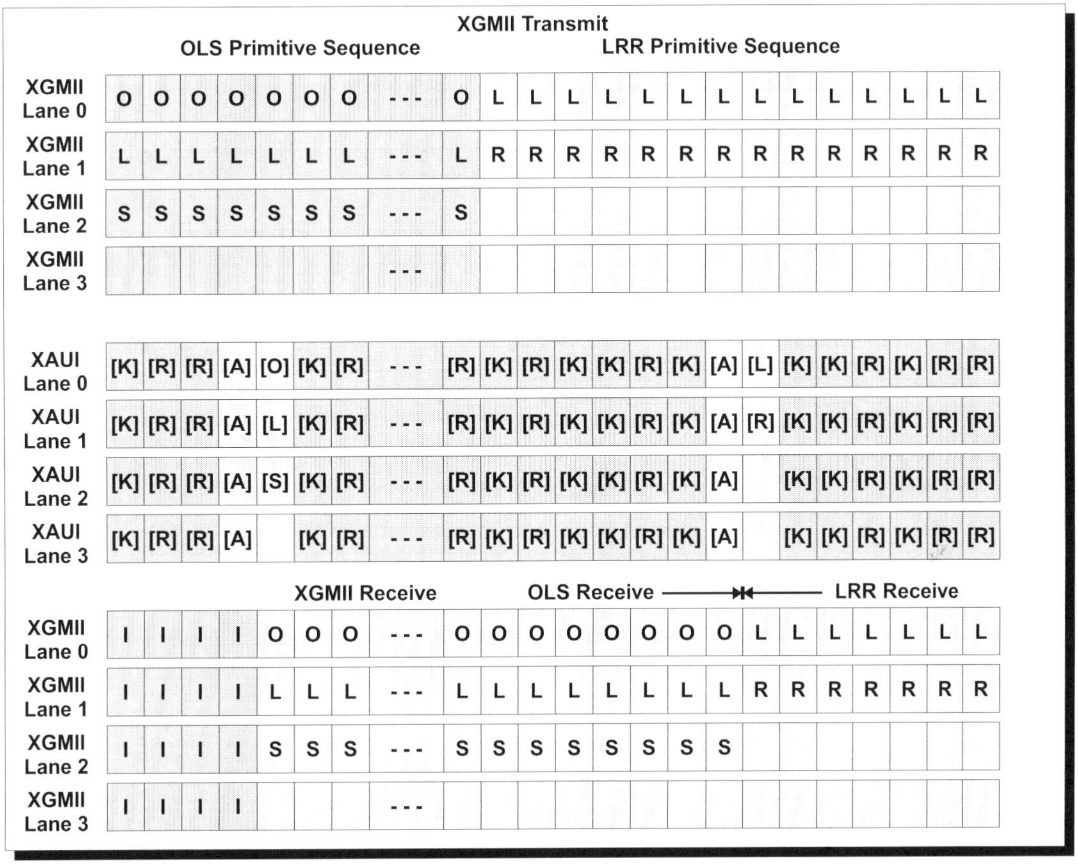

Figure 77. XAUI Primitive Sequence Changes

The 64B/66B coding maps XGMII parallel information or XAUI four-lane serial information into 66-bit blocks for transmission. The first two bits of the block are used as a synchronization header while the remaining 64 bits are scrambled prior to transmission to limit run lengths with the code block.

Upon reception, the synchronization header is used to identify block alignment and the remaining 64 bits are descrambled. The descrambled block is then processed for transmission across XGMII or XAUI, depending on the design.

While this scheme is referred to as 64B/66B coding, that is somewhat of a misnomer because XGMII sends 32 data bits plus four control bits (a total of 36 bits) during each transfer (perhaps this really should have been called a 72B/66B coding scheme).

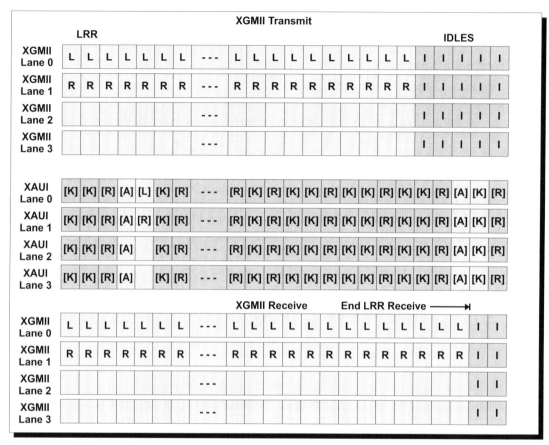

Figure 78. XAUI Primitive Sequence Transmission Ends

11.3.1 Block Sync Header

The first two bits of each block are a sync header used for block synchronization. If the block contains all data characters, these two bits are set to '01'b. If the block contains any control or special characters, the first two bits are set to '10'b. Values of '00'b and '11'b are not valid in the sync header. The two bits in the sync header are the only two bits in the 66-bit block that are always guaranteed to contain a transition.

11.3.2 Special Character Representation in the 64-Bit Block

If the XGMII characters in the block contain one or more control or special characters, special handling is required to create the 64-bit block. This is necessary because XGMII control characters consist of eight data bits plus the control bit (nine bits in total). To accommodate this, blocks containing control characters are encoded prior to scrambling in order to fit the necessary number of characters into the 64-bit block.

FC-2 Frame																		
IDLE [K]	IDLE [R]	SOFi3	Frame Header (6 Words)										Data Field (0-528 Words)		CRC	EOFt	IDLE [A]	IDLE [K]

Lane 0

K28.5	K28.0	K27.7	Dxx.y	Dxx.y	Dxx.y	Dxx.y	Dxx.y	Dxx.y	Dxx.y	Dxx.y	Dxx.y	Dxx.y	D21.4	K28.3	K28.5

Lane 1

K28.5	K28.0	D21.5	Dxx.y	Dxx.y	Dxx.y	Dxx.y	Dxx.y	Dxx.y	Dxx.y	Dxx.y	Dxx.y	Dxx.y	D21.3	K28.3	K28.5

Lane 2

K28.5	K28.0	D22.2	Dxx.y	Dxx.y	Dxx.y	Dxx.y	Dxx.y	Dxx.y	Dxx.y	Dxx.y	Dxx.y	Dxx.y	D21.3	K28.3	K28.5

Lane 3

K28.5	K28.0	D22.2	Dxx.y	Dxx.y	Dxx.y	Dxx.y	Dxx.y	Dxx.y	Dxx.y	Dxx.y	Dxx.y	Dxx.y	K29.7	K28.3	K28.5

Figure 79. XAUI Frame Transmission

The two bits in the sync header are set to '10'b if any control characters are present in the block. The next eight bits of the block (the first byte) contain the Block Type field. The value in this field identifies the content of the remainder of the block as shown in Table 19.

Block Type Field Value	Block Contents
x'1E'	Eight Control Characters
x'2D'	Four Control Characters/Ordered Set
x'33'	Four Control Characters/Start-of-Frame
x'4B'	Ordered Set/Four Control Characters
x'55'	Ordered Set/Ordered Set
x'66'	Ordered Set/Start-of-Frame
x'78'	Start-of-Frame/Data Word
x'B4'	End-of-Frame/Four Control Characters
x'FF'	Data Word/End-of-Frame
x'87', x'99', x'AA', x'CC', x'D2', x'E1'	Not used by 10-Gigabit Fibre Channel

Table 19. Block Type Field Values

The Block Type field uses eight of the 64 bits available in the block leaving, 56 bits for representing the characters that make up the block. Control characters are represented by either four-bit or seven-bit values in the block. This allows the eight-bit Block Type Field and eight seven-bit control character representations to be contained within the 64-bit block. The block representations for control characters are shown in Table 20 on page 156.

Control Character	Notation	XGMII Control Code	8B/10B Notation	Representation
Idle	/I/	x'07'	K28.0, K28.3, K28.5	'000 0000'b
Start	/S/	x'FB'	K27.7	implicit
Terminate	/T/	x'FD'	K29.7	implicit
Error	/E/	x'FE'	K30.7	'001 1110'b
Primitive Sequence Ordered Set	/Q/	x'9C'	K28.4	'0000'b
Reserved 0	/R/	x'1C'	K28.0	'010 1101'b
Reserved 1	-	x'3C'	K28.1	'011 0011'b
Reserved 2	/A/	x'7C'	K28.3	'100 1011'b
Reserved 3	/K/	x'BC'	K28.5	'101 0101'b
Reserved 4	-	x'DC'	K28.6	'110 0110'b
Reserved 5	-	x'F7'	K23.7	'111 1000'b
Primitive Signal Ordered Set	/Fsig/	x'5C'	K28.2	'1111'b

Table 20. Control Character Representation in 64-Bit Block

Putting this all together, Table 21 shows the formats of the various blocks. Data characters are identified with 'D' in the table, control characters with 'C', Ordered Sets with 'O', Start-of-Frame with 'S', and End-of-Frame with 'T'. When looking at this table, keep in mind that control characters may span byte boundaries within the block.

XGMII Data		66-Bit Block Format								
Word 0	Word 1	S	D_0	D_1	D_2	D_3	D_4	D_5	D_6	D_7
$D_0D_1D_2D_3$	$D_4D_5D_6D_7$	01	D_0	D_1	D_2	D_3	D_4	D_5	D_6	D_7
$C_0C_1C_2C_3$	$C_4C_5C_6C_7$	10	x'1E'	C_0	C_1	C_2	C_3 C_4	C_5	C_6	C_7
$C_0C_1C_2C_3$	$O_4D_5D_6D_7$	10	x'2D'	C_0	C_1	C_2	C_3 O_4	D_5	D_6	D_7
$C_0C_1C_2C_3$	$S_4D_5D_6D_7$	10	x'33'	C_0	C_1	C_2	C_3	D_5	D_6	D_7
$O_0D_1D_2D_3$	$S_4D_5D_6D_7$	10	x'66'	D_1	D_2	D_3	O_0	D_5	D_6	D_7
$O_0D_1D_2D_3$	$O_4D_5D_6D_7$	10	x'55'	D_1	D_2	D_3	O_0 O_4	D_5	D_6	D_7
$S_0D_1D_2D_3$	$D_4D_5D_6D_7$	10	x'78'	D_1	D_2	D_3	D_4	D_5	D_6	D_7
$O_0D_1D_2D_3$	$C_4C_5C_6C_7$	10	x'4B'	D_1	D_2	D_3	O_0 C_4	C_5	C_6	C_7
$D_0D_1D_2T_3$	$C_4C_5C_6C_7$	10	x'B4'	D_1	D_2	D_3	C_4	C_5	C_6	C_7
$D_0D_1D_2D_3$	$D_4D_5D_6T_7$	10	x'FF'	D_0	D_1	D_2	D_3	D_4	D_5	D_6

Table 21. 66-Bit Block Formats

When a Primitive Sequence or Primitive Signal Ordered Set is contained in the block, the Block Field identifies which word, or words, contains the Ordered Set(s). In this case, the special character associated with the Ordered Set is replaced with a four-bit value; '0000'b for a Primitive Sequence Ordered Set, or '1111'b for a Primitive Signal Ordered Set. This abbreviated representation allows two Ordered Sets to be indicated in the 56 bits available.

11.3.3 64-Bit Scrambler

Before the 64-bit portion of the block is transmitted, it is scrambled to limit the run lengths of transmitted bits. The scrambler is based on the following polynomial:

$$G(x) = 1 + x^{39} + x^{58}$$

The block sync header is not passed through the scrambler. This ensures that the bit transition used for block synchronization is preserved.

An illustration of the scrambler is shown in Figure 80.

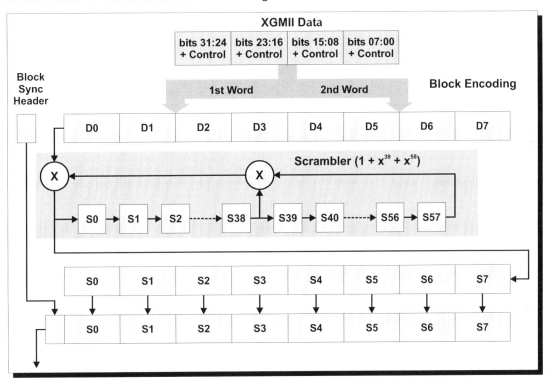

Figure 80. 64-Bit Block Scrambler

When serial data is received, the receiver must obtain block synchronization before blocks can be processed. Once this has been accomplished, receive blocks are descrambled (using the same polynomial), decoded and transferred across XGMII one word at a time. The receive process is shown in Figure 81 on page 158.

11.4 10.51875-Gigabit Serial Link Specifications

Multiple physical variants are specified to carry 64B/66B encoded data at 10.51875 gigabits per second using single-mode and multimode optical fiber. No electrical variants are defined

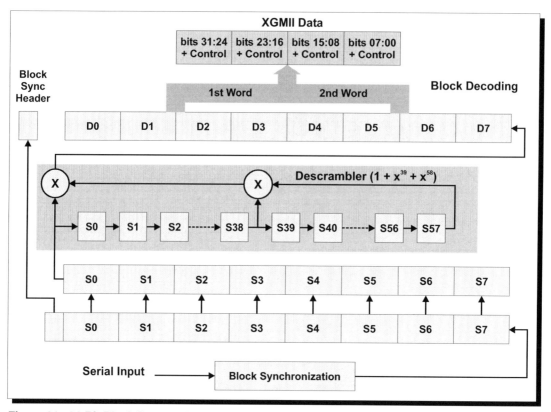

Figure 81. 64-Bit Block Descrambler

for operation at this signaling rate. Key characteristics of these variants are summarized in Table 22 on page 159.

11.5 4-Lane Link Specifications

10-Gigabit Fibre Channel defines multiple four-lane variants that carry XAUI signaling 3.1875 gigabaud using 8B/10B encoding) over short to intermediate distances using either optical fiber or electrical cabling. This section highlights the key specifications for these physical links.

4-Fiber Optical (1200-Mx-SN4P-S). 1200-Mx-SN4P-S defines a four-lane optical fiber link using four separate optical fibers. The fibers may be standard 50 um multimode optical fiber (M5), high-bandwidth 50 um multimode optical fiber (M5E), and 62.5 um multimode optical fiber (M6). Specifications for the 50 um variants are shown in Table 23 on page 160.

10-Gigabit Single-Lane Optical Links				
	1200-SM-LL-L	1200-M5-SN-S	1200-M5E-SN-S	1200-M6-SN-S
Data rate (MB/sec.)	1200	1200	1200	1200
Nominal bit rate (Mbaud)	10,200	10,200	10,200	10,200
Tolerance	(+/-) 100 ppm	(+/-) 100 ppm	(+/-) 100 ppm	(+/-) 100 ppm
Transmitter				
Type	Laser	Laser	Laser	Laser
Sprectral center wavelength	1260 - 1355 nm.	840 - 860 nm.	840 - 860 nm.	840 - 860 nm.
Spectral width RMS	.05 - 0.2	0.2 - 0.3	0.2 - 0.3	0.2 - 0.3
Launched power (average)	0.5 dBm	-1.0 dBm	-1.0 dBm	-1.0 dBm
Optical modulation amplitude	-3.9 dBm	-4.76	-4.76	-4.76
Receiver				
Sensitivity (max rcvd power)	0.5 dBm	-1.0 dBm	-1.0 dBm	-1.0 dBm
Optical modulation amplitude	0.0477 mw -13.23 dBm	0.0636 mw -11.98 dBm	0.0636 mw -11.98 dBm	0.0636 mw -11.98 dBm
Cable Plant				
Fiber core diameter	9 um.	50 um.		
Operating range (typical)	2m - 10km	82m	300m	33m
Optical fiber modal bandwidth	n/a	500 MHz/km	2000 MHz/km	200 MHz/km
Link loss budget	9.4 dB	7.5 dB	7.5 dB	7.5 dB

Table 22. 10-Gigabit Single-Lane Optical Links

11.5.1 4-Lane Optical Wavelength Division Multiplexing (1200-M5/M5E-SN4-S)

The 1200-M5-SN4-S variant uses wavelength division multiplexing to transmit four XAUI lanes via one optical fiber. Data for each lane is transmitted using a different wavelength laser operating in the 770-860 nm. range as shown in the far right column of Table 23 on page 160.

11.5.2 4-Lane Electrical (1200-DF-EL-S)

One electrical variant is based on four lanes using XAUI signaling (3.1875 gigabaud per lane with 8B/10B encoding). As with other Fibre Channel electrical links, distances are not defined as part of the specification (distance is determined by characteristics of the cables). However, a distance of 15 meters should be achievable at 3.1875 gigabaud.

Key characteristics of the 10-gigabit electrical variant are listed in Table 24 on page 160.

10-Gigabit 4-Lane Multimode Optical Links (50 um)				
	1200-M5-SN4P-S	**1200-M5E-SN4P-S**	**1200-M5-SN4-S**	**1200-M5E-SN4-S**
Data rate (MB/sec.)	1200	1200	1200	1200
Nominal bit rate (Mbaud)	4 * 3.1875	4 * 3.1875	4 * 3.1875 (WDM)	4 * 3.1875 (WDM)
Tolerance	(+/-) 100 ppm	(+/-) 100 ppm	(+/-) 100 ppm	(+/-) 100 ppm
Transmitter				
Type	Laser	Laser	Laser	Laser
Sprectral center wavelength	830 - 860 nm.	830 - 860 nm.	L0=772.5-783.6 nm. L1=795.2-806.5 nm. L2=819.4-830.8 nm. L3=845.0-856.6 nm.	L0=772.5-783.6 nm. L1=795.2-806.5 nm. L2=819.4-830.8 nm. L3=845.0-856.6 nm.
Spectral width RMS	0.85 nm. (max)	0.85 nm. (max)	0.5 nm. (max)	0.5 nm. (max)
Launched power (average)	-3 dBm	-3 dBm	0.5 dBm / Lane	0.5 dBm / Lane
Optical modulation amplitude	-6 dBm (min)	-6 dBm (min)	237 mW (min) -6.25 dBm (min)	237 mW (min) -6.25 dBm (min)
Receiver				
Sensitivity (max rcvd power)	0 dBm	0 dBm	0.5 dBm / Lane	0.5 dBm / Lane
Optical modulation amplitude	-12.5 dBm (max)	-12.5 dBm (max)	-12.5 dBm (max)	-12.5 dBm (max)
Cable Plant				
Fiber core diameter	50 μm	50 μm	50 μm	50 μm
Operating range (typical)	0.5m - 300m	0.5m - 500m	0.5m - 300m	0.5m - 550m
Optical fiber modal bandwidth	500 MHz/km	2,000 MHz/km	500 MHz/km	2,000 MHz/km
Link loss budget	7.5 dB	7.5 dB	8.0 dB	8.0 dB

Table 23. 10-Gigabit 4-Lane Multimode Optical Links (50 um)

10-Gigabit Electrical Link Specifications		
		1200-DF-EL-S
Data rate (MB/sec.)		1200
Nominal bit rate (Gigabaud)		3.1875
Tolerance		+/-100 ppm
Cable impedance		100Ω
Transmitter		
Amplitude	(max)	1500 mV (p-p)
	(min)	550 mV (p-p)
Eye mask amplitude	(Y1)	0.2
	(Y2)	0.1
Rise/Fall time (20-80%)	(max)	128 ps
	(min)	60 ps
Receiver		
Eye mask amplitude	(Y1)	200 mV
	(Y2)	1000 mV
Eye mask jitter	(X1)	0.285 UI
	(X2)	0.5 UI
Differential skew		100 ps.

Table 24. 10-Gigabit Electrical Link

11.6 Chapter Summary

10-Gigabit Fibre Channel

- 10-Gigabit Fibre Channel (10GFC) continues speed evolution
  - First Fibre Channel implementations were 262 Mbps (25 MB/s) and 531 Mbps (50 MB/s)
  - First widespread adoption occurred at 1 Gbps speed (100 MB/s)
  - Current products are at 2 Gbps (200 MB/s) and moving to 4 Gbps
- 10-Gigabit Fibre Channel standard was approved in 2003
  - Limited implementations to date
  - Primarily for inter-switch links (ISLs)

10GFC Highlights

- Goal was to develop 10-gigabit technology jointly with IEEE 10-gigabit Ethernet
  - One set of low-cost physical components
- Provide 12X the existing 1-gigabit bandwidth
  - 1,275 megabytes per second (1.275 Gbps)
- Minimize impact of Fibre Channel architecture and designs
  - Confine changes to FC-0 and FC-1
  - Minimize changes to FC-2 and above
- 10 GFC is also referred to as "FC Base10"

Four-Lane Interfaces

- 10GFC specifies four-lane physical interfaces
  - Transmission word is striped across the four lanes (1 byte per lane)
  - Each lane operates at 3.1875 Gbps (12.750 Gbps total)
  - Uses existing 8B/10B coding
- Four-lane multimode optical links
  - Four separate fibers, one per lane
  - Wavelength division multiplexed link with four channels in a single fiber
  - Distances of 300m with standard 50 um fiber or 500m with high-bandwidth 50 um fiber
- Four-lane electrical interface
  - Distances of a few meters

Single-Lane Interfaces

- 10GFC also specifies single-lane interfaces
  - Single data stream at 10.51875 gigabits per second
  - Only optical links are defined at this rate
- 9 um single-mode optical links
  - Long-wavelength laser (1310 nm)
  - Up to 10 km distance
- 50 um multimode optical links
  - Shortwave laser (850 nm)
  - 82 meters using standard 50 um fiber
  - 300 meters using high-bandwidth fiber
- Uses new 64B/66B coding scheme

10GFC Internal Interfaces

- Two new internal/external interfaces have been defined:
- 10-Gigabit Media Independent Interface (XGMII)
  - Internal or inter-chip interface
- 10-Gigabit Attachment Unit Interface (XAUI)
  - Internal or external interface
  - Provides the basis for four-lane physical interfaces

XGMII

- 10-Gigabit Media Independent Interface (XGMII)
- Provides a 1,275 MB/s short-distance interface
  - Distance limited to about 7 cm.
- 36-bit wide synchronous interface
  - Four 8-bit bytes + one control bit per byte
  - Control bit allows control characters to be sent
- Data is clocked on both edges of a 159.375 MHz clock
- Control characters are used to signal:
  - Idle
  - Start-of-Frame and End-of-Frame
  - Primitive Signals and Primitive Sequences

XAUI

- 10-Gigabit Attachment Unit Interface (XAUI)
- Transmission word is striped across four serial lanes
  - Each lane operates at 3.1875 Gbps
  - Uses existing 8B/10B encoding
  - Can use either optical or electrical signaling
- Ordered Sets are used to signal:
  - Idle
  - Start-of-Frame and End-of-Frame
  - Primitive Signals and Primitive Sequences

XAUI Synchronization

- XAUI receiver needs to determine character position in data stream
- Searches for the comma pattern
  - '001 1111'b or '110 0000'b
  - This is a unique bit combination in 8B/10B
  - Occurs as the first seven bits of K28.5
- Sync [K] Ordered Set is transmitted during Idle intervals to facilitate character synchronization at the receiver
  - Sync is a column of K28.5 characters
  - Facilitates synchronization on each lane

XAUI Inter-Lane Skew

- Data on the XAUI lanes may become skewed
  - Characters on each line arrive at different times due to variations in components and cables
- Align [A] Ordered Set facilitates deskew at receiver
  - Align is a column of K28.3 characters
- Align is sent every 16 to 31 columns during the Idle stream
  - Align interval is varied by a random number of columns
  - Prevents misalignment by one whole interval

XAUI Clock Elasticity

- XAUI signals may be repeated by intermediate entities
  - Each entity contains its own clock (oscillator)
- Need to compensate for oscillator tolerances
  - Original sender's oscillator vs. retransmitter's oscillator
- Compensation is accomplished by inserting or deleting Skip [R] Ordered Set
  - Skip is a column of K28.0 characters
  - Skip may always be deleted if necessary
  - Skip may be inserted into the Idle stream

Idle Stream Randomization

- To minimize electromagnetic interference, the Idle stream is randomized
  - This produces an idle stream with no fixed spectrum
- A random number generator is used to control Idle stream Ordered Sets
  - Align [A] is sent every 16 to 31 columns
  - If a frame is being transmitted when Align [A] is due, [A] is sent immediately after the frame
  - Sync [K] and Skip [R] are sent when Align is not being sent
  - Selection of Sync [K] or Skip [R] is also randomized to minimize noise

XAUI Primitives

- Primitive Signals are inserted into the Idle stream
  - Transmitted in place of the next [A], [S], or [R] Ordered Set
- Primitive Sequences are only signalled after an Align [A] column
  - Transmitted once after each Align [A] column for as long as the Primitive Sequence is active
  - If the Primitive Sequence changes, the Ordered Set for the new Primitive Sequence is transmitted after the next Align [A]
  - When the Primitive Sequence ends, normal Idle stream transmission resumes

12. FC-2 Concepts

Fibre Channel's FC-0 and FC-1 levels define physical interface and data link functions necessary to physically send transmission characters from one port to another. Beginning with the FC-2 level, the standard defines the content and structure of information being delivered, and how that delivery is controlled and managed. Figure 82 illustrates the relationship of FC-2 to the other Fibre Channel levels.

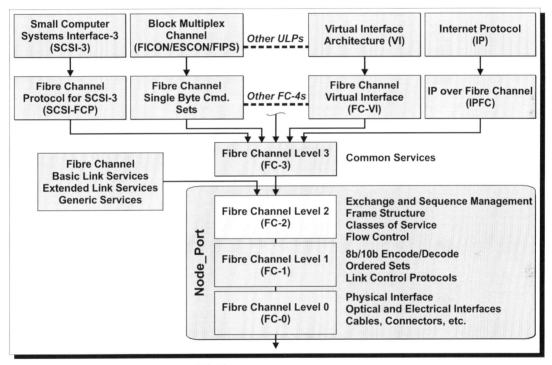

Figure 82. Fibre Channel Level 2 (FC-2)

Fibre Channel's FC-2 level is a major element of the Fibre Channel transport architecture and provides a multi-tiered approach to the control and management of information delivery. The four tiers of this structure are:

- A *login session*, between two ports enabling higher-level transactions to take place between those ports. The login session can be established by an explicit login process, or may be implicitly established in some environments. The Fibre Channel standard doesn't use the term session to refer to this level, rather, referring to it as being *"logged-in."*

- The *Exchange*, consisting of one or more related Information Units (such as command, data, and status) between two ports. The Exchange may represent an entire transaction, a portion of an transaction, or even multiple transactions. Each FC-4 protocol mapping defines how that particular protocol uses the Exchange mechanism.

- Each Information Unit is delivered by using a *Sequence* of one or more frames. Because the standard limits the size of a frame, the entire Information Unit may not fit within one frame. If this is the case, it is necessary to segment the Information Unit and use a Sequence of frames to deliver it.

- *Frames* transport data from one port to another. Frames can be thought of as envelopes used to carry information across the Fibre Channel interface.

This arrangement treats every transaction as the exchange of one or more Information Units, with each Information Unit delivered using a Sequence of one or more frames. An illustration of this relationship is shown in Figure 83.

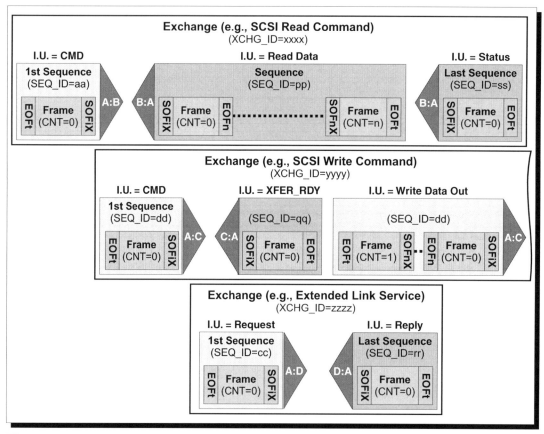

Figure 83. Exchange, Sequence, and Frame Relationship

In this example, the Exchange could represent a SCSI task, a portion of block multiplex channel program, a portion of an Internet Protocol FTP transaction, or one of Fibre Channel's own built-in functions, depending upon the upper-level protocol in use.

Each Information Unit is a portion of that operation, such as the command, data, status, request, response, or other protocol data unit and each is delivered using a single Sequence of frames. The content and function of the Information Units is defined by the FC-4 protocol mapping or Fibre Channel's definition of protocols such as the Extended Link Services protocol.

The Exchange, Sequence, and frame constructs are defined and managed by FC-2. The login session is managed above the FC-2 level by a higher-level process that is not defined by the standard (although the standard does specify the login actions required and provides the mechanisms to perform those actions).

12.1 Session Management - Login and Logout

Before any FC-4 upper-level protocol transactions (anything other than Fibre Channel's Link Services) can be performed between a pair of ports, it is necessary to establish a login session between the two ports. This is done by the login process that allows the ports to exchange information used during subsequent communications.

The login process may be performed by an explicit exchange of frames with the other port, or in some cases, login may be implicit when the ports already know all the necessary information through some means outside of the standard.

Information communicated during the login process includes identification of both the port and node, various FC-2 level capabilities, and the granting of credit allowing the other port to send a specified number of frames.

The login process may be performed as part of initialization, or when the first communication is desired with another port. Once the login session has been performed, it persists until a logout occurs, or other conditions cause the session to be terminated. Ports that need to communicate with more than one other port may be logged in with multiple ports concurrently. As long as the session is active with the other port, normal I/O operations may take place. In some applications, the login session may last from power-on to power-off (for example, a SCSI initiator and its associated disk drives).

If the current login session is ended for any reason, current I/O operations with the other port are terminated and new I/O operations are prohibited until a new login session is established.

12.2 Exchange

The Fibre Channel Exchange is the mechanism that two Fibre Channel ports use to identify and manage a set of related Information Units. The Information Units may represent an entire transaction (command, data, and status) or just a portion of a transaction. Each FC-4 protocol mapping specifies how that protocol uses Fibre Channel's Exchange mechanism.

The Exchange is described in more detail in *Exchange Management* on page 173.

12.3 Information Units

Each protocol, such as SCSI, block multiplex channel, IPI, or TCP/IP, has its own protocol-specific information that must be delivered to another port to perform a transaction. These "protocol data units" are called *Information Units* by Fibre Channel. The structure of the Information Units, their content, and the rules governing their use are specified by the Fibre Channel FC-4 protocol mapping for that particular protocol.

When an FC-4 process wants to send an Information Unit, it makes a delivery request to the next lower level, FC-3. Currently, there are no FC-3 functions defined and FC-3 simply converts the Information Unit delivery request to a Sequence delivery request and passes it to the FC-2 level. As a result, there is a one-to-one correspondence between FC-4 Information Units and FC-2 Sequences.

12.4 Sequence

When a higher-level process wishes to send information to another port, it makes a request to the FC-2 level to deliver that information saying, in effect, "deliver this chunk of information to the other port." The FC-2 level performs the Information Unit delivery by packaging the information into a Sequence of frames.

The standard limits the amount of data that can be put in a frame to 2112 bytes maximum. When the higher-level Information Unit is larger than what will fit into a single frame, FC-2 segments the Information Unit and delivers it using a Sequence of frames (details about the use and management of Sequences can be found in *Sequence Management* on page 189).

When the frames associated with the Sequence are received by the other port, they are reassembled back into the original Information Unit and delivered to the higher-level process (identified by the type field in the frame header) at the receiving port. An illustration of this delivery model is shown in Figure 84.

From the higher-level process perspective, a request was made to deliver the Information Unit at the sending port and the Information Unit was delivered by the receiving port. The higher-level processes (identified by the type field in the frame header) at both the sending and receiving ports understand the content and meaning of the Information Unit, but are not aware of the details of the actual delivery process such as segmentation and reassembly.

From FC-2's perspective, a request is made to deliver an Information Unit. FC-2 controls packaging the information in a Sequence of frames and managing the flow of those frames, but is unaware of the meaning of the information being delivered.

When the higher-level process makes an FC-2 Sequence request, it provides the Information Unit to be delivered and associated session, Exchange, and Sequence parameter information. These parameters could be thought of as an "Information Unit header". FC-2 uses this parameter information to fill in fields in the frame headers of the frame or frames used to deliver the Information Unit.

An illustration of this relationship between the Exchange parameters, Sequence parameters, Information Unit and the frame header is shown in Figure 85.

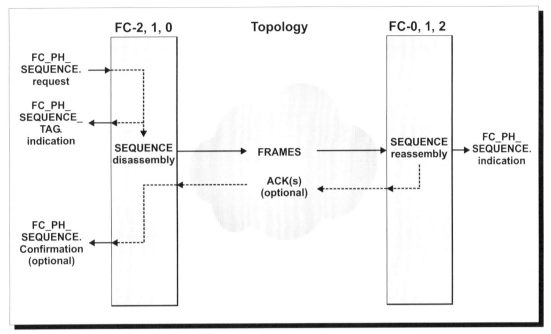

Figure 84. FC-2 Service Interface

The Information Unit may contain a single information set (and its associated information category and offset) or multiple information sets with multiple information categories and offsets. As FC-2 processes each information set within the Information Unit, the information category value for that information set is used in the information category field of the frame header. The offset value associated with each information set is used to supply the initial value of the parameter field (if used) for that information set.

Each information set results in one or more frames within the Sequence. Different information sets cannot be combined in the same frame because there is only one information category associated with each frame.

12.5 Frame

The frame is the basic information carrier in Fibre Channel. Other than Ordered Sets (that only communicate low-level link conditions), all information is contained in frames. The frame could be viewed as an envelope or container, providing a structure to transport information.

Each frame begins with a Start-of-Frame (SOF) delimiter Ordered Set and ends with an End-of-Frame (EOF) delimiter Ordered Set. In between these two delimiters is the frame content.

The first part of the frame content is the frame header. The frame header provides control information about the frame itself, or the information contained within the frame. The size of the frame header is fixed at 24 bytes and contains items such as:

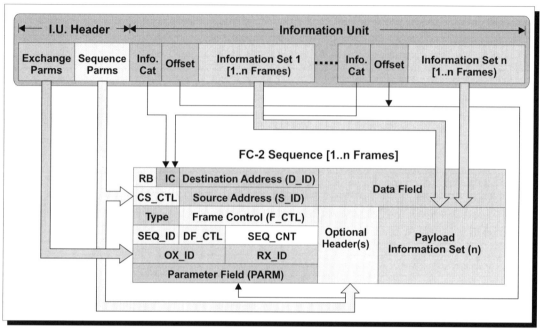

Figure 85. Information Unit

- the addresses of the destination (D_ID) and source (S_ID) ports,
- what type of protocol is carried by the frame (Type),
- what Exchange this frame belongs to (OX_ID and RX_ID),
- what Sequence this frame belongs to (SEQ_ID),
- other information needed for control.

Following the frame header is the data field of the frame. The data field contains information the frame is delivering, called the payload. In some cases, the data field may also contain extensions to the frame header (called optional headers).

The size of the data field is variable in four-byte increments and depends on the amount of information in the frame. To limit frames to a manageable size, the maximum size of the data field is limited to 2112 bytes.

Following the data field is a four-byte field containing check characters that allow the frame contents to be verified. The checking scheme uses a cyclic redundancy check and these characters are usually referred to as the CRC.

The CRC is followed by the End-of-Frame delimiter identifying the end of the frame.

Frames are discussed further in *Frame Structure* on page 201.

12.6 Flow Control and Credit

When a frame is ready for transmission, it is sent through the encoder (FC-1), to the serializer (FC-0), and finally out the transmit fibre where it is routed by the interconnecting topology to the receiver.

When the frame arrives at the receiver, it is received, deserialized, decoded, and stored in a receive buffer where it is processed by the receiving port. If another frame arrives while the receiver is processing the first frame, a second receive buffer is needed to hold the new frame.

Unless the receiver is capable of processing frames as fast as the transmitter is capable of sending them, it is possible for all of the receive buffers to fill up with received frames. If the transmitter should send another frame at this point, the receiver may not have a receive buffer available and the frame may be lost.

To prevent this kind of error condition, Fibre Channel provides a two-level flow control mechanism that allows the receiver to control when the transmitter may send frames. The receiving port controls the frame transmission by giving the sending port permission to send one or more frames to that particular receiving port. That permission is called credit.

Credit is granted during the login process and applies to the session between the two ports. The credit value is decremented when a frame is sent and replenished when a response is received. If the available credit reaches zero, the credit is exhausted and frame transmission with that particular port is suspended until the credit is replenished to a non-zero value.

The first level of flow control is used between a transmitter and the port at the other end of the link or circuit. This level of flow control is called buffer-to-buffer flow control, and uses buffer-to-buffer credit, because it controls the flow of frames between the sending port's transmit buffers and the next port's receiving buffers. Depending on the topology, the next port may be another node port (point-to-point and arbitrated loop) or a fabric port (arbitrated loop and fabric). In the point-to-point and fabric topologies, a single buffer-to-buffer credit value is used. In the arbitrated loop topology, separate buffer-to-buffer credit values may be used for each other port in the loop.

The second level of the flow control mechanism is used between the source node port and the destination node port and is called end-to-end flow control (and uses end-to-end credit). End-to-end flow control is always managed between a specific pair of node ports, so a node port may have many different end-to-end credit values, each for a different destination node port.

Figure 86 on page 170 illustrates how the two levels of flow control are used in a fabric topology. Buffer-to-buffer flow control regulates the flow of frames into and out of the fabric, allowing the fabric to manage congestion. End-to-end flow control manages the flow of frames between a specific pair of node ports and allows the receiving port to control which source node ports are allowed to send frames to the receiver (and how many frames).

Full details of the flow control mechanisms are described in *Flow Control* on page 257.

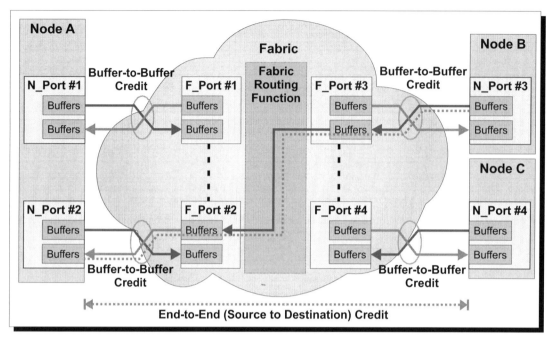

Figure 86. Buffer-to-Buffer and End-to-End Credit

12.7 Classes of Service

Due to its high data rate and flexible architecture, Fibre Channel provides the ability to carry many different types of information. Whether that information is traditional I/O activity, network traffic, or even real-time information such as video, it is being carried by Fibre Channel today.

Different types of information have different delivery requirements. Some applications, such as transaction processing, have sporadic traffic patterns and require reliable delivery of the information. Others, such as a video stream, have a time-sensitive traffic pattern and may be willing to sacrifice reliable delivery if necessary to assure on-time delivery.

To accommodate the different delivery requirements, Fibre Channel associates a set of delivery characteristics with each Sequence called the *class of service.* The class of service specifies a set of attributes that control how the delivery of that particular Sequence, and all frames in the Sequence, is handled. These attributes include items such as:

- Should a connection be established to reserve bandwidth?
- Is confirmation of delivery, or notification of non-delivery, desired?
- Which flow control mechanisms should be used?
- What should be done in the case of error?

Class of service characteristics are covered later in *Classes of Service* on page 273.

12.8 Chapter Summary

FC-2 Scope

- FC-2 is the largest part of the FC-PH standard and covers the:
  - Management of login sessions between ports
  - Management of transactions by use of the Exchange
  - Transfer of Information Units by use of a Sequence of frames
  - Frame formats and structure
  - Acknowledgement and flow control
  - Classes of service
  - Error processing

Session Management

- Ports must establish a login session before performing upper-level (FC-4) transactions
  - Performed using Extended Link Services protocol
- During login, the ports exchange information used during the session
  - Service parameters define each port's capabilities
  - Port names establish the identity of the ports
- Login is long lasting and may span multiple Exchanges
- If communication is no longer desired, logout ends the session

The Exchange

- The Exchange identifies and manages a set of related Sequences between two ports
  - During the Exchange, the ports exchange one or more Information Units
  - Each protocol defines how the Exchange is used by that protocol
- The Exchange may represent:
  - An entire transaction,
  - A portion of a transaction, or even
  - Multiple transactions
- Every frame is part of an Exchange as identified by the Originator and Responder (OX_ID and RX_ID) fields in the frame header

The Sequence

- The Sequence identifies and manages a set of related frames between two ports
- Every Information Unit is delivered using a Sequence of one or more frames
  - If the Information Unit fits in one frame, a single-frame Sequence is used, otherwise
  - The Information Unit is segmented by the sending port, and reassembled by the receiving port
- Every frame is part of a Sequence as identified by the Sequence_ID (SEQ_ID) field in the frame header

The Frame

- The frame is the basic carrier of information
  - Other than Ordered Sets, all information is delivered in frames
- Frames begin with a Start-of-Frame (SOF) Ordered Set delimiter
- Frames end with an End-of-Frame (EOF) Ordered Set delimiter
- In between is the frame content:
  - The frame header contains control information associated with the frame
  - The data field
  - Check characters (CRC) used to validate the frame's content

Flow Control

- Flow control is used to pace frame transmission
- Allows the receiver to control when the sender is permitted to send a frame
- Prevents the sender from overrunning the receiver
- The receiver gives the sender permission to send a specified number of frames
- That permission is called credit
  - Credit is granted during login, or
  - When an arbitrated loop circuit is opened

Levels of Flow Control

- Two levels of flow control are used
  - A link-level mechanism called Buffer-to-Buffer flow control
  - A source to destination port mechanism called End-to-End flow control
- This allows control of frames on both the link and between the two end ports
- End-to-end flow control also provides delivery confirmation

Classes of Service

- Fibre Channel can carry different types of traffic
  - Real-time, video
  - Transaction processing data
  - Archival data streams
- These data types have different delivery requirements
- Different classes of service address the differing delivery requirements
  - Should bandwidth be reserved, and if so, how much?
  - Is confirmation of delivery, or notification of non-deliverability desired?
  - How is the flow of frames managed?

13. Exchange Management

Fibre Channel provides the Exchange as a way to identify and manage a set of related Information Units. The Exchange may represent an entire transaction, a portion of an transaction, or even multiple transactions. The standard ties the ability to perform an Exchange to the presence, or absence, of a login session between the two ports as follows:

- Basic Link Services can always be performed prior to the establishment of a login session between two ports.

- Extended Link Service transactions can, in many case, be performed prior to the establishment of a login session between the ports although some Extended Link Service transactions require establishment of a login session before they will be accepted.

- Transactions associated with an FC-4 mapped protocol (or FC-4 defined link services) require establishment of a login session before those transactions can be performed.

The login session may be established implicitly (that is, by some means outside the standard, including prior knowledge), or explicitly by use of the PLOGI Extended Link Service request.

Subject to the login session requirements listed above, a port may originate or respond to Exchanges. A port that originates an Exchange is referred to as the Exchange originator, the port that responds to an Exchange is the Exchange responder.

A port may have multiple open Exchanges (the maximum number of active Exchanges a port is capable of supporting is implementation dependent). When a port has multiple open Exchanges, those Exchanges may be with one other port, or multiple other ports (subject to login session requirements).

During an Exchange, one or more Information Units are transported to or from the other port. Each Information Unit is delivered using a single Sequence. The number of frames in a Sequence depends upon the size of the Information Unit. A high-level illustration of two Exchanges and their associated Sequences is shown in Figure 87 on page 174.

13.1 Exchange Operation

So that a port can identify the beginning and end of an Exchange, the first and last Information Units of the Exchange (and the Sequences used to deliver them) are identified by the higher-level protocol. These indications are needed because the port has no knowledge of the content or significance of the information being transported.

The Exchange is considered open from the beginning of processing the first Sequence of the Exchange until completion of processing the last Sequence of the Exchange or the Exchange is abnormally ended.

Within an Exchange, Information Units may be sent in one direction only (from the Exchange originator to the Exchange responder), or in both directions. If Information Units are sent in

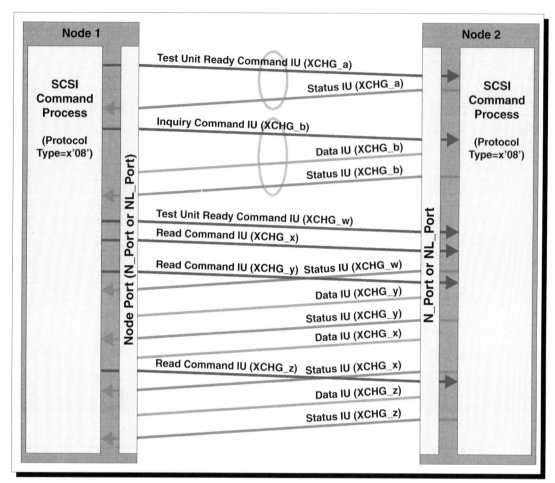

Figure 87. Fibre Channel Exchange

one direction only, the Exchange is a uni-directional Exchange. If Information Units are sent in both directions during the course of the Exchange, the Exchange is bi-directional.

Sequences within an Exchange are processed one at a time. The first Sequence is processed, then the second Sequence, and so on until the last Sequence is processed and the Exchange is complete. The number of Sequences in an Exchange and the content of each Sequence is determined by the higher-level protocol transaction being performed.

When the Exchange is created, the Exchange originator has the initiative to send the first Sequence. When that Sequence is completed, the Exchange originator may transfer control to the Exchange responder so that the responder can send a Sequence in return. This transfer of control is referred to as transferring Sequence Initiative. Depending upon the requirements of the higher-level protocol, Sequence Initiative may be transferred one or more times between the originator and responder ports. It is also possible that the Exchange originator may not transfer the initiative at all.

Because only one of the two ports can have the Sequence Initiative, there is only one active Sequence within an Exchange at any point in time (and that Sequence is being used to deliver an Information Unit from one port to another), the Exchange is half-duplex. Architecting the Exchange as half-duplex provides a mechanism for emulating the behavior associated with half-duplex protocols (this is especially true of traditional bus-oriented I/O interfaces that by their very nature can only be transporting one unit of information in one direction at a time).

A diagram of the Exchange operation within each of the ports is shown in Figure 88. Note that there is a separate instance of this illustration for every open Exchange in the port.

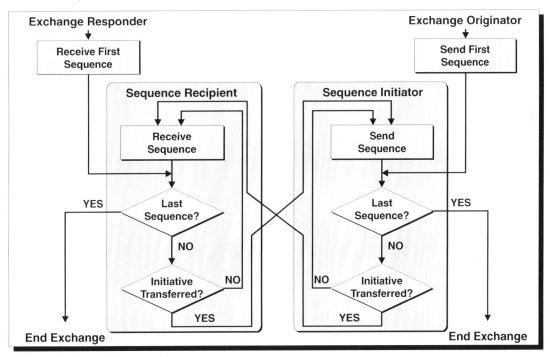

Figure 88. Exchange Flow Diagram

13.2 Exchange Identification

A port may have more than one Exchange open simultaneously. This allows for more efficient utilization of the port and link by allowing the port to multiplex between Exchanges and take advantage of periods of inactivity that normally occur during an Exchange.

When multiple Exchanges are active at the same time, some means to identify, or tag, each Exchange is needed so that when an event occurs, that event can be associated with the correct Exchange. Existing protocols that support disconnected operations or command queueing have developed their own protocol-dependent techniques for handling the identification of open operations by means of an address (allowing a single open operation per address), or assigning a unique identifier or tag value to each open operation.

Fibre Channel provides an identifier, called the Exchange_ID, that can be assigned to each Exchange to provide a way to link subsequent frames or events to the Exchange. This identifier is provided at the FC-2 level and is independent of the higher-level protocol or process.

13.2.1 Originator Exchange Identification (OX_ID)

When a port wants to begin a new transaction with another port, it has to originate an Exchange because all frame transmission (and, therefore, information transfer) occurs within the context of an open Exchange. The port that originates the Exchange is called the Exchange originator (the other port is called the Exchange responder).

Originating an Exchange does not involve explicit communication with the other port. The Exchange originator simply assigns an Originator Exchange_ID (OX_ID), creates the necessary control structures the originator needs to manage the transaction, and sends the first Sequence of the Exchange to the Exchange responder. The control information maintained by the port varies from one implementation to another, but may include memory address pointers, transfer byte counts, status and sense buffer pointers, frame header templates, and so forth.

The standard does not require that the originator assign an OX_ID if the higher-level protocol does not require this kind of identification for tracking, or if some other mechanism is available to accomplish the same result (while the standard does not require assignment of an OX_ID, individual protocol mappings may). To indicate that an OX_ID has not been assigned, a value of x'FFFF' is used.

When an OX_ID is assigned it must be unique to the originator or originator-responder pair to provide an unambiguous identification at the originator. The originator may use a single set of Exchange identifiers for all ports that it has open Exchanges with, or use a separate set of identifiers for each port. The intent of the standard is simply to provide an architected mechanism available for the port's use.

Once the Exchange is created, and the OX_ID assigned (or a value of x'FFFF' is used), the originator can begin transferring the first Sequence to the Exchange responder. For identification purposes, the originator's OX_ID is included in every frame in the Exchange, whether sent by the originator or responder.

When multiple originators communicate with the same responder, it is possible that they may assign duplicate OX_ID values (in fact, if the originators are using the same protocol chip the assignment algorithm is the same and duplicates are likely). In order for the responder to uniquely identify the transaction, the responder must qualify the OX_ID with the source address identifier (S_ID) of the originator. The responder can either use the combination of S_ID and OX_ID, or, it may wish to assign an identifier of its own to the transaction.

13.2.2 Responder Exchange Identification (RX_ID)

When the Exchange responder receives the first frame of the new Exchange, it has to create control structures of its own to manage the transaction. When it does this, it may want to assign its own identifier to the transaction, called the Responder Exchange_ID, or RX_ID. This identifier is in addition to the originator's Exchange identifier. Assigning an RX_ID may help the responder process subsequent Sequences associated with that Exchange, especially if the responder can have multiple Exchanges open at the same time.

The standard does not require that the responder assign an RX_ID if the protocol does not require this kind of tracking, or if some other mechanism is available to accomplish the same result (while the standard does not require assignment of an RX_ID, individual protocol mappings may). To indicate that an RX_ID has not been assigned, a value of x'FFFF' is used.

When an RX_ID is assigned it must be unique to the responder or originator-responder pair. This allows the responder to use a single set of identifiers for all ports that it has open Exchanges with, or use a separate set of identifiers for each port. Again, the intent of the standard is simply to provide an architected identification mechanism that the port may use.

When the responder sends a frame to the originator for an Exchange, the responder returns the originator's OX_ID and includes its own assigned RX_ID (or x'FFFF' if an RX_ID was not assigned) in every frame sent for that Exchange.

If the responder does not assign an RX_ID, it is still possible for multiple Exchanges to exist between the originator and responder. It simply means that the responder has to use the concatenation of the originator's S_ID and OX_ID fields to identify the transaction.

13.2.3 Exchange_ID Interlock

Some applications require that the responder assign an RX_ID value before the Exchange is allowed to proceed. When this condition occurs, it is called Exchange_ID interlock, or X_ID interlock for short.

When X_ID interlock is being used, the originator sends the first frame of the first Sequence of the Exchange and then waits for a response to that frame (an ACK or other reply). When the responder sends the response to the first frame, it provides the assigned RX_ID value in the frame header of the response frame (the OX_ID is copied from the first frame of the Sequence). From this point on, every frame of the Exchange contains both the OX_ID and RX_ID values assigned.

13.3 Exchange Multiplexing

Because a port can have multiple Exchanges open at the same time, the port may want to multiplex among them to take advantage of natural breaks in the Exchange processing to work on other Exchanges. For an example of Exchange multiplexing see Figure 89 on page 178.

When multiplexing between Exchanges, the state information for the current Exchange is stored in the control structures associated with that Exchange (the state of the Exchange is saved). When the transaction is subsequently resumed, the Exchange state information is re-

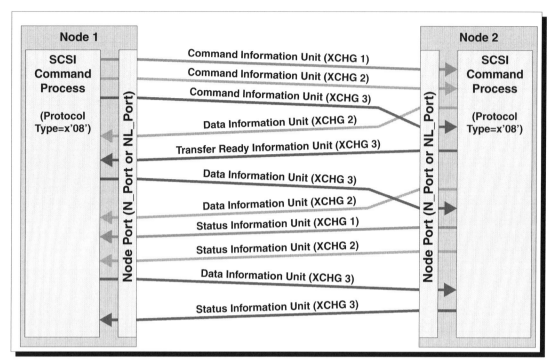

Figure 89. Exchange Multiplexing

stored allowing the Exchange to continue. Saving the state of one Exchange and restoring the state of a different one is referred to as a context switch.

Context switches can potentially occur as frequently as individual frames, and it is important to minimize the time required to perform a context switch if maximum performance is to be achieved. The Exchange identifiers offer one technique for minimizing the amount of time required for context switching.

The standard does not define the specific values to be used for the OX_ID and RX_ID (other than uniqueness requirements) and these two fields can be assigned any value of the ports' choosing. The value assigned to the Exchange_ID can be used to facilitate frame processing associated with an Exchange by using the Exchange_ID itself as a pointer into the data structure used to hold the control (or context) information for that Exchange.

Using this technique, when the originator creates a new Exchange it locates an available entry in its Exchange context table, assigns that entry to the new Exchange, and builds the necessary context structures to store the state or context information associated with that Exchange. The pointer to the control information is used as the OX_ID value and is present in every frame of that Exchange. When a frame is received by the originator it can use the OX_ID in the received frame to address the context information associated with that particular Exchange.

Chapter 13. Exchange Management

The responder can use this same approach. When the responder receives the first frame of a new Exchange, it needs to allocate an entry in its Exchange context table to hold the necessary information pertaining to that Exchange. When it locates an available entry in its context table, it can assign the pointer to that entry as the RX_ID. When a frame is received by the responder, it can use the RX_ID value in the received frame to address the context information associated with that particular Exchange.

Having separate identifiers for use by both the originator and responder can greatly simplify and speed up context switching that occurs as frames associated with different Exchanges are received. When the originator receives a frame, it uses the OX_ID value as a pointer to its context information associated with that Exchange, and when the responder receives a frame, it uses the RX_ID value as its pointer. An example of this use of the OX_ID and RX_ID values is shown in Figure 90.

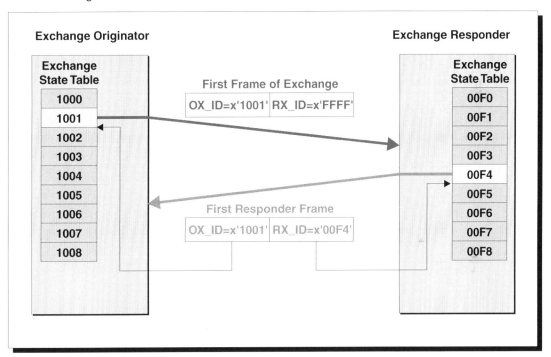

Figure 90. Use of OX_ID and RX_ID to Index into Exchange Context Structures

13.4 Exchange Origination

An Exchange may be originated before login is complete to perform Extended Link Service transactions (in fact, login is an Extended Link Service itself). When this is done, the Exchange uses the default login parameters and special Extended Link Services rules.

To originate an upper-level protocol Exchange, the following conditions must be met:

- The originating node port must have successfully completed N_Port Login (PLOGI) with the destination port (PLOGI is not required for many of Fibre Channel's Extended Link Services).

- The originating node port must have a unique Originator Exchange_ID (OX_ID) available not currently in use with the destination port.

- The originating node port has Exchange resources available to support the Exchange (e.g., an available Exchange Status Block (ESB), etc.).

- The originating node port is able to initiate a new Sequence (has an available SEQ_ID and any necessary resources).

The first Sequence of the Exchange is uniquely identified by setting the First_Sequence bit (located in the F_CTL field of the frame header) of every frame within that Sequence. This bit alerts the receiving port that a new Exchange is being originated and it is time to create the necessary Exchange control blocks. The First_Sequence bit is set in all frames of the Sequence so that the receiving port knows to create the Exchange control structures, even if one or more frames are lost due to a transmission error or the frames are delivered out-of-order.

When the originator transmits the first frame of the first Sequence of the Exchange, the RX_ID value is set to x'FFFF', indicating that the RX_ID is unassigned (after all, the responder doesn't even know the Exchange exists yet). If X_ID interlock is used, the originator waits for the responder to acknowledge and provide an RX_ID before sending subsequent frames for that Exchange. If X_ID interlock is not used, the originator may continue to send additional frames of that Sequence.

When an acknowledged class of service is used for the first Sequence of the Exchange (any class except Class-3), the originator must wait for at least one ACK from the responder before beginning the second Sequence of the Exchange. This protects against the case where the entire first Sequence of the Exchange is lost due to a transmission error.

13.5 Sequence Initiative

Within an Exchange, Information Units may flow in one direction only (from the originator to the responder), or in both directions.

When all Sequences in the Exchange are sent only from the originator to the responder, the Exchange is a uni-directional Exchange.

If Sequences within an Exchange are sent from the originator to the responder, and from the responder to the originator, the Exchange is referred to as a bidirectional Exchange. To prevent potential ambiguity regarding the timing relationships of Sequences and provide a means to support half-duplex protocols, only one port is permitted to send a Sequence within an Exchange at any point in time.

The originator of the Exchange has the initiative to send the first Sequence of that Exchange, because Exchanges are never created unless there is one or more Information Units to send. This is referred to as 'holding the Sequence Initiative' because the port can initiate one or more Sequences. In a uni-directional Exchange, the Exchange originator holds the Sequence Initiative for the entire duration of the Exchange.

In a bidirectional Exchange, the Sequence Initiative is transferred back and forth between the two ports as necessary to allow each port one or more opportunities to send Sequences. The upper-level protocol, and FC-4 mapping of that protocol, define when the Sequence Initiative is transferred and how many Sequences may be sent while holding the initiative.

A port currently sending a Sequence is referred to as the Sequence initiator. The current Sequence initiator controls which of the two node ports will be allowed to send the next Sequence for that Exchange. If the Sequence initiator has one or more additional Sequences ready to send for the Exchange, it holds the Sequence Initiative to send the next Sequence. If the Sequence initiator does not wish to send another Sequence for that Exchange at this time, it may transfer the Sequence Initiative to the Sequence recipient by setting the Sequence Initiative bit in the F_CTL field of the last frame of the current Sequence (it may be set in earlier frames of that Sequence as an advance indication, but is only meaningful in the last frame).

13.5.1 Sequence Initiative Transfer

In a confirmed class of service (e.g., Class-1, Class-2, or Class-F), the Sequence initiator does not consider the Sequence Initiative successfully transferred until it receives an ACK with one of the Sequence terminating End-of-Frame delimiters (EOFdt or EOFt) and the Sequence Initiative bit is set in the ACK confirming the transfer of initiative.

It is possible a transmission error could interfere with the transfer of initiative. If the last frame of the Sequence indicating Sequence Initiative is being transferred is lost due to a transmission error, the Sequence delivery failed and the transfer of Sequence Initiative does not occur.

If the ACK to the last frame indicating the transfer of initiative is lost due to a transmission error, the current Sequence initiator does not consider the initiative transferred, but the Sequence recipient does because it sent the required ACK. In this case, both ports believe they have the Sequence Initiative. When the Sequence transferring the initiative times out due to the lost ACK, the port transferring the initiative can determine the state of the initiative and whether the Sequence was delivered correctly, by reading the Exchange Status Block (ESB) of the other port.

In Class-3, the Sequence Initiative is considered transferred when the last data frame of the Sequence is sent and the Sequence Initiative bit of the F_CTL field in the frame header is set.

If the frame transferring the initiative is lost due to a transmission error, neither port believes it has the initiative. In this case, the Sequence recipient will timeout waiting for the missing frame. When the Sequence timeout occurs the higher-level process is notified so that the appropriate recovery action can be taken.

13.6 Mixing Classes of Service Within an Exchange

Multiple classes of service may be used for different Sequences during the same Exchange. When the request is made to FC-2 to deliver a Sequence, that request specifies which class of service should be used for that Sequence.

The upper-level process may wish to mix classes of service within an Exchange to take advantage of the different delivery characteristics for specific Sequences. When different classes of service are used within the same Exchange, Class-3 cannot be mixed with any other class of service (Class-3 is the only unacknowledged class of service).

13.7 Exchange Errors

Because the Exchange is primarily a mechanism for identifying and tracking Sequences, there are very few Exchange-related error conditions defined at the port level.

Data Frame Received While Holding the Sequence Initiative. Because only one port can hold Sequence Initiative for an Exchange at any point in time, an error results if the port currently holding the Sequence Initiative receives a data frame for that Exchange from the other port.

When this happens and the received frame is a Class-1, Class-2, or Class-F frame, the receiving port sends a Port Reject (P_RJT) to the other port indicating Exchange Error.

If this condition occurs and the received frame is a Class-3 frame, the received frame and all subsequent frames for that Exchange are discarded without processing, no P_RJT is sent, and the Exchange is abnormally terminated.

Class-3 Combined With Any Other Class of Service. If Class-3 is mixed with any other class of service in the same Exchange, an Exchange error occurs and the Exchange is abnormally terminated.

Streamed Sequences in Different Classes of Service. When streamed Sequences occur (*Streamed Sequences* on page 194), the streamed Sequences must all use the same class of service.

Extended Link Service (ELS) Timeout. Many Extended Link Service (ELS) requests require a response Sequence. To detect missing response Sequences, expected responses must be received within two times R_A_TOV. If this does not occur, the Exchange is abnormally terminated.

Two Active Sequences for the Same Exchange. Because only one Sequence can be active for an Exchange at a time, if a port begins transmission of a new Sequence for the Exchange before completing transmission of the previous Sequence, an Exchange error occurs.

13.8 Exchange Termination

Either the originator or responder can terminate the Exchange normally by setting the Last_Sequence bit in the last frame of the last Sequence of the Exchange (the Last_Sequence bit can be set in earlier frames in the Sequence as well to provide advance notification). Upon successful completion of the last Sequence of the Exchange, the Exchange is also completed and the OX_ID, RX_ID, and Exchange Status Block (ESB) are freed and available for reuse.

An Exchange may be abnormally terminated by either the originator or responder by one of the following methods or occurrences:

* Timeout of the last Sequence of the Exchange

- Using the Abort Sequence (ABTS) Basic Link Service with the Last_Sequence bit set (see *Abort Sequence (ABTS)* on page 311)

- N_Port Logout, either explicit or implicit

13.9 Exchange Error Policies

There are four Exchange error policies that specify how a Sequence delivery failure should be handled within an Exchange. The Exchange originator specifies the error policy in effect for a given Exchange by setting the Abort Sequence Condition bits in the F_CTL field of the frame header of the first data frame of the first Sequence of the Exchange.

The action specified by the error policy in effect for that Exchange is invoked when the Sequence initiator or Sequence recipient detects a Sequence delivery failure during the Exchange. For more information about the conditions that constitute a Sequence delivery failure, refer to *FC-2 Sequence Errors* on page 298.

13.9.1 Recovery Boundary

The basic unit of error recovery in Fibre Channel is the Sequence, not the frame. All error recovery is performed at either the Sequence or Exchange level. The decision to make the Sequence the recovery boundary is based on several considerations.

When a higher-level process wishes to send information, it makes a Sequence delivery request to the FC-2 level. The FC-2 level processes the Sequence request and segments the information into one or more frames. The number of frames in the resultant Sequence, the size of the data field, and the data boundaries of the individual frames are not known to the higher level that originated the request (segmentation and reassembly is completely transparent above the FC-2 level). Because the higher-level process does not have visibility or knowledge of the individual frames, it cannot manage retransmission at any level below that of the original Sequence delivery request.

While the FC-2 level has knowledge of the individual frames, it may not be reasonable to require FC-2 to perform frame retransmission. If FC-2 is going to retransmit individual frames in an attempt to recover from errors, then FC-2 will need to remember how to reconstruct (or keep a copy of) every outstanding frame that has been sent, but not yet confirmed. In the case of small configurations over limited distances, keeping a copy of frames until delivery has been confirmed may be possible because the number of outstanding frames can be kept small.

When the configuration is large or the distance between ports is substantial, the number of frames that can be in transit soon precludes keeping copies of all frames in transit.

For example, it takes light approximately 50 µs to travel 10 km. If a port begins sending frames to another port at the end of a 10 km. link it will take 100 µs. for the first frame to arrive at the other port and an acknowledgment to return. If the frames each have a data field of 128 bytes, the time to transmit a single frame is approximately 1.88 µs. With a 100 µs. round trip time, the port could send approximately 53 frames before the first acknowledgment is received. That means 53 individual frames worth of information to hold while waiting for confirmation.

However, Fibre Channel is capable of distances greater than 100 km. (by cascading links or fabric elements) to support applications such as off-site backup and archival, remote disaster recovery sites, and wide-area networks linking different locations together. For these types of applications, the distances may be hundreds of kilometers and the number of frames in transit may number into the thousands. Clearly, in this case, keeping a copy of every outstanding frame is not practical.

When all of these considerations were taken into account, it was realized that even if the port could do frame level retransmission there would still be situations where higher-level Sequence recovery would be required. To keep the port design simple the decision was to move error recovery up to the higher-level (that only knows about Sequences).

While Fibre Channel supports error recovery at the Sequence level, some upper-level FC-4 protocol mappings may specify that error recovery take place at the Exchange level.

13.9.2 Abort, Discard Multiple Sequences

In the Abort, Discard Multiple Sequence policy, the Sequence recipient delivers Sequences to the higher-level process in the order transmitted provided that the previous Sequence of the Exchange, if any, was deliverable.

Support of this error policy is required for Class-1, Class-2, Class-3 Sequences.

When this error policy is in effect, if a Sequence is non-deliverable, it and all subsequent Sequences for that Exchange are discarded until the Abort Sequence (ABTS) protocol has been completed. The ABTS protocol provides a mechanism for the two ports to synchronize their processing to the last delivered Sequence so that the failed Sequence and all subsequent Sequences can be resent by the upper-level process, if desired.

There is no attempt by the FC-2 level to retransmit individual frames and recover from the error, nor does the FC-2 level attempt to retransmit the failed Sequence. Any retransmission of failed or discarded Sequences will be performed by the higher-level process.

This error policy may be used by protocols in which later Sequences have a dependency on prior Sequences.

13.9.3 Abort, Discard a Single Sequence

In the Abort, Discard a Single Sequence policy, the Sequence recipient delivers Sequences to the higher-level process in the order that Sequences are completed without regard to the deliverability of previous Sequences in that Exchange.

Support of this error policy is required for Class-1, Class-2, Class-3 Sequences.

When this error policy is in effect, if a Sequence is non-deliverable, subsequent Sequences for that Exchange are still be delivered to the upper-level process. The failed Sequence is aborted using the Abort Sequence (ABTS) protocol. Upon completion of the ABTS protocol, the failed Sequence may be retransmitted by the upper-level process.

This error policy may be used by protocols where individual Sequences are not dependent upon one another, or the upper-level process will manage the retransmission and correct ordering of the Sequences.

13.9.4 Process Policy with Infinite Buffers

In the process policy with infinite buffers, frames are delivered to the upper-level process in the order received. This policy is only applicable to Class-1 service and uses a single ACK_0 at the end of the Sequence to confirm delivery of the entire Sequence. Support of this error policy is optional and indicated during N_Port Login (PLOGI).

The Sequence recipient may use the received Sequence, even if Sequence delivery was not successful.

This error policy may be used by real-time applications such as data logging or video transmission where Sequence retransmission may not be applicable because of the time sensitive nature of the data.

13.9.5 Discard Multiple Sequences with Immediate Retransmission

In the discard multiple Sequences with immediate retransmission policy, the Sequence recipient delivers Sequences to the higher-level process in the order transmitted provided that the previous Sequence of the Exchange, if any, was deliverable.

When this error policy is in effect, if a Sequence is non-deliverable, it and all subsequent Sequences for that Exchange are discarded until a Sequence with the retransmission bit in the F_CTL field of the frame header set is received, or the ABTS protocol has been completed.

This error policy is a special case of the Abort, discard multiple Sequences error policy and is only applicable to an Exchange where all transmission is in Class-1.

13.10 Exchange Status Block (ESB)

Associated with each Exchange is an Exchange Status Block (ESB) used to retain information about the current status of the Exchange. This information may be used to determine the current status of the Exchange, and may be used during error recovery processing to determine which Sequences were successfully delivered. Both the originator and responder maintain separate Exchange Status Blocks. The format of the Exchange Status Block is shown in Table 25 on page 186. A breakdown of the Exchange Status (E_STAT) bits in the Exchange Status Block is shown in Table 26 on page 186.

The contents of the Exchange Status Block can be retrieved by issuing a Read Exchange Concise Extended Link Service request (see *Read Exchange Concise (REC)* on page 369).

The number of Sequence Status Block (SSB) entries in the Exchange Status Block should be at least two greater than the number of open Sequences per Exchange value communicated during the login process. The information on completed Sequences is preserved until the number of Sequences in the Exchange exceeds the number of Sequence Status Block entries in the Exchange Status Block. At that time, the oldest entry may be deleted from the Exchange Status Block and all earlier entries shifted down to make room for the newest entry. The entries in the Sequence Status Block portion of the Exchange Status Block are preserved until they are replaced by newer entries or the Exchange is terminated.

Word	Bits 31-24	Bits 23-16	Bits 15-8	Bits 7-0
0	Originator Exchange_ID (OX_ID)		Responder Exchange_ID (RX_ID)	
1	reserved	Originator N_Port ID (Address)		
2	reserved	Responder N_Port ID (Address)		
3	Exchange Status bits (E_STAT) - see Table 26 on page 186			
4	reserved - 4 bytes			
5 to 32	Service Parameters (of the other Nx_Port) - 112 bytes - - - Service Parameters (of the other Nx_Port) - 112 bytes			
33 to 34	Oldest Sequence Status (1st 8 bytes of the Sequence Status Block) see Table 27 on page 199 Sequence Status Block (continued)			
35 to n-2	Next Oldest Sequence Status (1st 8 bytes of the Sequence Status Block) Sequence Status Block (continued)			
n-1 to n	Newest Sequence Status (1st 8 bytes of the Sequence Status Block) Sequence Status Block (continued)			

Table 25. Exchange Status Block (ESB)

Bit	Description	Value
31	ESB Owner	0 = Exchange originator 1 = Exchange responder
30	Sequence Initiative	0 = Other Port holds the initiative 1 = This Port holds the initiative
29	Completion	0 = Exchange is still open 1 = Exchange is complete
28	Ending Condition	0 = Exchange ended normally 1 = Exchange ended abnormally
27	Error Type	0 = Exchange aborted 1 = Exchange abnormally terminated
26	Recovery Qualifier	0 = None 1 = Recovery Qualifier active
25-24	Exchange Error Policy	00 = Abort, Discard multiple Sequences 01 = Abort, Discard a single Sequence 10 = Process with infinite buffers 11 = Discard multiple Sequences with immediate retransmission
23*	Originator X_ID Invalid	0 = Originator X_ID valid 1 = Originator X_ID invalid
22*	Responder X_ID Invalid	0 = Responder X_ID valid 1 = Responder X_ID invalid
21-00	reserved	
* Bits 23-22 reflect the completion condition of the newest Sequence Status Block contained in the ESB		

Table 26. Exchange Status Bits (E_STAT)

13.11 Chapter Summary

Exchange

- Exchange identifies and manages a set of related Sequences between two node ports
  - Created when the first Sequence of the transaction is processed
  - Ends when the last Sequence is processed
- Sequences within an Exchange are processed sequentially
  - First Sequence is processed,
  - Then the second,
  - And so forth until the last Sequence
- Only one Sequence is active at a time
  - Therefore, the Exchange is a half-duplex construct

Exchange Identification

- Ports may have more than one Exchange open at a time
  - Allows for more efficient link usage
  - Port can multiplex between Exchanges
  - This behavior is required by some protocols, such as SCSI
- When multiple Exchanges can occur, each needs to be identified
  - When an event occurs, which operation is it for?
- Existing protocols may have their own protocol-specific mechanism
- Fibre Channel provides a protocol-independent mechanism called the Exchange_ID (or X_ID)

Originator X_ID

- When a port begins a new transaction, it creates an Exchange
  - Created within the port, no communication with the other port
  - Information transfer subsequently occurs within the Exchange
- The originator assigns an identifier called the Originator Exchange_ID, or OX_ID
- Unique identifier at the originator to allow tracking frames within the Exchange

Responder Exchange_ID

- The responder becomes aware of the new Exchange when it receives the first frame
- Has to create control structures to manage the transaction
  - Memory pointers, data buffers, etc.
- Responder may assign a responder Exchange_ID (RX_ID), if desired
  - RX_ID may help responder manage the transaction
  - Could point to the context for the Exchange
- If no Exchange_ID is assigned, x'FFFF' is used
- Responder puts both the OX_ID and RX_ID in every frame of Exchange

Exchange Multiplexing

- The Exchange IDs can facilitate Exchange multiplexing
- Use the OX_ID and RX_ID as pointers to the control structures for the Exchange
- Originator assigns the pointer to its structure as the OX_ID
- Responder assigns the pointer to its structure as the RX_ID
- Each frame carries its own pointer to the control structures at each port

Exchange Origination

- To originate an Exchange (other than link services), the following conditions must be met:
  - The originator port must have successfully completed login with the other port
  - The originator has a valid OX_ID available
  - The originator has the resources available to support the Exchange
  - The originator is able to initiate a Sequence
- If all of these conditions are met, the originator can start the Exchange

Sequence Initiative

- Within an Exchange, information may flow in one direction only or in both
- If only one direction, the Exchange is uni-directional
- If both directions, the Exchange is bi-directional
  - Only one active Sequence is allowed
  - One of the ports has the initiative to send the next Sequence for that Exchange
  - This is called the Sequence Initiative
- Explicitly passed between the ports on the last frame of the Sequence when control is transferred

Mixing Classes of Service

- Multiple classes of service can be used within the same Exchange
- Allows accommodation of different data characteristics
  - Class-2 or 3 for single-frame Sequences
  - Class-1 for the data phase
- Cannot mix protocols within an Exchange
  - Send a SCSI command, get an IP packet?
  - Not prohibited by the standards, but this seems illogical

Error Recovery Boundary

- The recovery boundary in Fibre Channel is the Sequence or Exchange
  - NOT the frame
- The higher-level process requests transfer of an Information Unit (Sequence)
  - The port segments the Information Unit into a Sequence of frames
  - The higher level has no visibility to individual frames and cannot retransmit specific frames

Error Recovery Boundary

- Once the port sends a frame, it may not have the ability to retransmit it
  - Hundreds, or even thousands of frames could have been sent since the error frame
  - The port would have to remember information on every one in case a retry was needed
- This would complicate the port design significantly
- Therefore, recovery is moved up to the Sequence level
- The higher level has the original Information Unit and can ask to have it retransmitted

Exchange Error Policies

- Fibre Channel defines four error policies for Exchanges. They are:
  - Abort, discard multiple Sequences. Abort the failed Sequence and discard all subsequent ones of the Exchange
  - Abort, discard a single Sequence. Abort the failed Sequence, but use others of the Exchange
  - Process policy. Use the failed Sequence, even though it may be incomplete or have errors
  - Discard multiple Sequences with immediate retransmission. Discard all Sequences after the point of failure and retry beginning with the failed Sequence.

Exchange Errors

- If a port holds the Sequence Initiative for an Exchange and receives a data frame for the same Exchange
- If Class-3 is mixed with any other class of service in the same Exchange
- If an Extended Link Service request fails to receive an expected response within 2*R_A_TOV
- If streamed Sequences do not use the same Class of Service
- If a port begins transmitting a new Sequence for an Exchange before completing transmission of the previous Sequence

---

14. Sequence Management

To transport an Information Unit, an upper-level protocol or higher-level process makes a sequence request to the port to deliver the information. The port accomplishes the delivery by using a Sequence of one or more frames.

The maximum amount of data that can be carried in the data field of a single frame is limited to 2112 bytes. While some Information Units will fit into the data field of a single frame, larger Information Units will need to be packaged into a Sequence containing multiple frames.

14.1 Segmentation and Reassembly

Transporting large Information Units is handled by segmenting the Information Unit and delivering it with a multi-frame Sequence. When the frames arrive at the receiver, they are reassembled back into the original Information Unit. Segmentation and reassembly is performed by the FC-2 level and is transparent to the higher levels (they simply request that the Information Unit be delivered, the sending and receiving FC-2 take care of the segmentation and reassembly). An illustration of the segmentation and reassembly process is shown in Figure 91.

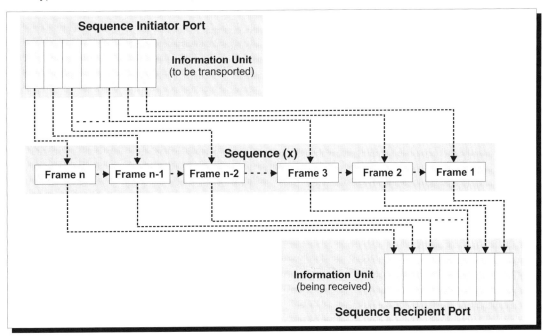

Figure 91. Segmentation and Reassembly

When information is transported from a sending port to a receiving port, the architectural model assumes the sender places the data in a buffer and requests the port to deliver it. The sending port takes the data from the buffer, segments it if necessary, and packages the data into frames for transmission. At the receiving port, frames are validated, and the data in the frames is reassembled into a reassembly buffer. After the entire Sequence has been reassembled, the higher level is notified that the data is now available for processing. This basic assumption about the segmentation and reassembly process separates the transmission of the data from the actual processing of the data by the receiver. If a sender sends the data in the Information Unit out-of-order, or the topology delivers the frames out-of-order, the receiver will not use the received data until the entire Information Unit has been reassembled.

Memory locations associated with the sender's and receiver's buffers are never communicated as a part of the Fibre Channel protocol, so there is no way to directly reference a memory location in either port's buffers. Instead, Fibre Channel uses a concept of relative offset, or displacement, that indicates the location, relative to the beginning of the buffer, where the data should be placed. By sending the relative offset value in the parameter field of each frame header, the receiver can determine where the data should be stored in its reassembly buffer by adding the relative offset value to the base address assigned to that particular operation.

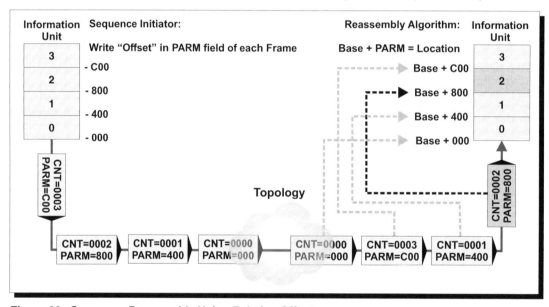

Figure 92. Sequence Reassembly Using Relative Offset

Fibre Channel's segmentation and reassembly capabilities are extremely powerful to accommodate a wide variety of applications and environments. For example, the transmitter may send data out-of-order, or from non-contiguous locations, to improve performance or perform scatter-gather types of operations. The fabric topology may deliver individual frames out-of-order in some situations. The segmentation and reassembly mechanisms present in Fibre Channel can accommodate such behaviors while still correctly reassembling the information.

14.2 Open Sequences and Active Sequences

When a Sequence is being sent from one port to another, each port has its own view about when that Sequence is open due to the frame transit time in the interconnecting topology.

14.2.1 Open and Active at the Sequence Initiator

The node port sending a Sequence is called the Sequence initiator. From the Sequence initiator's perspective, the Sequence is both *open* and *active* when the frame initiating the Sequence (the frame with a SOFc1, SOFi1, SOFi2 or SOFi3 delimiter) is sent. The Sequence remains *active* until the last data frame of the Sequence is sent (the one having the End_Sequence bit in the F_CTL field set).

Following transmission of the last data frame of the Sequence, the Sequence may remain *open* while waiting for confirmation of delivery of the frames of that Sequence. For those classes of service that provide confirmation of delivery (Class-1, Class-2, and Class-F), the Sequence remains open until an ACK with one of the terminating delimiters is received (EOFdt or EOFt) or the Sequence is abnormally terminated (see *Sequence Completion* on page 196).

Where no confirmation of delivery is expected (Class-3), the Sequence is considered no longer open when the last frame of the Sequence is sent (the frame with the EOFt delimiter).

14.2.2 Open and Active at the Sequence Recipient

The node port that receives a Sequence is called the Sequence recipient. From the Sequence recipient's standpoint, the Sequence is considered both *open* and *active* when any data frame for the Sequence is received (it does not have to be the initiating frame).

A Sequence remains *open* and *active* in Class-1, Class-2 or Class-F until an ACK with one of the Sequence-terminating delimiters is sent (EOFdt or EOFt). In Class-3, the Sequence remains *open* and *active* until all data frames up to the frame containing the EOFt delimiter have been received, or is abnormally terminated (see *Sequence Completion* on page 196).

14.3 Sequence Identification (SEQ_ID)

A node port may have multiple Sequences open at the same time. This could occur if the port has multiple open Exchanges. To reassemble each Sequence correctly, it is necessary to provide an identifier for each Sequence. This identifier is called the Sequence_ID (SEQ_ID for short) and is sent in the header of every frame of that Sequence (the frame header also carries the originator and responder Exchange identifiers). An illustration of interleaving frames of different Sequences is shown in Figure 93. While this example shows multiplexing occurring within the topology, both Sequences could originate from the same source port.

SEQ_ID is not qualified by Exchange identifiers. To prevent ambiguity during the processing and reassembly of Sequences, it is necessary that the SEQ_ID is unique between the Sequence initiator and Sequence recipient port pair. Because the SEQ_ID is not an extension of the Exchange identifiers, there is no way to determine which specific SEQ_ID will be used for the next Sequence. The following example may help illustrate why this occurs:

- SEQ_ID values 1, 2, and 3 are used for Exchange 1

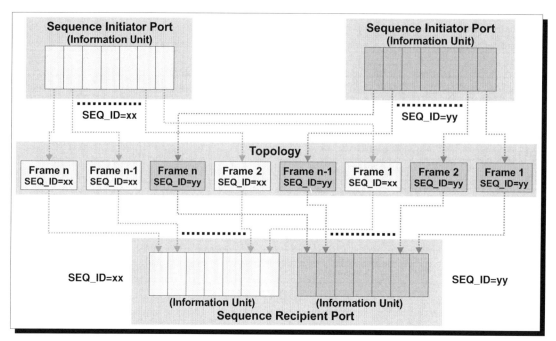

Figure 93. Frame Multiplexing

- Exchange 2 is started and uses SEQ_ID values 4 and 5
- When the next Sequence is sent for Exchange 1, the next available SEQ_ID value is 6
- Sequences 1, 2, and 3 are complete
- Exchange 2 uses SEQ_ID 1 for the next Sequence

In this example, Exchange 1 used SEQ_ID values 1, 2, 3, and 6. Exchange 2 used SEQ_ID values 4, 5, and 1. As can be seen, the SEQ_ID values cannot be used to determine the order of Sequences within an Exchange, nor can the SEQ_ID be used to determine if all Sequences associated with the Exchange have been received.

It can be argued that the SEQ_ID should have been treated as an extension of the Exchange identifiers and required to be assigned in increasing order within the Exchange (Exchange 1 uses SEQ_ID 1, 2, 3, etc.; Exchange 2 uses SEQ_ID 1, 2, 3, etc.). This would have provided enhanced Sequence handling capabilities. Unfortunately, this is not the way the standard defines the usage of the SEQ_ID.

14.3.1 Sequence_ID Reuse

To prevent reassembly errors in the case of transmission errors, consecutive Sequences in the same Exchange are required to have different SEQ_ID values (if there is a transfer of Sequence Initiative between the two Sequences, the Sequences are not considered consecutive). This requirement exists in case the end of the first Sequence and the beginning of the next Sequence are both lost due to transmission errors. If the SEQ_IDs of the two Sequences were the same, it is possible for the two fragments to appear as a single Sequence resulting in a possible undetected reassembly error. By requiring different SEQ_ID values, the two fragments are identifiable as different Sequences, both of which are incomplete.

14.4 Frame Identification–Sequence Count (SEQ_CNT)

Within a Sequence, each frame is consecutively numbered by the Sequence initiator. This sequential number is contained in the Sequence Count (SEQ_CNT) field of the frame header and provides a mechanism for the Sequence recipient to verify that all frames of the Sequence have been received.

The first frame of the first Sequence of an Exchange transmitted by either the originator or rc sponder is required to have a SEQ_CNT of x'0000'. The SEQ_CNT of each subsequent frame of that Sequence is incremented by +1.

When the next Sequence of the Exchange is sent, the SEQ_CNT may either restart at x'0000', or continue to increment by +1 from the last frame of the prior Sequence (this is called Continuously Increasing Sequence Count, or CISC). Continuously Increasing Sequence Count is required under some conditions as is discussed in *Streamed Sequences* on page 194.

While the SEQ_CNT of frames sent by the Sequence initiator will increment by +1, frames may not arrive in the same order at the Sequence recipient. This could occur if the topology delivers the frames out of order or retransmission of a frame due to a busy condition.

When the Sequence recipient receives any frame of the Sequence, it begins processing that Sequence and remembers the Sequence count of any received frames. When the frame with the Start-of-Frame delimiter initiating the Sequence is received, the SEQ_CNT of the first frame of the Sequence is known. When the frame with the End_Sequence bit is received, the SEQ_CNT of the last data frame of the Sequence is known. The entire Sequence consists of all frames with that SEQ_ID having SEQ_CNTs between that of the first and last frames.

14.4.1 Sequence Count Wrap

A very large Sequence could contain more frames than the SEQ_CNT field is able to count. It is also possible that, due to the use of continuously increasing Sequence count, a SEQ_CNT of x'FFFF' is reached before the end of the Sequence. If either of these cases occur, the SEQ_CNT may be allowed to wrap from x'FFFF' to x'0000', provided that it doesn't result in two active frames having the same SEQ_ID and SEQ_CNT.

To prevent duplication of the Sequence qualifiers, the SEQ_CNT can't be reused within a Sequence if that value has previously been used and the frame with the prior usage is still active. A frame is no longer active after an acknowledgment is received, or enough time has elapsed so that it can no longer possibly be delivered to the other port (this time is called the Resource_Allocation Timeout Value, or R_A_TOV).

14.4.2 Sequence Count (SEQ_CNT) in Response Frames

When an acknowledgment, reject, or busy response is sent to a frame, the OX_ID, RX_ID, and SEQ_ID of the response are set to the values present in the original frame. The SEQ_CNT is handled as follows:

- When an ACK_1, P_BSY, F_BSY, P_RJT, or F_RJT response is sent, SEQ_CNT is set to the value of the original frame. This allows the response to be associated with the correct data frame.

- When ACK_0 is sent in response to an entire Sequence, SEQ_CNT is set to the count of the last frame of the Sequence (the frame with End_Sequence set in the F_CTL field).

14.5 Streamed Sequences

When the Sequence initiator completes transmission of the current Sequence and has another Sequence to send for the same Exchange, it may either wait for confirmation of delivery of the prior Sequence before initiating the next Sequence, or proceed without waiting for confirmation. If the port begins the next Sequence prior to confirmation of the prior Sequence, the new Sequence is a streamed Sequence. If the port waits for confirmation of the prior Sequence before beginning the next Sequence, the new Sequence is a non-streamed Sequence.

Streamed Sequences must use the same class of service. If streamed sequences use different classes of service, it is considered an Exchange error.

14.5.1 Streamed Sequence SEQ_CNT Management

When streamed Sequences occur, the first frame of each streamed Sequence is required to use continuously increasing Sequence count from the last frame of the prior Sequence. An example of continuously increasing Sequence count is shown in Figure 94 (the operation shown in the example is a SCSI read-type command).

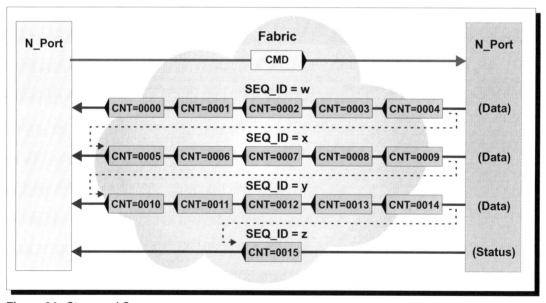

Figure 94. Streamed Sequences

14.5.2 Streamed Sequence SEQ_ID Management

During N_Port Login (PLOGI), the Sequence recipient indicates how many open Sequences it is capable of handling per Exchange. This value represents the maximum number of Sequences that can be streamed at any point in time.

The Sequence initiator is not allowed to initiate a new Sequence if the oldest open Sequence occurred more than the "open Sequences per Exchange" value Sequences ago. The "open Sequences per Exchange" value is communicated during the N_Port Login process. If the open Sequences per Exchange value from login is 3 and Sequences 11-93-22 have been sent, the Sequence initiator is not allowed to initiate another Sequence for that Exchange until Sequence 11 is complete, even if Sequences 93 and 22 are complete.

When streamed Sequences occur, the number of different SEQ_ID values that must be used before reusing a value is the number of "open Sequences per Exchange" value +1. That is, if the Sequence recipient reports during login that it can support three open Sequences per Exchange, then at least four different SEQ_ID values must be used before repeating a value.

14.6 Sequence Initiation

To initiate a Sequence, the initiating node port must:

- Hold the Sequence Initiative for the Exchange (the exchange originator implicitly has the initiative to send the first sequence of the exchange).
- Have a SEQ_ID available for use. The SEQ_ID must not currently be in use between the initiating port and the intended Sequence recipient.
- The SEQ_ID must meet the rules regarding SEQ_ID reuse (see *Sequence_ID Reuse* on page 192 and *Streamed Sequence SEQ_ID Management* on page 195).
- The total number of active Sequences (for all Exchanges) with the intended Sequence recipient must not exceed any of the following (all are indicated by the Sequence recipient during N_Port Login):
    - The total concurrent Sequences allowed by the Sequence recipient
    - The number of concurrent Sequences allowed for the intended class of service
    - The number of open Sequences per Exchange
- As long as the Sequence is open, the Sequence recipient maintains a Sequence Status Block (SSB). The format of the Sequence Status Block is shown in *Sequence Status Block (SSB)* on page 199.

Once a Sequence has been initiated, the SEQ_ID must be unique between the Sequence initiator and Sequence recipient until the Sequence has completed, or a Recovery Qualifier has been established during the Abort Sequence (ABTS) protocol (see *Abort Sequence (ABTS)* on page 311).

14.7 Frame Transmission Within a Sequence

When a Sequence consists of multiple frames, all frames in the Sequence are transmitted in the same class of service. Mixing classes of service within a Sequence is not allowed.

A SEQ_ID value must be assigned to each Sequence by the Sequence initiator and be present in the frame header of each frame in that Sequence. Each frame within the Sequence must contain the assigned, or reassigned, or unassigned OX_ID and RX_ID values.

Each frame in the Sequence indicates whether it was sent from the Exchange originator or responder as well as the Sequence initiator or recipient. These indications are carried in the frame header by the Exchange Context and Sequence Context bits in the F_CTL field (see *Bit 23: Exchange Context* on page 212 and *Bit 22: Sequence Context* on page 212).

Every frame in the Sequence must have a Sequence count that follows the applicable rules for SEQ_CNT (see *Frame Identification–Sequence Count (SEQ_CNT)* on page 193).

The data field of a transmitted Class-2, Class-3, or Class-1 connect frame cannot be larger than the receive data field size of the fabric (if present) or the Sequence recipient (i.e., the Sequence initiator can't send a frame larger than can be processed). The maximum receive data field size of the fabric is reported during fabric login. The maximum receive data field size of the Sequence recipient node port is reported during N_Port Login.

Frame transmission must observe the applicable flow control rules (see *Flow Control* on page 257). Failure to follow the flow control rules is a violation of the standard and may result in lost frames due to overrun conditions.

The next frame of a Sequence must be transmitted within the Error_Detect Timeout Value (E_D_TOV) of the previous frame of the Sequence. If the port is unable to send the frame within the allotted time period, a Sequence Error is detected.

14.8 Sequence Completion

The Sequence initiator identifies the last frame of a Sequence by setting the End_Sequence bit in the F_CTL field of the frame header. However, sending the last data frame does not necessarily indicate that the Sequence is complete because the Sequence initiator may need to wait for delivery confirmation. The following sections describe when the Sequence initiator and recipient consider the Sequence complete and deliverable to the upper level for processing.

14.8.1 Sequence Complete at Sequence Initiator

The Sequence initiator considers the Sequence complete protocol when:

- In Class-1, the Sequence initiator considers the Sequence complete when it receives the final ACK for the Sequence (an ACK with the EOFt or EOFdt End-of-Frame delimiter).

- In Class-2 or Class-F, the Sequence initiator considers the Sequence complete when it receives the final ACK for the Sequence (an ACK with the EOFt End-of-Frame delimiter) whether all ACKs for the Sequence have been received or not. The Sequence recipient will not send the final ACK until it has received all frames in the Sequence. Because the

ACKs may be delivered out-of-order, the Sequence initiator must account for all ACKs associated with the Sequence before reusing the SEQ_ID.

- In Class-3, the Sequence initiator considers the Sequence complete when:
  - all frames of the Sequence have been sent.
  - it has received a Basic Accept to an ABTS (using the ABTS to confirm Sequence delivery rather than aborting the Sequence. See *Abort Sequence (ABTS)* on page 311).
  - it has received LS_ACC to a Read Exchange Concise that confirms deliverability of the Sequence (see *Read Exchange Concise (REC)* on page 369).

14.8.2 Sequence Completion and Deliverability at the Sequence Recipient

The conditions necessary for the Sequence recipient to consider a Sequence complete and deliverable to the upper level for processing vary depending upon the class of service.

Class-1 Sequence. The Sequence recipient considers a Class-1 Sequence complete when all data frames of the Sequence have been received correctly, no Sequence errors have been detected, and all acknowledgments, if any, prior to the acknowledgment of the last data frame received have been transmitted.

Whether the completed Sequence is deliverable to the upper level depends on the Exchange error policy and status of prior Sequences within the Exchange.

- If the Exchange error policy is Discard Multiple Sequences, the current Sequence is deliverable if it is complete and the previous Sequence of the Exchange, if any, is deliverable. Under this error policy, the current Sequence is not deliverable unless the previous Sequence was deliverable.
- If the Exchange error policy is Discard a Single Sequence, then the current Sequence is deliverable when it is complete.

If the Sequence is complete and deliverable, the acknowledgment to the last data frame is sent with the End_Sequence bit set. The acknowledgment to the last data frame must use the appropriate Sequence terminating End-of-Frame delimiter (EOFt or EOFdt).

Class-2 or Class-F Sequence. The Sequence recipient considers a Class-2 or Class-F Sequence complete when all data frames of the Sequence have been received correctly, no Sequence errors have been detected, and all acknowledgments, if any, prior to the acknowledgment of the last data frame received have been transmitted. The final ACK is not sent until deliverability of the completed Sequence is determined.

If all prior frames of the Sequence have been received when the last data frame of the Sequence (End_Sequence) is received, the Sequence recipient determines deliverability and transmits the final ACK with End_Sequence set and an EOFt End-of-Frame delimiter.

If all prior frames of the Sequence have not been received when the last data frame of the Sequence (End_Sequence) is received (possibly as a result of the out-of-order frame delivery by the topology), the action taken depends on whether an Exchange event has occurred.

An Exchange event occurs when:

- Sequence Initiative is being transferred (F_CTL bit 16=1).
- The Continue Sequence Condition indicates the next Sequence is delayed (F_CTL bits 7:6=b'11').
- The Exchange_ID is being invalidated (Invalidate X_ID, F_CTL bit 14=1).
- This is the Last_Sequence of the Exchange (F_CTL bit 20=1).
- The End_Connection (F_CTL bit 18) is set.

If an Exchange event has not occurred, the Sequence recipient may save the Continue Sequence Condition bits and transmit an ACK to the last frame with the End_Sequence and Continue Sequence Condition bits set to zeros and an EOFn End-of-Frame delimiter. When the last missing frame of the Sequence has been received and the Sequence is complete, deliverability can be determined and the final ACK is sent containing the End_Sequence bit and saved Continue Sequence Condition bits with an EOFt delimiter.

If an Exchange event has occurred, the Sequence recipient must withhold transmission of the ACK to the last data frame until the Sequence is complete, then determine deliverability and send the ACK to the last data frame.

Whether the completed Sequence is deliverable to the upper-level depends on the Exchange error policy and status of prior Sequences within the Exchange.

- If the Exchange error policy is Abort, Discard Multiple Sequences, the current Sequence is deliverable if it is complete and all previous Sequences of the Exchange, if any, are also complete and have been delivered. If streamed Sequences have occurred, it is possible for this Sequence to be complete, but due to out-of-order frame delivery, prior Sequences are still open. Deliverability of the current Sequence cannot be determined until the prior Sequences are complete and have been delivered.
- If the Exchange error policy is Abort, Discard a Single Sequence, then the current Sequence is deliverable when it is complete, all previous Sequences of the Exchange are complete, and those that were deliverable have been delivered.

Class-3 Sequence. The Sequence recipient considers a Class-3 Sequence complete when all data frames of the Sequence have been received correctly, no Sequence errors have been detected, and the last data frame is terminated by EOFt.

Whether the completed Sequence is deliverable to the upper-level depends on the Exchange error policy and status of prior Sequences within the Exchange.

- If the Exchange error policy is Abort, Discard Multiple Sequences, the current Sequence is deliverable if it is complete and all previous Sequences of the Exchange, if any, are also complete and have been delivered. If streamed Sequences have occurred, it is possible for this Sequence to be complete, but due to out-of-order frame delivery, prior Sequences are still open. Deliverability of the current Sequence cannot be determined until the prior Sequences are complete and have been delivered.
- If the Exchange error policy is Abort, Discard a Single Sequence, then the current Sequence is deliverable when it is complete, all previous Sequences of the Exchange are complete, and those that were deliverable have been delivered.

14.9 Sequence Status Block (SSB)

The Sequence recipient maintains a Sequence Status Block (SSB) for each active Sequence (see Table 27 on page 199). The Sequence Status Block is used to track the progress of the Sequence on a frame-by-frame basis. The contents of the Sequence Status Block can be retrieved by the Sequence initiator through use of the Read Exchange Concise Extended Link Service request (see *Read Exchange Concise (REC)* on page 369).

Word	Bits 31-24	Bits 23-16	Bits 15-8	Bits 7-0
0	SEQ_ID	Reserved	Lowest SEQ_CNT	
1	Highest SEQ_CNT		S_STAT (see Table 28 on page 199)	
2	Error SEQ_CNT		OX_ID (Frame header word 4, bits 31:16)	
3	RX_ID		Reserved	

Table 27. Sequence Status Block

The format of the S_STAT field is shown in Table 28.

Bit	Description	Value
15	Sequence Context	1 = Sequence recipient, 0 = Sequence initiator
14	Open	1 = Sequence is Open, 0 = Sequence not Open
13	Active	1 = Sequence is Active, 0 = Sequence is not Active
12	Ending Condition	1 = Sequence ended abnormally, 0 = Sequence ended normally
11-10	ACK - Abort Sequence Condition	00 = Continue 01 = Abort Sequence requested 10 = Stop Sequence requested 11 = Abort with retransmission requested
9	ABTS Protocol performed	0 = Abort Sequence (ABTS) not completed 1 = Abort Sequence (ABTS) completed by recipient
8	Retransmission performed	0 = Retransmission not completed 1 = Retransmission completed by recipient
7	Sequence Timeout	0 = Sequence not timed-out 1 = Sequence timed-out by recipient (E_D_TOV)
6	P_RJT transmitted	1 = P_RJT transmitted, 0 = P_RJT not transmitted
5-4	Class of Service	00 = Reserved 01 = Class-1 10 = Class-2 11 = Class-3
3	ACK (EOFt) transmitted	1 = ACK (EOFt) transmitted, 0 = ACK (EOFt) not transmitted
2-0	reserved	

Table 28. Sequence Status Bits (S_STAT)

14.10 Chapter Summary

Segmentation/Reassembly

- All Information Units are delivered by using a Sequence of frames
- If the Information Unit fits in one frame, a single-frame Sequence is used, otherwise
- A multi-frame Sequence is necessary
  - When a multi-frame Sequence is needed, the port segments the Information Unit
  - The receiving port reassembles the frames back into the original Information Unit
- Segmentation is transparent to the higher-level that requested delivery of the Information Unit

Sequence Identification

- A port may have multiple Sequences open at the same time, for example, the port has multiple open Exchanges
- It is necessary to identify each so that frames can be associated with the correct Sequence
- This is done with the Sequence_ID, or SEQ_ID
- SEQ_ID is not an extension of the Exchange_ID, it is simply a Sequence identifier
- SEQ_IDs may be assigned in an arbitrary order by the port
  - There is no implication about the order of Sequences in the SEQ_ID value

Sequence Count

- As each frame of a Sequence is sent, it is numbered with a sequential count
- This is called the Sequence count, or SEQ_CNT
- The SEQ_CNT indicates the position of the frame in the Sequence
  - Used to verify that every frame of the Sequence has been received
  - Used in acknowledgments to indicate which frame is being acknowledged
  - May be used for reassembly

Streamed Sequences

- After a Sequence has been sent, the port may have another Sequence for the same destination (and Exchange)
- It could wait for confirmation that the prior Sequence was delivered before sending the next one, or
- It could send the next Sequence without waiting for confirmation of the previous Sequence
  - This is referred to as streamed Sequences
  - Streamed Sequences require continuously increasing sequence count (CISC)

Frame Transmission Rules

- When a Sequence consists of multiple frames, all frames are sent in the same class of service
- Required fields must be provided. Each frame:
  - The OX_ID and RX_ID, if assigned
  - The SEQ_ID of the Sequence to which it belongs
  - The SEQ_CNT indicating which frame of the Sequence it is
- The frame can't be larger than the receiver is capable of receiving
- The next frame of a Sequence must be transmitted within an allocated amount of time called E_D_TOV

Sequence Completion

- The Sequence initiator considers the Sequence complete when:
  - All frames have been sent and acknowledged (if applicable to the class of service), or
  - All frames have been sent, if unacknowledged class of service
- The Sequence recipient considers the Sequence complete when:
  - All frames have been received and final ACK sent (if acknowledged class of service), or
  - All frames have been received (if unacknowledged class of service), or
  - At least one frame has been received and a timeout occurs

15. Frame Structure

All information transferred in Fibre Channel is packaged in a data structure called a frame (networks generally use the term packet for this type of structure, but some networks also use the term frame, as in frame relay).

Structuring information in this manner provides a package that can be conveniently routed from one port to another. The structure of the Fibre Channel frame is similar to that used by other packetized interfaces and consists of a Start-of-Frame delimiter that identifies the beginning of the frame, a frame header with control information about the frame, a data field, CRC check characters to validate that the frame was received correctly, and an End-of-Frame delimiter. An illustration of the layout of the frame is shown in Figure 95.

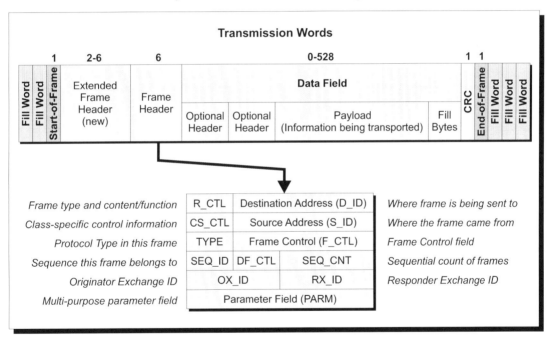

Figure 95. Fibre Channel Frame Structure

To limit the size of transmit and receive buffers in the ports, the number of characters that can be present in the data field portion of the frame is limited to 2112 bytes. Arriving at the optimal size for this upper limit is a compromise between the amount of data transferred per frame and the overhead associated with each frame (the frame delimiters, header, and check characters).

While the maximum amount of data that can be present in the data field is fixed by the standard, there is no minimum amount. The data field portion of a frame is a variable-length field and will be just large enough to hold the information being transported. Because frames are made up of transmission words, the data field must consist of an integral number of transmission words, and therefore the number of bytes present in the data field is always a multiple of four. To accommodate the case where the length of the data itself is not a multiple of four, up to three fill bytes may be present at the end of the data field. When this is the case, two control bits in the Frame Control field (F_CTL) indicate the presence of the fill bytes. Through this mechanism, the amount of data in the Information Unit being transported by the Sequence can be byte oriented.

Fibre Channel defines two basic frame types, Frame Type-0 (FT-0) and Frame Type-1 (FT-1) that are identified by bits in the Routing_Control field of the frame header.

- When the frame is FT-0, it is defined as a Link Control frame and the length of the data field is zero bytes. Link Control frames are used for link control functions such as Acknowledgment, Busy and Rejects, as well as providing a limited number of link control commands.

- If the frame type is FT-1, then it is defined as a Data frame and the data field may be any number of words between zero and 528 (0 and 2112 bytes). Data frames are used for FC-4 device data, extended link data, FC-4 link data, video data, and basic link data.

Frames are preceded and followed by a minimum of six transmission words at the originating node port. Once frame transmission begins, Start-of-Frame immediately follows the last IDLE or other fill word and the frame is transmitted without interruption. When frame transmission is completed, the first IDLE or other fill word immediately follows the End-of-Frame delimiter.

15.1 Start-of-Frame Delimiter

The Start-of-Frame delimiter identifies the beginning of a frame and prepares the receiving port to begin reception of the frame. Other than receiving the Start-of-Frame delimiter, the receiving port has no indication of the impending arrival of the frame. Descriptions of each of the Start-of-Frame delimiters and the Ordered Sets associated with them can be found in *Start-of-Frame (SOF)* on page 112.

The Fibre Channel standard is explicit regarding the use of the Start-of-Frame delimiters, requiring that the correct delimiter be used at the appropriate time. Use of an incorrect, or inappropriate for the conditions, Start-of-Frame delimiter is an error.

All switching and routing of information occurs between the end of one frame and the start of the next. The End-of-Frame delimiter forces the link's running disparity negative. Every transmission word that occurs between frames also results in the running disparity being negative at the end of the word. Therefore, when a Start-of-Frame is received, the link's running disparity should be negative, otherwise, a link error has occurred.

The position of the frame within the Sequence dictates which frame delimiters are used. Table 29 on page 203 summarizes delimiter usage for Sequences with differing numbers of frames.

Sequence Size	First Data Frame of Sequence	Middle Data Frames of Sequence	Last Data Frame of Sequence
Single frame Sequence	SOFc1, SOFi1, SOFi2, SOFi3, EOFn EOFt (in Class-3 only)		
Two frame Sequence	SOFc1, SOFi1, SOFi2, SOFi3, EOFn		SOFn1, SOFn2, SOFn3, EOFn, EOFt (in Class-3 only)
Three frame or greater Sequence	SOFc1, SOFi1, SOFi2, SOFi3, EOFn	SOFn1, SOFn2, SOFn3, EOFn	SOFn1, SOFn2, SOFn3, EOFn, EOFt (in Class-3 only)

Table 29. Frame Delimiter Usage

15.2 Extended Frame Headers

Recently, Fibre Channel introduced a new class of frame headers called extended headers. When one or more extended header is present, it follows the start-of-frame and precedes the standard frame header to provide additional information required in specific environments.

An extended header is identified using values in the R_CTL field. All extended headers have the R_CTL field as the first byte and the values used for extended headers do not conflict with the normal values found in this field. Table 31 on page 207 includes the R_CTL field values used by the extended headers (x'50' to x'52').

When an extended header is inserted by a switch or router, the frame CRC must be recomputed (the CRC includes all of the frame content between the SOF and EOF). When frame scrambling is being used (see *Frame Scrambling* on page 229), the scrambling seed is initialized at the SOF and frame words (including any extended headers) are scrambled.

When extended headers are present, the maximum frame size remains the same. Because of this, the size of the data field may need to be reduced in order for the frame to accommodate extended headers. Many node ports support a receive data field size of 2,048 bytes rather than the 2,112 byte maximum allowed by the standard (a difference of 64 bytes). All fabrics support maximum size frames. In many cases, it will be possible for a switch or router to add or remove extended headers without exceeding the maximum frame size.

15.2.1 Virtual Fabric Tagging Header (VFT_Header)

If a node port supports communicating with multiple virtual fabrics through the same physical link, frames need to be tagged to identify the virtual fabric to which they belong. This function is performed by the Virtual Fabric Tagging Header (VFT_Header).

When the VFT_Header header is present, it follows the start-of-frame delimiter and precedes any other extended headers such as the IFR_Header (see *Inter-Fabric Routing Header (IFR_Header)* on page 205) and the standard frame header.

The format of the VFT_Header is shown in Table 30 on page 204.

Word	31:24	23:16	15:08	07:00

0	R_CTL = x'50'	bits 23:22 = Version (b'00') bits 21:18 = Type (b'0000') bits 17:16 = Reserved	bits 15:13 = Priority
			bits 12:01 = Fabric ID (F_ID)
			  x'000' = Reserved
			  x'001' - x'EFF' = Available for Fabric IDs
			  x'F00' - x'FEE' = Reserved
			  x'FEF' = Control Virtual Fabric ID
			  x'FF0' - x'FFE' = Reserved
			  x'FFF' = Shall not be used as a Fabric ID
			bit 00 = Reserved	

1	Hop Count	Reserved		

Table 30. Virtual Fabric Tagging (VFT) Header Format

- The Version field indicates the version of the VFT_Header format (initially b'00').
- The Type field specifies the type of tagged frame and is currently set to b'0000'.
- The Priority field enables a priority, or Quality-of-Service, value to be associated with tagged frames.
- The Fabric ID field indicates the fabric that the frame is associated with (each virtual fabric has an assigned identifier called the Fabric ID)
- The hop count field specifies the number of remaining hops that may be traversed before the frame is dropped. When a switch retransmits a tagged frame, it decrements the hop count value by one. If a switch receives a tagged frame and the hop count is 1, the frame is discarded. The suggested initial default value for the hop count is 16.

The format of a frame with a VFT_Header is shown in Figure 96. Note that when the VFT_Header is present, the space available for the data field is decreased by two words.

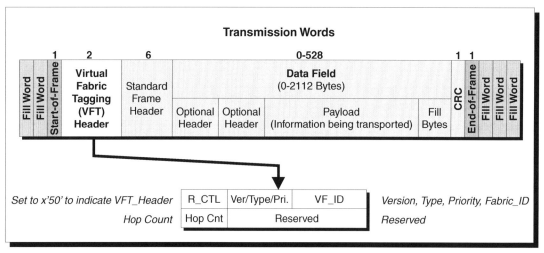

Figure 96. Frame with Virtual Fabric Tagging (VFT) Header

15.2.2 Inter-Fabric Routing Header (IFR_Header)

The Inter-Fabric Routing Header is used between fabric routers to carry Fabric identification information. the IFR header uses a value of x'51' in the R_CTL field and is two words (eight bytes) long. Node ports should not encounter frames with an IFR header present.

The format of a frame with an IFR header present is shown in Figure 97 on page 205.

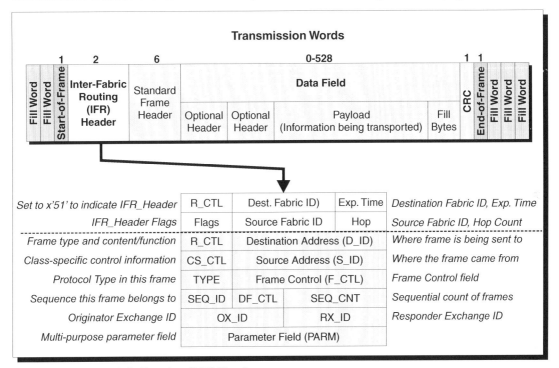

Figure 97. Inter-Fabric Routing (IFR) Header

15.2.3 Encapsulation (ENC) Header

Routers may need to forward frames from one router to another through a legacy fabric. When this is done, an Encapsulation (ENC) extended header may inserted after the SOF and before any other headers. The ENC header is created by copying the standard frame header, setting the R_CTL field to x'52' to identify this as an ENC extended header, setting the destination address to the address of the next hop router and the source address to the address of the sending router.

Because the ENC header has the same format as a standard frame header, existing switches are able to forward the frame normally.

15.3 Standard Frame Header

The frame header is a 24-byte (six word) structure containing control and addressing information associated with the frame. The layout of the frame header was shown earlier in Figure 95 on page 201.

The frame header is transmitted immediately following the Start-of-Frame delimiter beginning with word 0, bits 31-24 (the R_CTL field) followed by the Destination_ID (starting with bits 23-16, then bits 15-8, followed by bits 7-0). After word 0 is transmitted, word 1 is sent, again the most significant byte is sent first, the least significant byte of the word last. This process continues until all six words of the frame header have been transmitted. At this point, the data field (if any) is sent followed by the CRC and End-of-Frame delimiter.

15.3.1 Routing Control Field (R_CTL)

The R_CTL field (word 0, bits 31-24) consists of two sub-fields, the Routing Bits and the Information field. These two fields, serve to define the category (and in some cases, the function) of frame. Table 31 on page 207 decodes the routing bits and information field.

Bits 31-28: Routing Bits (R_Bits). The routing bits identify the category of frame. The intention is that these four bits can provide a quick decode that the receiving port can use to determine how the frame is to be processed (routed). The routing bits work in conjunction with the information field and type bits to fully define the frame processing.

Bits 27-24: Information Field (INFO). Once the category of frame has been determined from the routing bits, the information field provides further definition for that particular category of frame.

When a frame is an FC-4 Device_Data frame (R_Bits=x'0') or Video_Data frame (R_Bits=x'4'), the information field specifies the information category of the payload. The information category enables the recipient of the frame to determine how to interpret the payload (i.e, does the frame contain a command, data, status, or other category of information). Information category values are assigned to upper-level protocol information during the FC-4 protocol mapping.

When a frame is an Extended Link Data (R_Bits=x'2') or FC-4 Link Data (R_Bits=x'3') the information field identifies whether this frame is link service data (INFO=x'1'), a link service request (INFO=x'2'), or a link service reply (INFO=x'3').

When a frame is a Basic Link Data frame (R_Bits=x'8'), the information field specifies the specific Basic Link Service request or reply being communicated.

When a frame is a Link Control frame (R_Bits=x'C'), the information field specifies the link control function is associated with the frame.

Fibre Channel allows more than one kind (category) of information to be sent within the same Sequence of FC-4 Device_Data frames. This means that during a given Sequence, it is possible to have different information categories in the frames. A series of consecutive frames with the same information category are viewed as a single instance of that information category. If there are fill bytes associated with that particular information category, they can only be present on the last frame of the information category.

Frame Type	R_CTL		Description	Abbrev.
	R_Bits (0:3)	INFO (4:7)		
Data	x'0' FC-4 Device Data	x'0'	Uncategorized Information	
		x'1'	Solicited Data	
		x'2'	Unsolicited Control	
		x'3'	Solicited Control	
		x'4'	Unsolicited Data	
		x'5'	Data Descriptor	
		x'6'	Unsolicited Command	
		x'7'	Command Status	
		Others	Unspecified	
	x'2' Extended Link Data	x'1'	Extended Link Service Solicited Data	
		x'2'	Extended Link Service Unsolicited Control (Command or Request)	
		x'3'	Extended Link Service Solicited Control (Reply)	
	x'3' FC-4 Link Data	x'2'	FC-4 Link Service Unsolicited Control (Command or Request)	
		x'3'	FC-4 Link Service Solicited Control (Reply)	
	x'4' Video Data	(note)	Video_Data (note: Info bits same as FC-4 Device Data frames)	
	x'5' Extended Hdr.	x'0'	Virtual Fabric Tagging (VFT) Extended Header	
		x'1'	Inter-Fabric Routing (IFR) Extended Header	
		x'2'	Encapsulation (ENC) Extended Header	
	x'8' Basic Link Data	x'0'	see No Operation (NOP) on page 310	NOP
		x'1'	see Abort Sequence (ABTS) on page 311	ABTS
		x'2'	see Remove Connection (RMC) on page 315	RMC
		x'3'	Reserved	
		x'4'	see Basic_Accept (BA_ACC) on page 309	BA_ACC
		x'5'	see Basic Reject (BA_RJT) on page 309	BA_RJT
		x'6'	see Preempted (PRMT) on page 315	PRMT
		Others	Reserved	
Link Control	x'C' Link Control	x'0'	Acknowledgment (see ACK_1 on page 241)	ACK_1
		x'1'	Acknowledgment (see ACK_0 on page 242)	ACK_0
		x'2'	N_Port Reject (see N_Port Reject (P_RJT) and Fabric Reject (F_RJT) on page 248)	P_RJT
		x'3'	Fabric Reject (see N_Port Reject (P_RJT) and Fabric Reject (F_RJT) on page 248)	F_RJT
		x'4'	N_Port Busy (see N_Port Busy (P_BSY) on page 247)	P_BSY
		x'5'	Fabric Busy to Data Frame (see Fabric Busy (F_BSY) on page 245)	F_BSY
		x'6'	Fabric Busy to Link_Control Frame (see Fabric Busy (F_BSY) on page 245)	F_BSY
		x'7'	Link Credit Reset (see Link Credit Reset (LCR) on page 253)	LCR
		x'8'	Notify (see Notify (NTY) on page 254)	NTY
		x'9'	End (see End (END) on page 254)	END
		Others	Reserved	

Table 31. Routing Control (R_CTL) Field Decode

15.3.2 Destination_ID and Source_ID

Every Fibre Channel port has a native address identifier called the N_Port Identifier, or N_Port ID. This address is unique within the attached topology and is used to route frames to that port and verify that the frames were delivered to the correct port.

A node port acquires its N_Port ID during the topology initialization process, during login, or by other means.

- In a fabric topology, the N_Port normally acquires its address from the fabric during the fabric login (FLOGI) process.

- In a point-to-point topology, one of the N_Ports assigns an address to the other during the N_Port Login (PLOGI) process.

- In an arbitrated loop topology, the least-significant byte of the address is acquired during the loop initialization process and the upper two bytes are either set to zeros, or assigned during a subsequent fabric login.

The standard also allows a node port to obtain its address identifier by other means not defined by the standard (for example, through the use of address switches).

In addition to its N_Port ID, a node port may optionally have one or more alias address identifiers. The alias address identifier may be unique to the port, or shared by multiple ports. An example of a shared alias address identifier might be the creation of a group address associated with multiple node ports.

When a node port transmits a frame, it places the address identifier of the destination port in the Destination_ID (D_ID) field and its own address in the Source_ID (S_ID) field of the frame header. When a node port receives a frame, it compares the destination identifier field to its own address, or addresses if alias addresses are in use, to ensure the frame was delivered to the correct destination.

An N_Port address identifier of x'00 00 00' indicates an N_Port does not have an address identifier (is unidentified). When an N_Port is unidentified, it behaves as follows:

- It shall accept frames with any destination address identifier

- It shall not reject a frame (P_RJT) with a reason code of *"Invalid D_ID"*

- It shall reject frames other than Basic and Extended Link Services with a reason code of *"Login required"*

Address identifiers from x'FF FF F0' through x'FF FF FF' are reserved by the standard for use by Fibre Channel architected services and functions. These addresses are referred to as "well-known addresses" because they are assigned by the standard. The well-known addresses are listed in Table 198 on page 479 and the function associated with each is described in *Fibre Channel Services* on page 479.

15.3.3 Class Specific Control (CS_CTL)

The class specific control field provides multiple functions, depending on the class of service and the setting of bit 17 in the F_CTL field as shown in Table 32.

Class of Service	F_CTL bit 17	Description
Class-1	0	Class-1/6 connection options
	1	Class-1/6 Priority and Preemption
Class-2/3	0	Class-2/3 delivery preference
	1	Class-2/3 Priority and Preemption

Table 32. Class-Specific Control Field Usage

Class-1 Connection Options. When bit 17 of the F_CTL field is zero for a Class-1/6 connect request frame (SOFc1 delimiter), the CS_CTL field contains Class-1/6 connection options as shown in Table 33. These options are described in *Class-1* on page 273.

Bit	Abbr.	Description
31		Obsolete (was Class-1 dedicated Simplex)
30	SCR	0 = Stacked Connect Request not Requested 1 = Stacked Connect Request Requested (see *Node Port Behavior During a Class-1 Connection* on page 276). Only meaningful on the connect request frame (SOFc1).
29		Obsolete (was Camp-On Request)
28		Obsolete (was Buffered Class-1).
27-24		Reserved

Table 33. Class-Specific Control Field, Class-1

Class-1/6 Priority/Preemption. When bit 17 of the F_CTL field is one for a Class-1/6 connect request frame (SOFc1 delimiter), the CS_CTL field contains the priority of the connection request, and whether this request should preempt an existing lower-priority Class-1/6 connection, if present. The priority value and preemption flag are shown by Table 34 on page 209.

Bits	Description
31-25	Priority value
24	0 = No Preemption 1 = Preemption

Table 34. Class-1 Priority/Preemption

Class-2/3 Delivery Preference. When bit 17 of the F_CTL field is zero for a Class-2/3 frame, the CS_CTL field indicates the delivery preference for the frame as shown in Table 35. Preference is described in *Class-2 Priority and Preemption* on page 285 and *Class-3 Priority and Preemption* on page 287.

Class-2/3 Priority and Preemption. When bit 17 of the F_CTL field is set to one for a Class-2/3 frame, the CS_CTL field contains the priority value and whether this frame should preempt

Bit	Abbr.	Description
31	PREF	0 = Frame is delivered with no Preference 1 = Frame may be delivered with Preference
30		Reserved for additional Preference function
29-24	DSCP	Delivery preference (Differentiated Services Code Point - DSCP)

Table 35. Class-3 and Class-3 Delivery Preference

an existing lower-priority Class-1/6 connection, if present. The priority value and preemption flag are shown in Table 34 on page 209.

Bits	Description
31-25	Priority value
24	0 = No Preemption 1 = Preemption

Table 36. Class-2 and Class-3 Priority/Preemption

15.3.4 Type Field

Interpretation of the type field depends on whether the frame is a link control frame or a Fibre Channel data frame and the value of the Routing Bits (R_Bits).

When the frame is a data frame, the type field identifies the type of protocol being carried by the frame. As different protocols are mapped to Fibre Channel is assigned a type value, or range of values.

If the frame is an FC-4 Device Data frame (R_Bits = x'0'), the type field is interpreted as shown in Table 37. Type values have been assigned to several Fibre Channel standards documents in case they need to implement a document-specific protocol (e.g., the FC-SW and FC-AL standards).

Type Field	Protocol Service
x'00'	Reserved (Basic Link Services
x'01'	Reserved (Extended Link Services)
x'02'-x'03'	Reserved
x'04'	ISO/IEC 8802-2 LLC (in order)
x'05'	Internet Protocol (IP) over Fibre Channel (IETF RFC 4338)
x'06'-x'07'	Reserved
x'08'	Small Computer System Interface (SCSI) Fibre Channel Protocol (SCSI-FCP)
x'09'	Small Computer System Interface (SCSI) Generic Packetized Protocol (SCSI-GPP)
x'0A'-x'0F'	Reserved - SCSI
x'10'	Reserved - IPI-3

Table 37. Type Field Decode for FC-4 Device Data and FC-4 Link Data Frames (Part 1 of 2)

Type Field	Protocol Service
x'11'	IPI-3 Master
x'12'	IPI-3 Slave
x'13'	IPI-3 Peer
x'14'-x'17'	Reserved
x'18'	Reserved - Single-Byte Command Code Sets (SBCCS)
x'19'	Single-Byte Command Code Sets (SBCCS) - Channel (obsoleted by FC-FS)
x'1A'	Single-Byte Command Code Sets (SBCCS) - Control Unit (obsoleted by FC-FS)
x'1B'	Single-Byte Command Code Sets-2 (FC-SB-3) - Channel
x'1C'	Single-Byte Command Code Sets-2 (FC-SB-3) - Control Unit
x'1D'-x'1F'	Reserved - Single-Byte Command Code Sets (SBCCS)
x'20'	Fibre Channel Common Transport (FC-CT) Generic Services (see FC-GS-x)
x'21'	Reserved
x'22'	Switched Fabric Internal Link Services (FC-SW)
x'23'	Reserved for FC-AL (if needed)
x'24'	Simple Network Management Protocol (SNMP) Generic Services
x'25'	Inter-Fabric Routing (IFR) Services
x'26'-x'27'	Reserved - Fabric Services
x'28'-x'2F'	Reserved
x'30'-x'33'	Reserved - Scalable Coherent Interface (SCI)
x'34'-x'3F'	Reserved
x'40'	High-Performance Parallel Interface Framing Protocol (HiPPI-FP)
x'41'-x'47'	Reserved - High-Performance Parallel Interface (HIPPI)
x'48'	MIL-STD-1553 (FC-AE)
x'49'	ASM (FC-AE)
x'4A-x'4F'	Reserved for FC-AE
x'50'	BBL Control (FC-BB)
x'51'	BBL FDDI Encapsulated LAN PDU (FC-BB)
x'52'	BBL 802.3 Encapsulated LAN PDU (FC-BB)
x'53'-x'57'	Reserved for FC-BB
x'58'	Fibre Channel Virtual Interface (FC-VI)
x'59-x'5F'	Reserved
x'60'	FC-AV Container
x'61'-x'63'	Reserved for FC-AV
x'64'-x'DF'	Reserved
x'E0'-x'FF'	Vendor Unique

Table 37. Type Field Decode for FC-4 Device Data and FC-4 Link Data Frames (Part 2 of 2)

If the frame is an Extended Link Data frame (R_Bits = x'2') and the type field is x'01', the frame is an Extended Link Service frame. Type field values of x'20' through x'CF' are reserved for

Extended Link Data frames while values from x'D0' through x'FF' are available for vendor-unique Extended Link functions.

If the frame is a Video_Data frame (R_Bits = x'4'), type field values of x'00' through x'CF' are reserved and values from x'D0' through x'FF' are available for vendor unique assignment.

If the frame is a Basic Link Data frame (R_Bits = x'8') and the type field is x'00', the frame is a Basic Link Service frame. Type field values of x'20' through x'CF' are reserved for Basic Link Data frames while values from x'D0' through x'FF' are available for vendor-unique Basic Link functions.

If the frame is a link control frame (R_Bits = x'C'), the type field is reserved except when the link control frame is a fabric busy (F_BSY) sent in response to another link control frame. In this special case, the INFO field (word 0, bits 27-24) of the busied link control frame are copied into bits 27-24 of the type field of the fabric busy. This allows the originating port to reconstruct the original link control frame from the fabric busy.

15.3.5 Frame Control Field (F_CTL)

The frame control field is a 24-bit field containing miscellaneous frame control information. Most of the information in this field consists of single-bit, or double-bit indications. A breakdown of the fields in this frame is shown in Table 38 on page 213.

Bit 23: Exchange Context. This bit indicates whether this frame was sent by the originator or responder of the Exchange. When set to zero, this frame was sent by the Exchange originator. When set to one, this frame was sent by the Exchange responder.

Bit 22: Sequence Context. This bit indicates whether this frame was sent by the Sequence initiator or Sequence recipient. When set to zero, this frame was sent by the Sequence initiator. When set to one, this frame was sent by the Sequence recipient.

Bit 21: First_Sequence. This bit is set to one in every frame of the first Sequence of the Exchange and to zero in all frames of other Sequences within that Exchange. This bit notifies the recipient that a new Exchange is in progress and that the recipient should do whatever processing is necessary to process the new Exchange.

Bit 20: Last_Sequence. This bit is set to a one in the last data frame of the last Sequence of an Exchange to indicate that the Exchange has completed. It may be set to one in prior frames of the last Sequence of the Exchange, if desired as an early indication, but is not meaningful until the last frame. This bit is set to zero in all frames that are not part of the last Sequence of the Exchange.

Bit 19: End_Sequence. The End_Sequence bit is set to one in the last data frame of the Sequence to indicate that the Sequence is complete.

In Class-1, this bit is also set in the acknowledgment sent in response to the last data frame of the Sequence and confirms that the Sequence recipient recognized the last data frame.

Word 2, bit(s)	Control Field	Description
23	Exchange Context	0 = Originator of Exchange 1 = Responder of Exchange
22	Sequence Context	0 = Sequence Initiator 1 = Sequence Recipient
21	First_Sequence	0 = Not the First Sequence of the Exchange 1 = First Sequence of the Exchange
20	Last_Sequence	0 = Not the Last Sequence of the Exchange 1 = Last Sequence of the Exchange
19	End_Sequence	0 = Not the last Data frame of the Sequence 1 = Last Data frame of the Sequence
18	End_Connection (Class-1)	0 = Connection active 1 = End Class-1 Connection pending
17	CS_CTL/Priority Enable	0 = CS_CTL field contains Class-specific information 1 = CS_CTL field contains frame priority
16	Sequence Initiative	0 = Sequence Initiative Held 1 = Sequence Initiative Transferred
15	Obsolete (was X_ID Reassigned)	0 = X_ID assignment retained 1 = X_ID reassigned
14	Obsolete (was Invalidate X_ID)	0 = X_ID assignment retained 1 = invalidate X_ID
13:12	ACK_Form	00 = No Assistance provided 01 = ACK_1 required 10 = Reserved 11 = ACK_0 required
11:10	Obsolete	
9	Retransmitted Sequence	0 = Original Sequence transmission 1 = Sequence retransmission
8	Unidirectional Transmit (Class-1/6)	0 = Bidirectional transmission 1 = Unidirectional transmission

7-6	Continue Sequence
	Condition
		Last Data Frame - Sequence Initiator
		  00 = Next Sequence to follow-no information
		  01 = Next Sequence to follow-immediately
		  10 = Next Sequence to follow-soon
		  11 = Next Sequence to follow-delayed

Table 38. Frame Control (F_CTL) Fields (Part 1 of 2)

Word 2, bit(s)	Control Field	Description
5-4	Abort Sequence Condition	In an ACK or RJT frame from Sequence recipient: 00 = Continue Sequence 01 = Abort Sequence, perform Abort Sequence (ABTS) 10 = Stop Sequence 11 = Immediate Sequence retransmission requested Exchange error policy in the 1st data frame of the Exchange (from the Sequence initiator) 00 = Abort, Discard multiple Sequences 01 = Abort, Discard a single Sequence 10 = Process policy with infinite buffers 11 = Discard multiple Sequences with immediate retransmission
3	Relative Offset Present	0 = Parameter field does not contain a relative offset 1 = Parameter field contains a relative offset
2	Exchange Reassembly	Reserved for Exchange reassembly
1-0	Fill Data Bytes	End of Data field - number of bytes of fill 00 = 0 bytes of fill 01 = 1 byte of fill (last byte of data field) 10 = 2 bytes of fill (last two bytes of data field) 11 = 3 bytes of fill (last three bytes of data field)

Table 38. Frame Control (F_CTL) Fields (Part 2 of 2)

In Class-2 or Class-F, this bit is also set in the acknowledgment to the last data frame received by the Sequence recipient (which may not be the last frame transmitted if the topology delivers frames out-of-order).

Bit 18: End_Connection. The End_Connection bit is set to one in the last data frame of a Sequence to indicate that the node port is initiating a Class-1 disconnection. The node port sending the End_Connection is requesting the receiving port to respond with an acknowledge with the End-of-Frame disconnect terminate (EOFdt) when the receiving port has completed all active Sequences. This bit also requests the receiving port not to initiate any new Sequences during the current connection. For more information on the management of Class-1 connections, refer to *Class-1* on page 273.

Bit 17: Obsolete (was Chained_Sequence). This bit was removed and reclaimed by FC-PH2 and is now reserved.

Bit 16: Sequence Initiative. When a port originates an Exchange, it has the initiative to send the first Sequence. On completion of this Sequence, the originator may either hold the Sequence Initiative to send another Sequence, or transfer the initiative so that the other port in the Exchange may send a Sequence. Within any particular Exchange, there is exactly one Sequence Initiative bit associated with that Exchange, and one or the other of the two ports will be holding that initiative at any time.

A port that currently has the Sequence Initiative for an Exchange may originate one or more Sequences for that Exchange. A port that does not have the Sequence Initiative is prohibited from originating any Sequences within that Exchange until it receives the Sequence Initiative.

The Exchange is architected to be a half-duplex construct in order to emulate half-duplex protocols that may be mapped to Fibre Channel. The Sequence Initiative bit is the mechanism for enforcing half-duplex behavior at the Exchange level because only one port is allowed to send a Sequence for a that Exchange at a time.

Sequence Initiative transfer is initiated by setting the Sequence Initiative bit to one in the last data frame of a Sequence. In Class-1, Class-2, or Class-F the transfer is considered complete when an acknowledgment to the last data frame (End_Sequence = 1) is received and the Sequence Initiative bit is set to one in the acknowledgment. In Class-3, the transfer is considered complete when the last data frame of the Sequence (End_Sequence = 1) is sent and the Sequence Initiative bit is set to one.

Bit 15: Obsolete (was X_ID Reassigned).

Bit 14: Obsolete (was Invalidate X_ID).

Bits 13-12: ACK_Form. These two bits allow the Sequence initiator (the port that is sending the Sequence) to direct the Sequence recipient which acknowledgment policy to use for the Sequence. This enables ports capable of both ACK_0 and ACK_1 to specify which should be used on a Sequence-by-Sequence basis. These bits relieve the Sequence recipient from having to refer to the acknowledgment capabilities of the Sequence initiator to determine how to acknowledge frames within the Sequence.

Bit 11: Obsolete (was Data Compression).

Bit 10: Obsolete (was Data Encryption).

Bit 9: Retransmitted Sequence. Bit 9 is only meaningful during Class-1 operations when the Exchange error policy specified in the F_CTL field of the first frame in the Exchange is specified as Discard multiple Sequences with immediate retransmission (F_CTL bits 5-4 set to '11').

When the Sequence initiator receives an ACK with the abort Sequence condition bits (F_CTL bits 5-4) set to '11', and all prior Sequences are complete, the Sequence initiator may begin retransmission of the indicated Sequence. If all prior Sequences are not complete (for example an ACK is missing) the Sequence initiator is not permitted to begin Sequence retransmission until it has determined that the prior Sequences were delivered successfully. It may determine this by use of the Read Exchange Concise Extended Link Service request, or by other means.

When a Sequence is retransmitted under these conditions, every frame of the Sequence has bit 9 set to differentiate the frame from the original Sequence transmission.

Bit 8: Unidirectional Transmit. Unidirectional Transmit is meaningful on the connect frame (SOFc1) of a Class-1 operation. When this bit is set to zero, the connection is bidirectional and the connection recipient may begin transmission of Sequences immediately after the connection is established (subject to Sequence Initiative and flow control constraints). When this bit is set to a one, the connection is unidirectional and the connection recipient is not allowed to transmit data frames during that connection.

If a unidirectional Class-1 connection was established by the SOFc1 frame, the connection initiator may later change the connection to bidirectional by setting bit 8 to a zero in either the first or last data frame of a Sequence.

The connection recipient can request that a unidirectional Class-1 connection be changed to a bidirectional connection by setting bit 8 equal to a one in an ACK frame. Once it does this, it must set bit 8 to a one in all subsequent ACKs of that connection. Even though the connection recipient is requesting the connection be changed to a bidirectional one, the connection initiator may, or may not, choose to honor that request.

Bits 7-6: Continue Sequence Condition. The Continue Sequence Condition bits are informational bits that may be set at the end of Sequence to provide information regarding when the next Sequence may be expected. The four decodes associated with these bits do not identify specific time intervals and are only meaningful by mutual understanding between the ports. There is no definition of what immediately, soon, or delayed mean in terms of absolute time.

Bits 7 and 6 are meaningful at two different times:

- The first is when the End_Sequence bit is set to one and the Sequence Initiative is not transferred. In this case, the Sequence initiator is holding the initiative and using the bits to provide information regarding when the next Sequence may be sent.

- The second case where these bits have meaning is when the Sequence recipient acknowledges the last frame of a Sequence that transfers Sequence Initiative. In this case, the bits indicate when the Sequence following the transfer of initiative may be expected.

These bits were intended to facilitate the management of resources within the port and decide whether a Class-1 connection should be maintained or terminated. These bits could also be used in an arbitrated loop topology to assist in deciding whether to close the current loop circuit or not, although this use is not commonplace.

Bits 5-4: Abort Sequence Condition. The Abort Sequence Condition bits have two distinct uses.

In the first data frame of the Exchange only, these bits specify the error policy that applies to that Exchange. Fibre Channel defines four error policies that can be applied to an Exchange. The error policies are listed in Table 39. Details of the behavior of each of the error policies is covered in *Exchange Error Policies* on page 183.

In an acknowledge frame, bits 5-4 indicate what action the Sequence initiator should take with regards to continuing transmission of that Sequence. These actions are listed in Table 40 on page 217.

F_CTL Bits (5:4)	Meaning in First Frame of the Exchange
b'00'	Abort, discard multiple Sequences
b'01'	Abort, discard a single Sequence
b'10'	Process policy with infinite buffers
b'11'	Discard multiple Sequences with immediate retransmission

Table 39. Exchange Error Policy

F_CTL Bits (5:4)	Meaning in Acknowledge Frame
b'00'	Continue Sequence. No error or abnormal condition has been detected and transmission of the Sequence should continue
b'01'	Abort Sequence requested. The Sequence recipient has detected an error or other abnormal condition and is requesting that the Sequence initiator abort the Sequence
b'10'	Stop Sequence. A condition has occurred at the Sequence recipient such that the Sequence initiator should end the current Sequence as soon as possible. This request does not necessarily indicate an error and the Sequence should not be aborted. Frame sent following the frame receiving the acknowledge with stop Sequence indicated may or may not be processed by the Sequence recipient
b'11'	Discard multiple Sequences with immediate retransmission. These bits indicate that the recipient has detected an error during a Class-1 connection when the Exchange error policy is Discard multiple Sequences with immediate retransmission and is requesting a retransmission of the failed Sequence

Table 40. Continue Sequence Condition Bits

Further discussion of Exchange error policy, and the management of errors can be found in *Error Detection and Recovery* on page 293.

Bit 3: Relative Offset Present. When bit 3 is set on a data frame, this bit indicates that the parameter field of the frame header (see *Parameter Field* on page 222) contains a valid relative offset value. When bit 3 is set to zero, the parameter field does not contain a relative offset. Bit 3 is only meaningful on data frames and is ignored on ACK, Link_Response, and Basic Link_Data frames.

Bit 2: reserved for Exchange_Reassembly. Bit 2 is set to a zero by the Sequence initiator to indicate that the payload in this data frame is associated with an Exchange between a single pair of node ports. This means that reassembly of the Sequences associated with that Exchange can be managed within a single destination port.

Setting bit 2 to a one is reserved for future use and indicates that the payload in this frame is associated with an Exchange that may span multiple ports, and therefore reassembly in not limited to a single destination port. Because this is a reserved function, bit 2 cannot be set to one within the scope of existing standards.

Bits 1-0: Fill Data Bytes. When bits 1:0 are non-zero in a data frame, it indicates that one or more fill bytes are present in the last word of the payload of this frame. When fill bytes are present, they are ignored by the recipient (other than for CRC calculations). Fill bytes may be any valid data character at the discretion of the transmitting port.

The standard states that *"Bits 1-0 shall only be meaningful on the last data frame of a series of consecutive data frames of a single Information Category within a single Sequence."* This statement is ambiguous, as fill bytes should only be present in the data frame that contains the highest relative offset of a single information category.

If one considers how a Sequence should be reassembled in the receiver's reassembly buffer, any fill bytes associated with an Information Category should be located at the highest offset into the buffer. If the frames transporting that Information Category contain information in a random relative offset fashion, the last data frame of the Information Category may not contain the highest relative offset.

15.3.6 F_CTL Bit Interactions

Table 41 on page 219 summarizes the usage of the F_CTL bits for data frames at different points in an Exchange.

15.3.7 Sequence_ID Field (SEQ_ID)

The Sequence_ID is an eight-bit field used to identify and track all frames within a Sequence between a source and destination port pair. All frames within the same Sequence have the same SEQ_ID. This provides a mechanism that the Sequence recipient can use to associate those frames during the reassembly process.

As long as the Sequence is open, the SEQ_ID must be a unique value between the pair of ports (that is, the combination of S_ID, D_ID, and SEQ_ID must be unique). Having duplicate Sequences with the same SEQ_ID open between a pair of ports creates an ambiguity as to which Sequence a given frame belongs and could result in reassembly errors.

While the SEQ_ID must be unique between a port pair, there is no requirement that SEQ_ID values be assigned in any numerical order. That is, the SEQ_ID values can be assigned in a completely arbitrary manner by the Sequence initiator. As a result, the SEQ_ID cannot be used to infer anything about the order of Sequences within an Exchange.

Furthermore, the SEQ_ID is not qualified by the Exchange identifiers (to be discussed shortly in *Originator and Responder Exchange_ID (OX_ID, RX_ID)* on page 222). This means that the SEQ_ID uniqueness must be maintained across Exchanges between the port pair.

If the Sequence initiator completes the current Sequence and starts a new Sequence for the same Exchange before receiving the final ACK for the first Sequence (in Class-1, Class-2 or Class-F), or before the R_A_TOV timeout value has expired for all frames in a Class-3 Sequence, the new Sequence is termed a streamed Sequence. With streamed Sequences additional Sequence management rules must be observed to ensure the integrity of the streamed

F_CTL bit value during?	23 - Exchange Context	22 - Sequence Context	21 - First_Sequence	20 - Last_Sequence	19 - End-Sequence	18 - End_Connection	17 - Reserved per FC-PH2	16 - Sequence Initiative	15 - Obsolete	14 - Obsolete	13:12 - ACK Assistance	11 - Reserved per FC-FS	10 - Reserved per FC-FS	9 - Retransmitted Seq.	8 - Unidirectional Transmit	7:6 - Continue Seq. Condition	5:4 - Abort Seq. Condition	3 - Relative Offset Present	2 - Exchange Reassembly	1:0 - Fill Data Bytes
First Sequence of Exchange																				
Connect Request (SOFc1)	0	0	1	0	VL	0	0	A	0	0	V	0	0	V	V	VL	V	V	0	IC
1st Frame of Sequence	0	0	1	0	0	*	0	A	0	0	V	0	0	V	V	*	V	V	0	IC
Middle Frame in Sequence	0	0	1	0	0	*	0	A	0	0	V	0	0	V	*	*	*	V	0	IC
Last Frame of Sequence	0	0	1	0	1	V1	0	V	0	0	V	0	0	V	V	V	*	V	0	IC
1st and Last Frame of Sequence	0	0	1	0	1	V1	0	V	0	0	V	0	0	V	V	V	V	V	0	IC
Middle Sequence of Exchange																				
Connect Request (SOFc1)	V	V	0	0	VL	0	0	A	0	0	V	0	0	V	V	VL	*	V	0	IC
1st Frame of Sequence	V	V	0	0	0	*	0	A	0	0	V	0	0	V	V	*	*	V	0	IC
Middle Frame in Sequence	V	V	0	0	0	*	0	A	0	0	V	0	0	V	*	*	*	V	0	IC
Last Frame of Sequence	V	V	0	0	1	V1	0	V	0	0	V	0	0	V	V	V	*	V	0	IC
1st and Last Frame of Sequence	V	V	0	0	1	V1	0	V	0	0	V	0	0	V	V	V	*	V	0	IC
Last Sequence of Exchange																				
Connect Request (SOFc1)	V	V	0	A	VL	0	0	A	0	0	V	0	0	V	V	VL	*	V	0	IC
1st Frame of Sequence	V	V	0	A	0	*	0	A	0	0	V	0	0	V	V	*	*	V	0	IC
Middle Frame in Sequence	V	V	0	A	0	*	0	A	0	0	V	0	0	V	*	*	*	V	0	IC
Last Frame of Sequence	V	V	0	1	1	V1	0	V	0	0	V	0	0	V	V	V	*	V	0	IC
1st and Last Frame of Sequence	V	V	0	1	1	V1	0	V	0	0	V	0	0	V	V	V	*	V	0	IC
First and Last Sequence of Exchange																				
Connect Request (SOFc1)	0	0	1	A	VL	0	0	A	0	0	V	0	0	V	V	VL	V	V	0	IC
1st Frame of Sequence	0	0	1	A	0	*	0	A	0	0	V	0	0	V	V	*	V	V	0	IC
Middle Frame in Sequence	0	0	1	A	0	*	0	A	0	0	V	0	0	V	*	*	*	V	0	IC
Last Frame of Sequence	0	0	1	1	1	V1	0	V	0	0	V	0	0	V	V	V	*	V	0	IC
1st and Last Frame of Sequence	0	0	1	1	1	V1	0	V	0	0	V	0	0	V	V	V	V	V	0	IC

* = bit is not meaningful

A = bit is Allowed to be set

F = Meaningful on the first and following Data frames of a Sequence until at least one ACK is received for Sequence

IC = bits are valid on the last frame of the Information Category (see *Bits 1-0: Fill Data Bytes* on page 218)

V = bit is Valid during this frame

VL = bit is Valid if the SOFc1 is also the Last frame of the Sequence (i.e., a single-frame Sequence)

V1 = bit is Valid during this frame only in Class-1

Table 41. F_CTL Bit Settings for Data Frames

Sequences. These rules have to do with the assignment of SEQ_ID and SEQ_CNT values and are discussed further in *Streamed Sequences* on page 194.

Because of the size of the SEQ_ID field, the number of open Sequences between any given pair of ports is limited to 256 at any time.

15.3.8 Data Field Control (DF_CTL)

The Data_Field Control is an eight-bit field that indicates the presence of one or more optional headers at the beginning of the data field of the frame. Optional headers are used for information that may be required by some applications or protocol mappings but do not need to be present in every frame. Each protocol mapping specifies the use of any optional headers required by that protocol. A summary of the DF_CTL field is shown in Table 42.

Bit 22 of the DF_CTL field was initially associated with the Expiration_Security header. This header has been withdrawn in FC-PH2 and is no longer part of the current standard.

Bit	Description
23	Reserved for Extended Frame header
22	Reserved (was Expiration Security header that was removed by FC-PH2)
21	0 = No Network header present 1 = Network header present
20	0 = No Association header present 1 = Association header present
19-18	Reserved

17-16	Device header
	  00 = No Device header present
	  01 = 16-byte Device header present
	  10 = 32-byte Device header present
	  11 = 64-byte Device header present

Table 42. Data Field Control (DF_CTL)

When one or more optional headers is present, they occur at the beginning of the frame data field immediately following the frame header and in the order listed in Table 42. That is, the Network_Header precedes the Association_Header which precedes the Device_Header. When an optional header is present, it reduces the amount of space available in the data field, because the optional headers and payload share the data field. When the maximum size of the data field was being determined, it was decided to allow (a nominal value of) 64 bytes for the optional headers and 2,048 bytes for the payload. This resulted in a total size of 2,112 bytes, the architected maximum data field size allowed in a Fibre Channel frame.

If an optional header is not present, no space is reserved for it in the data field of the frame. Rather, the next optional header (or payload if no additional optional headers are present) occupies the first available word in the data field.

Positioning the optional headers at the beginning of the data field and assigning them fixed sizes and order facilitates hardware processing of the optional headers when appropriate. One way to view the optional headers is as an optional extension of the frame header.

The optional headers, and their corresponding bits in the DF_CTL field are only meaningful for FC-4 Device_Data or Video_Data frames and are discussed in more detail in *Optional Headers* on page 223.

15.3.9 Sequence Count (SEQ_CNT)

The Sequence Count is a 16-bit field that is used to indicate the sequential order of frame transmission within a Sequence or multiple consecutive Sequences within the same Exchange. The Sequence recipient may use the SEQ_CNT to:

- Determine the order of frame transmission for Sequence reassembly.
- Confirm that all frames within the Sequence have been received.
- Detect a lost or missing frame.

The Sequence Count of the first frame of the first Sequence of the Exchange transmitted by either the originator or responder is x'0000'. The Sequence count of each successive frame in that Sequence is incremented by one. Therefore, for the first Sequence of the Exchange, the Sequence Count will begin at x'0000', the next frame will be SEQ_CNT=x'0001', then SEQ_CNT=x'0002', and so on.

If, at the end of the current Sequence, the Sequence initiator retains the Sequence Initiative and begins sending a new Sequence for the same Exchange while the previous Sequence is still open (waiting for an acknowledgment, or R_A_TOV time period in the case of Class-3) the new Sequence is called a streamed Sequence and has special rules for the assignment of SEQ_ID and SEQ_CNT values.

When streamed Sequences occur, the SEQ_CNT continues to increment across Sequence boundaries. If the last frame of the prior Sequence ended with SEQ_CNT=x'1234', the first frame of the streamed Sequence begins with SEQ_CNT='1235'. This behavior is referred to as continuously increasing SEQ_CNT and helps ensure streamed Sequences can be properly reassembled under error conditions (or, at least that the error can be reliably detected).

When streamed Sequences do not occur, the Sequence initiator may restart the SEQ_CNT at x'0000' for the first frame of the new Sequence, or use a continuously increasing SEQ_CNT.

When continuously increasing SEQ_CNT is used, the first frame of the Sequence no longer begins with a count of x'0000'. To positively identify the first frame of a Sequence, the Start-of-Frame delimiter is used to provide an indication that is independent of the Sequence count.

If the SEQ_CNT reaches x'FFFF' and there is still more information to send, the SEQ_CNT is allowed to wrap to x'0000' subject to some restrictions. When allowing the SEQ_CNT to wrap, care must be taken to ensure that wrapping does not result in two outstanding frames having the same SEQ_ID and SEQ_CNT values at the same time as this could lead to reassembly problems. Therefore, it is necessary to ensure that the prior usage of the SEQ_CNT is no longer active before reusing the value. This can be determined by receipt of an acknowledgment confirming delivery of that frame, or expiration of the R_A_TOV timeout (the R_A_TOV timeout is set to a value that ensures a frame cannot possibly still be in transit). Subject to these restrictions, the SEQ_CNT can continue to wrap indefinitely, if desired.

The SEQ_ID and SEQ_CNT values used in Acknowledgments and Link_Response frames is the same value that was present in the frame being responded to. These values are simply copied from the header of the original frame.

15.3.10 Originator and Responder Exchange_ID (OX_ID, RX_ID)

When a port originates an Exchange, it normally assigns an identifier to that Exchange. Once an Originator Exchange_ID (OX_ID) has been assigned to an Exchange, it is used in every frame of that Exchange, whether the frame is a data frame or link control frame sent by either the originator or responder of the Exchange.

When a port responds to an Exchange, it may assign an identifier of its own called the RX_ID. Once a Responder Exchange_ID has been assigned, it is placed in every frame of the Exchange sent by the Exchange responder and echoed back in every frame sent by the Exchange originator.

15.3.11 Parameter Field

The parameter field has several uses determined by the frame type.

For Device_Data frames, the parameter field may be used to carry a relative offset value indicating the offset of the first byte of data in the payload relative to the upper-level protocol defined buffer for that Information Category. The presence of a relative offset value in the parameter field is indicated by bit 3 of the F_CTL field set to a one (see *Bit 3: Relative Offset Present* on page 217). Use of relative offset is optional in the standard and support of this option is indicated during the N_Port Login process.

The parameter field is a 32-bit field indicating the relative offset value in bytes. This limits the maximum relative offset to 2^{32} bytes. When the relative offset is used, it can provide a powerful technique for the reassembly of Sequences because each frame carries its own data pointer in the parameter field allowing reassembly to take place even if the Sequence consists of variable-sized frames, or frames received out-of-order.

One side effect of the use of relative offset is that if effectively limits the maximum Sequence size to 2^{32} bytes plus one frame because there is no way to specify offset values larger than this within a Sequence. In most practical applications this is not a serious constraint because a new Sequence can be started to continue the transfer, if needed.

For Link_Control frames, use of the parameter field depends on the type of Link_Control Frame. For acknowledgments, the parameter field is used to indicate the number of frames that are being acknowledged (see *Acknowledge (ACK)* on page 239). For Port Busy and Port and Fabric Rejects, the parameter field contains an action and reason code associated with the response (see *N_Port Reject (P_RJT) and Fabric Reject (F_RJT)* on page 248 and *N_Port Busy (P_BSY)* on page 247).

15.4 Data Field

The frame's data field is a variable-length field that contains optional header information, the payload, and if necessary, from one to three fill bytes.

The standard limits the size of the data field to a maximum of 2112 bytes. This value represents a compromise between frame buffering and latency requirements and transmission efficiency (larger frames require larger buffers and reduce the opportunities for multiplexing, smaller frames are less efficient because they have the same fixed overhead as larger frames but deliver less data).

While that data field cannot exceed 2112 bytes, the standard allows individual ports to implement data field capabilities smaller than this size. This could be done to reduce cost by reducing the size of the buffers, or because of application-specific needs. However, to ensure a common level of capability, the minimum size data field that a port must be capable of receiving is set at 128 bytes (with 256 bytes recommended). The actual receive data field size capability implemented by a port must be a multiple of four bytes (word-sized) is communicated during the login process (see *Fibre Channel Session Management* on page 403).

When the frame contains one or more optional headers, those headers occur at the beginning of the data field, immediately following the frame header. Because the maximum size of the data field is fixed, the optional headers reduce the amount of space available for the payload.

The payload contains the information being transported by the frame and is determined by the higher-level service or FC-4 upper-level protocol. The size of the upper-level protocol Information Unit is not required to be a multiple of four bytes (the standard supports byte-boundary Information Units). When the upper-level information is not a multiple of four bytes, one or more fill bytes are required to pad the information to the next word boundary (the payload is always a multiple of four bytes). Bits 1:0 of the F_CTL field identify the presence, and number of fill bytes at the end of the payload.

Because the data field is variable length, although always a multiple of four, how does the receiving port determine the actual size of a frame? There is no length field in the frame header. Rather, the receiving port knows the frame size when it recognizes the End-of-Frame delimiter (or any other Ordered Set, for that matter).

15.5 Optional Headers

Optional headers provide a set of architected extensions to the frame header. To avoid unnecessary overhead, it is desirable to minimize the size of the frame header because it represents overhead associated with every frame sent. For applications requiring additional header information optional headers provide a way to extend the frame header. When optional headers are present, they are located at the beginning of the data field, preceding the frame's payload.

There are four optional headers defined. They are the Encapsulating Security Payload (ESP) optional header, Network_Header, Association_Header, and Device_Header.

15.5.1 Encapsulating Security Payload (ESP) Optional Header

The ESP optional header is used to provide frame integrity and confidentiality through the use of cryptographic techniques.

Frame integrity is provided by a cryptographic integrity check value (ICV) computed over the contents of the frame header (with the values of the D_ID, S_ID and CS_CTL assumed to be zeros for the computation), optional headers (including the ESP header) and the frame payload. The D_ID, S_ID and CS_CTL fields are excluded from the integrity check as these values may be modified by inter-fabric routers or other devices performing address translation.

Frame confidentiality protects the frame's payload through encryption.

The ESP header provides parameters necessary to provide integrity and confidentiality and consists of two parts; an ESP header and an ESP trailer. Table 43 shows the format of a frame when an ESP header is present.

Word	31:24	23:16	15:08	07:00
Frame Header	R_CTL	Destination_ID (D_ID)		
	CS_CTL	Source_ID (S_ID)		
	TYPE	Frame Control (F_CTL)		
	SEQ_ID	DF_CTL	SEQ_CNT	
	OX_ID		RX_ID	
	Parameter (PARM)			
ESP Header	Security Parameter Index (SPI			
	ESP Sequence Number			
	Other Optional Headers (if present)			
	Payload (variable length)			
	Fill Bytes (if present)			
ESP Trailer	ESP Padding (2 - 254 bytes)			
			Pad Length	Not Meaningful
	Integrity Check Value (ICV) (Does not cover D_ID, S_ID or CS_CTL)			
	Frame CRC			

Table 43. Frame Format with ESP Optional Header Present

ESP Header. The ESP Header contains a Security Parameter Index (SPI) value that is used to locate security parameters associated with this frame. The SPI may be used as an index into a security associations database containing the encryption algorithm and key necessary to unencrypt the frame. The ESP Sequence Number is used to prevent replay of the frame.

ESP Trailer. Block-oriented encryption schemes create encrypted blocks of fixed sizes to help mask the content. The ESP Padding field enables the frame to padded out to the appropriate block size. The size of the ESP Padding is specified by the Pad Length field.

The Integrity Check Value (ICV) contains a cryptographic value (signature) computed over the contents of the frame header (with the values of the D_ID, S_ID and CS_CTL assumed as zeros for the computation), optional headers, including the ESP header and the frame payload. The ICV does not include the ESP trailer or frame CRC.

15.5.2 Network Optional Header

The Network header consists of two eight-byte fields and is present in the data field of the frame when DF_CTL bit 21 is set to a one. This optional header is used when communications takes place between a Fibre Channel node port and a non-Fibre Channel network node, such as an Ethernet port. It may also be used when forwarding information between Fibre Channel networks consisting of two or more Fibre Channel fabrics. The format of the Network header is shown in Table 44.

Bits 63-60	Bits 59 - 00
D_NAA	Network Destination Address
S_NAA	Network Source Address

Table 44. Network_Header

The destination network address authority (D_NAA) and source network address authority (S_NAA) fields identify what type of network address is present in bits 59-00. Typically this field represents the administering or registration authority responsible for assigning network addresses. The values in bits 63-60 correspond to the address types shown in Table 45:

Bits 63-60	Network Address Authority (NAA)
x'0'	Ignored
x'1'	IEEE 48-bit Universal Lan Address (ULA) - the 48-bit Media Access Control (MAC) address
x'2'	IEEE Extended - Fibre Channel extension to IEEE 48-bit Universal Lan Address (ULA)
x'3'	Locally Assigned
x'4'	Internet Protocol (IP) 32-bit address
x'5'-x'B'	Reserved
x'C'	CCITT - 60-bit Individual Address (CCITT is now known as ITU-T)
x'D'	Reserved
x'E'	CCITT - 60-bit Group Address (CCITT is now known as ITU-T)
x'F'	Reserved

Table 45. Network Address Authority

When the designated address is less than 60-bits in length, it is right-aligned in the Network Destination Address or Network Source Address field with unused higher-order bits reserved.

For a discussion of use of the network optional header, refer to *IP Over Fibre Channel (IPFC)* on page 591.

15.5.3 Association Optional Header

The Association_Header is a 32-byte optional header that provides two separate functions, the Process_Associator and Operation_Associator. This header is present in the data field of the frame when DF_CTL bit 20 is set to a one. When this header is present, it follows the ESP and Network_Header (if present), and precedes the Device_Header and payload of the frame. The format of the Association_Header is shown in Table 46.

Word	Bits 31-28	Bits 27-00
0	Validity Bits	Originator Process_Associator (most significant 3 bytes)
1		Originator Process_Associator (least significant 4 bytes)
2		Responder Process_Associator (most significant 3 bytes)
3		Responder Process_Associator (least significant 4 bytes)
4		Originator Operation_Associator (most significant word)
5		Originator Operation_Associator (least significant word)
6		Responder Operation_Associator (most significant word)
7		Responder Operation_Associator (least significant word)

Table 46. Association_Header

Validity bits in word 0, bits 31-28 indicate which fields in the Association_Header contain valid information.

Bit	Bits 27-00
31	1 = Originator Process_Associator meaningful 0 = Originator Process_Associator not meaningful
30	1 = Responder Process_Associator meaningful 0 = Responder Process_Associator not meaningful
29	1 = Originator Operation_Associator meaningful 0 = Originator Operation_Associator not meaningful
28	1 = Responder Operation_Associator meaningful 0 = Responder Operation_Associator not meaningful
27-25	Reserved
24	1 = Multicast Process_Associator (FC-PH3) 0 = Unicast Process_Associator (FC-PH3)

Table 47. Association_Header Validity Bits

Process_Associator. The Process_Associator is used to identify a process, or group of processes within the Node containing the node port. These processes could be logical processes such as software processes, virtual machine instances, or logical system partitions, or physical processes such as a multiprocessor configuration. Use of the Process_Associator is optional and determined by the FC-4 protocol mapping or specific application. An example illustrating the use of the Process_Associator is shown in Figure 98 on page 227.

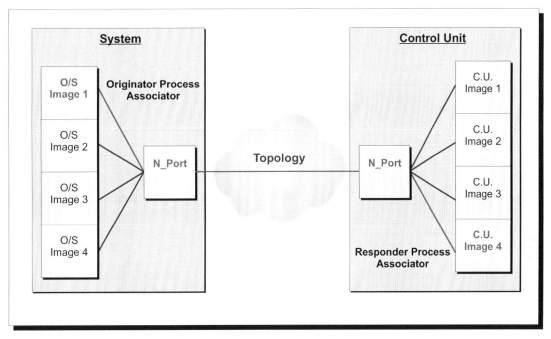

Figure 98. Use of the Process_Associator

While use of the Process_Associator is protocol or application specific and the contents are completely implementation dependent, there are a few rules governing its use.

Once a Process_Associator has been established, it applies to all node ports within the node that have access to the related process, and it cannot be changed for the duration of that Exchange. Therefore the minimum scope of the Process_Associator is the Exchange. A node port is not required to remember the Process_Associator after a logout with the other port, therefore, the maximum scope of the Process_Associator is the login session.

Operation_Associator. The Operation_Associator is used to identify an operation within the node (the Exchange_ID normally identifies a transaction, or portion of the complete transaction, within a port).

The Operation_Associator may be used by protocols that allow an operation to use more than one port during the operation. When this occurs, that portion of the operation that occurs as a transaction within a single port is identified using the Exchange_ID, the entire operation is identified by using the Operation_Associator.

While use of the Operation_Associator is protocol or application specific and the contents of the associator are completely implementation dependent, the standards do provide rules governing its use.

15.5.4 Device Optional Header

The Device_Header is an optional header provided for use by an FC-4 protocol mapping, if that FC-4 has need for a protocol-specific header.

The Device_Header may be either 0, 16, 32, or 64 bytes long with the content and usage defined by the FC-4 mapping. When the Device_Header is present, it follows the Network_Header and Association_Header (if present) and precedes the payload. The presence and size of the Device_Header is specified by DF_CTL, bits 17-16.

15.6 Cyclic Redundancy Check (CRC)

The CRC is used to validate that the frame header and data field were received correctly. The CRC immediately follows the data field and precedes the End-of-Frame delimiter (it does not include the SOF and EOF delimiters). The CRC used by Fibre Channel is the same as that used by the FDDI interface as computed using the following 32-bit polynomial:

$$X^{32}+X^{26}+X^{23}+X^{22}+X^{16}+X^{12}+X^{11}+X^{10}+X^{8}+X^{7}+X^{5}+X^{4}+X^{2}+X+1$$

The CRC is calculated, and checked, on the 32-bit data word that exists prior to encoding or after decoding (not on the encoded data).

15.7 End-of-Frame Delimiter Usage

The End-of-Frame delimiter identifies the normal ending of a frame and informs the receiving port to end reception of the frame. Other than receiving an End-of-Frame delimiter, the receiving port may have no prior knowledge regarding the actual size of the frame.

In addition to identifying the end of a frame, the End-of-Frame delimiter provides information about the position of the frame within the Sequence and whether a Class-1 connection is being removed. Because the class of service was specified by the Start-of-Frame delimiter, the End-of-Frame delimiters do not specifically identify the class of service. For a description of each End-of-Frame delimiter, see *End-of-Frame (EOF)* on page 113 (Ordered Sets for each End-of-Frame delimiter are listed in Table 11 on page 114).

The Fibre Channel standard is explicit regarding the correct use of the End-of-Frame delimiters, requiring that the correct delimiter be used at the appropriate time. Use of an incorrect, or inappropriate, End-of-Frame delimiter is an error.

- The last data frame of a Class-1, Class-2 or Class-F Sequence uses the EOFn delimiter. The End_Sequence bit in the F_CTL field of the frame header identifies this as the last frame of the Sequence. The appropriate Sequence terminating delimiter (EOFt or EOFdt) is used on a subsequent ACK frame.

- The last data frame of a Class-3 Sequence uses the EOFt delimiter in addition to setting the End_Sequence bit in the F_CTL field of the frame header.

- If a frame cannot be completed successfully by the sender, EOFa should used to indicate an aborted frame.

- Otherwise, EOFn is used to signal the end of the frame.

Chapter 15. Frame Structure

As mentioned earlier, all switching and frame routing occurs between the end of one frame and the start of the next. The End-of-Frame delimiter forces the link's running disparity negative to prevent possible running disparity errors when switching occurs.

15.8 Frame Scrambling

Frame scrambling is used to reduce the probability of long runs of repeating patterns appearing on the link. While the 8b/10b coding scheme transforms frame words into transmission words, it does not prevent repeating patterns. If a frame payload consists of repeating characters, the encoded data will consist of repeating characters.

The physical interface specifications (Fibre Channel's FC-0 level) specify when scrambling is to be used. While scrambling is not used for link speeds of 4 Gbps and slower, it may be required for some links operating at 8.5 Gbps and faster.

When scrambling is used, all frame words between the Start-of-Frame and End-of-Frame delimiters are scrambled, including any extended headers, the standard frame header, the data field, and CRC. The sender scrambles the frame data before it is encoded by the 8b/10b encoder and the receiver unscrambles the data after it is decoded and before processing the frame content. Scrambling and unscrambling both use exactly the same algorithm and logic.

The scrambling algorithm is based on the equivalent of a linear feedback shift register implementing the following polynomial:

$$G(x) = x^{58} + x^{39} + 1$$

An example of a serial implementation of the scrambler algorithm is shown in Figure 99.

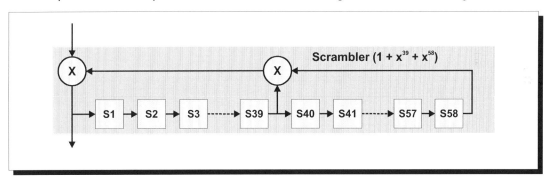

Figure 99. Frame Scrambler (Serial Implementation)

When a SOF is transmitted, the 58-bit scrambler seed is initialized to the low-order 58 bits of x'029438798327338'. For each frame word to be scrambled, the frame word is XOR'd with bits 58:27 of the seed and the result is XOR'd with bits 39:08 of the seed to form the scrambled word. After each word is scrambled, bits 58:33 of the seed are set from bits 26:01 of the seed, and bits 32:01 of the seed are set from the scrambled word as shown in Figure 100. This process continues for each frame word until the EOF is reached. An example of a parallel implementation of the scrambling algorithm is shown in Figure 100 on page 230.

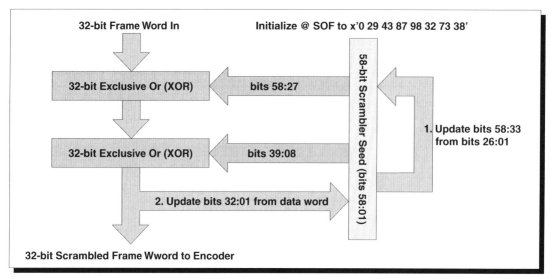

Figure 100. Frame Scrambler (Parallel Implementation)

15.8.1 Frame Scrambling Example

Table 48 provides an example of the result of frame scrambling.

Word		Unscrambled Frame Word	Scrambled Frame Word
		<SOF>	<SOF>
0		x'060405EF'	x'036480EF'
1		x'000404E8'	x'7C9E03E9'
2	Frame Header	x'08290000'	x'0FF007D8'
3		x'00000000'	x'F59F1A4C'
4		x'8018FFFF'	x'CDF237F6'
5		x'00000000'	x'FE25D775C'
6		x'00000000'	x'91714751'
7		x'00000000'	x'2E7F35AA'
8		x'00000002'	x'FE0D2A22'
9	FCP_CMND Payload	x'12018300'	x'D830F3EB'
10		x'20000000'	x'E6FAE951'
11		x'00000000'	x'DBF10F2B'
12		x'00000000'	x'1D0DB668'
13		x'00000020'	x'AA79D18B'
14	Frame CRC	x'AA92695C'	x'38AB00D5'
		<EOF>	<EOF>

Table 48. Frame Scrambling Example

15.8.2 Transmit Data Path

The transmit data path, including the scrambler, is shown in Figure 101. When scrambling is supported, it may by bypassed for some link rates if scrambling is not specified for that speed.

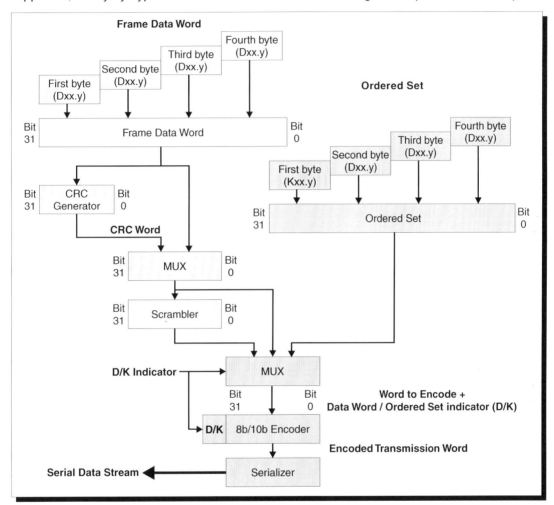

Figure 101. Transmit Data Path

15.8.3 Receive Data Path

The receive data path, including the scrambler, is shown in Figure 102. When scrambling is supported, it may by bypassed for some link rates if scrambling is not specified for that speed.

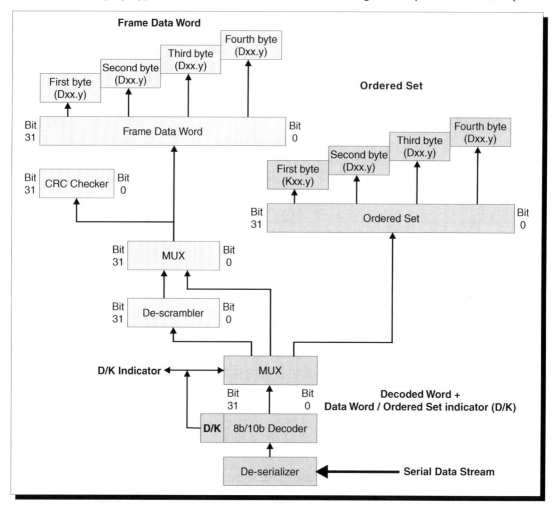

Figure 102. Receive Data Path

15.9 Chapter Summary

Frames

- All information transferred in Fibre Channel is transferred in frames
- Each frame:
  - Begins with a Start-of-Frame delimiter and ends with an End-of-Frame delimiter
  - Contains a header
  - May contain a data field
  - Contains CRC to validate the contents
- The amount of data per frame is limited to 2112 bytes (528 words)
  - Limit the size of buffers
  - Allow for efficient switching and multiplexing

Start-of-Frame Delimiter

- Start-of-Frame (SOF) identifies the beginning of a frame
- Prepares the receiver for frame reception
- The correct SOF must be used for the current conditions
  - Class of service
  - Position within the Sequence
  - Connection established, or not
- Incorrect delimiter usage is an error

Frame Header

- Frame header contains control information about the frame:
  - Frame type
  - Destination address
  - Source address
  - OX_ID, RX_ID, SEQ_ID, SEQ_CNT
  - Type of protocol being carried in the frame
- The header is always 24 bytes (6 words) long
- The data field, if any, immediately follows the header

Routing Control (R_CTL)

- The first 8 bits of the header are the routing control (R_CTL) field
- Defines the type of frame and its contents
- 1st four bits are the Routing bits (R_BITS)
  - Identifies the frame type
- 2nd four bits are called the information field, or information category (IC) field
  - Define the contents of the frame, or
  - Identify the function of the frame
- See Table 31 on page 207 for details

Addresses (D_ID/S_ID)

- The header contains two 24-bit address fields,
  - The Destination_ID (D_ID)
  - The Source_ID (S_ID)
- These are used to route the frame and verify correct delivery
- Addresses may be one of:
  - A normal address - variously referred to as the N_Port ID (FC-PH/FC-FS), Native address identifier (FC-AL), or Port Identifier (FC-GS-3)
  - Well-known address identifier
  - Alias address identifier

Class-Specific Control (CS_CTL)

- The Class-specific control field has two uses:
- If F_CTL bit 17 is set, this field contains a Priority value
  - Fabric can deliver frames based on priority
  - Ports can process frames based on priority
- If F_CTL bit 17 is zero, this field contains a delivery "preference" value
  - deliver via the fastest path, or
  - deliver via the most secure path, etc.

Type Field

- The type field specifies what type of protocol is carried by the frame
- As each protocol is mapped to Fibre Channel, it is assigned a type value
- Some common Type field values are:
  - x'00' and x'01' = Link services
  - x'05' = IP over Fibre Channel
  - x'08' = SCSI Fibre Channel Protocol (FCP)
  - x'20' = FC-CT, used when communicating with the Name Server
- Refer to Table 37 on page 210 for a complete listing

Frame Control (F_CTL)

- The F_CTL field holds miscellaneous control bits associated with the frame, such as:
  - The context of the frame (from the originator or responder of the Exchange, from the Sequence initiator or recipient)
  - If this frame is part of the first or last Sequence of the Exchange
  - If this is the last data frame of the Sequence
  - If Sequence Initiative is being transferred
- Refer to Table 38 on page 213 for a detailed list

Sequence_ID (SEQ_ID)

- The SEQ_ID field identifies which Sequence this frame belongs to
- Used to identify and track the frames in a Sequence
- As long as the Sequence is open, the SEQ_ID must be unique between a pair of ports
  - Because this is an 8-bit field only 256 open Sequences between a pair of ports in each direction
- SEQ_ID values are not necessarily assigned in order
- The following series of SEQ_ID values is valid:
  - x'10', x'11', x'37', x'09'

Data Field Control (DF_CTL)

- A frame may have one or more optional headers at the beginning of the data field
  - Could be viewed as extensions to the frame header
- DF_CTL indicates whether optional headers are present
- Optional headers are:
  - Encapsulating Security Payload (ESP)
  - Network header
  - Association header
  - Device header

Sequence Count (SEQ_CNT)

- SEQ_CNT identifies the position of the frame within the Sequence
  - SEQ_CNT increments by +1 as each frame of the Sequence is sent
- SEQ_CNT starts at x'0000' for the first frame of the first Sequence of the Exchange
- When streamed Sequences occur, the SEQ_CNT continues to increment across Sequence boundaries
  - Called continuously increasing SEQ_CNT
- When streamed Sequences do not occur, SEQ_CNT can restart at x'0000' or continuously increase

Exchange_ID (OX_ID,RX_ID)

- The Exchange IDs identify which Exchange the frame belongs to
- The originator assigns the OX_ID
  - It is present in every frame of the Exchange
- The responder may assign an RX_ID
  - That is present in every subsequent frame of the Exchange
- The OX_ID and RX_ID may be related to control blocks
  - Facilitate context efficient Exchange multiplexing

Parameter Field (PARM)

- Parameter field is the last field in the frame header and has several uses
- It may contain a relative offset value
  - An offset value, or displacement of the first byte of data in the frame,
  - Relative to an upper-level protocol buffer
  - For example SCSI uses this field as the offset into the data buffer for the command (like the SCSI data pointers)
- For link control frames it has the reason code and explanation
- May contain other "parameters" depending on the specific frame

Frame Data Field

- The data field is a variable size field
- May be from 0 to 2112 bytes in 4-byte increments
- Data field is not padded out to a fixed size (other than word boundaries)
- Ports may implement smaller receive data fields than 2112 bytes
  - Save the cost of buffers
  - Simplify memory management (2048 rather than 2112)
  - Actual supported value is communicated during login

Data Field Contents

- The data field may contain one, or more, optional headers,
  - DF_CTL identifies whether optional headers are present
  - Optional headers are in fixed order and have fixed sizes to facilitate hardware processing
  - When present, optional headers reduce the space available for the payload
- Followed by the payload,
  - The information being sent to the other port
- And, if necessary, up to three fill bytes to align the CRC on a word boundary

Optional Headers

- Optional headers provide a set of architected extensions to the frame header
  - Carry information not needed in the header of every frame
- Four headers are defined:
  - Encapsulating Security Payload (ESP)
  - Network header
  - Association header
  - Device header
- When present, they appear in this order before the payload. If not present, no space is reserved

Encapsulating Security Payload (ESP)

- Provides integrity and confidentiality protection for frames
- Consists of an ESP header and ESP trailer
  - A "wrapper" around an encrypted payload
- ESP header contains Security Parameter Index
  - Pointer to security session parameters
  - Identifying encryption algorithm and key
- Integrity Check Value (ICV)
  - Digital hash of frame using session key
  - Ensures that frame content has not been altered
  - Does not include D_ID, S_ID or CS_CTL

Network Optional Header

- Network header used when routing outside of Fibre Channel
  - For example, bridging to a network environment
- May need to hold up to two network addresses
  - The type of network source address (4-bits) and the address itself (60-bits), and
  - The type of network destination address (4-bits) and the address itself (60-bits)
- These are used for routing between the two environments
- See Table 44 on page 225 and Table 45 on page 225

Association Optional Header

- The association header has two functions put in to support mainframe requirements
- The Process_Associator identifies a process behind the port
  - System process, virtual machine, Logical image or partition (LPAR)
- The Operation_Associator may be used to locate resources associated with an operation
  - When the Exchange is not sufficient
  - For example, when dynamic multi-pathing during an operation)

Device Optional Header

- The device header is provided in case an FC-4 mapping needs additional header information
  - May be 0, 16, 32, or 64 bytes
  - Length is specified by two bits in the DF_CTL field
- Not used by any of the common FC-4 mappings
  - Is used by the mapping of the Virtual Interface Architecture to Fibre Channel (FC-VI)

CRC

- The CRC is a 32-bit check word that validates the frame contents were received correctly
  - CRC generation and checking is on the unencoded (8-bit) data
- The sender begins CRC generation with the frame header and continues through the end of the data field
- The receiver begins checking with the header and continues until the End-of-Frame delimiter is detected
- At that time, the frame has been processed from the header through the CRC itself

End-of-Frame

- The End-of-Frame delimiter identifies the end of the frame
- It also identifies the final frame of a Sequence
- In Class-1, the End-of-Frame is used to end the connection
- Running disparity is forced negative by the End-of-Frame delimiter
  - All switching and frame routing occurs between the end of one frame and the start of the next
  - The link's running disparity is at a known state both before and after the switch occurs

Extended Headers

- Standards have defined three extended headers
  - Provide additional information required in some environments
- Occur after the SOF and before the standard frame header
- Identified by their R_CTL field values:
  - x'50' = Virtual Fabric Tagging (VFT) header
  - x'51' = Inter-Fabric Routing (IFR) header
  - x'52' = Encapsulation (ENC) header

Virtual Fabric Tagging (VFT) Header

- Ports may support communication with multiple virtual fabrics
  - Using a single physical link
  - Node port needs to maintain a separate context for each virtual fabric
- Frames need to tagged to identify the fabric to which they belong
  - Tagging is done using the VFT Header
- VFT Header is an Extended Header
  - After the SOF and before any other headers (including the standard frame header)
  - Presence is indicated by R_CTL field value
  - R_CTL field value = x'50'

Inter-Fabric Routing (IFR) Header

- Used by routers to forward frames between fabrics
  - IFR header contains source and destination Fabric IDs
  - Inserted by the ingress router
  - Removed by the egress router
- IFR Header should not be received by a node port or switch
- Presence is indicated by R_CTL field value
  - R_CTL field value = x'51'

Encapsulation (ENC) Header

- Used by routers to route frames through an existing fabric
- ENC header has same structure and format as the standard frame header
  - Precedes standard frame header
  - R_CTL field = x'52'
  - Router sets destination ID to next hop router
  - Sets source ID to this hop router's address
- Provides a way to supply D_ID and S_ID while still preserving original frame header
- Node ports should not encounter the ENC header

Frame Scrambling

- The frame content may be scrambled
  - Reduces the probability of long strings of repeated characters
  - Aids in signal recovery on faster links (8 Gbs and faster)
- Frame data words are XOR'd with a seed value
  - Scrambling seed is initialized at the SOF
  - Scrambling seed is updated for every word using a specified algorithm
- Transmitter and receiver follow exactly the same process
  - XORing a word with the same seed twice produces the original word

FC-2 Data Rate Calculation (1 Gbps)

- To deliver 100 MB/sec., must deliver 800 Mbs
- After encoding, 800 Mbits = 1000 Mbaud (8b/10b)
- Every frame has 60 bytes of overhead (120 with ACK)
- For a 2048 byte payload, 2168 characters are sent (payload+frame overhead+ACK)
- The efficiency is 2048/2168 or 94.5%
- The raw link rate is 106.25 MB/s (1 Gbps)
- Multiplying 106.25 MB/sec by 94.5% gives a data rate of 100.37 MB/sec.

16. Link Control Frames

Fibre Channel defines multiple link control functions that are used to manage the link and provide confirmation of delivery or notification of non-delivery. These functions are implemented using link control (FT-0) frames (all other operations use data frames that are FT-1).

Link control frames provide three different types of function. They are:

- Link continue frames that provide acknowledgment of delivery of data frames.
- Link response frames that provide notification a frame has been rejected or could not be processed due to a busy condition.
- Link control commands used to initiate a low-level action at the destination port.

When a port sends data frames in Class-1, Class-2 or Class-F, it must provide sufficient resources to receive link control frames in response to those data frames. A node port is not allowed to send a busy response to a link control frame because this could lead to endless repetition (I'm busy. I'm busy to your busy. I'm busy to your busy to my busy, etc.). If the node port fails to provide the necessary resources and a link control frame is received, it will be lost and the associated Sequence delivery fails.

When a port sends a link control frame in response to a received data frame, the link control frame may receive a fabric busy response if the fabric is unable to deliver the link control frame. If a fabric busy response is received to a link control frame, the link control frame can be reconstructed from the fabric busy. This relieves the node port from having to save the link control frame in case retransmission is required due to a fabric busy condition.

16.1 Acknowledge (ACK)

The acknowledgment (ACK) frame is used by all classes of service except Class-3. ACK provides three primary functions. They are:

1. to confirm successful frame delivery to the designated recipient.
2. to provide a flow control function between the two node ports by indicating the Sequence recipient's readiness to receive one or more additional frames from the Sequence initiator (the additional frames do not necessarily have to be part of the current Sequence). This flow control function of the ACK is discussed later in *End-to-End Flow Control (EE_Credit)* on page 268.
3. to allow the Sequence recipient to signal other conditions associated with the Sequence.

ACK confirms successful frame delivery to the destination port and frame acceptance by the destination port. ACK does not imply successful delivery to a higher-level process.

Each data frame in the Sequence is acknowledged only once—multiple ACKs for the same data frame are not allowed.

ACKs are considered part of the Sequence, even though they are sent by the Sequence recipient. The class of service used for the ACK is the same as was used for the original data frame and the OX_ID, RX_ID, and SEQ_ID must all match the values used for the data frames in that Sequence.

When an ACK is sent, the frame header of the ACK indicates the frame, or group of frames, being acknowledged. The D_ID, S_ID, OX_ID, RX_ID, SEQ_ID, and SEQ_CNT fields provide the necessary context information.

The Sequence initiator does not consider the Sequence complete until the final ACK is received. Successful transmission and reception of the final ACK completes the Sequence. Therefore, the final ACK uses the appropriate Sequence terminating End-of-Frame delimiter (EOFt or EOFdt) for the class of service in use. If the final ACK is lost due to a transmission error, the Sequence fails to complete and a Sequence timeout occurs.

Fibre Channel provides two acknowledgment policies that can be used to provide confirmation of delivery. Those policies are ACK_1 and ACK_0.

- **ACK_1** is the default behavior required by the standard and provides one acknowledgment per data frame. (Draft amendment-2 modified FC-PH to allow either ACK_1 or ACK_0 as the default.)

- **ACK_0** is an optional behavior that provides one acknowledgment for all previous frames of the Sequence.

If a port supports Class-1 or Class-2 it must support either ACK_1 or ACK_0 behavior. The option to use ACK_0 as the default (after N_Port Login) was added by an amendment to the standard so that Class-3 only designs could provide delivery confirmation at the Sequence level (ACK_0) without having to implement the full ACK processing necessary to support ACK_1 operation. If a port supports Class-F, it must support ACK_0.

16.1.1 Fabric Busy to an ACK

If an ACK receives a fabric busy (F_BSY), the ACK is not retransmitted. This should only occur in Class-2 operation as a result of severe fabric congestion.

The reason the ACK is not retransmitted is that the fabric does not return F_BSY immediately. Rather, it attempts to deliver the frame for up to the Error_Detect Timeout value (E_D_TOV). By the time the ACK could be retransmitted, the Sequence initiator has already detected a Sequence timeout as a result of the missing ACK.

16.1.2 ACK Use of the Parameter Field

In an ACK, the parameter field indicates the number of frames being acknowledged and whether all previous ACKs of the Sequence have been sent.

Bits 15-0 of the parameter field are set to x'00 00' for an ACK_0 and x'00 01' for an ACK_1.

Bit 16 of the parameter field of an ACK is defined as the history bit. When the history bit is set to zero, it indicates that all previous ACKs of that Sequence have been sent. When the history bit is set to one, it indicates that at least one previous ACK has not been sent.

When the history bit is set to zero, the Sequence initiator knows that the Sequence recipient has sent an ACK to all prior frames of the Sequence, whether the ACK has been received or not. Because of this, the Sequence initiator knows that those prior frames are no longer occupying a receive buffer in the recipient and the Sequence initiator can send additional frames as if the ACKs had been received. This can help prevent starvation if one or more ACKs is lost due to a transmission error.

While the standard allows use of the history bit to manage flow control in the event of loss of one or more ACKs, it does not relieve the Sequence initiator of accounting for all ACKs in a Class-2 Sequence. In Class-2, there is the possibility of out-of-order delivery of ACKs, therefore the prior ACKs may still arrive at a later time.

16.1.3 ACK_1

ACK_1 is the default acknowledgment policy for those ports supporting Class-1, Class-2 or Class-F service. When ACK_1 is used, one ACK_1 is sent by the Sequence recipient in response to each data frame received without error. An example of ACK_1 behavior is shown in Figure 103.

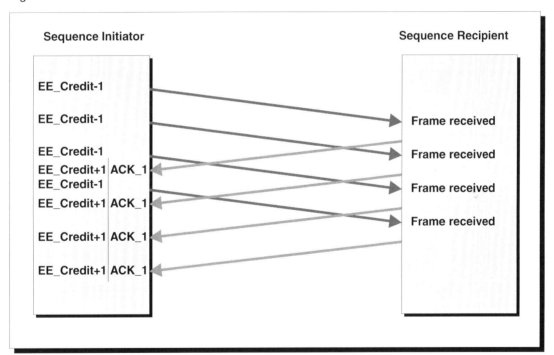

Figure 103. ACK_1 Operation

ACK_1 frames should be sent in the same order as the corresponding data frames are received, even if the data frames are received out-of-order. Withholding ACKs withholds replenishment of the Sequence initiator's permission to send additional frames and may result in degraded performance at the Sequence initiator. This condition could arise from the following scenarios:

- The Sequence initiator has exhausted its credit and is waiting for one or more ACKs to replenish the credit.

- The Sequence recipient is withholding ACKs for frames it has received while waiting for a missing previous frame that has not yet been received.

- The missing frame arrives, the Sequence recipient sends ACKs for all of the frames and the Sequence initiator can resume frame transmission. However, due to the withheld ACKs, there was a period of time when the Sequence initiator was unable to send any frames, degrading performance. (If the missing frame never arrives, the Sequence times-out and a Sequence error results.)

16.1.4 ACK_0

ACK_0 is an optional acknowledgment policy for those ports supporting Class-1 or Class-2 service. Support of ACK_0 is indicated by the port during the N_Port Login process. When ACK_0 is used, one ACK_0 is sent by the Sequence recipient to acknowledge that all prior data frames of the Sequence have been received without error. An example of ACK_0 behavior is shown in shown in Figure 104.

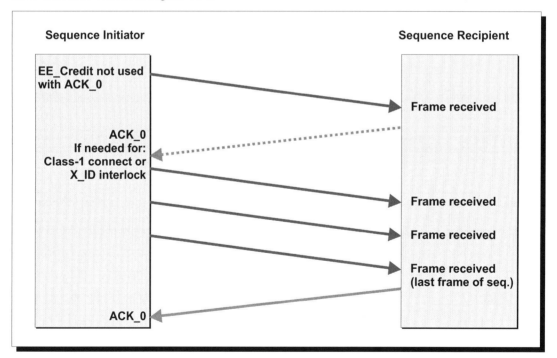

Figure 104. ACK_0 Operation

Normally, a single ACK_0 is sent at the end of the Sequence confirming delivery of the entire Sequence and ending the Sequence. However, there are two exception conditions where an ACK_0 is sent prior to the end of the Sequence:

- The first is to respond to a Class-1 connect request (SOFc1).

- The second is to perform X_ID interlock (see *Exchange_ID Interlock* on page 177).

When ACK_0 is used for a Class-1 Sequence, the Sequence recipient is assumed to have a sufficient number of buffers available to receive the entire Sequence (sometimes referred to as infinite buffers). Because ACK_0 is not sent until the end of the Sequence (other than the two exception cases listed earlier), the Sequence recipient has no way to replenish the Sequence initiator's permission to send frames during the Sequence. The Sequence initiator simply assumes that enough buffers are available. In most cases, the higher-level protocol limits the Sequence size to a value manageable by the Sequence recipient.

When ACK_0 is used for Class-2, there is an additional flow control mechanism used that allows frame transfer to be paced by the Sequence recipient (see *Buffer-to-Buffer Flow Control (BB_Credit)* on page 263.

16.1.5 ACK Precedence and ACK Generation Assistance

When both the Sequence initiator and recipient support use of ACK_0, it should be used to minimize the amount of link activity. If ACK_0 is not supported by both ports, ACK_1 is used.

When both ports support multiple ACK behaviors, the Sequence initiator may have a preference for which ACK behavior is used for a particular Sequence. FC-PH2 added the ACK_Form bits (bit 13-12 of F_CTL in the frame header) to allow the Sequence initiator to override the default precedence order.

16.1.6 Additional Functions Performed using ACK

In addition to confirming frame delivery and providing a flow control function between the two node ports, the ACK may be used by the Sequence recipient to perform additional functions or signal the Sequence initiator of other conditions. Among them are:

- The Exchange responder sends an ACK to provide an RX_ID to the Exchange originator, perhaps to establish X_ID Interlock.

- The Sequence recipient informs the Sequence initiator via the Abort Sequence Condition bits (bits 5-4 in F_CTL in the frame header) what action to take regarding the continued transmission of the Sequence. The Sequence recipient can request that the Sequence initiator:

  - Continue sending the Sequence bits 5-4 = x'00').

  - Abort the Sequence (bits 5-4 = x'01') by using the Abort Sequence (ABTS) protocol.

  - Stop the Sequence (bits 5-4 = x'10') by setting END_Sequence in the next data frame of the Sequence.

  - Begin immediate retransmission of the Sequence (bits 5-4 = x'11').

- The Sequence recipient ends a Class-1, Class-2 or Class-F Sequence by using the appropriate Sequence terminating delimiter (EOFt or EOFdt) on the final ACK of the Sequence.
- The Sequence recipient confirms that a Class-1 connection has been established by sending an ACK to the Class-1 connect frame (SOFc1).
- The Sequence recipient requests the removal of a Class-1 connection by using an EOFdt delimiter on the last ACK of the Sequence.
- The Sequence recipient uses the ACK to perform X_ID reassignment.

16.1.7 ACK Generation

In most designs, ACKs are generated by the port hardware. This is done to provide a timely response to received data frames. To minimize hardware complexity, the generation of ACKs is kept as simple as possible.

The Start-of-Frame delimiter for all ACK frames is SOFnx (where "x" matches the class of service of the corresponding data frame).

The frame header is set as follows (other bits may be set depending upon conditions present):

- R_CTL is set to indicate the ACK form.
  - ACK_1 = x'C0'
  - ACK_0 = x'C1'
- The destination and source ID fields (D_ID and S_ID) are swapped.
- The type field is set to zeros.
- F_CTL is updated as follows:
  - The Exchange and Sequence Context bits in F_CTL (bits 23 and 22) are inverted.
  - The Abort Sequence Condition bits in F_CTL (bits 5-4) are set to direct the Sequence initiator what action to take regarding continued transmission of this Sequence.
- The OX_ID, RX_ID, and SEQ_ID are copied from the corresponding data frame.
- The SEQ_CNT is set to the SEQ_CNT of the highest data frame being acknowledged.
- The parameter field is set as follows:
  - The History bit (bit 16) is set to zero if all previous ACKs of this Sequence have been transmitted. Otherwise this bit is set to one.
  - Bits 15-0 indicate the number of frames being acknowledged. Zero indicates all prior frames of the Sequence (ACK_0) and one indicates one frame (ACK_1).

The data field is not present (its length is zero bytes) in an ACK.

The CRC is calculated on the information in the frame header and immediately follows the frame header.

The End-of-Frame delimiter indicates if this is the last frame of the Sequence (EOFt or EOFdt) or an intermediate frame (EOFn).

16.2 Fabric Busy (F_BSY)

When the fabric is unable to deliver a valid frame due to a busy condition within the fabric or at the destination node port, it returns a fabric busy to the sender of the frame. Whether the fabric is allowed to return a busy indication to a particular frame depends on the received frame and class of service.

- In Class-1, the fabric is only allowed to return F_BSY to the Class-1 connect frame (the connect frame uses the SOFc1 delimiter). Once the Class-1 connection has been established, the fabric is not allowed to return a busy to any of the subsequent frames during that connection. When F_BSY is returned to a Class-1 connect frame, the F_BSY uses the SOFn1 Start-of-Frame delimiter and the EOFdt End-of-Frame delimiter.

- In Class-2 and Class-F operations, the fabric is allowed to return F_BSY to any frame.

- In Class-3, F_BSY is not allowed to any frame.

There are two different R_CTL field values used for F_BSY depending on whether the F_BSY is in response to a link control frame (FT-0) or a data frame (FT-1).

- If F_BSY is in response to a link control frame, R_CTL of the frame header is set to x'C6'.

- If F_BSY is in response to a data frame, R_CTL of the frame header is set to x'C5'.

Differentiating F_BSY responses in this manner allows a node port receiving F_BSY to internally route the frame for appropriate processing.

When the fabric sends F_BSY it provides a reason code in bits 31-28 of the type field in the frame header. If F_BSY is in response to a link control frame, bits 27-24 of R_CTL are copied into bits 27-24 of the type field. Table 49 on page 246 summarizes the F_BSY reason codes.

To prevent needless or endless repetition of busy indications, F_BSY cannot be sent in response to another busy (F_BSY or P_BSY) frame. Instead, the fabric discards the busy frame.

Fabric busy conditions are expected to be an unusual event. The fabric determines how long to wait before returning F_BSY and provides the attached node ports with an Error_Detect Timeout Value (E_D_TOV) that assures the F_BSY is returned before the Sequence timesout. In many cases, F_BSY may result in Sequence delivery failures, either due to the node port's inability to retransmit the busied frame or the standard prohibiting retransmission of the busied frame (e.g., ACKs receiving F_BSY are not retransmitted).

16.2.1 Node Port Processing of F_BSY to Data Frame

When a node port receives F_BSY in response to a data frame, it may retransmit the data frame, if it is able. It is up to the implementation to decide which data frames will be retransmitted as a result of receiving F_BSY, and how many times the frame is retransmitted if additional F_BSY is received in response to retransmission.

The standard doesn't require a node port to have the ability to retransmit data frames that receives F_BSY at all. It could simply consider the frame undeliverable and let the Sequence fail. Or, the port may attempt retransmission of specific frames, such as the first frame of the Sequence, but not others.

R_CTL	Type Field	F_BSY is in Response to:	Reason for the Fabric Busy (F_BSY)
x'C5'	x'1x'	Data frame (see note 1)	The fabric is busy
	x'3x'	Data frame (see note 1)	The destination Nx_Port is busy with a Class-1 connection
x'C6'	x'10'	ACK_1	The fabric is busy (the ACK_1 is not retransmitted)
	x'11'	ACK_0	The fabric is busy (the ACK_0 is not retransmitted)
	x'12'	P_RJT	The fabric is busy
	x'13'	F_RJT	The fabric is busy
	x'17'	Link Credit Reset (LCR)	The fabric is busy
	x'18'	Notify (NTY)	The fabric is busy
	x'19'	End (END)	The fabric is busy
	x'30'	ACK_1	The destination Nx_Port is engaged in a Class-1 connection (the ACK_1 is not retransmitted)
	x'31'	ACK_0	The destination Nx_Port is engaged in a Class-1 connection (the ACK_0 is not retransmitted)
	x'32'	P_RJT	The destination Nx_Port is engaged in a Class-1 connection
	x'33'	F_RJT	The destination Nx_Port is engaged in a Class-1 connection
	x'37'	Link Credit Reset (LCR)	The destination Nx_Port is engaged in a Class-1 connection
	x'38'	Notify (NTY)	The destination Nx_Port is engaged in a Class-1 connection
	x'39'	End (END)	The destination Nx_Port is engaged in a Class-1 connection
	Others		reserved
1. Type field bits 27-24 for F_BSY to a data frame are the same as in the original data frame.			

Table 49. F_BSY Reason Codes

If the node port was required to be able to retransmit any data frame it had sent, it would need to save sufficient information to allow reconstruction of any frames in transit. In a large configuration this could amount to saving information for possibly thousands of frames. Clearly, this is not practical in most applications.

If a node port exhausts is ability to retry the data frame, it notifies the higher-level process that the Sequence delivery failed. Depending on the Exchange error policy in effect for the Sequence, the higher-level process may decide to abort the Sequence, or even the Exchange.

16.2.2 Node Port Processing of F_BSY to Link Control Frame

When a node port receives F_BSY in response to a link control frame (other than an ACK) it reconstructs the original link control frame from the F_BSY and retransmits it. If a node port receives F_BSY in response to an ACK in Class-2, the F_BSY is discarded and the ACK is not retransmitted.

Reconstruction of the original link control frame is possible because the information necessary is present in the F_BSY (the only information from the original link control frame destroyed is the type field). The node port simply:

- Moves bits 27-24 of the type field to bits 27-24 of R_CTL. This changes the link control frame back to its original function.

- Swaps the destination and source ID fields (D_ID and S_ID).

- Inverts the Exchange and Sequence context bits in F_CTL (bits 23 and 22).

The reconstructed link control frame (with recalculated CRC) can then be retransmitted.

16.3 N_Port Busy (P_BSY)

When the node port is temporarily unable to accept a valid frame due to a busy condition within the port it returns N_Port busy (P_BSY) to the sender of the frame. Whether the node port is allowed to return a busy indication to a particular frame depends on the received frame and class of service.

- In Class-1, the node port can only return P_BSY to the Class-1 connect frame (the connect frame uses the SOFc1 delimiter). Once the Class-1 connection is been established, the node port is not allowed to return a busy to any of the subsequent frames during that connection. When a P_BSY is returned to a Class-1 connect frame, the P_BSY uses the SOFn1 Start-of-Frame delimiter and the EOFdt End-of-Frame delimiter.

- In Class-2 operations, the node port may return P_BSY to any data frame.

- In Class-3, P_BSY is not allowed to any frame.

P_BSY may only be sent in response to data frames. A node port is not allowed to send P_BSY in response to a link control frame—it must process a link control frame for each unacknowledged data frame. P_BSY cannot be sent in response to another busy (that would be a P_BSY to a link control frame). If the port cannot process the received busy, it is discarded.

P_BSY conditions are expected to be an unusual event and may result in Sequence delivery failures due to the sending node port's possible inability to retransmit the busied frame.

16.3.1 P_BSY Action and Reason Codes

When the node port returns P_BSY, it provides an action and reason code in the parameter field of the frame header.

The action code is stored in bits 31-24 of the parameter field and is set to x'01' to indicate that the Sequence terminated, or x'02' if the Sequence is still active. The reason code in bits 23-16, identifies why the P_BSY was sent.

Bits 15-8 are reserved and bits 7-0 may be used for vendor unique information.

Table 50 on page 248 summarizes the P_BSY reason codes.

Parameter Field Bits				Explanation
Action Code **31-24**	**Reason Code** **23-16**	**Reserved** **15-8**	**Vendor Unique** **7-0**	
x'01'	x'01'	x'00'		The Sequence is terminated, the physical Nx_Port is busy.
	x'03'	x'00'		The Sequence is terminated, a required resource is busy.
	x'07'	x'00'		The Sequence is terminated, one or more Nx_Ports in the multicast group responded with a busy (Partial Multicast Busy).
	x'FF'	x'00'	vendor unique	The Sequence is terminated, vendor unique busy, see bits 7-0.
x'02'	x'01'	x'00'		The Sequence is not terminated, the physical Nx_Port is busy.
	x'03'	x'00'		The Sequence is not terminated, a required resource is busy.
	x'07'	x'00'		The Sequence is not terminated, one or more Nx_Ports in the multicast group responded with a busy (Partial Multicast Busy).
	x'FF'	x'00'	vendor unique	The Sequence is not terminated, vendor unique busy, see bits 7-0.
Other	Other			Reserved

Table 50. P_BSY Action and Reason Codes

16.4 N_Port Reject (P_RJT) and Fabric Reject (F_RJT)

N_Port reject (P_RJT) and fabric reject (F_RJT) provide notification that a valid Class-1 or Class-2 frame could not be processed by the node port or fabric. There are numerous reason why a reject may be sent. The reason for a particular reject is contained in the reason code sub-field of the parameter field of the reject link control frame.

The node port or fabric may send a reject in response to any data frame.

The fabric may send a reject in response to a link control frame only for the following reasons:

- The class of service indicated in the link control frame is not supported by the fabric.
- The destination or source ID (D_ID or S_ID) is invalid.
- The node port is not available temporarily.
- The node port is not available permanently.
- Fabric login is required.

The node port may send a reject in response to a link control frame only for the following reason:

- An unexpected ACK was received.

If a node port detects an error in a link control frame for a valid Exchange, it should initiate the Abort Sequence (ABTS) protocol and not transmit a reject. If a node port detects an error in a link control frame for an unidentified or invalid Exchange, it discards the link control frame and ignores the error. A reject frame is not allowed in response to another reject frame.

If a rejectable condition is detected on a Class-3 frame, the frame is discarded and no reject is sent. A Sequence error is detected as a result of the missing frame.

If a frame within a Sequence is rejected, the Sequence will either be abnormally terminated or aborted. If the RJT frame ends with EOFt or EOFdt, the port sending the RJT has terminated the Sequence. In Class-1, terminating the Sequence is only allowed in response to the connect frame (SOFc1). In Class-2, the rejecting port is only allowed to terminate the Sequence in response to an interlocked data frame associated with X_ID assignment or reassignment. Otherwise, the EOFn End-of-Frame delimiter is used and the Sequence is not terminated by the RJT.

When a node port receives RJT with an EOFn End-of-Frame delimiter, it performs the Abort Sequence (ABTS) protocol.

16.4.1 Reject Action and Reason Codes

When a node port or the fabric returns a reject, it provides an action and reason code in the parameter field of the frame header.

The action code is stored in bits 31-24 of the parameter field and is set to x'01' that the Sequence may be retryable if the condition indicated by the reason code in bits 23-16 is changed or corrected. When the action code is set to x'02' the Sequence cannot be retried and further recovery, such as abort Sequence, may be required.

Bits 15-8 are reserved and bits 7-0 may be used for vendor unique information.

The parameter field organization is the same as used for the P_RJT discussed earlier. Table 51 on page 250 summarizes the reject action and reason codes.

16.5 Creation of ACK, F_BSY, P_BSY, F_RJT, and RJT

The format of ACK, F_BSY, P_BSY, F_RJT, and P_RJT frames is arranged to simplify the processing required to create the response frame. All of these response frames are created by manipulation of the header of the frame being responded to. The data field of the received frame, if any, is discarded (all link control frames have a zero-length data field) and a new CRC calculated on the header.

The SOFn1, SOFn2 or SOFi Start-of-Frame delimiter is used (same as the class of service of the frame) for all ACK, F_BSY, P_BSY, F_RJT, and P_RJT frames.

The End-of-Frame delimiter depends on whether the Sequence is terminated by the response or is still open following the ACK, F_BSY, P_BSY, F_RJT, and P_RJT. If the Sequence is terminated, the appropriate Sequence terminating delimiter is used (EOFt or EOFdt).

Action Code 31-24	Reason Code 23-16	F_RJT P_RJT	Explanation	Retry ?
x'01'	x'01'	F_RJT P_RJT	Invalid D_ID: F_RJT - The fabric is unable to locate the destination Nx_Port Address. P_RJT - The node port that received this frame does not recognize the D_ID as its own.	Y
x'01'	x'02'	F_RJT P_RJT	Invalid S_ID: F_RJT - The S_ID does not match the Nx_Port ID assigned by the fabric. P_RJT - The destination node port does not recognize the S_ID as valid.	Y
x'01'	x'03'	F_RJT	Nx_Port not available, temporary: The node port specified is a valid destination address, but the node port is not functionally available. The node port is on-line and may be performing a Link Recovery protocol, for example.	Y
x'01'	x'04'	F_RJT	Nx_Port not available, permanent: The node port specified by the D_ID is a valid destination address, but the node port is not functionally available. The node port is offline or powered down.	Y
x'01'	x'05'	F_RJT P_RJT	Class of service not supported: The class of service specified by the frame being rejected is not supported.	Y
x'02'	x'06'	F_RJT P_RJT	Delimiter usage error: The SOF or EOF is not appropriate for the current conditions. For example, a SOFc1 is received when a Class-1 connection is already established.	N
x'02'	x'07'	F_RJT P_RJT	Type not supported: The type field of the frame being rejected is not supported by the port sending the reject.	N
x'02'	x'08'	P_RJT	Invalid link control: The command specified in the Information Category bits within R_CTL is invalid or not supported as a link control frame.	N
x'02'	x'09'	P_RJT	Invalid R_CTL field: R_CTL is invalid or inconsistent with the other frame header fields or conditions present.	N
x'02'	x'0A'	P_RJT	Invalid F_CTL field: F_CTL is invalid or inconsistent with the other frame header fields or conditions present.	N
x'02'	x'0B'	P_RJT	Invalid OX_ID: The OX_ID field is invalid or inconsistent with the other frame header fields or conditions present.	N
x'02'	x'0C'	P_RJT	Invalid RX_ID: The RX_ID field is invalid or inconsistent with the other frame header fields or conditions present.	N
x'02'	x'0D'	P_RJT	Invalid SEQ_ID: The SEQ_ID field is invalid or inconsistent with the other frame header fields or conditions present.	N
x'02'	x'0E'	P_RJT	Invalid DF_CTL: The DF_CTL field is invalid.	N

Table 51. P_RJT and F_RJT Action and Reason Codes (Part 1 of 3)

Action Code 31-24	Reason Code 23-16	F_RJT P_RJT	Explanation	Retry ?
x'02'	x'0F'	P_RJT	Invalid SEQ_CNT: The SEQ_CNT field is invalid or inconsistent with the other frame header fields or conditions present. This reject is not used to indicate out-of-order or missing data frames.	N
x'02'	x'10'	P_RJT	Invalid Parameter Field: The parameter field is incorrectly specified or invalid.	N
x'02'	x'11'	P_RJT	Exchange Error: An error has been detected in the identified Exchange (OX_ID). This could indicate data frame transmission without Sequence Initiative.	N
x'02'	x'12'	P_RJT	Protocol Error: An error has been detected that violates the rules of FC-2 signaling protocol and is not specified by other error codes.	N
x'02'	x'13'	F_RJT P_RJT	Incorrect Length: The frame being rejected is an incorrect length for the conditions present (e.g., a link control frame with a non-zero length data field).	N
x'02'	x'14'	P_RJT	Unexpected ACK: An ACK was received from an unexpected S_ID. The ACK was received from a logged-in port but was not for an open Sequence or Exchange.	N
x'02'	x'15'	F_RJT	Class of service not supported by x'FF FF FE': The class of service specified by the frame being rejected is not supported.	N
x'01'	x'16'	F_RJT P_RJT	Login required: An Exchange is being initiated before login has been performed.	Y
x'01'	x'17'	P_RJT	Excessive Sequences attempted: A new Sequence was initiated by a node port that exceeded the capability of the Sequence recipient as specified during node port login.	Y
x'01'	x'18'	P_RJT	Unable to establish Exchange: A new Exchange was initiated by a node port that exceeded the capability of the responder.	Y
x'01'	x'19'		Obsolete (was Expiration_Security_Header not supported)	
x'02'	x'1A'	F_RJT	Fabric path not available: The speed of the source and destination node ports does not match. Other fabric characteristics related to multiple fabric elements may also use this reason code.	N
x'02'	x'1B'		Obsolete (was Class-4 Invalid VC_ID)	
x'02'	x'1C'	F_RJT P_RJT	Invalid CS_CTL:	N
	x'1D'		Obsolete (was Class-4 Insufficient Resources for VC	
x'02'	x'1E'		Obsolete (was Dedicated Simplex not supported)	
x'02'	x'1F'	F_RJT P_RJT	Invalid Class of Service:	N
x'02'	x'20'	F_RJT	Preemption Request Rejected:	N

Table 51. P_RJT and F_RJT Action and Reason Codes (Part 2 of 3)

Action Code 31-24	Reason Code 23-16	F_RJT P_RJT	Explanation	Retry ?
x'02'	x'21'	F_RJT	Preemption not enabled:	N
x'02'	x'22'	F_RJT	Multicast error:	N
x'02'	x'23'	F_RJT	Multicast error terminate:	N
x'01'	x'24'	P_RJT	Process Login required:	R
x'02'	x'25'	F_RJT	Invalid attachment state:	N
x'01' x'02'	x'FF'		Vendor unique, retryable or non-retryable	Y/N
Others	Others		reserved	

Table 51. P_RJT and F_RJT Action and Reason Codes (Part 3 of 3)

The steps used are:

1. The Start-of-Frame delimiter is set to SOFnx, where "x" is the same as the class of service of the frame being busied.

2. R_CTL is set to indicate which response is being generated:
   - x'C0', for ACK_1
   - x'C1', for ACK_0
   - x'C2', for P_RJT
   - x'C3', for F_RJT
   - x'C4', for P_BSY
   - x'C5' for F_BSY to a data frame
   - x'C6' for F_BSY to a link control frame

3. The destination and source ID fields (D_ID and S_ID) are swapped (the source of the received frame becomes the destination of the response).

4. If F_BSY is being sent, bits 31-28 of the type field are set to indicate the F_BSY reason, otherwise, the type field is set to x'00'.
   - If the F_BSY is in response to a link control frame, bits 27-24 of R_CTL of the link control frame are copied to bits 27-24 of the type field.

5. In F_CTL,
   - the Exchange Context and Sequence Context bits (23-22) are inverted.
   - if this is an ACK, the Abort Sequence Condition bits (5-4) are set to inform the Sequence initiator what action to take regarding continued transmission of this Sequence.
   - if this is an ACK, other bits in F_CTL may be set as well.

6. All other header fields, and bits not specifically mentioned, are copied from the frame being responded to.

7. The data field, if any, is discarded.

8. The CRC is recalculated.

9. The appropriate End-of-Frame delimiter is selected as follows:

- In Class-1, if F_BSY is in response to a Class-1 connect request frame (SOFc1), the EOFdt End-of-Frame delimiter is used, otherwise EOFn is used.

- If P_BSY, and the action code indicates that the Sequence is terminated, the appropriate Sequence terminating End-of-Frame delimiter is used (EOFt or EOFdt), otherwise EOFn is used.

- If F_RJT or P_RJT, and the sender of the reject has terminated the Sequence, the appropriate Sequence terminating End-of-Frame delimiter is used (EOFt or EOFdt), otherwise EOFn is used.

16.6 Link Credit Reset (LCR)

Link Credit Reset (LCR) is a link control command used to reset the end-to-end credit between a pair of node ports to the login value. LCR is normally only issued in Class-2 and is sent by a node port to a specific destination node port to recover from lost end-to-end credit conditions that may result from lost ACKs due to transmission errors. Because LCR is used to recover from out of credit conditions, it is not subject to end-to-end credit and can be sent even if the end-to-end credit is zero.

After sending LCR, the node port waits for R_A_TOV before initiating any new Sequences with the destination port. This ensures that any frames associated with open Sequences from the issuing port to the LCR recipient have been purged.

When LCR is received by the destination port, the end-to-end credit with the port sending the LCR is reset to its login value and any data frames present in the destination port's receive buffers for the port issuing the LCR are discarded.

Because frames may be discarded as a result LCR, all active Sequences (of any class of service initiated by the port issuing LCR to the destination port are abnormally terminated. Any Exchange and Sequence error recovery that may be necessary is performed by the higher-level processes.

While LCR does not remove a Class-1 connection, if a connection exists when the decision is made to send LCR, it should be removed prior to sending LCR. This is due to the fact that Class-1 frames may be discarded as a result of LCR. LCR is not intended to be used to recover from out-of-credit conditions during Class-1 operations—that is accomplished by using the Link Reset protocol.

LCR is one of the rare cases where a frame is not considered a part of any Exchange or Sequence. All fields in the frame header other than R_CTL, D_ID, and S_ID are reserved (set to zero by the issuing port and not checked by the receiving port). The SOFn2 Start-of-Frame and EOFn End-of-Frame delimiters are used. Because the OX_ID, RX_ID, and SEQ_ID are all set to zero, they may potentially conflict with an existing Exchange.

There is no expected reply to LCR, although it may receive F_BSY or F_RJT from the fabric. LCR may also receive P_RJT with a reason code of "Invalid D_ID", or "Class not supported".

16.7 Notify (NTY)

Notify (NTY) is a link control command sent by the fabric to a node port currently involved in a Class-1 connection to inform the node port that a Class-1 Camp-on connection request exists at its fabric port. This is a request by the fabric for the node port to begin the end connection protocol on the current connection so the pending connection can be made.

NTY is sent using Class-2 delimiters and is only allowed if the destination node port supports Class-1 intermix. There is no reply to NTY.

NTY is not considered to be part of any Exchange or Sequence. All fields in the frame header other than R_CTL, D_ID, and S_ID are reserved (set to zero by the issuing port and not checked by the receiving port). The SOFn2 Start-of-Frame and EOFn End-of-Frame delimiters are used. The D_ID is the address of the destination node port, the S_ID is the address of the Fabric Controller (x'FF FF FD').

Like other link control commands, Notify NTY may be sent without regard to end-to-end credit and does not participate in end-to-end flow control.

16.8 End (END)

End has been obsoleted by FC-FS.

Chapter Summary

Link Control Frames

- Link control frames provide three functions
  - Link continue frames (acknowledgments)
  - Link response frames (reject or busy)
  - Link control commands that initiate a low-level action at the destination port
- No data field is present in link control frames
- All the necessary information is contained in the frame header

Acknowledge (ACK)

- Used during Class-1, Class-2 and Class-F operations
  - Not used by Class-3
- Confirms successful delivery to the correct recipient
- Provides end-to-end flow control
  - Indicates the Sequence recipient's readiness to receive another frame
- Each frame is acknowledged only once

ACK Policies

- Fibre Channel provides two different acknowledgment policies
  - ACK_1 is the default with one ACK per frame
  - ACK_0 allows a Sequence to be acknowledged with a single ACK_0
- ACK_1 is the default prior to N_Port Login
  - ACK_1 is required for Class-F
- Either ACK_1 or ACK_0 can be used as the default after N_Port Login
  - Use of ACK_0 as the default was added by FC-PH amendment 2

ACK Generation

- ACK are simple to create from the header of the received frame
  - R_CTL is set to x'C0' for ACK_1 or x'C1' for ACK_0
  - The D_ID and S_ID fields are swapped
  - The Type field is set to zero
  - The Exchange and Sequence context bits in F_CTL are inverted
  - The OX_ID, RX_ID, SEQ_ID are copied from the data frame
  - The SEQ_CNT is set equal to the SEQ_CNT of the highest frame being acknowledged
  - The parameter field is set to indicate the number of frames being acknowledged

Reject (P_RJT or F_RJT)

- A port rejects a frame to provide notification that a valid frame could not be processed
  - Frame was received correctly (no CRC error)
- RJT provides an action and reason code
- The action code indicates if the frame may be retried once the condition is corrected
- The reason code specifies why the reject was sent, for example
  - Wrong destination address
  - Unsupported class of service, etc.

Fabric/Port Busy (F_BSY/P_BSY)

- F_BSY is returned when the fabric is unable to deliver a frame due to a busy condition
- P_BSY is returned when a node port is temporarily busy and unable to process a frame
- When F_BSY/P_BSY is sent, the fabric/port provides a reason code
- F_BSY/P_BSY does not apply to all frames:
  - In Class-1/6, busy is only allowed on the connect request frame
  - In Class-2 or Class-F any frame may receive busy
  - In Class-3 busy is not sent. If a frame can't be delivered, it is discarded without notification

17. Flow Control

One of the goals of Fibre Channel is to provide reliable delivery of information from sender to receiver. One way to enhance reliable delivery is to ensure the physical layer (FC-0) and encode layers (FC-1) provide a data link with a low bit-error rate. However, simply minimizing the number of bit-level transmission errors in not enough. One must also ensure consistent and reliable frame delivery. Flow control is one mechanism that provides this reliability.

When a port sends a frame, the frame is built in a transmit buffer, then bytes that make up the frame are encoded, serialized, and transmitted on the transmit fiber. When the frame arrives at the receiving port at the end of that fiber, the bits are deserialized, decoded, and the frame is temporarily held in a receive buffer. Figure 105 illustrates how frames are transferred from the transmit buffers in a sending port to the receive buffers in a receiving port.

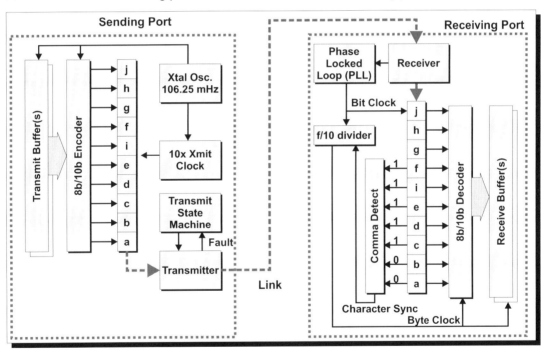

Figure 105. Transmit and Receive Buffers

To improve performance, most ports provide more than one transmit and receive buffer. Multiple transmit buffers allows a port to build new frames while previous frames are being transmitted. Multiple receive buffers allow a port to continue receiving new frames while previously received frames are being processed.

As frames arrive at a receiving port, they occupy available receive buffers while awaiting processing. If frames arrive faster than a receiving port is able to process them, the available receive buffers will fill up. If all available receive buffers are full and another frame arrives, there is no place to store the frame and it will be discarded (a condition commonly referred to as a buffer overrun). Discarded frames are undesirable because they result in Sequence delivery failures and the resulting error recovery processing.

17.1 Credit

To prevent buffer overrun, Fiber Channel provides flow control mechanisms, called credit, to regulate the flow of frames from a sending port to a receiving port. Credit is permission granted by a receiving port to a sending port to send a specified number of frames. An example how credit is used to control frame transmission is shown in Figure 106.

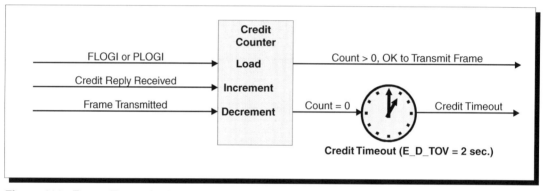

Figure 106. Frame Transmission and Credit

A receiving port gives the sending port credit during login (or through dynamic signaling on an arbitrated loop). This allows the sending port to transmit one or more frames (each credit is permission to send one frame). When a frame is sent (actually, the SOF), the available credit is decremented by one. If the available credit reaches zero, no more frames can be sent until the credit is replenished (becomes non-zero).

When a frame arrives at a receiving port, it occupies one of the available receive buffers. As the frame is processed and the receive buffer becomes available, the receiving port sends a response to the sender indicating it is ready to receive another frame. This indication replenishes the available credit allowing another frame to be sent. In this manner, the rate of frame transmission is regulated by the receiving port based on the availability of buffers to hold received frames.

The optimal amount of credit that is required depends on the link speed and distance. It takes light approximately 5 nsec. to propagate through each meter of optical fiber. If two ports are connected by a 10 km. optical link, it will take approximately 50 μsec. for the frame to travel from one end of the optical fiber to the other end. The receiving port processes the received frame and generates a response (that takes another 50 μsec. to reach the sending port). The result is a round-trip time of approximately 100 μsec.

Figure 107 shows how round trip delays and the credit values can affect performance. In this example, the sending port has a credit of one. When the sending port transmits a frame, it decrements its available credit to zero. It must wait for the frame to reach the other port, be processed, and a response to be returned. With a round-trip delay of 100 μsec., the sending port will only be able to transmit a frame once every 100 usec., or 10,000 frames per second. If each frame transfers 2,048 bytes of payload, the effective link throughput is approximately 20.48 megabytes per second (2,048 bytes per frame x 10,000 frames per second).

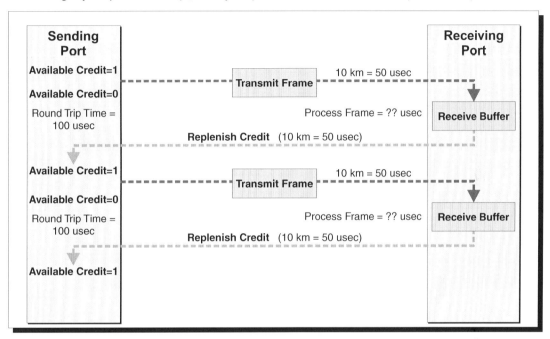

Figure 107. Timing Example for Credit=1

This is not very efficient, and, the situation becomes even worse on faster links, longer-distance links, when smaller frames are sent, or through complex topologies that contribute significant delivery latencies. What is needed is a way to achieve higher performance while still preventing the overrun of receive buffers. This is provided by the use of larger credit values in order to enable frame streaming.

17.1.1 Credit and Frame Streaming

If a sending port can send more than one frame without having to wait for a response to each, performance can be improved. This behavior is referred to as frame streaming and is key to achieving high performance over long links.

If the time required to transmit a series of frames is greater than the round-trip time, the sender will receive the response to the first frame before the last frame is sent and the available credit never reaches zero. An example of how a larger available credit allows frame streaming is shown in Figure 108. In this example, the sender has a credit of four. This enables the sender to send up to four frames based on the available credit (it is not necessary to wait for a response to each frame before sending the next frame). When sufficient credit is available, the response to the first frame is received before the available credit reaches zero and frame transmission can continue without interruption.

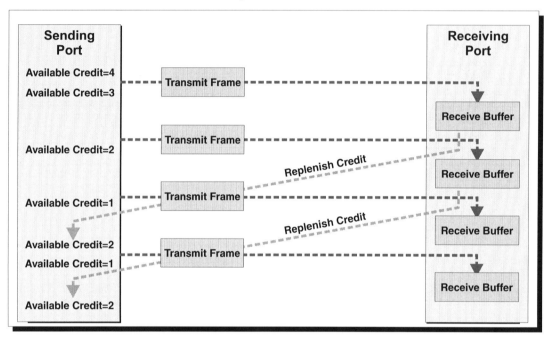

Figure 108. Frame Transmission and Credit

17.1.2 Determining the Optimal Credit Value

The optimal amount of credit is determined by the distance (or latency, to be more precise), the processing time at the receiving port, link signaling rate, and the size of the frames being transmitted. The formula to determine the optimal credit is:

Credit = (Round_Trip_Time + Receiving_Port_Processing_Time)/Frame_Transmission_Time

Using the 10 km. link discussed earlier, the round-trip time is 100 μsec. Assuming a processing time of 10 μsec. per frame at the receiving port and a 10 μsec. frame transmission time (both based on a 2,048 byte frame and 200 MB/sec), this formula yields the following result:

$$(100 \ \mu sec. + 10 \ \mu sec.) / 10 \ \mu sec. = 11 \ Credits$$

This formula is dependent on three key parameters; the round trip time (the distance), the frame processing time, and the frame transmission time. If any of these parameters change, the optimal credit value changes. For example, if the link distance is increased to 30 km, the round-trip time is increased by a factor of three to 300 μsec. and the amount of available credit necessary to obtain full link utilization when transmitting 2,048 byte frames increases to 16.

$$(300 \text{ μsec.} + 10 \text{ μsec.}) / 10 \text{ μsec.} = 31 \text{ Credits}$$

When shorter frames are sent (i.e., 128 bytes), each frame requires less transmission time. If 128 byte frames are sent over a 10 km. link, the round trip time doesn't change (it is determined by the speed of light through the fiber), but the frame transmission time is now approximately 0.85 μsec. Again, assuming the receiving port requires one frame time for processing, the formula becomes:

$$(100 \text{ μsec.} + 0.85 \text{ μsec.}) / 0.85 \text{ μsec.} = 118.6 \text{ Credits}$$

Table 52 summarizes the number of frames in transit for different combinations of frame data field sizes and link distances for 100 MB/sec. links. For longer distances or higher speeds, the values scale in a linear fashion. A 100 km. link operating at 100 MB/sec. could have 1,155 32-byte frames in transit. For a 10 km. link operating at 200 MB/sec., the number of 32 byte frames in transit could be 2,310. The values shown in Table 52 do not include time that may be required for the receiving port to process received frames, nor for the source port to process responses. These times need to be added to the values in the table to obtain the total round trip time and optimal credit values.

Data Field Size	Frame Time on a 100 MB/sec link (usec.)	Potential Number of Frames in Transit for a 1 gigabit Link (each km is equivalent to 10 usec. round trip)									
		1 km.	2 km.	3 km.	4 km.	5 km.	6 km.	7 km.	8 km.	9 km.	10 km.
32	0.87	11.56	23.1	34.7	46.2	57.8	69.31	80.9	92.4	104.0	115.5
64	1.17	8.6	17.1	25.7	34.3	42.9	51.4	60.0	68.6	77.1	86.7
128	1.77	5.7	11.3	17.0	22.6	28.3	33.9	29.6	45.2	50.9	56.5
256	2.97	3.4	6.7	10.1	13.5	16.8	20.2	23.5	26.9	30.3	33.6
512	5.38	1.9	3.7	5,6	7.4	9.3	11.1	13.0	14.9	16.7	18.6
1024	10.20	1.0	2.0	2.9	3.9	4.9	5.9	6.9	7.8	8.8	9.8
2048	19.84	0.5	1.0	1.5	2.0	2.5	3.0	3.5	4.0	4.5	5.0

Table 52. Number of Frames in Transit for Various Data Field Sizes vs. Link Distances

Note that while the number of credits needed to maintain full link utilization increases as the frame size decreases, the amount of memory required remains essentially the same. If the round trip time is 120 usec., a sending port operating at 1062.5 megabaud can transmit 12,750 bytes in this amount of time. Whether those bytes are used to send 2,048 byte frames or 128 byte frames is secondary (ignoring the overhead associated with each frame).

17.2 Different Types of Flow Control

The obvious place to apply flow control is at the link level to control the flow of frames from the transmit buffers to the receive buffers in the port at the opposite end of the link. This level of flow control is called buffer-to-buffer flow control and uses buffer-to-buffer credit.

Because buffer-to-buffer flow control is a link-level flow control, it applies individually to both fibers of every link in the entire system. When buffer-to-buffer flow control is used, no port is permitted to send a frame on any link unless there is a buffer to hold that frame at the receiving end of the link. As a result, buffer-to-buffer flow control is sufficient to prevent buffer overruns and the associated frame loss. Buffer-to-buffer flow control is described in detail in *Buffer-to-Buffer Flow Control (BB_Credit)* on page 263.

However, buffer-to-buffer flow control does not provide a way for a destination port to control frame transmission by a source port unless the ports are directly connected in a point-to-point or arbitrated loop configuration. In a fabric topology, buffer-to-buffer flow control provides a mechanism to control the flow of frames between the node port and fabric port, but not between the two node ports.

This level of flow control is provided by a second mechanism called end-to-end flow control that uses end-to-end credit. End-to-end flow control is described in *End-to-End Flow Control (EE_Credit)* on page 268.

Figure 109 illustrates the scope of each type of flow control.

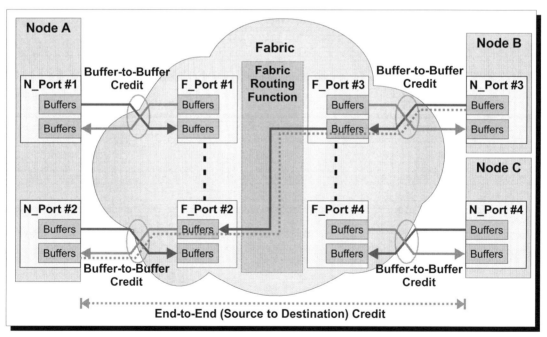

Figure 109. Flow Control Between Two Node Ports Connected via a Fabric

17.2.1 Obtaining Credit

Credit is obtained during N_Port and fabric login (this is called the login credit and is used to initialize the available credit value between the ports). On an arbitrated loop, credit is granted both during the login process and dynamically when a loop circuit is opened.

Prior to login with the other port, there is a set of default service parameters, including credit that enable the login to be performed and actual credit values established.

17.3 Buffer-to-Buffer Flow Control (BB_Credit)

Buffer-to-buffer flow control is a link-level flow control mechanism available for managing the rate of frame transmission between two ports on a link or arbitrated loop circuit. The actual ports involved in buffer-to-buffer flow control depend on the interconnection topology.

17.3.1 Buffer-to-Buffer Flow Control Protocol

The purpose of buffer-to-buffer flow control is to prevent overrunning a receiver's buffers by controlling a sending port's permission to transmit a frame beginning with any of the following Start-of-Frame delimiters:

- Start-of-Frame connect Class-1 (SOFc1)
- Start-of-Frame initiate or Start-of-Frame normal Class-2 (SOFi2 or SOFn2)
- Start-of-Frame initiate or Start-of-Frame normal Class-3 (SOFi3 or SOFn3)
- Start-of-Frame fabric (SOFf) on an inter-switch link when using buffer-to-buffer flow control on that link.

In order to transmit a frame beginning with one of the above SOF delimiters, the available BB_Credit must be greater than zero. Transmitting one of the applicable frame types when the available BB_Credit is zero is a violation of the protocol and may result in frame loss due to lack of a receive buffer at the other port.

When a sending port begins frame transmission and transmits one of the listed SOF delimiters, the available BB_Credit is decremented. If the port is unable to complete frame transmission, the frame is terminated with an End-of-Frame abort (EOFa). If the available BB_Credit is non-zero, additional frames may be sent until the available BB_Credit is zero, provided the following conditions are met:

- Certain frames may also be subject to end-to-end credit. If that is the case, the available end-to-end credit must also be non-zero.
- Streamed Sequence restrictions may prevent data frame transmission across Sequence boundaries, even if credit is available.

When a receiving port recognizes one of the listed SOF delimiters, it owes the sending port an R_RDY when the receive buffer associated with the frame becomes available. This is true even if the received Start-of-Frame is not associated with a valid frame. This includes the following conditions (there may be others as well):

- A frame beginning with one of the above SOF delimiters has an 8b/10b error during the frame content.

- A frame beginning with one of the above SOF delimiters has a CRC error.

- A frame beginning with one of the above SOF delimiters has frame content that results in a rejectable condition (whether a reject is actually sent or not is irrelevant).

- A frame beginning with one of the above SOF delimiters is terminated with an inappropriate EOF.

- A frame beginning with one of the above SOF delimiters is terminated with an EOFa, EOFni, EOFdti.

- A frame beginning with one of the above SOF delimiters contains fewer than seven words of frame content between the SOF and EOF.

- A frame beginning with one of the above SOF delimiters exceeds the size of the receive data buffer.

- A frame beginning with one of the above SOF delimiters is terminated by an Ordered Set other than a valid EOF (note that any Ordered Set terminates the frame).

When a receiver ready (R_RDY) Primitive Signal is received, the available BB_Credit value is incremented. Unless the alternate BB_Credit management model is in use, the available BB_Credit is not permitted to increment past the login BB_Credit value (see the discussion of the *Alternate BB_Credit Management Model* on page 264).

R_RDY only applies to the link on which it is received and is not propagated through a fabric. Receipt of R_RDY indicates the port at the other end of the link is ready to receive another frame. It does not mean that the frame associated with that receive buffer was valid (a frame with a CRC error is discarded without processing and results in the receive buffer being freed and an R_RDY sent).

17.3.2 Alternate BB_Credit Management Model

The alternate BB_Credit management model is used in the arbitrated loop topology to manage the flow of frames between the two ports participating in the current loop circuit. This model differs from the standard model in the following areas:

- Login BB_Credit is used with the following changes:
  - Prior to login, the available BB_Credit is assumed to be zero.
  - The login BB_Credit granted to another port may be zero.
  - A port may assume the login BB_Credit is zero, even if another port granted a non-zero value during login. The port is not obligated to remember or use the login credit.
  - A separate login BB_Credit may be received from each port in the loop.
- When a loop circuit is opened, the following actions occur:
  - The login BB_Credit for the specific ports are used to initialize the available BB_Credit for that loop circuit, which may be zero.
  - One or more R_RDYs is sent by each port to indicate the number of receive buffers available. The dynamic signaling of BB_Credit allows ports with zero available BB_Credit to begin frame transmission.

- If a loop circuit is opened with a port that granted a login BB_Credit of zero and the port does not have any available receive buffers, it may close the loop circuit without sending an R_RDY.
- When the loop circuit is closed, the following occurs:
  - Available BB_Credit is set to zero (it is re-established when a loop circuit is opened).
  - Any outstanding R_RDYs are not transmitted.

Use of the alternate BB_Credit management model is required in arbitrated loop environments. While use of the alternate does not appear to be specifically prohibited in other topologies, it is not clear how it might be used. Support of the alternate BB_Credit model is indicated during the login process.

17.3.3 Obtaining Buffer-to-Buffer Credit

The means by which buffer-to-buffer credit is established depends on the topology.

- Buffer-to-buffer credit (BB_Credit) is granted during the N_Port Login (PLOGI) in a point-to-point topology or when logging in with an NL_Port on the same arbitrated loop.
- Buffer-to-buffer credit is granted during Fabric Login (FLOGI) in a fabric topology or on a public arbitrated loop.
- Buffer-to-buffer credit is also granted dynamically when a circuit is opened between two ports on an arbitrated loop by transmitting one R_RDY for each available buffer.
- Buffer-to-buffer credit is granted during the Exchange Link Parameters (ELP) switch internal link service between two E_Ports, or between an E_Port and a B_Port.

Prior to N_Port Login or Fabric Login in a non-loop topology or Exchange Link Parameters on an inter-switch link, the buffer-to-buffer credit is one. This allows the login or Exchange Link Parameters request to be sent.

Prior to N_Port Login or Fabric Login on an arbitrated loop, the buffer-to-buffer credit is zero. Credit to perform the login is granted when the loop circuit is opened via the dynamic signaling protocol using R_RDYs.

17.3.4 Buffer-to-Buffer Credit Recovery

Due to transmission errors, one or more frames or R_RDY Primitive Signals can be corrupted such that it is not recognized by the receiver. A frame error that causes the SOF to be corrupted may result in the receiving port failing to recognize the frame and generate the subsequent R_RDY. Similarly, a transmission error that causes an R_RDY to become corrupted may result in the receiving port failing to recognize the R_RDY. Both of these conditions may result in the loss of use of one receive buffer because the available BB_Credit is not replenished.

Over an extended period of time, enough credits could be lost to cause the link performance to degrade without any explicit error indication. The user would simply perceive that operations seemed to be taking longer, but examination of the link statistics would not necessarily reveal an excessive number of errors.

To prevent link degradation due to lost Buffer-to-Buffer credit conditions, the standards provide multiple methods to enable credit recovery.

Buffer-to-Buffer Credit Recovery by Link Reset. Lost BB_Credit can be recovered in a point-to-point or fabric environment by use of the Link Reset protocol (which restores the available BB_Credit back to the login BB_Credit) or by performing a relogin. Fabric login does not cause existing N_Port Logins to be removed, but N_Port Login (as might be used in a point-to-point environment) terminates all open Exchanges. The Link Reset protocol may cause one or more frames to be discarded by the receiving port and can result in potential Sequence delivery failures.

One of the problems associated with using link reset as a credit recovery mechanism is determining when credit recovery is required. If one waits until the credit is exhausted for E_D_TOV (a clear indication of a credit problem), performance may have been seriously degraded for an extended time. On the other hand, issuing link reset when one simply suspects a credit problem may result in lost frames and errors.

Due to the potentially disruptive nature of link reset or relogin, this method is not desirable during normal operation unless other methods do not exist or are not usable.

Buffer-to-Buffer Credit Recovery by BB_SCx. The Fibre Channel Framing and Signaling document (FC-FS) adds a new method for BB_Credit recovery that does not require a link reset. This avoids the potential disruption and lost frames that may occur when the link is reset. It also provides a method to detect lost BB_Credit and dynamically recover the lost credit without interrupting normal frame transmission.

When this BB_Credit recovery method is used, a BB_Credit recovery parameter (BB_SC_N) is communicated during Fabric Login (FLOGI) in the fabric topology, or N_Port Login (PLOGI) in the point-to-point topology (this method is not needed on an arbitrated loop topology - see *Buffer-to-Buffer Credit Recovery on an Arbitrated Loop* on page 267). If the two ports indicate different BB_SC_N values during login, the larger of the two values is used by both ports.

BB_SC_N is used to compute a value based on the following formula:

$$\text{Computed Value} = 2^{\text{BB\_SC\_N}}$$

The computed value specifies the number of frames to be sent between BB_SCs (Buffer-to-Buffer State Change - SOF) Primitive Signals, and the number of R_RDYs sent between BB_SCr (Buffer-to-Buffer State Change - R_RDY) Primitive Signals.

For example, if BB_SC_N equals three, the computed value is:

$$\text{Computed Value} = 2^3$$

In this case, each port will send BB_SCs after every eight frames that are subject to buffer-to-buffer flow control. Each port will also send BB_SCr after every eight R_RDYs. BB_SCs and BB_SCr establish checkpoints every BB_SC_N frames and R_RDYs allowing the receiving port to detect lost frames and lost R_RDYs.

Each port maintains a count of the number of frames received between the completion of login and receipt of the first BB_SCs as well as between successive occurrences of BB_SCs. When the count of the number of frames reaches the computed value determined by BB_SC_N, it wraps back to zero and starts over. If the count of the number of frames received is not zero when BB_SCs is received, one or more frames has been lost.

If computed value is eight, but only seven frames have been received since the last BB_SCs, the receiving port knows that one frame was transmitted by the sending port, but not recognized by the receiving port. The sending port decremented its available buffer-to-buffer credit when the frame was sent and now requires an R_RDY from the receiving port to replenish its available credit. In this case, the receiving port generates one R_RDY to replenish the credit for the lost frame. The formula for determining the number of R_RDYs to send is:

$$\text{BB\_Credits lost by other port} = (2^{BB\_SC\_N} - \text{BB\_Fames received}) \text{ modulo } 2^{BB\_SC\_N}$$

When BB_SCs is received and any necessary R_RDYs transmitted, the frame count is set to zero in preparation for the next interval.

Likewise, each port maintains a count of the number of R_RDYs received between completion of login and receipt of the first BB_SCr as sell as between successive occurrences of BB_SCr. When the count of the number of R_RDYs reaches the computed value based on BB_SC_N, it wraps back to zero and starts over. If the count of the number of R_RDYs received is not zero when BB_SCr is received, one or more R_RDYs has been lost.

If the computed value based on BB_SC_N is eight, but only seven R_RDYs have been received since the last BB_SCr, the R_RDY counter in the port will be seven and the port knows that one R_RDY has been lost. In this case, it can increment its available BB_Credit by one to recover the lost R_RDY. The formula for determining the number of BB_Credits to recover is:

$$\text{BB\_Credits lost} = (2^{BB\_SC\_N} - \text{R\_RDYs received}) \text{ modulo } 2^{BB\_SC\_N}$$

When BB_SCr is received and any necessary available credit adjustments made, the R_RDY count is set to zero in preparation for the next interval.

Because it is possible for a BB_SCs or BB_SCr Ordered Set to be lost due to transmission errors the recovery mechanism needs to accommodate this possibility as well. This is the reason the formulas for determining the number of lost frames and lost R_RDYs uses the modulo of the computed value. By doing this, the determination that occurs on the next BB_SCs or BB_SCr will correctly determine the number of lost frames or lost R_RDYs in two measurement intervals. The only error condition not detected by this scheme is if all the frames or R_RDYs are lost between BB_SCs or BB_SCr Ordered Sets.

Buffer-to-Buffer Credit Recovery on an Arbitrated Loop. In the arbitrated loop topology, lost BB_Credit is automatically recovered when the current loop circuit is closed and a new loop circuit opened. This is due to the fact that the available BB_Credit is established when a new loop circuit is opened based on the login credit and dynamic signaling using the R_RDY Primitive Signal.

If one or more frames or R_RDYs are corrupted and not recognized by the receiving port, performance may be adversely affected for the remainder of that loop circuit, but not subsequent loop circuits. As a result, no explicit method beyond the normal behavior is necessary to provide credit recovery on the arbitrated loop.

17.4 End-to-End Flow Control (EE_Credit)

End-to-end flow control is a source node port to destination node port flow control mechanism that is available for managing the rate of frame transmission between two node ports.

17.4.1 End-to-End Flow Control Protocol

The purpose of end-to-end flow control is to manage data frame (FT-1) transmission between node ports. End-to-end credit (EE_Credit) is managed on a per-port basis and is granted during N_Port Login (PLOGI) with the associated port. This credit is referred to as the login EE_Credit and is used to initialize the available EE_Credit for that port.

Sequence Initiator. The Sequence initiator observes the following behavior for frames subject to end-to-end flow control (end-to-end flow control does not apply when ACK_0 is used).

Certain frames may also be subject to buffer-to-buffer credit. If that is the case, the available buffer-to-buffer credit must also be non-zero. In addition, streamed Sequence restrictions may prevent data frame transmission across Sequence boundaries, even if credit is available.

1. The Sequence initiator is not allowed to transmit a frame subject to end-to-end flow control unless the login EE_Credit and available EE_Credit are both greater than zero (and, if applicable, the BB_Credit is greater than zero).

2. At the end of N_Port Login available EE_Credit is set to the login EE_Credit value.

3. In Class-1 or Class-6, the available EE_Credit is set to the login EE_Credit-1 when the connect request frame (SOFc1) is sent and decremented as each subsequent Class-1 or Class-6 data frame is sent.

4. In Class-2 or Class-F, the available EE_Credit is decremented as each Class-2 data frame is sent.

5. If ACK_1 with the history bit=1, F_BSY to a data frame, F_RJT, P_BSY, or P_RJT is received, the available EE_Credit is incremented by +1.

6. If ACK_1 is received and the history bit=0, available EE_Credit is incremented by +1 for the ACK_1 and each unacknowledged data frame with a SEQ_CNT lower than the ACK. If an ACK with a lower SEQ_CNT arrives later, available EE_Credit is not incremented.

7. If ACK_1 terminated with EOFt or EOFdt is received, the available EE_Credit is incremented by +1 for each unacknowledged data frame with a SEQ_CNT lower than the ACK_1. If one of those ACKs with a lower SEQ_CNT arrives later, the available EE_Credit is not incremented.

In no case is the available EE_Credit value allowed to exceed the login EE_Credit value.

17.4.2 End-to-End Credit Recovery

Due to transmission errors, it is possible for one or more ACK or other link control frames to be lost or corrupted such that they are not recognized by the receiver. This may cause loss of end-to-end credits at the node port because the available EE_Credit is not replenished. There are several mechanisms that allow lost EE_Credit to be recovered. Among them are:

1. At the end of N_Port Login available EE_Credit is set to the login EE_Credit value.

2. When a dedicated connection is removed, or a virtual circuit is deactivated EE_Credit for any unacknowledged frames can be recovered.

3. The Sequence initiator can recover EE_Credit when an ACK_1 with the history bit=0 is received and previous frames of that Sequence are unacknowledged.

4. The Sequence initiator can recover EE_Credit when the Sequence is terminated, either normally or abnormally. The amount of EE_Credit that is recovered is equal to the number of unacknowledged frames associated with that Sequence.

5. The available EE_Credit is set to the login EE_Credit when a Link Credit Reset (LCR) link control frame is sent or received.

17.4.3 Estimate Credit Procedure

The Fibre Channel standards provide a measurement procedure that enables two ports to estimate the number of frames in transit and adjust credit values based on the round trip time. An illustration of the estimate credit procedure is shown in figure 110 on page 269.

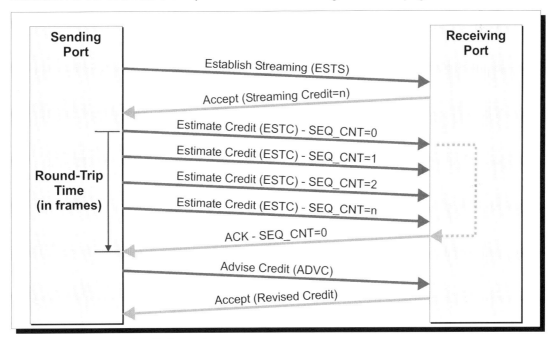

Figure 110. Estimate Credit Procedure

This procedure is only applicable to the end-to-end flow mechanism and probably only makes sense when a connection is established. Use of this procedure, or a similar mechanism, in a connectionless mode of operation may not provide consistent results due to the non-deterministic delivery latency of connectionless operation.

The estimating process consists of three steps:

1. The first is to establish a temporary credit value between the two ports sufficient to allow frames to be streamed to the destination without exhausting the available credit. This is done by use of the Establish Streaming Credit (ESTS) Extended Link Service request (described in *Establish Streaming (ESTS)* on page 335).

2. In the second step, the node port transmits a stream of frames until the first acknowledgment is received. This is done using the Estimate Credit (ESTC) Extended Link Service request (see *Estimate Credit (ESTC)* on page 336). At this point, the node port can determine how many frames have been sent (i.e., the round-trip time).

3. In the final step, the node port advises the other port of the credit it is requesting based on the number of frames in transit discovered in step 2. The advisement is done with the Advise Credit (ADVC) request (*Advise Credit (ADVC)* on page 321).

17.5 Chapter Summary

Flow Control

- Flow control is used to pace the flow of frames between a sending and receiving port
- Receiving ports have one or more receive buffers
- When a frame is received, it occupies a receive buffer
- If all available receive buffers fill there is no place to store another frame
  - If another frame arrives, it may be lost
- Flow control allows the receiver to pace the rate of frame transmission based on buffer availability

Credit

- A receiving port gives a sending port permission to send a specified number of frames
- That permission is called credit
  - When a frame is sent, the credit is decremented (consumed)
  - When a reply is received, the credit is incremented (replenished)
- As long as a port has available credit, it may send additional frames
- If the credit is exhausted, frame transmission is suspended until the credit is replenished

Obtaining Credit

- Credit may be obtained either of two ways:
  - During the login process - referred to as login credit
  - On an arbitrated loop credit is also granted dynamically when a loop circuit is opened

Credit and Frame Streaming

- In addition to preventing overrun of receive buffers, credit can improve link performance
- Credit allows the sender to begin transmission of a series of frames without having to wait for a response to each
  - This helps mask the effect of distance on long links
- If the credit were one,
  - The sender could send a frame and then would have to wait for a reply
  - Then send another frame and wait
  - This can be very inefficient

Credit and Long Links

- Light travels through optical fiber at about 5 nsec. per meter, or 50 usec for 10 km.
  - If a frame is sent on a 10 km. link it will take a minimum of 100 usec for a response to return
- If the credit is one, the maximum number of frames that can be sent is 10,000 per second
  - If each frame has a payload of 2048 bytes, the throughput is just over 20 MBs (10% utilization of a 2 Gbps link)
- If the credit is increased to 2, twice as many frames can be sent (20% utilization)
- When the credit reaches about 10, the link is fully utilized and additional credit doesn't help

Estimate End-to-End Credit Procedure

- Performance on long links can be improved by increasing the credit
- The link itself holds some number of frames
  - A 2k byte frame is about 4 km.long (at 1 Gbps)
- The estimate credit procedure allows the credit to be adjusted based on the number of frames in transit
- The ports setup to stream frames and count how many frames are sent before a response is received
- Then, the credit can be revised to take into account the number of frames in transit

Buffer-to-Buffer Flow Control

- Buffer-to-buffer flow control is a link-level flow control
  - Each frame sent decrements the available buffer-to-buffer credit
  - Each receiver ready (R_RDY) received increments the available credit
- Used for the following frames:
  - Class-1 connect request frame
  - All Class-2 and Class-3 frames
- Does not apply to:
  - Class-1 frames after the connection is established

Topology Dependencies

- Buffer-to-buffer flow control manages different ports depending on the topology
- In the point-to-point topology:
  - It manages the flow between the two N_Ports
- On an arbitrated loop:
  - It manages the flow between the two ports in the loop circuit
  - Which can be two NL_Ports or an NL_Port and an FL_Port
- In a fabric topology:
  - It manages the flow between the N_Port and F_Port

Alternate BB_Credit

- On an arbitrated loop, an alternate BB_Credit model is used
- A login credit of zero can be used
  - Zero credit can be granted during login
  - Zero credit can be assumed, even if the other port grants credit
- Dynamic signaling is also used to provide credit when the loop circuit is opened
  - R_RDYs are sent to notify the other port of the credit for that loop circuit

BB_Credit Recovery

- Frames or R_RDYs may be lost due to transmission errors
  - Can result in loss of available buffers
  - May result in performance degradation
- Point-to-point links
  - Historical recovery was to reset the link (LR)
  - Reset could cause frame loss
- New non-disruptive recovery added in FC-FS
  - Uses BB_SCs and BB_SCr Primitive Signals
  - BB_SCs transmitted every "n" frames
  - BB_SCr transmitted every "n" R_RDYs
- BB_Credit recovery on loop is inherent in the loop protocols

End-to-End Credit

- Manages the flow of frames between two Node Ports
- Applies to:
  - All Class-1and Class-2 frames, except when ACK_0 is used
  - All Class-F frames
  - Does not apply to Class-3 frames
- The port maintains a separate available EE_Credit count for each other Node Port
  - The available credit for that port is decremented when a frame is sent to the port
  - Updated when ACK, BSY, or RJT is received

18. Classes of Service

To support the needs of a wide variety of applications and data types, Fibre Channel has defined multiple delivery options referred to as *classes of service*. Each class of service provides a specific set of delivery attributes such as:

- Is a connection established? If so, how much bandwidth is reserved for that connection?
- Is in-order frame delivery guaranteed?
- Is the delivery latency deterministic?
- Is confirmation of delivery or notification of non-delivery provided?
- How is flow control managed?

The answers to these basic questions form the basis for the different classes of service provided. Table 53 summarizes the characteristics of each class of service.

Attribute	Class-1/6	Class-2/F	Class-3
Connection Oriented (reserves a path)?	Yes	No	No
Bandwidth Reservation?	Yes	No	No
Guaranteed Latency	Yes	No	No
Guaranteed Delivery Order?	Yes	No	No
Delivery Confirmation (ACK)?	Yes	Yes	No
Frame Multiplexing with Different Ports?	No (with Intermix)	Yes	Yes
End-to-End Flow Control	Yes	Yes	No
Link-Level Flow Control	SOFc1 only	Yes	Yes
Usage	Very Limited	Some (e.g., FICON)	Common

Table 53. Class of Service Comparison

18.1 Class-1

Class-1 is a connection-oriented class of service, that establishes a dedicated connection allocating full-bandwidth between a pair of node ports. Class-1 provides confirmation of delivery or notification of non-deliverability between the source and destination ports.

When a Class-1 connection is established, the route between the connection initiator and connection recipient is allocated and a circuit created between the two node ports. All Class-1 frames transmitted during the connection are routed via the circuit allocated when the connection was established. This ensures in-order frame delivery during the Class-1 connection. Because the route is fixed for the duration of the circuit and reserved for the exclusive use of the two node ports, the delivery latency is deterministic. The combination of guaranteed bandwidth, in-order frame delivery, and deterministic latency make Class-1 well suited to high-bandwidth, real-time applications such as video or data streaming.

Class-1 connections are always established and removed on Sequence boundaries. A connection is always established at the beginning of a Sequence (in fact the SOFc1 frame delimiter used to establish the Class-1 connection implicitly initiates a Sequence). A connection is removed at the end of a Sequence by the terminating frame of that Sequence. During a single Class-1 connection, one or more Sequences may be transmitted between the two node ports. The connection may be a short as a single Sequence, or as long as multiple Exchanges depending upon the two node ports.

An example of a Class-1 connection in a fabric environment is illustrated in Figure 111. Note that while the Class-1 connection allocates a dedicated path between the pair of node ports, frame transmission between other pairs of ports is still possible.

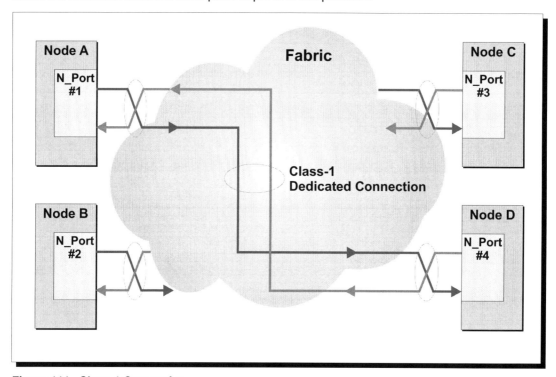

Figure 111. Class-1 Connection

18.1.1 Establishing a Class-1 Connection

The connection initiator requests a Class-1 connection at the beginning of a Sequence by transmitting the first frame of the Sequence using the Start-of-Frame connect Class-1 delimiter (SOFc1). Following transmission of the connect request frame, the connection initiator waits for an acknowledge (ACK) from the connection recipient indicating that the connection has been established (connections always begin on Sequence boundaries).

The connect request frame is treated as a connectionless frame and is subject to buffer-to-buffer flow control (once the connection is established, buffer-to-buffer flow control is not used. An example of the Class-1 connection setup protocol is shown at the top of Figure 112.

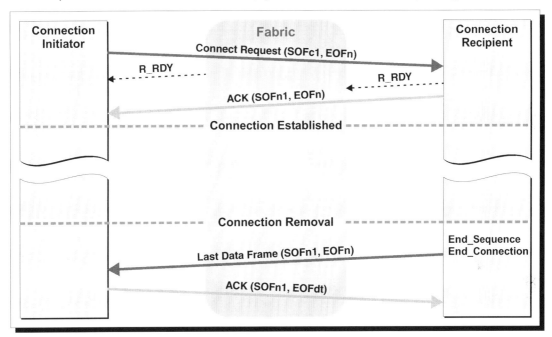

Figure 112. Class-1 Connection Setup and Removal

If a fabric is present, it allocates a dedicated path between the connection initiator and the node port identified by the D_ID field of the connect request frame. Resources allocated to the path are dedicated to that connection and not available for other traffic. If the fabric is unable to establish the connection, it sends a F_RJT or F_BSY response to the connect request frame.

If priority is enabled, the connection initiator indicates the priority associated with that connection in the CS_CTL field of the frame header of the connect request frame.

The path allocated by the fabric is determined solely by the fabric and is not controllable by, or visible to node ports. The method by which the fabric determines the path depends on the implementation of a particular fabric and is not defined by the standard. Letting the fabric manage the path allocation relieves the node port of having to maintain routing information.

If no fabric is present, the same protocol is followed by the connection initiator and connection recipient (except F_RJT and F_BSY cannot occur). In an arbitrated loop topology, the connection initiator must win arbitration and open a loop circuit with the connection recipient before sending the connect request frame.

When the connection recipient identified by the D_ID field in the connect request frame accepts the connection request, it sends a reply indicating whether the connect request was accepted. The connection recipient may send:

- An ACK frame confirming delivery and acceptance of the connection request.
- If the connection recipient is busy and cannot process the connect request, P_BSY may be returned. The connection is not considered established and the P_BSY uses an End-of-Frame disconnect terminate (EOFdt) delimiter to remove the fabric's connection.
- If the connection recipient detects a reject condition on the connect request frame, P_RJT may be returned with a reason code explaining why P_RJT was sent. The connection is not considered established and the P_RJT uses an End-of-Frame disconnect terminate (EOFdt) delimiter to remove the fabric's connection.

When the connection is established, available end-to-end credit is reinitialized from the login end-to-end credit. If the connection recipient does not have sufficient receive buffers to satisfy the login end-to-end credit with the connection initiator when the connect frame is received, it may need to delay transmission of the ACK until the required receive buffers are available.

Once the connection initiator receives the ACK to the connect request frame, the connection is considered established and frame transmission can continue.

18.1.2 Node Port Behavior During a Class-1 Connection

While a Class-1 connection exists the two node ports send frames only to each other, except when intermix is supported and in use (see *Class-1 with Intermix* on page 278).

All frames sent during a Class-1 connection must contain the correct D_ID and S_ID and use the appropriate Start-of-Frame and End-of-Frame delimiters.

- Start-of-Frame initiate Class-1 (SOFi1) is used for the first data frame of each Sequence, Start-of-Frame normal Class-1 (SOFn1) for subsequent frames within the Sequence (once the connection is established SOFc1 is not allowed).
- End-of-Frame terminate (EOFt) is used for the final ACK of each Sequence, EOFn for any previous frames (EOFdt is used only when the connection is being removed and is described in *Removing a Class-1 Connection* on page 277).

Frame transmission during a Class-1 connection is controlled using the end-to-end flow control mechanism. End-to-end credit is granted during the N_Port Login process that occurs before Class-1 operations begin.

As frames are sent, the available end-to-end credit for the other node port is decremented. If the available end-to-end credit is exhausted, frame transmission is suspended until the credit is replenished. Credit is replenished by receipt of ACK frames.

Busy is not permitted during a Class-1 connection. By definition, Class-1 guarantees full link bandwidth and busy is an indication that the necessary bandwidth is not available. Busy may occur on the connect frame if the fabric or destination port is unable to accept the connect frame at that point in time.

During a Class-1 connection, the two node ports may originate multiple Exchanges and initiate multiple Sequences with each other. A given Exchange may span multiple Class-1 connections. The duration of the connection is determined by a higher-level process, but is at least one Sequence.

It is possible for a port involved in a Class-1 connection to have open Exchanges with other ports, if those Exchanges were in existence prior to the Class-1 connection. A port that supports intermix (see *Class-1 with Intermix* on page 278) may originate or respond to Exchanges with other node ports during the Class-1 connection.

18.1.3 Topology Behavior During a Class-1 Connection

A fabric may reject (F_RJT) or busy (F_BSY) a Class-1 connection request frame, but once the connection is established, the fabric (nor any other topology) does not interfere with frame transmission, generate responses to those frames, or participate in the flow control governing frame transmission between the two node ports.

The topology must guarantee that the full link bandwidth is available to the two node ports for the duration of the Class-1 connection.

The interconnecting topology must provide in-order frame delivery during a Class-1 connection. Point-to-point and arbitrated loop inherently provide in-order delivery; the fabric must ensure that frames are delivered to the destination port in the same order as transmitted.

18.1.4 Removing a Class-1 Connection

When the connection is no longer needed, the current Sequence initiator can begin the process of removing the connection (either port could be the Sequence initiator at this time). The Sequence initiator sets the End_Connection bit in the F_CTL field of the last data frame of a Sequence (connections always end on Sequence boundaries).

When the Sequence recipient receives the data frame with End_Connection set, it prepares to remove the connection. When all prior ACKs for the Sequence have been sent, the Sequence recipient sends the final ACK using the End-of-Frame disconnect terminate (EOFdt) delimiter.

When the fabric forwards the ACK with the EOFdt, it removes the Class-1 connection and frees the resources that had been used by the connection.

When the Sequence initiator receives the ACK with the EOFdt delimiter, delivery of the last data frame, and the request to end the connection is confirmed. The connection removal process is shown at the bottom of Figure 112 on page 275.

18.1.5 Connection Recovery

Certain error conditions may result in the state of an existing or pending Class-1 connection may be ambiguous or unknown. When this occurs, the link reset protocol is used to remove the connection and return to a known state.

Some examples of conditions indicating the state of a Class-1 connection is ambiguous are (the list is intended to be exhaustive):

- A node port believes it has a Class-1 connection with node port (x) and receives a SOFc1 from node port (y)

- A node port believes it has a Class-1 connection with node port (x) and receives a SOFi1 from node port (y) when intermix is not in use

- A node port believes it has a Class-1 connection with node port (x) and receives a SOFn1 from node port (y) when intermix is not in use

- If the last active Sequence during a Class-1 connection times out, a Link Timeout error is detected and the link reset protocol is used to end the existing connection.

- If a node port is not engaged in a Class-1 connection and receives an invalid frame beginning with a SOFc1, it discards the frame and performs the link reset protocol.

18.1.6 Class-1 Priority and Preemption

Class-1 establishes a dedicated connection between a pair of node ports. The connection reserves a full-bandwidth path between the ports for those two ports' exclusive use.

There may be many Class-1 connection requests pending in a fabric. With the addition of priority, Class-1 connection requests can be prioritized. This allows the fabric to examine pending connection requests and process higher-priority request first. Class-1 priority is enabled by setting F_CTL bit 17 to one and placing the priority value in bits 31-25 of the CS_CTL field. A value of '0000 000'b indicates no priority has been assigned. The remaining values indicated the priority of the frame in increasing order (i.e., a value of '0000 001'b has lower priority than a value of '0000 010'b).

Sometimes it is desirable to preempt (interrupt and remove) an existing Class-1 connection to allow a higher-priority connection to be established. This may be accomplished by also setting the preemption bit in the CS_CTL field (bit 24). When preemption is enabled and the current connection request has higher priority than the existing connection, the existing connection is interrupted and removed without following the normal removal process and a Preempted (PRMT) Basic Link Service is sent to the ports associated with the preempted connection.

18.1.7 Class-1 with Intermix

Intermix is an optional feature that may be provided by node ports and topologies that support Class-1 operation. Intermix allows a node port that has a Class-1 connection active to send or receive (intermix) Class-2 or Class-3 frames interleaved with Class-1 frames. The Class-2 or Class-3 frames may be sent or received with the other node port involved in the Class-1 connection, or any other node port.

Intermix allows a port (and the fabric) to use unused Class-1 bandwidth for Class-2 and Class-3 frames. Class-1 frames take priority over Class-2 and Class-3 frames, and the fabric has to ensure that the full Class-1 bandwidth is available to support the dedicated connection. An example of intermix is shown in Figure 113.

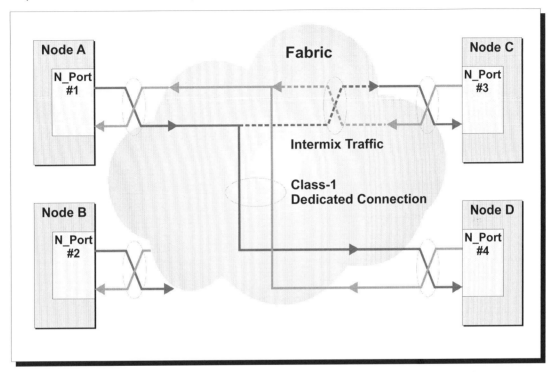

Figure 113. Class-1 Connection with Intermix

A node port indicates support for intermix during the fabric and N_Port Login processes. If a fabric is present, the fabric must also indicate support of intermix in its LS_ACC reply to the fabric login from the node port or intermix is not functional.

18.1.8 Class-1 Stacked Connect Requests

Stacked connect requests is an optional feature that may be provided by the fabric in support of Class-1 operations. When stacked connect requests is available, it allows a node port to send one or more Class-1 connect request frames (SOFc1) whether a connection is pending, established, or complete.

If multiple connection requests are pending and priority is not enabled, the fabric may process them in any order. This allows the fabric to complete the first available connection without regard to the order in which the connection requests were received. If priority is enabled, the connection initiator indicates the priority associated with that connection in the CS_CTL field of the frame header in the connect request frame.

Because a node port uses the E_D_TOV timeout value to time a connect request (it is part of a Sequence and E_D_TOV is used to detect Sequence timeouts), the fabric must ensure that a response is provided before E_D_TOV or an error will occur. If the fabric is unable to process a stacked connect request within E_D_TOV, it may send F_BSY to the connect request frame.

If neither F_BSY or ACK is received by the node port within E_D_TOV, it detects a Sequence timeout and initiates the connection recovery protocol (using LR/LRR).

To use stacked connect requests, intermix must also be supported because connection requests can be sent even while an existing connection is in effect. Support of both functions can be determined during fabric login (FLOGI) as described in *Fabric Login Session Management* on page 427. Figure 114 provides an illustration of Class-1 stacked connect requests.

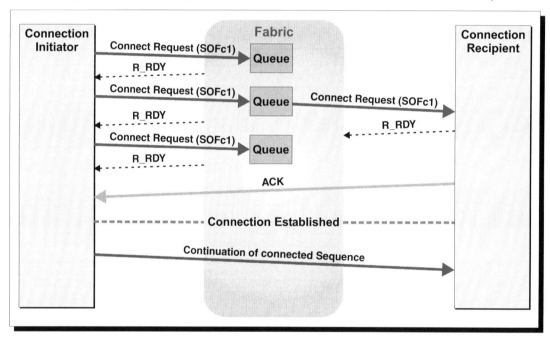

Figure 114. Class-1 Stacked Connect Requests

A node port can determine the status of the stacked connect by using the Read Connection Status (RCS) Extended Link Service request described by *Read Connection Status (RCS)* on page 368.

Due to the timings involved, there are two methods of implementing stacked connect requests. They are transparent mode and lock-down mode.

Transparent Mode. In transparent mode, when the SOFc1 connect request is delivered to the destination port, the return path has already been established. This behavior is the same as would be during normal Class-1 connection.

This means that the connection recipient can begin frame transmission immediately following transmission of the ACK to the connect request frame.

Lock-Down Mode. In lock-down mode, when the SOFc1 connect request frame is delivered to the destination port, the return path may not have been established (it will be established on the ACK).

When lock-down mode is active, the connection recipient cannot begin frame transmission immediately following the ACK to the connect request frame (SOFc1).

To inform the connection recipient this mode is in effect, the connection initiator sets Unidirectional Transmit in the F_CTL field (bit 8) to inhibit the connection recipient from transmitting data frames after the ACK to the connect request is sent (link control frames can still be sent).

Determining Which Mode is Functional. When a node port logs in with the fabric (FLOGI) it requests either, or both, stacked connect modes by setting word 0 bits 29 (transparent mode) and 28 (lock-down mode) of the Class-1 service parameters. If the fabric supports either mode, it will set the corresponding bit in the LS_ACC reply to the FLOGI. If neither mode is supported by the fabric, word 0 bits 29-28 of the Class-1 service parameter field will be set to b'00'. If transparent mode is supported and functional, word 0 bit 29 is set. If lock-down mode is supported and functional, word 0 bit 28 is set. If the fabric supports both modes and the node port requests both, the fabric will only enable one mode (both modes can't be active at the same time).

Changes to Stacked Connect Requests in FC-PH2. FC-PH2 modified the operation of stacked connect requests to enhance the control and error detection capabilities.

Prior to these changes, once the node port had completed fabric login and determined that stacked connect request was functional, stacked connect request was operational for every connection request. Furthermore, the connection initiator timed the connection process and expected a response within E_D_TOV. This meant that E_D_TOV had to be set large enough to cover both the frame transit time and the connection processing time.

The first change to stacked connect request alters how a node port indicates to the fabric that it wants a stacked connect request. In FC-PH, this was done during fabric login and applied to all Class-1 connection requests. In FC-PH2, the request for stacked connection is made as part of the connect request frame itself and applies only to that individual connection. Consequently, the Class-1 stacked connect request login parameters provided by the node port during fabric login are not used. The fabric indicates which mode of stacked connect request is supported in its response to the fabric login.

When a node port sends a connect request frame, the stacked connect request is indicated by bit 30 of the class specific control (CS_CTL) field of the frame header (see *Class Specific Control (CS_CTL)* on page 208). This allows the node port to control the connection mode on a connection-by-connection basis.

The second change to stacked connect requests was the addition of the connection request timeout value (CR_TOV). This defined the amount of time that the fabric was allowed to queue the connect request, and separated the connect time from the frame transit and response time defined by E_D_TOV. The use of CR_TOV is described in *Connection Request Timeout Value (CR_TOV)* on page 294.

18.1.9 Unidirectional Class-1 Connection

When the connection initiator sends the Class-1 connect request frame (SOFc1), it indicates if the data frame transmission will be unidirectional or bidirectional. This is done by setting the Unidirectional Transmit bit in the F_CTL of the connect request frame header (bit 8) to one.

If the dedicated connection is bidirectional, the connection recipient may begin frame transmission immediately after transmitting ACK to the connect request frame. If the dedicated connection is unidirectional, the connection recipient can only send link control frames (e.g., ACK).

The connection initiator can change a unidirectional dedicated connection into a bidirectional connection by setting the Unidirectional Transmit bit to zero on either the first or last data frame of a Sequence (it is not meaningful on other frames of the Sequence).

The connection recipient may request that the connection initiator change a unidirectional connection into a bidirectional one by setting Unidirectional Transmit to zero in an ACK frame. Once the bit has been set to zero in an ACK frame, it must be set to zero in all subsequent ACKs during that connection. While the connection recipient may request that the connection be changed to bidirectional, the connection initiator is under no obligation to do so.

18.1.10 Responses to a Connect Request

The connection initiator may receive several responses to the connect request frame:

- If ACK is received from the connection recipient, the dedicated connection has been established. If more than one stacked connect request is pending, the S_ID field of the ACK identifies which connection request was honored.

- If F_BSY is received, the connection could not be established by the fabric within the allotted amount of time. The connection initiator should retransmit the request.

- If F_RJT is received, the fabric could not process the frame. The F_RJT reason code identifies why the frame could not be processed.

- If P_BSY is received, the connection recipient was busy and could not process the connect request frame. The connection initiator should retransmit the request.

- If P_RJT is received, the connection recipient could not process the frame. The P_RJT reason code identifies why the frame could not be processed.

- If no response is received within the allowed time, the connection request has timed-out. The allowed amount of time is:

  - For stacked connect request, transparent mode: CR_TOV + E_D_TOV

  - For stacked connect request, lock-down mode: 2*CR_TOV + E_D_TOV

18.2 Class-2

Class-2 is a connectionless class of service with confirmation of delivery, or notification of non-deliverability of frames.

No bandwidth is allocated or guaranteed when using Class-2. This means the Class-2 frames will be forwarded or delivered as bandwidth permits, but may be delayed in transit due to congestion or other traffic. In a fabric topology, it is the responsibility of the fabric to provide appropriate congestion control to prevent bandwidth hogging and starvation of ports.

The delivery latency of a Class-2 frame in a busy topology may not be deterministic because frame delivery is subject to available bandwidth. This makes Class-2 more appropriate for asynchronous or bursty traffic that can tolerate the potential delays.

No connection is established in Class-2, and the fabric forwards each frame on a frame-by-frame basis using its internal forwards algorithms. Successive frames may be routed over different paths due to congestion or other considerations, and consequently, frames may be received out of order by the recipient (a node port can request in-order frame delivery when it logs in with the fabric).

Because no connection is established in Class-2 (unless the topology itself creates a circuit), frames may be sent to different destinations, one after another. The fabric will route each frame to the appropriate destination. It is also possible that a port may be transmitting a frame to one destination while simultaneously receiving a frame from a different port.

An example of Class-2 operation showing the frame multiplexing in a fabric environment is illustrated in Figure 115.

Class-2 is a connectionless service between two ports with confirmation of delivery or notification of non-deliverability. Because Class-2 is connectionless, a node port may send consecutive frames to different destinations. Frame multiplexing is discussed further in *Frame Multiplexing* on page 516.

Because Class-2 is connectionless, there is no connect delimiter or connection setup protocol. Class-2 frames initiating a Sequence use the Start-of-Frame initiate Class-2 (SOFi2) delimiter. Subsequent frames in a Sequence use the Start-of-Frame normal Class-2 (SOFn2) delimiter.

Frames within a Sequence may arrive out-of-order at the Sequence recipient if the topology does not preserve frames ordering. If streamed Sequences occur (see *Streamed Sequences* on page 194), it is possible for frames from different Sequences to arrive at the Sequence recipient out-of-order and intermixed. ACK frames sent by the Sequence recipient may arrive at the Sequence initiator out-of-order as well.

Likewise, there is no disconnect delimiter or connection tear-down protocol. The last frame of the Sequence uses the End-of-Frame terminate (EOFt) delimiter. Prior frames use the End-of-Frame normal (EOFn) delimiter.

The Sequence initiator identifies the last data frame of the Sequence by setting the End_Sequence bit in the F_CTL field of the frame header. This frame uses the EOFn End-of-Frame delimiter. When the Sequence recipient sends the final ACK of the Sequence, it sets End_Sequence and uses the EOFt delimiter. The final ACK sent by the Sequence recipient

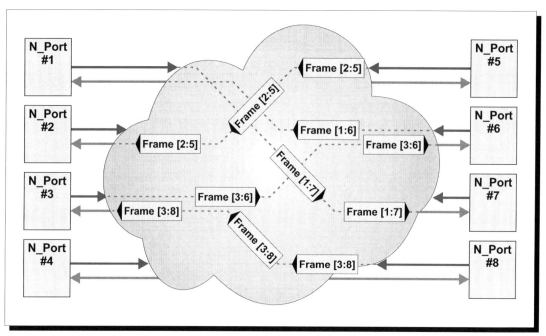

Figure 115. Class-2, 3 and F Frame Multiplexing

may not necessarily be the ACK to the last data frame if data frames arrive at the Sequence recipient out-of-order.

18.2.1 Class-2 Flow Control

Class-2 frames use both buffer-to-buffer and end-to-end flow control to manage the flow of frames. An example of Class-2 operation illustrating the use of both flow control mechanisms is shown in Figure 116.

18.2.2 Class-2 Delivery Preference

Because Class-2 is a connectionless class of service, no bandwidth or path is reserved for frame delivery. To provide Quality-of-Service (QoS) attributes for Class-2, delivery preference may be used. Class-2 delivery preference is enabled by setting both F_CTL bit 17 to zero and CS_CTL bit 31 to one and providing a Differentiated Services Code Point (DSCP) value in bits 29-24 of CS_CTL.

Differentiated Services Code Points are a set of values defining policies to differentiate traffic flows. The default value of '000000'b indicates a best effort QoS. Other values are defined in RFC 2597, 'Assured Forwarding PHB Group' and RFC 2598, 'An Expedited Forwarding PHB'.

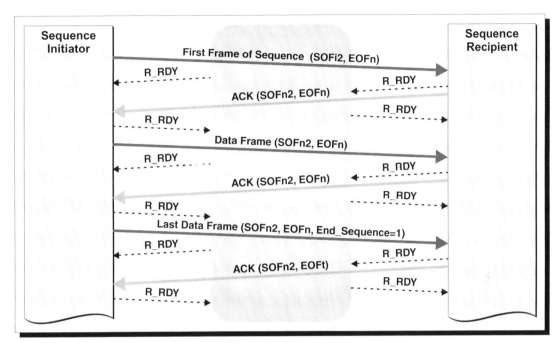

Figure 116. Class-2 Operation

18.2.3 Class-2 Priority and Preemption

When priority is enabled for Class-2, the priority can be used to forward higher priority frames ahead of lower-priority frames. The can help ensure the timely delivery of important traffic. Priority is enabled by setting F_CTL bit 17 to one and providing the priority value in bits 31-25 of the CS_CTL field.

It may be desirable to preempt (interrupt and remove) an existing Class-1 connection to allow higher-priority Class-2 frames to be delivered. This may be accomplished by also setting the preemption bit in the CS_CTL field (bit 24). When preemption is enabled and the Class-2 frame has higher priority than the existing connection, the existing connection is interrupted and removed without following the normal removal process and a Preempted (PRMT) Basic Link Service is sent to the ports associated with the preempted connection.

18.3 Class-3

Class-3 is a connectionless class of service providing a datagram-like delivery service with no confirmation of delivery, or notification of non-deliverability of frames. If a frame cannot be delivered or processed, it is discarded without notification.

No bandwidth is allocated or guaranteed when using Class-3. This means the Class-3 frames will be forwarded or delivered as bandwidth permits, but may be delayed in transit due to congestion or other traffic. In a fabric topology, it is the responsibility of the fabric to provide appropriate congestion control to prevent bandwidth hogging and starvation of ports.

The delivery latency of a Class-3 frame in a busy topology may not be deterministic because frame delivery is subject to available bandwidth. This makes Class-3 more appropriate for asynchronous or bursty traffic that can tolerate the potential delays.

No connection is established in Class-3, and the fabric routes each frame on a frame-by-frame basis using its internal forwards algorithms. Successive frames may be routed over different paths due to congestion or other considerations, and consequently, frames may be received out of order by the recipient (a node port can request in-order delivery during fabric login).

Because no connection is established in Class-3 (unless the topology itself creates a circuit), frames may be sent to different destinations, one after another. The fabric will route each frame to the appropriate destination. It is also possible that a port may be transmitting a frame to one destination while simultaneously receiving a frame from a different port.

Other than not providing confirmation of delivery or notification of non-delivery, Class-3 operations are identical to the Class-2 operation shown earlier in Figure 115 on page 284.

Class-3 is a connectionless datagram service with no confirmation of delivery or notification of non-deliverability. There are no busy or reject responses sent by either the fabric or receiving port to received frames. If a frame cannot be processed, it is discarded without notification and the Sequence delivery fails due to the missing frame or Sequence timeout.

Because Class-3 is connectionless, a node port may send consecutive frames to different destinations as described in *Frame Multiplexing* on page 516.

Like Class-2, there is no connect delimiter or connection setup protocol. Class-3 frames that initiate a Sequence use the Start-of-Frame initiate Class-3 (SOFi3) delimiter. Subsequent frames in a Sequence use the Start-of-Frame normal Class-3 (SOFn3) delimiters.

Frames within a Sequence may arrive out-of-order at the Sequence recipient if the topology reorders the frames. If streamed Sequences occur (see *Streamed Sequences* on page 194), frames from different Sequences may arrive at the recipient out-of-order and intermixed.

There is no disconnect delimiter or connection tear-down protocol. The Sequence initiator identifies the last data frame of the Sequence by setting End_Sequence in the F_CTL field of the frame header. and using the EOFt End-of-Frame delimiter.

18.3.1 Class-3 Flow Control

18.3.2 Class-3 frames use only buffer-to-buffer flow control to manage the flow of frames. Figure 117 on page 287 shows an example of Class-3 operation and the use of buffer-to-buffer flow control. This flow control mechanism is sufficient to prevent buffer overrun conditions, but does not allow a receiving port control over which source port is allowed to send frames.

18.3.3 Class-3 Delivery Preference

Because Class-3 is a connectionless class of service, no bandwidth or path is reserved for frame delivery. To provide Quality-of-Service (QoS) attributes for Class-3, delivery preference

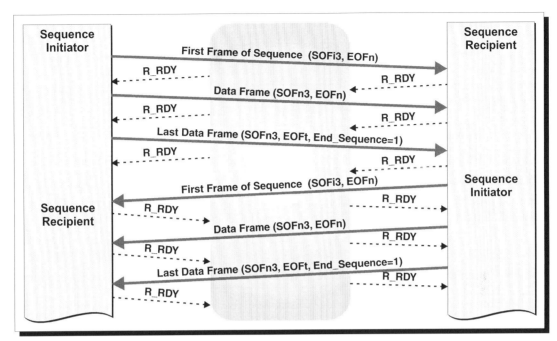

Figure 117. Class-3 Operation

may be used. Class-3 delivery preference is enabled by setting both F_CTL bit 17 to zero and CS_CTL bit 31 to one and providing a Differentiated Services Code Point (DSCP) value in bits 29:24 of CS_CTL.

Differentiated Services Code Points are a set of values defining policies to differentiate traffic flows. The default value of '000000'b indicates a best effort QoS. Other values are defined in RFC 2597, 'Assured Forwarding PHB Group' and RFC 2598, 'An Expedited Forwarding PHB'.

18.3.4 Class-3 Priority and Preemption

When priority is enabled for Class-3, the priority can be used to forward higher priority frames ahead of lower-priority frames. The can help ensure the timely delivery of important traffic. Priority is enabled by setting F_CTL bit 17 to one and providing a priority value in bits 31:25 of the CS_CTL field.

It may be desirable to preempt (interrupt and remove) an existing Class-1 connection to allow higher-priority Class-3 frames to be delivered. This may be accomplished by also setting the preemption bit in the CS_CTL field (bit 24). When preemption is enabled and the Class-3 frame has higher priority than the existing connection, the existing connection is interrupted and removed without following the normal removal process and a Preempted (PRMT) Basic Link Service is sent to the ports associated with the preempted connection.

18.3.5 Class-3 Error Considerations

When Class-3 is used, there is no delivery confirmation or notification of non-deliverability provided to the sender. Class-3 is best suited to those applications that do not require delivery confirmation, or provide any needed confirmation at a higher-level. The higher-level confirmation may be provided by the FC-4 protocol being transported (e.g., TCP/IP provides confirmation at the TCP level).

Due to the absence of delivery confirmation, responsibility for determining correct delivery of a Sequence shifts from the Sequence initiator to the Sequence recipient. In the other classes of service, the final ACK confirms delivery of the Sequence. Absence of the final ACK, or receipt of a busy or reject, provides notification of non-deliverability of the Sequence. In either case, the Sequence initiator is responsible for determining whether the Sequence was delivered.

The Sequence initiator considers the Sequence complete when the last frame of the Sequence is transmitted In Class-3. The Sequence initiator doesn't know if the Sequence was received correctly by the recipient. Before delivery to the higher-level process by the Sequence recipient, a determination is made as to whether the Sequence was received correctly.

When the Sequence initiator considers a Sequence complete is important because, once the Sequence initiator considers the Sequence complete, it no longer has to preserve data buffers used to hold the Sequence. Without higher-level control, the Sequence information may be deleted by the sender after the last frame is sent. If an error is subsequently detected by the Sequence recipient, the sending port may no longer have access to the necessary data.

18.3.6 Class-3 Multicast

When supported by the topology, Class-3 may be used for multicast or broadcast operations. Because there is no confirmation of delivery or notification of non-deliverability, when Class-3 is used for multicast, it is referred to as unreliable multicast, or Class-3 multicast (for a reliable multicast service, see *Class-6* on page 288).

18.4 Class-6

Class-6 is a variation of Class-1 providing a reliable one-to-many multicast service with delivery confirmation or notification of non-deliverability. Class-6 uses the same frame delimiters as Class-1 and follows observes all Class-1 rules and behaviors. Class-6 differs from Class-1 only in the processing of responses from members of the multicast group.

In Class-6, a multicast server (see *Multicast Server* on page 488) consolidates the responses from members of the multicast group and creates a single response to the multicast initiator. This behavior is shown in the description of the multicast server in Figure 154 on page 489.

18.4.1 Establishing a Class-6 Multicast Connection

Before a node port can use Class-6 multicast, it must have completed N_Port Login (PLOGI) with the multicast server and all members of the multicast group. The Class-1 service parameters established by the login process are used to control Class-6 operations.

When a port wishes to perform a Class-6 multicast, it sends a connect request frame (using the SOFc1 and EOFn delimiters) to the address of the multicast group. This requests the fabric to establish Class-1 connections between the multicast initiator and all the ports in the multicast group. The connect request can use any available options available for Class-1 connections such as stacked connect requests, and priority and preemption. After transmitting the connect request frame, the multicast initiator waits for a response before sending additional frames associated with that connect request.

All Class-6 connections are unidirectional connections and only the connection initiator is permitted to send data frames. To indicate a unidirectional connection, the connection initiator set Unidirectional Transmit (F_CTL bit 8) in the connect request frame.

If priority or preemption is enabled, the multicast initiator indicates the priority associated with that connection in the priority field of the frame header in the connect request frame (see *Class-1 Priority and Preemption* on page 278).

The fabric forwards the connect request frame unchanged to each member of the multicast group. The connect request frame, and all multicast frames, are not altered by the fabric.

When each member of the multicast group receives the connect request frame (indicated by the SOFc1 delimiter), it processes the connect request following normal Class-1 connection rules. If priority is enabled, the priority associated with the connection is contained in the priority field of the frame header of the connect request frame.

If the destination port accepts the connect request, it sends a normal acknowledgment (ACK). When the fabric detects a frame with a source address of a multicast group, it forwards that frame to the multicast server at well-known address x'FF FF F5'.

The multicast server waits for ACK from all members of the multicast group, and when all ACKs have been received, sends a single ACK to the multicast initiator to indicate the multicast connection has been established and multicast operations can begin. The ACK, or any other response frame generated by the multicast server, uses the RX_ID supplied by the multicast server when the multicast initiator logged in with the multicast server. This is different from normal operations, where the responder node port assigns the RX_ID (in a manner of speaking, the multicast server is the responder in Class-6).

If the multicast server detects the connect request was unsuccessful, it returns a busy or reject response to the multicast connect request frame and indicates the reason for the response.

- If any member of the multicast group is not able to receive frames, the multicast server sends P_RJT to the multicast initiator.

- If one or more members of the multicast group returns P_BSY to the connect request from the multicast server, the multicast server returns P_BSY with a reason code of "partial multicast busy" (see Table 50 on page 248).

- If one or more members of the multicast group returns P_RJT to the connect request from the multicast server or all ACKs have not been received within E_D_TOV, the multicast server returns P_RJT with an explanation of "multicast error".

- If one or more members of the multicast group returns ACK, P_BSY, or P_RJT with an EOFdt delimiter to the connect request from the multicast server, the multicast server returns reject with an explanation of "multicast error terminate". This reject uses EOFdt.

- If one or more members of a multicast group initiates the Link Reset (LR) Primitive Sequence, the fabric initiates Link Reset with all other members of the group, including the multicast initiator (see *Link Reset Protocol and Link Recovery States* on page 133).

18.4.2 Behavior During a Class-6 Connection

Once a multicast connection is established, the multicast initiator may transmit frames to the multicast group using the group address as the destination address in the frame header

The fabric forwards frames addressed to the multicast group to every member of the multicast group. The fabric does not alter the frames in any way, and they are delivered to the multicast destination node ports exactly as received by the fabric (the D_ID field is the multicast group address, the S_ID is the multicast initiator's address). The destination port must recognize the multicast group address as a valid alias address.

Because multicast is a unidirectional transmit operation, the multicast initiator never transfers Sequence Initiative when Class-6 multicast is used. The destination ports are only permitted to send link control frames during a Class-6 multicast.

18.4.3 Ending a Class-6 Connection

The Class-6 multicast initiator begins the process of ending the multicast connection by sending the last frame of the final Sequence with End_Connection in the F_CTL field set to one. The multicast server forwards this frame to all members of the multicast group. As each member completes processing the Sequence it sends the final ACK with End_Connection set to one and uses the EOFdt delimiter. This ends the connection between the multicast server and that particular destination port. When all destination ports have completed the final Sequence and replied with the final ACK, the multicast server sends a final ACK to the multicast initiator with End_Connection set to one and terminated with the EOFdt delimiter.

If the connection to one member of a multicast group is preempted, the effect on the remaining ports is implementation dependent (the connections may remain, or may be preempted).

18.4.4 Class-6 Multicast Flow Control

Class-6 flow control occurs between the multicast initiator and multicast group following normal Class-1 flow control rules. The multicast connect request frame uses the SOFc1 delimiter and observes both buffer-to-buffer and end-to-end flow control. Once the connection is established, only end-to-end flow control is used.

The multicast initiator maintains flow control with the multicast group address. When the multicast initiator sends a frame to the multicast group address, end-to-end credit (and buffer-to-buffer credit if this is the connect frame) is decremented. When the multicast server sends a response to the multicast initiator, the end-to-end credit is replenished. The multicast initiator does not maintain flow control with the individual destination ports (because all multicast frames are sent to the multicast group address).

Chapter 18. Classes of Service

18.5 Chapter Summary

Classes of Service

- Different types of data may have different delivery needs in regards to:
  - Bandwidth allocations (all, some, none)
  - Delivery latency (deterministic, non-deterministic)
  - Delivery confirmation (acknowledgment)
  - Frame delivery order
  - Flow control (buffer-to-buffer, end-to-end, or both)
- Fibre Channel has defined combinations of these characteristics referred to as classes of service
  - Class-1, Class-2, Class-3 and Class-F have been defined

Class-1

- Class-1 is a connection-oriented service with confirmation of delivery or notification of non-delivery
  - The connection reserves full bandwidth between the ports (dedicated connection)
  - Connections are always established and removed on Sequence boundaries
  - Multiple Sequences or Exchanges can occur within a single Class-1 connection
- In-order frame delivery is guaranteed
- Delivery latency is deterministic

Class-1 (continued)

- Fabric login is required (unless only communicating on the same arbitrated loop)
- Login with the other node port is required
- End-to-end flow control is used for all frames
  - Except when ACK_0 is used
- Buffer-to-buffer flow control is only used on the connect request frame (SOFc1)
- Busy may be returned only to the connect request frame
  - Once the connection is established busy is not allowed
- Reject may be returned on any frame

Class-1 Service with Intermix

- A Class-1 dedicated connection makes a port busy for the duration of that connection
  - Communication with other ports in not possible while the connection is active
- Intermix is an optional feature that can alleviate this condition
  - Intermix allows limited connectionless frames even while a connection is established
  - Intermix frames are handled as bandwidth is available
  - The dedicated connection frames have higher priority than the intermix frames
  - Only usable if both the node port and fabric support its use

Stacked Connect Requests

- Stacked connect requests is a Class-1 optional feature
- Allows multiple connection requests to be sent to the fabric
  - The fabric queues the requests
  - Process the first it is able to complete
  - The order of the requests is irrelevant
- Prevents a port from getting hung up trying to connect to a busy destination

Class-6

- Class-6 is a variation of Class-1
  - Uses Class-1 frame delimiters
  - Observes all Class-1 rules and behavior
- Provides reliable multicast with acknowledgement
- Requires a special fabric that supports the Multicast Server
  - ACKs from multicast recipients are routed to the multicast server
  - Multicast server sends a single ACK to the multicast originator
- Primary application is avionics industry

Class-1/6 Priority and Preemption

- Priority assigns priority to Class-1/6 connections
  - Priority value is in the CS_CTL field and enabled by F_CTL bit 17
- Preemption allows a new connection to preempt an existing connection
  - Based on the priority of the connections
  - Also the Preemption bit in the CS_CTL field
  - When a connection is preempted, the ports are notified with the Preempted Basic Link Service

Class-2

- Class-2 is a connectionless service with confirmation of delivery, or notification of non delivery
  - There is no connection setup or tear down
- Frames are routed individually by the fabric
- No bandwidth is reserved, it is used as needed to route frames
- The order of frame delivery is not guaranteed
  - In-order can be requested at login
- The delivery latency is not deterministic
  - Frames can be delayed in transit due to congestion

Class-2 (continued)

- Fabric login is required (unless only communicating on the same arbitrated loop)
- Login with the other node port is required
- Flow control
  - End-to-end flow control is used on every frame (except when ACK_0 is used)
  - Buffer-to-buffer flow control is used on every frame
- Responses
  - F_BSY or P_BSY may be returned to any frame
  - RJT may be returned to any frame

Class-3

- Class-3 is a connectionless service with NO confirmation of delivery, or notification of non delivery
  - There is no connection setup or tear down
- Frames are routed individually by the fabric
- No bandwidth is reserved, it is used as needed to route frames
- The order of frame delivery is not guaranteed
  - In-order can be requested at login
- The delivery latency is not deterministic
  - Frames can be delayed in transit due to congestion

Class-3 (continued)

- Fabric login is required (unless only communicating on the same arbitrated loop)
- Login with the other node port is optional
- Flow control
  - There is no end-to-end flow control (Class-3 does not use ACKs)
  - Buffer-to-buffer flow control is used on every frame
- Responses
  - No ACKs, BSYs, or RJTs from the destination port
  - If a frame can't be delivered or processed, it is discarded without notification

Class-2/3 Priority and Preemption

- Provides Quality of Service (QoS) and Priority to Classes 2 and 3
- Priority is enabled by F_CTL bit 17
  - When Priority is enabled, CS_CTL contains the priority value
  - Can also preempt Class-1/6 connections
- When Priority is not enabled, CS_CTL contains a preference value
  - Preference values represent different types of service delivery policies
  - A value of x'00' indicates best-effort delivery

19. Error Detection and Recovery

Error detection and recovery in Fibre Channel can be more complicated than was the case on some earlier interfaces. This is due to the more complex nature of the interface and the associated lower-level protocols associated with the FC-0, FC-1, and FC-2 levels. In addition, error detection and recovery are complicated by the fact that information can be in an indeterminate state while it is in transit. When a port sends a frame to another port, there is a period of ambiguity as to whether the frame was received correctly by the other port until confirmation of delivery is received.

The Fibre Channel architecture provides ample checking at each of the levels to ensure that the function performed at that level was correct, and perhaps examining the error mechanisms at each level is the most practical approach.

19.1 Timer Values

Timers are a common mechanism to detect when an expected event or condition failed to occur, or lasted longer than it should have. In many cases, timeouts provide the only practical means to detect some error conditions. For example, a port sends a frame to another port and expects a response in return. What if that response never comes? How long should the port wait before deciding that something has gone wrong and an error has occurred?

To keep the design of Fibre Channel port as simple as possible, the number of different timers specified by the standard has been kept to a minimum. There is a short timer used to detect link-level failures called the Receiver-Transmitter Timeout value, a medium length timer used to detect frame and Sequence level errors called the Error_Detect Timeout value (E_D_TOV), and a long duration timer used to determine worst-case conditions called the Resource_Allocation Timeout value (R_A_TOV).

19.1.1 Receiver-Transmitter Timeout Value (R_T_TOV)

The Receiver-Transmitter timeout value (R_T_TOV) is used to time events on the link such as Loss-of-Synchronization and expected responses to link-level protocols (such as occur during the Link Reset protocol).

This timer is measuring events on a single link that are generally controlled by hardware in the link control facility, so a reasonable value for the timer can readily be determined suitable for all supported link configurations. The value specified by the standard is 100 ms.

19.1.2 Error Detect Timeout Value (E_D_TOV)

The E_D_TOV timeout value times events and responses at the Sequence level. Because frames and their associated responses may traverse the fabric and involve processing by both the sending and receiving ports (both of which may have other work they are currently engaged in), this timer value needs to be much larger.

Because frames and ACKs may traverse a very complex and widespread fabric, it is not practical to set a value for E_D_TOV short enough to facilitate timely error detection and yet still provide adequate time for frame delivery in a complex fabric environment. To accommodate different environments, the Fibre Channel fabric determines the appropriate value for E_D_TOV in a fabric environment and informs the node port of the value during fabric login.

By letting the fabric determine the E_D_TOV value, it can be scaled according to the anticipated frame delivery time in that particular fabric. The generally accepted default value for E_D_TOV is two seconds (after all, if a frame hasn't be delivered and an expected ACK received within two seconds, it is likely that something really is wrong).

19.1.3 Resource Allocation Timeout Value (R_A_TOV)

The R_A_TOV timeout value defines how long resources associated with a failed Sequence or Exchange should be locked out from reuse following a Sequence delivery failure. The value is set long enough to ensure that any frames in transit have either been delivered, or never will be delivered.

This timeout value is also used to determine how long a port waits for a response to a link service request before an error is detected. A long timeout value is appropriate in this case because link service processing is frequently performed in firmware or software (that may be in the middle of error recovery processing as it is).

The minimum value for R_A_TOV is 2 times E_D_TOV. The generally accepted default value used for R_A_TOV is 10 seconds.

19.1.4 Connection Request Timeout Value (CR_TOV)

FC-PH2 added a fourth timer to the three defined by the original standard. This new timer is the connection request timeout value, or CR_TOV.

The connect request timeout defines how long the fabric can hold a Class-1 stacked connect request. The purpose of this timer is to allow separation of the connection queueing time in the fabric from the error detect time defined by E_D_TOV. Prior to this change, E_D_TOV timed the total amount of time from when the connection initiator sent the connect request frame until ACK (or F_BSY) was received for that frame. This change allows separation of the connection queueing time from the frame transit time.

Figure 118 on page 295 illustrates the relationship of CR_TOV and E_D_TOV during establishment of a dedicated connection for both the transparent and lock-down modes of stacked connect requests.

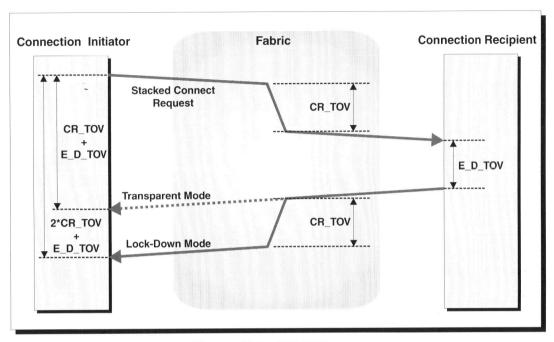

Figure 118. Connection Request Timeout Value (CR_TOV)

19.2 Link Error Status Block (LESB)

The Link Error Status Block is used to record link-level errors detected by a node port and may be used to assist in determining the integrity of the node port and attached link. The contents of the Link Error Status Block can be retrieved by use of the Read Link Status (RLS) Extended Link Service request (described on *Read Link Error Status Block (RLS)* on page 370). The layout of the Link Error Status Block is shown in Table 54.

Word	Description
0	Link Failure Count
1	Loss-of-Synchronization Count
2	Loss-of-Signal Count
3	Primitive Sequence Protocol Error Count
4	Invalid Transmission Word Count
5	Invalid CRC Count

Table 54. Link Error Status Block (LESB)

While the contents of the Link Error Status Block can be retrieved by use of the RLS Extended Link Service request, there is no mechanism defined to reset the contents of the LESB. Therefore, the contents simply continue to increment until the counter rolls over, at which point the count continues from zero.

19.3 FC-0 Link Errors

FC-0 level errors are primarily associated with the quality of the received signal or timeout of link-level protocols. The FC-0 link error conditions and associated actions are:

- Loss-of-Synchronization for less than R_T_TOV (see *Loss-of-Synchronization State* on page 128)

- Loss-of-Synchronization for greater than R_T_TOV (see *Link Failure Protocol and Link Failure States* on page 138)

- Loss-of-Signal (see *Link Failure Protocol and Link Failure States* on page 138)

- Link Reset Protocol timeout greater than R_T_TOV see (*Link Reset Protocol and Link Recovery States* on page 133). This causes termination of all open Class-1 and Class-6 Sequences and may cause frames to be discarded in Class-2, Class-3 and Class-F.

Figure 119 illustrates the link-level error conditions.

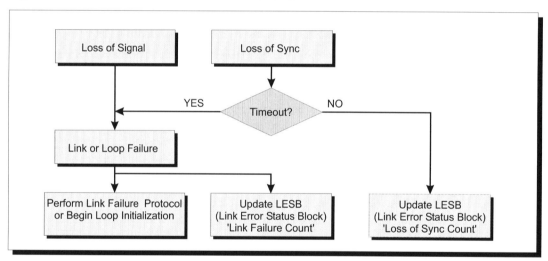

Figure 119. Link-Level Errors

19.4 FC-1 Level Errors

The FC-1 level provides error checking and detection of the encoded data stream based on invalid transmission characters or running disparity conditions.

If an invalid transmission character is received or the running disparity is incorrect, a code violation error is detected and the Invalid Transmission Word count field of the Link Error Status Block (LESB) is incremented.

If the disparity is incorrect at the beginning of an Ordered Set, an "invalid beginning disparity" error is detected. All Ordered Sets, except for the End-of-Frame delimiters should begin with negative running disparity when the K28.5 character is received.

Normally, the only place the K28.5 character occurs is as the first character of an Ordered Set (note that this is not the case for 10 gigabit Fibre Channel). If K28.5 is detected in any other byte position, an "invalid special code alignment condition" is detected (sometimes also referred to as a "misplaced special character" error).

If an invalid transmission word error occurs during frame reception, the frame is invalid and the data field may or may not be used depending upon the Exchange error policy in effect. Because it may not be possible to identify the character or characters in the frame are in error, most implementations have chosen to discard invalid frames without using the header or data field. When a Class-1 dedicated connection or arbitrated loop circuit exists, it may be possible to assume certain conditions relative to the invalid frame for the purposes of error recovery.

19.4.1 Primitive Sequence Protocol Error

If a node port is in the Active (AC) state and receives a Link Reset Response (LRR) Primitive Sequence, a Primitive Sequence Protocol error is detected and recorded in the Link Error Status Block (LESB).

19.5 FC-2 Invalid Frame Conditions

A frame may be considered invalid for several reasons. In general, invalid frames are discarded without processing. Under some conditions, such as during a Class-1 dedicated connection or during an arbitrated loop circuit, it may be possible to infer information about the invalid frame for the purposes of error recovery.

The following conditions result in an invalid frame condition:

- No receive buffer is available to receive the frame
- An Ordered Set, other than one of the defined End-of-Frame delimiters is detected during frame reception
- A frame is terminated with the End-of-Frame abort (EOFa) delimiter
- A CRC error is detected
- An invalid transmission word is detected within the frame

A summary of these error conditions is shown in Figure 120 on page 298.

19.6 FC-2 Link Timeout Errors

In Class-1, a link timeout is detected when a Sequence timeout has occurred on all active Sequences (conditions for detecting a Sequence timeout are described in *Sequence Timeout* on page 298).

In Class-1, Class-2 and Class-3 a link timeout error is detected when one or more R_RDY Primitive Signals are not received within E_D_TOV after the buffer-to-buffer credit count has reached zero.

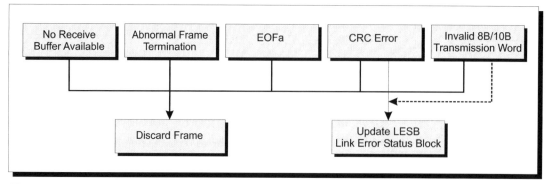

Figure 120. Invalid Frame Conditions

Recovery from a link timeout is accomplished by performing the Link Reset protocol as described in *Link Failure Protocol and Link Failure States* on page 138.

19.7 FC-2 Sequence Errors

During the transmission or reception of a Sequence, either the Sequence initiator or recipient may detect that an error has occurred. The primary methods of error detection are:

- Detection of a missing frame based on a timeout (E_D_TOV)
- Detection of a missing frame based on SEQ_CNT
- Detection of a missing frame based on Continuously Increasing Relative Offset
- Detection of a rejectable condition within a frame (P_RJT)
- Reception of a reject frame (F_RJT or P_RJT)
- Detection of an internal malfunction

Following detection of a Sequence error, the action taken depends on the class of service, the error detected, and the Exchange error policy in effect for the Exchange containing the failed Sequence. Discussion of error actions begins with *Sequence Error Processing - Class-1, Class-2 and Class-F* on page 300. A simplified overview of Sequence level errors is presented in Figure 121 on page 299.

19.7.1 Sequence Timeout

Both the Sequence initiator and Sequence recipient may use a timer to ensure that the next expected event within a Sequence occurs within the allowable time period. The time value used to time for occurrence of the next expected Sequence event is the Error_Detect timeout value (E_D_TOV). This timer is discussed in *Error Detect Timeout Value (E_D_TOV)* on page 294.

When the Sequence initiator transmits a data frame in Class-1, Class-2 or Class-F it expects a response to that data frame (ACK, RJT, or BSY) within E_D_TOV. Other events may occur that cause the Sequence initiator to stop timing the expected event. Examples of these other

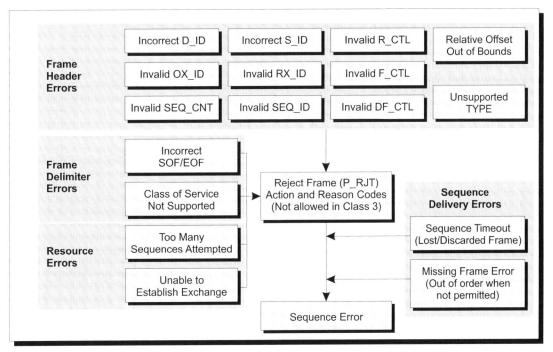

Figure 121. Sequence Errors

events are Link Credit Reset (that terminates open Exchanges), Abort Sequence (ABTS) or N_Port logout (LOGO).

When the Sequence recipient receives the last data frame of a Sequence, it verifies that all frames have been received correctly before sending the final ACK (EOFt or EOFdt) of that Sequence.

A Sequence timeout is detected if the E_D_TOV timeout period expires for an expected event before the Sequence is complete.

The action taken by the Sequence initiator or recipient upon detection of a Sequence timeout is dependent upon the class of service and Exchange error policy in effort for the Exchange containing the failed Sequence. These actions are described beginning with *Processing Common to all Discard Error Policies* on page 300 and continuing through *Abort, Discard a Single Sequence* on page 303.

19.7.2 Detection of Missing Frames

The following list summarizes conditions that indicate a missing frame:

1. In a Class-1 Sequence, a frame is received with a SEQ_CNT that is not +1 greater than the previous frame of the Sequence. For this check, x'0000' is considered +1 greater than x'FFFF' to accommodate a wrap of the SEQ_CNT within the Sequence.

---

2. In a Class-1 Sequence, the next expected frame of the Sequence is not received within E_D_TOV.

3. In a Class-2, Class-3 or Class-F Sequence, with out-of-order delivery, a potentially missing frame is identified when the SEQ_CNT of a received frame is not +1 greater than the previous frame of that Sequence. If the potentially missing frame is not received within E_D_TOV, a missing frame error is detected.

4. In a Class-2 or Class-F Sequence with in-order delivery, a potentially missing frame is identified when the SEQ_CNT of a received frame is not +1 greater than the previous frame of that Sequence. If the potentially missing frame is not received within E_D_TOV, a missing frame error is detected. The potentially missing frame could have received a fabric busy or port busy and will be retransmitted later. This check does not apply to Class-3 because frames are never busied in Class-3.

5. In a Class-3 Sequence with in-order delivery, a frame is received with a SEQ_CNT that is not +1 greater than the previous frame of the Sequence. For this check, x'0000' is considered +1 greater than x'FFFF' to allow a wrap of the SEQ_CNT within the Sequence.

6. In any class of service with in-order delivery, a frame is received that has an SOFnx delimiter (where "x" is the class of service) for a Sequence that is not active (the first frame of the Sequence was lost).

7. In any class of service with in-order delivery, a frame is received initiating a new Sequence in an Exchange and the last frame of the prior Sequence has not been received (the last frame of the previous Sequence was lost).

8. In any class of service with in-order delivery when continuously increasing relative offset is used, a frame is received that has a relative offset not equal to the offset of the last byte of the previous frame in that Sequence +1.

19.7.3 Sequence Error Processing - Class-1, Class-2 and Class-F

Processing of Sequence errors in Class-1, Class-2 and Class-F frequently relies on the use of ACK or RJT to report a Sequence error to the Sequence initiator and begin the error processing. None of the link control frames used in these classes of service are available in Class-3 so error processing of Class-3 Sequences is discussed separately in *Sequence Errors - Class-3* on page 304.

Processing Common to all Discard Error Policies. The following actions are taken by the Sequence recipient upon detection of, or following detection of a Sequence error:

• When the discard policy is in effect for the Exchange and a Sequence error is detected by the Sequence recipient, the data field of the frame in error and all subsequent frames of the Sequence (or Sequences if Discard Multiple) is discarded. In all cases, except a stop Sequence condition (Abort Sequence Condition bits in the F_CTL = b'10'), the entire Sequence is discarded. While the data field of received frames is discarded, the frame header is still processed for valid frames received.

• If the Sequence recipient receives a data frame for a Sequence and the recipient wishes to stop the transmission of that Sequence without aborting the Sequence, it can send an

ACK with the Abort Sequence Condition bits in the F_CTL = b'10', indicating stop Sequence. This is not considered an error and the Sequence may use the received portion of the Sequence.

- If the Sequence recipient detects an error within a valid frame of a Sequence it transmits P_RJT with a reason code indicating why P_RJT was sent (see Table 51 on page 250).

- If the Sequence recipient receives a data frame for an active Sequence and it had previously rejected one of more data frames of that Sequence, it continues to indicate that error to the Sequence initiator by setting the Abort Sequence Condition bits in the F_CTL field of subsequent ACKs in the same manner as it would for a missing frame.

- If the Sequence recipient transmits an ACK with the Abort Sequence Condition bits set, or has sent a P_RJT, it posts that information in the Sequence Status Block (SSB) (see *Sequence Status Block (SSB)* on page 199).

The following actions are taken by the Sequence initiator upon receipt of P_RJT or F_RJT, or upon detection of, or following detection of a Sequence error:

- If the Sequence initiator receives a P_RJT or F_RJT it aborts the Sequence by transmitting the Abort Sequence (ABTS) Basic Link Service, unless the Sequence has already been terminated by the Sequence recipient through use of an EOFt or EOFdt End-of-Frame delimiter on the RJT.

- If the Sequence initiator receives an ACK with the Abort Sequence Condition bits requesting stop Sequence (Abort Sequence Condition bits in the F_CTL = b'10'), it ends the Sequence by setting the End_Sequence bit in the next data frame of the Sequence. If the last data frame of the Sequence has already been sent, the FC-4 process is notified but no other action is taken. If the Sequence is still active, but the Sequence initiator does not have a data frame available for transmission, it may send a NOP Basic Link Service frame as part of the active Sequence to indicate End_Sequence.

- If the Sequence initiator detects a missing frame or internal error that prevents normal completion of the Sequence, receives an ACK with a detected rejectable condition, or receives an ACK requesting that the Sequence be aborted (Abort Sequence Condition bits in the F_CTL = b'01'), it aborts the Sequence by transmitting an Abort Sequence (ABTS) Basic Link Service command (see *Abort Sequence (ABTS)* on page 311).

- If the Sequence initiator detects a Sequence timeout (see *Sequence Timeout* on page 298) in Class-1 and end-to-end credit is available, the Sequence initiator can read the Sequence and Exchange status from the Sequence recipient to determine the status of the Sequence (i.e., was the Sequence correctly processed by the Sequence recipient, but the final ACK lost in transmission?). If Sequence delivery has failed, the Sequence initiator may abort the Sequence using Abort Sequence (ABTS).

  If no end-to-end credit is available, or all active Sequences have timed out, the Sequence initiator performs the Link Reset Protocol using the LR Primitive Sequence (see *Link Reset Protocol and Link Recovery States* on page 133).

- If the Sequence initiator detects a Sequence timeout (see *Sequence Timeout* on page 298) in Class-2 and end-to-end credit is available, the Sequence initiator can read the Sequence and Exchange status from the Sequence recipient to determine the status of the Sequence. If Sequence delivery has failed, the Sequence initiator aborts the Sequence using Abort Sequence (ABTS).

If no end-to-end credit is available, the Sequence initiator transmits a Link Credit Reset link control frame (see *Link Credit Reset (LCR)* on page 253) to the recipient which abnormally terminates all active Sequences between the port pair.

Abort, Discard Multiple Sequences - Class-1 and Class-F. If the Sequence recipient detects a missing frame error or internal malfunction in Class-1 for an Exchange with the Abort, Discard Multiple Sequences error policy in effect, it requests that the Sequence be aborted by setting the Abort Sequence Condition bits in the F_CTL field of the frame header to b'01' in the ACK corresponding to the frame during which the missing frame error was detected.

For errors other than missing frame, the Sequence recipient sets the Abort Sequence Condition bits in the F_CTL field of the frame header to b'01' in any subsequent ACKs transmitted. The Sequence recipient may continue to send ACKs for subsequent frames of the Sequence, or any subsequent streamed Sequences, until Abort Sequence (ABTS) is received.

If an ACK is transmitted for the last data frame of the Sequence, the End_Sequence, End_Connection, Sequence Initiative, Invalidate X_ID (F_CTL bits 19, 18, 16, and 14) are ignored and those bits are set to zero in the ACK, along with the Abort Sequence Condition bits in the F_CTL field of the frame header set to b'01'.

Abort, Discard Multiple Sequences - Class-2. If the Sequence recipient detects a missing frame error, transmits a P_RJT, or detects internal malfunction in Class-2 for an Exchange with the Discard Multiple Sequences error policy in effect, it requests that the Sequence be aborted by setting the Abort Sequence Condition bits in the F_CTL field of the frame header to b'01' in the ACK corresponding to the frame during which the missing frame error was detected.

For errors other than missing frame, the Sequence recipient sets the Abort Sequence Condition bits in the F_CTL field of the frame header to b'01' in any subsequent ACKs transmitted. The Sequence recipient may continue to send ACKs for subsequent frames of the Sequence, or any subsequent streamed Sequences, until Abort Sequence (ABTS) is received.

If an ACK is transmitted for the last data frame of the Sequence, normal Sequence completion rules apply in addition to setting the Abort Sequence Condition bits in the F_CTL field of the frame header set to b'01'.

Discard Multiple Sequences with Immediate Retransmission. This error policy is only applicable to Class-1 operations. If the Sequence recipient detects a missing frame error or internal malfunction for an Exchange with the Discard Multiple Sequences with Immediate Retransmission error policy in effect, it requests that the Sequence be aborted and immediately retransmitted by setting the Abort Sequence Condition bits in the F_CTL field of the frame header to b'11' in the ACK corresponding to the frame during which the missing frame error was detected.

If the Sequence recipient detects a missing frame error or internal malfunction in Class-1 for an Exchange with the Discard Multiple Sequences with Immediate Retransmission error policy in effect and the Sequence recipient is not able to transmit an ACK with the same SEQ_ID as the Sequence that requires retransmission, the Sequence observes the behavior described previously in *Abort, Discard Multiple Sequences - Class-1 and Class-F* on page 302 and requests that the Sequence be aborted (without retransmission) by setting the Abort Sequence Condition bits in the F_CTL field of the frame header to b'01' in any subsequent ACKs transmitted.

For errors other than missing frame, the Sequence recipient sets the Abort Sequence Condition bits in the F_CTL field of the frame header to b'11' in any subsequent ACKs transmitted. The Sequence recipient may continue to send ACKs for subsequent frames of the Sequence, or any subsequent streamed Sequences, until a new Sequence (SOFix) is received with the retransmission bit in the F_CTL field set, or an Abort Sequence (ABTS) is received.

If the Sequence recipient transmits an ACK for the last data frame of the Sequence, the End_Sequence, End_Connection, Sequence Initiative, and Invalidate X_ID (F_CTL bits 19, 18, 16, and 14) bits are ignored in the data frame and those bits are set to zero in the ACK, and the Abort Sequence Condition bits in the F_CTL field of the frame header set to b'11'.

If the Sequence recipient is not able to support the Discard Multiple Sequences with Immediate Retransmission error policy, it follows the behavior described in *Abort, Discard Multiple Sequences - Class-1 and Class-F* on page 302.

If the Sequence initiator receives an ACK with the Abort Sequence Condition bits in the F_CTL field of the frame header to b'11' requesting that the Sequence be retransmitted, it will begin retransmission of the first non-deliverable Sequence (as indicated by the SEQ_ID of the first ACK requesting retransmission) by initiating a new Sequence with the retransmission bit set in the F_CTL field of the frame header.

The Sequence initiator will continue to set the retransmission bit until it receives at least one ACK indicating that the retransmitted Sequence has been successfully initiated by the Sequence recipient.

If the Sequence initiator is uncertain of the correct Sequence at which to begin retransmission, it may issue a Read Exchange Concise (REC) Extended Link Service request to determine which Sequences have been delivered or abort the Sequence using Abort Sequence (ABTS).

Abort, Discard a Single Sequence. If the Sequence recipient detects a missing frame error or internal malfunction in Class-1, Class-2 or Class-F for an Exchange with the Abort, discard a single Sequence error policy in effect, it requests that the Sequence be aborted by setting the Abort Sequence Condition bits in the F_CTL field of the frame header to b'01' in the ACK corresponding to the frame at which the missing frame error was detected.

For errors other than missing frame, the Sequence recipient sets the Abort Sequence Condition bits in the F_CTL field of the frame header to b'01' in any subsequent ACKs transmitted for that Sequence. The Sequence recipient may continue to send ACKs for subsequent frames of the Sequence, or any subsequent streamed Sequences (Abort Sequence is not indicated in the streamed Sequences), until the requested Abort Sequence (ABTS) is received.

If the final ACK of the Sequence is transmitted, End_Sequence, End_Connection, Sequence Initiative, and Invalidate X_ID (F_CTL bits 19, 18, 16, and 14) of the data frame are ignored and those bits are set to zero in the ACK along with the Abort Sequence Condition bits in the F_CTL field of the frame header set to b'01'.

Process with Infinite Buffers Error Policy. When the Process policy is in effect for the Exchange, the Sequence recipient ignores errors detected on intermediate frames or timeout errors and does not request Abort Sequence (ABTS) as a result of those errors. Even though Abort Sequence (ABTS) is not requested, the error is reported to the upper-level process of the Sequence recipient.

If the Sequence recipient detects an internal error related to a Sequence, or detects that the first or last frame of a Sequence is missing, it requests that the Sequence by aborted by setting the Abort Sequence Condition bits in the F_CTL field of the frame header to b'01' in any subsequent ACKs and responding as described in *Abort, Discard a Single Sequence* on page 303.

If the Sequence recipient detects an error within a valid frame of a Sequence it transmits P_RJT with a reason code indicating why the P_RJT was sent (see Table 51 on page 250).

The process policy is only applicable to Class-1 operations using ACK_0.

19.7.4 Sequence Errors - Class-3

Errors within a Class-3 Sequence can only be detected by the Sequence recipient because there are no acknowledgments or rejects in Class-3.

When either of the discard error policies is in effect for the Exchange, the Sequence recipient behaves in the same manner as described for Class-1 and Class-2 except that no ACKs are transmitted in response to received frames, or to signal an Abort Sequence condition.

The Sequence recipient discards frames received for one or more Sequences of the affected Exchange after the error depending on whether discard multiple Sequences or discard a single Sequence is in effect. If the discard multiple Sequences policy is in effect, the Sequence recipient continues to discard Sequences for the Exchange until the Exchange is terminated.

The upper-level recovery process may retransmit the entire Sequence, or only that portion of the Sequence following the point of error detection.

Errors that occur during Class-3 operation can be detected in one of the following methods:

1. In a Class-3 Sequence, with out-of-order delivery, a potentially missing frame is identified when the SEQ_CNT of a received frame is not +1 greater than the previous frame of that Sequence. If the potentially missing frame is not received within E_D_TOV, a missing frame error is detected.

2. In a Class-3 Sequence with in-order delivery, a frame is received with a SEQ_CNT that is not +1 greater than the previous frame of the Sequence. For this check, x'0000' is considered to be +1 greater than x'FFFF' to accommodate a SEQ_CNT wrap in the Sequence.

3. In any class of service with in-order delivery, a frame is received that has an SOFnx delimiter (where "x" is the class of service) for an Sequence that is not active (the first frame of the Sequence was lost).

4. In any class of service with in-order delivery, a frame is received initiating a new Sequence in an Exchange and the last frame of the prior Sequence has not been received (the last frame of the previous Sequence was lost).

5. In any class of service with in-order delivery when continuously increasing relative offset is used, a frame is received that has a relative offset not equal to the offset of the last byte of the previous frame in that Sequence +1.

In Class-3 service, notification of the Sequence error, if necessary, is the responsibility of the upper-level protocol process in the Sequence recipient.

19.8 FC-2 Exchange Errors

Most error detection occurs at the Sequence level and there are a rather limited number of Exchange errors. A search of the standard revealed only the following explicit Exchange errors:

- If the current Sequence initiator receives a data frame for an Exchange while it holds the Sequence Initiative an Exchange error is detected. In Class-1, Class-2 or Class-F, the Sequence initiator sends a P_RJT in response to the received data frame. In Class-3, the received data frame is discarded.

- If streamed Sequences in the Exchange use different classes of service.

- If the originator of an Extended Link Service request or FC-4 link service request does not receive an expected reply Sequence within two times R_A_TOV, it detects an Exchange error and aborts the Exchange.

19.9 Chapter Summary

Timers

- Receiver-Transmitter Timeout Value (R_T_TOV)
  - Times Loss-of-Synchronization, link-level protocols
- Error Detect Timeout Value (E_D_TOV)
  - General timer for missing events,
  - Lost frames, lost ACKs, etc.
- Resource Allocation Timeout Value (R_A_TOV)
  - Long timer for reuse of resources
  - Defines latest time frames can be delivered
- Connection Request Timeout Value (CR_TOV)
  - Times Class-1/Class-6 connection request

FC-0/1 Errors

- FC-0 provides only basic error checks
- Loss-of-Synchronization
  - Temporary if <R_T_TOV (100 msec.)
  - Link failure if >R_T_TOV
- Loss-of-Signal
- FC-1 adds encoding and link-level errors
  - Invalid transmission word
  - Invalid 8b/10b transmission character
  - Incorrect disparity
  - Misplaced special character
- Link Reset protocol timeout (LR/LRR)

FC-2 Sequence Errors

- FC-2 is primarily concerned with Sequence delivery
  - Missing frame timeout (E_D_TOV)
  - Missing ACK timeout (E_D_TOV)
  - Missing frame detected (SEQ_CNT)
  - Missing frame detected (Relative Offset)
  - Detection of rejectable condition (P_RJT)
  - Reception of a reject (P_RJT or F_RJT)
  - Detection of an internal malfunction
- Recovery occurs at the Sequence or Exchange level
  - Individual frames are not retransmitted!

Exchange Error Policy

- Sequence error results in one of the following, depending on the Exchange error policy
  - The failed Sequence is processed
  - The failed Sequence is aborted, subsequent Sequences of the Exchange are used
  - The failed Sequence is aborted, subsequent Sequences of the Exchange are not used
  - The failed Sequence and any subsequent Sequences are discarded; retransmission is begun with the failed Sequence
- The error policy used is defined by the FC-4 protocol mapping

Class-3 Errors

- Class-3 transfers the burden of error detection to the Sequence recipient
  - No ACKs or RJTs are sent to indicate delivery failure
  - Errors may be detected by missing frames or timeouts
- Upper-level protocol process must handle Sequence delivery failures
  - Abort the Sequence
  - Abort the Exchange
  - Request retransmission of the Sequence

Exchange Errors

- Most error detection is at the Sequence level
- Exchange error conditions are limited:
  - If Sequence initiator receives a data frame while it holds Sequence Initiative
  - If streamed Sequences within an Exchange use different classes of service
  - If the originator of an Extended Link Service does not receive an expected reply within 2 times R_A_TOV

20. Basic Link Services

Link services provide architected functions available to users of the Fibre Channel port. In most cases, link services will be used by a port driver or adapter function as necessary. Figure 122 illustrates how the Link Services relate to the architected Fibre Channel levels.

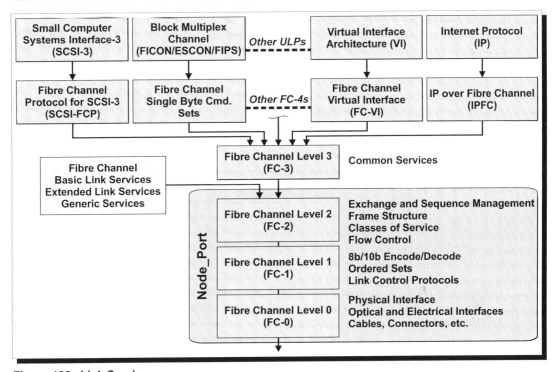

Figure 122. Link Services

Link service frames are categorized as link data frames and follow the flow control and response rules defined for device data frames (with the exception of the Abort Sequence Basic Link Service). They are subject to buffer-to-buffer and end-to-end credit as appropriate for the class of service being used and may receive busy and reject responses, as applicable.

If link service frames are sent prior to N_Port Login, they use the default login parameters as listed in *Default Service Parameters* on page 425. Following N_Port Login, the login service parameters are used.

Optional headers are not allowed in link service frames. Therefore, the DF_CTL field must be x'00' and the link service payload, if any, begins immediately following the frame header

(FC-PH allowed use of the Expiration_Security header in extended or FC-4 link service frames, but this optional header has been removed in FC-PH3 and is no longer applicable).

There are three types of link services defined, depending upon the type of function provided and whether the frame contains a payload or not. They are Basic Link Services, Extended Link Services (described in *Extended Link Services* on page 317), and FC-4 Link Services.

20.1 Basic Link Service Overview

Basic Link Services provide a set of basic control functions that can be used within the context of an existing Exchange to perform simple control functions or pass control information between two ports involved in that Exchange. Table 55 lists the Basic Link Service frames.

Frame Type	R_CTL		Description	Abbrev.
	R_Bits	INFO		
Data (FT-1)	x'8'	x'0'	No Operation (see *No Operation (NOP)* on page 310)	NOP
		x'1'	Abort Sequence (see *Abort Sequence (ABTS)* on page 311)	ABTS
		x'2'	Remove Connection (see *Remove Connection (RMC)* on page 315)	RMC
		x'3'	Reserved	
		x'4'	Basic Accept (see *Basic_Accept (BA_ACC)* on page 309)	BA_ACC
		x'5'	Basic Reject (see *Basic Reject (BA_RJT)* on page 309)	BA_RJT
		x'6'	Preempted (FC-PH3) (see *Preempted (PRMT)* on page 315)	PRMT
		Others	Reserved	

Table 55. Basic Link Service Frames

N_Port Login is not required prior to using a Basic Link Service and a Basic Link Service may be used following an implicit or explicit logout.

While the standard requires that a node port support all Basic Link Service commands, there are cases that arise where a node port may not implement all Basic Link Service commands.

- The Remove Connection (RMC) Basic Link Service command is only applicable to Class-1 and Class-6 operation.

- The Preempted (PRMT) Basic Link Service command is only applicable to Class-1 and Class-6 operation.

- Some profile-defined environments may prohibit use of one or more Basic Link Services in the specific environment (e.g., the Private Loop Direct Attach profile prohibits the use of NOP and RMC). That does not relieve a port from complying with requirements stated in the standard, if standards compliance is claimed.

Basic Link Service commands consist of a single frame request that may be inserted into an existing Sequence associated with the Exchange or sent as a separate Sequence. When a Basic Link Service request is inserted into an existing Sequence, it is considered part of the

Sequence, but is not considered a separate information category (it is not included in the number of information categories per Sequence login parameter).

The Basic Link Service command is contained within the R_CTL field of the frame header and the payload length of the request frame is zero. The type field of the frame header is set to x'00' for both the Basic Link Service request and reply frames.

20.2 Basic Link Service Replies

There are two responses to a Basic Link Service request; Basic_Accept and Basic_Reject.

20.2.1 Basic_Accept (BA_ACC)

Basic_Accept is a single-frame response that notifies the sender of a Basic Link Service command that the command has been completed by the recipient and returns information, where applicable.

The D_ID field of the BA_ACC identifies the source of the Basic Link Service request being accepted. The S_ID field identifies the destination of the Basic Link Service request and source of the BA_ACC.

The payload length is zero, except when the BA_ACC is in response to an ABTS. See *Abort Sequence (ABTS)* on page 311 for a description of the payload when the BA_ACC is in response to an ABTS.

20.2.2 Basic Reject (BA_RJT)

Basic Reject is a single-frame response that notifies the sender of a Basic Link Service command that the command request has been rejected. A four-byte reason code is supplied in the first four bytes of the payload of the BA_RJT frame to identify the reason the request was rejected. Table 56 illustrates the format of the BA_RJT payload.

Word	31:24	23:16	15:08	07:00
0	Reserved	Reason Code	Reason Explanation	Vendor Unique

Table 56. Basic Reject (BA_RJT) Payload Formal

Reason codes identify why BA_RJT was returned and are listed in Table 57 on page 310.

The port may also provide an explanation providing additional information in the third byte of the reject payload if the BA_RJT is in response to the Abort Sequence (ABTS) Basic Link Service. Reason code explanations are listed in Table 58 on page 310.

The OX_ID and RX_ID fields of the BA_RJT are set to match the Exchange in which the Basic Link Service request was received. The SEQ_ID follows normal Sequence identifier assignment rules.

The D_ID field of the BA_RJT identifies the source of the Basic Link Service request being rejected. The S_ID field identifies the destination of the Basic Link Service request and source of the BA_RJT.

Reason Code	Description
x'01'	Invalid Command Code - the command code in bits 27:24 of the R_CTL field is invalid
x'03'	Logical Error - the command is invalid or logically inconsistent for the current conditions
x'05'	Logical Busy - the port is unable to perform the request at this time
x'07'	Protocol Error - an error has been detected that violates FC-2 protocols and is not covered by another reason code
x'09'	Unable to Perform Command Request - the recipient is unable to perform the request at this time (it may be initializing or performing error recovery, for example)
others	reserved
x'FF'	Vendor Unique error (see bits 7:0)

Table 57. Basic Reject (BA_RJT) Reason Codes

Reason Code Explanation	Description	Applicable Commands
x'00'	No additional information	ABTS
x'03'	Invalid OX_ID - RX_ID Combination	ABTS
x'05'	Sequence Aborted, no Sequence information provided	ABTS
others	reserved	

Table 58. Basic Reject (BA_RJT) Reason Code Explanations

20.3 No Operation (NOP)

The NOP Basic Link Service performs no operation of its own, but may be used to carry control bits between the Sequence initiator and recipient. The NOP uses delimiters appropriate to the current conditions, including class of service and Sequence initiation and termination.

There is no payload associated with the NOP, however the frame delimiters are examined by both the fabric and destination port and the F_CTL field is examined by the destination port.

NOP may be used to perform the following functions (all of which would be unusual):

- To initiate a Class-1 or Class-6 connection by using the SOFc1 Start-of-Frame delimiter

- To initiate Sequences, terminate Sequences, or transfer Sequence Initiative when there are no data frames to send

- Terminate a Class-1 or Class-6 connection by using the End_Connection protocol

There is no reply Sequence to NOP (other than ACK, F_RJT, P_RJT, F_BSY, P_BSY, R_RDY, or VC_RDY as applicable to the class of service).

20.4 Abort Sequence (ABTS)

The Abort Sequence Basic Link Service may be used to abort a Sequence or the entire Exchange containing the Sequence. The Exchange and Sequence are identified by the OX_ID, RX_ID, and SEQ_ID fields in the frame header of the ABTS command.

Because ABTS is used during error recovery, normal requirements for frame transmission are relaxed so ABTS can be sent under abnormal conditions. This allows ABTS to be sent even if:

- The available end-to-end credit (EE_Credit) is zero
- The Sequence initiator does not hold the Sequence Initiative for the Exchange
- There is no Sequence open
- The maximum concurrent Sequences allowed by the login parameters are in use
- The port is the connection recipient in a unidirectional Class-1 connection

Sequence Initiative and End_Sequence are always set in the ABTS frame to allow the ABTS recipient to generate a reply Sequence (Basic Accept).

When ABTS is sent within an open Sequence, other F_CTL bits in the ABTS frame header, such as First_Sequence, are set to match those used in the data frames of the Sequence containing the ABTS.

The E_D_TOV and R_A_TOV timers are reset when ABTS is transmitted and used to time the reply to the ABTS.

Following transmission of ABTS, the node port considers the Exchange to be in an indeterminate state and does not transmit any Sequences or provide notification of Sequence arrival for that Exchange until a reply to the ABTS is received and processed, including any recovery that may be needed.

20.4.1 Aborting a Sequence with ABTS

The Sequence initiator may request that the Sequence recipient abort one or more Sequences of an Exchange by transmitting ABTS as part of the open Sequence being aborted.

The SEQ_ID field in the frame header of the ABTS is set to the same SEQ_ID as was used for the last Sequence transmitted by the Sequence initiator. The delimiters used for the ABTS use the same class of service as the Sequence being aborted.

20.4.2 Aborting an Exchange with ABTS

When ABTS is used to abort an Exchange, the ABTS may be transmitted by either the Sequence initiator or recipient of the last Sequence as either a part of the open Sequence or in a new Sequence.

ABTS is considered a continuation of the last Sequence, or the Sequence in error. If the last Sequence is still open and the Sequence initiator transmits ABTS, the SEQ_ID of the open Sequence is used in the ABTS frame. The SEQ_CNT is incremented by +1 from the SEQ_CNT of the last data frame transmitted for the Sequence (i.e., the ABTS follows the normal SEQ_ID and SEQ_CNT rules).

If ABTS is transmitted as a new Sequence, the transmitting port may use any SEQ_ID available for use with the destination port (SEQ_ID uniqueness rules must be observed) and the SEQ_CNT may be either continuously increasing from the last data frame of the previous Sequence or x'0000'.

Because the Sequence recipient may transmit ABTS, even though it does not have the Sequence Initiative for the Exchange, the Sequence initiator may receive ABTS while it still holds the initiative. If this occurs, the Sequence initiator aborts the Exchange by setting the Last_Sequence bit to one in the BA_ACC to the ABTS.

20.4.3 ABTS BA_ACC Reply

The expected reply to ABTS is a Basic Accept (BA_ACC) frame indicating the action taken by the ABTS recipient.

When ABTS is received, the ABTS recipient may abort no Sequences, one Sequence, multiple Sequences, or the entire Exchange depending upon the status of each Sequence within the Exchange and the Exchange error policy in effect for the Exchange (see *Exchange Error Policies* on page 183).

Depending upon the Exchange error policy, data frames for deliverable Sequences within the Exchange received after ABTS may be processed prior to transmission of the BA_ACC reply to the ABTS.

The format of the BA_ACC in reply to ABTS is shown in Table 59. The SEQ_ID validity bit indicates if the ABTS recipient has information regarding the last deliverable Sequence.

Size (bytes)	Description

1	SEQ_ID validity
	    x'00' - SEQ_ID field is invalid
	    x'80' - SEQ_ID field is valid

1	SEQ_ID of the last Sequence deliverable to the higher-level process, if valid is set
2	reserved
2	OX_ID of target Exchange
2	RX_ID of target Exchange
2	Low SEQ_CNT
2	High SEQ_CNT

Table 59. Basic Accept (BA_ACC) Payload in Response to ABTS

No Sequences Aborted. To indicate that the Sequence containing the ABTS is the last deliverable Sequence and nothing was aborted by the ABTS recipient, the following values are set:

- SEQ_ID Validity = valid (information on the last deliverable Sequence is available)
- SEQ_ID = the SEQ_ID of the Sequence containing the ABTS frame
- Low SEQ_CNT = High SEQ_CNT = SEQ_CNT of the ABTS frame

One or More Sequences Aborted, Information on Last Deliverable Sequence. In order to indicate that the ABTS recipient has information on the last deliverable Sequence but one or more subsequent Sequences were aborted, the following values are set (if the Exchange was aborted, Last_Sequence is set in the F_CTL field of the BA_ACC frame header). The Low SEQ_CNT and High SEQ_CNT values define the Recovery Qualifier range, if one has been established.

- SEQ_ID Validity = valid (information on the last deliverable Sequence is available)
- SEQ_ID = the SEQ_ID of the last deliverable Sequence received from the ABTS initiator
- Low SEQ_CNT = the SEQ_CNT of the last data frame of the last deliverable Sequence, or x'0000' if the Exchange was aborted
- High SEQ_CNT = SEQ_CNT of the ABTS frame, or x'FFFF' if the Exchange was aborted

One or More Sequences Aborted, No Information on Last Deliverable Sequence. To indicate that the ABTS recipient does not have information regarding the last deliverable Sequence and has aborted one or more subsequent Sequences, the following values are set (if the Exchange was aborted, Last_Sequence is set in the F_CTL field of the BA_ACC frame header). The Low SEQ_CNT and High SEQ_CNT values define the Recovery Qualifier range, if one has been established.

- SEQ_ID Validity = invalid (information on the last deliverable Sequence is not available)
- SEQ_ID = invalid (not meaningful)
- Low SEQ_CNT = x'0000'
- High SEQ_CNT = SEQ_CNT of the ABTS frame, or x'FFFF' if the Exchange was aborted

20.4.4 Recovery Qualifier

When a Sequence is aborted in a connectionless class of service (Class-2 or Class-3), it is possible that one or more frames associated with the aborted Sequence may still be in transit in the topology. If a new Sequence is initiated between the Sequence initiator and Sequence responder of the aborted Sequence and that Sequence has the same SEQ_ID and SEQ_CNT values as the frames still in transit from the aborted Sequence, reassembly errors could result should those frames ultimately arrive at the Sequence recipient.

To prevent this from occurring, when a Sequence is aborted in Class-2 or Class-3, a Recovery Qualifier may be established identifying the SEQ_ID and a range of SEQ_CNT values that cannot be reused because they may still be in transit.

While the Recovery Qualifier is active, the Sequence initiator is not allowed to originate any data frames that fall within the Recovery Qualifier range. Furthermore, any frames received by either the Sequence initiator or Sequence recipient that fall within the Recovery Qualifier range are assumed to be part of the aborted Sequence and are discarded without processing.

The Recovery Qualifier remains in effect long enough to ensure that all frames associated with the aborted Sequence have either been discarded or can no longer possibly be delivered. The time value used is the Resource_Allocation timeout value (R_A_TOV) discussed in *Resource Allocation Timeout Value (R_A_TOV)* on page 294.

Once R_A_TOV has expired for the aborted Sequence, the Sequence initiator transmits a Reinstate Recovery Qualifier (RRQ) Extended Link Service command to inform the Sequence recipient that the affected SEQ_ID and SEQ_CNT range can now be reused. The Reinstate Recovery Qualifier Extended Link Service is described on *Reinstate Recovery Qualifier (RRQ)* on page 373.

20.4.5 ABTS Example, Exchange Aborted

Figure 123 on page 314 illustrates use of ABTS to abort an Exchange. In this case, the ABTS recipient sets Last_Sequence = 1 to indicate that the Exchange is being aborted.

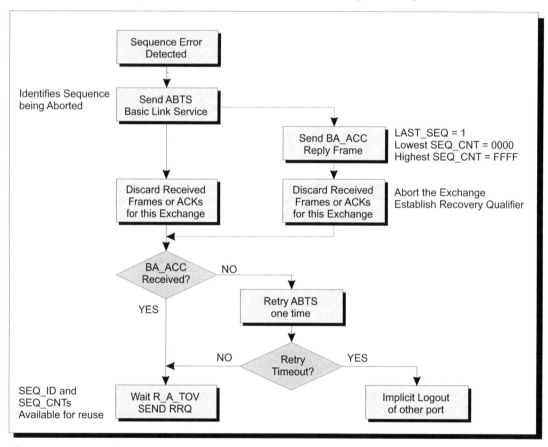

Figure 123. Abort Sequence-Last Sequence (ABTS-LS) Protocol

20.5 Remove Connection (RMC)

The Remove Connection Basic Link Service may be used to request an immediate Class-1 disconnection, without observing the normal disconnection protocol. The destination is requested to respond with an ACK frame using the EOFdt end-to-frame delimiter.

RMC results in termination of open Sequences in both the ports engaged in the Class-1 connection and should not be used in lieu of the normal disconnection process.

There is no reply Sequence to RMC (other than the requested ACK, F_RJT, or P_RJT).

20.6 Preempted (PRMT)

The Preempted Basic Link Service frame was added in FC-PH3 as part of the preemption protocol. PRMT is used by the fabric to notify the node port that the connection in which this node port is engaged has been preempted and no longer exists. All open Sequences associated with that connection are abnormally terminated as a result of the preemption.

The D_ID field of the PRMT is set to the address of the node port being notified of the preemption. The S_ID field is set to the S_ID field of the SOFc1 connect-request frame that caused the preemption.

There is no reply Sequence to PRMT (other than ACK or P_RJT).

20.7 Chapter Summary

Basic Link Services

- The standard defines a small set of basic services
  - No Operation (NOP)
  - Abort Sequence (ABTS)
  - Remove Connection (RMC)
  - Preempted (PRMT)
- All may be issued within an existing Sequence
- ABTS is the only commonly used service
  - Used to abort a failed Sequence or Exchange
- The data field is zero bytes on all Basic Link Services
  - All necessary information is in the frame header

No Operation (NOP)

- Performs no operation
- May be used to initiate a Class-1 connection (using the SOFc1 delimiter)
- May be used to transfer bits to Sequence recipient
  - Sequence Initiative
  - End_Sequence
  - Last_Sequence

Abort Sequence (ABTS)

- Used to abort a failed Sequence or Exchange
- Sent by the Sequence initiator
  - Within an existing Sequence
  - As a separate Sequence
- May be requested by the Sequence recipient
  - In an ACK or RJT
- Normal response is Basic Accept (BA_ACC)
  - May indicate that the Exchange was aborted by setting Last_Sequence

Remove Connection (RMC)

- Requests immediate Class-1 connection removal
- Does not follow normal removal protocol
  - Recipient replies with ACK using EOFdt
  - Results in termination of open Sequences

Preempted (PRMT)

- Added by FC-PH3
- Notifies a node port that its Class-1 connection has been preempted
  - Removed due to a higher-priority connect request

21. Extended Link Services

Extended Link Services provide a set of protocol-independent Fibre Channel functions that can be used by a port to perform a specified function or service at another port. Extended Link Services are described in the Fibre Channel Link Services (FC-LS) standard.

Each Extended Link Service (ELS) operation is performed using a separate Exchange. An Extended Link Service operation normally consists of a request (or command) Sequence with a transfer of Sequence Initiative and a reply (or response) Sequence that ends the Exchange. Each Sequence consists of one or more frames and observes normal Sequence identification and management rules.

An illustration of the Extended Link Service protocol is shown in Figure 124.

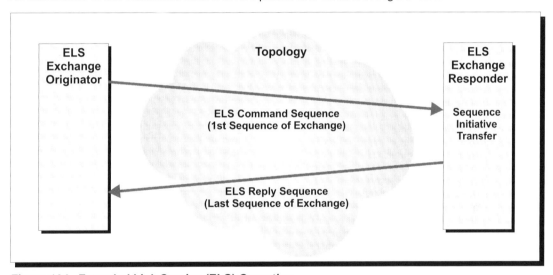

Figure 124. Extended Link Service (ELS) Operation

The type field in the frame header is set to x'01' for both the request and reply Sequences to indicate the Extended Link Service protocol.

The R_CTL field in the frame header of the request Sequence is set to x'22' (Link Data Frame, Unsolicited Control). The First_Sequence of Exchange bit (bit 21) is set to one in the F_CTL field and the Exchange Error Policy (bits 5:4 of F_CTL) is set to Abort, Discard Multiple (b'00').

If a reply Sequence is expected, the Last_Sequence of Exchange bit (bit 20) is set to zero and Sequence Initiative is transferred (bit 16 is set to one). If no reply Sequence is expected, the Last_Sequence of Exchange bit (bit 20) is set to one and the setting of the Sequence Initiative bit is not defined.

The R_CTL field in the frame header of the reply Sequence is set to x'23' (Link Data Frame, Solicited Control). The Last_Sequence of Exchange bit (bit 20) is set to one in the F_CTL field and the setting of the Sequence Initiative bit is not defined.

Extended Link Services may use any class of service available between the two ports and observes normal class of service and flow control rules defined for that class of service.

Bits 31:24 (the first byte) of the first word of the Extended Link Service request Sequence contains the command. The remaining three bytes of the first word contain command-specific parameters defined by the specific Extended Link Service request. Table 60 illustrates the format of the Extended Link Service command request.

Word	31:24	23:16	15:8	7:0
0	ELS Command	ELS specific parameters		
1 to n	ELS specific parameters (if present)			

Table 60. ELS Request Sequence Format

21.1 Link Service Accept (LS_ACC)

Most Extended Link Service requests result in a reply Sequence (although there are some exceptions). Bits 31:24 (the first byte) of the first word of the Extended Link Service reply Sequence indicates if the request was accepted (LS_ACC) or rejected (LS_RJT). The remaining three bytes of the word contain command-specific parameters defined by the specific Extended Link Service request. Additional words may return function-specific information.

The LS_ACC reply Sequence notifies the originator of an ELS request that the request has completed and may return information appropriate to the request. Any information returned follows the ELS reply code in the first word of the first frame of the Sequence. Table 61 illustrates the general format of the LS_ACC reply.

Word	31:24	23:16	15:8	7:0
0	LS_ACC = x'02'	ELS specific information		
1 to n	ELS specific information (if present)			

Table 61. Link Service Accept (LS_ACC) Reply Format

21.2 Support of Extended Link Services

The standard only requires support of the Fabric Login (FLOGI), N_Port Login (PLOGI), Logout (LOGO), and Reinstate Recovery Qualifier (RRQ) Extended Link Service commands and replies. Support of other link service requests is optional, although some technical reports may require support of certain Extended Link Services for functional or interoperability reasons.

While a port is not required to generate PLOGI, it must be capable of responding to one, if received. If a port that does not generate PLOGI is used in a point-to-point configuration and the Port_Name is greater than the other node port's name, the other node port may timeout waiting to receive a PLOGI request. This may result in a non-functional configuration.

21.3 ELS Command Codes

Table 62 lists the Extended Link Service requests and replies and the page where each is described. Because new Extended Link Services are being defined as an ongoing part of the standards development process, the reader should consult the most recent versions of the appropriate standards for a complete and current listing.

Code (hex)	Abbrev.	Extended Link Service	Reply Seq?	PLOGI Req'd?	Ref. Page
01	LS_RJT	Link Service Reject (LS_RJT)	n/a	n/a	400
02	LS_ACC	Link Service Accept (LS_ACC)	n/a	n/a	318
03	PLOGI	N_Port Login (PLOGI)	Yes	No	357
04	FLOGI	Fabric Login (FLOGI)	Yes	No	343
05	LOGO	Logout (LOGO)	Yes	No	352
06	ABTX	Obsolete (was Abort Exchange)			
07	RCS	Read Connection Status (RCS)	Yes	Yes	368
08		Obsolete (was Read Exchange Status Block - RES)			
09		Obsolete (was Read Sequence Status Block - RSS)			
0A	RSI	Request Sequence Initiative (RSI)	Yes	Yes	389
0B	ESTS	Establish Streaming (ESTS)	Yes	Yes	335
0C	ESTC	Estimate Credit (ESTC)	No	Yes	336
0D	ADVC	Advise Credit (ADVC)	Yes	Yes	321
0E	RTV	Read Timeout Value (RTV)	Yes	Yes	371
0F	RLS	Read Link Error Status Block (RLS)	Yes	Yes	370
x10	ECHO	Echo (ECHO)	Yes	No	334
11	TEST	Test	No	Yes	395
12	RRQ	Reinstate Recovery Qualifier (RRQ)	Yes	Yes	373
13	REC	Read Exchange Concise (REC)	Yes	Yes	369
14		Reserved (some implementations may have used this for the FCP SRR FC-4 Link Service)			
15:1F		Reserved			
20	PRLI	Process Login (PRLI)	Yes	Yes	360
21	PRLO	Process Logout (PRLO)	Yes	Yes	364
22		Obsolete (was State Change Notification - SCN)			
23	TPLS	Test Process Login State (TPLS)	Yes	Yes	396
24	TPRLO	Third-Party Process Logout (TPRLO)	Yes	Yes	398
25		Obsolete (was Login Control List Management - LCLM)			
26:2F		Reserved			
30	GAID	Get Alias_ID (GAID)	Yes	No	347
31	FACT	Fabric Activate Alias_ID (FACT)	Yes	No	340
32	FDACT	Fabric Deactivate Alias_ID (FDACT)	Yes	No	342
33	NACT	N_Port Activate Alias_ID (NACT)	Yes	No	355
34	NDACT	N_Port Deactivate Alias_ID (NDACT)	Yes	No	356
35:3F		Reserved			
40		Obsolete (was Quality of Service Request - QoSR)			

Table 62. Extended Link Services (Part 1 of 2)

Code (hex)	Abbrev.	Extended Link Service	Reply Seq?	PLOGI Req'd?	Ref. Page
41		Obsolete (was Read Virtual Circuit Status - RVCS)			
42:4F		Reserved			
50	PDISC	Discover N_Port Service Parameters (PDISC)	Yes	Yes	333
51	FDISC	Discover Fabric Service Parameters (FDISC)	Yes	Yes	332
52	ADISC	Discover Address (ADISC)	Yes	Yes	331
53		Obsolete (was Report Node Capabilities - RNC)			
54		Obsolete (was FC Address Resolution Protocol (FARP) Request)			
55		Obsolete (was FC Address Resolution Protocol (FARP) Reply)			
56		Obsolete (was Read Port Status Block - RPS)			
57		Obsolete (was Read Port List - RPL)			
58	RPBC	Report Port Buffer Conditions (RPBC)	Yes	Yes	383
59:5F		Reserved			
60	FAN	Fabric Address Notification (FAN)	No	No	341
61	RSCN	Registered State Change Notification (RSCN)	Yes	No	379
62	SCR	State Change Registration (SCR)	Yes	No	394
63	RFNT	Report Node FC-4 Types (RNFT)	Yes	Yes	381
64:67		Reserved			
68	CSR	Clock Synchronization Request (CSR)	Yes	No	328
69	CSU	Clock Synchronization Update (CSU)	No	No	331
6A:6F		Reserved			
70	LINIT	Loop Initialize (LINIT)	Yes	No	353
71		Obsolete (was Loop Port Control - LPC)			
72	LSTS	Loop Status (LSTS)	Yes	No	354
73:76		Reserved			
77		Vendor Specific (was Read Topology Information - RTIN)			
78	RNID	Request Node-Identification Data (RNID)	Yes	No	385
79	RLIR	Registered Link-Incident Report (RLIR)	Yes	Yes	374
7A	LIRR	Link-Incident Record Registration (LIRR)	Yes	Yes	350
7B	SRL	Scan Remote Loop (SRL)	Yes	Yes	390
7C	SBRP	Set Bit-Error Reporting Parameters (SBRP)	Yes	Yes	391
7D	RPSC	Report Port Speed Capabilities (RPSC)	Yes	Yes	384
7E	QSA	Query Security Attributes (QSA)	Yes	No	367
7F	EVFP	Exchange Virtual Fabrics Parameters (EVFP)	Yes	n/a	337
80	LKA	Link Keep Alive (LKA)	Yes	No	351
81:8F		Reserved			
90	AUTH_ELS	Authentication (AUTH_ELS) Link Service	Yes	No	322
91:96		Reserved			
97	RFCN	Registered Fabric Change Notification (RFCN)	Yes	n/a	372
A0:A6		Reserved for Fast Fabric Initialization (FFI)			
A7:FF		Reserved			

Table 62. Extended Link Services (Part 2 of 2)

21.4 Advise Credit (ADVC)

The Advise Credit (ADVC) request is used to inform the destination port of the amount of end-to-end credit the source port is requesting. The Extended Link Service request contains the node port's PLOGI service parameters, except that the end-to-end credit fields represent the amount of credit desired, rather than the amount being granted.

21.4.1 Advise Credit (ADVC) Request

The format of the ADVC Extended Link Service request is shown in Table 63 (see *N_Port Login (PLOGI)* on page 357 for a description of the login service parameters).

Word	Bits 31:24	Bits 23:16	Bits 15:8	Bits 7:0
0	Command = x'0D'	x'00'	x'00'	x'00'
1 to 4	Common Service Parameters (16 bytes)			
5 to 6	N_Port Name (8 bytes)			
7 to 8	Node Name (8 bytes)			
9 to 12	Class-1 Service Parameters (16 bytes)			
13 to 17	Class-2 Service Parameters (16 bytes7)			
18 to 21	Class-3 Service Parameters (16 bytes)			
22 to 25	Obsolete (was Class-4 Service Parameters) (16 bytes)			
26 to 29	Vendor Version Level (16 bytes)			

Table 63. Advise Credit (ADVC) Request Sequence

While ADVC is intended primarily to support the estimate credit protocol described in the *Estimate Credit Procedure* on page 269, it may be used for other purposes as well.

21.4.2 Advise Credit (ADVC) Reply

The LS_ACC reply contains the revised end-to-end credit as indicated by the appropriate class-specific service parameters and follows the same format as the ADVC request (with the exception of the first word, which is equal to x'02 00 00 00').

The revised credit may equal the amount requested in the ADVC Extended Link Service request or be less, depending upon the buffer management mechanism of the sending port. The class validity bit designates which end-to-end credit values are being revised. The revised end-to-end credit replaces the current login credit for the port sending the LS_ACC reply.

21.5 Authentication (AUTH_ELS) Link Service

Node ports use the AUTH_ELS to perform authentication with the fabric and with other node ports. The request is sent from a node port to the fabric login address (x'FF FF FE') or to another node port using protocol type x'01' (Extended Link Services).

The formats of all of the AUTH_ELS link service request is shown in Table 64.

Word	31:24	23:16	15:08	07:00
0	**Command Code:** AUTH_ELS = x'90'	AUTH Flags (see Table 66 on page 323)	AUTH Message Code (see Table 65 on page 322)	Protocol Version
1	Message Length in bytes(4 bytes)			
2	Transaction Identifier (4 bytes)			
3:n	Message Payload (variable)			

Table 64. AUTH_ELS Request Format

21.5.1 AUTH_ELS Message Codes

The purpose of the AUTH_ELS link service is to deliver authentication messages. The message is identified by the AUTH Message Codes listed in Table 65.

Message Code Value	AUTH Message Description
x'01' - x'09'	Reserved for legacy implementations
x'0A'	AUTH_Reject (see *AUTH_Reject Message Payload* on page 324)
x'0B'	AUTH_Negotiate (see *AUTH_Negotiate Message Payload* on page 323)
x'0C'	AUTH_Done (see *AUTH_Done Message Payload* on page 323)
x'10'	DHCHAP_Challenge (see *DHCHAP_Challenge Message Payload* on page 324)
x'11'	DHCHAP_Reply (see *DHCHAP_Reply Message Payload* on page 325)
x'12'	DHCHAP_Success (see *DHCHAP_Success Message Payload* on page 325)
x'13'	FCAP_Request (see *FCAP_Request Message Payload* on page 325)
x'14'	FCAP_Acknowledge (see *FCAP_Acknowledge Message Payload* on page 326)
x'15'	FCAP_Confirm (see *FCAP_Confirm Message Payload* on page 326)
x'16'	FCPAP_Init (see *FCPAP_Init Message Payload* on page 327)
x'17'	FCPAP_Accept (see *FCPAP_Accept Message Payload* on page 327)
x'18'	FCPAP_Complete (see *FCPAP_Complete Message Payload* on page 327)
x'FO' - x'FE'	Vendor specific
other values	Reserved

Table 65. AUTH Message Codes

AUTH Flags. The AUTH Flags are described in Table 66 on page 323.

Bit	AUTH_ELS Description
7	1 = More fragments to follow, 0 = No more fragments
6	Concatenation Flag
5:1	Reserved
0	Sequence Number

Table 66. AUTH Flags

21.5.2 AUTH_Negotiate Message Payload

The AUTH_Negotiate message transfers a list of usable authentication protocols from the authentication initiator to the authentication responder. Protocols are listed in the order of most desirable to least desirable. Table 67 shows the format of the AUTH_Negotiate message.

Word	31:24	23:16	15:08	07:00
0:1	Authentication Initiator Name (8 bytes)			
2	Number of Usable Authentication Protocols in list (4 bytes)			
	Authentication Protocol #1 Parameter Length (4 bytes)			
	Authentication Protocol #1 Protocol Identifier (4 bytes)			
	x'00 00 00 01' = DH-CHAP x'00 00 00 02' = FCAP x'00 00 00 03' = FCPAP		x'00 00 00 04' = IKEv2 x'00 00 00 05' = IKEvv2-AUTH others = Vendor specific or reserved	
	Parameter 1 Tag = x'00 01' (HashList)		Parameter 1 Word Count (number of Hash Functions included)	
	Parameter 1 Value = Hash Function Identifier (4 bytes for each identifier included) x'00 00 00 05' = MD5 Hash Function x'00 00 00 06' = SHA-1 Hash Function			
	Parameter 2 Tag = x'00 02' (DHgIDList)		Parameter 2 Word Count (number of DH groups included)	
	Parameter 2 Value = Diffe-Hellman Group Identifier (4 bytes for each identifier included)			
	x'00 00 00 00' = Null x'00 00 00 01' = DH Group 1,024 x'00 00 00 02' = DH Group 1,280 x'00 00 00 03' = DH Group 1,536 x'00 00 00 04' = DH Group 2,048		x'00 00 00 05' = DH Group 3,072 x'00 00 00 06' = DH Group 4,096 x'00 00 00 07' = DH Group 6,144 x'00 00 00 08' = DH Group 8,192 other values = reserved	

Table 67. AUTH_Negotiate Message Format

21.5.3 AUTH_Done Message Payload

The AUTH_Done message completes the transaction for some authentication protocols. The AUTH_Done message has no Message Payload.

21.5.4 AUTH_Reject Message Payload

The AUTH_Reject message indicates rejection of a received authentication message. The format of the AUTH_Reject message is shown in Table 68.

Word	31:24	23:16	15:08	07:00
0	Reason Code: x'01' = Auth. Failure x'02' = Logical Error	Reason Code Explanation	Reserved	

Table 68. AUTH_Reject Message Format

AUTH_Reject Reason Code Explanations are listed in Table 69.

Value	Reason Code Explanation
x'01'	Authentication Mechanism Not Usable
x'02'	DH Group Not Usable
x'03'	Hash Function Not Usable
x'04'	Authentication Transaction Already Started
x'05'	Authentication Failed
x'06'	Incorrect Payload
x'07'	Incorrect Authentication Protocol Message
x'08'	Restart Authentication Protocol
x'09'	AUTH Concatenation not Supported
x'0A'	Unsupported protocol Version
others	Reserved

Table 69. AUTH_Reject Reason Code Explanations

21.5.5 DHCHAP_Challenge Message Payload

The DHCHAP_Challenge message is sent from an authentication responder to the authentication initiator when DH-CHAP has been selected from the AUTH_Negotiate message. The format of the DHCHAP_Challenge message is shown in Table 70.

Word	31:24	23:16	15:08	07:00
0	Authentication Responder Name (variable)			
	Hash Identifier (4 bytes - see Table 67 on page 323)			
	DH Group Identifier (4 bytes - see Table 67 on page 323)			
	Challenge Value Length (4 bytes)			
	Challenge Value (variable)			
	DH Value Length (4 bytes)			
	DH Value (variable)			

Table 70. DHCHAP_Challenge Message Format

21.5.6 DHCHAP_Reply Message Payload

The DHCHAP_Reply message is sent from the authentication initiator to the authentication responder in reply to a challenge message. The format is shown in Table 71.

Word	31:24	23:16	15:08	07:00
	Response Value Length (4 bytes)			
	Response Value (variable)			
	DH Value Length (4 bytes)			
	DH Value (variable)			
	Challenge Value Length (4 bytes)			
	Challenge Value (variable)			

Table 71. DHCHAP_Reply Message Format

21.5.7 DHCHAP_Success Message Payload

The DHCHAP_Success message is sent to indicate a successful response to a challenge. The format is shown in Table 72.

Word	31:24	23:16	15:08	07:00
0	Response Value Length (4 bytes)			
1:n	Response Value (variable)			

Table 72. DHCHAP_Success Message Format

21.5.8 FCAP_Request Message Payload

The FCAP_Request message is sent from the authentication responder to the authentication initiator. The format of the FCAP_Request message is shown in Table 73.

Word	31:24	23:16	15:08	07:00
Cert.	Responder Certificate Identifier: x'00 01' = FCAP X.509 Certificate other values = reserved		Responder Certificate Length (2 bytes)	
	Responder Certificate Data (variable)			
Nonce	Authentication Responder Nonce Identifier: x'00 01' = Binary String		Authentication Responder Nonce Length (2 bytes = x'01 00')	
	Authentication Responder Nonce Value (256 bytes)			
	Hash Identifier (4 bytes - see Table 67 on page 323)			
	DH Group Identifier (4 bytes - see Table 67 on page 323)			

Table 73. FCAP_Request Message Format

21.5.9 FCAP_Acknowledge Message Payload

The FCAP_Acknowledge message is sent from the authentication initiator to the authentication responder. The format of the FCAP_Acknowledge message is shown in Table 74.

Word	31:24	23:16	15:08	07:00
Nonce	Authentication Initiator Nonce Identifier: x'00 01' = Binary String		Authentication Initiator Nonce Length (256 bytes)	
	Authentication Initiator Nonce Value (256 bytes)			
Sig.	Authentication Initiator Signature Identifier: x'00 01' = SHA-1		Authentication Initiator Signature Length (2 bytes = x'00 80')	
	Authentication Initiator Signature Value (128 bytes)			
Cert.	Authentication Initiator Certificate Identifier: x'00 01' = FCAP X.509 Certificate other values = reserved		Authentication Initiator Certificate Length (2 bytes)	
	Authentication Initiator Certificate Data (variable)			
DH Value	DH Value Length (4 bytes)			
	DH Value (variable)			

Table 74. FCAP_Acknowledge Message Format

21.5.10 FCAP_Confirm Message Payload

The FCAP_Confirm message is sent from the authentication responder to the authentication initiator. The format of the FCAP_Confirm message is shown in Table 75.

Word	31:24	23:16	15:08	07:00
Sig.	Authentication Responder Signature ID: x'00 01' = SHA-1		Authentication Responder Signature Length (2 bytes = x'00 80')	
	Authentication Initiator Signature Value (128 bytes)			
DH Value	DH Value Length (4 bytes)			
	DH Value (variable)			

Table 75. FCAP_Confirm Message Format

21.5.11 FCPAP_Init Message Payload

The FCPAP_Init message is sent from the authentication responder to the authentication initiator. The format of the FCPAP_Init message is shown in Table 76.

Word	31:24	23:16	15:08	07:00
	Authentication Responder Name (variable)			
	Authentication Data Length (4 bytes)			
	Authentication Data Value (variable)			
Salt	SRP Salt Length (4 bytes)			
	SRP Salt Value (variable)			
	Hash Identifier (4 bytes)			
	DH Group Identifier (4 bytes)			

Table 76. FCPAP_Init Message Format

21.5.12 FCPAP_Accept Message Payload

The FCPAP_Accept message is sent from the authentication initiator to the authentication responder. The format of the FCPAP_Accept message is shown in Table 77.

Word	31:24	23:16	15:08	07:00
	Authentication Data Length (4 bytes)			
	Authentication Data Value (variable)			
Hash	Hash Length (4 bytes)			
	Hash Value (variable)			
Salt	SRP Salt Length (4 bytes)			
	SRP Salt Value (variable)			

Table 77. FCPAP_Accept Message Format

21.5.13 FCPAP_Complete Message Payload

The FCPAP_Complete message is sent from the authentication initiator to the authentication responder. The format of the FCPAP_Complete message is shown in Table 78.

Word	31:24	23:16	15:08	07:00
Hash	Hash Length (4 bytes)			
	Hash Value (variable)			

Table 78. FCPAP_Complete Message Format

21.6 Clock Synchronization Request (CSR)

The Clock Synchronization Request Extended Link Service request is sent to the Clock Synchronization Server (at address x'FF FF F5') or the Fabric Controller (at address x'FF FF FD') to request the destination either send or quit sending periodic Clock Synchronization Updates (CSU).

21.6.1 Clock Synchronization Request (CSR) Request

The format of the CSR Extended Link Service request is shown in Table 79.

Word	Bits 31:24	Bits 23:16	Bits 15:8	Bits 7:0
0	Command = x'68'	x'00'	x'00'	x'00'
1	Clock Sync Mode	CS_Accuracy	CS_Implemented_MSB	CS_Implemented_LSB
2	CS_Update_Period			

Table 79. Clock Synchronization Request (CSR) Request Sequence

Clock Sync Mode (word 1, bits 31:24). The value in this field specifies the clock synchronization mode and indicates which fields contain valid information as shown in Table 80.

Value	When sent to the Clock Sync Server	When sent to the Fabric Controller
x'00'	Enable clock synchronization service to this client. The following fields are not meaningful in the CSR request. CS_Accuracy CS_Implemented_MSB CS_Implemented_LSB CS_Update_Period	Return Quality of Service parameters. The following fields are not meaningful in the CSR request: CS_Accuracy CS_Implemented_MSB CS_Implemented_LSB CS_Update_Period
x'01'	Enable clock synchronization service to this client. The following fields contain the requested Quality of Service parameters. CS_Accuracy CS_Implemented_MSB CS_Implemented_LSB CS_Update_Period	Return Quality of Service parameters. The following fields contain the requested Quality of Service parameters. CS_Accuracy CS_Implemented_MSB CS_Implemented_LSB CS_Update_Period
x'FF'	Disable clock synchronization service to this client.	Reserved
Other values	Reserved	Reserved

Table 80. Clock Sync Mode

CS_Accuracy (word 1, bits 23:16). This field indicates the requested accuracy of the clock synchronization value as it leaves the server port. The byte contains two values, the CS_Accuracy_Mantissa (bits 23:21) and CS_Accuracy_ Exponent (bits 20:16).

Specifically, the request is that the Clock Count value is always within the range of:

$$T\_reference \pm (0.5 + CS\_Accuracy\_Mantissa * 2^{-4}) * 2^{(CS\_Accuracy\_Exponent-30)}$$

where:

- T_reference is the clock reference value internal to the server
- CS_Accuracy_Mantissa is a value from '000'b to '111'b
- CS_Accuracy_Exponent is a value from '00000'b to '11111'b

Example #1: If CS_Accuracy Mantissa = '001'b and the Exponent = '01011'b, then the Clock Synchronization value as it exits the server is requested to be within the range of:

$$T\_reference \pm 1.073 \ \mu sec.$$

Example #2: If CS_Accuracy Mantissa = '111'b and the Exponent = '11000'b, then the Clock Synchronization value as it exits the server is requested to be within the range of:

$$T\_reference \pm 14.65 \ msec$$

CS_Implemented_MSB (word 1, bits 15:08). This field contains a value within the range of 0 to 63. This value indicates the bit position of the most significant bit (MSB) requested from the 64-bit Clock Count field. For example, a value of '110111'b (55 decimal) indicates the client requests that the highest bit containing meaningful information be bit 55 of the Clock Count field (the most significant bit of byte 1).

CS_Implemented_LSB (word 1, bits 07:00). This field contains a value within the range of 0 to 63. This value indicates the bit position of the least significant bit (LSB) requested from the 64-bit Clock Count field. For example, a value of '001000'b (16 decimal) indicates the client requests that the lowest bit containing meaningful information be bit 16 of the Clock Count field (the least-significant bit of byte 6).

CS_Update_Period (word 2). This field contains a value that represents the time, in microseconds, between consecutive updates from the Clock Synchronization server.

21.6.2 Clock Synchronization Request (CSR) LS_ACC Reply

The format of the LS_ACC reply is shown in Table 81.

Word	Bits 31:24	Bits 23:16	Bits 15:8	Bits 7:0
0	LS_ACC = x'02'	x'00'	x'00'	x'00'
1	Clock Sync Mode	CS_Accuracy	CS_Implemented_MSB	CS_Implemented_LSB
2	CS_Update_Period			

Table 81. Clock Synchronization Request (CSR) LS_ACC Reply

Clock Sync Mode (word 1, bits 31:24). The value in this field specifies the clock synchronization mode. A value of x'00' indicates Clock Synchronization service is enabled to this client, a value of x'FF' indicates Clock Synchronization service is disabled to this client, other values are reserved.

CS_Accuracy (word 1, bits 23:16). This field indicates the accuracy of the clock synchronization value as it leaves the server port. The byte contains two values, the CS_Accuracy_Mantissa (bits 23:21) and CS_Accuracy_ Exponent (bits 20:16).

CS_Implemented_MSB (word 1, bits 15:08). This field contains a value within the range of 0 to 63. This value indicates the bit position of the most significant bit (MSB) from the 64-bit Clock Count field. For example, a value of '110111'b (55 decimal) indicates that the highest bit containing meaningful information be bit 55 of the Clock Count field (the most significant bit of byte 1).

CS_Implemented_LSB (word 1, bits 07:00). This field contains a value within the range of 0 to 63. This value indicates the bit position of the least significant bit (LSB) from the 64-bit Clock Count field. For example, a value of '001000'b (16 decimal) indicates that the lowest bit containing meaningful information be bit 16 of the Clock Count field (the least-significant bit of byte 6).

CS_Update_Period (word 2). This field contains a value that represents the time, in microseconds, between consecutive updates from the Clock Synchronization server.

21.7 Clock Synchronization Update (CSU)

The Clock Synchronization Update Extended Link Service request is used by the Clock Synchronization Server at address x'FF FF F6' to distribute clock information to the destination node port.

The CSU request uses information category value '0001'b in bits 03:00 of the R_CTL field (R_CTL = x'21'). This is different from every other Extended Link Service request. Because there is no reply Sequence to the CSU request, both the First_Sequence of Exchange (bit 21) and Last_Sequence of Exchange (bit 20) bits of the F_CTL field in the frame header are set.

21.7.1 Clock Synchronization Update (CSU) Request

The format of the CSU Extended Link Service request is shown in Table 82. There is no reply Sequence to the CSU request.

Word	Bits 31:24	Bits 23:16	Bits 15:8	Bits 7:0
0	Command = x'69'	reserved		
1	(MSB)	Clock Count (8 bytes)		
2				(LSB)

Table 82. Clock Synchronization Update (CSU) Request Sequence

21.8 Discover Address (ADISC)

The Discover Address link service command was added by FC-PH2 and allows a pair of node ports to exchange addresses and identifiers. ADISC allows confirmation of the identity of an NL_Port on an arbitrated loop following potential configuration changes or as part of confirmation or recovery processes.

21.8.1 Discover Address (ADISC) Request

The format of the ADISC request is shown in Table 83.

Word	Bits 31:24	Bits 23:16	Bits 15:8	Bits 7:0
0	x'52'	x'00'	x'00'	x'00'
1	Reserved	Hard address of originator		
2 to 3	Port_Name of originator (8 bytes)			
4 to 5	Node_Name of originator (8 bytes)			
6	Reserved	N_Port ID of originator		

Table 83. Address Discover (ADISC) Request Sequence

21.8.2 Discover Address (ADISC) Reply

The format of the LS_ACC reply is identical except the ADISC command code is replaced with the LS_ACC code (x'02 00 00 00') and the informational fields are provided by the responder.

21.9 Discover Fabric Service Parameters (FDISC)

FDISK performs one of two functions depending on the S_ID value used in the FDISK request.

When the S_ID of the FDISC request is zero, the FDISC request transfers an N_Port name and node name, and requests assignment and login of an additional N_Port_ID. This shall only be done by an N_Port with at least one N_Port_ID that is currently logged in with the Fabric. Assigning an additional N_Port_ID does not modify the service parameters between the two ports. This function is referred to as N_Port ID Virtualization, or NPIV.

When the S_ID of the FDISC request is set to a previously-assigned N_Port_ID, the FDISC contains the N_Port name and node name corresponding to that N_Port_ID. The interchange of FDISC information does not modify the login state or service parameters between the two ports. Service parameters in the request are ignored and no error condition are reported.

The destination address used by the FDISC request is the fabric login address (x'FF FF FE').

21.9.1 Discover Fabric Service Parameter (FDISC) Request

The FDISC request Sequence is identical to that of fabric login (FLOGI) with the exception of the command code as shown in Table 84 (see *Login Service Parameters* on page 413).

Word	Bits 31:24	Bits 23:16	Bits 15:8	Bits 7:0
0	Command = x'51'	x'00'	x'00'	x'00'
1 to 4	Common Service Parameters (16 bytes)			
5 to 6	N_Port Name (8 bytes)			
7 to 8	Node Name (8 bytes)			
9 to 12	Class-1 Service Parameters (16 bytes)			
13 to 16	Class-2 Service Parameters (16 bytes)			
17 to 20	Class-3 Service Parameters (16 bytes)			
21 to 24	Obsolete (was Class-4 Service Parameters) (16 bytes)			
25 to 28	Vendor Version Level (16 bytes)			

Table 84. Fabric Discover (FDISC) Request Sequence

21.9.2 Discover Fabric Service Parameter (FDISC) Reply

If the S_ID field of the FDISC request is set to zero, the D_ID field of the LS_ACC reply is set to the additional N_Port ID being assigned and an implicit fabric login to have occurred.

If the S_ID field of the FDISC request is non-zero and is currently logged in, the fabric replies with LS_ACC with the D_ID set to the S_ID from the request. The format of the LS_ACC reply Sequence is identical to that returned in response to a successful fabric login (FLOGI).

If the S_ID field of the FDISC request is set to zero and no N_Port ID is logged in, or set to a non-zero N_Port ID that is not currently logged in, the fabric port replies with F_RJT with a reason code of "Login required". If the FDISC is received in Class-3, the request is discarded.

21.10 Discover N_Port Service Parameters (PDISC)

The Discover N_Port Service Parameters Extended Link Service command allows a node port to test the current login state and exchange service parameters with another node port without affecting the login state or operating parameters between the two node ports.

Note: While PLOGI also exchanges service parameters, it implicitly logs out the prior session and establishes a new one. As a result of the implicit logout, all open Exchanges between the node ports are abnormally terminated when the new PLOGI is received.

21.10.1 Port Discover (PDISC) Request

The format of the PDISC command is identical to that of N_Port Login (PLOGI) with the exception of the command code and is shown in Table 85.

Word	Bits 31:24	Bits 23:16	Bits 15:8	Bits 7:0
0	Command = x'50'	x'00'	x'00'	x'00'
1 to 4	Common Service Parameters (16 bytes)			
5 to 6	N_Port Name (8 bytes)			
7 to 8	Node Name (8 bytes)			
9 to 12	Class-1 Service Parameters (16 bytes)			
13 to 16	Class-2 Service Parameters (16 bytes)			
17 to 20	Class-3 Service Parameters (16 bytes)			
21 to 24	Obsolete (was Class-4 Service Parameters) (16 bytes)			
25 to 28	Vendor Version Level (16 bytes)			

Table 85. N_Port Discover (PDISC) Request Sequence

21.10.2 Port Discover (PDISC) Reply

If PDISC is received by a node port and the node port is currently logged in (PLOGI) with the originator, the node port replies with LS_ACC. The format of the LS_ACC reply Sequence is identical to that returned in response to a successful PLOGI request.

If a Link Reset (LR) or arbitrated loop initialization occurs following receipt of PDISC, but before the LS_ACC reply is sent, no LS_ACC reply is sent. If a Link Reset (LR) or arbitrated loop initialization (LIP) occurs between transmission of the PDISC request and reception of the LS_ACC reply, the LS_ACC is ignored.

If PDISC is received and the node port is not currently logged-in (PLOGI) with the originator, the node port replies with LS_RJT with a reason code of "Unable to supply requested data".

21.11 Echo (ECHO)

The Echo Extended Link Service request is a single-frame request Sequence requesting that the recipient return the Echo data to the originator in a single-frame LS_ACC reply Sequence.

21.11.1 Echo (ECHO) Request

The format of the ECHO Extended Link Service request is shown in Table 86.

Word	Bits 31:24	Bits 23:16	Bits 15:8	Bits 7:0
0	Command = x'10'	x'00'	x'00'	x'00'
1 to n	ECHO data, must not exceed the (maximum receive data field size allowed per login - 4)			

Table 86. Echo (ECHO) Request Sequence

21.11.2 Echo (ECHO) Reply

The ECHO reply is identical to the ECHO request with the first word replaced by x'02 00 00 00' to indicate this is an Extended Link Service LS_ACC reply.

21.12 Establish Streaming (ESTS)

The Establish Streaming Extended Link Service request is used to request a temporary allocation of end-to-end credit, known as the streaming credit, from the destination port. The value should be large enough to allow continuous frame streaming from the originating node port to the destination node port.

The SOF delimiter of the Sequence used for the ESTS request identifies the class of service for which the credit is being requested.

The recipient of the ESTC Extended Link Service request grants the streaming credit in the LS ACC reply to the ESTC Extended Link Service request. The format of the reply consists of the node port's login service parameters, with the streaming credit granted in the class specific service parameters identified with the class validity bit set to one. The other service parameter fields in the LS_ACC reply are ignored.

21.12.1 Establish Streaming (ESTS) Request

The format of the ESTS Extended Link Service request is shown in Table 87.

Word	Bits 31:24	Bits 23:16	Bits 15:8	Bits 7:0
0	Command = x'0B'	x'00'	x'00'	x'00'

Table 87. Establish Streaming (ESTS) Request Sequence

21.12.2 Establish Streaming (ESTS) Reply

The LS_ACC reply contains the end-to-end streaming credit as indicated by the appropriate class specific service parameters and follows the same format as the ESTS request (with the exception of the first word which is equal to x'02 00 00 00').

The credit granted may equal the amount requested in the ESTS request or less, depending upon the buffer management mechanism of the responder port. The class validity bit designates which end-to-end credit values are being revised.

21.13 Estimate Credit (ESTC)

The Estimate Credit Extended Link Service is used to estimate the number of frames in transit between the originating port and the destination port. Once this value is determined, it may be used to revise the end-to-end credit between the two ports based on the number of frames in transit (i.e., the distance or delay between the ports. Refer to *Estimate Credit Procedure* on page 269 for additional information).

The ESTC Extended Link Service request Sequence transmits a Sequence of frames until the first acknowledgment is received. At this time, the transmitting port can determine the number of frames that can be in transit between itself and the receiving port. The Start-of-Frame delimiter identifies the class of service for which the credit is being estimated.

21.13.1 Estimate Credit (ESTC) Request

The format of the ESTC Extended Link Service request is shown in Table 88. Because there is no reply Sequence to this request, the request sets the Last_Sequence bit in the F_CTL field of the frame header to end the Exchange at the end of the ESTC request Sequence.

Word	Bits 31:24	Bits 23:16	Bits 15:8	Bits 7:0
0	Command = x'0C'	x'00'	x'00'	x'00'
1 to n	Any data, must not exceed the (maximum receive data field size allowed per login - 4)			

Table 88. Estimate Credit (ESTC) Request Sequence

21.13.2 Estimate Credit (ESTC) Reply

There is no reply Sequence to the Estimate Credit Extended Link Service request. Because there is no reply, the recipient cannot send LS_RJT in response to the ESTC request.

21.14 Exchange Virtual Fabrics Parameters (EVFP)

The Exchange Virtual Fabrics Parameters Extended Link Service enables a virtual fabric capable node port to exchange parameters with the associated virtual fabrics.

21.14.1 Exchange Virtual Fabric Parameters (EVFP) Request

The format of the EVFP Extended Link Service request is shown in Table 89. The LS_ACC reply Sequence uses the same format with the exception of the Command field.

When sent by an N_Port, the source address is x'FF FF F0', the address of the N_Port Controller and the destination address is x'FF FF FE'. When sent by an F_Port, the source address is x'FF FF FE' and the destination address is x'FF FF F0'.

Word	Bits 31:24	Bits 23:16	Bits 15:8	Bits 7:0
0	Command = x'7F'	x'00'	x'00'	x'00'
1	Protocol Version (shall be x'01')	**Message Code:** x'01' = EVFP_SYNC x'02' = EVFP_COMMIT others = Reserved	Transaction Identifier	
2:3n	Core N_Port Name / Core Switch Name			
4	Reserved		Message Payload Length (20 + Message Payload length)	
5:n	Message Payload (not present for EVFP_COMMIT Message)			

Table 89. Exchange Virtual Fabric Parameters (EVFP) Request and Reply Sequences

EVFP Message Code. The EVFP Message Code field identifies the message being communicated by this EVFP transaction.

Transaction Identifier. The Transaction Identifier identifies a specific transaction between the N_Port and F_Port. The Transaction Identifier is assigned by the EVFP originator and is contained in each subsequent message of the entire transaction. The transaction may require multiple EVFP operations and their associated Exchanges.

Core N_Port / Core Switch_Name. If the originating port is an N_Port, this field is set to the Core N_Port Name. Because an N_Port may use different N_Port names for each fabric, this parameter provides a way to identify the physical N_Port across multiple virtual fabrics.

If the originating port is an F_Port, this field is set to the Core Switch_Name. Because each virtual fabric may use a different Fabric_Name, this parameter provides a way to identify the physical fabric.

Payload Length. This field specifies the total number of bytes in the EVFP payload.

21.14.2 EVFP_SYNC Message Payload

The EVFP_SYNC message enables a node port and fabric port to communicate a list of virtual fabric related descriptors. The format of the EVFP_SYNC Message Payload is shown in Table 90. Descriptors #1 through 3 are required in all EVFP_SYNC messages, others are optional.

Word	Bits 31:24	Bits 23:16	Bits 15:8	Bits 7:0
	Descriptor #1: Tagging Administrative Status (Required)			
0	Descriptor Control = x'01'	Descriptor Type = x'01'	Descriptor Length = x'0004'	
1	Administrative Tagging Mode (also see Table 91): x'0000 0001' = [OFF] The FC_Port shall not perform VFT Tagging x'0000 0002' = [ON] The FC_Port may perform VFT Tagging if the peer does not prohibit it x'0000 0003' = [AUTO] The FC_Port may perform VFT Tagging if the peer requests it			
	Descriptor #2: Port VF_ID (Required)			
2	Descriptor Control = x'01'	Descriptor Type = x'02'	Descriptor Length = x'0004'	
3	Port Flags (reserved shall be set to x'0000')		Port VF_ID	
	Descriptor #3: Locally-Enabled VF_ID List (Required)			
4	Descriptor Control = x'01'	Descriptor Type = x'03'	Descriptor Length = x'0200'	
5:132	VF_ID Bitmap (4096 entries corresponding to VFT_IDs x'000' through x'FFF'			
133:m	Descriptor #m			
m:n	Descriptor #n			

Table 90. Exchange Virtual Fabric Parameters (EVFP) Message Payload

Administrative Tagging Mode. The Administrative Tagging Mode field specifies how VFT Tagging is negotiated between the peer FC_Ports. Table 91 illustrates the possible behaviors.

		Peer Tagging Mode		
		OFF	ON	AUTO
Local	OFF	Non-Tagging	Non-Tagging	Non-Tagging
Tagging	ON	Non-Tagging	Tagging	Tagging
Mode	AUTO	Non-Tagging	Tagging	Non-Tagging

Table 91. Tagging Mode Negotiation

General Descriptor Format. All descriptors share the same common format shown in Table 92 on page 338.

Word	Bits 31:24	Bits 23:16	Bits 15:8	Bits 7:0
0	Descriptor Control	Descriptor Type	Descriptor Length	
1:n	Descriptor Value			

Table 92. Exchange Virtual Fabric Parameters (EVFP) Message Payload

Descriptor Control. The Descriptor Control value provides a mechanism to indicate how the recipient should respond if a descriptor is not supported. Descriptor Control codes are shown in Table 93.

Value	Description
x'01'	**Critical:** Abort the EVFP transaction if the descriptor is not supported.
x'02'	**Non-Critical:** Skip the descriptor if it is not supported and continue the EVFP transaction.
others	Reserved

Table 93. EVFP Descriptor Control Codes

Descriptor Type. The Descriptor Type field identifies the descriptor as shown in Table 94.

Value	Descriptor Type
x'01'	Tagging Administrative Status Descriptor
x'02'	Port VF_ID Descriptor
x'03'	Locally-Enabled VF_ID List Descriptor
x'F0':x'FE'	Vendor Unique Descriptor
others	Reserved

Table 94. EVFP Descriptor Types

Descriptor Length. This field specifies the number of bytes in the Descriptor Value field.

21.14.3 Exchange Virtual Fabric Parameters (EVFP) LS_RJT Reply

If the EVFP recipient is unable to perform the operation, it responds with LS_RJT containing the Reason Code and Reason Code Explanations as shown in Table 95.

Error Condition	Reason Code	Explanation
EVFP ELS not supported	Command not supported	No additional explanation
EVFP collision	Command already in progress	No additional explanation
Protocol Version not supported	Protocol Error	No additional explanation
EVFP_COMMIT before EVFP_SYNC	Logical Error	No additional explanation
Insufficient Resources	Unable to Perform Command Request	No additional explanation
Invalid Payload Message	Protocol Error	No additional explanation

Table 95. EVFP LS_RJT Reply Sequence

21.15 Fabric Activate Alias_ID (FACT)

Fabric Activate Alias_ID is sent to the Fabric Controller to request that the Fabric Controller activate the specified alias address identifier for the designated node ports.

21.15.1 Fabric Activate Alias_ID (FACT) Request

The format of the FACT request is shown in Table 96.

Word	Bits 31:24	Bits 23:16	Bits 15:8	Bits 7:0
0	Command = x'31'	x'00'	x'00'	x'00'
1	Reserved	Alias_ID		
2	NP_List_Length (number of entries in the following N_Port list)			
3	Reserved	N_Port ID		
4 to (n-1)	Reserved	N_Port ID		
n	Reserved	N_Port ID		

Table 96. Fabric Activate Alias_ID (FACT) Request Sequence

21.15.2 Fabric Activate Alias_ID (FACT) Request

The expected reply is LS_ACC with no additional information.

21.16 Fabric Address Notification (FAN)

Fabric Address Notification (FAN) was added by the Fabric Loop Attach (FLA) technical report and incorporated into the FC-FS standard to provide a mechanism for a fabric FL_Port to notify public NL_Ports (NL_Ports that had completed Fabric Login) of the FL_Port's address, Port_Name, and Fabric_Name.

The original purpose of FAN was to allow the FL_Port to provide information to public NL_Ports on an arbitrated loop following loop initialization. The public NL_Ports could use this information to verify the identity and address of the FL_Port before resuming Exchanges that were in progress prior to the loop initialization.

If a public NL_Port receives FAN and the Loop Fabric Address, Fabric Port_Name, or Fabric_Name do not match it current fabric login session, the fabric is implicitly logged out and a new fabric login is required. A public NL_Port that fails to receive FAN within an implementation dependent timeout period following loop initialization may use FDISC to discover the fabric identity or relogin with the fabric.

21.16.1 Fabric Address Notification (FAN) Request

FAN is sent by the FL_Port using a Source_ID (S_ID) of x'FF FF FE' to each NL_Port currently logged in with that FL_Port. The format of the FAN request is shown in Table 97.

Word	Bits 31:24	Bits 23:16	Bits 15:8	Bits 7:0
0	Command = x'60'	x'00'	x'00'	x'00'
1	Reserved	Loop Fabric Address		
2:3	Fabric Port_Name			
4:5	Fabric_Name			

Table 97. Fabric Address Notification (FAN) Request Sequence

21.16.2 Fabric Address Notification (FAN) Reply

There is no reply Sequence to FAN.

> NOTE – Although FC-FS indicates that LS_RJT could be sent, this appears to be an error. If the FAN request Sequence sets the Last_Sequence bit in the F_CTL field, no response is possible. If the Last_Sequence bit is not set, a reply is required.

21.17 Fabric Deactivate Alias_ID (FDACT)

Fabric Deactivate Alias_ID is sent to the Fabric Controller by the Alias Server to request that the Fabric Controller activate the specified alias address identifier for the designated node ports.

21.17.1 Fabric Deactivate Alias_ID (FDACT) Request

The format of the FDACT request is shown in Table 98.

Word	Bits 31:24	Bits 23:16	Bits 15:8	Bits 7:0
0	Command = x'32'	x'00'	x'00'	x'00'
1	Reserved	Alias_ID		
2	NP_List_Length (number of entries in the following N_Port list)			
3	Reserved	N_Port ID		
4:(n-1)	Reserved	N_Port ID		
n	Reserved	N_Port ID		

Table 98. Fabric Deactivate Alias_ID (FDACT) Request Sequence

21.17.2 Fabric Deactivate Alias_ID (FDACT) Reply

The expected reply is LS_ACC with no additional information.

21.18 Fabric Login (FLOGI)

Fabric login is used by a node port to determine if a fabric is present and, if so, exchange service parameters with the fabric. Fabric login is required for all classes of service and is mandatory for N_Ports and optional for NL_Ports.

Fabric login is performed by a node port following initial link or loop initialization and before communicating with other node ports. The node port performs explicit fabric login by transmitting the FLOGI Extended Link Service request to the well-known address x'FF FF FE'. This address is assigned to the fabric port associated with the link to which the node port is connected.

As is the case with all Extended Link Services, a new Exchange is created for the FLOGI Extended Link Service request and normal Exchange and Sequence management rules apply.

When an N_Port first attempts fabric login, it uses a source identifier (S_ID) of x'00 00 00' meaning that the port is unidentified. When an NL_Port first attempts fabric login, it uses a source identifier of x'00 00 AL_PA' (AL_PA is the one-byte arbitrated loop physical address obtained during loop initialization).

The FLOGI command contains the node port's service parameters, and the LS_ACC reply contains the fabric's service parameters. The service parameters establish the operating environment between the node port and the fabric including parameters such as the maximum size frame that can be received by each port and the buffer-to-buffer credit between the node port and fabric port.

21.18.1 Fabric Login (FLOGI) Request

The FLOGI request Sequence contains the node port's service parameters. For details of the service parameters, refer to *Login Service Parameters* on page 413. The format of the FLOGI request is shown in Table 99 on page 343.

Word	Bits 31:24	Bits 23:16	Bits 15:8	Bits 7:0
0	Command = x'04'	x'00'	x'00'	x'00'
1 to 4	Common Service Parameters (16 bytes)			
5 to 6	N_Port Name (8 bytes			
7 to 8	Node Name (8 bytes)			
9 to 12	Class-1 Service Parameters (16 bytes)			
13 to 16	Class-2 Service Parameters (16 bytes)			
17 to 20	Class-3 Service Parameters (16 bytes)			
21 to 24	Obsolete (was Class-4 Service Parameters) (16 bytes)			
25 to 28	Vendor Version Level (16 bytes)			

Table 99. Fabric Login (FLOGI) Request Sequence

21.18.2 Fabric Login (FLOGI) Reply

The LS_ACC reply is identical to the FLOGI request except the command code is replaced with the LS_ACC code (x'02 00 00 00') and the service parameters are the fabric's.

The response to the FLOGI indicates whether a fabric is present. If a fabric is present and an LS_ACC reply is received, fabric login is complete. In the LS_ACC, the fabric may optionally assign or confirm the N_Port identifier (address) of the node port that initiated the FLOGI.

21.18.3 Responses to Initial Fabric Login

When an N_Port first attempts fabric login it uses an S_ID of x'00 00 00' and does not know if a fabric is present (when an NL_Port first attempts fabric login, it uses a source identifier of x'00 00 AL_PA'). Several responses to the FLOGI are possible. These responses, and corresponding actions that should be taken by the node port, are listed below.

1. An R_RDY is normally received in response to the Class-1 connect request frame or Class-2 or Class-3 frame used to send the FLOGI command. This is normal buffer-to-buffer flow control and the FLOGI originator should wait for the reply Sequence.

2. If ACK_1 with a D_ID of x'00 00 00' (or x'00 00 AL_PA for an NL_Port) and S_ID of x'FF FF FE' is received, the FLOGI frame has been received by the F_Port or N_Port (if in a point-to-point topology, the FLOGI is received by the other N_Port). The FLOGI originator should wait for the reply Sequence.

3. If LS_ACC with a S_ID of x'FF FF FE' is received and the OX_ID is the same as the OX_ID of the FLOGI command, there are two possibilities:

   • If the Common Service parameters indicate the response came from a fabric, FLOGI is complete and the LS_ACC contains the fabric's service parameters. The D_ID field of the LS_ACC contains the N_Port ID (address) that has been assigned by the fabric.

   • If the Common Service parameters indicate the response came from an N_Port, no fabric is present and N_Port Login (PLOGI) should be performed.

4. If F_BSY or P_BSY with a D_ID of x'00 00 00' (or x'00 00 AL_PA for an NL_Port) and S_ID of x'FF FF FE' is received, the FLOGI recipient is busy. The FLOGI originator should retry the FLOGI later.

5. If F_RJT or P_RJT with a D_ID of x'00 00 00' (or x'00 00 AL_PA for an NL_Port) and S_ID of x'FF FF FE' is received, the FLOGI recipient has rejected the frame. The FLOGI originator should examine the reason code and take the appropriate action.

   • If the reason code is "Class of service not supported" the FLOGI originator should try a different class of service. If all supported classes of service have been attempted, the classes of service are incompatible and operations are not possible.

   • If F_RJT is received and the reason code is "Invalid S_ID" the FLOGI originator should attempt FLOGI with a source address identifier other than zeros. The fabric does not support address assignment.

   • For other reason codes, the appropriate action should be taken.

---

6. If an N_Port receives FLOGI with a D_ID of x'FF FF FE' and S_ID of x'00 00 00', the N_Port is in the point-to-point topology and the N_Port should reply with LS_ACC.

The Common Service parameters field of the LS_ACC contains the same information as was received in the FLOGI, except that the N_Port/F_Port bit is set to '0' to indicate that the LS_ACC was transmitted by an N_Port.

The LS_ACC contains the Port_Name and Node_Name of the receiving N_Port and all classes of service are marked invalid.

The N_Port makes a decision on what action to take next by comparing the value of its Port_Name with value of the Port_Name in the received FLOGI.

- If this port's name is lower, it waits for N_Port Login (PLOGI) from the attached N_Port.

- If this port's name is higher, it initiates N_Port Login PLOGI with the attached N_Port.

7. If LS_RJT with an S_ID of x'FF FF FE' is received, the FLOGI may be retried if the condition indicated by the reason code can be corrected.

8. If no reply is received within E_D_TOV, an error has occurred and Abort Sequence (ABTS) should be performed prior to attempting FLOGI again.

21.18.4 Responses to Subsequent Fabric Logins

After a node port has completed fabric login, it may need to relogin at some point. This could occur immediately following receipt of LS_ACC from the fabric if the fabric does not support address assignment, or later as a result of error conditions.

When the node port performs a subsequent FLOGI, it does not use an S_ID of x'00 00 00' (or x'00 00 AL_PA for an NL_Port). Rather it uses the S_ID that was assigned to the port prior to the FLOGI, or if none was assigned, a value of the port's choosing. (FLOGI was first attempted with an S_ID of zeros and the fabric rejected the FLOGI with a reason code of "Invalid S_ID" indicating that the fabric does not support address assignment.)

In this case, receipt of FLOGI sent by another N_Port cannot occur because the FLOGI originator knows that a fabric is present as a result of completion of the previous FLOGI. However, other responses to the FLOGI are possible. These responses, and corresponding actions that should be taken by the N_Port, are listed below.

1. An R_RDY is normally received in response to the Class-1 connect request frame or Class-2 or Class-3 frame used to send the FLOGI command. This is normal buffer-to-buffer flow control and the FLOGI originator should wait for the reply Sequence.

2. If ACK_1 with a D_ID the same as that used by the N_Port and S_ID of x'FF FF FE' is received, the FLOGI frame has been received by the F_Port or N_Port (if in a point-to-point topology, the FLOGI is received by the other N_Port). The FLOGI originator should wait for the reply Sequence.

3. If LS_ACC with a D_ID the same as that used by the N_Port and S_ID of x'FF FF FE' is received and the OX_ID is the same as the OX_ID of the FLOGI command, the FLOGI is complete and the LS_ACC contains the fabric's service parameters.

4. If F_BSY or P_BSY with a D_ID the same as that used by the N_Port and S_ID of x'FF FF FE' is received, the FLOGI recipient is busy. The FLOGI originator should retry the FLOGI later.

5. If F_RJT or P_RJT with a D_ID the same as that used by the N_Port and S_ID of x'FF FF FE' is received, the FLOGI recipient has rejected the frame. The FLOGI originator should examine the reason code and take the appropriate action.

   - If the reason code is "Class of service not supported" the FLOGI originator should try a different class of service. If all supported classes of service have been attempted, the classes of service are incompatible and operations are not possible.

   - If F_RJT is received and the reason code is "Invalid S_ID" the FLOGI originator should attempt FLOGI with a source address identifier other than zeros. The fabric does not support address assignment.

   - For other reason codes, the appropriate action should be taken.

6. If LS_RJT with a D_ID the same as that used by the N_Port and S_ID of x'FF FF FE' is received, the FLOGI may be retried if the condition indicated by the reason code can be corrected.

7. If no reply is received within E_D_TOV, an error has occurred and Abort Sequence (ABTS) should be performed prior to attempting the FLOGI again.

21.19 Get Alias_ID (GAID)

The Get Alias_ID request is sent from the Alias Server to the Fabric Controller to request an alias address identifier.

The request includes the alias group service parameters so the Fabric Controller can verify that the proposed service parameters do not conflict with the fabric's service parameters.

The request also includes a list of node ports that will be included in the alias group. The list of node ports is included so the fabric can verify its ability to support an alias group consisting of the listed ports. Some fabrics may not be able to support group operations such as multicast operations that span domain boundaries.

21.19.1 Get Alias_ID (GAID) Request

The format of the Get Alias_ID (GAID) request is shown in Table 136.

Word	Bits 31:24	Bits 23:16	Bits 15:8	Bits 7:0
0	Command = x'30'	x'00'	x'00'	x'00'
1	Alias Flags	Alias_Class		
2	Alias_Qualifier (8 bytes)			
3				
4 to 23	Alias Service Parameters (80 bytes)			
24	NP_List_Length (number of entries in the following N_Port list)			
25	Reserved	N_Port ID		
26:(n-1)	Reserved	N_Port ID		
n	Reserved	N_Port ID		

Table 100. Get Alias_ID (GAID) Request Sequence

Alias Flags. The alias flags byte identifies the type of alias group referenced by this alias token and specifies options for the alias group.

Alias Group Type (word 1, bits 31:28). The high-order four bits of the alias flags byte identifies the alias group type. The Alias Group Type values are shown in Table 101.

bits 31:28	Description
b'0000'	Reserved
b'0001'	Multicast Group
b'0010'	Hunt Group
Others	Reserved

Table 101. GAID Alias Group Type

Send to Initiator (word 1, bit 27). When set to one, this bit indicates that the initiator of a frame is eligible to receive a copy of the frame if it is a member of the group. When this bit is set to zero, the initiator of the frame is not considered a member of the group.

Reserved (word 1, bits 26:25). These bits are reserved.

Multicast Group IPA - MG_IPA (word 1, bit 24). When set to one, this bit indicates that the Initial Process_Associator (IPA) associated with this multicast group is a Multicast Group IPA. When this condition exists, the responder Process_Associator is set equal to the Alias_Qualifier for the multicast group and bit 24 of the association header is set to one indicating that this IPA is a multicast IPA.

Alias_Class. The alias class field is used to identify the multicast class or hunt group identifier. This can be used to define and identify multicast groups based on the protocol type and/or routing bits in the routing control field of the frame header. The values that can be used in the type and routing bits fields are the same as the values defined for use in the frame header.

Type (word 1, bits 23:16). This field contains the type value that is used to qualify frames for multicasting. When this field is set to a non-zero value, only frames of the specified type are multicast to members of the multicast group. A value of all ones in this field (x'FF') is interpreted to mean that the multicast group includes all type values.

This field is not meaningful for hunt groups.

Routing Bits (word 1, bits 15:12). This field contains the routing bit value that is used to further qualify frames for multicasting. When this field is set to a non-zero value, only frames with the specified routing bits are multicast to members of the multicast group. A value of all ones in this field ('1111'b) is interpreted to mean that the multicast group includes all routing bit values.

This field is not meaningful for hunt groups.

Hunt Group ID (word 1, bits 11:00). This field may be used by the common controlling entity associated with a hunt group to identify that hunt group. This may be useful when the common controlling entity is associated with more than one hunt group.

This field is reserved for multicast groups.

Alias_Qualifier (words 2:3). For a multicast group, this 64-bit field is used to further qualify frames for multicasting. The alias qualifier is defined as follows:

- **All Zeroes:** The alias qualifier is unknown and a unique value may be assigned by the Alias Server. If the Alias Server is unable to assign the alias qualifier, it rejects the request.

- **All Ones:** For multicast, all ones indicates that all alias qualifiers for the associated alias class may be processed. This value is reserved for hunt groups.

- **All Other Values:** The alias qualifier is assigned by the FC-4 identified by the alias class type value. The meaning of the value assigned is defined by the associated FC-4.

Alias Service Parameters (words 4:23). The alias service parameters define the service parameters to be used for all operations with the alias group. The alias service parameters is an 80-byte field containing the Common Service parameters (16 bytes) and class specific service parameters (16 bytes per class). The format of the alias service parameters is the same as that supplied during N_Port Login (see *Login Service Parameters* on page 413).

The service parameters are established when the alias group is created and apply to the implicit login performed when a node port is added to the alias group using the N_Port Activate Alias_ID (NACT) Extended Link Service.

If a hunt group is being created, the Class-specific service parameters indicate which classes of service are valid.

21.19.2 Get Alias_ID (GAID) LS_ACC Reply

The normal reply to GAID is LS_ACC containing the Alias_ID assigned by the Fabric Controller. The format of the GAID LS_ACC reply is shown in Table 111 on page 354.

Word	Bits 31:24	Bits 23:16	Bits 15:8	Bits 7:0
0	LS_ACC = x'02'	x'00'	x'00'	x'00'
1	Reserved	Alias_ID		

Table 102. Get Alias_ID (GAID) LS_ACC Reply

21.20 Link-Incident Record Registration (LIRR)

The Link-Incident Record Registration Extended Link Service is used to request that the recipient add the requesting port to the list of ports that should receive a Registered Link-Incident Report (RLIR). When a node port is registering with a fabric, the request is sent to the Management Server at well-known address x'FF FF FA'.

If logout (either explicit or implicit) occurs between the LIRR requestor and recipient, the registration is cleared and the requestor is no longer eligible to receive Registered Link-Incident Reports (for any FC-4 protocol type) from the recipient port. If Process Login (PRLI) is required by the associated FC-4 protocol, a process logout (either explicit or implicit) clears the registration for that protocol type.

21.20.1 Link-Incident Record Registration (LIRR) Request

The format of the LIRR Extended Link Service request is shown in Table 103.

Word	Bits 31:24	Bits 23:16	Bits 15:8	Bits 7:0
0	Command = x'7A'	x'00'	x'00'	x'00'
1	Registration Function	Link-Incident Record Registration Type	Reserved	

Table 103. Link-Incident Record Registration (LIRR) Request Sequence

Word 1, Bits 31:24, Registration Function. These bits are defined as shown in Table 104.

x'00'	Reserved.
x'01'	**Set Registration.** Register the source port to receive RLIR notifications
x'03:FE'	Reserved.
x'FF'	**Clear Registration.** Remove the source port from receiving RLIR notifications

Table 104. LIRR Registration Functions

Link-Incident Record Registration Type (word 1, bits 23:16). This field contains the FC-4 protocol type for which the requestor wishes to receive RLIR notifications.

21.20.2 Link-Incident Record Registration (LIRR) Reply

The expected reply is LS_ACC with no additional information.

If the recipient does not support the Link-Incident Record Registration request, it may send LS_RJT with a reason code of "command not supported."

If the recipient cannot perform the requested registration, it may send LS_RJT with a reason code of "unable to perform command request".

21.21 Link Keep Alive (LKA)

The Link Keep Alive Extended Link Service request is used to generate traffic and confirm that a link is still operational and not terminated due to lack of traffic. The primary application of this ELS is on an extended-distance link that is passing through a non-Fibre Channel network. This may be necessary because some environments (e.g., TCP) may terminate connections that have not had activity for some period of time.

21.21.1 Link Keep Alive (LKA) Request

The format of the LKA Extended Link Service request is shown in Table 105. Both the source and destination ID fields are set to x'FF FF FD', the address of the local Fabric Controller and the remote peer Fabric Controller.

Word	Bits 31:24	Bits 23:16	Bits 15:8	Bits 7:0
0	Command = x'80'	x'00'	x'00'	x'00'

Table 105. Link Keep Alive (LKA) Request Sequence

21.21.2 Link Keep Alive (LKA) Reply

The LKA LS_ACC reply format is shown in Table 106.

Word	Bits 31:24	Bits 23:16	Bits 15:8	Bits 7:0
0	Command = x'02'	x'00'	x'00'	x'00'

Table 106. Link Keep Alive (LKA) LS_ACC Reply Sequence

21.22 Logout (LOGO)

Logout is used to end the login session between two node ports or a node port and the fabric port. When the logout occurs between two node ports, any open or active Exchanges or Sequences in the current session are terminated by the logout and any resources associated with that session are released. When logout occurs between a node port and the fabric, open or active Exchanges or Sequences are not terminated provided the node port relogs-in with the fabric before open or active Exchanges and Sequences time out and the node port receives the same N_Port identifier from the fabric.

LOGO may be used to relinquish an address that was acquired using FDISC when N_Port ID Virtualization (NPIV) is being used.

A node port performs an explicit logout by transmitting the LOGO Extended Link Service request to the destination port using a new Exchange created for the LOGO. The destination address used is the address of the other node port or the fabric login server (x'FF FF FE'). Normal Exchange and Sequence management rules apply, including flow control applicable to the class of service used.

21.22.1 Logout (LOGO) Request

The format of the LOGO command is shown in Table 107.

Word	Bits 31:24	Bits 23:16	Bits 15:8	Bits 7:0
0	x'05'	x'00'	x'00'	x'00'
1	Reserved	N_Port Identifier (That is being logged out. This may be different from the S_ID in the frame header if the port's address has changed)		
2 and 3	Port_Name of the LOGO originator (8 bytes)			

Table 107. N_Port Logout (LOGO) Request Sequence

21.22.2 Logout (LOGO) Reply

The expected response to the LOGO is an LS_ACC reply. There are no parameters associated with the LS_ACC.

Receipt of an LS_ACC reply from the destination port indicates the LOGO was accepted and is complete at the destination port.

21.23 Loop Initialize (LINIT)

Loop Initialize was added by the Fabric Loop Attach (FLA) technical report to provide a mechanism for a node port to request that an FL_Port begin loop initialization on a remote arbitrated loop. The LINIT is sent to the Loop Fabric Address of the FL_Port associated with the destination loop. The LINIT Extended Link Service request contains information specifying the parameters the receiving FL_Port should use in the loop initialization.

21.23.1 Loop Initialize (LINIT) Request

The format of the LINIT Extended Link Service request is shown in Table 108.

Word	Bits 31:24	Bits 23:16	Bits 15:8	Bits 7:0
0	Command = x'70'	x'00'	x'00'	x'00'
1	Reserved	Initialization Function	LIP Byte 3	LIP Byte 4

Table 108. Loop Initialize (LINIT) Request Sequence

Initialization Function (word 1, bits 23:16). The function to be performed is as follows:

x'00' **Normal initialization.** The fabric determines the best method by which to accomplish the loop initialization.

x'01' **Force Login.** The L_Bit is set in the LISA Sequence of the loop initialization to force all affected NL_Ports to relogin with the fabric and other node ports.

x'02:FF' **Reserved.**

21.23.2 Loop Initialize (LINIT) Reply

The expected reply to the LINIT Extended Link Service is LS_ACC. LS_ACC is not sent by a fabric until the FL_Port has completed loop initialization, transitioned to the Monitoring state, and sent any required FAN Extended Link Services. The format of the LINIT LS_ACC reply is shown in Table 109.

Word	Bits 31:24	Bits 23:16	Bits 15:8	Bits 7:0
0	LS_ACC = x'02'	x'00'	x'00'	x'00'
1	Reserved			LINIT Status

Table 109. Loop Initialize (LINIT) LS_ACC Reply

LINIT Status (word 1, bits 07:00). The status of the LINIT command is defined as follows:

x'00' **Reserved.**

x'01' **Success.** The requested function was completed successfully.

x'02' **Failure.** The requested function could not be completed.

x'03:FF' **Reserved.**

21.24 Loop Status (LSTS)

Loop Status was added by the Fabric Loop Attach (FLA) technical report to provide a mechanism for a node port to determine the status of a remote arbitrated loop. The LSTS request is sent to the Loop Fabric Address of the FL_Port associated with the destination loop. The format of the LSTS Extended Link Service request is shown in Table 110.

Word	Bits 31:24	Bits 23:16	Bits 15:8	Bits 7:0
0	Command = x'72'	x'00'	x'00'	x'00'

Table 110. Loop Status (LSTS) Request Sequence

The format of the LS_ACC to the Loop Status request is shown in Table 111.

Word	Bits 31:24	Bits 23:16	Bits 15:8	Bits 7:0
0	LS_ACC = x'02'	x'00'	x'00'	x'00'
1	Reserved	Failed Receiver	FLA Compliance Level: x'00' = Reserved x'01' = FLA Level A x'02' = FLA Level B others = Reserved	Loop State (see Table 112)
2:5	Current Public Loop Devices bit map (16 bytes)			
6:9	Current Private Loop Devices bit map (16 bytes)			
10:41	AL_PA Positional Map (128 bytes)			

Table 111. Loop Status (LSTS) LS_ACC Reply

Failed Receiver. This field contains the AL_PA of the port that has reported a loop failure. This field is only valid if the Loop State field indicates Loop Failure. If the point of the failure cannot be determined, this field is set to x'F7'.

Loop State. This field identifies the state of the remote loop as shown in Table 112.

Value	Description
x'00'	Reserved
x'01'	**Online.** The loop is not Initializing and no failure has been detected.
x'02'	**Loop Failure.** A loop failure has been detected and the AL_PA of the port reporting the failure (if available) is contained in the Failed Receiver field.
x'03'	**Initialization Failure.** The FL_Port has been unable to complete loop initialization.
x'04'	**Initializing.** The loop is currently performing loop initialization.
x'05:FF'	Reserved.

Table 112. Loop State

21.25 N_Port Activate Alias_ID (NACT)

N_Port Activate Alias_ID is sent to a node port by the Alias Server to request that the node port activate the specified alias address identifier and perform an implicit N_Port Login with the specified alias address identifier using the service parameters provided.

If the alias token indicates that the alias address identifier is for a multicast group, only the Common Service parameters and Class-3 service parameters are applicable. If the alias address if for a hunt group, all Class-specific service parameters may be used.

The node port sends LS_ACC if it can satisfy the following conditions:

- it can support the alias class specified in the alias token
- it can support the alias group service parameters
- it has assigned the received Alias_ID as an alias address identifier for this port

21.25.1 N_Port Activate Alias_ID (NACT) Request

The format of the NACT request is shown in Table 113. See the description of the Get Alias_ID Extended Link Service (*Get Alias_ID (GAID)* on page 347) for a description of the Alias Flags, Alias_Class, Alias_ID, and Alias Service Parameters.

Word	Bits 31:24	Bits 23:16	Bits 15:8	Bits 7:0
0	Command = x'33'	x'00'	x'00'	x'00'
1	Alias Flags	Alias_Class		
2	Alias_Qualifier (8 bytes)			
3				
4	Reserved	Alias_ID		
5 to 24	Alias Service Parameters (80 bytes)			

Table 113. N_Port Activate Alias_ID (NACT) Request Sequence

21.25.2 N_Port Activate Alias_ID (NACT) Reply

The expected reply to NACT is LS_ACC with no additional information.

21.26 N_Port Deactivate Alias_ID (NDACT)

N_Port Deactivate Alias_ID is sent to a node port by the Alias Server to request that the node port deactivate the specified alias address identifier.

21.26.1 N_Port Deactivate Alias_ID (NDACT) Request

The format of the NDACT request is shown in Table 114.

Word	Bits 31:24	Bits 23:16	Bits 15:8	Bits 7:0
0	Command = x'32'	x'00'	x'00'	x'00'
1	Reserved	Alias_ID		

Table 114. N_Port Deactivate Alias_ID (NDACT) Request Sequence

21.26.2 N_Port Deactivate Alias_ID (NDACT) Reply

The expected reply is LS_ACC with no additional information.

21.27 N_Port Login (PLOGI)

N_Port Login allows two node ports to establish a session and exchange identities and service parameters. PLOGI is performed following completion of the fabric login process and prior to FC-4 level operations with the destination port.

21.27.1 N_Port Login (PLOGI) Request

The format of the PLOGI contains the node port's service parameters. The format of the PLOGI command is shown in Table 115.

Word	Bits 31:24	Bits 23:16	Bits 15:8	Bits 7:0
0	Command = x'03'	x'00'	x'00'	x'00'
1 to 4	Common Service Parameters (16 bytes)			
5 to 6	N_Port Name (8 bytes)			
7 to 8	Node_Name (8 bytes)			
9 to 12	Class-1 Service Parameters (16 bytes)			
13 to 16	Class-2 Service Parameters (16 bytes)			
17 to 20	Class-3 Service Parameters (16 bytes)			
21 to 24	Obsolete (was Class-4 Service Parameters) (16 bytes)			
25 to 28	Vendor Version Level (16 bytes)			

Table 115. N_Port Login (PLOGI) Request Sequence

21.27.2 N_Port Login (PLOGI) Reply

Several responses may occur as a result of the PLOGI request.

Responses to N_Port Login (Fabric Present). Responses to PLOGI and corresponding actions that should be taken by the node port, are summarized below.

1. An R_RDY is normally received in response to the Class-1 connect request frame or Class-2 or Class-3 frame used to send the PLOGI command. This is normal buffer-to-buffer flow control and the PLOGI originator should increment the available BB_Credit and wait for the reply Sequence.

2. If ACK_1 with the D_ID of the PLOGI originator and S_ID of the PLOGI responder is received, the PLOGI frame has been received by the other node port. The PLOGI originator should update the available EE_Credit and wait for the reply Sequence.

3. If LS_ACC with the D_ID of the PLOGI originator and S_ID of the PLOGI responder is received and the OX_ID is the same as the OX_ID of the PLOGI command, the PLOGI is complete and the LS_ACC contains the other port's service parameters.

4. If F_BSY with the D_ID of the PLOGI originator and S_ID of the PLOGI responder is received, the fabric is busy. The PLOGI originator should update the available EE_Credit and retry the PLOGI later.

5. If F_RJT with the D_ID of the PLOGI originator and S_ID of the PLOGI responder is received, the fabric has rejected the PLOGI frame. The PLOGI originator should update the available EE_Credit and take the appropriate action indicated by the reject reason code and explanation.

   - If the reject reason code explanation is "Class not supported" the login originator should retry the login using a different class of service.

   - If the reject reason code explanation is "Invalid D_ID" the login originator should determine the address for the destination and retry the login.

   - For other reason codes the login should be retried if the condition indicated by the reject reason code can be corrected.

6. If P_BSY with the D_ID of the PLOGI originator and S_ID of the PLOGI responder is received, the destination node port is busy. The PLOGI originator should update the available EE_Credit and retry the PLOGI later.

7. If P_RJT with the D_ID of the PLOGI originator and S_ID of the PLOGI responder is received, the destination node port has rejected the PLOGI frame. The PLOGI originator should update the available EE_Credit and take the appropriate action indicated by the reject reason code and explanation.

   - If the reject reason code explanation is "Class not supported" the login originator should retry the login using a different class of service.

   - For other reason codes the login should be retried, if the condition indicated by the reject reason code can be corrected.

8. If LS_RJT with the D_ID of the PLOGI originator and S_ID of the PLOGI responder is received, the PLOGI may be retried if the condition indicated by the reason code can be corrected.

9. If no reply is received within E_D_TOV, an error has occurred and Abort Sequence (ABTS) should be performed prior to attempting the PLOGI again.

Responses to N_Port Login (Fabric not Present). The responses to PLOGI, and corresponding actions that should be taken by the N_Port, are somewhat different when no fabric is present and are listed below.

1. An R_RDY is normally received in response to the Class-1 connect request frame or Class-2 or Class-3 frame used to send the PLOGI command. The R_RDY is a normal buffer-to-buffer flow control signal and the PLOGI originator should increment the available BB_Credit and wait for the reply Sequence.

2. If ACK_1 with the D_ID of the PLOGI originator and S_ID of the PLOGI responder is received, the PLOGI frame has been received by the other node port. The PLOGI originator should update the EE_Credit and wait for the reply Sequence.

3. If LS_ACC with the D_ID of the PLOGI originator and S_ID of the PLOGI responder is received and the OX_ID is the same as the OX_ID of the PLOGI command, the PLOGI is complete and the LS_ACC contains the other port's service parameters.

4. If P_BSY with the D_ID of the PLOGI originator and S_ID of the PLOGI responder is received, the destination node port is busy. The PLOGI originator should update the available EE_Credit and retry the PLOGI later.

5. If P_RJT with the D_ID of the PLOGI originator and S_ID of the PLOGI responder is received, the destination node port has rejected the PLOGI frame. The PLOGI originator should update the available EE_Credit and take the appropriate action indicated by the reject reason code and explanation.

   - If the reject reason code explanation is "Class not supported" the login originator should retry the login using a different class of service.

   - For other reason codes, if the condition indicated by the reject reason code can be corrected, the login should be retried.

6. If LS_RJT with the D_ID of the PLOGI originator and S_ID of the PLOGI responder is received, the PLOGI may be retried if the condition indicated by the reason code can be corrected.

7. If PLOGI is received, the two node ports have attempted login simultaneously in a point-to-point or arbitrated loop topology. The node port makes a decision on what action to take next by comparing its Port_Name with the Port_Name in the received PLOGI.

   - If this node port's value is lower, it processes the received PLOGI.

   - If this node port's value is higher, it replies to the received PLOGI with LS_RJT with a reason code explanation of "Command already in progress (x'19')."

8. If no reply is received within E_D_TOV, an error has occurred and Abort Sequence (ABTS) should be performed prior to attempting the PLOGI again.

21.28 Process Login (PRLI)

The PRLI Extended Link Service request is used to communicate one or more process service parameter pages from the PRLI originator to the PRLI responder port. Each service parameter page contains service parameters for a single image pair (pair of processes) and may be for a specific FC-4 protocol type, or for all FC-4 protocol types between the image pair.

21.28.1 Process Login (PRLI) Request

The format of the Process Login request is shown in Table 116.

Word	Bits 31:24	Bits 23:16	Bits 15:8	Bits 7:0
0	Command = x'20'	Page Length = x'10'	Payload Length	
1:4	Service Parameter Page (16 bytes)			
-	- - -			
n	Service Parameter Page (16 bytes)			

Table 116. Process Login (PRLI) Request Sequence

Page Length (word 0, bits 23:16). The page length in byte 1 of word 0 is set to x'10' indicating that each Service Parameter page is 16 bytes long.

Payload Length (word 0, bits 15:00). The payload length field specifies the number of bytes in the PRLI request and is equal to (number of pages x 16) + 4 bytes. Because the request will always include word 0 and at least one Service Parameter page, the minimum request length is 20 bytes. The maximum size of the request length is 65,532 bytes and is always a multiple of four bytes.

21.28.2 PRLI Request Service Parameter Page

Each of the Service Parameter pages contains parameters for a single image pair and may be associated with a single FC-4 protocol type or common to all FC-4 protocol types between the image pair. The format of the Service Parameter page is shown in Table 117 on page 360.

Word	Bits 31:24	Bits 23:16	Bits 15:8	Bits 7:0
0	Type Code	Type Code Extension	PRLI Flags	
1	Originator Process_Associator (if present)			
2	Responder Process_Associator (if present)			
3	FC-4 Type or Common Service Parameters			

Table 117. Service Parameter Page Format

Type Code (word 0, bits 31:24). The Type Code field identifies the FC-4 protocol type to which this service parameter page applies (for a listing of the type code values, *'Type Field Decode for FC-4 Device Data and FC-4 Link Data Frames' on page 210*). If the type code is set to x'00' the service parameter page is common to all FC-4 protocol type codes.

Type Code Extension (word 0, bits 23:16). This field is reserved for future use.

PRLI Flags (word 0, bits 15:00). These bits are defined as shown in Table 118.

Bit 15	**Originator Process_Associator Validity.** When this bit is set to one, the originator Process_Associator is valid. When this bit is zero, the originator Process_Associator is not meaningful.
Bit 14	**Responder Process_Associator Validity.** When this bit is set to one, the responder Process_Associator is valid. When this bit is zero, the responder Process_Associator is not meaningful.
Bit 13	**Establish Image Pair.** When this bit is set to one, the PRLI originator is requesting the establishment of an image pair and exchanging service parameters for that image pair relationship. When this bit is set to zero, the request is for the exchange of service parameters, but not the establishment of a new image pair.
Bit 12:00	Reserved.

Table 118. PRLI Flags

Service Parameters (word 3, bits 31:00). This field contains the FC-4 protocol mapping defined service parameters. There are no Common Service parameters defined (type code in word 0, byte 0 equal to x'00').

21.28.3 Process Login (PRLI) Reply

The expected reply Sequence is either LS_ACC or LS_RJT.

The PRLI LS_ACC is used to respond to one or more service parameter pages contained in the PRLI Extended Link Service request. Each service parameter response page contains a service parameter response for a single image pair (pair of processes) and may be for a specific FC-4 protocol type, or for all FC-4 protocol types between the image pair. The format of the Process Login LS_ACC is shown in Table 116 on page 360.

Word	Bits 31:24	Bits 23:16	Bits 15:8	Bits 7:0
0	LS_ACC = x'02'	Page Length = x'10'	Payload Length	
1:4	Service Parameter Response Page (16 bytes)			
-	- - -			
n	Service Parameter Response Page (16 bytes)			

Table 119. Process Login (PRLI) LS_ACC

Page Length (word 0, bits 23:16). The page length in byte 1 of word 0 is set to x'10' indicating that each Service Parameter Response page is 16 bytes long.

Payload Length (word 0, bits 15:00). The payload length field specifies the number of bytes in the PRLI LS_ACC and is equal to (number of pages x 16) + 4 bytes. Because the reply will always include word 0 and at least one Service Parameter Response page, the minimum reply length is 20 bytes. The maximum size of the reply length is 65,532 bytes and is always a multiple of four bytes.

21.28.4 PRLI Service Parameter Response Page

Each of the Service Parameter Response pages contains parameters for a single image pair and may be associated with a single FC-4 protocol type or common to all FC-4 protocol types between the image pair. The number of Service Parameter Response pages must match the number of Service Parameter pages in the PRLI request. The format of the Service Parameter Response page is shown in Table 120.

Word	Bits 31:24	Bits 23:16	Bits 15:8	Bits 7:0
0	Type Code	Type Code Extension	PRLI Response Flags	
1	Originator Process_Associator (if present)			
2	Responder Process_Associator (if present)			
3	FC-4 Type or Common Service Parameters			

Table 120. Service Parameter Response Page Format

Type Code (word 0, bits 31:24). The Type Code field identifies the FC-4 protocol type to which this service parameter response page applies (for a listing of the type code values, see *Type Field Decode for FC-4 Device Data and FC-4 Link Data Frames* on page 210). If the type code is set to x'00' the service parameter page is common to all FC-4 protocol type codes.

Type Code Extension (word 0, bits 23:16). This field is reserved for future use.

PRLI Response Flags (word 0, bits 15:00). These bits are defined as shown in Table 121 on page 363.

Service Parameter Response (word 3, bits 31:00). This field contains the FC-4 protocol mapping defined service parameters. There are no Common Service parameters defined (type code in word 0, byte 0 equal to x'00').

bit 15	**Originator Process_Associator Validity.** When this bit is set to one, the originator Process_Associator is valid. When this bit is zero, the originator Process_Associator is not meaningful.
bit 14	**Responder Process_Associator Validity.** When this bit is set to one, the responder Process_Associator is valid. When this bit is zero, the responder Process_Associator is not meaningful.
bit 13	**Image Pair Established.** When this bit is set to one, the image pair requested in the corresponding PRLI has been established. When this bit is zero, the image pair was not established and the Response Code (word 0, bits 11:08) provides additional information.
bit 12	**Reserved.**
bits 11:08	**Response Code.** This field contains a value indicating the result of the corresponding PRLI request. These bits are interpreted as follows:
	'0000'b Reserved
	'0001'b Request executed.
	'0010'b The responder image has no resources available for establishing the image pairs between the specified and destination node ports. The PRLI request may be retried.
	'0011'b Initialization is not complete for the responder image. The PRLI request may be retried.
	'0100'b The responder image corresponding to the Responder Process_Associator specified in the does not exist. The request should not be retried.
	'0101'b The responder image has a predefined configuration that precludes establishing this image pair. The PRLI request should not be retried.
	'0110'b The PRLI request was executed conditionally. Some service parameters could not be set to the requested state. See the Service Parameter Response field for additional information.
	'0111'b The destination node port is unable to process requests containing multiple Service Parameter pages. The request should be retried with a single Service Parameter page.
	'1000'b Service Parameters are invalid.
	'1001:1111'b Reserved
bits 07:00	**Reserved.**

Table 121. PRLI Response Code

21.29 Process Logout (PRLO)

Process Logout provides a mechanism to terminate an existing session between an image pair and frees up the resources associated with the terminated session. The PRLO request allows one or more image pairs to be terminated with a single request.

21.29.1 Process Logout (PRLO) Request

The PRLO Extended Link Service request is used to transfer one or more logout parameter pages from the PRLO originator to the PRLO responder port. Each logout parameter page contains logout parameters for a single image pair (pair of processes) and may be for a specific FC-4 protocol type, or for all FC-4 protocol types between the image pair. The format of the Process Logout request is shown in Table 122.

Word	Bits 31:24	Bits 23:16	Bits 15:8	Bits 7:0
0	Command = x'21'	Page Length = x'10'	Payload Length	
1:4	Logout Parameter Page (16 bytes)			
-	- - -			
n	Logout Parameter Page (16 bytes)			

Table 122. Process Logout (PRLO) Request Sequence

Page Length (word 0, bits 23:16). The page length in byte 1 of word 0 is set to x'10' indicating that each Logout Parameter page is 16 bytes long.

Payload Length (word 0, bits 15:00). The payload length field specifies the number of bytes in the PRLO request and is equal to (number of pages x 16) + 4 bytes. Because the request will always include word 0 and at least one Logout Parameter page, the minimum request length is 20 bytes. The maximum size of the request length is 65,532 bytes and is always a multiple of four bytes.

21.29.2 PRLO Logout Parameter Page

Each Logout Parameter page contains parameters for a single image pair. The Logout Parameter page may be associated with a single FC-4 protocol type or common to all FC-4 protocol types between the image pair. Table 123 shows the format of the Logout Parameter page.

Word	Bits 31:24	Bits 23:16	Bits 15:8	Bits 7:0
0	Type Code	Type Code Extension	PRLO Flags	
1	Originator Process_Associator (if present)			
2	Responder Process_Associator (if present)			
3	Reserved			

Table 123. Logout Parameter Page Format

Type Code (word 0, bits 31:24). The Type Code field identifies the FC-4 protocol type to which this logout parameter page applies (for a listing of the type code values, see *Type Field Decode for FC-4 Device Data and FC-4 Link Data Frames* on page 210). If the type code is set to x'00' the logout parameter page is common to all FC-4 protocol type codes.

Type Code Extension (word 0, bits 23:16). This field is reserved for future use.

PRLO Flags (word 0, bits 15:00). These bits are defined as shown in Table 124.

Bit 15	**Originator Process_Associator Validity.** When this bit is set to one, the originator Process_Associator is valid. When this bit is zero, the originator Process_Associator is not meaningful.
Bit 14	**Responder Process_Associator Validity.** When this bit is set to one, the responder Process_Associator is valid. When this bit is zero, the responder Process_Associator is not meaningful.
Bit 13:00	Reserved.

Table 124. PRLO Flags

21.29.3 Process Logout (PRLO) Reply

The expected reply Sequence is either LS_ACC or LS_RJT.

The PRLO LS_ACC is used to respond to one or more logout parameter pages contained in the PRLO Extended Link Service request. Each service parameter response page contains a service parameter response for a single image pair (pair of processes) and may be for a specific FC-4 protocol type, or for all FC-4 protocol types between the image pair. The format of the Process Logout LS_ACC is shown in Table 125.

Word	Bits 31:24	Bits 23:16	Bits 15:8	Bits 7:0
0	LS_ACC = x'02'	Page Length = x'10'	Payload Length	
1:4	Logout Parameter Response Page (16 bytes)			
-	- - -			
n	Logout Parameter Response Page (16 bytes)			

Table 125. Process Login (PRLO) LS_ACC

Page Length (word 0, bits 23:16). The page length in byte 1 of word 0 is set to x'10' indicating that each Logout Parameter Response page is 16 bytes long.

Payload Length (word 0, bits 15:00). The payload length field specifies the number of bytes in the PRLO LS_ACC and is equal to (number of pages x 16) + 4 bytes. Because the LS_ACC always includes word 0 and at least one Logout Parameter Response page, the minimum LS_ACC length is 20 bytes. The maximum size of the LS_ACC is 65,532 bytes and is always a multiple of four bytes.

PRLO Logout Parameter Response Page. Each of the Logout Parameter Response pages contains parameters for a single image pair and may be associated with a single FC-4 protocol type or common to all FC-4 protocol types between the image pair. The number of Logout

Parameter Response pages must match the number of Logout Parameter pages in the PRLO request. The format of the Logout Parameter Response page is shown in Table 126.

Word	Bits 31:24	Bits 23:16	Bits 15:8	Bits 7:0
0	Type Code	Type Code Extension (reserved)	PRLO Response Flags	
1	Originator Process_Associator (if present)			
2	Responder Process_Associator (if present)			
3	Reserved			

Table 126. Logout Parameter Response Page Format

Type Code (word 0, bits 31:24). The Type Code field identifies the FC-4 protocol type to which this logout parameter response page applies (for a listing of the type code values, *Type Field Decode for FC-4 Device Data and FC-4 Link Data Frames* on page 210). If the type code is set to x'00' the logout parameter page is common to all FC-4 protocol type codes.

PRLO Response Flags (word 0, bits 15:00). See Table 127.

bit 15	**Originator Process_Associator Validity.** If this bit is set to one, the originator Process_Associator is valid. If zero, the originator Process_Associator is not meaningful.
bit 14	**Responder Process_Associator Validity.** If this bit is set to one, the responder Process_Associator is valid. If zero, the responder Process_Associator is not meaningful.
bit 13:12	**Reserved.**
bits 11:08	**Response Code.** This field contains a value indicating the result of the corresponding PRLO request. These bits are interpreted as follows: '0000'b — Reserved '0001'b — Request executed. '0010:0011'b — Reserved '0100'b — The responder image corresponding to the Responder Process_Associator specified in the PRLO request and the PRLO LS_ACC does not exist. The PRLO request should not be retried. '0101:0110'b — Reserved '0111'b — The destination node port is unable to process PRLO requests containing multiple Service Parameter pages. The PRLO request should be retried with a single Service Parameter page. '1000'b — Service Parameters invalid. '1001:1111'b — Reserved
bits 07:00	**Reserved.**

Table 127. PRLO Response Flags

21.30 Query Security Attributes (QSA)

Query Security Attributes (QSA) provides a method for a node port to determine the security attributes of the fabric. In addition, the QSA also performs an implicit registration to receive an Registered Fabric Change Notification (RFCN) if the security attributes of the fabric change (see *Registered Fabric Change Notification (RFCN)* on page 372).

QSA is sent from a node port to the fabric controller (at address x'FF FF FD').

The format of a QSA extended link service request is shown in Table 128.

Word	31:24	23:16	15:08	07:00
0	Command = x'7E'	x'00'	x'00'	x'00'
1	Revision (currently x'00 00 00 02')			
2	**Enforced Security Attribute Registration Mask**			
	Bit	Description		
	31:2	Reserved		
	1	**Insistent Domain_ID Change Notification.** When set to one indicates that change notification is required for the Insistent Domain_ID Enforced Security Attribute.		
	0	**Fabric Binding Change Notification.** When set to one indicates that change notification is required for the Fabric Binding Enforced Security Attribute.		
3	**Extended Security Attribute Registration Mask**			
	Bit	Description		
	31:1	Reserved		
	0	Vendor Specific		

Table 128. Query Security Attributes (QSA) Request

LS_ACC to QSA follows the same format as the request except that the first byte of the payload contains x'02' and the mask fields indicate the policies being enforced by the fabric (e.g., when set in an LS_ACC reply, word 2, bit 1 indicates the fabric is currently enforcing Insistent Domain_ID Change Notification).

> NOTE – Version 1 of the QSA request did not contain words 2 and 3 (the response is still the same). Notification of changes in fabric attributes was implicitly communicated by fabric logout (OLS).

21.31 Read Connection Status (RCS)

The Read Connection Status Extended Link Service request is used to request the Fabric Controller to return the status of the current dedicated connection for the specified node port. A port may use the RCS Extended Link Service request to determine the connection status of other node ports attached to the fabric.

21.31.1 Read Connection Status (RCS) Request

The RCS Extended Link Service request is sent to the Fabric Controller at well-known address x'FF FF FD' (see *Fabric Controller* on page 483).

The format of the RCS Extended Link Service request is shown in Table 129.

Word	Bits 31:24	Bits 23:16	Bits 15:8	Bits 7:0
0	Command = x'07'	x'00'	x'00'	x'00'
1	Reserved	N_Port Identifier		

Table 129. Read Connection Status (RCS) Request Sequence

21.31.2 Read Connection Status (RCS) Reply

The LS_ACC reply to the RCS Extended Link Service request contains the connection status for the designated node port. The format of the RCS LS_ACC reply is shown in Table 130.

Word	Bits 31:24	Bits 23:16	Bits 15:8	Bits 7:0
0	LS_ACC = x'02'	x'00'	x'00'	x'00'
1	Connection Status	N_Port Identifier		

Table 130. Read Connection Status (RCS) LS_ACC Reply

Connection Status (word 1, bits 31:24). This field is defined as shown in Table 131.

Bit	Description
31	Connect request delivered to the destination N_Port
30	One or more connect requests stacked
29	Connection established
28	Intermix is functional with the destination N_Port
27:24	Reserved

Table 131. RCS Connection Status

21.32 Read Exchange Concise (REC)

The function of REC is to provide Exchange status information enabling the requestor to determine the status of the specified Exchange. In addition, REC allows a node port to retrieve Exchange information for an Exchange originated by another node port.

The target Exchange is specified by the S_ID, OX_ID, and RX_ID identifiers in the request. The receiving port can locate the Exchange Status Block (ESB) using the S_ID and OX_ID, or RX_ID if assigned.

Read Exchange Concise (REC) Request. The format of the REC extended link service request is shown in Table 132.

Word	Bits 31-24	Bits 23-16	Bits 15-8	Bits 7-0
0	Command = x'13'	x'00'	x'00'	x'00'
1	Reserved	Exchange Originator S_ID		
2	OX_ID		RX_ID	

Table 132. Read Exchange Concise (REC) Request

Read Exchange Concise (REC) Reply. The accept reply to the REC request contains Exchange information as shown in Table 133. Bits 30 (Sequence Initiative) and 29 (Exchange_Completion) of the Exchange Status Block (E_STAT) must be valid, the setting of other bits in E_STAT is optional. The Data Transfer Count is the number of bytes received from the upper-level protocol and transmitted, or the number of bytes received and delivered to the upper-level protocol.

Word	Bits 31-24	Bits 23-16	Bits 15-8	Bits 7-0
0	LS Accept = x'02'	x'00'	x'00'	x'00'
1	OX_ID		RX_ID	
2	Reserved	Exchange Originator N_Port ID		
3	Reserved	Exchange Responder N_Port ID		
4	Data Transfer Count			
5	Exchange Status, E_STAT (see Table 26 on page 186)			

Table 133. Read Exchange Concise (REC) Accept Reply

21.33 Read Link Error Status Block (RLS)

The Read Link Error Status Block Extended Link Service requests the destination node port or fabric port to return the current contents of the Link Error Status Block (LESB) associated with the designated N_Port ID.

The Link Error Status Block contains information regarding the number of link errors, link failures, loss-of-synchronization, Loss-of-Signal, and 8b/10b invalid characters that have been detected. This information may assist in determining the link condition for maintenance purposes.

While the Read Link Error Status Block request provides a means to read the contents of the Link Error Status Block, the standard does not provide a mechanism to reset the contents. The event counters in the Link Error Status Block increment until they wrap, then continue to increment from zero.

21.33.1 Read Link Error Status Block (RLS) Request

The RLS Extended Link Service request is sent to the desired node port, or the fabric port at the well-known address x'FF FF FE' (the address used to access the attached fabric port).

The format of the RLS Extended Link Service request is shown in Table 134.

Word	Bits 31:24	Bits 23:16	Bits 15:8	Bits 7:0
0	Command = x'0F'	x'00'	x'00'	x'00'
1	Reserved	N_Port Identifier		

Table 134. Read Link Error Status Block (RLS) Request Sequence

21.33.2 Read Link Error Status Block (RLS) Reply

The LS_ACC reply to the RLS Extended Link Service contains the Link Error Status Block for the designated port as shown in Table 135.

Word	Bits 31:24	Bits 23:16	Bits 15:8	Bits 7:0
0	LS_ACC = x'02'	x'00'	x'00'	x'00'
1 to 6	Link Error Status Block (see *Link Error Status Block (LESB)* on page 295 for the format of the status block)			

Table 135. Read Link Error Status Block (RLS) LS_ACC Reply

21.34 Read Timeout Value (RTV)

The Read Timeout Value link service Extended Link Service request is used to request the destination node port or fabric port return the Resource_Allocation and the Error_Detect time-out values.

21.34.1 Read Timeout Value (RTV) Request

The RTV Extended Link Service request is sent to the desired node port, or the fabric port at the well-known address x'FF FF FE' (the address used to access the attached fabric port).

The format of the RTV Extended Link Service request is shown in Table 136.

Word	Bits 31:24	Bits 23:16	Bits 15:8	Bits 7:0
0	Command = x'0E'	x'00'	x'00'	x'00'

Table 136. Read Timeout Value (RTV) Request Sequence

21.34.2 Read Timeout Value (RTV) Reply

The LS_ACC reply to the RTV Extended Link Service request contains the Resource Allocation Timeout Value (R_A_TOV) and Error Detect Timeout Value (E_D_TOV) values at the designated port as shown in Table 137. In an apparent oversight, the reply does not include the C_R_TOV timer added by FC-PH3.

FC-PH3 added one word to the RTV LS_ACC reply to report the resolution of the E_D_TOV timer. When word 3, bit 26 is zero (the default in the original standard), the E_D_TOV timer uses increments of 1 msec. When word 3, bit 26 is one, the E_D_TOV timer uses increments of 1 nsec.

Word	Bits 31:24	Bits 23:16	Bits 15:8	Bits 7:0
0	LS_ACC = x'02'	x'00'	x'00'	x'00'
1	Resource_Allocation Timeout Value (see *Resource Allocation Timeout Value (R_A_TOV)* on page 294)			
2	Error_Detect Timeout Value (see *Error Detect Timeout Value (E_D_TOV)* on page 294)			
3	Timeout Qualifier (added in FC-PH3) bits 31:27 = reserved bit 26 = E_D_TOV resolution: zero = 1 msec. intervals, one = 1 nsec. intervals bits 25:00 = reserved			

Table 137. Read Timeout Value (RTV) LS_ACC Reply

21.35 Registered Fabric Change Notification (RFCN)

If a node port registers to be notified when fabric security attributes change (see *Query Security Attributes (QSA)* on page 367), the Fabric Controller sends an RFCN extended link service when a change occurs.

The format of the RFCN request is shown in Table 138. There is no reply sequence to RFCN.

Word	31:24		23:16	15:08	07:00
0	Command = x'97'		x'00'	x'00'	x'00'
1	Revision (currently x'00 00 00 02')				
2	**Change Flags**				
	Bit	Description			
	31:1	Reserved			
	0	**Fabric Security Attributes.** When set to one, a change is occurring in a Fabric Security Attribute (i.e., the Fabric Binding or the Insistent Domain_ID Attributes) for which change notification has been registered.			

Table 138. Registered Fabric Change Notification (RFCN) Request

21.36 Reinstate Recovery Qualifier (RRQ)

The Reinstate Recovery Qualifier Extended Link Service request is used to reenable resources that are locked as the result of establishing a Recovery Qualifier.

A recovery qualifier may be established as the result of the Abort Sequence (ABTS) protocols to ensure that any frames associated with the aborted Sequence or Exchange have been purged from the system before the Sequence qualifiers are reused. This is accomplished by locking those resources from reuse until R_A_TOV has expired.

RRQ notifies the destination node port that Sequence qualifiers associated with the recovery qualifier identified in the RRQ request are now available for reuse. If the Exchange had been aborted, the Exchange Status Block (ESB) is available for immediate reuse.

The Reinstate Recovery Qualifier Extended Link Service request is transmitted by the port that initiated and successfully completed the original ABTS protocol. A new Exchange is used for the RRQ and its associated reply, not the one that was previously aborted or contained the aborted Sequence.

21.36.1 Reinstate Recover Qualifier (RRQ) Request

The format of the Reinstate Recovery Qualifier request is shown in Table 139.

Word	Bits 31:24	Bits 23:16	Bits 15:8	Bits 7:0
0	Command = x'12'	x'00'	x'00'	x'00'
1	Reserved	Exchange Originator S_ID		
2	OX_ID		RX_ID	
3 to 10	Association header (32 bytes - may be optionally required)			

Table 139. Reinstate Recovery Qualifier (RRQ) Request Sequence

21.36.2 Reinstate Recover Qualifier (RRQ) Reply

The expected reply to the RRQ request is LS_ACC.

If RRQ is received from a port that was not the originator or responder of the Exchange identified in the RRQ request, the RRQ Extended Link Service request is rejected.

21.37 Registered Link-Incident Report (RLIR)

The Registered Link-Incident Report (RLIR) Extended Link Service request provides a mechanism for a node port to send error information (an incident record) to another node port. Ports that wish to receive incident records must register their interest using the Link-Incident Record Registration (LIRR) Extended Link Service (see *Link-Incident Record Registration (LIRR) on page 350*).

A link incident occurs as the result of an FC-4 specific condition detected at a port. Each FC-4 protocol mapping that wishes to use this reporting mechanism must define the conditions that result in a link incident. The format of the information reported for a specific FC-4 condition is also defined by the FC-4 protocol mapping.

Multiple ports may register to receive information for the same FC-4 protocol type. When this occurs, the port sends the incident record to one or more of the registered destinations. The means by which the port selects the destination or destinations is not defined by the standard.

21.37.1 Registered Link-Incident Report (RLIR) Request

The format of the Registered Link-Incident Report (RLIR) Extended Link Service request is shown in Table 140.

Word	Bits 31:24	Bits 23:16	Bits 15:8	Bits 7:0
0	Command = x'79'	x'00'	x'00'	x'00'
1	Link-Incident Record FC-4 Format (Type)	Common Link-Incident Record Length	Common Link-Incident Descriptor Length	Specific Link-Incident Record Length
2 to n	Common Link-Incident Record (16 or 64 bytes)			
n +1	Common Link-Incident Descriptor			
n +1	Incident Qualifier (IQ)	Incident Code (ID)	E_Port Address Identifier (EPAI)	
n + 2 to max	Specific Link-Incident Record			

Table 140. Registered Link-Incident Report (RLIR) Request Sequence

Link-Incident Record Format (word 1, bits 31:24). This field identifies the FC-4 protocol type associated with this link-incident record. The value of x'00' is reserved.

Common Link-Incident Record Length (word 1, bits 23:16). This field specifies the length of the common link-incident record (if present). A value of x'10' indicates 16 bytes of common link-incident record are present, and a value of x'40' indicates 64 bytes of common link-incident record are present.

Link Descriptor Length (word 1, bits 15:08). This field specifies the length of the link-incident descriptor. Currently, this field is required to specify four bytes.

Specific Link-Incident Record Length (word 1, bits 07:00). This field specifies the length of the FC-4 specific link-incident record, if present. A value of x'00' indicates that no FC-4 specific link-incident record is present. The minimum value of this field is 0 bytes, the maximum value is 252 bytes. This field is required to be a multiple of four bytes.

Common Link-Incident Record (words 2:n). The common link-incident record always contains the Port_Name and Node_Name of the port associated with the incident record and may contain information about the attached port and associated operation. The format of the common link-incident record is shown in Table 141 on page 375.

Word	Bits 31:24	Bits 23:16	Bits 15:8	Bits 7:0
0	Incident Port's Port_Name (mandatory)			
1				
2	Incident Port's Node_Name (mandatory)			
3				
4	Incident Port Type	Incident Port Identifier		
5	Connected Port Port_Name			
6				
7	Connected Port Node_Name or Fabric_Name			
8				
9	Fabric_Name			
10				
11	Incident Port Physical Port number			
12	Transaction ID			
13	Reserved			Time Stamp Format
14	Time Stamp			
15				

Table 141. Common Link-Incident Record

Incident Port's Port_Name (words 0:1). This mandatory field contains the Port_Name of the port associated with this link-incident report.

Incident Port's Node_Name (words 2:3). This mandatory field contains the Node_Name of the node associated with this link-incident report.

Incident Port Type (words 4, bits 31:24). This optional field identifies the type of port associated with this incident report. The values used to identify the different port types are listed in Table 142 on page 376. If the port type is unknown or not reported, the port type is set to x'00'.

Incident Port Identifier (word 4, bits 23:00). This optional field contains the N_Port Identifier (address) of the port associated with the link-incident report. If the port does not have an identifier, or if the identifier is unknown, this field is set to x'00 00 00'.

Connected Port's Port_Name (words 5:6). This optional field contains the Port_Name of the port connected to the port associated with this link-incident report.

Port Type	Description
x'00'	Unknown
x'01'	N_Port
x'02'	NL_Port
x'81'	F_Port
x'82'	FL_Port
x'84'	E_Port
x'85'	B_Port
Other values	Reserved

Table 142. Port Types

- If the incident port is an L_Port in a private loop, the connected port is the port associated with the link incident, if known.

- If the incident port is an L_Port in a public loop, the connected port shall be the FL_Port.

- If the incident port is an N_Port connected to a fabric, the connected port is the F_Port.

- If the incident port is an FL_Port, the connected port is the port associated with the link incident, if known.

- If the connected port's Port_Name is unknown or unspecified, the Connected Port Port_Name field may be zero.

Connected Port's Node_Name or Fabric_Name (words 7:8). This optional field contains the Port_Name or Fabric_Name of the port connected to the port associated with this link-incident report.

Fabric_Name (words 9:10). This optional field contains the Fabric_Name received in the response to the FLOGI when the incident port logged in with the fabric. If the incident port is a private NL_Port (i.e., did not perform FLOGI) or the port has not yet completed fabric login, this field is set to zeros.

Incident Port Physical Port Number (word 11). This optional field contains a vendor-specific identifier that allows the physical port associated with this incident report to be identified.

Transaction ID (word 12). This optional field contains a 32-bit value that starts at one and increments by one for each link-incident record generated by the reporting node. Applications receiving link-incident records may use this value to eliminate duplicates or detect missing records. The value of zero is used to indicate the Transaction ID is unknown or not unspecified.

Time Stamp Format (word 13, bits 7:0). This optional field specifies the format of the subsequent time stamp as listed in Table 143 on page 377.

Time Stamp (words 14:15). This optional field contains a time stamp in the specified format. If the Time Stamp Format is x'00', the contents of this field are not specified and may contain any value.

Time Stamp Format	Description
x'00'	The time stamp field is not specified or unknown
x'01'	Time Server: The 64 bit time stamp is reported in units of seconds and fractions of a second using the value obtained from the Time Server.
x'02'	Clock synchronization format: The 64 bit time stamp is reported as defined for the Clock Synchronization Update (CSU) ELS.
Other values	Reserved

Table 143. Time Stamp Formats

21.37.2 Common Link-Incident Descriptor

The common link-incident descriptor provides additional information about how the link-incident record should be interpreted.

Incident Qualifier (IQ) (word 1, bits 31:24). This field further identifies how the link-incident record should be interpreted. See Table 144 for a description of this field.

Bit	Description
Bit 31	**Reserved.**
Bit 30	**Reserved.**
Bit 29	**Switch.** When equal to one, this bit indicates that the node identified by the incident node descriptor is a switch node. When equal to zero, the node is not a switch node.
Bit 28	**Expansion Port.** When Bit 29 is equal to one, this bit identifies the type of switch port. If this bit is equal to one, the port is an E_Port. When equal to zero, the port is not an E_Port (i.e., F_Port or FL_Port).
Bits 27:26	**Reporting Status Order.** These two bits identify the status of the link associated with the incident report. The values associated with these two bits are: '00'b *Informational Report.* This report is informational only. '01'b *Link Degraded but Operational.* The link is not in the Link Failure or Offline state as a result of event associated with this link-incident report. '10'b *Link Not Operational.* The link is in the Link Failure or Offline state as a result of event associated with this link-incident report. '11'b *Reserved.*
Bit 25	**Subassembly Type.** When set to one, this bit specifies that the type of subassembly associated with this report is a laser.When zero, the subassembly is not a laser.
Bit 24	**FRU Identification.** When set to one, this bit indicates that the Specific Link-Incident Record identifies a Field Replaceable Unit (FRU). When set to zero, a FRU is not identified by the Specific Link-Incident Record.

Table 144. RLIR Incident Qualifier

Incident Code (IC) (word 1, bits 23:16). This field identifies the type of incident being reported. The values in this field are defined in Table 145 on page 378.

Expansion Port Address Identifier - EPAI (word 1, bits 15:00). When bits two and three of the Incident Qualifier (IQ) field are both ones, this field contains the Domain and Area address identifiers (x'dd aa') of the other E_Port on this inter-switch link.

Value	Description
x'00'	Reserved
x'01'	**Implicit Incident.** A condition that has occurred within the node has affected the associated link. This may cause a link-incident to be recognized by the attached node.
x'02'	**Bit-Error Rate Threshold Exceeded.** The number of code-violation errors has exceeded a threshold rate.
x'03'	**Link Failure.** A Loss-of-Signal error or Loss-of-Synchronization for greater than R_T_TOV has been recognized.
x'04'	**Link Failure - Not Operational Primitive Sequence (NOS) Recognized.** The NOS sequence has been recognized by the associated node.
x'05'	**Link Failure - Primitive Sequence Timeout.** The associated node has detected a timeout of the Link Reset Protocol (LR/LRR) or has timed out while in the NOS Receive state and after NOS is no longer recognized.
x'06'	**Link Failure - Invalid Primitive Sequence for Port State.** The port has received LR or LRR while in the Wait for OLS state.
x'07'	**Link Failure - Loop Initialization Time Out.** The incident port failed to complete arbitrated loop initialization within the specified amount of time.
x'08'	**Link Failure - Receiving LIP(F8).** The incident port is receiving the Loop Failure LIP(F8).
Others	Reserved

Table 145. RLIR Incident Codes

21.37.3 Specific Link-Incident Record Data

The format of this field is defined by each FC-4 protocol type that uses link-incident reporting. Refer to the appropriate FC-4 protocol mapping document for a description of this field.

21.37.4 Registered Link-Incident Report (RLIR) Reply

The normal response to an RLIR request is LS_ACC with no additional information.

If the recipient N_Port or L_Port does not support the RLIR ELS, it replies with an LS_RJT with a reason code of "Command not supported".

If the recipient N_Port or L_Port cannot accept the specified Link-Incident Record type, it replies with an LS_RJT with a reason code of "Unable to perform command request".

If the recipient N_Port or L_Port is not logged in with the requesting port it shall reply with an LS_RJT with a reason code of "Unable to perform command request" and a reason code explanation of "N_Port Login required".

21.38 Registered State Change Notification (RSCN)

Registered State Change Notification (RSCN) indicates that an event has occurred that may have affected the login state of the designated port, area, or domain or the ability to communicate with the designated port, area, or domain.

When a node port receives RSCN, it may verify the condition of the login state of the indicated port by using of an appropriate link service. For example, the node port login state can be determined by using an appropriate Fibre Channel link service, such as the NOP Basic Link Service or some other means. The state of the process login can be determined by using the Test Process Login State (TPLS) Extended Link Service request.

21.38.1 Registered State Change Notification (RSCN) Request

The format of the Registered State Change Notification request is shown in Table 146. The number of Affected N_Port ID Pages present depends on the number of state-change events being reported.

Word	Bits 31:24	Bits 23:16	Bits 15:8	Bits 7:0
0	Command = x'61'	Page Length = x'04'	Payload Length	
1	1st Affected N_Port ID Page (4 bytes)			
- - -	- - -			
n	nth Affected N_Port ID Page (4 bytes)			

Table 146. Registered State Change Notification (RSCN) Request Sequence

Page Length (word 0, bits 23:16). The page length in byte 1 of word 0 is set to x'04' to indicate that each affected N_Port ID page is 4 bytes long.

Payload Length (word 0, bits 15:00). The payload length field specifies the number of bytes in the RSCN request Sequence and is always a multiple of four (the request is always an integral number of words). Because the request Sequence always includes word 0 and at least one affected N_Port ID page, the minimum request Sequence length is eight bytes. The maximum size of the request Sequence length is 65,532 bytes.

Affected N_Port ID Page (words 1:n). Each of the Affected N_Port ID Pages contains a single N_Port Identifier that identifies a specific node port that has experienced a potential state change event. The Affected N_Port ID cannot be x'FF FF FF' (the well-known broadcast address) or x'00 00 00' (which indicates that the port is unidentified). The format of the Affected N_Port ID Page entry is shown in Table 147.

Word	Bits 31:24	Bits 23:16	Bits 15:8	Bits 7:0
0	Address Format	N_Port Identifier		

Table 147. Affected N_Port ID Page Format

Address Format (bits 31:24). The address format field identifies the type RSCN event that has occurred and the nature of the value present in the N_Port Identifier field of the Affected N_Port ID page as shown in Table 148.

Bits		Description
7:6	Reserved	
5:2	**RSCN Event Qualifier:**	
	b'0000'	Event is not specified.
	b'0001'	Changed Name Server Object: An object maintained by the Name Server has changed state for the port, area or domain indicated by the N_Port Identifier field.
	b'0010'	Changed Port Attribute: An internal state of the port specified by the N_Port Identifier field has changed. The change of state is identified in a protocol specific manner.
	b'0011'	Changed Service Object: An object maintained by the service identified by the well-known address contained in the N_Port Identifier field has changed state.
	b'0100'	Changed Switch Configuration: The switch configuration has changed for the area or domain specified by the N_Port Identifier field.
1:0	**Format of the N_Port Identifier field for this event:**	
	b'00'	Port Address: Bits 23:00 contain the 24-bit address identifier of the affected port.
	b'01'	Area Address: Bits 23:08 contain the Domain+Area identifier of the affected area. Bits 7:0 are set to zeros. Any links and ports within the area may be affected.
	b'10'	Domain Address: Bits 23:16 contain the Domain identifier of the affected domain. Bits 15:00 are set to zeros. Any links and ports within the domain may be affected.
	b'11'	Fabric Address: The event has affected the entire fabric. Bits 23:00 are set to zeros.

Table 148. RSCN Event Qualifier and Address Format

21.38.2 Registered State Change Notification (RSCN) Reply

The expected reply to RSCN is LS_ACC with no additional information or LS_RJT.

21.39 Report Node FC-4 Types (RNFT)

The Report Node FC-4 Types (RNFT) Extended Link Service requests the recipient to return a list of supported FC-4 protocol types. It may be used any time after completion of N_Port Login (PLOGI) to verify that the remote node port supports a given FC-4 protocol.

21.39.1 Report Node FC-4 Types (RNFT) Request

The format of the Report Node FC-4 Types (RNFT) request is shown in Table 149.

Word	Bits 31:24	Bits 23:16	Bits 15:8	Bits 7:0
0	Command = x'63'	x'00'	Maximum Size	
1	reserved			Index

Table 149. *Report Node FC-4 Types (RNFT) Request Sequence*

Maximum Size (word 0, bits 15:00). This field contains a 16-bit value that specifies the maximum length of the LS_ACC reply that the originator can accept. A value of zero indicates the RNFT LS_ACC may be any size.

Index (word 1, bits 07:00). The Index is an 8-bit value that specifies the index to the first FC-4 entry to be returned in the RNFT reply.

Each FC-4 protocol supported by the responder has an index in the range from zero to (List Length – 1) that should be used to specify a subset of the entries when the entire list does not fit into one reply. The index of the entry for a particular FC-4 Type may change at any time.

21.39.2 Report Node FC-4 Types (RNFT) Reply

The normal response is an LS_ACC Sequence containing a list of supported FC-4 protocol types. The format of the Report Node FC-4 Types (RNFT) LS_ACC is shown in Table 150.

Word	Bits 31:24	Bits 23:16	Bits 15:8	Bits 7:0
0	LS_ACC = x'02'	x'00'	Payload Length (M)	
1	reserved	List Length	Reserved	Index
2	1st FC-4 Type (1)	1st FC-4 Qualifier (1)		
- - -		- - -		
n	nth FC-4 Type (n)	nth FC-4 Qualifier (n)		

Table 150. *Report Node FC-4 Types (RNFT) Reply*

Payload Length (word 0, bits 15:00). This field contains a 16-bit value that specifies the length (M) of the RNFT LS_ACC reply in bytes where M = 8 + N*4 (where N is the number of FC-4 entries in the LS_ACC reply).

List Length (word 1, bits 31:24). This field contains an 8-bit value that specifies the total number of FC-4 protocols supported by the responder.

If List Length exceeds (Index + N) the originator may request additional records with another RNFT in which the Index value is increased by N.

Index (word 1, bits 07:00). The Index field contains an 8-bit value that specifies the index of the first FC-4 Entry returned in the RNFT reply.

FC-4 Type (word n, bits 31:24). This field contains the FC-4 Type value of a FC-4 protocol that is supported by the sending node port.

FC-4 Qualifier (word n, bits 23:00). The FC-4 Qualifier may be used to distinguish between two protocols that use the same FC-4 Type code.

- For FC-4 type codes which are reserved or assigned for specific use by the standards (x'00' - x'DF'), the value of the FC-4 Qualifier is zero.
- For vendor-specific FC-4 Type codes (x'E0' through x'FF'), the FC-4 Qualifier is selected from one of the 24-bit Company_ID values assigned by the IEEE registration authority to the organization that defines that vendor-specific FC-4 protocol, and that Company_ID shall be used to qualify that FC-4 TYPE in all implementations.

  It is up to the organization that defines a vendor-specific FC-4 protocol to ensure that the protocol has a unique qualified FC-4 Type.

21.39.3 LS_RJT Reply

A specific FC-4 may require that its N_Ports support RNFT and, therefore, may conclude that a remote N_Port that returns LS_RJT with reason code explanation of "Request not supported" does not support that FC-4.

21.40 Report Port Buffer Conditions (RPBC)

The Report Port Buffer Capabilities (RPBC) Extended Link Service provides a method for ports to exchange information about buffer capabilities available for processing ELS requests and replies.

21.40.1 Report Port Buffer Capabilities (RPBC) Request

The request is sent to a destination node port. The format of the RPBC Extended Link Service request is shown in Table 151.

Word	Bits 31:24	Bits 23:16	Bits 15:8	Bits 7:0
0	Command = x'58'	Reserved		
1	Port Buffer Capabilities: bit 31: Multi-Frame ELS supported bits 30-12: Reserved bits 11-0: ELS Receive Data Field size			
2	Reserved	Obsolete (was Originator S_ID)		

Table 151. Report Port Buffer Capabilities (RPBC) Request Sequence

21.40.2 Report Port Buffer Capabilities (RPBC) Reply

The normal response to an RPBC request is an LS_ACC reply Sequence containing ELS buffer capabilities. The format of the LS_ACC reply Sequence is shown in Table 152.

Word	Bits 31:24	Bits 23:16	Bits 15:8	Bits 7:0
0	LS_ACC = x'02'	x'00'	x'00'	Flag
1	Port Buffer Capabilities bit 31: Multi-Frame ELS supported bits 30-12: Reserved bits 11-0: ELS Receive Data Field size			

Table 152. Report Port Buffer Capabilities (RPBC) Reply Sequence

LS_RJT Reply. If the recipient Port does not support the RPBC ELS, it replies with an LS_RJT reply Sequence with a reason code of "Command not supported".

21.41 Report Port Speed Capabilities (RPSC)

The Report Port Speed Capabilities (RPSC) Extended Link Service requests the destination port to report its current operating speed as well as all supported speeds.

21.41.1 Report Port Speed Capabilities (RPSC) Request

The request is sent to a destination node port or the domain controller for the associated fabric port (at address x'FF FC Domain_ID). The format of the RPSC request is shown in Table 153.

Word	Bits 31:24	Bits 23:16	Bits 15:8	Bits 7:0
0	Command = x'7D'	x'00'	x'00'	Flag

Table 153. Report Port Speed Capabilities (RPSC) Request Sequence

21.41.2 Report Port Speed Capabilities (RPSC) Reply

The normal response to an RSPC request is an LS_ACC reply Sequence containing a list of supported speeds and the current operating speed for each port associated with the RSPC recipient.The format of the LS_ACC reply Sequence is shown in Table 154.

Word	Bits 31:24	Bits 23:16	Bits 15:8	Bits 7:0
0	LS_ACC = x'02'	reserved	Number of Entries in reply	
1	Port Speed Capabilities (Port 1) bit 31: 1 gigabit capable bit 30: 2 gigabit capable bit 29: 4 gigabit capable bit 28: 10 gigabit capable bit 27: 8 gigabit capable bit 26: 16 gigabit capable bits 25:17: reserved bit 16: Speed capability unknown		Port Operating Speed (Port 1) bit 15: 1 gigabit operation bit 14: 2 gigabit operation bit 13: 4 gigabit operation bit 12: 10 gigabit operation bit 11: 8 gigabit operation bit 10: 16 gigabit operation bits 9:02: reserved bit 01: Operating speed unknown bit 00: Operating speed not established	
- - -	- - -		- - -	
n	Port Speed Capabilities (Port n) bit 31: 1 gigabit capable bit 30: 2 gigabit capable bit 29: 4 gigabit capable bit 28: 10 gigabit capable bit 27: 8 gigabit capable bit 26: 16 gigabit capable bits 25:17: reserved bit 16: Speed capability unknown		Port Operating Speed (Port n) bit 15: 1 gigabit operation bit 14: 2 gigabit operation bit 13: 4 gigabit operation bit 12: 10 gigabit operation bit 11: 8 gigabit operation bit 10: 16 gigabit operation bits 9:02: reserved bit 01: Operating speed unknown bit 00: Operating speed not established	

Table 154. Report Port Speed Capabilities (RPSC) LS_ACC Reply

21.42 Request Node-Identification Data (RNID)

The Request Node-Identification Data (RNID) Extended Link Service request is used to acquire node-identification data. Node-identification data provides information about the associated node and is normally used for configuration discovery and management purposes.

RNID may be sent directly to a specified node port or the Fabric Controller (at well-known address x'FF FF FD') in a fabric topology. When RNID is sent to the Fabric Controller, the reply contains node identification data for the instance of the Fabric Controller to which the requesting node port is attached.

A RNID request may be for common node identification data (Port_Name and Node_Name), FC-4 specific information, or topology information. FC-4 specific information allows each FC-4 protocol mapping to return different node identification data.

Through use of the RNID ELS, a switch may obtain node-identification data for all nodes attached to that switch's F_Ports, FL_Ports, or E_Ports. Management applications may use this data to discover the configuration.

21.42.1 Request Node-Identification Data (RNID) Request

The format of the Request Node-Identification Data Extended Link Service request is shown in Table 155.

The request may be for either common node-identification data (Port_Name and Node_Name) or FC-4 specific identification data. The information to be returned is specified in the node identification data format field (word 1, bits 31:24) of the request.

- The node-identification data field is set to x'00' when requesting common node-identification data.

- The node-identification data format is set to the FC-4 type value (as listed in Table 37 on page 210) when requesting FC-4 specific node-identification data.

- The node-identification data format is set to x'DF' when requesting topology information.

Word	Bits 31:24	Bits 23:16	Bits 15:8	Bits 7:0
0	Command = x'78'	x'00'	x'00'	x'00'
1	Node-identification data format	Reserved		

Table 155. Request Node-Identification Data (RNID) Request Sequence

21.42.2 Request Node Identification Data (RNID) Reply

The format of the LS_ACC reply to the RNID Extended Link Service request is shown in Table 156 on page 386. The reply may contain common node-identification data, FC-4 specific node-identification information, or topology information depending on the request.

Node-Identification Data Format (word 1, bits 31:24). This field identifies the format of the FC-4 specific node-identification data, if present. A value of x'00' indicates that only common

Word	Bits 31:24	Bits 23:16	Bits 15:8	Bits 7:0
0	LS_ACC = x'02'	x'00'	x'00'	x'00'
1	Node-identification data format	Common Node-identification data length (x'00' or x'10')	Reserved	FC-4 Specific Node-identification data length
2:5	Common Node-Identification Data (16 bytes if present)			
2:n or 6:n	FC-4 Specific Node-Identification Data (if present)			

Table 156. Request Node-Identification Data (RNID) LS_ACC Reply

node-identification data is present. A value of x'DF' indicates topology information is present. Other values indicate FC-4 specific node-identification data is present.

Common Node-Identification Data Length (word 1, bits 23:16). This field specifies the length of the common node-identification data (if present). A value of x'00' indicates that no common node-identification data is present. A value of x'10' indicates that 16 bytes of common node-identification data is present.

FC-4 Specific Node-Identification Data Length (word 1, Bits 07:00). This field specifies the length of the FC-4 specific node-identification data, if present. A value of x'00' indicates that no FC-4 specific node-identification data is present. The minimum value of this field is 0 bytes, the maximum value is 252 bytes. This field is required to be a multiple of four bytes.

21.42.3 Node-Identification Data

Node-identification data may be either common or FC-4 specific node-identification data. The format of common node-identification data is shown in Table 157.

Word	Bits 31:24	Bits 23:16	Bits 15:8	Bits 7:0
2	N_Port Name			
3				
4	Node_Name or Fabric_Name			
5				

Table 157. Common Node-Identification Data

FC-4 specific node-identification data is defined by each FC-4 protocol mapping that supports node-identification. It may contain information such as:

- Validity flags
- Node type (e.g., SCSI target, SCSI initiator, SBCCS channel, SBCCS control unit, etc.)
- Product model number/type number
- Plant of manufacture
- Serial number or Sequence number

21.42.4 Topology Information

When the RNID request is for topology information, the responder returns information about attached nodes. When topology information is returned, the format of the topology information data is shown in Table 158.

Word	Bits 31:24	Bits 23:16	Bits 15:8	Bits 7:0
0	LS_ACC = x'02'	x'00'	x'00'	x'00'
1	Node-identification data format (x'DF')	Common Node-identification data length (shall be x'10')	Reserved	FC-4 Specific Node-identification data length (x'34')
2:5	Common Node-Identification Data (16 bytes)			
6:9	Vendor Unique			
10	Associated Type			
11	Physical Port Number			
12	Number of Attached Nodes			
13	Node Management	IP Version	UDP/TCP Port	
14:17	IP Address of management entity (16 bytes)			
18	Reserved		Vendor Specific	

Table 158. Topology Identification Data

Vendor Unique (words 6:9). This field may contain vendor-unique information.

Associated Type (word 10). This field identifies the type of entity supplying the topology identification data. The values are shown in Table 159 on page 387.

Value	Entity Type
x'00 00 00 01'	Unknown
x'00 00 00 02'	Other (none of the following)
x'00 00 00 03'	Hub
x'00 00 00 04'	Switch
x'00 00 00 05'	Gateway
x'00 00 00 06'	Converter (bridge)
x'00 00 00 07'	Host bus adapter (plugable Fibre Channel adapter card)
x'00 00 00 08'	Proxy agent
x'00 00 00 09'	Storage device (disk, CD, tape, etc.)
x'00 00 00 0A'	Host system
x'00 00 00 0B'	Storage subsystem (RAID, library, etc.)
x'00 00 00 0C'	Module
x'00 00 00 0D'	Software driver
Other Values	Reserved

Table 159. Associated Type Values

Physical Port Number (word 11). This field identifies the physical port on the entity this topology identification information is associated with.

Number of Attached Nodes (word 12). This field identifies how many nodes are attached to this physical port (e.g., number of NL_Ports attached to an FL_Port).

Node Management (word 13, bits 31:24). This field specifies protocols available for managing the node (values not listed are reserved).

- x'00' indicates the node supports management using IP/UDP/SNMP
- x'01' indicates the node supports management using IP/TCP/Telnet
- x'02' indicates the node supports management using IP/TCP/HTTP
- x'03' indicates the node supports management using IP/TCP/HTTPS

IP Version (word 13, bits 23:16). This field contains the IP version supported by the management entity, if present. A value of x'00' indicates no IP support, x'01' indicates IP version 4, x'02' indicates IP version 6. Other values are reserved.

UDP/TCP Port (word 7, bits 15:00). This field contains the UDP or TCP port associated with the management entity, if present.

IP Address of Management Entity (words 14:17). This field contains the IP address of the management entity, if present.

Reserved (word 18, bits 31:16). These bytes are reserved.

Vendor Specific (word 18, bits 15:00). This field may contain vendor-specific information.

21.43 Request Sequence Initiative (RSI)

The Request Sequence Initiative Extended Link Service request is used to request that the Sequence Initiative for the designated Exchange be passed as soon as possible.

A new Exchange is used for the RSI and its associated reply, not the one for which the Sequence Initiative transfer is being requested. RSI is only accepted from either the originator or responder of the designated Exchange and the LS_ACC reply is sent following the transfer of initiative for the designated Exchange.

21.43.1 Request Sequence Initiative (RSI) Request

The format of the Request Sequence Initiative Extended Link Service request is shown in Table 160.

Word	Bits 31:24	Bits 23:16	Bits 15:8	Bits 7:0
0	Command = x'12'	x'00'	x'00'	x'00'
1	Reserved	Exchange Originator S_ID		
2	OX_ID		RX_ID	
3 to 10	Association header (32 bytes - may be optionally required)			

Table 160. Request Sequence Initiative (RSI) Request Sequence

21.43.2 Request Sequence Initiative (RSI) Reply

When RSI is received, the Sequence initiator transfers the initiative by one of the following methods:

- If the Sequence Initiative has already been transferred for the designated Exchange, reply to the RSI with LS_ACC.
- If the designated Sequence is active, the Sequence is terminated by transmitting a data frame with the End_Sequence and Sequence Initiative bits set to one.
- If the designated Sequence is active and there are no data frames to send for that Sequence, a NOP Basic Link Service frame is sent with the End_Sequence and Sequence Initiative bits set to one.
- If there are no Sequences, a new Sequence consisting of the NOP Basic Link Service frame is sent with the End_Sequence and Sequence Initiative bits set to one.

21.44 Scan Remote Loop (SRL)

The Scan Remote Loop (SRL) Extended Link Service requests a switch to scan attached loops to determine if any ports have been disabled or removed from the loop.

If the switch determines any ports currently logged in with the fabric have been removed or disabled, it updates the Name Server and sends an RSCN to all registered node ports.

The SRL request indicates whether the switch should scan all attached loops or just a single loop. If a single loop is to be scanned the request contains the FL_Port Identifier of the loop to be scanned.

21.44.1 Scan Remote Loop (SRL) Request

The format of the Scan Remote Loop Extended Link Service request is shown in Table 161.

Word	Bits 31:24	Bits 23:16	Bits 15:8	Bits 7:0
0	Command = x'7B'	Reserved		
1	Flag	Address Identifier of the FL_Port		

Table 161. Scan Remote Loop (SRL) Request Sequence

Flag (word 1, bits 31:24). This field is interpreted as follows:

bits 7:1   Reserved

bit 0:   Scan indicated FL_Port: If this bit is set to zero, all FL_Ports within the domain shall be scanned. If this bit is set to one, then only the loop attached to the FL_Port addressed in the address identifier of the FL_Port field shall be scanned.

Address Identifier of the FL_Port (word 1, bits 23:00). When bit 0 of the Flag field is set to one, this field contains the address identifier of the FL_Port. When bit 0 of the Flag field is set to one, this field is ignored.

21.44.2 Scan Remote Loop (SRL) Reply

The expected reply to the Scan Remote Loop request is LS_ACC with no further information.

21.45 Set Bit-Error Reporting Parameters (SBRP)

The Set Bit-Error Reporting Parameters request communicates a set of bit-error rate reporting parameters to a specified port or all ports within a specified domain within the fabric. To set parameters for a specified domain, SBRP is sent to the domain controller at x'FF FC dd'.

Three parameters are associated with the bit-error rate threshold: the error interval, the error window, and the bit-error rate threshold. (see *Bit-Error Rate Thresholding* on page 48 for a description of how these values are used).

The error interval is the time period over which bit error bursts are integrated to produce a single reported error. Many error conditions result in error bursts rather than a single error. To prevent a single error burst from being reported as multiple errors, all errors occurring within the error interval are considered to be a single error.

An error window is composed of one or more error intervals. The number of intervals in error occurring in an error window are counted and compared to a value derived from the bit-error rate threshold. If the count is equal or greater than derived value, a Registered Link-Incident Report (see *Registered Link-Incident Report (RLIR)* on page 374) is generated with an Incident Code specifying bit-error rate threshold exceeded. At the end of the error window, the count is reset to zero and the bit-error rate threshold process is repeated.

21.45.1 Set Bit-Error Reporting Parameters (SBRP) Request

The format of the SBRP Extended Link Service request is shown in Table 162.

Word	Bits 31:24	Bits 23:16	Bits 15:8	Bits 7:0
0	Command = x'7C'	x'00'	x'00'	x'00'
1	Set/Report/Default Flags			
2	Error Window Value		Error Interval Value	
	Error Threshold			

Table 162. Set Bit-Error Reporting Parameters (SBRP) Request Sequence

Reporting Flags (word 1, bits 31:00). The Reporting Flags specify the function requested by this SBRP request (bits 31:02 are reserved).

  Bit 0 = Set Error Reporting Parameters: When set to one, this bit requests that the destination set the error window, the error interval, and the bit-error rate threshold parameters to the values contained in this request. If the destination is a Domain Controller, the request is for the switch to set all switch ports to the requested values.

  Bit 1 = Report Error Reporting Parameters: When set to one, this bit requests that the destination return the active parameters currently being enforced.

Error Window Value (word 1, bits 21:16). This field consists of a 4-bit exponent value in bits 31:28 and a 12-bit base value in bits 27:16. The value in the exponent portion (bits 31:28) defines the scale of the time value contained in the base portion of this field (bits 27:16) as shown in table Table 163.

Exponent Value	Time Scale
b'0000'	10^0 seconds (1 second)
b'0001'	10^{-1} seconds (.1 second, or 100 msec.)
b'0010'	10^{-2} seconds (.01 second, or 10 msec.)
b'0011'	10^{-3} seconds (.001 second, or 1 msec.)
b'0100'	10^{-4} seconds (.0001 second, or 100 usec.)
b'0101'	10^{-5} seconds (.00001 second, or 10 usec.)
b'0110'	10^{-6} seconds (.000001 second, or 1 usec.)
b'0111'	10^{-7} seconds (.0000001 second, or 100 nsec.)
b'1000'	10^{-8} seconds (.00000001 second, or 10 nsec.)
b'1001'	10^{-9} seconds (.000000001 second, or 1 nsec.)
b'1010'	10^{-10} seconds (.0000000001 second, or 100 psec.)
b'1011'	10^{-11} seconds (.00000000001 second, or 10 psec.)
b'1100'	10^{-12} seconds (.000000000001 second, or 1 psec.)
b'1101'	10^{-13} seconds (.0000000000001 second)
b'1110'	10^{-14} seconds (.00000000000001 second)
b'1111'	10^{-15} seconds (.000000000000001 second)

Table 163. Exponent Values for SBRP

For example, an exponent field value of b'0101' specifies that the time scale is 10^{-5} seconds (.00001 seconds or 10 usec.). If the base value is x'001', the resulting time is 10 usec.

The Error Window has a tolerance of -0 to +1 of the maximum Error Interval.

Error Interval (word 2, bits 15:12). This field consists of a 4-bit exponent value in bits 15:12 and a 12-bit base value in bits 11:00.

The value in the exponent portion (bits 15:12) defines the scale of the time value contained in the base portion of this field (bits 11:00) as shown in table Table 163. The error interval has a tolerance of plus or minus 50%.

Error Threshold (Word 3). The error threshold field specifies a multiplier used in determining when RLIR should be generated to report a "bit-error rate threshold exceeded" condition. The value used to determine the threshold is based on this field and the current speed of the port.

First, the operating speed of the port (in gigabits per second) is rounded to an integer number (i.e., 1, 2, 4, or 10 gigabits per second). This number is then multiplied by the error threshold value to obtain the actual value used in the comparison.

For example, if the error threshold is set to x'00 00 01 00' (256 decimal) on a 1-gigabit per second link the comparison value is 256 * 1, or 256. The same error threshold value on a 2-gigabit link results in a comparison value of 256 * 2, or 512. On a 10-gigabit link the same value results in a comparison value of 256 * 10, or 2560.

21.45.2 Set Bit-Error Reporting Parameters (SBRP) Reply

The expected response to SBRP is an LS_ACC reply as shown in Table 164. The formats of the error window value, error interval value and error threshold fields are the same as described previously for the SBRP request.

Word	Bits 31:24	Bits 23:16	Bits 15:8	Bits 7:0
0	LS_ACC = x'02'	x'00'	x'00'	x'00'
1	Bit 31 = SBRP Request Accepted. Bits 30:00 are reserved			
2	Error Window Value		Error Interval Value	
	Error Threshold			

Table 164. Set Bit-Error Reporting Parameters (SBRP) Reply

SBRP Request Accepted (word 1, bit 31). This bit indicates if the SBRP recipient accepted the parameters provided in the SBRP request. Note that while the standard calls this bit SBRP Request Accepted, when the bit is set it really means the SBRP request was Rejected.

- When a request to set the reporting parameters is indicated (SBRP request word 1, bit 0 is set to one) and the recipient can accept the requested parameters, it sets this bit to zero (Accepted) and returns the requested error window, interval and threshold parameters in words 2 and 3.

- When a request to set the reporting parameters is indicated (SBRP request word 1, bit 0 is set to one) and the recipient cannot accept the requested parameters, it sets the SBRP Request Accepted bit to one (Rejected) and returns those parameters that were acceptable in words 2 and 3 (values unenforceable by the recipient are set to zero).

- When a request to report the parameters is indicated (SBRP request word 1, bit 1 is set to one) the recipient sets the SBRP Request Accepted bit to zero (Accepted) and reports the current bit-error rate reporting parameters being enforced. If no bit-error rate reporting is being enforced, words 2 and 3 are set to zeros.

- When a request to report the default parameters is indicated (SBRP request word 1, bit 2 is set) the recipient sets the SBRP Request Accepted bit to zero (Accepted) and returns the default bit-error rate reporting parameters it is capable of enforcing.

21.46 State Change Registration (SCR)

A node port sends a State Change Registration request to the Fabric Controller at well-known address x'FF FF FD', or directly to a destination node port, to request the destination to add the originating node port to the list of node ports registered to receive RSCN.

21.46.1 State Change Registration (SCR) Request

The format of the State Change Registration request is shown in Table 165.

Word	Bits 31:24	Bits 23:16	Bits 15:8	Bits 7:0
0	Command = x'62'	x'00'	x'00'	x'00'
1	Reserved	Reserved	Reserved	Registration Function

Table 165. State Change Registration (SCR) Request Sequence

The registration functions are defined as shown in Table 166.

Value	Description
x'00'	**Reserved.**
x'01'	**Fabric detected registration.** Register to receive all fabric detected state change events.
x'02'	**N_Port detected registration.** Register to receive all state change notifications resulting from receipt of a node-port-generated RSCN sent to the Fabric Controller.
x'03'	**Full registration.** Register to receive all RSCN requests issued. The RSCN request shall return all affected N_Port ID pages.
x'04:FE'	**Reserved.**
x'FF'	**Clear** any current registrations for the originating node port.

Table 166. SCR Registration Functions

21.46.2 State Change Registration (SCR) Reply

The expected reply to SCR is LS_ACC with no additional information or LS_RJT.

21.47 Test

The Test Extended Link Service request is used to perform diagnostic or test operations at the recipient port. The Test Extended Link Service request is transmitted as a single-frame Sequence from the Exchange originator to the responder.

21.47.1 Test (TEST) Request

The format of the TEST Extended Link Service request is shown in Table 167.

Word	Bits 31:24	Bits 23:16	Bits 15:8	Bits 7:0
0	Command = x'11'	x'00'	x'00'	x'00'
1	TEST data (must not exceed the maximum receive data field size allowed per login - 4)			

Table 167. Test (TEST) Request Sequence

21.47.2 Test (TEST) Reply

There is no reply Sequence to the Test request Sequence.

21.48 Test Process Login State (TPLS)

The Test Process Login State Extended Link Service allows a node port to determine the process login state of an image pair with another node port. TPLS may be issued following certain error conditions or as a result of receiving a state change notification (see *Registered State Change Notification* on page 441).

21.48.1 Test Process Login State (TPLS) Request

The TPLS Extended Link Service request is used to transfer one or more Image Pair ID pages from the originator to the responder port. Each Image Pair ID page identifies a single image pair (pair of processes). The image pair is identified by the concatenation of the S_ID, Originator Process_Associator, D_ID, Responder Process_Associator. The format of the TPLS request is shown in Table 168.

Word	Bits 31:24	Bits 23:16	Bits 15:8	Bits 7:0
0	Command = x'23'	Page Length = x'10'	Payload Length	
1:4	1st Image Pair ID Page (16 bytes)			
-	- - -			
n	nth Image Pair ID Page (16 bytes)			

Table 168. Test Process Login State (TPLS) Request Sequence

Page Length (word 0, bits 23:16). The page length in byte 1 of word 0 is set to x'10' to indicate that each Image Pair ID page is 16 bytes long.

Payload Length (word 0, bits 15:00). The payload length specifies the number of bytes in the request and is equal to (number of pages x 16) + 4 bytes. Because the request will always include word 0 and at least one Image Pair ID page, the minimum request length is 20 bytes. The maximum size of the request length is 65,532 bytes and is always a multiple of four bytes.

Image Pair ID Page (words 1:n). Each of the Image Pair ID pages contains parameters to identify a single image pair and may be associated with a single FC-4 protocol type or common to all FC-4 protocol types between the image pair. The format of the Image Pair ID page is shown in Table 169 on page 396.

Word	Bits 31:24	Bits 23:16	Bits 15:8	Bits 7:0
0	Reserved		TPLS Flags	
1	Originator Process_Associator (if present)			
2	Responder Process_Associator (if present)			
3	Reserved			

Table 169. TPLS Image Pair ID Page Format

21.48.2 Test Process Login State (TPLS) Reply

The LS_ACC transfers one or more response pages. Each response page contains the state of a single image pair. The image pair is identified by the S_ID, Originator Process Associator, D_ID and Responder Process Associator. The format of the LS_ACC is shown in Table 170.

Word	Bits 31:24	Bits 23:16	Bits 15:8	Bits 7:0
0	LS_ACC = x'02'	Page Length = x'10'	Payload Length	
1:4	1st TPLS Response Page (16 bytes)			
-	- - -			
n	nth TPLS Response Page (16 bytes)			

Table 170. Test Process Login State (TPLS) LS_ACC

Payload Length. The payload length specifies the number of bytes in the TPLS LS_ACC and is equal to (number of pages x 16) + 4 bytes. Because the reply will always include word 0 and at least one TPLS Response page, the minimum length is 20 bytes.

TPLS Response Page. Each of the TPLS Response pages contains parameters to identify the state of a single image pair. The TPLS Response page format is shown in Table 171.

Word	Bits 31:24	Bits 23:16	Bits 15:8	Bits 7:0
0	Reserved		TPLS Response Flags	
1	Originator Process_Associator (if present)			
2	Responder Process_Associator (if present)			
3	Bit 0: Image Pair State, other bits are reserved			

Table 171. TPLS Response Page Format

bit 15:	When set to one, the originator Process_Associator is valid. When this bit is zero, the originator Process_Associator is not meaningful.	
bit 14:	When this bit is set to one, the responder Process_Associator is valid. When this bit is zero, the responder Process_Associator is not meaningful.	
bit 13:12	Reserved.	
bits 11:08	TPLS Response Code. This field indicates the result of the corresponding TPLS request.	
	'0000'b	Reserved
	'0001'b	Request executed
	'0010:0110'b	Reserved
	'0111'b	The destination node port is unable to process TPLS requests containing multiple image pair ID pages.
	'1000:1111'b	Reserved
bits 07:00	Reserved.	

Table 172. TPLS Response Flags

21.49 Third-Party Process Logout (TPRLO)

Third-Party Process Logout allows a node port to invalidate all image pairs associated with the specified FC-4 protocol type and Process_Associators existing between two other node ports. The effect of the TPRLO is the same as if process logout (PRLO) had been performed for all image pairs of the specified FC-4 protocol type and Process_Associators by one of the parties in the image pair. TPRLO provides a means for a third party to end process login sessions of another port and would normally be used to free resources associated with a failed port.

21.49.1 Third-Party Process Logout (TPRLO) Request

A TPRLO request is used to transfer one or more TPRLO Logout pages from the originator to the responder port. Each Logout page identifies a Process_Associator (if used), the specific FC-4 protocol type, and the N_Port ID associated with the process logins to be removed. The format of the Third-Party Process Logout request is shown in Table 173.

Word	Bits 31:24	Bits 23:16	Bits 15:8	Bits 7:0
0	Command = x'24'	Page Length = x'10'	Payload Length	
1:4	1st TPRLO Logout Parameter Page (16 bytes)			
-	- - -			
n	nth TPRLO Logout Parameter Page (16 bytes)			

Table 173. Third-Party Process Logout (TPRLO) Request Sequence

Payload Length (word 0, bits 15:00). The payload length specifies the number of bytes in the TPRLO request and is equal to (number of pages x 16) + 4 bytes. Because a request will always include word 0 and at least one TPRLO logout parameter page, the minimum request length is 20 bytes. The maximum request length is 65,532 bytes (always a multiple of four).

TPRLO Logout Parameter Page (words 1:n). Each Logout Parameter page contains parameters to identify one or more image pairs and may be associated with a single FC-4 protocol type, common to all FC-4 protocol types between the specified image pair, or global to all specified image pairs. The format of the Logout Parameter page is shown in Table 174 on page 398.

Word	Bits 31:24	Bits 23:16	Bits 15:8	Bits 7:0
0	Type Code	Type Code Extension	TPRLO Flags (see Table 175 on page 399)	
1	Third-Party Originator Process_Associator (if present)			
2	Responder Process_Associator (if present)			
3	Reserved	Third-Party Originator N_Port ID		

Table 174. TPRLO Logout Parameter Page Format

The TPRLO Flags provide additional information as described in Table 175 on page 399.

bit 15:	Originator Process_Associator Validity. When this bit is set to one, the originator Process_Associator is valid. When this bit is zero, the originator Process_Associator is not meaningful.
bit 14:	Responder Process_Associator Validity. When this bit is set to one, the responder Process_Associator is valid. When this bit is zero, the responder Process_Associator is not meaningful.
bit 13:	Third-party Originator N_Port validity. When set to one, this bit indicates that word 3, bits 23:00 (Third-Party Originator N_Port ID) are meaningful.
bit 12:	Global process logout. When set to one, this bit indicates that all image pairs for all node ports of the specified FC-4 protocol shall be invalidated. When this bit is set only one logout parameter page is permitted in the TPRLO request.
bits 11:00:	Reserved.

Table 175. TPRLO Flags

When the Global Process Logout bit is set to 1 (bit 12), it indicates that all image pairs for all node ports of the specified FC-4 protocol type be invalidated. If the global process logout bit in the TPRLO Flags is set, only one logout parameter page is permitted in the request.

21.49.2 Third-Party Process Logout (TPRLO) Reply

The TPLS LS_ACC is used to transfer one or more TPRLO response pages in response to a TPRLO request. Each TPRLO response page contains the results of a single TPRLO Logout Parameter page request. The format of the LS_ACC is shown in Table 176.

Word	Bits 31:24	Bits 23:16	Bits 15:8	Bits 7:0
0	LS_ACC = x'02'	Page Length = x'10'	Payload Length	
1:4	1st TPRLO Response Page (16 bytes)			
-	- - -			
n	nth TPRLO Response Page (16 bytes)			

Table 176. Third Party Process Logout (TPRLO) LS_ACC

Page Length (word 0, bits 23:16). The page length in byte 1 of word 0 is set to x'10' to indicate that each TPRLO Response page is 16 bytes long.

Payload Length (word 0, bits 15:00). The payload length field specifies the number of bytes in the TPRLO LS_ACC and is equal to (number of pages x 16) + 4 bytes. The reply always includes word 0 and at least one TPRLO Response page, the minimum reply length is 20 bytes. The maximum size of the reply length is 65,532 bytes and is always a multiple of four bytes.

TPRLO Response Page (words 1:n). The format of each of the TPRLO response pages is the same as the response page for a PRLO request as shown in *PRLO Logout Parameter Response Page* on page 365.

21.50 Link Service Reject (LS_RJT)

The link service reject (LS_RJT) reply Sequence notifies the originator of an ELS request that the request has not been accepted. LS_RJT may be sent as a reply to any request that allows a reply Sequence. LS_RJT provides a reason code and explanation in the second word of the reply Sequence. Table 177 illustrates the format of the LS_RJT reply.

Word	31:24	23:16	15:8	7:0
0	LS_RJT = x'01'	x'00'	x'00'	x'00'
1	Reserved	Reason Code	Reason Explanation	Vendor Unique

Table 177. Extended Link Service Reject (LS_RJT) Format

Reason codes indicating why LS_RJT was sent are listed in Table 178 on page 400.

Reason Code	Description
x'01'	Invalid ELS Command Code - the command code in bits 31:24 of the ELS command word is invalid
x'03'	Logical Error - the command is invalid or logically inconsistent for the current conditions
x'05'	Logical Busy - the port is unable to perform the request at this time
x'07'	Protocol Error - an error has been detected that violates FC-2 protocols and is not covered by another reason code
x'09'	Unable to perform command request - the recipient is unable to perform the request at this time (it may be initializing or performing error recovery, for example)
x'0B'	Command not supported - the recipient does not support the ELS command
others	Reserved
x'FF'	Vendor Unique error (see bits 7:0)

Table 178. Link Service Reject (LS_RJT) Reason Codes

Further information about why an ELS request was rejected is provided by the reason code explanations listed in Table 179 on page 400. This table also indicates which explanations are applicable to each ELS request.

Reason Code Explanation	Description	Applicable Commands
x'00'	No additional information	
x'01'	Service Parameter error - options	FLOGI, PLOGI
x'03'	Service Parameter error - Initiator Control	FLOGI, PLOGI
x'05'	Service Parameter error - Recipient Control	FLOGI, PLOGI
x'07'	Service Parameter error - Receive data field size	FLOGI, PLOGI
x'09'	Service Parameter error - Concurrent Sequences	FLOGI, PLOGI
x'0B'	Service Parameter error - Credit	FLOGI, PLOGI
x'0D'	Invalid Nx_Port/Fx_Port Name	FLOGI, PLOGI
x'0E'	Invalid Node/Fabric Name	FLOGI, PLOGI

Table 179. Link Service Reject (LS_RJT) Reason Code Explanations (Part 1 of 2)

Reason Code Explanation	Description	Applicable Commands
x'0F'	Invalid Common Service parameters	FLOGI, PLOGI
x'11'	Invalid Association header	RRQ, RSI
x'13'	Association header required	RRQ, RSI
x'15'	Invalid originator S_ID	RRQ, RSI
x'17'	Invalid OX_ID-RX_ID combination	RRQ, RSI
x'19'	Command (request) already in progress	PLOGI, RSI
x'1E'	N_Port Login Required	ADISC, ADVC, ESTS, LIRR, PDISC, PRLO, RLIR, RNFT, RNID, TPLS, TPRLO
x'1F'	Invalid N_Port identifier	RCS, RLS
x'21'	Obsolete (was Invalid SEQ_ID)	
x'23'	Obsolete (was Attempt to abort invalid Exchange)	
x'25'	Obsolete (was Attempt to abort inactive Exchange)	
x'27'	Obsolete (was Recovery Qualifier required)	
x'29'	Insufficient resources to support login	FLOGI, PLOGI
x'2A'	Unable to supply requested data	ADVC, ESTC, RCS, RLS, RNID, RTV
x'2C'	Command (request) not supported	ADVC, ESTS, FACT, FDACT, GAID, LIRR, NACT, NDACT, PRLI, PRLO, TPLS, TPRLO, RLIR, RNFT
x'2D'	Invalid payload length	FLOGI, PLOGI
x'30'	No Alias IDs available for this alias type	GAID
x'31'	Alias ID cannot be activated (no resources avail.)	FACT, NACT
x'32'	Alias ID cannot be activated (invalid Alias ID)	FACT, NACT
x'33'	Alias ID cannot be deactivated (doesn't exist)	FCACT, NDACT
x'34'	Alias ID cannot be deactivated (resource problem)	FCACT, NDACT
x'35'	Service Parameter conflict	NACT
x'36'	Invalid Alias_Token	GAID
x'37'	Unsupported Alias_Token	NACT
x'38'	Alias Group cannot be formed	GAID
x'40'	Obsolete (was Class-4 QoS parameter error)	
x'41'	Obsolete (was Class-4 VC_ID not found)	
x'42'	Obsolete (was Class-4 Insufficient resources to support a connection)	
x'44'	Obsolete (was Invalid Port_Name/Node_Name)	
Other values	reserved	

Table 179. Link Service Reject (LS_RJT) Reason Code Explanations (Part 2 of 2)

21.51 Chapter Summary

Extended Link Services (ELS)

- Provide a set of protocol-independent functions
- Used for link management and control
  - Not used for I/O commands
  - Several can be used prior to N_Port Login
- Operate within a separate Exchange
  - Observe normal Exchange rules
- Normally use a request/reply protocol
  - Command (request) Sequence
  - Reply (LS_ACC or LS_RJT) Sequence
- Usually implemented as firmware routines

ELS Protocol

- First word of request contains ELS command
  - Remainder of the request may contain function-specific information
- Accept (LS_ACC) response
  - Indicates command request was accepted and is complete
  - May contain requested information in reply
- Link Service Reject (LS_RJT)
  - Indicates command request was not accepted
  - Returns a reason code and explanation

ELS Commands - Login Related

- Fabric Login (FLOGI)
- Discover Fabric Service Parameters (FDISC)
- Fabric Address Notification (FAN)
- Exchange Virtual Fabric Parameters (EVFP)
- N_Port Login (PLOGI)
- Discover N_Port Service Parameters (PDISC)
- Address Discover (ADISC)
- Logout (LOGO)
- Process Login (PRLI)
- Process Logout (PRLO)
- Third-Party Process Logout (TPRLO)
- Test Process Login State (TPLS)
- State Change Registration (SCR)
- Registered State Change Notification (RSCN)

ELS Commands - Status Conditions

- Status Retrieval:
  - Read Link Error Status Block (RLS)
  - Read Connection Status (RCS)
  - Read Exchange Concise (REC)
  - Read Timeout Value (RTV)
  - Read Port Buffer Conditions (RPBC)
  - Report Node FC-4 Types (RNFT)
  - Report Port Speed Capabilities (RPSC)
  - Request Node Identification Data (RNID)
- Set Bit-Error Reporting Parameters (SBRP)

ELS Commands - General

- Link Incident Records:
  - Link Incident Record Registration (LIRR)
  - Registered Link Incident Record (RLIR)
- Arbitrated Loop:
  - Loop Init (LINIT)
  - Loop Status (LSTS)
  - Scan Remote Loop (SRL)
- Reinstate Recovery Qualifier (RRQ)
- Request Sequence Initiative (RSI)
- Test (TEST)
- Echo (ECHO)

ELS Commands - Services

- Security:
  - Authentication ELS (AUTH_ELS)
  - Query Security Attributes (QSA)
  - Reg. Fabric Change Notification (RFCN)
- Estimate End-to-End Credit:
  - Estimate Credit (ESTC)
  - Establish Streaming (ESTS)
  - Advise Credit (ADVC)
- Alias_ID:
  - Get Alias_ID (GAID)
  - Fabric Activate Alias_ID (FACT)
  - Fabric Deactivate Alias_ID (FDACT)
  - N_Port Activate Alias_ID (NACT)
  - N_Port Deactivate Alias_ID (NDACT)

22. Fibre Channel Session Management

Fibre Channel provides three levels of login session management to establish identity and operating parameters between Fibre Channel entities. The login session could be between a node port and the fabric, two node ports, or processes associated with the node ports.

When a login session is established, the two ports involved exchange information used to manage and control subsequent communications during that session. The information exchanged identifies the port, node, fabric, or a process associated with the port or node. In addition, login exchanges parameters that may be used to control the use of features, options, or capabilities during the session.

Fibre Channel defines three different levels of login; fabric login, N_Port Login, and process login. The following figure illustrates the scope of the login levels.

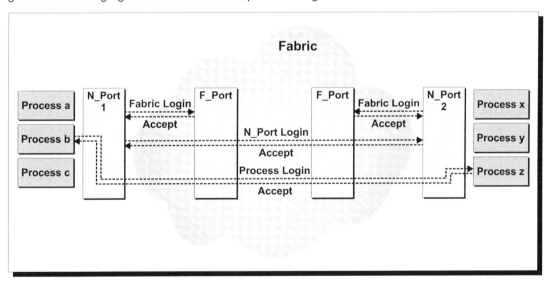

Figure 125. Fibre Channel Logins

The login process may be explicit, in which case the two ports use Fibre Channel Extended Link Services to perform the login, or it can be implicit when the necessary information is known by a means outside of the standard.

When explicit login is used, it is performed by using Extended Link Service commands. These commands operate as normal Fibre Channel Exchanges and follow normal Exchange and Sequence management rules, including applicable buffer-to-buffer and end-to-end flow control. Normal Start-of-Frame and End-of-Frame delimiters are used as appropriate for the class of service in use by the login link service Exchange. Because the classes of service supported by the other port may not be known, it may be necessary to attempt a fabric or N_Port Login command multiple times, each using a different class of service.

Login sessions are normally long-lived and may last for multiple Exchanges. In some applications the login session may be established as a part of initialization and lasts until the system or peripheral is powered off. In other applications the login session may last only for the duration of an operation or group of operations. The duration of the login session is managed by an upper-level process outside the scope of the Fibre Channel standard.

If a port or process no longer desires communications with another port or process, the session may be ended by logging out with that port. Logout may be an explicit action using Extended Link Services or link-level protocols, or an implicit action performed within the port. When logout occurs, the session with the other port or process is ended, any open or active Exchanges and Sequences associated with that port or process are terminated, and any resources used to hold the service parameters of the other port or process may be freed.

Fabric Login (FLOGI). Fabric login is used by a node port to establish a session with the fabric and is necessary before any frames can be sent through the fabric by a node port. Fabric login is required for all N_Ports and optional for NL_Ports (if an NL_Port does not perform fabric login, it cannot use the fabric to communicate with other node ports).

Fabric login is performed using the FLOGI Extended Link Service command. During fabric login the node port and fabric exchange service parameters and identify themselves to each other. In its LS_ACC to the fabric login, the fabric assigns an address to the node port.

N_Port Login (PLOGI). N_Port Login is used to establish a session between two node ports and is necessary before any upper-level (FC-4) commands or operations can be performed. N_Port Login is applicable to both N_Ports and NL_Ports.

N_Port login is performed using the PLOGI Extended Link Service command. During N_Port Login, the two node ports exchange service parameters and identify themselves to each other.

Process Login (PRLI). Process login is used to establish a session between a process at one node port and a process at another node port. Use of process login is specified by each FC-4 protocol mapping.

Process login is performed using the PRLI Extended Link Service command. During PRLI, the two processes exchange service parameters defined by the FC-4 protocol mapping.

22.0.1 State Change Notification

State change notification is a mechanism that allows interested node ports to receive a notification when the login state of other ports changes, or the ability to reach another port changes. If a node port wants to receive state change notifications, it must register its interest with the Fabric Controller or other node port using State Change Registration (SCR).

22.1 Chapter Summary

Session Management

- Fibre Channel provides three levels of session management
  - Node port to fabric login (FLOGI)
  - Node port to node port login (PLOGI)
  - FC-4 process to FC-4 process login (PRLI)
- Session is normally long-lived
- Exchange parameters used during the associated session
  - Performed using Extended Link Services
- Logout ends session if no longer needed

Fabric Login (FLOGI)

- Required before a node port can use the fabric
- Performed using FLOGI Extended Link Service
  - Payload contains node port's service parameters
  - LS_ACC contains fabric's service parameters
  - LS_ACC contains node port's address
- Explicit logout using LOGO Extended Link Service
- Implicit logout
  - Implicit logout if the link is reinitialized (OLS)
  - Implicit logout if a new FLOGI occurs
  - Implicit logout when certain errors occur

N_Port Login (PLOGI)

- Establishes session between two node ports
- Required before upper-level protocol operations are allowed
- Performed using PLOGI Extended Link Service
  - Payload contains node port's service parameters
  - LS_ACC contains other node port's service parameters
- Session may be ended by
  - Logout (LOGO)
  - Certain error conditions

Process Login (PRLI)

- Establishes session between FC-4 processes
- Use is defined by associated FC-4
  - SCSI FCP requires Process Login
  - Exchange FC-4 service parameters
- Session may be ended by:
  - Process Logout (PRLO)
  - A third party using Third-Party Process Logout (TPRLO)
  - Certain error conditions
- State of process login can be verified by use of Test Process Login State (TPLS)

State Change Notification

- Notify other ports when login state changes at a designated node port
  - Other ports can then verify login state
- Sent by node port, or fabric on behalf of the node port
- Original State Change Notification (SCN) ELS now obsolete
  - No way for interested ports to register their interest
- Replaced by Registered State Change Notification (RSCN)
  - Interested node ports register by sending State Change Registration (SCR)

23. Fibre Channel Names

Fibre Channel names provide a means to uniquely identify Fibre Channel nodes, ports, and fabrics independent of upper-level protocol or operating system environments. The Fibre Channel name is a 64-bit identifier that can be created using different formats specified by the standard. Some formats ensure that the resulting name is unique worldwide. In this case, the name is referred to as a Worldwide Name (WWN). Other name formats do not ensure worldwide uniqueness, resulting in what is referred to simply as a Fibre Channel Name (FCN).

When a Fibre Channel name is associated with a port it is called a Port_Name. When a Fibre Channel name is associated with a node it is referred to as a Node_Name, and when associated with a fabric, it is a Fabric_Name (while individual switches have Switch_Names, the fabric has a single name). When the names are worldwide unique they are frequently referred to as the Worldwide Port_Name (WWPN), Worldwide Node_Name (WWNN), or Worldwide Fabric_Name.

The first four bits of the name identify the name format. The standard refers to these bits as the Name Assignment Authority, or NAA. When a new naming method is added to the standard, a four-bit value is assigned to that specific naming method to ensure that the NAA field is unique among the various name formats.

The use of the remaining bits of the name are determined by the format identified in the NAA field. Table 180 lists the assigned NAA values and their associated name formats.

NAA bits 63-60	Name bits 59-00	Type
x'0'	Ignored	
x'1'	IEEE Name (see *IEEE Name (Format 1)* on page 408)	WWN
x'2'	IEEE Extended Name (see *IEEE Extended Name (Format 2)* on page 409)	WWN
x'3'	Locally Assigned (see *Locally Assigned Name (Format 3)* on page 409)	FCN
x'4'	Internet Protocol Name (see *IP Name (Format 4)* on page 409)	WWN
x'5'	IEEE Registered (see *IEEE Registered Name (Format 5)* on page 410)	WWN
x'6'	IEEE Registered Extended (see *IEEE Registered Extended Name (Format 6)* on page 410)	WWN
x'7'-x'B'	Reserved	
x'C' to x'F'	EUI-64 Mapped (see *EUI-64 Mapped (Formats C-F)* on page 411)	WWN

Table 180. Fibre Channel Name Formats

Names are communicated when a login session is established between node ports, or between a node port and the Fabric. This allows the ports to establish the identity of the other port prior to performing subsequent operations with that port. Fibre Channel names may also be communicated at other times, such as after potential configuration changes, to confirm the identity of the ports, node, or fabric.

The name may be used in the Network_Header as a network address when bridging or routing between Fibre Channel and non-Fibre Channel networks (see *Network Optional Header* on page 225).

Several formats of Fibre Channel names are based on the 48-bit IEEE 802.1A Universal Lan MAC Address (ULA) used by many networks. When used within a Fibre Channel name, the 48-bit MAC address is used as an identifier for a node, port, or fabric; it is not an address for frame routing. An illustration of the format of the 48-bit Universal Lan MAC Address (ULA) is shown in Figure 126.

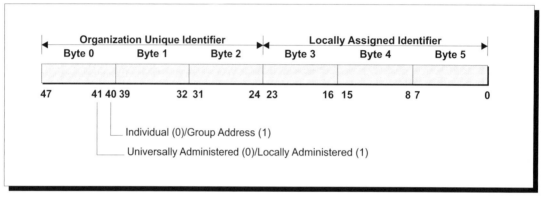

Figure 126. IEEE 48-bit MAC Address Format

The least significant bit of the first byte of the IEEE Organizational Unique Identifier (bit 40) corresponds to the Individual/Group address bit defined by IEEE 802.1A and must be zero when used in a Fibre Channel name. The Universally or Locally Administered Address (bit 41) also must be zero when used in a Fibre Channel name.

23.1 IEEE Name (Format 1)

The IEEE name (format 1) is based directly on the 48-bit Universal Lan MAC address and may be assigned to a node, port, or fabric. The 48-bit MAC address is placed in the low-order 48 bits (6 bytes) of the 64-bit (8 byte) Fibre Channel name as shown in Table 181.

Word	Bits 31-24	Bits 23-16	Bits 15-8	Bits 7-0
0	x'1'	Zeros (12 bits)	IEEE Organizational Unique ID (OUI)	
1	OUI (continued)	Locally Assigned Identifier		

Table 181. IEEE Name Format

Using an IEEE name format may simplify bridging or routing when the Fibre Channel port communicates with a non-Fibre Channel port in a network environment. This allows the lower-order 48 bits to be extracted and used as a network MAC address in the network portion of the configuration. In fact, some network applications require that this name format be used for a node port supporting network protocols (see *IP Over Fibre Channel (IPFC)* on page 591).

23.2 IEEE Extended Name (Format 2)

The IEEE Extended name format is a Fibre Channel unique extension of the format 1 name based on the 48-bit IEEE 802.1A Universal Lan MAC Address (ULA). The IEEE Extended name makes use of the 12 bits that were set to zeros in the format 1 IEEE name described in *IEEE Name (Format 1)* on page 408 to identify the ports associated with a single node or fabric as shown in Table 182.

Word	Bits 31-24	Bits 23-16	Bits 15-8	Bits 7-0
0	x'2'	Node_Port or F_Port Identifier	IEEE Organizational Unique ID (OUI)	
1	OUI (continued)	Locally Assigned Identifier		

Table 182. IEEE Extended Name Format

The IEEE Extended name (format 2) contains a port identifier field and may only be used as a Node_Port or Fabric_Port name, not as a node or fabric name. Normally, this format would be used to identify ports associated with a node or fabric having an IEEE name (format 1).

23.3 Locally Assigned Name (Format 3)

In the Locally Assigned name (format 3) all bits except the NAA field are assigned by the vendor. This name format may be assigned to any of the Fibre Channel entities — Node, Node_Port, Fabric_Port, or Fabric.

When a Locally Assigned name is used, each vendor is responsible for ensuring that the name is unique within the domain of the fabric or other interconnecting topology. Name uniqueness between different vendor's products is not guaranteed by this name format.

The format of the Locally Assigned name is shown in Table 183.

Word	Bits 31-24	Bits 23-16	Bits 15-8	Bits 7-0
0	NAA x'3'	Locally Assigned		
1	Locally Assigned			

Table 183. Locally Assigned Name Format

23.4 IP Name (Format 4)

A unique 32-bit Internet Protocol (IP) address may be used as the basis for the IP name assigned to a Node. Using an IP name format may simplify bridging or routing when the Fibre

Channel port communicates with a non-Fibre Channel port in an IP environment, because the Fibre Channel name and the IP address are the same.

The format of the IP name is shown in Table 184.

Word	Bits 31-24	Bits 23-16	Bits 15-8	Bits 7-0
0	NAA x'4'	Reserved		
1	IP Address			

Table 184. IP Name Format

23.5 IEEE Registered Name (Format 5)

This name format was added by FC-PH3 to increase the number of vendor-specified identifiers beyond what was possible with the IEEE name format (NAA=x'1'). This name format may be used by a node, port, Fabric or other object.

The IEEE name (format 1) requires 12 bits of the name field be set to zeros, allowing only 24 bits for vendor assignment. The IEEE Registered name (format 5) still uses the IEEE assigned Organization Unique Identifier (OUI) to ensure uniqueness, while allowing a vendor to assign all remaining 36 bits as a vendor-specific identifier (VSID).

While this name format increases the number of Fibre Channel names per Organization Unique Identifier, it does not readily map to a 48-bit network MAC address. Consequently, use of this format may not be allowed for nodes and ports that support network protocols such as IP over Fibre Channel.

The format of the IEEE Registered name is shown in Table 185.

Word	Bits 31-24	Bits 23-16	Bits 15-8	Bits 7-0
0	NAA x'5'	IEEE Organizational Unique ID (OUI)		VSID (35:32)
1	Vendor-Specific Identifier - VSID (31:00)			

Table 185. IEEE Registered Name Format

23.6 IEEE Registered Extended Name (Format 6)

The IEEE Registered Extended name format was also added by FC-PH3 to further increase the number of vendor-specified identifiers by adding a 64-bit extension to the IEEE registered format.

While this name format may be assigned to any Fibre Channel related object, there is no way to communicate the vendor-specified extension field using the existing link services, such as login, because the name fields are limited to 64 bits total.

This name format also does not readily map to a 48-bit network MAC address and use of this format may not be allowed for nodes and ports that support network protocols such as IP over Fibre Channel.

The format of the IEEE Registered Extended name is shown in Table 186.

Word	Bits 31-24	Bits 23-16	Bits 15-8	Bits 7-0
0	NAA x'6'	IEEE Organizational Unique ID (OUI)		VSID (35:32)
1	Vendor-Specific Identifier - VSID (31.00)			
2	Vendor-Specified Identifier Extension (63:32)			
3	Vendor-Specified Identifier Extension (31:00)			

Table 186. IEEE Registered Extended Name Format

23.7 EUI-64 Mapped (Formats C-F)

The IEEE has defined an expanded version of the 48-bit LAN MAC address called the 64-bit extended unique identifier (EUI-64). The EUI-64 identifier consists of a 24-bit Organizational Unique Identifier (OUI) followed by a 40-bit vendor-specific value. Fibre Channel provides support for this identifier through a mapping of the EUI format to the Fibre Channel name format.

Obviously, the EUI-64 identifier cannot map directly to a 64-bit Fibre Channel name because the first four bits of the Fibre Channel name are the NAA field identifying the name format. In the Organizational Unique Identifier (OUI), there are two bits that are not applicable to Fibre Channel usage, the "Universally Administered/Locally Administered" and "Individual/Group Address" bits (see Figure 126 on page 408). These bits are always b'00' when used in a Fibre Channel context and are omitted by the mapping, reducing the OUI field to 22 bits instead of 24 bits. When converting from an EUI-64 Mapped name format to a true EUI-64, these two bits are inserted into the OUI with their values set to b'00'.

In the EUI-6 Mapped name, bits 31:30 of the NAA field are set to b'11' and the remaining two bits of the NAA field are set from bits 21:20 of the (modified) OUI resulting in NAA values from b'1100' to b'1111' (formats x'C' through x'F') as shown in Table 187.

Word	Bits 31:30	Bits29-24	Bits 23-16	Bits 15-8	Bits 7-0
0	NAA b'11'	IEEE Organizational Unique ID (OUI) bits 21:00			VSID (39:32)
1	Vendor-Specified Identifier Extension (31:00)				

Table 187. IEEE Registered Extended Name Format

23.8 Chapter Summary

Fibre Channel Names

- Each node, port, and fabric has a name
- Used to identify the entity
  - Even if address changes due to reconfiguration
- Name is a unique 64-bit value
  - May be worldwide unique (Worldwide Name, WWN)
  - May only be fabric unique (Fibre Channel Name, FCN)
- Name is communicated during login
  - May be communicated during other Extended Link Services to verify login session

Name Uniqueness

- Uniqueness is ensured by registering part of the name
  - IEEE provides such a registration service
  - Originally for network interface card 48-bit Media Access Control (MAC) addresses
- IEEE assigns 24-bit Organization Unique Identifier (OUI)
  - Company assigns remaining 24-bits
- Fibre Channel provides several formats for mapping the 48-bit value into the 64-bit name field
- Name may also be locally assigned
  - Company is responsible for ensuring uniqueness

24. Login Service Parameters

When a node port logs in with another node port or the fabric, the two ports exchange information specifying their FC-2 capabilities. This information is referred to as the service parameters and is used by the ports to determine which FC-2 options, features, and capabilities can be used between the ports during that login session.

Service parameters are present in the payload of login requests (either N_Port Login or fabric login) and the LS_ACC reply to the login request. Service parameters are also communicated by the FDISC and PDISC Extended Link Service request and reply Sequences. An illustration of the format of the login payload, both request and LS_ACC, is shown in Figure 127.

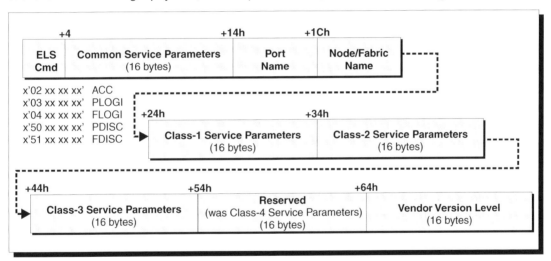

Figure 127. N_Port or Fabric Login Request and LS_ACC

24.1 Common Service Parameters

The Common Service parameters apply to all classes of service supported by the port. The format of the Common Service parameters for both the fabric port and node port is shown in Figure 128 on page 414. The Common Service parameters for the node port vary depending upon whether the node port is performing Fabric Login (FLOGI) or N_Port Login (PLOGI).

Table 188 on page 415 summarizes the Common Service parameters and indicates when each login operation and class of service applies.

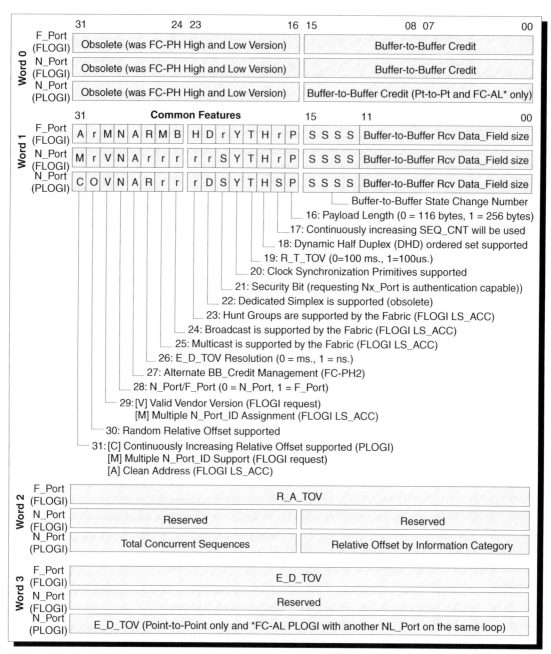

Figure 128. Login Common Service Parameters

Word	bit(s)	Description	PLOGI Class-1	PLOGI Class-2	PLOGI Class-3	FLOGI Class-1	FLOGI Class-2	FLOGI Class-3
0	31-24	Obsolete (was Highest Version Supported)	y	y	y	y	y	y
	23-16	Obsolete (was Lowest Version Supported)	y	y	y	y	y	y
	15-0	Buffer-to-Buffer Credit	1	1	1	y	y	y
1	31	Continuously Increasing Relative Offset (PLOGI only)	y	y	y	n	n	n
		Multiple N_Port_ID Support (FLOGI request only)	n	n	n	y	y	y
		Clean Address (FLOGI LS_ACC only)	n	n	n	y	y	y
	30	Random Relative Offset	y	y	y	n	n	n
	29	Valid Vendor Version Level	y	y	y	y	y	y
		Multiple N_Port_ID Assignment - NPIV (in FLOGI LS_ACC)	n	n	n	y	y	y
	28	0 = N_Port / 1 = F_Port (or FL_Port)	y	y	y	y	y	y
	27	Alternate BB_Credit Management	y	y	y	y	y	y
	26	E_D_TOV Resolution	y	y	y	n	n	n
	25	Multicast supported (in FLOGI LS_ACC)	n	n	n	y	y	y
	24	Broadcast supported (in FLOGI LS_ACC)	n	n	n	y	y	y
	23	Hunt Group supported (in FLOGI LS_ACC)	n	n	n	y	y	y
	22	Dedicated Simplex (obsolete)	y	y	y	n	n	n
	21	Security Bit (authentication supported/required)	y	y	y	y	y	y
	20	Clock Synchronization Primitives (SYN) supported	1	1	1	y	y	y
	19	R_T_TOV value (0 = 100 ms., 1 = 100 us.)	1	1	1	y	y	y
	18	Dynamic Half Duplex	y	y	y	y	y	y
	17	SEQ_CNT	y	y	y	n	n	n
	16	Payload Length	y	y	y	y	y	y
	15-12	Buffer-to-Buffer State Change Number (BB_SC_N)	1	1	1	y	y	y
	11-00	Buffer-to-Buffer Receive Data_Field Size	y	y	y	y	y	y
2	31-00	Resource Allocation Time-out Value (R_A_TOV)	1	1	1	y	y	y
	31-16	N_Port Total Concurrent Sequences	y	y	y	n	n	n
	15-00	Relative Offset by Information Category	y	y	y	n	n	n
3	31-00	Error Detect Time-out Value (E_D_TOV)	1	1	1	y	y	y

1. Valid during PLOGI only in the point-to-point topology or when logging in with another node port on the same arbitrated loop.

Table 188. Common Service Parameter Applicability

Word 0, bits 31-24: Obsolete (was Highest Version). This field formerly contained a value identifying the latest version of the standard supported as shown in Table 189.

Version	FC-PH Version Level
x'00'	None
x'06'	FC-PH, version 4.0
x'07'	FC-PH, version 4.1
x'08'	FC-PH, version 4.2
x'09'	FC-PH, version 4.3
x'10'	FC-PH2
x'20'	FC-PH3
Other values	Reserved

Table 189. FC-PH Version Levels

Word 0, bits 23-16: Obsolete (was Lowest Version). This field formerly contained a value identifying the earliest version of the standard supported by the port.

Word 0, bits 15-00: Buffer-to-Buffer Credit. This field is the buffer-to-buffer credit value being granted and represents the total number of buffers available to hold Class-1/6 connect request (SOFc1), Class-2, or Class-3 frames. During PLOGI, this value is only valid in point-to-point and arbitrated loop topologies. In an arbitrated loop, this value is only valid when logging in with another NL_Port on the same loop.

Word 1, bit 31: Continuously Increasing Relative Offset. When set to "1" during a PLOGI request or LS_ACC to a PLOGI, this bit indicates the node port supports the use of continuously increasing relative offset for the information categories specified in *Word 2, bits 15-00: Relative Offset by Information Category* on page 418.

Continuously increasing relative offset requires that the parameter fields of successive frames within a single information category begin with the parameter field value of the prior frame of the information category + the payload length of the prior frame of the information category +1.

Indicating support of this capability applies both as a Sequence initiator and Sequence recipient, although use of continuously increasing relative offset is not required as a Sequence initiator, even if both ports support it.

Word 1, bit 31: Multiple N_Port ID Support. When this bit is set to "1" by a node port in a FLOGI request, the node port is indicating it is capable of requesting multiple N_Port IDs by use of the FDISC Extended Link Service (NPIV).

Word 1, bit 31: Clean Address. When this bit is set to "1" by the Fabric in LS_ACC to a FLOGI, the fabric is indicating the node port can begin using the supplied N_Port ID immediately, even if it is different from the address identifier the node port had prior to the FLOGI. Normally, a node port is required to wait R_A_TOV following an address change before originating frames using a new N_Port identifier.

Word 1, bit 30: Random Relative Offset. when set to "1", the node port supports the use of random relative offset for the information categories specified in *Word 2, bits 15- 00: Relative Offset by Information Category* on page 418.

Random relative offset allows the parameter fields of successive frames to use random values that may increase, decrease, or otherwise fluctuate within a Sequence.

Indicating support of this capability applies both as a Sequence initiator and Sequence recipient, although use of random relative offset is not required as a Sequence initiator, even if both ports support it.

Word 1, bit 29: Valid Vendor Version Level. when set to "1", this bit indicates that the Vendor Version Level field contains valid information.

Word 1, bit 29: Multiple N_Port_ID Assignment. when set to "1" by the Fabric in a LS_ACC to FLOGI, this bit indicates that the Fabric is capable of assigning multiple N_Port_IDs in response to an FDISC Extended Link Service (NPIV).

Word 1, bit 28: N_Port / F_Port. when set to "1", this bit indicates the port supplying the service parameters is a fabric port. A value of "0" means the port is a node port.

Word 1, bit 27: Alternate BB_Credit Management. When set to "1", this bit indicates the port is capable of supporting the arbitrated loop Alternate BB_Credit management model. The arbitrated loop topology requires use of the Alternate BB_Credit model.

Word 1, bit 26: E_D_TOV Resolution. when set to "1", this bit indicates the E_D_TOV value is expressed in nanoseconds. A value of "0" indicates that the E_D_TOV value is expressed in milliseconds.

Word 1, bit 25: Multicast. When set to "1" by the Fabric in LS_ACC, this bit indicates the Fabric supports multicast. When set to "0", multicast is not supported.

Word 1, bit 24: Broadcast. When set to "1" by the Fabric in LS_ACC, this bit indicates the Fabric supports broadcast. When set to "0", broadcast is not supported.

Word 1, bit 23: Hunt Groups. When set to "1" by the Fabric in LS_ACC, this bit indicates the Fabric supports hunt groups. When set to "0", hunt groups are not supported.

Word 1, bits 22: Dedicated Simplex (obsolete).

Word 1, bit 21: Security Bit. When set to "1" by a node port in an FLOGI or PLOGI request, this bit indicates the node port is capable of performing authentication.

When set to "1" by the Fabric in an LS_ACC to FLOGI, this bit indicates that the fabric requires the node port to perform authentication.

When set to "1" by a node port in an LS_ACC to PLOGI, this bit indicates that the recipient node port requires the originating node port to perform authentication.

Word 1, bit 20: Clock Synchronization Primitives Support. When set to "1", the SYNx, SYNy, and SYNz clock synchronization Primitive Signals are supported.

Word 1, bit 19: R_T_TOV Value. When set to "1", this bit indicates the R_T_TOV value is 100 usec. When set to "0", R_T_TOV is 100 msec.

Word 1, bit 18: Dynamic Half Duplex. When this bit is set to "1", the NL_Port supports use of the Dynamic Half Duplex Primitive Signal. This bit is only applicable to arbitrated loop environments supporting FC-AL2.

Word 1, bit 17: Sequence Count. When set to "0", normal Sequence count rules apply. When set to "1", the node port is indicating it will transmit all frames within an Exchange using continuously increasing Sequence count.

The first frame of the first Sequence of the Exchange begins with SEQ_CNT x'0000' as per normal rules. Subsequent frames transmitted within that Exchange increase SEQ_CNT by +1 as each frame is transmitted. The incrementing SEQ_CNT continues across Sequence boundaries, even if Sequence Initiative is transferred to the other port. Frames sent by the other port have no effect on the SEQ_CNT used by the port.

Word 1, bit 16: Payload Length. When set to "1", the FLOGI payload is 256 bytes. If this bit is set to a "0", the length is 116 bytes.

Word 1, bits 15-12: Buffer-to-Buffer State Change Number (BB_SC_N). When Buffer-to-Buffer credit recovery is supported (see *Buffer-to-Buffer Credit Recovery* on page 265), this field contains the value specifying the number of frames between BB_SCs Primitive Signals and the number of R_RDYs between BB_SCr Primitive Signals.

When Buffer-to-Buffer credit recovery is not supported, this field contains zeros.

Word 1, bits 11-00: Buffer-to-Buffer Receive Data_Field Size. This field is a binary value that represents the largest data field size for a connect-request (SOFc1), Class-2, or Class-3 frame that the port is able to receive. Values less than 256, greater than 2112, or not a multiple of 4 are invalid.

Word 2, bits 31-00: R_A_TOV. During fabric login, this field contains the Resource Allocation timeout value (R_A_TOV) expressed in milliseconds.

Word 2, bits 31-16: Total Concurrent Sequences. During N_Port Login, this field contains the total number of concurrent Sequences of all classes that a node port is capable of supporting as a Sequence recipient. This number must be less than, or equal to, the sum of the number of concurrent Sequences specified in the Class-specific service parameters for all classes of service.

Word 2, bits 15-00: Relative Offset by Information Category. During N_Port Login, this field identifies the information categories for which the use of relative offset, either continuously increasing or random, is supported. Table 190 on page 419 lists usage of the bits in this field. When a bit is set, support is indicated as both Sequence initiator and recipient.

Bit 15:	Relative Offset is supported for Information Category 15
Bit 14:	Relative Offset is supported for Information Category 14
Bit 13:	Relative Offset is supported for Information Category 13
Bit 12:	Relative Offset is supported for Information Category 12
Bit 11:	Relative Offset is supported for Information Category 11
Bit 10:	Relative Offset is supported for Information Category 10
Bit 09:	Relative Offset is supported for Information Category 9
Bit 08:	Relative Offset is supported for Information Category 8
Bit 07:	Relative Offset is supported for Information Category 7 (Command Status)
Bit 06:	Relative Offset is supported for Information Category 6 (Unsolicited Command)
Bit 05:	Relative Offset is supported for Information Category 5 (Data Descriptor)
Bit 04:	Relative Offset is supported for Information Category 4 (Unsolicited Data)
Bit 03:	Relative Offset is supported for Information Category 3 (Solicited Control)
Bit 02:	Relative Offset is supported for Information Category 2 (Unsolicited Control)
Bit 01:	Relative Offset is supported for Information Category 1 (Solicited Data)
Bit 00:	Relative Offset is supported for Information Category 0 (Uncategorized Data)

Table 190. Relative Offset by Information Category

Word 3, bits 31-00: Point-to-Point E_D_TOV Value. E_D_TOV is the error detect time-out value provided by the fabric during fabric login or a node port during PLOGI in a point-to-point topology or with another NL_Port on the same arbitrated loop.

24.2 Port_Name

This is the eight-byte name assigned to this node port or fabric port and used for identification purposes. It uses one of the formats described in *Fibre Channel Names* on page 407.

24.3 Node_Name or Fabric_Name

This is the eight-byte name assigned to the node or fabric that contains this node port or fabric port and used for identification purposes. It uses one of the formats described in *Fibre Channel Names* on page 407.

24.4 Class-Specific Service Parameters

The Class-specific service parameters specify the capabilities of the fabric or node port for each class of service. Table 191 on page 420 summarizes the Class-specific service parameters and indicates when each login operation and class of service is applicable.

The format of the Class-specific service parameters are shown in Figure 129 on page 421. Note that the Class-specific service parameters for the node port vary depending on whether the node port is performing fabric login (FLOGI) or N_Port Login (PLOGI).

Word	bit(s)	Description	Class-1/6	Class-2	Class-3	Class-1/6	Class-2	Class-3
			PLOGI			**FLOGI**		
0	31	Class Valid	y	y	y	y	y	y
	30	Intermix Mode	y	n	n	y	n	n
	29-28	Stacked Connect Request (removed by FC-PH3)	n	n	n	n	n	n
	27	Sequential Delivery	n	n	n	n	y	y
	26	Obsolete (was Dedicated Simplex)	-	n	n	n	n	n
	25	Camp-On	n	n	n	y	n	n
	24	Obsolete (Buffered Class-1)	-	n	n	n	n	n
	23	Priority	y	y	n	y	y	n
		Initiator Control						
	15-14	X_ID Reassignment	y	y	n	n	n	n
	13-12	Initial Process_Associator	y	y	y	n	n	n
	11	ACK_0 Capable	y	y	n	n	n	n
	10	Obsolete	-	-	-	-	-	-
	9	ACK Generation Assistance	y	y	n	n	n	n
	8	Obsolete	-	-	-	-	-	-
	7-6	Obsolete	-	-	-	-	-	-
	5	Obsolete	-	-	-	-	-	-
	4	Clock Synchronization Capable	y	y	y	y	y	y
		Recipient Control						
1	31	ACK_0 Capable	y	y	n	n	n	n
	30	Obsolete	-	-	-	-	-	-
	29	X_ID Interlock	y	y	n	n	n	n
	28-27	Error Policy Supported	y	y	y	n	n	n
	25-24	Categories per Sequence	y	y	y	n	n	n
	23	Obsolete	-	-	-	-	-	-
	22-21	Obsolete	-	-	-	-	-	-
	20	Obsolete	-	-	-	-	-	-
	19	Clock Synchronization Capable	y	y	y	y	y	y
	18-16	Reserved - Fabric Specific	y	y	y	y	y	y
	15-0	Receive Data Field Size	y	y	y	n	n	n
2	31-16	Concurrent Sequences	y	y	y	n	n	n
	14-0	N_Port End-to-End Credit	y	y	n	n	n	n
3	31-16	Open Sequences per Exchange	y	y	y	n	n	n

Table 191. Class-Specific Service Parameter Applicability

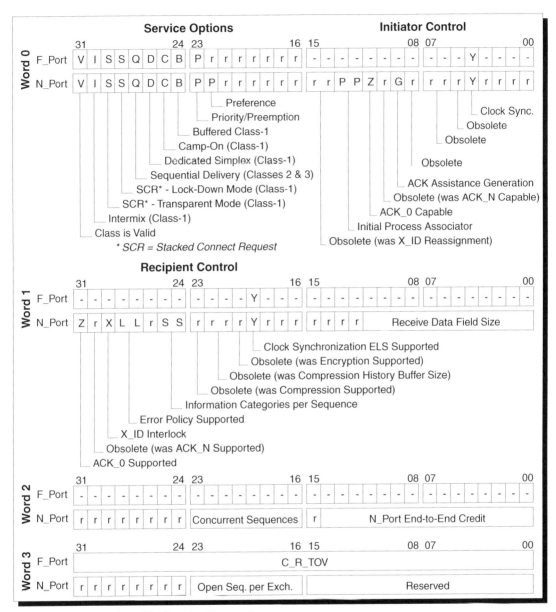

Figure 129. Class-Specific Service Parameters

Word 0, bit 31: Class Validity. When set to "1", the corresponding class of service is supported. When set to "0", the class is not supported.

Word 0, bit 30: Intermix Mode. When set to "1" in the Class-1 service parameters, inter-mix is supported by the node port and support of intermix is requested from the fabric. When set to "1" in the LS_ACC reply to fabric login (FLOGI), this bit indicates Dedicated Simplex is functional.

Word 0, bit 29: Stacked Connect Request Transparent Mode. When set to "1" in the Class-1 service parameters during fabric login, stacked connect request-transparent mode is being requested by the node port. When set by the fabric, stacked connect re-quest-transparent mode is supported and functional. While a node port may request both modes, the fabric will not indicate that more than one mode is functional.

Word 0, bit 28: Stacked Connect Request Lock-Down Mode. When set to "1" in the Class-1 service parameters during fabric login, stacked connect request lock-down mode is being requested by the node port. When set by the fabric, stacked connect re-quest lock-down mode is supported by the fabric and functional. While a node port may request both modes, the fabric will not indicate that more than one mode is functional.

Word 0, bit 27: Sequential Delivery. When set to "1" in the Class-2 or Class-3 Class-specific service parameters by a node port during fabric login, the node port is request-ing sequential frame delivery for the corresponding class of service. When set to "1" by the fabric in the LS_ACC to the FLOGI, it indicates that the fabric will provide in-order frame delivery for that class of service.

Word 0, bit 26: Obsolete (was Dedicated Simplex). when set to "1" in the Class-1 ser-vice parameters during FLOGI, this bit indicates the node port is requesting support for Dedicated Simplex connections. When set to "1" in the LS_ACC reply to the fabric log-in, this bit indicates that Dedicated Simplex is functional.

Word 0, bit 25: Camp-On. when set to "1" in the Class-1 service parameters during FLOGI, this bit indicates the node port is requesting support for Camp-On connections. When set to "1" in the LS_ACC reply to fabric login, it indicates Camp-On is functional.

Word 0, bit 24: Obsolete (was Buffered Class-1).

Word 0, bit 23: Priority. when set to "1" in during FLOGI, this bit indicates the node port is requesting support for Priority/Preemption. When set to "1" in the LS_ACC reply to the fabric login, this bit indicates that Priority/Preemption is functional.

Word 0, bits 15-14: X_ID Reassignment. These two bits indicate that when the node port is the Sequence initiator it may reassign its X_ID (either the OX_ID or RX_ID de-pending upon whether the node port is the Exchange originator or responder) at certain Sequence boundaries. Bits 15-14 are encoded as shown in Table 192 on page 423.

Word 0, bits 13-12: Initial Process_Associator. These two bits are used to indicate the node port requires an Association header at certain Sequence boundaries. Bits 13-12 are encoded as shown in Table 193 on page 423.

'00'b	X_ID reassignment not supported
'01'b	X_ID reassignment supported
'10'b	Reserved
'11'b	X_ID reassignment required (and supported)

Table 192. X_ID Reassignment Login Bits

'00'b	Initial Process_Associator not supported
'01'b	Initial Process_Associator supported
'10'b	Reserved
'11'b	Initial Process_Associator required (and supported)

Table 193. Initial Process_Associator Login Bits

Word 0, bit 11: ACK_0 Capable. when set to "1" in the Class-1 or Class-2 service parameters during PLOGI, this bit indicates that when the node port is the Sequence initiator it is capable of supporting ACK_0. For ACK_0 to be functional, the other node port must indicate ACK_0 support in word 1, bit 31 of the LS_ACC reply to the PLOGI.

Word 0, bit 10: Obsolete.

Word 0, bit 9: ACK Generation Assistance. when set to "1" in the Class-1 or Class-2 service parameters during PLOGI, this bit indicates that when the node port is the Sequence initiator it is capable of generating the ACK_Form bits of the F_CTL field.

Word 0, bit 8-5: Obsolete.

Word 0, bit 4: Clock Synchronization Capable. when set to "1" during PLOGI, this bit indicates that when this node port is the Sequence initiator it has clock synchronization capability. For clock synchronization to be functional, the other node port must indicate clock synchronization support in word 1, bit 19 of the LS_ACC reply to the PLOGI.

Word 1, bit 31: ACK_0 Supported. when set to "1" in Class-1 or Class-2 service parameters during PLOGI, this bit indicates that when the node port is the Sequence recipient it is capable of supporting ACK_0. For ACK_0 to be functional, the other node port must indicate ACK_0 capability in word 0, bit 11 of the LS_ACC reply to the PLOGI.

Word 1, bit 30: Obsolete.

Word 1, bit 29: X_ID Interlock. when set to "1" in the Class-1 or Class-2 service parameters during PLOGI, this bit indicates that when the node port is the Sequence recipient it requires that interlock be used during X_ID assignment or reassignment.

Word 1, bits 28-27: Exchange Error Policy. These two bits indicate the Exchange error policies supported when the node port is the Sequence recipient (see *Exchange Error Policies* on page 183). The Exchange originator will specify the policy for an Exchange in the F_CTL field of the first frame of the first Sequence of the Exchange. Bits 28-27 are encoded as shown in Table 194.

'00'b	Only the discard policy is supported
'01'b	Reserved
'10'b	Both discard and process are supported
'11'b	Reserved

Table 194. Exchange Error Policy Login Bits

Word 1, bits 25-24: Information Categories per Sequence. These two bits specify the number of information categories per Sequence that are supported when the node port is the Sequence recipient. Bits 26-25 are encoded as shown in Table 195 on page 424.

'00'b	1 Category per Sequence
'01'b	2 Categories per Sequence
'10'b	Reserved
'11'b	More than 2 Categories per Sequence

Table 195. Information Categories per Sequence Login Bits

Word 1, bit 23-20: Obsolete.

Word 1, bit 19: Clock Synchronization Capable. when set to "1" during PLOGI, this bit indicates that when this node port is the Sequence recipient it has clock synchronization capability. For clock synchronization to be functional, the other node port must indicate clock synchronization support in word 0, bit 4 of the LS_ACC reply to the PLOGI.

Word 1, bits 10-0: Receive Data Field Size. This field is a binary value specifying the largest data field that the node port is capable of receiving in this class of service. The value must be a multiple of four and cannot exceed 2112 bytes. FC-PH specified the minimum value as 128 bytes; this was increased to 256 bytes by FC-PH3.

Word 2, bits 23-16: Concurrent Sequences. This field is a binary value specifying the maximum number of concurrent Sequences that the node port is capable of supporting for this class of service. The total of all Class-specific concurrent Sequences cannot exceed the total concurrent Sequences field in the Common Service parameters.

Word 2, bits 14-0: N_Port End-to-End Credit. This field is a binary value specifying the end-to-end credit being granted to the other node port for this class of service.

Word 3, bits 31-00: CR_TOV. During fabric login, this field specifies the CR_TOV value in milliseconds. CR_TOV is applicable to Class-1 operations only.

Word 3, bits 23-16: Open Sequences per Exchange. During N_Port Login, this field is a binary value specifying the maximum number of open Sequences the node port is capable of supporting for a single Exchange in this class of service. This parameter controls the ability of the Sequence initiator to stream Sequences and determines how may Sequences may be open at any point.

Word 3, bits 15-00: Class-6 Multicast RX_ID. During N_Port Login, this field contains the RX_ID that shall be used by the multicast server when acknowledging the Class-6 multicast connection initiator.

24.5 Vendor Version Level

This field is used to identify vendor-specific deviations from the Fibre Channel versions specified in the Common Service parameters. The field is only meaningful if the Vendor Version Valid bit in the Common Service parameters is set to a "1". The format of the Vendor Version Level is shown in Table 196.

Word	Bits 31-24	Bits 23-16	Bits 15-8	Bits 7-0
0	Vendor Identification Code		Vendor-specific versions supported	
1	Vendor-specific versions supported by the N_Port (continued)			
2	Reserved for vendor-specific use			
3	Reserved for vendor-specific use			

Table 196. Vendor Version Level

24.6 Default Service Parameters

Prior to login or following a logout, the port uses a default set of service parameters allow subsequent communications using link services. The default login parameters are:

- Receive Data Field size = 128 bytes
- Buffer-to-Buffer Credit = 1 (N_Port or F_Port), or 0 (NL_Port or FL_Port)
- End-to-End Credit = 1 (if applicable to the class of service)
- ACK Policy = ACK_1 (if applicable to the class of service)
- Total Concurrent Sequences = 1
- Concurrent Sequences per Class = 1
- X_ID Interlock = required (if applicable to the class of service)
- X_ID Reassignment = not allowed
- Error Policy = discard multiple Sequences
- Relative Offset = not used
- E_D_TOV resolution = 0 (msec.)
- BB_SC_N = '0000'b

In addition, no optional features or functions can be used until login has been completed.

24.7 Chapter Summary

Service Parameters

- Communicate a port's FC-2 capabilities
- Service parameters consist of:
  - Common Service parameters (common to all classes of service)
  - Class-specific service parameters (one set for each class of service)
- Service parameters are exchanged during:
  - Fabric Login (FLOGI)
  - N_Port Login (PLOGI)
  - Fabric Discover (FDISC) and Port Discover (PDISC)
- Does not define FC-4 capabilities such as protocols supported

Common Service Parameters

- Defines Class-independent parameters
  - Buffer-to-Buffer credit
  - Support of Buffer-to-Buffer credit recovery
  - Support of relative offset (continuous, random, for which information categories)
  - Node Port or Fabric Port
  - Alternate BB_Credit model supported
  - Dynamic Half Duplex (DHD) supported
  - Buffer-to-Buffer receive data field size
  - Total concurrent Sequences (all classes of service)
  - Timeout values (E_D_TOV, R_A_TOV)

Class-Specific Parameters

- Defines parameters for each class of service
  - Is class of service supported?
  - Intermix supported (Class-1)
  - Sequential delivery (requested/provided)
  - Dedicated Simplex (Class-1) - obsolete
  - Camp-on (Class-1)
  - Buffered Class-1 (obsolete)
  - Priority and Preemption
  - End-to-End Credit
  - Open Sequences per Exchange

Class-Specific Parameters

- Sequence Initiator capabilities
  - X_ID Reassignment supported
  - ACK_0 Capable
  - ACK Generation Assistance provided
  - Clock Synchronization capable
- Sequence Recipient capabilities
  - ACK_0 capable
  - X_ID Interlock
  - Error policies supported
  - Information Categories per Sequence
  - Clock Synchronization Capable
  - Receive data field size for this class

Default Service Parameters

- Receive Data Field size = 128 bytes
- Buffer-to-Buffer Credit = 1 (N_Port or F_Port), or 0 (NL_Port or FL_Port)
- End-to-End Credit = 1 (if applicable)
- ACK Policy = ACK_1 (if applicable)
- Total Concurrent Sequences = 1
- Concurrent Sequences per Class = 1
- X_ID Interlock = required (if applicable)
- X_ID Reassignment = not allowed
- Error Policy = discard multiple Sequences
- Relative Offset = not used

Default Service Parameters (cont.)

- R_A_TOV = 10,000 (msec.)
- E_D_TOV = 2,000 (msec.)
- E_D_TOV resolution = 0 (msec.)
- BB_SC_N = '0000'b

25. Fabric Login Session Management

Fabric login is used by a node port to detect if a fabric is present and, if so, establish a session with the fabric by communicating identities and exchanging service parameters. Fabric login is also the mechanism whereby the fabric assigns an address to a node port. Fabric login is required before the fabric will accept frames for delivery to other node ports.

In a point-to-point or fabric topology, fabric login is performed following link initialization and before other communication with other node ports is attempted. When the node port attempts fabric login, it does not know if there is a fabric present, or if the port is in a point-to-point configuration. Fabric login provides a mechanism for the node port to determine the topology through the response received to the login attempt.

On an arbitrated loop, fabric login may be performed following loop initialization. Unlike the other topologies, an NL_Port is not required to perform fabric login (see *Fabric Login Requirements* on page 429).

25.1 Establishing a Fabric Login Session

Fabric login may be either explicit or implicit. A node port performs explicit Fabric login by transmitting the FLOGI Extended Link Service request (see *Fabric Login (FLOGI)* on page 343) to the well-known address of the fabric login server (x'FF FF FE').

If this is the first time that an N_Port has performed FLOGI, it uses x'00 00 00' as its source address. If the N_Port had previously completed FLOGI, the port uses its current address in the FLOGI request.

If this is the first time that an NL_Port has performed FLOGI, it uses x'00 00 AL_PA' as its source address (where AL_PA is the arbitrated loop physical address acquired by the NL_Port during loop initialization. If the NL_Port had previously completed FLOGI, the port uses its current address in the FLOGI request.

As with all Extended Link Services, a new Exchange is created for the FLOGI Extended Link Service request and normal Exchange and Sequence management rules apply, including flow control applicable to the class of service used. A diagram of a FLOGI operation is provided by Figure 130 on page 428.

Because a node port does not know which classes of service are supported by the fabric, the port could possibly receive F_RJT with a reason code of "Class of Service Not Supported". If this occurs, the node port should retry the fabric login using a different class of service. If all supported classes of service have been tried and the fabric login is unsuccessful, the port and fabric are incompatible.

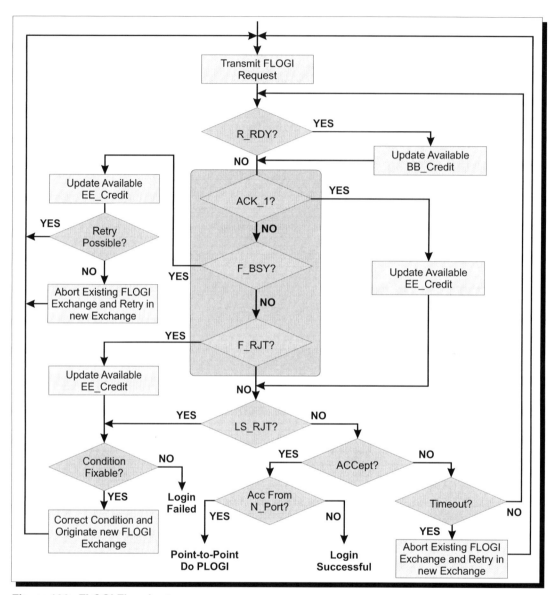

Figure 130. FLOGI Flowchart

During Fabric login, service parameters are exchanged between the node port and fabric. Service parameters contain the Port_Name, Node_Name or Fabric_Name, and FC-2 capability information. The service parameters establish the operating parameters used between the node port and fabric during the login session (see *Login Service Parameters* on page 413).

Service parameters define the port's capabilities, such as the maximum frame data field size that can be received by each port, buffer-to-buffer credit, etc.

The response to the FLOGI indicates if a fabric is present. If a fabric is present and an LS_ACC reply is received, the fabric login process is complete. In the LS_ACC, the fabric assigns (or confirms) the N_Port identifier (address) of the node port that initiated the FLOGI and returns the fabric's service parameters. A description of the service parameters is found in *Login Service Parameters* on page 413.

25.1.1 Fabric Login Requirements

N_Ports are required to perform fabric login to determine the topology. If the N_Port is in a point-to-point topology, FLOGI is accepted and the service parameters indicate that the attached port is an N_Port. In this case, the two N_Ports perform N_Port Login.

Fabric login is optional for NL_Ports. If an NL_Port does not perform fabric login, it is referred to as a Private NL_Port. If the NL_Port performs fabric login, it is referred to as a public port.

Private NL_Port. An NL_Port that does not perform fabric login is referred to as a Private NL_Port. Private NL_Ports can only communicate with other NL_Ports on the same arbitrated loop. Because a private port has not logged in with the fabric, it is not part of the fabric's address space and cannot send or receive frames via the fabric.

Private NL_Port addresses are of the form x'00 00 AL_PA', where AL_PA is the arbitrated loop physical address acquired by the port during loop initialization.

Public NL_Ports. Public NL_Ports perform fabric login if a fabric port is present in the loop. If the fabric login is successful, the NL_Port becomes part of the fabric address space and can send and receive frames with other node ports (N_Ports or NL_Ports) via the fabric. If the fabric login is not successful, or no fabric port is present in the loop, the NL_Port reverts to private NL_Port behavior.

Public NL_Port addresses are of the form x'xx xx AL_PA' where the upper 16 bits of the address are assigned by the fabric, non-zero, and the same for all public ports on that loop.

25.2 N_Port ID Virtualization (NPIV)

N_Port ID virtualization is an optional feature that enables an N_Port to acquire multiple addresses from the fabric. Each address is associated with a unique N_Port context and has the appearance of being a separate N_Port to other ports in the fabric.

25.2.1 N_Port ID Virtualization Address Acquisition

When N_Port ID virtualization is used, the N_Port performs a normal Fabric Login (FLOGI) to acquire its initial N_Port ID (address). Once fabric login has been successfully completed, an N_Port may acquire additional addresses using the Fabric Discover (FDISC) extended link service shown by Figure 131 on page 430 (the source ID in the FDISC request is all zeros). The FLOGI and each FDISC presents a unique Port_Name (WWPN) to the fabric.

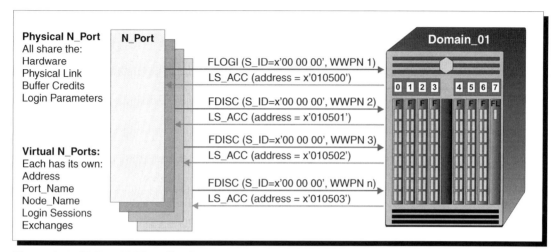

Physical N_Port
All share the:
Hardware
Physical Link
Buffer Credits
Login Parameters

Virtual N_Ports:
Each has its own:
Address
Port_Name
Node_Name
Login Sessions
Exchanges

N_Port

FLOGI (S_ID=x'00 00 00', WWPN 1)
LS_ACC (address = x'010500')

FDISC (S_ID=x'00 00 00', WWPN 2)
LS_ACC (address = x'010501')

FDISC (S_ID=x'00 00 00', WWPN 3)
LS_ACC (address = x'010502')

FDISC (S_ID=x'00 00 00', WWPN n)
LS_ACC (address = x'010503')

Domain_01

0 1 2 3   4 5 6 7

Figure 131. N_Port ID Virtualization

An N_Port may relinquish an address by performing Logout (LOGO) with the fabric. The logout specifies the address and Port_Name of the address being relinquished. If all assigned addresses are relinquished, it is necessary for the N_Port to perform another FLOGI to acquire addresses.

25.2.2 N_Port Virtualization Link Considerations

Because the virtual N_Ports share the same physical link, link events can affect multiple N_Port IDs. All of the N_Port IDs on a link share the same buffer-to-buffer credit (BB_Credit). When one N_Port ID sends a frame, the available BB_Credit for that link is decremented. When R_RDY is received, the available BB_Credit for that link is incremented. If the available BB_Credit is zero no frames can be sent by any N_Port ID on that link.

If a Link Reset occurs (LR/LRR), the available BB_Credit for that link is restored to the FLOGI values. In addition, frames may be discarded for any N_Port ID associated with that link.

If a Link Failure (NOS) or Link Initialization (OLS) occurs all N_Port IDs associated with that link are implicitly logged-out from the fabric and it is necessary to re-login using FLOGI and re-acquire the additional N_Port IDs using FDISC in order to continue.

25.3 Terminating an Existing Fabric Login Session

Prior to FC-FS, there was no explicit fabric logout. If a node port (N_Port or NL_Port) initiated a new fabric login, the FLOGI causes an implicit logout of the prior session and establishment of a new session. FC-FS added the ability to explicitly logout from the fabric by sending a LOGO extended link service request to address x'FF FF FE'.

Non-Loop Implicit Fabric Logout. If an N_Port or F_Port wishes to terminate the current fabric login session, it may cause an implicit fabric logout by transmitting the offline (OLS) Primitive Sequence (note that this does not apply to NL_Ports or FL_Ports).

If an N_Port or F_Port enters the link failure protocol (by either transmitting or receiving the NOS Primitive Sequence), an implicit fabric logout occurs.

Arbitrated Loop Implicit Fabric Logout. If an FL_Port wishes to terminate current fabric login sessions with attached Public NL_Ports, it may begin loop initialization and set the L-Bit (login required bit) in the LISA loop initialization sequence.

If an NL_Port or FL_Port detects a loop failure, an attempt is made to reinitialize the loop, but an implicit fabric logout does not occur.

25.4 Actions on Implicit Fabric Logout and Relogin

If an implicit fabric logout occurs, the node port does not originate or accept communications from other node ports through the fabric until fabric relogin has been completed. During the relogin, the node port may discover one of the following conditions has occurred (both implicitly end current login sessions with other node ports).

- If the node port's identifier (address) has changed, the node port does not initiate or accept communications with other node ports through the fabric until it has explicitly logged out with each and performed N_Port Login (PLOGI) to reestablish login sessions with those ports.
- If the fabric port's Port_Name or the Fabric_Name has changed since the last fabric login, the fabric has been reconfigured or the node port is no longer attached to the same fabric. The action taken depends on the level of the standard implemented by the node port and fabric.

  Prior to the FC-FS standard, the node port waited for R_A_TOV before initiating or accepting communication with other node ports through the fabric. After R_A_TOV expires, the node port logs out and performs N_Port Login (PLOGI) with node ports it had been logged in with previously.

  FC-FS added a new bit in the Fabric Login (FLOGI) LS_ACC service parameters called the Clean Address bit (see *Word 1, bit 31: Clean Address* on page 416). When this bit is set, the node port may begin using the new address immediately without waiting for R_A_TOV to expire.

If neither condition occurs, the node port can continue open Sequences and Exchanges.

25.5 Determining the State of a Fabric Login Session

Sometimes events may occur that result in a node port being unable to determine the current state of its fabric login session. The Fabric Discover (FDISC) Extended Link Service (*Discover Fabric Service Parameters (FDISC)* on page 332) with a non-zero S_ID enables a node port to determine its current fabric login status and determine the service parameters of the fabric.

A node port may also simply choose to send a new Fabric Login (FLOGI) request. Unlike N_Port Login (PLOGI) and Process Login (PRLI), initiating a new fabric login does not result in termination of open Sequences and Exchanges (unless the node port is assigned a different address or the Fabric_Name or fabric port's Port_Name has changed).

25.6 Chapter Summary

Fabric Login (FLOGI)

- FLOGI is issued by a node port to:
  - Determine if a fabric is present
  - Establish a session with the fabric
  - Exchange service parameters with the fabric
- FLOGI is mandatory for N_Ports
  - FLOGI is optional for NL_Ports (not required for those that don't intend to use the fabric)
- FLOGI assigns the node port's address
  - Assigns all 24 bits to an N_Port
  - Assigns upper 16 bits to an NL_Port (lower 8 bits are the AL_PA)

N_Port ID Virtualization (NPIV)

- N_Port virtualization enables an N_Port to acquire multiple N_Port IDs (addresses)
  - Each address has the appearance of a separate N_Port to other ports
  - Separate WWPN is used for each address
  - Each address maintains a separate context
- The initial address is acquired using FLOGI
  - Additional addresses are acquired by FDISC
- An address can be relinquished using LOGO
- All virtual N_Ports share the same physical link
  - BB_Credit is shared by all virtual N_Ports
  - Link Reset, Link Initialization or Link Failure affects all virtual N_Ports on that link

Fabric Logout and Relogin

- Logout can occur explicitly or implicitly
- Explicit logout uses LOGO ELS sent to x'FF FF FE'
- Implicit logout occurs when:
  - A new FLOGI occurs
  - OLS or NOS is received or transmitted
- When a re-login occurs
  - If the port is assigned the same address, PLOGI sessions are still in effect and operations can continue
  - If the port is assigned a different address, PLOGI sessions are abnormally terminated

Fabric Address Notification (FAN)

- Added by the Fabric Loop Attach (FLA) technical report
- Provides mechanism for FL_Port to notify NL_Ports of:
  - FL_Port's address
  - FL_Port's name
  - Fabric's name
- Allows NL_Port to verify configuration following loop initialization
  - If FL_Port's identifiers have changed, the prior session is implicitly logged out

Fabric Discover (FDISC)

- FDISC has two different uses
- If the S_ID = Port's address, used to verify the current login information, especially the:
  - FL_Port's address
  - FL_Port's name
  - Fabric's name
  - Avoids the implicit logout associated with a new FLOGI
- If the S_ID = x'000000', N_Port is requesting another N_Port ID
  - See N_Port ID Virtualization (NPIV)

26. N_Port Login Session Management

N_Port Login provides a mechanism to establish and manage a session between two node ports (N_Ports or NL_Ports). Login is required before a node port will accept operations (other than basic or Extended Link Service requests) from another node port. If a node port receives a request (other than a Basic Link Service request or selected Extended Link Service requests) from another node port, the request is rejected with P_RJT (Class-1 or Class-2) or discarded (Class-3).

26.1 Establishing a Node Port Login Session

N_Port Login is optional for Class-3 and required by all other classes of service. Class-3 is excepted by the standard because it is used for broadcast and it is unreasonable to require a port to log in with every other port prior to performing a broadcast. However, in practice, explicit N_Port Login is required before performing any FC-4 operations, just as with the other classes of service.

N_Port Login may be either explicit or implicit. A node port performs explicit N_Port Login by transmitting the PLOGI Extended Link Service request to the destination port (see *N_Port Login (PLOGI)* on page 357).

As with all Extended Link Services, a new Exchange is created for the PLOGI Extended Link Service request and normal Exchange and Sequence management rules apply, including flow control applicable to the class of service used. A flow diagram of a PLOGI operation is provided by Figure 132 on page 434.

Because a node port does not know which classes of service are supported by the destination, the port may receive P_RJT with a reason code explanation of "Class of Service Not Supported". If this occurs, the node port should retry the N_Port Login using a different class of service. If all supported classes of service have been tried and the N_Port Login is unsuccessful, the two ports are incompatible.

If the two node ports are connected through a fabric, both node ports must have successfully completed fabric login before the node ports can communicate. In addition, the parameters governing the fabric login session may constrain the parameters available during the N_Port Login operation (e.g., classes of service).

During explicit N_Port Login, service parameters are exchanged between the two node ports. Service parameters contain the Port_Name, Node_Name, and the port's FC-2 capability information. The service parameters establish the operating parameters used between the ports during the login session (see *Login Service Parameters* on page 413). Service parameters

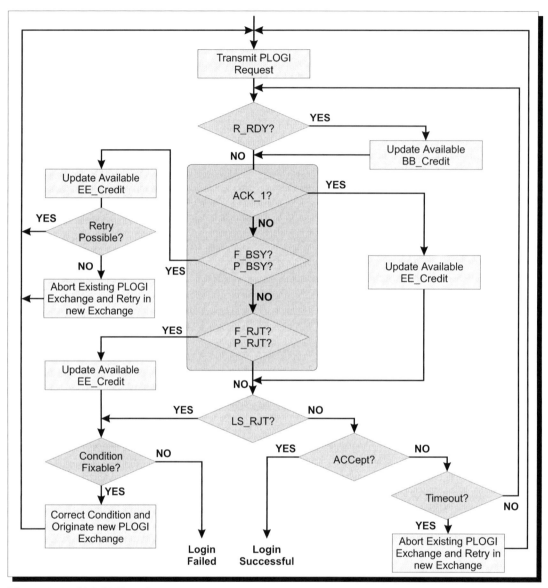

Figure 132. PLOGI Flowchart

provide information, including items such as the maximum size of frame that can be received by each port, end-to-end credit, etc.

Receipt of an LS_ACC reply from the destination node port indicates the PLOGI request was accepted and is complete at the destination port. The LS_ACC reply contains the other port's service parameters completing the exchange of parameters between the two ports.

In a point-to-point topology, N_Port Login is used to assign N_Port identifiers (addresses) to the two node ports. N_Port Login also establishes the login buffer-to-buffer credit value between the two ports.

In an arbitrated loop topology, N_Port Login with another node port on the same loop establishes the login buffer-to-buffer credit value between the two node ports.

26.2 Terminating an Existing Node Port Login Session

An existing N_Port Login session may be ended explicitly by using the Logout (LOGO) Extended Link Service request, or implicitly due to events that affect the login session.

When a logout occurs, either explicitly or implicitly, any open Sequences and Exchanges between the two node ports are abnormally terminated and any resources associated with those session are freed. If upper-level protocol operations are in progress, those operations are terminated when the logout occurs.

26.2.1 Explicit N_Port Logout

The Logout (LOGO) Extended Link Service command provides a mechanism for explicitly ending an existing login session between two node ports (see *Logout (LOGO)* on page 352 for a description of the LOGO Extended Link Service). Processing of the LOGO Extended Link Service is similar to that shown in Figure 132 on page 434.

26.2.2 Implicit N_Port Logout

There are events and conditions that may cause an existing login session to end without use of the LOGO Extended Link Service. This is referred to as an implicit logout. These conditions may result in a LOGO being sent by the affected port, or the affected port may simply remove the login session without notifying the other port.

Reset is one example of an event that may cause implicit logout of other node ports. When the affected port is reset (e.g., power-on reset), information regarding current login sessions is reset and all existing Exchanges are abnormally terminated.

If a point-to-point link to another node port fails or is reinitialized, an implicit logout occurs with the other port and a new N_Port Login is required. This occurs if the node port enters the link failure or link initialization protocols. Arbitrated loop initialization does not result in a logout.

If a node port's address changes for any reason, any existing login sessions are abnormally terminated. This could occur if an arbitrated loop port is unable to acquire its previous address during loop initialization, or it a port initiates a new fabric login and receives a different address from the fabric.

Receipt of PLOGI from a port that is already logged in ends the prior login session by causing an implicit logout before establishing the new login session. Any open or active Exchanges or

Sequences in the prior session are terminated by the implicit logout and any resources associated with the prior session are released.

26.3 Determining the State of a Login Session

Sometimes events occur that may result in a node port being unable to determine the current state of a login session. This could occur as a result of events occurring on the link, such as arbitrated loop initialization or receipt of a state change notification.

While a node port could simply perform N_Port Login by sending a PLOGI request, establishing new login session results in an implicit logout of the prior session. This causes any open Sequences or Exchanges associated with that prior session to be abnormally terminated. To avoid termination of operations in progress it is desirable to be able to verify the state of existing login sessions without causing an implicit logout.

There are two Extended Link Services enabling a node port to determine the status of existing login sessions and verify the identity of the other port without affecting the current login state.

- The Discover N_Port Service Parameters (PDISC) Extended Link Service command allows a node port to determine the current login status and exchange service parameters with the other port (see *Discover N_Port Service Parameters (PDISC)* on page 333).

- The Discover Address (ADISC) Extended Link Service provides a means for a port to discover the identity of another port and whether that port was able to acquire its desired address (some topologies allow a hard address to be provided to the port by switches, jumper, or other means). For a description of the ADISC Extended Link Service, see *Discover Address (ADISC)* on page 331.

26.4 PLOGI Trace Example

Figure 133 is an analyzer trace of a PLOGI operation. For details of the Common and Class specific service parameters, refer to *Login Service Parameters* on page 413.

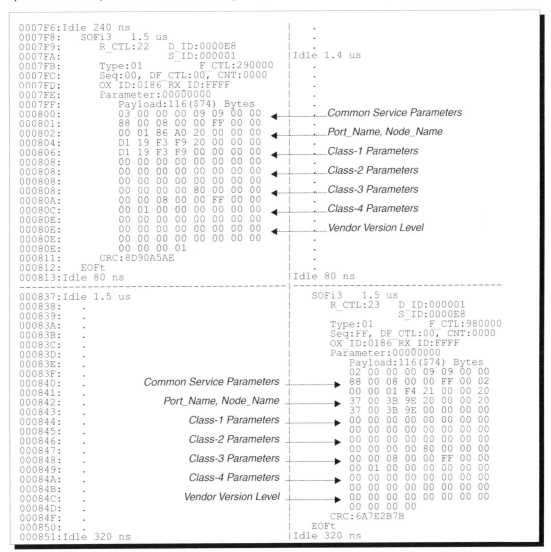

Figure 133. PLOGI Trace Example

26.5 Chapter Summary

N_Port Login (PLOGI)

- PLOGI establishes a session between two node ports
  - Exchanges service parameters and names
  - Issued in a separate Exchange
- May receive P_RJT with "Class not Supported"
  - Should retry login using a different class of service
- In point-to-point topology, PLOGI also assigns addresses

Logout (LOGO)

- Logout ends a session between two node ports
- Terminates all open Exchanges between the ports
- May be explicit:
  - Using LOGO Extended Link Service
- May be implicit:
  - Due to error conditions
  - At the port's choice (to free login resources, for example)

Port Discover (PDISC)

- Extended Link Service added by FC-PH2
- Exchanges service parameters with another node port without doing PLOGI
  - Avoid implicit logout associated with PLOGI
- Allows a node port to:
  - Verify the identity of another node port
  - Determine if the other port's service parameters have changed
- Primary application is in arbitrated loop
  - Verify the configuration following a loop initialization

Address Discover (ADISC)

- Extended Link Service added by FC-PH2
- Allows a node port to:
  - Verify the identity of another node port
  - Determine if the other node port's address matches its hard address, if used
- Primary application is in arbitrated loop
  - Verify the configuration following a loop initialization

27. Process Login

Process login is used to establish and manage a session between an FC-4 level process in an originator port and a corresponding FC-4 process in the responder port. When an FC-4 process login session is established, service parameters may be exchanged to control subsequent communication during the session.

The use of process login is dependent on the FC-4 protocol mapping for a specific upper-level protocol and is defined during the FC-4 mapping process. The process login Extended Link Services described in this chapter provide a generic mechanism to support the process login while leaving the definition of the service parameters up to the specific FC-4 protocol mapping.

Process login establishes a session between two FC-4 processes at the node ports. This relationship is referred to as an image pair (a logical process or image at one node port and a logical process or image at the other node port). The processes involved could be system processes, system images such as the mainframe logical partitions, control unit images, FC-4 processes, or other processes. When the process login in performed, the two ports may optionally exchange Process_Associators that can subsequently be used to identify a specific process at both the originator and responder ports.

Figure 125 on page 403 illustrates a relationship between process b in node port 1 and process z in node port 2. Process login provides a mechanism to establish the relationship between the two processes (in effect establishing a binding between the two processes). If desired, the processes can be identified by assigning a Process_Associator to each of the processes. The Process_Associators can subsequently be used during operations between the two processes to validate that the operation should be performed.

Process login may also be performed between the FC-4 protocol mappings in the ports to establish FC-4 dependent options or parameters. The SCSI Fibre Channel Protocol (FCP) mapping requires the use of PRLI to communicate FCP-defined parameters (see *SCSI FCP Process Login* on page 573).

Use of PRLI is optional from FC-2's perspective but may be required by a specific upper-level protocol, as is the case of the SCSI-FCP protocol mapping. PRLI may be accomplished implicitly by a means outside of the standard, or explicitly by use of the PRLI Extended Link Service request.

The Test Process Login Extended Link Service request (see *Test Process Login State (TPLS)* on page 396) provides a means to determine the current process login state between an image pair.

27.1 Chapter Summary

Process Login (PRLI)

■ Optional service to establish a session between two FC-4 processes
  • Referred to as an "image pair"
  • Binds the two processes
  • Process is protocol specific (type field)
  • May have multiple image pairs for a single protocol (requires use of Process_Associators)
■ FC-4 protocol defines use of process login
  • SCSI-3 FCP mapping requires process login
  • Communicate FC-4 specific service parameters

Process Logout (PRLO)

■ Logs out a session between two FC-4 processes
■ Removes one or more image pairs
  • Removes binding between the processes
  • Terminates any open Exchanges between the image pair

Test Process Login State (TPLS)

■ Allows a node port to determine the process login state
■ May be used during error recovery
■ May be triggered by a State Change Notification
■ If process login state matches expected state, resume operation,
  • Otherwise, relogin to establish new session

Third-Party Process Logout (TPRLO)

■ Allows a third party to log out a session between two FC-4 processes
■ Removes one or more image pairs
  • Terminates any open Exchanges between the image pair
■ May be used during error recovery
  • In multi-originator environments
  • Free up resources associated with a failed port in the image pair

28. Registered State Change Notification

Registered State Change Notification (RSCN) is an Extended Link Service mechanism that provides notification to interested node ports when events occur that may affect the login state or ability to communicate with an affected node port. This mechanism would normally be used by SCSI-FCP initiators to receive notifications of events that may have affected target devices or FC-SB-2 channels to receive notifications of events that may have affected control units.

Ports interested in receiving RSCN notifications must explicitly register to receive notifications using the State Change Registration (SCR) Extended Link Service request. The registration request may be sent to the Fabric Controller or directly to specific node ports. The Fabric Controller or affected node port will then send RSCN to registered node ports when a state change event occurs.

When a node port registers to receive RSCN notifications, it may register to receive notification of all state change events, only those events detected by the fabric, or only those events detected by the affected node port.

RSCN is sent to a node port if all the following conditions are met:

- The node port has registered to receive RSCN (see *State Change Registration (SCR)* on page 394),
- The node port is currently logged in with the fabric (or other port, if registered directly with the other node port),
- The node port has not gone offline since it last registered to receive RSCN,
- The node port supports Class-2 or Class-3 (if the destination port supports Class-3, RSCN is sent in Class-3, otherwise Class-2 is used),
- The registration function requested in the SCR matches the RSCN type,
- The affected N_Port ID is different from the registered port's identifier
- One of the following conditions is met:
  - The RSCN is a fabric format notification
  - The RSCN is a domain format notification
  - The RSCN is an area format notification and there is at least one active zone containing both the registrant port and affected port
  - The RSCN is a port format notification and there is at least one active zone containing both the registrant port and affected port
  - Zoning is not active

Receipt of an RSCN notification may cause recipient node ports currently logged-in with the affected port to verify the current status of their login session. If the current login session is still valid, operations with the affected port may continue. If the current login session is no longer valid, the recipient can attempt to relogin with the affected port, if possible. If it is not possible to re-establish a login session with the affected port, the RSCN recipient may perform an implicit logout in order to free resources associated with the affected node port.

Determination of the state of the current login state may be performed by using Extended Link Services such as Port Discover (PDISC), Fabric Discover (FDISC), Test Process Login State (TPLS), upper-level protocol actions, or by other means.

To prevent unexpected termination of existing Exchanges, a node port receiving RSCN should not perform N_Port Login (PLOGI) or Process Login (PRLI) without first determining login is required (performing a new PLOGI or PRLI causes an implicit logout of the existing session).

28.1 RSCN Issued by the Fabric Controller

The Fabric Controller sends RSCN to registered node ports upon detection of certain events associated with an affected port, area, or domain within the fabric. The Fabric Controller ensures that any fabric-associated resources (e.g., the Name Server) have been updated to reflect the associated event prior to sending RSCN to registered node ports.

To receive RSCN notifications from the Fabric Controller, a node port must remain logged-in with the fabric from the time the State Change Registration (SCR) ELS request is processed. If a registered node port is logged-out from the fabric or performs a new Fabric Login (FLOGI) any existing state change registration with the Fabric Controller is removed.

The Fabric Controller examines the type of event encountered and compares it with the registrations to determine which node ports have registered to receive this type of event. If the registration matches, the Fabric Controller sends RSCN to the node port; if the registration does not match, no RSCN is sent.

Transmission of RSCN by the Fabric Controller to registered node ports is determined by the type of event and may be limited by the current zoning configuration.

- If the RSCN is for a fabric-related event, it is sent to all registered node ports, regardless of zoning.
- If the RSCN is for an area-related event associated with an arbitrated loop, the RSCN is only sent to registered node ports that are not associated with that arbitrated loop (RSCN is not sent to node ports on the same arbitrated loop for area-related events).
- If the RSCN is for a port-related event, the Fabric Controller only sends RSCN to registered ports if the registered node port is a member of the same zone as the affected node port or zoning is not active.

When the Fabric Controller originates an RSCN request Sequence, the S_ID is that of the Fabric Controller (x'FF FF FD') and the D_ID is that of the specific node port to receive the RSCN.

If the Fabric Controller is associated with a multi-switch fabric, the Fabric Controller requests its associated domain controller to send an Inter-Switch RSCN (SW_RSCN) to all other domain controllers in the fabric. This ensures that RSCN notifications are sent to all registered node ports in the entire fabric.

Fabric Controller Originated Port-Related RSCN. The Fabric Controller originates a port-related RSCN (format 0: DD AA PP) upon detection of any of the following events:

- The Fabric Controller receives a fabric login (FLOGI) from a node port.
- An implicit fabric logout of the affected node port occurs (including Loss-of-Signal, receipt of NOS, OLS, or a new FLOGI from a port that had already completed FLOGI).
- The Fabric Controller receives an RSCN sent by the affected node port.
- The Name Server detects a change in the state of any registered object for the affected node port (a new object is registered, an existing object is de-registered, or an internal Name Server error has affected a registered object or entry). The Name Server requests the Fabric Controller to originate RSCN to registered ports.
- An NL_Port does not respond to a Fabric Address Notification (FAN) Extended Link Service request within E_D_TOV.
- An NL_Port does not accept an OPN from an FL_Port.
- The Fabric Controller detects any other state change event associated with the affected node port.
- The domain controller associated with this Fabric Controller receives a port-related Inter-Switch RSCN (SW_RSCN) from another domain controller.

Fabric Controller Originated Area-Related RSCN. The Fabric Controller originates an area-related RSCN (format 1: DD AA 00) upon detection of any of the following events:

- Loop initialization fails.
- A loop initialization has occurred and the FL_Port set the "L-bit" in the LISA initialization Sequence.
- The domain controller associated with this Fabric Controller receives an area-related Inter-Switch RSCN (SW_RSCN) from another domain controller.

Fabric Controller Originated Fabric-Related RSCN. The Fabric Controller originates a domain-related RSCN (format 2: DD 00 00) upon detection of any of the following events:

- A new switch is added to the fabric and successfully completes inter-switch link initialization or an existing switch is removed from the fabric
- A new inter-switch link becomes active or an existing inter-switch link becomes inactive.
- The path between the affected node port, area, domain and any other node port, area, or domain has changed. This could occur as the result of a change to the fabric's routing tables, the ability of the fabric to deliver frames in order, etc.
- The domain controller associated with this Fabric Controller receives a fabric-related Inter-Switch RSCN (SW_RSCN) from another domain controller.

28.1.1 Fabric Controller Initiative to Send RSCN

If the Fabric Controller detects additional RSCN events prior to sending a pending RSCN, those additional events may create the initiative to send additional RSCN notifications.

- If RSCN has already been sent and a new state change event occurs, the initiative to send a new RSCN is created.
- If RSCN has not been sent and the new state change event is identical to the pending event, the new event does not create the initiative to send a new RSCN.
- If RSCN has not been sent and the new state change event can be merged with the pending event, the Fabric Controller may either merge the new event into the pending event or send a new RSCN.
- If RSCN has not been sent and the new state change event cannot be merged with the pending event, the initiative to send a new RSCN is created.

The initiative to send RSCN is considered discharged when the Start-of-Frame (SOF) delimiter of the first frame of the RSCN request Sequence is transmitted by the Fabric Controller.

28.2 RSCN Issued by the Affected Node Port

A node port may originate a port-related RSCN as a result of any of the following conditions:

- An event has occurred that affects existing N_Port Logins.
- An event has occurred that affects existing process logins or affects the node port's ability to accept new process logins or events defined by an FC-4.
- A failure has occurred within node port.

The affected node port may send RSCN to the Fabric Controller (if present) or any node port that has registered directly with the affected node port to receive RSCN. Direct registration with the affected node port is performed using the State Change Registration (SCR) sent directly from the registrant port to the affected port.

28.2.1 Node Port Initiative to Send RSCN

It is possible for additional RSCN events to occur at an affected port. These additional events may create the initiative to send additional RSCN notifications.

- If the affected node port detects additional RSCN events prior to sending a pending RSCN, those additional events do not create the initiative to send additional RSCN notifications. One RSCN notification is sufficient for any number of events.
- If RSCN has already been sent and a new state change event occurs, the initiative to send a new RSCN is created.

These rules apply whether the affected node port is sending RSCN to the Fabric Controller or to registered node ports and apply on a per-port basis. If the node port had the initiative to send RSCN to multiple ports, it may have already sent RSCN to some ports, but not yet sent RSCN to others. The initiative to send RSCN is considered discharged when the Start-of-Frame (SOF) delimiter of the first frame of the RSCN request Sequence is transmitted.

28.3 Chapter Summary

State Change Notification

■ RSCN may indicate a new device is available or an existing device is no longer available
  • Port can initiate login with the new device, or
  • Port can verify the current login state of an existing device
■ Three Extended Link Service (ELS) commands
  • State Change Notification (SCN) - obsolete
  • State Change Registration (SCR)
  • Registered State Change Notification (RSCN)

State Change Registration (SCR)

■ Allows a port to register to be notified of state changes
  • SCR is normally sent to the Fabric Controller at address x'FF FF FD'
  • SCR may also be sent directly to the another node port
■ Registration may be for Fabric-generated RSCNs, Port-generated RSCNs, or both
■ Registration is not port specific
  • Registered port receives notification of all applicable state changes

Registered State Change Notification

■ Ports register to receive RSCN using State Change Registration (SCR)
■ A node port may originate RSCN as a result of a port-detected event
  • RSCN may be sent to the Fabric controller or directly to other registered node ports
■ Fabric Controller may originate RSCN
  • As a result of a fabric-detected event
  • RSCN is sent to all registered node ports

RSCN Formats (Formats 3, 2, 1)

■ The RSCN indicates the scope of the event
■ Format 3: the event affects the entire fabric
  • The active zone set (configuration) has changed
■ Format 2: the event affects the specified domain
  • The Domain_ID has changed
  • The routing database has changed and the affected domain has become accessible or inaccessible from the node port
■ Format 1: the event affects the specified area or arbitrated loop
  • Loop initialization failed

RSCN Formats (Format 0)

■ Format 0: an event has affected the specified port
  • A node port logs in or re-logs in with the fabric
  • A node port implicitly logs out (i.e., goes to the OFFLINE or LINK FAILURE state)
  • A node port deregisters with the name server
  • Name server registration information changes
  • An NL_Port does not respond to a FAN
  • An NL_Port does not accept an OPN from the FL_Port
  • Any other condition that indicates the node port is not responding

Criteria to Receive RSCN (part 1)

■ RSCN is sent if all of the following conditions are met:
■ The node port has registered to receive RSCN
■ The node port is currently logged-in with the fabric (or other node port if registered directly)
■ The node port has not gone offline since it last registered to receive RSCN
■ The node port supports Class-2 or Class-3
  • If the destination port supports Class-3, RSCN is sent in Class-3, otherwise Class-2 is used
■ The registration function requested in the SCR matches the RSCN type

Criteria to Receive RSCN (part 2)

- The affected N_Port ID is different from the registered port's identifier
- And, one of the following conditions is met:
  - The RSCN is a fabric format notification
  - The RSCN is a domain format notification
  - The RSCN is an area format notification and there is at least one zone containing the registrant port and affected port
  - The RSCN is a port format notification and there is at least one zone containing the registrant port and affected port
  - Zoning is not active
- RSCN is only issued after the name server database has been updated

29. Fibre Channel Security

During the initial development of Fibre Channel the generally held viewpoint was that its primary application would be as an I/O interface replacement. Because of this, the interface was designed to provide characteristics similar to existing I/O interfaces, such as the SCSI bus and ESCON. While these interfaces provided excellent performance characteristics, they were based on an underlying assumption of a trusted environment and provided minimal security. What security was provided was due to the controlled nature of I/O configurations and the ability to limit physical access to the configuration.

With the advent of Fibre Channel, it now became possible to create configurations that extended beyond the relative safety of the data center with its controlled physical access. As more systems and I/O devices were connected in increasingly complex configurations, the potential for unauthorized access became increasingly worrisome. While the exchange of names during login and the use of zoning provides a measure of access control, both are still based on a fundamental assumption of trust as there is no method to authenticate the identity of the ports.

The introduction of Fibre Channel to Internet Protocol (IP) gateways brought security issues to the forefront. Whereas Fibre Channel configurations had existed mostly in relatively secure environments, sending critical data via the Internet raised serious security concerns.

29.1 Types of Security Threats

Before planning a security strategy, it is important to understand the nature of potential security threats. Figure 134 on page 448 illustrates points where potential exposures may exist within a fabric. At each of these points, any of the following types of events could occur:

- **Unauthorized access:** an unauthorized entity gains access to services.
- **Impersonation:** an entity impersonates another entity in order to gain access to services authorized for the impersonated entity.
- **Man in the middle:** a entity is inserted into the path and modifies traffic between authorized entities.
- **Alteration:** an unauthorized entity alters data (e.g., frames, zoning, Name Server database, etc.)
- **Interception:** an entity intercepts sensitive traffic (e.g., passwords or financial data).
- **Denial of service:** an entity creates a traffic overload preventing authorized entities from accessing services.

The key issues to be addressed from a security standpoint are:

- **Authentication:** is the entity really as it claims to be? Access to many resources is based on Port_Names or addresses. If a port is able to "spoof" the identity of another port it may gain access to resources available to the other port.

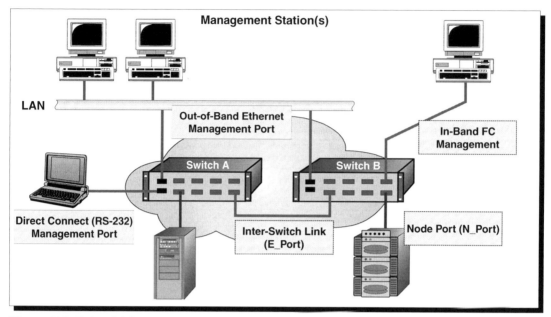

Figure 134. Potential Security Exposures

- **Authorization:** what resources is an entity authorized to have access to? What entities are allowed to attach to a given fabric, or to specific switches or ports on those switches?

- **Integrity:** has the content of a frame been altered in transit? Did the frame really come form the alleged sender?

- **Confidentiality:** how is sensitive information protected? If the traffic stream is intercepted can sensitive information be breached?

The security protocols address these areas and enable a more secure and robust environment in cases where that protection is needed. Security protocols are optional behaviors that may or may not be used depending upon the requirements of the configuration.

29.2 Authentication

Authentication protocols enable an entity, such as a switch or node port, to confirm the identity of other entities within the fabric. Without being able to confirm the identity of other entities, it is impossible to create a secure environment. Authentication is defined for node to switch (Nx_Port to Fx_Port), node to node (Nx_Port to Nx_Port), switch to switch (E_Port to E_Port), and switch to bridge (E_Port to B_Port).

Two entities may negotiate whether authentication is required, and if so, which authentication protocol will be used. This is done using the AUTH_ELS (see *Authentication (AUTH_ELS) Link Service* on page 322).

The authentication protocols enable entities to perform mutual authentication and optionally establish a shared session key that can be used to provide integrity and confidentiality for that session. Figure 135 on page 449 shows the basic authentication negotiation, authentication and security association establishment.

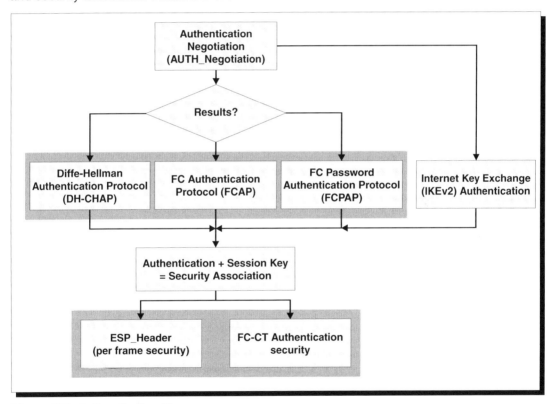

Figure 135. Authentication Flow

As can be seen from the Figure 135, there are four different authentication protocols defined, reflecting different methods of performing authentication.

29.2.1 Diffe-Hellmann Challenge Handshake Authentication Protocol (DH-CHAP)

The Diffe-Hellmann Challenge Handshake Authentication Protocol is a secret-based authentication method. With a secret-based authentication, entities that authenticate one another share a common secret. Each DH-CHAP entity has a unique name and is provided with a shared secret. In order to perform authentication, an entity must know the secret associated with the other entity or rely on a third party that knows the secret (e.g., a RADIUS server).

The DH-CHAP protocol provides for one entity to authenticate another, or for both entities to authenticate each other (bi-directional authentication). DH-CHAP also provides a method to create a session key that can be used to provide integrity when using the FC-CT Extended Preamble or integrity and confidentiality using the Encapsulated Security Protocol (ESP) optional header.

The DH-CHAP protocol consists of four required steps and an optional fifth step as shown in Figure 136 on page 450.

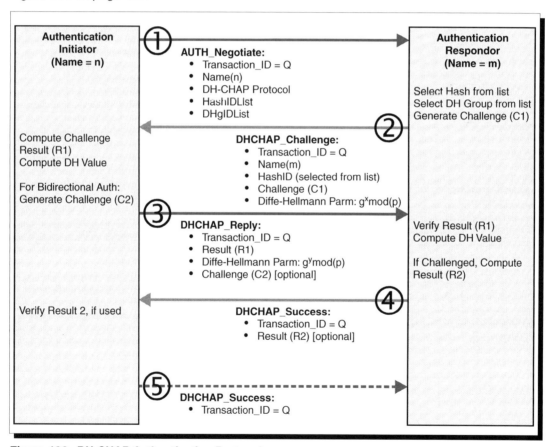

Figure 136. DH-CHAP Authentication Protocol

1. The authentication protocol begins when the authentication initiator sends an AUTH_Negotiate message to the authentication responder (see *AUTH_Negotiate Message Payload* on page 323). The message contains the authentication initiator's name, identifies DH-CHAP as one of the available authentication protocols and provides a list of usable hash functions (e.g., SHA-1, MD5, etc.) and Diffe-Hellmann group identifiers.

2. The authentication responder selects a hash function and Diffe-Hellmann group from the lists provided in the AUTH_Negotiate message and sends a DHCHAP_Challenge message identifying the selected hash function and Diffe-Hellmann group and containing a randomly selected challenge value and optional DH value (see *DHCHAP_Challenge Message Payload* on page 324). If responder selects a NULL DH group identifier, the protocol provides authentication, but does not create the session key needed to establish a security session.

3. The authentication initiator sends a DHCHAP_Reply message containing the result computed for the challenge, the initiator's DH value (unless the NULL DH group identifier was used) and an optional challenge to the responder if bidirectional authentication is desired (see *DHCHAP_Reply Message Payload* on page 325). The result is computed by performing a mathematical transform against the concatenation of the least significant byte of the Transaction Identifier, the initiator's secret and the received challenge.

4. If authentication succeeds, the authentication responder sends a DHCHAP_Success message (see *DHCHAP_Success Message Payload* on page 325). If the DHCHAP_Reply message contained a challenge to the responder, the responder computes the challenge result and includes it in the success message.

5. If a challenge was sent to the authentication responder in the DHCHAP_Reply message and the result contained in the DHCHAP_Success message is correct, the initiator sends a DHCHAP_Success message to the responder to complete the protocol.

29.2.2 Fibre Channel Certificate Authentication Protocol (FCAP)

The Fibre Channel Authentication Protocol is a certificate-based authentication method. With certificate-based authentication, entities that establish security relationships are certified by a trusted certificate authority. FCAP is based on the Internet Key Exchange (IKE) and IKEv2 authentication using certificates and signatures.

Each FCAP entity has a unique name, a certificate associated with that name, a private/public key pair corresponding to that certificate, and the certificate of the signing certificate authority.

The FCAP protocol provides for bi-directional authentication and creates a session key that can be used to provide integrity when using the FC-CT Extended Preamble or integrity and confidentiality using the Encapsulated Security Protocol (ESP) optional header.

The FCAP protocol consists of five steps as shown in Figure 137.

1. The authentication protocol begins when the authentication initiator sends an AUTH_Negotiate message to the authentication responder (see *AUTH_Negotiate Message Format* on page 323). The message contains the authentication initiator's name, identifies FCAP as one of the available authentication protocols and provides a set of authentica-

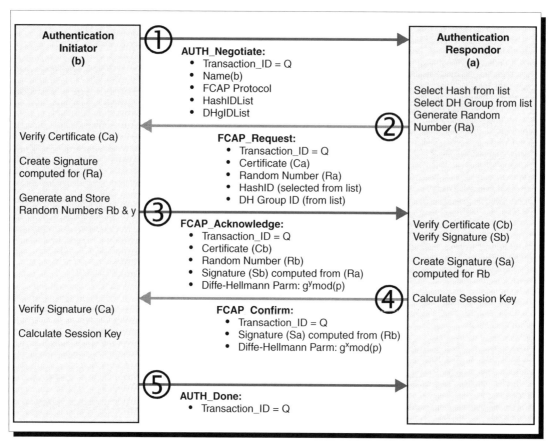

Figure 137. FCAP Authentication Protocol

tion parameters including a list of usable hash functions (e.g., SHA-1, MD5, etc.) and Diffe-Hellmann group identifiers.

2. The authentication responder selects a hash function and Diffe-Hellmann group from the lists provided in the AUTH_Negotiate message and sends a FCAP_Request message identifying the selected hash function and Diffe-Hellmann group and containing the responder's certificate (Ca) and a random number (Ra), called a nonce (see *FCAP_Request Message Payload* on page 325).

3. The authentication initiator verifies the received certificate (Ca) with the certificate of the certification authority. If the certificate verifies, the initiator sends a FCAP_Acknowledge message containing its certificate (Cb), its signature (Sb), a Diffe-Hellmann parameter and a new nonce (Rb) (see *FCAP_Acknowledge Message Format* on page 326).

The signature (Sb) is computed by performing a mathematical transform against the concatenation of the received nonce (Ra) concatenated with the Diffe-Hellmann parameter and then encrypted using the RSA private key of the authentication initiator.

4. The authentication responder verifies the received certificate (Cb) with the certificate of the certification authority. If the certificate verifies, the responder decrypts the signature (Sb) using the RSA public key of the initiator obtained from the received certificate (Cb).

   The responder verifies the signature (Sb) by performing a mathematical transform against the concatenation of its generated nonce (Ra) concatenated with the Diffe-Hellmann parameter. If the computed value and the received signature value are the same, the signature is verified.

   The authentication responder sends an FCAP_Confirm message containing its signature (Sa) computed by performing a mathematical transform against the concatenation of the received nonce (Rb) concatenated with the Diffe-Hellmann parameter and then encrypted using the RSA private key of the authentication responder (see *FCAP_Confirm Message Payload* on page 326).

5. The authentication initiator decrypts the signature (Sa) using the RSA public key of the responder obtained from the received certificate (Ca).

   The responder verifies the received signature (Sa) by performing a mathematical transform against the concatenation of its generated nonce (Rb) concatenated with the Diffe-Hellmann parameter. If the computed value and the received signature value are the same, the signature is verified and the initiator sends a AUTH_Done message to complete the protocol (see *AUTH_Done Message Payload* on page 323).

29.2.3 Fibre Channel Password Authentication Protocol (FCPAP)

The Fibre Channel Password Authentication (FCPAP) protocol is a password-based authentication method wherein each entity has a unique name and a password. Entities that establish security relationships have knowledge of the password-based credential material of other entities. FCPAP is based on the SRP algorithm (described in RFC 2945 and SRP-6).

The FCPAP protocol provides for bi-directional authentication and creates a session key that can be used to provide integrity when using the FC-CT Extended Preamble or integrity and confidentiality using the Encapsulated Security Protocol (ESP) optional header.

The FCAP protocol consists of five steps as shown in Figure 138 on page 454.

1. .The authentication protocol begins when the authentication initiator sends an AUTH_Negotiate message to the authentication responder (see *AUTH_Negotiate Message Payload* on page 323). The message contains the authentication initiator's name, identifics FCAP as one of the available authentication protocols and provides a set of authentication parameters including a list of usable hash functions (e.g., SHA-1, MD5, etc.) and Diffe-Hellmann group identifiers.

2. The authentication responder selects a hash function and Diffe-Hellmann group from the lists provided in the AUTH_Negotiate message. It selects the administratively configured salt (s_z) and pre-computed verifier (v_z) for the authentication initiator, selects a random

---

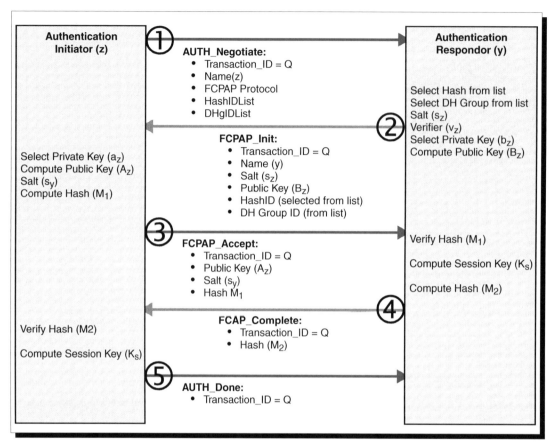

Figure 138. FCPAP Authentication Protocol

private key (b_z), computes a public key (B_z) and sends an FCPAP_Init message to the authentication initiator (see *FCPAP_Init Message Payload* on page 327).

3. The authentication initiator selects the administratively configured salt (s_y), a random private key (a_z), computes a public key (A_z), a hash (M_1) and sends an FCPAP_Accept message with the public key, hash and salt values (see *FCPAP_Accept Message Payload* on page 327).

4. The authentication responder verifies the received hash (M_1), computes a hash (M_2) and a session key (K_s). The authentication responder sends an FCPAP_Complete message containing hash (M_2) (see *FCPAP_Complete Message Payload* on page 327).

5. The authentication initiator verifies hash (M_2) and, if the verification is successful, computes a session key (K_s) and sends an AUTH_Done message to complete the protocol (see *AUTH_Done Message Payload* on page 323).

29.2.4 AUTH_ELS Message Fragmentation

Due to limitations in some node port implementations, it may not be possible to transfer the entire authentication message at once. Some node port implementations have limited buffer capabilities for receiving Extended Link Service frames. These node ports should set the Query Buffer Condition bit in the FLOGI and PLOGI common service parameters to indicate that a limitation exists and also support the Report Buffer Conditions (RPBC) extended link service that is then used to determine the ELS receive capabilities.

If the AUTH message is larger than the node port's ELS buffer capabilities, the message will have to be fragmented and delivered using multiple AUTH_ELS requests as shown in Figure 139 on page 455. Fragmentation does not occur for AUTH messages delivered using the AUTH_ILS or B_AUTH_ILS.

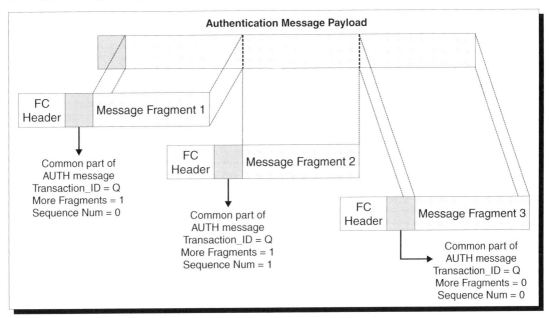

Figure 139. AUTH_ELS Message Fragmentation

29.3 Cryptographic Integrity and Confidentiality

The session key generated at the end of the Authentication protocols may be used to provide cryptographic integrity and confidentiality. Cryptographic integrity protects the integrity of frames by verifying that frames have not been altered. Cryptographic integrity does not mask the content of the frames or provide confidentiality.

Confidentiality uses encryption to ensure the integrity of frames and masks frame content to protect against disclosure.

Cryptographic integrity and confidentiality can be applied on a per-frame basis using the Fibre Channel Encapsulated Security Protocol (ESP) optional header and for the FC-CT protocol on a per-Information Unit basis using the FC-CT Extended Preamble.

29.3.1 Encapsulating Security Payload (ESP) Optional Header

The Encapsulating Security Payload (ESP) optional header (and associated trailer) is used to provide frame integrity and confidentiality through the use of cryptographic techniques. Presence of the ESP_Header and trailer are indicated using DF_CTL bit 22. When the ESP_Header is used, it must be present in every frame of the sequence. The format of a frame containing an ESP_Header and trailer is shown in Figure 140.

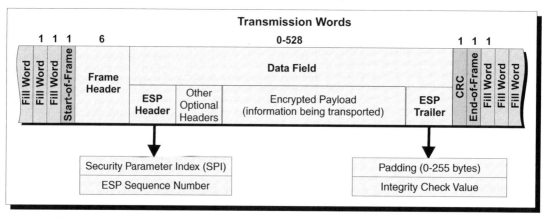

Figure 140. Frame with ESP_Header

Frame integrity is provided by a cryptographic integrity check value (ICV) computed over the contents of the frame header (with the values of the D_ID, S_ID and CS_CTL assumed to be zeros for the computation), optional headers (including the ESP header) and the frame payload. The D_ID, S_ID and CS_CTL fields are excluded from the integrity check as these values may be modified by inter-fabric routers or other devices performing address translation.

The ESP header provides the parameters necessary to provide integrity and confidentiality and consists of two parts; an ESP header and an ESP trailer.

ESP Header. The ESP Header contains a Security Parameter Index (SPI) value that is used to locate security parameters associated with this frame. The SPI may be used as an index into a security association database containing the encryption algorithm and key necessary to decrypt the frame. The ESP Sequence Number is used to prevent replay of the frame.

ESP Trailer. Block-oriented encryption schemes create encrypted blocks of fixed sizes to help mask the content. The ESP Padding field enables the frame to padded out to the appropriate block size. The size of the ESP Padding is specified by the Pad Length field.

The Integrity Check Value (ICV) contains a cryptographic value (signature) computed over the contents of the frame header (with the values of the D_ID, S_ID and CS_CTL assumed as zeros for the computation), optional headers, including the ESP header and the frame payload. The ICV does not include the ESP trailer or frame CRC.

Table 197 shows the format of a Fibre Channel frame when the ESP optional header and trailer are present.

Word	31:24	23:16	15:08	07:00
0	R_CTL	Destination_ID (D_ID)		
1	CS_CTL	Source_ID (S_ID)		
2	TYPE	Frame Control (F_CTL)		
3	SEQ_ID	DF_CTL	SEQ_CNT	
4	OX_ID		RX_ID	
5	Parameter (PARM)			
ESP Header	Security Parameter Index (SPI			
ESP Header	ESP Sequence Number			
Opt. Hdrs	Other Optional Headers (if present)			
Payload	Payload (variable length)			
Payload	Fill Bytes (if present)			
ESP Trailer	ESP Padding (2 - 254 bytes)			
ESP Trailer			Pad Length	Not Meaningful
ESP Trailer	Integrity Check Value (ICV)			
	Frame CRC			

Table 197. Frame with ESP Optional Header Present

29.3.2 FC-CT Integrity and Confidentiality

The Fibre Channel Common Transport protocol used to communicate with various services, such as the management server provides integrity (and optionally, confidentiality) by means of the FC-CT Extended Preamble.

29.4 Authorization

Several switch vendors have implemented authorization features to the composition and configuration of a fabric. These features consist of Fabric Binding, Switch Binding and Port Binding. A given switch may support all, some, or none of these features. Figure 141 shows a fabric using all of these features (in different combinations in different switches).

29.4.1 Fabric Binding

Fabric binding defines which switches are authorized to belong to a fabric and enables an administrator to prevent unauthorized switches from being added. If an unauthorized switch at-

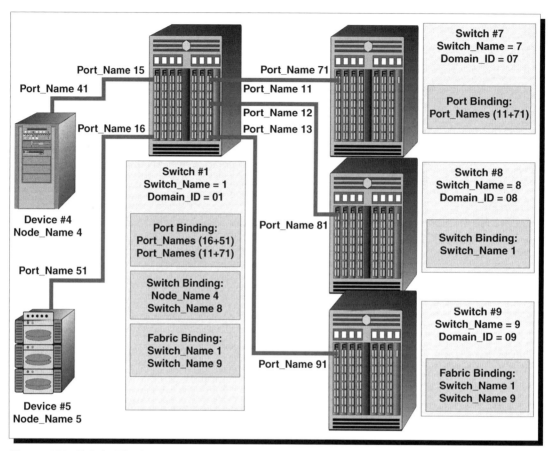

Figure 141. Fabric Binding, Switch Binding and Port Binding

tempts to join the fabric, the inter-switch link is isolated and the E_Port enters the "Invalid Attachment" state. Fabric binding can be enforced by examining switch names during the Exchange Link Parameters (ELP) operation.

Fabric binding uses a Switch Membership List to identify the switches that are authorized to join the fabric. In order to enforce fabric binding, each switch in the fabric must have access to this list to determine if a new switch should allowed to join the fabric.

Fabric binding does not specify which ports can be used for connections between switches. It simply specifies which switches are authorized to join the fabric.

29.4.2 Switch Binding

Switch binding defines which switches are authorized to connect to a given switch. Each switch maintains a list of the other switches that are allowed to connect to the switch. When a new ISL becomes active and Exchange Link Parameters (ELP) is performed, the switch examines its switch binding list. If the attached switch is on the list, the ISL can be used, otherwise, the E_Port enters the "Invalid Attachment" state and the ISL is isolated.

Whereas fabric binding information applies to the entire fabric, switch binding information only applies to a specific switch and does not need to be distributed outside of that switch.

29.4.3 Port Binding

Port binding specifies which node ports are authorized to connect to specific switch ports. This enables an administrator to define allowable node port attachments and prevent the attachment of unauthorized node ports or attachment of node ports to unauthorized switch ports.

When Port Binding is used, each switch maintains a list of switch ports and allowed node ports. When an attached node port performs Fabric Login (FLOGI), the switch port uses the list to determine if the node port is authorized to attach to the associated switch port. If so, the FLOGI can be accepted. Otherwise, FLOGI is rejected.

As with switch binding, port binding information only applies to a specific switch and does not need to be distributed outside of that switch.

29.5 Determining Fabric Security Attributes

Query Security Attributes (QSA) is an extended link service that may be sent from a node port to the fabric controller to determine security attributes supported by the fabric and register to be notified if the attributes change (notification is provided by the Registered Fabric Change Notification, RFCN).

29.5.1 Fabric Change Notification

If the Fabric Controller accepts a QSA request from a node port and a subsequent policy change modifies the state of a registered security attribute, the following steps occur:

1. The Fabric Controller sends LS_RJT to all QSA Requests from all node ports. The Reason Code = 'Logical Busy' and Reason Code Explanation = 'No Additional Explanation'.

2. The Fabric Controller sends a Registered Fabric Change Notification (RFCN) to the registered node port and implicitly logs out the node port from the Fabric.

3. The Fabric Controller waits for a minimum of 2 times RA_TOV to allow frames sent from the node port prior to the implicit fabric logout to reach their destinations.

4. The Fabric Controller allows the changed security attribute(s) to take effect.

5. The Fabric Controller accepts any subsequent QSA Requests from node ports.

29.6 Security Versus Zoning and Virtual Fabrics

Zoning limits the ability to discover (soft zoning) or access (hard zoning) node ports attached to fabric. Zoning does not affect access to well-known addresses such as the Name Server and Fabric Controller.

Virtual fabrics enable a single physical fabric to be partitioned into multiple virtual fabrics (also referred to as Virtual SANs or Logical SANs). Each virtual fabric has its own independent fabric services such as zoning, FSPF database and routing tables, Name Server and Fabric Controller. Virtual fabrics provide separate management domains and limit the scope of fabric events to a single virtual fabric.

Neither zoning or virtual fabrics explicitly define or limit which node ports or switches may be attached to a fabric or their associated connections. Neither provides mechanisms to authenticate the identity of the ports or verify the integrity of their messages. Malicious entities could gain access to services by impersonating the identity of another entity by using the name of an authorized port. Configuration integrity could be compromised by the intentional or accidental introduction of switches or node ports into an existing configuration. This could be especially disruptive in environments that rely of a predefined configuration such as FICON.

The Fibre Channel Security Protocols (FC-SP) standard builds upon the zoning and virtual fabric functions by adding mechanisms to provide authorization (fabric membership and physical connections), authentication (verification of the identity of node ports and switches and the integrity of their messages) and encryption (to protect the confidentiality of transmissions).

29.7 Chapter Summary

Security Background

- Fibre Channel was originally designed as a data center or campus interface
  - Replacement for existing I/O interfaces such as SCSI or ESCON
  - Security was provided by limiting physical access (same as SCSI and ESCON)
- External communications raise security concerns
  - May not be able to rely on physical security
  - IP extension poses a multitude of risks

Types of Security Threats

- Unauthorized access: attempt to access unauthorized resources
- Impersonation: impersonating another entity to gain access to their authorized resources
- Man in the middle: monitoring and/or modifying communications between authorized entities
- Alteration: altering communication or data between authorized entities
- Interception: intercepting confidential information such as passwords or credit card data
- Denial of service: Overloading an entity to the point that authorized users are denied access

Security, Zoning and Virtual Fabrics

- Zoning limits the ability to discover (soft zoning) or access (hard zoning) other ports
  - Does not limit access to well-known services
  - Does not provide authentication of entities
- Virtual fabrics provide isolation between instances of services
  - Separate Name Server, Fabric Controller, Zoning, FSPF Database and routing tables
- Security provides authorization, authentication and encryption
  - Which devices can join a fabric and which ports can connect to other ports
  - Means to authenticate the identity of entities
  - Encryption provides confidentiality

Authorization

- Fabric Binding specifies which switches are authorized to join a fabric
  - Specified by the Fabric Membership List
- Switch Binding specifies which switches are authorized to connect to a given switch
  - Specified by the Switch Connectivity List
- Port Binding specifies which ports are authorized to connect to other ports
  - Also specified by the Switch Connectivity List

Authentication

- Authentication enables an entity to verify the identity of another entity
  - Prevents impersonation by a third party
- Three different authentication methods defined
- Diffie-Hellman Challenge Handshake Authentication Protocol (DH-CHAP)
  - DH-CHAP is based on shared secrets
- Fibre Channel Authentication Protocol (FCAP)
  - FCAP is based on certificates
- Fibre Channel Password Authentication Protocol (FCPAP)
  - FCPAP is based on passwords

Fibre Channel Encryption

- Encryption protects data confidentiality
  - Only a recipient with the secret key can decrypt the data
  - Protects against interception and alteration
- Uses a new optional header called the Encapsulation Security Protocol Header
  - The ESP_Header occurs at the beginning of the (encrypted) data field
- An ESP_Trailer is at the end of the data field
  - Provides for integrity checking
  - Contains a cryptographic hash of the frame header and data field (except S_ID, D_ID and CS_CTL)
  - Protects against alteration

Query Security Attributes (QSA)

- QSA is an ELS that enables a node port to determine fabric security attributes
  - Insistent Domain_ID
  - Fabric Binding
- QSA is also used to register to be notified if the security attributes change
  - Notification is provided by RFCN
- QSA is sent to the Fabric Controller

Reg. Fabric Change Notification

- RFCN provides notification to node ports is fabric security attributes change
  - Node port must have registered using QSA
- If a security attribute changes:
  - Fabric Controller sends LS_RJT to all QSA requests from all node ports
  - Fabric Controller sends RFCN to registered node port(s)
  - Fabric logs out registered node port(s)
  - Fabric Controller waits at least 2 times RA_TOV to allow frames in transit to reach their destinations
  - Fabric Controller allows the new security attribute(s) to take effect
  - Fabric Controller now accepts QSA requests from node ports

30. Node Port Initialization

Fibre Channel standards do not provide a complete step-by-step definition of the actions a node port performs when it is first initialized or reinitialized. The standard does not provide this because the steps vary from one environment to another and depend on a number of implementation and functional factors.

This chapter discusses a number of disconnected topics from the standards and provides an initialization scenario that pulls together all of the various initialization-related actions.

> NOTE – This scenario simply reflects the opinion of the author and is not required by the standards or necessarily implemented as described.

30.1 Node and Node Port Initialization

When a node initializes in a Fibre Channel fabric environment, there are a number of steps the node and node port may perform. The potential actions include:

- Link speed negotiation
- Link initialization and determination of the port's operating mode (N_Port or NL_Port)
- Performing fabric login (FLOGI)
- Registering to receive state change notifications
- Registering to receive link incident records
- Registering information with the Name Server
- Retrieving information from the Name Server
- Logging in with other node ports (PLOGI)
- Performing Process Login (PRLI), if required
- Performing protocol-specific initialization actions

A diagram illustrating these actions is shown in Figure 142 on page 464. Most of the actions are optional or depend on the configuration, node function, or protocols supported.

30.2 Link Initialization and Speed Negotiation

The first step of the initialization process is to initialize the port, perform power-on self-test, if supported, and acquire link synchronization. A node port may begin link initialization and speed negotiation as a result of one of the following events (there may be other events that also cause link initialization depending on the port design):

- a power-on reset
- an internal or external input requesting link initialization (e.g., a request from the port management interface)

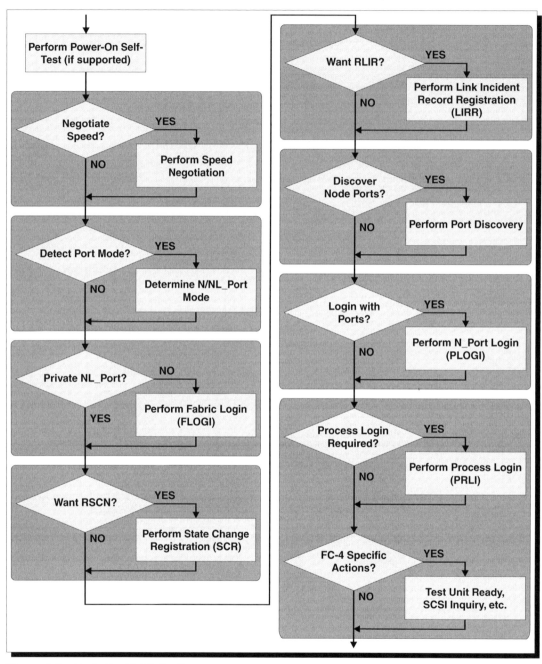

Figure 142. Node Port Initialization

- a transition to the Link Offline condition as defined in FC-PH and FC-FS
- loss of signal or loss of synchronization greater than R_T_TOV
- receiving an OLS, NOS, or LIP primitive sequence
- failure to complete a prior link initialization attempt

30.3 Speed Negotiation

If a Fibre Channel port is capable of operating at more than one link rate it may support auto-speed negotiation. When supported, speed negotiation allows the port to negotiate with the attached port to determine the highest mutually supported speed.

The procedure for speed negotiation is described in the Fibre Channel Framing and Signaling (FC-FS) standard. Support for speed negotiation is optional in the standard, and does not apply to ports that only support one link speed.

Even when a port is capable of multiple link speeds and speed negotiation, it may be configured to operate at a specific speed. Just because the connected ports are capable of operating at a higher speed, other infrastructure components such as cables, arbitrated loop hubs, or disk enclosures may not be capable of reliably operating at the higher rate.

30.4 Determining the Port Operating Mode

Some Fibre Channel node ports may be capable of operating as either an NL_Port or N_Port. If the port is capable of operating in either mode, it may perform procedures to determine the correct operating mode for that port.

In some cases, the node port may only be capable of operating in one mode or the other, and even if the port is capable of operating in both modes, it may be configured to operated in a specific mode.

The port operating mode determination procedure can be started once a port has acquired link synchronization. A flowchart of this is shown in Figure 143 on page 466.

30.4.1 Determination of Arbitrated Loop or Point-to-Point Mode

If a node port is loop capable, it first attempts the arbitrated loop initialization procedure (for a description of this process the reader is referred to the companion book in this series, *Fibre Channel Arbitrated Loop*).

If the node port is not loop capable (or configured for N_Port mode), it performs non-loop link initialization as defined in the FC-PH and FC-FS standards. An example of this behavior is shown in Figure 144 on page 467.

In this example, Port A is capable of both arbitrated loop mode (NL_Port) and point-to-point mode (N_Port). Port B is only capable of point-to-point mode. Port A first attempts arbitrated loop initialization. Because Port B is not loop capable, it does not recognize the LIP ordered set, and treats it as an idle. Port A times out waiting to receive LIP and detects a loop initialization failure.

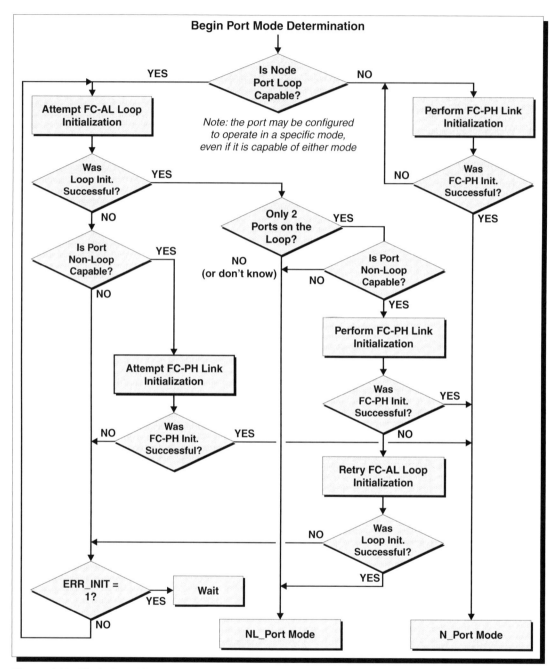

Figure 143. Node Port Mode Determination

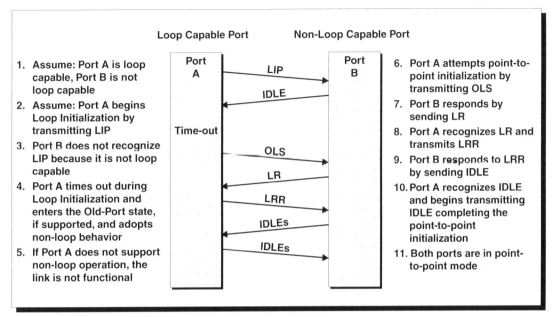

Figure 144. Loop Capable Port and Non-Loop Capable Port

Because Port A is also capable of point-to-point mode, it attempts non-loop initialization by transmitting the Offline Sequence (OLS). Port B recognizes the OLS and responds with Link Reset (LR). Port A then sends Link Reset Response (LRR). Port B sends IDLEs and Port A responds with IDLEs completing the point-to-point initialization.

30.4.2 Two-Ported Loop vs. Point-to-Point Mode

If the arbitrated loop initialization process is successful and there are only two ports on the loop, the two arbitrated loop ports may attempt to operate in N_Port mode. This is not required by the standards and the subject of controversy and debate.

The controversy stems from the overhead associated with the arbitrated loop protocols and the behavior NL_Ports exhibit when there are only two ports on the loop. If the NL_Ports repeatedly open and close loop circuits on a two-ported loop they may be incurring loop overheads needlessly. While this may not be a significant factor on short links, it may adversely affect performance on longer links.

If there are only two ports on the arbitrated loop and the NL_Ports behave appropriately in loop mode, there is no reason to ever close a loop circuit once it has been opened. If the loop circuit is left open indefinitely, there is no performance penalty associated with continuing to operate in arbitrated loop mode. If there are more than two ports on the loop, the loop circuit could still be left open until the current arbitration winner detects that another port is arbitrating. At that time, the loop circuit could be closed.

The problem with leaving the loop circuit open is that some NL_Port implementations may not behave as expected.

If the NL_Port is a half-duplex design, it normally cannot send and receive data frames during the same loop circuit. If the half-duplex port is opened, it prepares to receive frames and is unable to send any data frames during this loop circuit. If the loop circuit is left open indefinitely, the half-duplex port can never send any data frames. If a half-duplex port opens the loop circuit, it opens a half-duplex circuit preventing the open recipient from sending data frames.

Even if both NL_Ports are capable of full-duplex operation, they still may not behave as expected if the loop circuit is left open. While a port may be capable of sending or receiving data frames during a loop circuit, it may not be capable of supporting data transfers in both directions during the same loop circuit. This can occur if the port has single data-transfer function (such as a direct memory access, or DMA) that is initialized on a per-circuit basis.

The problem an NL_Port encounters on a two-ported loop is that there is no way to determine the capabilities of the other port. Consequently, most arbitrated loop ports default to opening and closing loop circuits as required.

Because of the ambiguity concerning the capabilities of the other port, a loop port may attempt to operate in point-to-point mode when there are only two ports on the loop. Therefore the decision to attempt point-to-point mode operation is more about determining the capabilities of the other port than the overhead of the loop protocols.

To determine if the other port is capable of non-loop mode operation, a node port may begin a new loop initialization by transmitting the Loop Initialization Primitive sequence (LIP). When it receives LIP, the port knows the other port has entered the initialization process. The node port may then transmit the Offline Sequence (OLS) to begin non-loop initialization (starting a new loop initialization is necessary because OLS is only recognized by a loop port during the loop initialization process).

If there is only one other port on the loop and that port is non-loop capable, it responds to OLS by transmitting Link Reset (LR). The node port responds to LR by transmitting Link Reset Response (LRR). The other port then transmits IDLEs and the node port responds by also transmitting IDLEs completing the point-to-point mode initialization. At this point the node port can assume N_Port behavior and perform fabric login (FLOGI).

If there is more than one other port on the loop, but that port was not detected for some reason (e.g., one or more loop ports in non-participating mode), the point-to-point initialization will not be successful.

When the loop port restarts loop initialization and transmits the Offline Sequence (OLS), the next port on the loop responds to OLS by sending Link Reset (LR), but the third port does not recognize LR while in the loop initialization process. The port that is transmitting OLS times out waiting for LR and assumes point-to-point mode is not supported by this configuration. It may then begin a third loop initialization to return to arbitrated loop mode. This initialization should complete successfully with the same results as the first loop initialization

30.5 Fabric Login (FLOGI)

After a node port completes link initialization and operating mode determination, it may perform fabric login. A flowchart of the fabric login process is shown in Figure 145 on page 470.

N_Ports (ports not operating in arbitrated loop mode) are required to perform fabric login (FLOGI). If the N_Port is connected in a point-to-point configuration, the fabric login (FLOGI) extended link service will be accepted with an indication in the accept that the port is connected to another N_Port. In this case, the ports continue the initialization in point-to-point mode.

If the FLOGI is accepted with an indication that the other port is an F_Port, the N_Port is connected in a fabric environment and continues with fabric related initialization activities.

If the fabric login is rejected with an indication that the class of service is not supported, the node port may retry fabric login using a higher-numbered class of service, if available. If no more classes of service are available, operation with the fabric is not possible because the port and fabric have no classes of service in common.

NL_Ports are not required to perform Fabric login (FLOGI). Whether to perform fabric login is an implementation decision, and not dictated by the standards.

If an NL_Port does not perform fabric login, it is referred to as a private NL_Port and is not part of the fabric address space.

If an NL_Port performs fabric login it is referred to as a public port. If a fabric is present and the fabric login is successful, the NL_Port becomes part of the fabric address space. If no fabric (FL_Port) is present, or the port is unable to complete the fabric login, the NL_Port behaves as a private NL_Port. Public NL_Ports attempt fabric login when they complete their power-on initialization processing, or following a loop initialization with the L_Bit (Login Required) bit set during the LISA loop initialization sequence.

A public NL_Port may determine that no fabric is present and bypass attempting fabric login. It may determine the presence of an FL_Port by examining the arbitrated loop position map (if available) or by detecting that an attempt to open the FL_Port failed. If the NL_Port does not attempt fabric login, it behaves as a private NL_Port.

30.6 State Change Registration (SCR)

Some ports may wish to receive notification when the login state of other ports in the fabric changes. Ports that want this type of notification can register to receive state change notifications. State changes occur when a new port logs in with the fabric (or performs a re-login), a port is disconnected from the fabric, the fabric receives the NOS or OLS primitive sequence, the fabric receives a state change notification from the node port, or other similar events.

A port that wants to receive state change notifications registers its interest by using the State Change Registration (SCR) extended link service. The SCR extended link service request is normally sent to the Fabric Controller at well-known address x'FF FF FD' (although the SCR request may also be sent directly to a specific port). If the Fabric Controller detects a state change event, it sends a Registered State Change Notification (RSCN) extended link service to all registered ports.

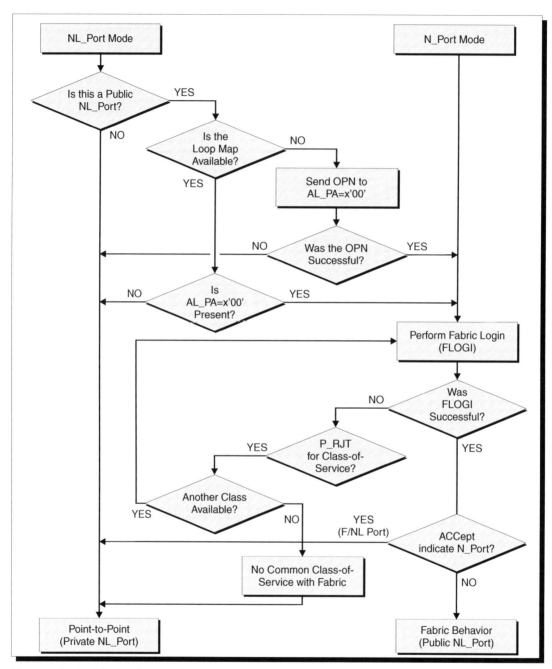

Figure 145. Fabric Login Flowchart

State change registration with the Fabric Controller is not port-specific — a port registers to be notified of all state changes. When a port receives an RSCN, the RSCN contains one or more addresses indicating ports that have had a state change event.

The RSCN recipient must examine the address of the affected port and determine if it is interested in the state of that port. If so, it may want to verify its current login state with the affected port, if possible, or release resources associated with that port if the port is no longer accessible. If the port in not interested in the affected port, the RSCN notification is accepted, but no further action is necessary.

30.7 Link Incident Record Registration (LIRR)

Some ports may wish to receive a notification when another port has a link incident record to report. A link incident record is error information that has been accumulated by a port and the port wishes to report that information to interested ports.

The fabric may contain one or more entities responsible for collecting and reporting error information. This may be a node running a management application.

If a port wishes to receive this type of information, it must register its interest by sending a Link Incident Record Registration (LIRR) extended link service request. The registration request is sent to the Management Server at address x'FF FF FA' or directly to a specific node port.

When a node supports link incident registration (i.e., it accepts the LIRR extended link service) and has a link incident record to report, it sends a Registered Link Incident Record (RLIR) extended link service to the Management Server and all registered node ports.

N_Port login is required prior to registering to receive link incident records from either the Management Server or a specific node port. The login session must be maintained for the entire time the port wishes to receive link incident records. If a port logs out with the Management Server or other port, the link incident registration is removed.

30.8 Port/Device Discovery

Many operating systems' input/output (I/O) architectures are based on the principle of device discovery. Discovery is needed when the I/O configuration of the system is not stored or predetermined. When the operating system is initialized, it discovers devices that are attached and assumes that those devices may be used. A flowchart showing how a port could discover available devices is shown in Figure 146 on page 472.

Device Discovery in a Point-to-Point Environment. Device discovery in the point-to-point topology is trivial as there can only be one other device. The address of that device is obtained during the PLOGI process that was used to determine the ports were connected in a point-to-point topology.

Device Discovery in an Arbitrated Loop. In an arbitrated loop topology, the loop initialization process may build a loop map (LILP and LIRP). When the loop map is available, it provides a list of ports on the loop.

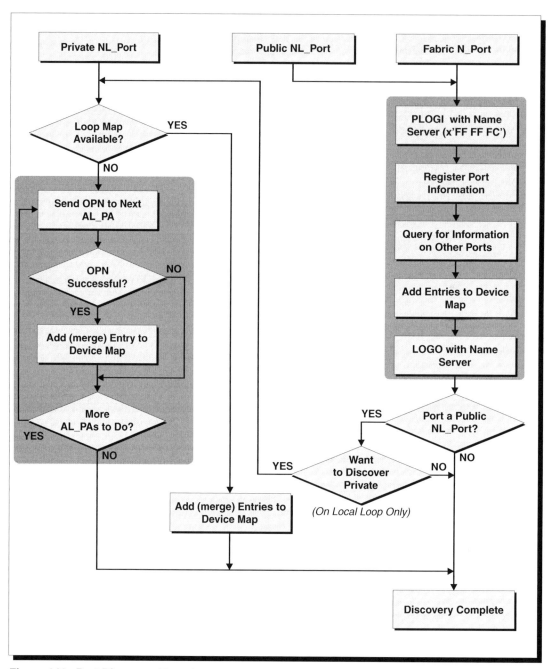

Figure 146. Port Discovery Flowchart

Some ports do not support building the loop map. If any port on the loop does not support this procedure, no loop map is available. In this case, a port may attempt to discover other ports on the loop by scanning all possible loop addresses (somewhat analogous to scanning a SCSI bus to detect attached devices).

The standard does not specify how a loop port discovers other ports on the same loop when no loop map is available. One possible approach is for a port to win arbitration and attempt to open a loop circuit with one of the AL_PAs. If the open is successful, a port has been discovered and represents a device that may be accessed. If the open is unsuccessful, no device exists at that AL_PA and scanning can proceed to the next AL_PA.

Ports operating in an environment based on device discovery need to make information regarding discovered ports available to the operating system. This is normally done by device driver software written specifically for that port and operating system combination.

Device Discovery in a Fabric Topology. Discovering other ports in a fabric topology is not as simple as looking at a loop map or scanning allowed addresses. The fabric provides a 24-bit address space with over 16 million possible addresses. Scanning is simply not practical. In this case, devices are normally discovered by querying the Fibre Channel Name Server (a sub-function of the Directory Server).

N_Ports and public NL_Ports login with the fabric and should register information with the Name Server. Because some NL_Ports implementations did not register information with the Name Server, many fabrics automatically register information during the fabric login process (this behavior is not required by the standards).

Because private NL_Ports do not login with the fabric, the Name Server may not contain information about private ports. In this case, public NL_Ports may need to use both the loop map, or scanning, and the Name Server to discover all devices. When both methods are used, the port must ensure it does not duplicate information when a port is discovered by both methods.

30.9 Name Server Registration

The Name Server provides a database that may contain information about node ports. Once information is registered with the Name Server, it can be retrieved or queried by other ports.

Some information may be registered in the Name Server database by the Fabric Login Server when a node port logs in with the fabric. Other information must be explicitly registered by the node port. As a part of its initialization processing, a node port should register information with the Name Server so it is available to other ports (registering information is required by some Fibre Channel technical reports).

30.10 Name Server Query

A node port may want to interrogate the Name Server database to retrieve information about other ports. For example, a SCSI initiator may request a list of all devices that have registered support of the SCSI protocol. If zoning is in effect, information returned by the Name Server is limited to other ports within the same zone(s) as the requestor.

Node ports must perform port login (PLOGI) with the Name Server before they can register or retrieve information from the Name Server database. When a port completes its registration or query operations, it should log out with the Name Server to free up login-related resources. Registered information is maintained in the Name Server after the logout as long as the associated port is still accessible by the fabric.

30.11 N_Port Login (PLOGI)

N_Port Login is required before performing operations using any protocol other than link services. N_Port login is performed using the PLOGI extended link service.

> NOTE – Note: The standards allow for an implicit login. In this case, the port implicitly knows the service parameters of the other port and uses those parameters. Implicit login is not permitted in most open environments.

The standard allows either port to initiate the PLOGI operation, or both ports could simultaneously attempt to login with each other. If this occurs, one of the ports will accept the PLOGI and the other will send LS_RJT with a reason code of 'command already in progress'. The decision to accept or reject the login is based on the Port_Names of the two node ports.

Some protocols may specify which node port initiates the N_Port login (PLOGI) extended link service. For example, the SCSI-FCP protocol assumes the SCSI initiator will originate the PLOGI and the SCSI target waits for that to occur. This allows the initiator to determine which ports it wishes to communicate with and initiate login with only those ports.

30.12 Process Login (PRLI)

Some protocols require Process Login (PRLI). Process Login may be required when the FC-4 protocol mapping contains optional behaviors that must be negotiated or agreed upon by the two ports. (The SCSI-3 FCP protocol requires process login to negotiate the use of optional FC-4 Information Units and behaviors before commands will be accepted.) Process Login may also be required when Initial Process Associators are used between the ports.

30.13 Protocol-Specific Initialization

After the preceding steps have been completed, a node port may need to perform additional protocol-specific actions. The actions taken depend on the protocol(s) being used by the node and node port. In addition, the actions may be different for different operating systems, even if they are using the same protocol. Finally, different actions may be taken depending on the function of the node (e.g., SCSI initiator vs. target, FC-SB-2 channel vs. FC-SB-2 control unit).

A SCSI initiator may send a TEST UNIT READY command to clear a pending unit attention condition at a target. If may then send a REPORT LUNs command to determine which logical unit numbers (LUNs) are supported by the target. The SCSI initiator may then send an INQUIRY command to obtain information about each logical unit (LUN).

30.14 Chapter Summary

Node Port Initialization

- Node port initialization consists of a number of different steps:
  - Link Initialization and port mode determination
  - Fabric login (FLOGI)
  - Registering to receive state change notifications (SCR)
  - Registering to receive link incident records
  - Registering with the Name Server
  - Querying the Name Server
  - Logging-in with other node ports (PLOGI)
  - Performing Process Login (PRLI)
  - Performing protocol-specific actions

Link Initialization

- If a port is capable of multiple link speeds, it may perform speed negotiation
  - Determine the highest mutually supported speed
- A port may be manually configured to operate at a specific speed
  - By setting configuration options or backplane wiring in a disk enclosure
- Once word synchronization is acquired, the port operating mode can be determined

Determine Port Mode

- If a port is capable of both N_Port and NL_Port modes, it must determine which mode to use
- Attempt loop initialization first
  - If unsuccessful, attempt non-loop initialization
- If loop initialization is successful, the port may want to attempt non-loop initialization if there is only one other port on the loop
  - Point-to-point mode may avoid overhead associated with the loop protocols
  - The port may also remain in loop mode and never close the loop circuit (also avoids the overhead)

Fabric Login

- Fabric login (FLOGI) gives a port access to the fabric
- Fabric login also assigns a port's address
  - All 24-bits for an N_Port
  - Upper 16-bits for an NL_Port (least significant 8 bits are the AL_PA acquired during loop initialization)
- Fabric login is mandatory for N_Ports
- Fabric login is optional for NL_Ports
  - NL_Port that does not perform fabric login is called a 'private' NL_Port
  - NL_Port that does perform fabric login is called a 'public' NL_Port

State Change Registration

- Some ports may wish to be notified when the login state of other ports change
  - For example: SCSI initiators, FICON channels, nodes with maintenance functions, etc.
- To receive state change notifications, a port must register using the State Change Registration (SCR) ELS
  - SCR is sent to the Fabric Controller or directly to the other node port
  - Port receives Registered State Change Notification (RSCN) when a state change occurs

Link Incident Records

- Some ports may wish to be notified when other ports have a link incident record to report
  - A record containing error information
- To receive link incident records, a port must register using Link Incident Record Registration (LIRR) extended link service
  - LIRR is sent to the Management Server or directly to the other node port
  - The port will then receive a Registered Link Incident Records (RLIR)

Port/Device Discovery

- In some environments, a system discovers the available devices
  - Most SCSI environments use a discovery process
- The means to discover devices depends on the Fibre Channel topology
  - In point-to-point discovery is trivial
  - In an arbitrated loop ports may use the loop map (if available) or scan the loop
  - In a fabric environment, ports are discovered by querying the Name Server

Name Server Registration

- Information must be registered with the Name Server to be available to other ports
- Some information may be registered as a result of Fabric login (FLOGI)
  - Port Address
  - Port_Name and Node_Name
  - Port type (N_Port or NL_Port)
  - Classes of service supported
- Other information must be explicitly registered
  - FC-4 protocols supported
  - FC-4 features and descriptors
- A node port must login with the Name Server in order to register information

Name Server Query

- A node port may query the Name Server to obtain information about other ports
  - Get a list of addresses of all ports that have registered support of the SCSI-FCP protocol
  - Get the address of the port with the designated Port_Name
- A node port must login with the Name Server in order to query the database
  - The port should logout when it is done to free up login resources
- Name Server operations use the Fibre Channel Common Transport (FC-CT) protocol

Process Login (PRLI)

- Some protocols or applications require the use of process login (PRLI)
- Process login is used to communicate FC-4 specific information
  - For example, support for use of optional Information Units
- Each FC-4 specifies if Process Login is used, and if so, for what purpose
  - Process Login is required by the SCSI_FCP protocol mapping

Protocol-Specific Actions

- Some protocols require additional initialization actions
  - SCSI initiators may send an INQUIRY command to determine the device class
  - FICON channels establish logical paths with the attach control units

31. FC-3: Common Services

Fibre Channel's FC-3 level is provided by the architecture to allow processing of a higher-level process Information Unit prior to transmission by the FC-2 level. The Information Unit may be associated with an FC-4 protocol mapping or other system processes. Figure 147 illustrates the relationship of FC-3 to the other levels of the standard.

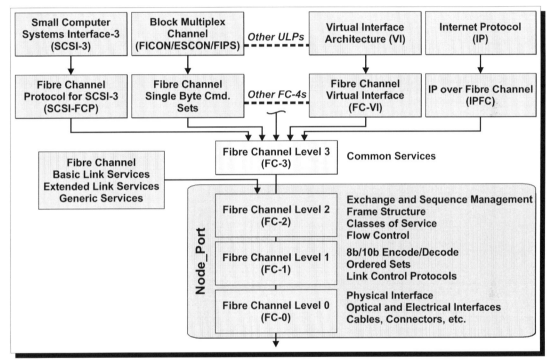

Figure 147. Fibre Channel Level 3 (FC-3)

In the Fibre Channel architecture the FC-4 level, or other higher-level process, makes a request to the FC-3 level to deliver an Information Unit. The FC-3 level may perform some operation or transformation on the Information Unit, such as encryption, then make one or more Sequence delivery requests to the FC-2 level. The requests made to the FC-2 level may be to a single FC-2 to deliver multiple Sequences, or to multiple FC-2s.

In the absence of any FC-3 level functions, Information Unit delivery requests are simply translated into Sequence delivery requests and passed to the FC-2 level.

31.1 Chapter Summary

FC-3 Common Services

- Placeholder for future functions
  - Operates between FC-4 Information Unit and FC-2 Sequence
- Transforms the FC-4 Information unit before delivery
  - Data Encryption
  - Data Compression
  - Data Translation
  - Data Striping
  - Multipathing
  - Mirroring
  - RAID
- No standardized functions today

32. Fibre Channel Services

In addition to specifying node port and topology behavior, Fibre Channel defines several generic services used to manage a Fibre Channel network. Most of generic services are optional and, when they are present, are usually only found in the switched fabric topology.

NOTE – The format and function of each of the services associated with both of these protocols is described in detail in the companion book in this series, *Fibre Channel Switched Fabric*. This section is intended to provide an overview of these services only.

32.1 Well-Known Addresses

Each generic service is assigned a specific address, referred to as its well-known address. If a given service is present, it will be at that well-known address. If a service is not present, the well-known address associated with that service is unused. Table 198 lists the services and corresponding well-known addresses.

Address Value	Description	See Page
x'FF FF FF'	Broadcast Address/Server	482
x'FF FF FE'	Fabric Port Login Server	483
x'FF FF FD'	Fabric Controller	483
x'FF FF FC'	Directory/Name Server	484
x'FF FF FB'	Time Server	485
x'FF FF FA'	Management Server	486
x'FF FF F9'	Obsolete (was Class-4 Quality of Service Facilitator - QoSF)	
x'FF FF F8'	Obsolete (was Alias Server)	
x'FF FF F7'	Obsolete (was Key Distribution Server)	
x'FF FF F6'	Clock Synchronization Server	
x'FF FF F5'	Multicast Server	488
x'FF FF F4'	Event Server	
x'FF FF F3'-x'FF FF F1'	Reserved	
x'FF FF F0'	N_Port Controller (used for Virtual Fabrics)	

Table 198. Well-Known Address Identifiers

32.2 Generic Services Implementation

The standards do not specify how a particular service is implemented. The service may be provided by a standalone node port attached to a switched fabric, arbitrated loop, or point-to-point topology or by an integrated node port in a device such as a Fibre Channel switch.

32.2.1 Services in a Switched Fabric Topology

Most Fibre Channel switches provide one or more generic services via an integrated node port contained within the switch itself. When the switch receives a request for one of the well-known addresses, it routes the request to the integrated node port for processing.

In a multi-switch fabric, services are normally implemented as distributed functions. Each switch contains an instance of the function and data associated with that instance. Collectively, the distributed instances provide a single consistent function to attached node ports, accessed using the well-known address assigned to that service. Internally, communication between the instances uses the Domain Controller address associated with each switch (x'FF FC xx').

An example of this type of distributed services implementation is shown in Figure 148.

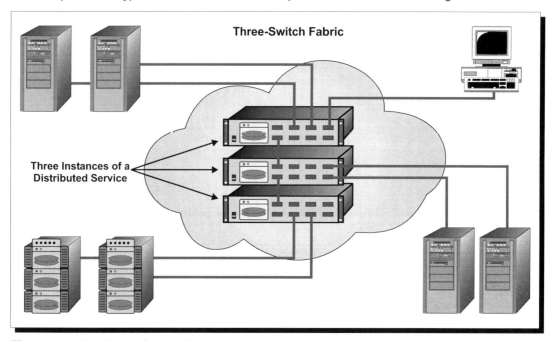

Figure 148. Distributed Service Provided by Fibre Channel Switches

While not common, one or more services could be provided by a standalone server attached to the fabric. The server could be a single system attached to the fabric or a set of distributed servers attached to the fabric. The server may be dedicated to providing one or more services, or it may provide services in addition to other functions by recognizing the well-known address as an alias address.

When a service is provided by a standalone server attached to the fabric in this manner, the fabric's forwarding function must know to route frames addressed to the well-known address of the service to the appropriate fabric port in order to reach the server.

To avoid availability and congestion problems that may result from having a single server, a well-known service may be implemented as a distributed function. There may be multiple instances of the service, with requests being routed to the nearest instance. If one of the servers should fail, requests can be routed to one of the remaining servers.

32.2.2 Services in a Arbitrated Loop Topology

While fully supported by the standards, well-known services are not normally found in a private arbitrated loop topology (one without a participating FL_Port).

The arbitrated loop standard does allow generic services to be provided by one of the node ports in the loop (referred to as an F/NL_Port). In this case, the F/NL_Port accepts open Ordered Sets sent to the address of the FL_Port (AL_PA=x'00') and recognizes the well-known address of the supported service or services.

In a public arbitrated loop (one with a participating FL_Port), any supported services are accessed at their well-known address via the fabric.

32.2.3 Services in a Point-to-Point Topology

It would be unusual to find any of the Fibre Channel services provided in a point-to-point topology although either of the two N_Ports could provide one or more services by supporting the service function and recognizing its associated well-known address as an alias address.

32.3 Fibre Channel Common Transport (FC-CT) Protocol

Communication with the generic services uses both the Extended Link Service protocol and the Fibre Channel Common Transport (FC-CT) protocol, depending on the function being performed.

The FC-CT protocol provides a simple protocol with a consistent format and behavior regardless of the service being accessed. The common transport protocol is used to access the following generic services.

- Directory Server (x'FF FF FC')
- Time Server (x'FF FF FB')
- Management Server (x'FF FF FA')
- Event Server (x'FF FF F4')

Each of these services appear as a node port to clients, regardless of how the actual service is implemented. In many cases, one or more services may be provided as a feature of a Fibre Channel switch, in other cases the service may be provided by a standalone server, or as an optional function of a server via an alias address. Because each service is accessed via its node port, client node ports must perform N_Port Login (PLOGI) with the well-known address of the service in order to access the associated services.

Fibre Channel Common Transport operations use normal Fibre Channel Exchange and Sequence mechanisms and may use any class of service supported by the client node port and generic service node port. In implementations where the service is provided as a distributed function within the fabric, Class-F service is used for server-to-server communications within the fabric.

Each generic service operation is an Exchange consisting of one or more Information Units. As with all protocols, each Information Unit is delivered using a Sequence of one or more frames (the actual number of frames depends on the size of the Information Unit). There are three Information Units in the FC-CT protocol:

- FC-CT Request: A request is sent from the client to the generic service provider. The request consists a of single FC-CT Information Unit containing the client request.

- FC-CT Response: A response is sent from the generic service provider to the client. The response transfers a single FC-CT Information Unit containing a response to the client request.

- FC-CT Unsolicited: An unsolicited Information Unit may be sent from a generic service provider to the client to provide notification of an event or condition encountered by the generic service provider.

The Fibre Channel Common Transport protocol is assigned protocol type x'20', Fibre Channel services. The routing bits in the R_CTL field are set to b'0000', FC-4 device data and the information category is normally set to b'0010' (unsolicited control) for the request and b'0011' (solicited control) for the response.

The error policy for the FC-CT protocol is to abort the failed Sequence and discard all subsequent Sequences of that Exchange (Abort, discard multiple Sequences).

32.3.1 FC-CT Protocol

The client originates an FC-CT Exchange, transmits the request Sequence (transferring Sequence Initiative), and waits for the response Sequence before sending the next request. This provides an interlocked, half-duplex operation with the server because only one Exchange and Sequence is open at a time. An illustration of an FC-CT operation is shown in Figure 149 on page 483.

32.4 Broadcast

Broadcast is an optional service located at well-known address x'FF FF FF'. When broadcast is supported, Class-3 frames sent to this address are broadcast to all operational node ports. Some Fibre Channel fabrics define a special broadcast zone that limits the scope of broadcast frames. When this is done, frames sent to the broadcast address are only delivered to ports that are members of this special broadcast zone.

Broadcast may be used by some upper-level protocols during normal operations. For example, some network protocols use broadcast to locate other ports using the Address Resolution Protocol (ARP). This allows one node port to locate another node port when only the IP address or name of the other port is known.

Broadcast is normally limited to Class-3 because there is no mechanism to handle the ACKs or other link control frame responses sent from recipient ports in the other classes of service. However, Class-6 provides a mechanism to perform reliable multicast and broadcast with ac-

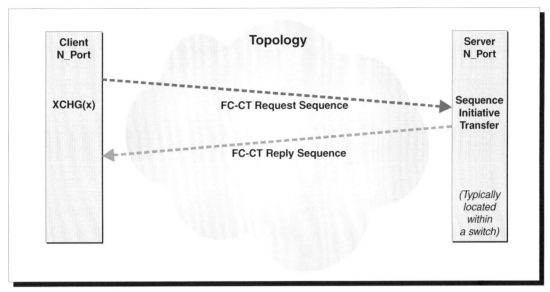

Figure 149. FC-CT Protocol

knowledgement. In order to use Class-6, a special Fibre Channel switch is required that provides the multicast server (see *Multicast Server* on page 488).

32.5 Fabric Login Server

Well-known address x'FF FF FE' is the destination address for fabric login requests. The fabric is required to support this address in order to accept Fabric Login (FLOGI) requests.This address is also used by some Extended Link Service requests associated with the fabric port. For this reason, address x'FF FF FE' is sometimes referred to as the link service facilitator.

The standards do not specify how the functions associated with this address are implemented. They may be part of the fabric port itself or processed by the switch controller associated with the fabric port. From the perspective of the attached node port, it doesn't matter as the protocol is the same in either case.

In addition to Fabric Login (FLOGI) requests, this address is used as the destination address for the Discover Fabric Service Parameters (FDISC), Read Link Error Status Block (LESB), and Read Timeout Values (RTV) Extended Link Service requests.

32.6 Fabric Controller

The Fabric Controller, located at well-known address x'FF FF FD', is responsible for managing initialization of the fabric, building and maintaining routing tables, generation of F_RJT link response frames, and managing internal operations of the fabric.

While the primary functions of the Fabric Controller pertain to initialization and internal operations of the fabric, the Fabric Controller may also support a number of Extended Link Services.

- When the fabric supports Class-1, the Fabric Controller responds to the Read Connection Status (RCS) Extended Link Service request (see *Read Connection Status (RCS)* on page 368) used to determine the status of a Class-1 connection or connection request.

- Node ports wishing to receive Registered State Change Notifications (RSCN) register with the Fabric Controller by sending a State Change Registration (SCR) Extended Link Service request (*State Change Registration (SCR)* on page 394) to the Fabric Controller.

- A node port may send a Registered State Change Notification (RSCN) Extended Link Service request (*Registered State Change Notification (RSCN)* on page 379) to the Fabric Controller for subsequent distribution to registered node ports.

- If the fabric supports multicast or hunt groups, the Fabric Controller may support the Get Alias ID (*Get Alias_ID (GAID)* on page 347), Fabric Activate Alias ID (*Fabric Activate Alias_ID (FACT)* on page 340), and Fabric Deactivate Alias ID (*Fabric Deactivate Alias_ID (FDACT)* on page 342) Extended Link Services.

32.7 Directory Server

The directory server is an optional service (at address x'FF FF FC') that provides directory services to node port clients. There are two sub-functions associated with the directory server, the Name Server and the IP Address Server. An illustration of the Directory Server and its two sub-services is shown in Figure 150 on page 485.

As with many well-known services, the directory server appears as a node port to its clients. Client node ports must N_Port Login (PLOGI) with the directory server in order to gain access to the directory services. Communication with the directory server uses the Fibre Channel Common Transport (FC-CT) protocol, can use any mutually supported class of service, and follows all normal Exchange and Sequence management rules.

32.7.1 Name Server

The Name Server (formerly known as the Simple Name Server) provides a database used to hold information about node ports. The Name Server provides a rich set of commands to register information in the database, remove information from the database, and query information in the database using many different query parameters.

Some information may be registered in the Name Server database when a node port logs in with the fabric using Fabric Login (FLOGI). Other information must be registered explicitly by the node port in order to appear in the database.

Node ports may query the Name Server to obtain information about other node ports. For example, a SCSI initiator may request a list of all node ports that support the SCSI FCP protocol. An example of a storage device registering support of an FC-4 protocol and a system sending a query for a list of ports supporting a specific protocol is shown in Figure 151 on page 486.

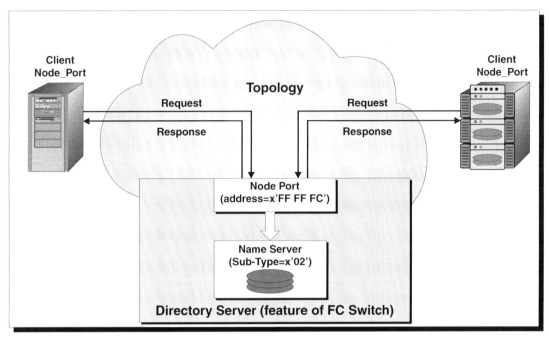

Figure 150. Directory Server

When zoning is in effect, responses to queries are filtered to provide only information about other ports within the same zone(s) as the requestor. In this manner, a system using a Name Server query to discover other ports will only receive information about ports within its zone(s).

32.7.2 IP Address Server

The IP address server provides a simplified database function for IP address resolution. The database consists of only Fibre Channel node port addresses and registered IP addresses. By providing one of the addresses, a client can retrieve the other.

32.8 Time Server

The time server, located at well-known address x'FF FF FB', is an optional service providing a fabric-wide time. Time maintained by the time server is intended for managing expiration timers or elapsed time values and is not intended to provide precise time synchronization.

As with many well-known services, the time server appears as a node port to its clients. Client node ports must perform N_Port Login (PLOGI) with the time server in order to gain access to the time services. Communication with the time server uses the Fibre Channel Common Transport (FC-CT) protocol, can use any mutually supported class of service, and follows all normal Exchange and Sequence management rules.

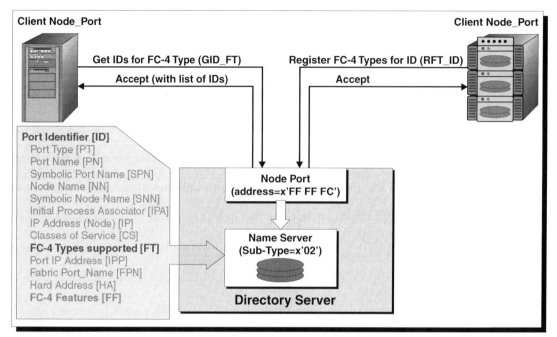

Figure 151. Name Server Registration and Query

Time maintained by the time server may be requested by client node ports using the time service request, Get_Time. This is the only command defined for the time server. An illustration of a Get Time operation is shown in Figure 149 on page 483.

If the time server is implemented as a distributed function, the standards require the individual servers to synchronize their times to within a maximum deviation of 2 seconds.

32.9 Management Server

The management server at the well-known address x'FF FF FA' is an optional service used to access management services. The normal client of the management server is a management application running in one of the nodes. The management application uses the management server to determine the fabric configuration, create and manage zones within the fabric, and access the Name Server database without zoning restrictions.

As with other generic services, the management server appears as a node port to clients. Client node ports must perform N_Port Login (PLOGI) with the management server to gain access to the management services. Communication with the management server uses the Fibre Channel Common Transport (FC-CT) protocol, can use any mutually supported class of service, and follows all normal Exchange and Sequence management rules.

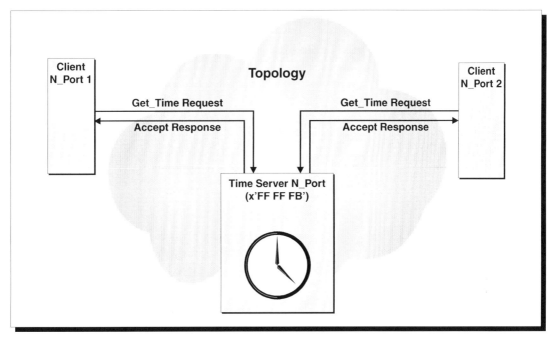

Figure 152. Time Server

32.9.1 Fabric Configuration Server

The fabric configuration server provides configuration information to management clients. This information identifies the interconnect elements (switches and managed hubs) within the fabric, platforms containing one or more nodes (each containing one or more node ports), and the connections between them.

Figure 153 on page 488 shows an example fabric consisting of three interconnect elements, two platforms containing two nodes each, several additional nodes and their associated ports.

32.9.2 Fabric Zone Server

The fabric zone server provides facilities for zone management and administration. By using fabric zone server commands, a management application can create or remove zones, add or remove members from the zone, group zones into zone sets, and activate a specific zone set. This allows the management application to control which node ports have access to other node ports when a specified zone set is active.

32.9.3 Unzoned Name Server

The Unzoned Name Server function of the management server provides read-only access to the entire Name Server database.

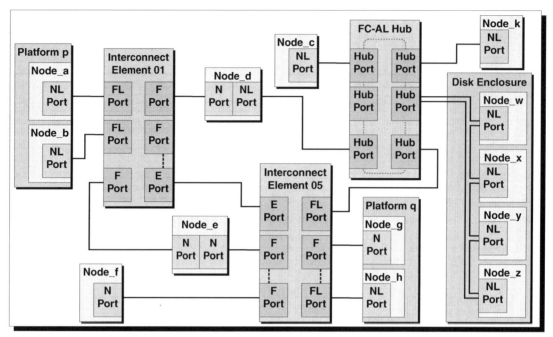

Figure 153. Fabric Configuration Server

Queries sent to the Name Server only return information about other node ports in the same zone(s) as the requestor. This limits the scope of information returned and provides soft-zoning by the Name Server (soft zoning limits available information but does not prevent access).

32.10 Clock Synchronization Server

The clock synchronization server is an optional service at address x'FF FF F6' used to distribute a master clock to client node ports.

If a node port wishes to receive clock synchronization information, it sends a Clock Synchronization Request (CSR) Extended Link Service request to the clock synchronization server (see *Clock Synchronization Request (CSR)* on page 328).

If the Clock Synchronization request is accepted, the clock synchronization server sends periodic Clock Synchronization Updates (CSU) to the node port. The CSU enables the node port to synchronize its clock to the master clock in the clock synchronization server.

32.11 Multicast Server

The multicast server at the well-known address x'FF FF F5' is an optional service that assists in providing Class-6 reliable multicast. Class-6 uses Class-1 delimiters and observes normal Class-1 rules. An illustration of a reliable multicast communication using the multicast server is shown in Figure 154 on page 489.

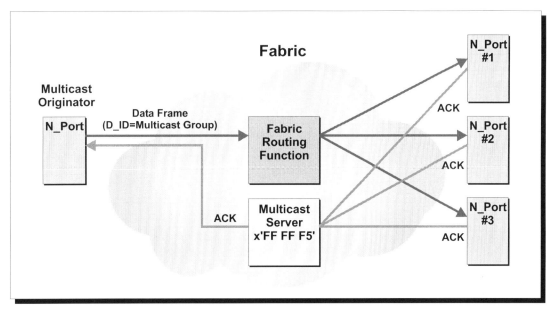

Figure 154. Reliable Multicast (Class-6)

When a Class-1 multicast frame is sent by the multicast originator, the fabric forwarding function sends a copy of the frame to every member of the multicast group. The fabric does not change the content of the multicast frame in any way (the destination address is that of the multicast group and the source address is the address of the originating port).

Each member of the multicast group responds to the received frame with ACK, BSY, or RJT as appropriate for the frame. Because the destination address of the frame is the address of the multicast group, each recipient must recognize this address as an alias address. When the ACK, BSY, or RJT is sent, the destination address is the address of the originating port and the source address is that of the multicast group (when link control frames are created, the source and destination addresses of the original frame are swapped).

When the fabric forwarding function recognizes a frame with a source address of a multicast group, it routes the frame to the multicast server for processing. The multicast server processes the ACK, BSY, or RJT responses from members of a multicast group and sends a single consolidated reply to the multicast originator.

If one or more of the multicast destination ports does not acknowledge receipt of a multicast frame, the multicast server sends a BSY or RJT response frame to the multicast originator indicating that the multicast frame delivery failed.

When the multicast operation is complete and the multicast originator indicates the end of the connection, the multicast server processes the final acknowledge (terminated with the EOFdt delimiter) from each member of the multicast group and, upon completion, sends a single response to the multicast originator (also terminated with the EOFdt delimiter).

32.12 Chapter Summary

Generic Services

- Fibre Channel defines several functions to provide various services to node port clients
  - Most of these services are optional
- Most of the services are only found in fabric configurations
  - Services may be provided by an F/NL_Port on an arbitrated loop (unusual)
  - Services may be provided by one of the N_Ports in a point-to-point topology (very unusual)
- Available services are usually provided as features of Fibre Channel switches
- Each service is assigned a "well-known" address by the standards

Distributed Services

- Many services are provided as standard features of Fibre Channel switches
  - The architecture allows separate node ports for the services but that isn't normally done
- In a multi-switch fabric, each switch has an instance of the supported services
  - Results in a distributed services structure
- Each instance of a service may need to communicate with other instances
  - Internal communications use Class-F service
  - Sent to the Domain Controller associated with that instance (x'FF FC xx') of the service

Common Transport Protocol

- Communication with the services uses two protocols
  - Extended Link Services protocol
  - Fibre Channel Common Transport (FC-CT)
- FC-CT is the protocol used for accessing the:
  - Name Server (x'FF FF FC')
  - Time Server (x'FF FF FB')
  - Management Server (x'FF FF FA')
  - Event Server (x'FF FF F4')
- FC-CT uses a simple request/response protocol
  - Response is either CT_ACC or CT_RJT

Broadcast

- Optional service that may be provided by the topology
- Originating node port sends a frame to address x'FF FF FF'
  - Class-3 only
  - Topology sends the frame to all other node ports
- Scope of the broadcast may be limited to a special "broadcast zone"
- Arbitrated loop requires special OPNr
  - OPNr conditions the other ports to receive and replicate (repeat) frames

Fabric Login Server

- Destination for Fabric Login (FLOGI) requests
  - Located at well-known address x'FF FF FE'
  - Required service in almost all environments
  - May not be provided if implicit FLOGI is used
- May be the recipient of other link service requests as well
  - For example, FDISC when N_Port ID Virtualization (NPIV) is used

Fabric Controller

- Required function in multi-switch fabrics
  - Located at address x'FF FF FD'
- Participates in normal fabric activities
  - Fabric and inter-switch link initialization
  - Routing table maintenance
- Provides State Change Notification support
- Performs Alias_ID Extended Link Services (if supported)
  - Get Alias_ID
  - Activate Alias_ID
  - Deactivate Alias_ID

Directory Server

- Provides directory services to client node ports
  - Optional service at address x'FF FF FC'
  - Required service in most open systems environments
- One directory sub-functions are defined
  - Name Server
- Name server provides a repository for information about nodes and node ports
  - Port_Name, port address, classes of service supported, FC-4's supported, etc.

Time Server

- Provides a fabric-wide time
  - Optional service at address x'FF FF FB'
  - This service is not supported by most Fibre Channel switches
- Supports a single command: Get Time
- Work is underway to re-architect the Time Server to use the Network Time Protocol (NTP)
  - Provide protocol enabling switches to co-ordinate their internal times

Management Server

- Provides management services to clients
  - Optional service at address x'FF FF FA'
  - Required in most open system environments
- Multiple sub-functions are currently defined:
  - Fabric configuration server provides access to information about the fabric configuration
  - Fabric zone server provides services for zone management
  - Unzoned Name Server provides read-only access to the entire Name Server database
  - Event Server provides event notification for fabric events
- There is a pending proposal to add a Lock Manager sub-function in the future

Clock Synchronization Server

- Specialized service to provide real-time clock synchronization services
  - Located at address x'FF FF F6'
  - This service is not supported by most Fibre Channel switches
- Clock synchronization uses Extended Link Services
  - Clients request clock updates using the Clock Synchronization Request (CSR)
  - Clock Synchronization server then sends periodic Clock Synchronization Updates (CSU) to the node port

Multicast Server

- Specialized service required by Class-6 reliable multicast
  - Located at address x'FF FF F5'
  - This service is not supported by most Fibre Channel switches
- Multicast originator sends Class-1 frame to the address of the multicast group
  - Fabric routing function forwards the frame to every member of the multicast group
- Each member of the multicast group responds with ACK, BSY, or RJT
  - Responses go to the multicast server
  - Multicast server creates a single response to the multicast originator

33. Topologies

Fibre Channel provides three distinct and one hybrid interconnection topologies. By having more than one interconnection option available, a particular application can choose the topology best suited to its requirements. Having multiple interconnect options differs from previous I/O interfaces, such as the Small Computer System Interface (SCSI) which originally provided only a multi-drop bus interconnection topology and limits users to the characteristics provided by that interconnect.

Fibre Channel supports a wide range of communications modes of operation, models of communication behavior, and interconnecting topologies. This allows Fibre Channel to be used in a wide range of applications having different communications needs. While a full discussion of communications modes and models is beyond the scope of this book, this chapter introduces the communication modes and models used by Fibre Channel.

33.1 Fibre Channel Topologies

A *topology* is a scheme for interconnecting Fibre Channel nodes. To provide flexibility and scalability, Fibre Channel supports three topologies as shown in Figure 155. They are: point-to-point, arbitrated loop, and switched fabric.

33.1.1 Topology Comparison

Each topology provides a unique set of attributes such as the number of ports that can be interconnected, the total bandwidth available to the ports, delivery latency, etc. Table 199 provides a brief summary comparing selected attributes of each topology.

While each topology provides dramatically different capabilities in regards to the number of ports that can be attached or the aggregate bandwidth available to the ports, they all share several characteristics.

- All topologies are expected to deliver error-free frames reliably to the correct recipient.
- All Fibre Channel topologies use separate transmit and receive fibers.
- All Fibre Channel topologies consist of one transmitter function connected to one receiver function (there are no multi-drop or multi-tap connections).
- As long as it is operational, a transmitter function is always transmitting a stream of serial information (this facilitates synchronization at the attached receiver along with providing an indication that the link is functional).
- All topologies allow the use of optical fiber, electrical transmission lines, or a combination of both.
- All topologies provide a scheme to assign addresses to the attached ports (no switches or jumpers are required).

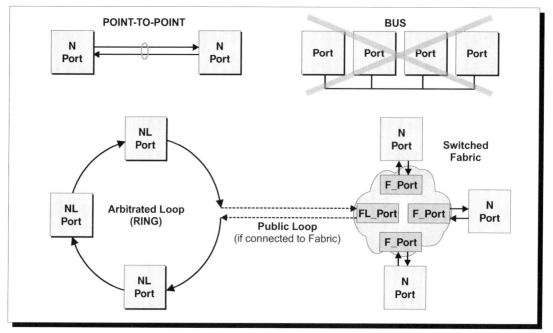

Figure 155. Fibre Channel Topologies

33.1.2 Point-to-Point Topology

The *point-to-point topology* is a direct connection between two ports. The connecting link is dedicated to the two ports and they have exclusive use of the full bandwidth provided. Because the link is dedicated to the two ports, no special protocol is required to manage access to the link. There is no need for the arbitration, selection, or disconnection protocols required by shared interconnect topologies such as the bus or loop. Eliminating these protocols reduces overhead and improves efficiency.

While the point-to-point topology is simple and efficient, it does not lend itself to larger configurations because each additional device requires another point-to-point link.

33.1.3 Arbitrated Loop Topology

Arbitrated loop is a shared-interconnect topology that provides more connectivity capabilities than the point-to-point topology. In the arbitrated loop, each port receives and retransmits signals to the next port in the ring. Because the signal is regenerated by each port, signal quality is restored and more ports can be attached to the arbitrated loop than would be possible using a point-to-point or multidrop bus topology.

The primary objective for the arbitrated loop is to provide low-cost connectivity for medium-sized configurations. In this respect, arbitrated loop fills the niche between point-to-point (limited in connectivity) and the switched fabric (more costly).

Attribute	Point-to-Point	Arbitrated Loop	Switched Fabric
Number of ports	2	2 to 127	Up to 2^{24}
Maximum bandwidth	Link rate times 2	Link rate times 2	Link rate times number of ports
Bandwidth allocation	Dedicated	Shared by all loop ports	Managed by fabric
Address assignment	N_Port Login	Loop initialization and Fabric Login	Fabric Login
Number of concurrent circuits	1	1	Number of port pairs (number of ports/2)
Effect of port failure	Point-to-point link fails	Loop fails (port bypass function required)	Link between switch and port fails
Concurrent maintenance	Link is down	May be disruptive to entire loop	Link between switch and port is down
Expansion	Add additional point-to-point links	Attach loop to fabric	Expand fabric
Redundancy/High-Availability	Add redundant port and point-to-point link	Use dual loops and dual-ported devices	Use redundant switches
Link rates supported	All	All (all devices on loop must be same rate)	All (fabric may support mixed rates)
Media types supported	All	All	All
Classes of service supported	All	Class-1, -2, -3	All
Frame delivery order	In order	In order	Not guaranteed
Access to interconnect medium	Dedicated	Arbitration	Dedicated
Cost per port	Port cost	Port cost + loop function (+ hub if used)	Port cost + fabric port

Table 199. Fibre Channel Topology Comparison

Because all ports share use of the arbitrated loop, available bandwidth is shared among the ports. In this respect, the arbitrated loop is similar to a multidrop bus such as the SCSI bus. To manage access to the loop, loop-specific protocols are used. These protocols allow a port to arbitrate for access to the loop, open and close loop circuits with other ports, and initialize the loop. These protocols use part of the bandwidth provided by the loop and may have an adverse effect on performance.

Each port in the loop and the links between the ports delays signals sent around the loop. Because of this, the size of the loop is usually limited to prevent excessive delays and the associated performance degradation. While the addressing capabilities of the arbitrated loop allow up to 127 ports to share the loop, most implementations will limit the actual number of ports to less than the maximum allowed.

The arbitrated loop (like other ring topologies) is subject to catastrophic failures. The failure of a single port or interconnection between ports can cause the entire loop to fail. This is because each port in the loop must successfully pass the signal to the next port. If any port is removed, powered off, or not functional, the loop is broken. To circumvent this, a bypass function is normally provided for each port. The port bypass function shunts the signal around a non-operational port so that the rest of the loop can continue to operate.

When a port is added to or removed from the loop, a temporary disruption occurs as the signal path is interrupted. This may cause a transient error when the loop is reconfigured or a port fails.

33.1.4 Switched Fabric Topology

Most large-scale Fibre Channel networks use the switched *fabric topology*. In this topology, information is routed from one port to another by means of a switch or group of interconnected switches referred to simply as a *fabric*. The switched fabric topology provides the most flexibility, highest aggregate bandwidth, and greatest connectivity of the Fibre Channel topologies.

The number of ports that can be attached in a switched fabric topology is only limited by the size of the fabric and 24-bit Fibre Channel address space. While an individual switch may be limited in the number of ports that can be attached, very large fabrics can be created by using multiple interconnected switches. Theoretically, a Fibre Channel switched fabric could contain over 16 million ports.

The switched fabric provides the potential for very high total bandwidth. Most switches allow multiple concurrent communications between different pairs of ports. For example, a switch with sixteen 100 MB/s ports is potentially capable of 1,600 MB/s of aggregate throughput (16 pairs of ports communicating at 100 MB/s each). Because of this, the aggregate bandwidth of the fabric increases as the size of the fabric grows.

The switched fabric topology also avoids the access control and management overheads associated with shared interconnects such as the arbitrated loop topology. Because each port has its own dedicated link to the switched fabric, no arbitration, selection, or disconnection protocols are required between the port and the switch. Avoiding these overheads improves the efficiency and performance of the fabric topology.

The switched fabric topology inherently provides isolation between devices. While a single port can cause an entire arbitrated loop to fail, the failure of a singe port in the fabric topology affects only that port. The inherent isolation of the fabric enhances the reliability of this topology and facilitates both configuration changes and concurrent maintenance activities.

33.1.5 Public Arbitrated Loop Topology

Fibre Channel also supports a public loop topology created by attaching one or more arbitrated loops to a fabric. Public arbitrated loops allow an implementation that takes advantage of each topology's strengths. The fabric provides the connectivity, ability to support complex configurations, and high aggregate bandwidth required by systems and disk array controllers. The arbitrated loop provides low-cost connectivity with shared bandwidth suitable for peripheral devices, such as disk drives, without the added cost of a fabric switch. Figure 156 on page 497 shows an example of a public arbitrated loop topology.

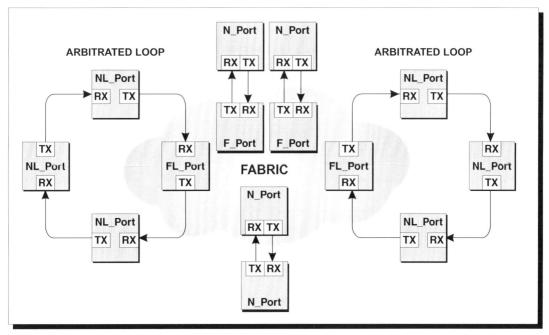

Figure 156. Public Arbitrated Loop Topology

33.1.6 Address Assignment

Each Fibre Channel topology provides a mechanism to assign addresses to attached node ports without the requirement for setting any switches or jumpers.

- In a point-to-point topology, one of the two N_Ports assigns an address to the other port when the two ports initiate a communication session by performing a port login.

- In a fabric topology, the fabric assigns an address to each N_Port when that N_Port initiates a communication session with the fabric by performing a fabric login.

- In an arbitrated loop topology, the low-order 8-bits of the 24-bit address, are assigned during the Loop Initialization process (the AL_PA) and the high-order bits default to x'00 00'. If the NL_Port performs Fabric Login (FLOGI), the fabric assigns the high-order 16 bits, leaving the AL_PA unchanged.

One of the consequences of letting the topology assign addresses is that any given port may receive a different address from one initialization to the next if the parameters that determine the address change (for example, the fabric or arbitrated loop configuration) is changed.

Addresses may change due to configuration changes and may pose a problem for some applications that rely on a fixed address as the means of identifying a particular entity. For those applications, Fibre Channel configurations may use switches or jumpers to set addresses.

33.2 Chapter Summary

Topologies

- Fibre Channel provides three different interconnection schemes, called topologies
- Point-to-Point
  - Direct connection between two ports
- Arbitrated Loop
  - Ring topology supporting up to 127 ports
  - Arbitration used for access control
  - Shared bandwidth among all ports on loop
- Switched Fabric
  - Switched topology supporting up to 2^{24} ports
  - Total bandwidth determined by fabric
- Fabric attached Arbitrated Loop (public loop)
  - One or more Arbitrated Loops connected to a fabric

Common Characteristics

- All topologies share several characteristics
  - The topology is expected to deliver error-free frames reliably to the correct recipient
  - All topologies use separate transmit and receive fibers
  - One transmitter is always connected to one receiver (no multi-drops)
  - Any of the media types may be used
  - As long as a port is operational information is sent on the transmit fibre
- All provide a mechanism to automatically assign addresses

Addressing

- Fibre Channel provides a much larger address space than traditional I/O interfaces
  - Not intended to replace the Internet
  - The address field is 24 bits (slightly over 16 million addresses)
- Address assignment may be performed
  - Automatically by the topology
  - Manually by the use of switches or jumpers in some applications
- Addresses are used to route information to the recipient
  - And, the recipient confirms correct routing by verifying the address of received frames

Address Assignment

- Point-to-Point topology
  - Assigned by one of the ports during port login
- Arbitrated Loop topology
  - Assigned during loop initialization
  - Least significant 8-bits only (most significant 16-bits = x'0000')
- Switched Fabric topology
  - Assigned during fabric login
- Fabric attached Arbitrated Loop (public loop)
  - Least significant 8-bits assigned during loop initialization (the AL_PA)
  - Most significant 16-bits assigned during fabric login (FLOGI)

34. Point-to-Point

The point-to-point topology is the simplest Fibre Channel topology and is fully specified by the FC-PH standard. In a point-to-point topology, one N_Port is connected directly to another N_Port by means of a link. Figure 157 illustrates two instances of the point-to-point topology.

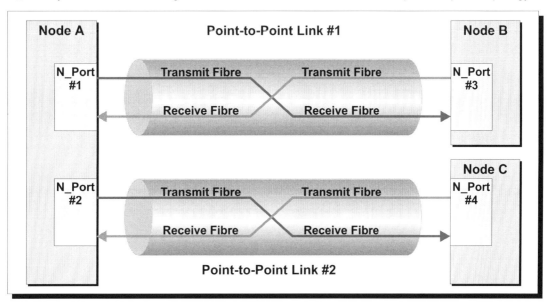

Figure 157. Point-to-Point Topology (Two Instances)

Because the link between the ports is dedicated to the exclusive use of the two ports, no special protocol is required to access use the link, and the two N_Ports have the full link bandwidth available to them.

All frames sent by a transmitter arrive at the receiver at the opposite end of the link after a deterministic time, and in the same order as sent (the time depends upon the length of the link).

No routing is required to deliver frames. Frames sent by a transmitter travel through the link to the associated receiver. Addressing is not really necessary to facilitate frame routing, but addresses are assigned anyway for consistency with the other topologies. While there is no frame routing at the link level in a point-to-point topology, a node with more than one N_Port has to make a choice about which N_Port to use and, thereby, performs a routing function.

If a point-to-point link fails, becomes disconnected, or one of the N_Ports is powered off, that link is no longer operational. However, in an environment with multiple point-to-point links, the failure of one link does not affect the operation of other point-to-point links.

34.1 Chapter Summary

Point-to-Point Topology

- Point-to-point is the simplest Fibre Channel topology
- One N_Port is connected directly to another N_Port using a link
- The two N_Ports have sole use of the link
  - No special protocol is required to access the link
- All of the link's bandwidth is available to the ports
- Frames always arrive at the receiver in the same order as they were sent
- The time for a frame to be delivered is deterministic

Point-to-Point Topology

- To expand a point-to-point topology, N_Ports are added to the node
  - Each N_Port enables one additional point-to-point connection
  - Each N_Port is part of a different addressing domain
  - Each point-to-point link is independent of other links
- The node is responsible for frame routing by selecting the correct N_Port

35. Arbitrated Loop

In addition to the point-to-point and switched fabric topologies, Fibre Channel provides a third topology called the arbitrated loop. The arbitrated loop is a ring-based topology that provides a middle ground between the point-to-point and fabric topologies. With the ability to connect up to 126 NL_Ports and a single FL_Port on a loop, it provides more connectivity than a point-to-point connection, but less than a fabric and is best suited for medium-sized configurations.

In an arbitrated loop, the transmit output of one port is connected to the receive input of the next port. The process of connecting transmit output to receive input continues until a closed loop is formed as shown in Figure 158. Each connection between transmitter and receiver can use any of the supported media types (optical or electrical) and the ports can be separated up to the distance capability of the media used.

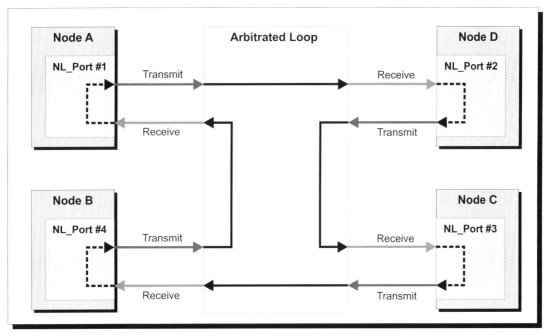

Figure 158. Arbitrated Loop Topology

As data is sent from one port to another, it is routed around the loop and repeated by intermediate ports until it arrives at the destination. The routing and repeating functions are unique to the arbitrated loop topology. Node ports with loop functionality are called NL_Ports, and fabric ports with loop functionality are called FL_Ports. When it is not necessary to distinguish between loop-capable and non loop-capable ports the term node port or fabric port may be used.

There is no master port in an arbitrated loop and control is distributed among the ports. To prevent multiple ports from sending frames at the same time, a port must arbitrate for access to the loop. This is necessary because in the arbitrated loop topology all ports share use of the loop and the bandwidth provided by the loop. In this regard, the arbitrated loop is similar to other shared-bandwidth interconnection schemes, such as the SCSI bus.

35.1 Arbitrated Loop Physical Addresses (AL_PA)

Within an arbitrated loop, ports are identified using a one-byte identifier called the Arbitrated Loop Physical Address, or AL_PA. The AL_PA is assigned during loop initialization and is used in loop-specific Ordered Sets when it is necessary to identify either one or two ports in the loop. The AL_PA value corresponds to the low-order byte of the port's 24-bit address identifier.

To preserve the running disparity on the link, AL_PA values are restricted to those characters that have neutral disparity after encoding. There are 134 neutral disparity characters in the 8b/10b encoding scheme. Seven of the neutral disparity characters (those between x'F0' and x'FF') are either reserved or have assigned special usage. The remaining 127 values (irregularly distributed between x'00' and x'EF') are available for use as AL_PA values by loop ports.

The number of available AL_PA values determines the maximum number of ports able to acquire an address and participate in loop operations. AL_PA x'00' is reserved for the FL_Port. The remaining 126 AL_PA values between x'01' and x'EF' are available for use by NL_Ports.

Io resolve simultaneous requests to use the loop, the AL_PA values are prioritized with the FL_Port (AL_PA x'00) having the highest priority and the NL_Ports (x'01' through x'EF') having decreasing priority. Normally, assigning priority to ports would result in higher-priority ports receiving more access to the loop than lower-priority ports. This unequal access to the loop is prevented by the access fairness protocol (see *Access Fairness* on page 508).

35.2 Loop Protocols

To support the operation of the arbitrated loop, several loop-specific protocols are used to:

- Initialize the arbitrated loop and assign addresses
- Arbitrate for access to the loop
- Open a loop circuit with another port in the loop
- Close a loop circuit when the two ports have completed their use of the loop
- Implement access fairness to prevent starvation of ports in the loop

Arbitrated loop protocols use loop-specific Ordered Sets. To process these Ordered Sets, most designs implement a function called the Loop Port State Machine (LPSM). The LPSM is normally implemented in hardware due to the speed at which the arbitrated loop protocols execute (at 100 MB/sec, an Ordered Set requires less than 40 nanoseconds).

The arbitrated loop standard contains a detailed specification of the behavior of the Loop Port State Machine as a way of defining the behavior of a loop port. A simplified illustration of the Loop Port State Machine and the Ordered Sets associated with the major state transitions is shown in Figure 159.

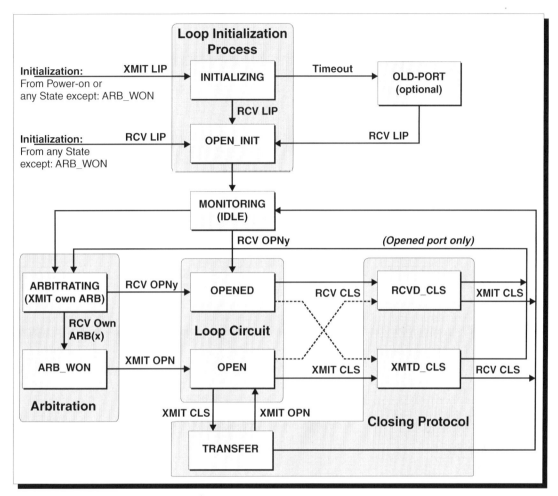

Figure 159. Loop Port State Machine

35.2.1 Loop Initialization

When a loop port is powered on or initialized, it executes the loop initialization protocol (Initializing and Open_Init states). The Initializing state suspends loop activity and transmits the Loop Initialization Primitive Sequence (LIP), causing all ports to enter the Open_Init state. When loop ports are in the Open_Init state, they are conditioned to send and receive initialization frames. This allows a loop port to send initialization frames to its downstream neighbor and receive initialization frames from its upstream neighbor. An illustration of the condition of the loop in the Open_Init state is shown in Figure 160 on page 504.

In the Open_Init state, a temporary Loop Initialization Master (LIM) is selected. The Loop Initialization Master originates a series of frames to perform address assignment in the loop. Ad-

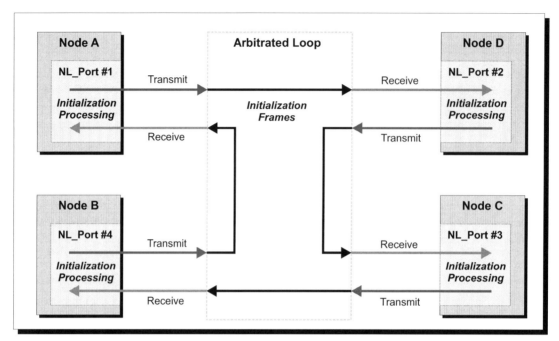

Figure 160. Arbitrated Loop Open Initialize State

dress assignment is done in four steps to allow ports that had an address before the loop initialization to reclaim their addresses before any new ports can acquire an address.

Loop initialization may build a positional map of the loop. The positional map provides a count of the number of ports in the loop, their addresses, and their relative position in the loop.

35.2.2 Arbitration

When a loop port wants to gain access to the loop it has to arbitrate. When the port wins arbitration, it can open a loop circuit with another port in the loop (a function similar to selecting a device on a bus interface). Once the loop circuit has been opened, the two ports can send and receive frames with each other.

When a port needs access to the loop, it enters the arbitrating state and begins sending an ARB(x) Ordered Set whenever it receives an IDLE or lower-priority ARB. The ARB(x) is a loop-specific Ordered Set that contains the arbitrated loop physical address (AL_PA) of the port that is arbitrating. When the arbitrating port receives its own ARB(x), it wins arbitration (to win arbitration, every other port in the loop had to allow the ARB(x) to pass). An illustration of the arbitration process is shown in Figure 161.

Unlike a SCSI bus, there is no separate arbitration phase in the loop. When a port arbitrates, it sends its ARB(x) whenever it receives an IDLE or lower-priority ARB (these words are referred to as fill words). Fill words occur even when there is a loop circuit open between other ports on the loop. IDLEs and ARBs exist between the frames and other Ordered Sets.

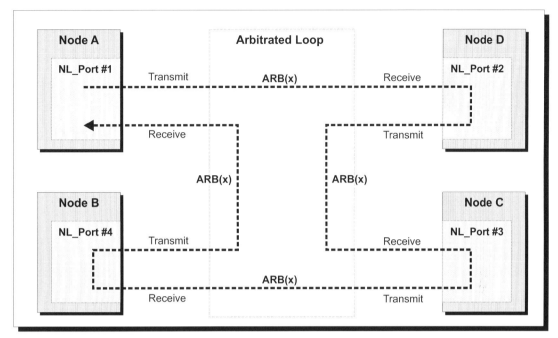

Figure 161. Arbitration

If the loop is idle when a port begins arbitration, it will receive its own ARB(x) after the ARB(x) has circled the loop, and it will win arbitration. If another port has already won arbitration, that port currently owns the loop and discards received ARB(x) Ordered Sets to prevent any other port from winning arbitration. Ports in the arbitrating state continue to send their ARB(x) at every fill word opportunity until they win arbitration, are opened, or the loop is initialized.

35.2.3 Opening a Loop Circuit

When a port is arbitrating and receives its own ARB(x), it wins arbitration, enters the Arbitration_Won state, sends an OPN Ordered Set with the AL_PA of the destination port to open a loop circuit with that port, and goes to the Open state. When the other port receives the OPN with its AL_PA in it, it enters the Opened state completing the loop circuit. The loop circuit may be for either full-duplex or half-duplex operation. To open a full-duplex circuit, the OPN(yx) Ordered Set is used, for a half-duplex circuit, the OPN(yy) Ordered Set is used.

After the loop circuit is opened, the arbitration winner and the port that was opened can send and receive frames with each other. When a loop circuit is opened between two ports in the loop, all other ports in the loop are acting as repeaters. This allows frames to pass through the intermediate ports on their way to the destination port. An illustration of a loop circuit between NL_Port 1 and NL_Port 3 is shown in Figure 162 on page 506.

In the example in Figure 162, NL_Port 1 wins arbitration and sends a full-duplex OPN(3,1) to NL_Port 3. When NL_Port 1 sends the OPN, it goes to the OPEN state and is conditioned for

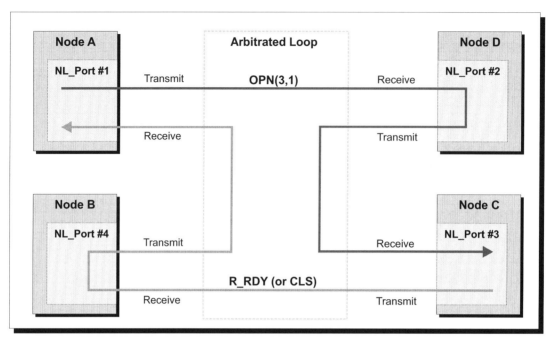

Figure 162. Opening a Loop Circuit

frame transmission and reception. Upon recognizing the OPN(3,1), NL_Port 3 goes to the Opened state, where it is conditioned for frame transmission and reception. NL_Port 3 indicates it is ready to receive a frame by sending an R_RDY Ordered Set (if NL_Port 3 is ready to receive multiple frames, it may send multiple R_RDY Ordered Sets).

Once a loop circuit has been opened between the two ports, the characteristics are very similar to that of a point-to-point circuit. The two ports in the loop circuit are conditioned to send and receive frames while all other ports in the loop are acting as repeaters for all frames and non-fill word Ordered Sets. Other loop ports may be arbitrating by replacing fill words, but this has no effect on communication between the two ports.

Because the arbitrated loop creates dynamic point-to-point-like circuits, it has many of the characteristics of a point-to-point topology. While a loop circuit is open, the two ports have full use of the available bandwidth of the loop, the ports can use full-duplex transmission and reception, and the time necessary for a frame to be delivered is deterministic.

35.2.4 Closing a Loop Circuit

When the two ports in a loop circuit complete their frame transmission, they may close the loop circuit to allow other ports to use the loop. The point at which the loop circuit is closed depends on the higher-level protocol, the operation in progress, and the design of the loop ports.

When a loop port finishes with the current loop circuit, it sends a CLS Ordered Set to the other port to signal that it has no more frames or other FC-2 level information to send, enters the

Transmitted_Close state, and waits for the other port to finish. When an open port receives a CLS Ordered Set, it enters the Received_Close state, finishes its frame transmission, sends a CLS of its own and enters the Monitoring state.

An illustration of the closing protocol is shown in Figure 163. In this example, NL_Port 1 finishes frame transmission and sends a CLS to NL_Port 3. When NL_Port 3 finishes, it sends a CLS to NL_Port 1 to indicate that it is done and returns to the Monitoring state.

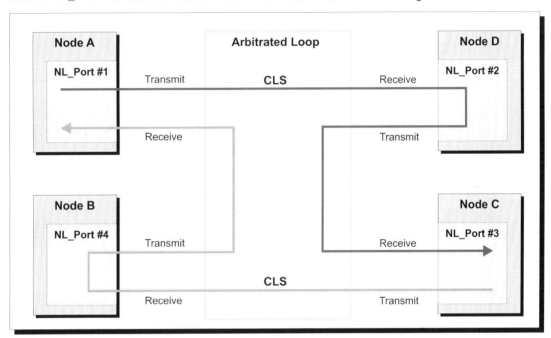

Figure 163. Closing Protocol

35.2.5 Transfer

The loop port that won arbitration may optionally close the current loop circuit and, without relinquishing control of the loop, open a new loop circuit. This is done using the Transfer state in the loop port state machine. Normally when the arbitration winner sends CLS it enters the Transmitted_Close state and waits for the other port to send CLS before entering the Monitoring state and relinquishing control of the loop. When transfer is used, the arbitration winner sends CLS and enters the Transfer state waiting for the other port to complete. When the other port is done it sends a CLS and returns to the Monitoring state. At this point, the arbitration winner (in the Transfer state) can send an OPN to open a new loop circuit. Because control of the loop was never relinquished, it is not necessary to arbitrate again.

The transfer protocol allows loop ports with frames for multiple destinations (such as the FL_Port or a SCSI initiator) to send the frames as efficiently as possible without forcing the port to incur the overhead having to arbitrate multiple times, once for each destination.

35.2.6 Access Fairness

When a shared interconnect is used to connect multiple ports, it is possible that one or more ports may monopolize the interconnect causing starvation at other ports. To prevent this, the arbitrated loop provides an access fairness protocol. The access fairness protocol ensures that each port needing access to the loop has an opportunity to win arbitration and use the loop. Access fairness is not time fairness; it does not dictate how long a port that has won arbitration is allowed to use the loop. Defining the length of time that a port can retain control of the loop is application-specific.

Access fairness functions by limiting when a port is allowed to arbitrate for access to the loop. Once a port has won arbitration and relinquished control of the loop it does not arbitrate again until all other *arbitrating* ports have had a chance to win arbitration. Ports that are not arbitrating do not affect the operation of this protocol.

When a port wins arbitration, it sets its access variable to false inhibiting the port from arbitrating again until it is notified that all other ports arbitrating for access to the loop have had a chance to win arbitration. In this way, each port that needs to access the loop wins arbitration once, then waits while other arbitrating ports have a chance to win arbitration also.

Once a port wins arbitration, it tests for other arbitrating ports by sending the ARB(F0) Ordered Set between frames and other Ordered Sets. If any other port is arbitrating, that port replaces the ARB(F0) with its own ARB(x). If the current arbitration winner receives an ARB(F0) back, it knows that no other port is arbitrating for access to the loop. The current arbitration winner then begins transmitting IDLE between frames and other Ordered Sets to notify any waiting ports that they may begin arbitrating again after retransmitting two IDLEs.

35.3 Loop Availability Considerations

One last point should be made before leaving the arbitrated loop topology, and that is in regards to failures. All ports in the loop are connected in series, with information flowing into one port, passing through it, and being sent to the next port. If any port in the loop fails, is removed, or powered off, the entire loop is broken.

Port Bypass Circuit. Most loop implementations provide a means to bypass a failing port or will use a redundant loop to provide the necessary robustness. Bypassing can be done within an enclosure (as is normally the case for a disk enclosure) or by the interconnect. When done by the interconnect, it is normally provided by an arbitrated loop hub.

Arbitrated Loop Hubs. Each loop port (or group of loop ports) connects to a hub port. The hub port detects when valid signal is present and automatically includes the attached port in the loop. If the hub does not detect a valid signal at an input, it automatically bypasses the associated loop port, allowing the rest of the loop to continue to operate. An example of an arbitrated loop incorporating a hub is shown in Figure 164 on page 509.

When a hub is used, loop ports connect to the hub rather than their neighbors. This changes the physical wiring of the loop into a star configuration with all the ports connected to the hub. This allows standard cables to be used because it is not necessary to physically separate the transmit and receive fibres, as would be required if the loop was physically wired as a loop.

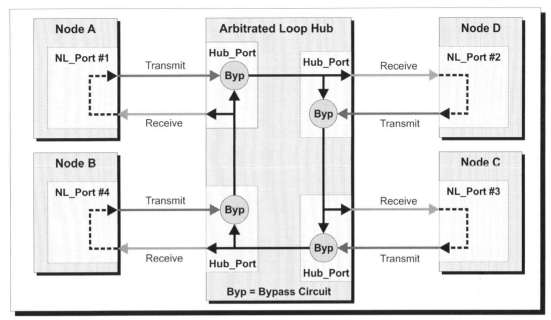

Figure 164. Arbitrated Loop with Hub

Hubs may provide additional flexibility by allowing a mixture of optical and electrical ports (or, even allowing each port to be configured individually). By providing one or two optical ports along with several electrical ports, hubs could be placed in wiring closets adjacent to the attached ports and cascaded over extended distances using the optical links.

Hubs may provide management capabilities by allowing individual hub ports to be monitored, enabled, or bypassed under control of a network management agent. Management functions may be performed in band, using Fibre Channel signaling, out of band using a separate network such as Ethernet, or a protocol-specific facility such as SCSI Enclosure Services (SES).

35.4 Loop Performance

Unlike the point-to point and fabric topologies, the arbitrated loop is a shared interconnect so it is necessary to arbitrate before frames can be sent. Because the time to win arbitration is affected by other activity in the loop, the arbitrated loop does not provide guaranteed bandwidth or latency when utilization is high.

Point-to-point provides dedicated bandwidth between the two N_Ports; the fabric allows multiple pairs of ports to communicate simultaneously and provides high aggregate bandwidth; but an arbitrated loop only permits one pair of ports to communicate at a time. The shared bandwidth behavior probably makes the arbitrated loop topology best suited to applications where multiple lower-speed devices can share a single interconnect (e.g., multiple disk drives).

35.5 Loop Switches

There are several limitations to the arbitrated loop topology. Each port adds latency to signals retransmitted around the loop. In large loops, the total delay can significantly affect performance. Another limitation is that only two ports can communicate at a time, other ports are blocked by the open loop circuit. If a port fails or corrupts the data stream it can affect traffic for other ports on the loop. A device that can alleviate these limitations is the loop switch.

A loop switch is a simple switching element that uses the loop protocols to control the switching function in a way that is totally transparent to attached devices. Loop switches are not fabric switches and do not provide services such as the Name Server. Node ports do not login with a loop switch. An example of an arbitrated loop with a loop switch is shown in Figure 165.

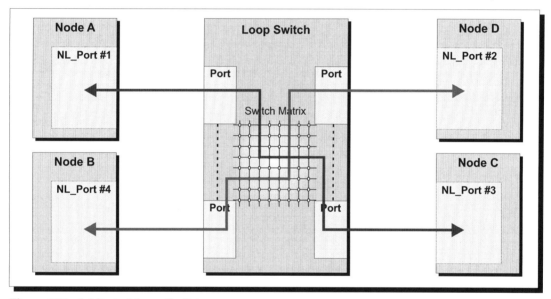

Figure 165. Arbitrated Loop Switch

When a loop port arbitrates, the loop switch returns the ARB(x) ordered set allowing the port to win arbitration. The loop port then transmits an OPN to open a loop circuit. The loop switch traps the OPN, examines the destination AL_PA and, if the destination is available, sets up the switching matrix and forwards the OPN to complete the loop circuit. If the destination is currently part of a different loop circuit, the loop switch can either delay forwarding the OPN or return a CLS ordered set (a CLS in response to an OPN is interpreted as a busy condition at the destination). The loop switch does not contain frame buffers or participate in flow control. Once the switching matrix is set up, frames simply flow through the switching matrix.

While loop switches are offered a standalone products, most will probably be incorporated within disk enclosures (now referred to as "Switched Bunch of Disks", or SBODs). The cost of incorporating a loop switch is not significantly higher than the cost of port bypass circuits while providing significant performance and availability benefits.

35.6 Chapter Summary

Arbitrated Loop

- Arbitrated loop provides capabilities in between the point-to-point and fabric topologies
  - More connectivity than point-to-point but less than the fabric
  - Shared bandwidth equal to a point-to-point link, but less than the fabric
  - Comparable to point-to-point in cost, but less expensive than the fabric
- The arbitrated loop function is a simple addition to an N_Port or F_Port
- Loop-capable ports have an 'L' added to their port types, e.g., NL_Ports or FL_Ports

Arbitrated Loop Physical Address

- Within a loop, ports are identified by using a one-byte address called the Arbitrated Loop Physical Address (AL_PA)
  - Corresponds to low-order byte of the 24-bit address
- To preserve the running disparity, AL_PA values are restricted to neutral-disparity characters
  - Provides one FL_Port at AL_PA x'00' (highest priority)
  - Up to 126 NL_Ports from AL_PA x'01' through x'EF' (lowest priority)
  - AL_PA values are irregularly distributed in this range

Arbitrated Loop Protocols

- All ports in the loop share use of the loop
- Only two ports can communicate at a time
- Arbitration is used to manage access to the loop
  - When a port requires the loop, it has to arbitrate
  - When it wins arbitration, it can open a loop circuit with another port to send and receive frames
  - When the ports are done, the loop circuit is closed, allowing other ports to use the loop
- Management of loop circuits is not unlike the management of a shared bus, like SCSI

Loop Port State Machine

- Most loop protocols are executed in hardware
  - Events happen at a 40 nanosecond rate
- Arbitrated loop standard defines a Loop Port State Machine (LPSM)
  - Describes behavior of a loop port
  - Defines loop protocol behavior
  - May be implemented directly from the standard, or modified to suit the design
- LPSM controls the:
- Entry to initialization, arbitration, and the opening and closing of loop circuits

Loop Initialization

- Loop initialization initializes the loop
  - Assigns AL_PA values to loop ports
  - Provides notification that the configuration may have changed
  - May be used to signal a loop failure
- Initiated by using the Loop Initialization Primitive (LIP) sequence
  - Forces all ports to the Open_Init state
  - Suspends non-initialization loop traffic
  - Initialization is not a reset!
  - Operations may resume after initialization
- Open_Init processing usually done in firmware

Arbitration

- Arbitration is used to manage access to the loop
- Prevents multiple ports from sending frames simultaneously
- When a port needs access to the loop it must first win arbitration
  - Sends ARB(x) Ordered Set whenever it receives IDLE or a lower-priority ARB
  - X = AL_PA of the loop port
  - When the port receives its own ARB(x), it wins
- Port can then open a loop circuit
- Arbitration occurs between frames, there is no separate arbitration phase

Opening a Loop Circuit

- When a port wins arbitration it opens a loop circuit before sending frames
- Conditions the other port for frame reception and transmission
- Loop circuit can be full-duplex or half-duplex
  - To open a full-duplex circuit, OPN(yx) is used
  - To open a half-duplex circuit, OPN(yy) is used
- When loop circuit is open, behavior is essentially point-to-point
  - All other ports are acting as repeaters

Closing a Loop Circuit

- When the two ports in the circuit finish, they close the loop circuit
- Frees the loop for other ports to win arbitration
- When a port is finished, it sends a CLS Ordered Set
- When a port receives a CLS it knows the other port is finished
- When a port has both sent and received a CLS, the loop circuit is closed

Transfer

- Transfer allows the arbitration winner to close the current loop circuit and open a new circuit without re-arbitrating
- Improves the efficiency of the loop for ports with frames for multiple destinations
  - FL_Port
  - Perhaps a SCSI initiator

Access Fairness

- Because AL_PA values are prioritized, it would be possible for high-priority ports to monopolize the loop
- Access fairness offsets the AL_PA priority
  - Limits when a port is allowed to arbitrate
- Once a port has won arbitration, it will not arbitrate again until:
  - All other arbitrating ports have had an opportunity to win arbitration
  - Arbitration winner tests for other arbitrating ports by sending ARB(F0)
  - If no other port is arbitrating, sends IDLE to notify ports that they can arbitrate again

Loop Availability

- All ports in the loop are in series
  - If any port fails, is removed, or is powered off, the loop is broken
- For high availability, a way to bypass a non-functional port or position is needed
  - Usually done with a port bypass circuit
  - Bypasses the point of failure so the rest of the loop continues to operate
  - Bypass function may be provided by a hub or within a disk enclosure
- May be controlled with loop-specific Ordered Sets or some other means

Arbitrated Loop Switches

- Loop topology has several limitations:
  - Each port adds latency to retransmitted signals
  - Only one pair or ports can communicate at a time
  - Any port can corrupt the data stream
- Loop switch provides a simple switching function
  - Driven by the arbitrated loop protocols
  - Transparent to the attached devices
- Often integrated into FC disk enclosures

36. Fibre Channel Fabric

While the point-to-point topology is simple and straightforward, it does not provide the connectivity necessary for many applications. The need for more connectivity led to the development of the second Fibre Channel topology, the switched fabric. Whereas point-to-point is limited to only two ports, the switched fabric provides the ability to connect up to 2^{24} ports (in excess of 16 million ports).

Switched fabric, or simply fabric, is a term used describe a switch or group of interconnected switches that delivers frames to a destination using on the destination address in the frame header. At its simplest, a fabric may consist of a single switch. In more complex forms, a fabric may consist of multiple interconnected switches, functioning as a single logical entity. Node ports see the fabric as a frame-forwarding mechanism and have no awareness of the internal structure of the fabric, paths within the fabric, or how the fabric implements its forwarding algorithms. A conceptual view of the fabric as seen by the node ports is shown in Figure 166.

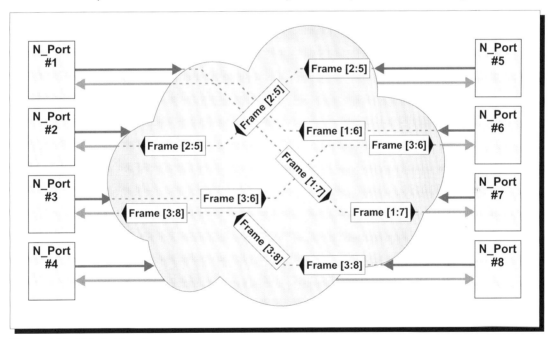

Figure 166. Fabric Topology

Looking deeper into the fabric reveals that each node port is connected via its associated link to a fabric port (either an F_Port or an FL_Port). Within the fabric, fabric ports are interconnected by a switching function that enables frames to be forwarded from one fabric port to another fabric port based on the destination address in the frame header. When a node port sends a frame to the fabric, the frame is received by the ingress fabric port, forwarded through the switching function to the appropriate egress fabric port, and from there to the destination node port. An illustration of this functional view of the fabric is shown in Figure 167.

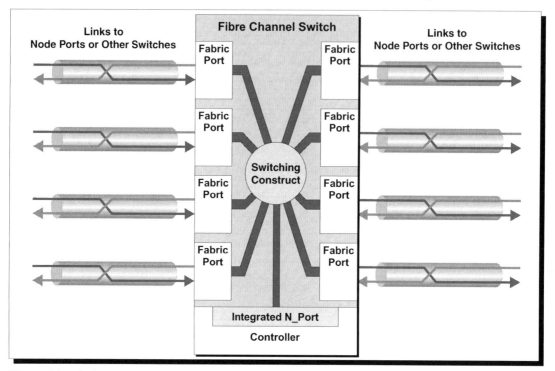

Figure 167. Switch Ports and Switching Function

Fabric ports provide a different function from node ports and they are different in design. Whereas a node port is the source or destination of information delivered by sequences of frames and is responsible for the segmentation and reassembly of those sequences, a fabric port is simply a forwarding mechanism participating in the delivery of frames. Other than examining the destination and source address fields (and perhaps checking the CRC of frames), neither the fabric ports nor fabric interprets the content of the frames being delivered.

The fact that the fabric does not interpret frames means that the fabric can deliver frames carrying different protocols. From the fabric's perspective, all frames are treated the same. The FC-4 protocols associated with source and destination node ports must understand how to interpret the individual protocols, but the fact that different protocols are being transported is completely transparent to the fabric.

The Fabric Controller manages the operation of the fabric and provides other supporting functions, such as communicating with other elements of the fabric to manage addresses or control routing or access privileges. The Fabric Controller also provides state change notifications, via RSCNs (see *Registered State Change Notification* on page 441).

36.1 Fabric Communication Modes

Two fundamental communication modes are associated with delivery of frames between node ports. The node ports can establish a connection to reserve a path between the ports (referred to as connection-oriented or circuit-switching mode) or they can simply transmit frames without establishing a prior connection (referred to as connectionless or frame-switching mode).

The Fibre Channel architecture supports both modes of operation through the different classes of service defined. Class-1 and Class-6 are connection-oriented modes while Class-2, Class-3 and Class-F are connectionless frame switching classes.

36.1.1 Connection-Oriented Mode (Class-1)

To reserve resources and establish a path between two ports, a connection may be established to support subsequent communications. Setting up the connection is a process that allocates a path between the two ports and reserves the resources to support communications along that path (A connection in this context is a logical reservation of resources along a path and is different from the physical connection associated with cables and connectors).

To establish the connection, a setup protocol is necessary because resources must be allocated to support the connection. When the connection is no longer needed, a removal protocol is used to remove the connection and free up the resources that were allocated to the connection. Both the setup and removal protocols require confirmation of the setup and removal and connection-oriented modes require delivery confirmation by the node ports.

Because the setup process reserves resources along a particular path, all frames transmitted during that connection follow that path. As a result, frames transmitted during that connection are delivered to the destination in the same order as transmitted.

When resources are allocated along a path, that allocation is for all of path the resources between the two ports In a full-speed (100 MB/s) Fibre Channel environment, a dedicated connection reserves a 100 MB/s bidirectional path between the two node ports as shown in.

Dedicated connections are provided by Fibre Channel's Class-1 service. The connection starts when the connection initiator begins a new Sequence using the Start-of-Frame connect Class-1 (SOFc1) delimiter. This delimiter instructs the fabric to attempt to establish a dedicated connection between the connection initiator (identified by the S_ID field in the frame header) and the connection recipient (identified by the D_ID field in the frame header).

While a dedicated connection exists, the time for frames to travel from the sending port to the receiving port is consistent because all resources along the path are dedicated to that connection. During the Class-1 connection, the node ports and all the resources in the path between the node ports are busy to other frames.

The switching function used to support a dedicated connection employs a switching construct that provides guaranteed bandwidth and latency to the connection. One example of a switching construct that provides this characteristic is the crossbar (or crosspoint) matrix.

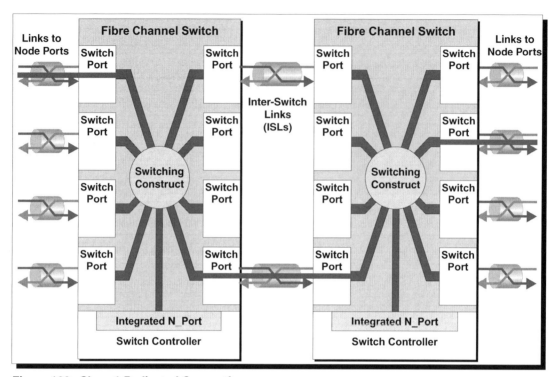

Figure 168. Class-1 Dedicated Connection

36.1.2 Connectionless Mode (Classes 2, 3 and F)

It is also possible for ports to communicate without establishing a connection or circuit before-hand. In this mode of communication, sometimes referred to as frame switching or packet switching, the ports simply send their frames and the interconnecting topology routes them to the correct destination (in network applications, this is referred to as packet switching).

During connectionless operation, no advance connection or circuit is set up and no resources are reserved. When a frame is transmitted, it is processed as bandwidth as resources permit. Consequently, there is no guarantee of the actual bandwidth available to the node port. If traffic in the path to the destination node port is light, the node port has access to all, or almost all the bandwidth. If the amount of traffic in the path to the destination node port is heavy, the port may have little or even none of the bandwidth, leading to busy conditions.

The amount of bandwidth available to a port, and the time required to deliver frames, is dependent on the utilization of the topology; throughput and latency may be less predictable.

Frame Multiplexing. Connectionless operation forwards frames on a frame-by-frame basis as bandwidth permits. It is possible for a node port to send a series of consecutive frames, each for a different destination. The fabric examines the destination ID in each connectionless frame to determine how to forward that particular frame.

When the fabric forwards a frame sent by a port, it uses only the path resources necessary to deliver that particular frame. A bidirectional path is not required to deliver connectionless frames. Resources on the reverse path are only used as needed for frames in the opposite direction. Depending on the topology, it is possible for a node port to send frames to one destination while receiving frames from a different source. Currently, the fabric topology is the only topology that permits this behavior as both point-to-point and arbitrated loop inherently allocate bidirectional circuits between a pair of ports (although an arbitrated loop circuit with the FL_Port allows frame multiplexing, just as if the loop port were directly attached to the fabric).

An example of frame multiplexing is shown in Figure 169 on page 517. In this example, N_Port A sends a series of frames to N_Ports B, C, and D. The fabric forwarding function routes each frame to the correct destination based on the address in the frame header. While N_Port A is sending frames, it may also be receiving frames. These frames could be from the same node port that N_Port A is sending to, or another node port.

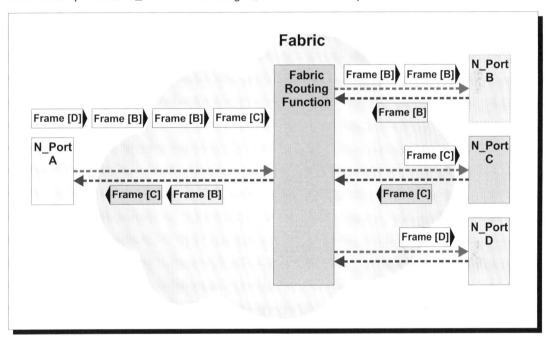

Figure 169. Frame Multiplexing

36.1.3 Mixed Mode Operation

In a connection-oriented mode of operation (such as Class-1), a node port is restricted to communicating with the other node port involved in that connection. This can lead to problems because the port is busy to other traffic. One approach to alleviating the inaccessibility that can result from using dedicated connections is to allow the node ports to use both connection and connectionless modes at the same time (circuit switching and frame switching), provided the connectionless operations do not interfere with the Class-1 frames.

To support both modes of operation simultaneously, Fibre Channel has defined a feature called intermix (described in *Class-1 with Intermix* on page 278) that allows a port to intermix connectionless frames onto a Class-1 connection. This allows the port to send or receive Class-2 or Class-3 frames as bandwidth is available. Intermix requires a fabric support and the ability for the node port to interleave both types of frames.

36.2 Frame Forwarding Within the Switching Element

When a node port wants to send frames to another node port, it places the destination address of the other node port in the frame header and sends those frames to the fabric. The fabric receives, switches, and delivers the frames based on the destination address. The fabric is responsible for selecting the path, or paths, that are used for the delivery of frames. The sending node port has no knowledge of available paths, nor does it have any control over the actual path used.

The decision to do all frame forwarding based on the destination address in the frame header relieves the node port from having to maintain any kind of routing table. All the sending node port needs to know is the address of the destination node port.

Allowing the fabric to select the actual path used to forward frames from the source port to the destination port enables the fabric to perform adaptive path selection based on traffic or congestion, or select an alternate path in the event of a failure. The adaptive path selection is not visible to the sending or receiving ports except as differences in the paths may affect latency or other delivery characteristics.

There are numerous designs that can be used within a switch to forward frames from one fabric port to another. The following sections explore some common techniques used by Fibre Channel switches. There are other techniques that could be used to forward frames within a switch that may be used in future Fibre Channel switches.

36.2.1 Crossbar Switch

The crossbar switch is an efficient switching mechanism with a long history reaching back to the early days of the telephone system. In a crossbar switch, an xy switching matrix is used to forward frames from one input port to one or more output ports. This switching matrix provides the ability to handle multiple concurrent transfers between different port pairs without interference, a characteristic that is referred to as non-blocking. An example of an eight-ported crossbar switch is shown in Figure 170.

In the crossbar switch, any input can be connected to any output by activating the appropriate switch point. For example to forward frames from input A to output D, the switch point at [A,D] is activated. If a reverse path is desired, then the switch point at [D,A] can also be activated. Because multiple switch points can be activated concurrently, the total throughput of the crossbar switch is equal to the number of port pairs. The eight-ported switch shown in Figure 170 is capable of eight concurrent transfers, or a total of 800 megabytes per second in a full-speed Fibre Channel environment.

Crossbar Input Buffering. Each input port requires at least one frame buffer to hold a received frame while the crossbar switch is set up to deliver that frame. As soon as the switch

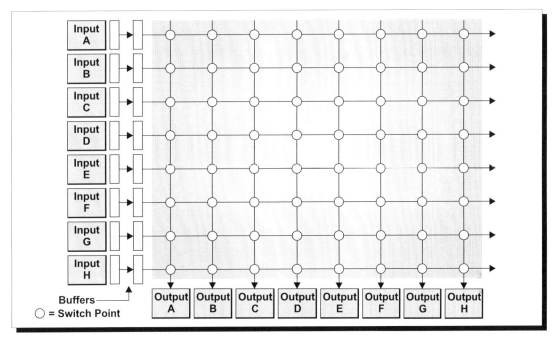

Figure 170. Eight-Ported Crossbar Switch

point is activated, the frame can be forwarded to the selected output port. It is not necessary to wait for the entire frame to be received before forwarding begins. It is simply necessary that the switch point be activated before forwarding occurs. To expedite the switching process, the destination address is contained in the first word of the frame header.

To improve performance on the link between the node port and the switch input port, it is desirable to have more than one input buffer available. This allows multiple frames to be in transit between the node port and the switch input port and improves link utilization.

Crossbar Connection Modes. The crossbar switch is capable of supporting both connection-oriented and connectionless modes of operation. An illustration of the crossbar switch with a dedicated connection between port A and port B and concurrent simultaneous connectionless frames (indicated by dashed lines) from port D to port G, port F to port E, and port G to port F is shown in Figure 171.

When a Class-1 service is used, appropriate switch points are activated when the connection is established and remain activated until the connection is removed. In normal Class-1 operation, two switch points are activated to provide a bidirectional circuit between the two ports. Once the connection is established and the appropriate switch points activated, frames can be routed directly from the input port to the output port, bypassing the input buffers, if desired. For this reason, buffer-to-buffer flow control is not used after the connection is established.

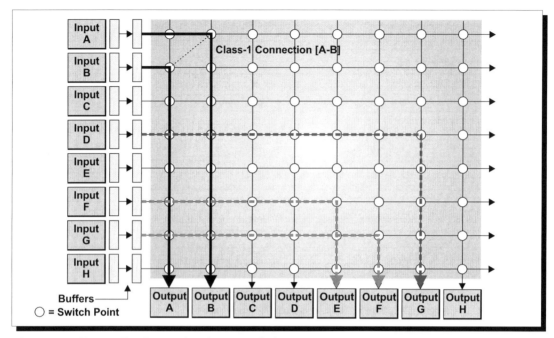

Figure 171. Forwarding Through a Crossbar Switch

When a connectionless class of service is used, the appropriate switch point is activated only for the duration of the frame or frames, being delivered from one port to another. If a frame is being sent from input port F to output port B, the switch point [F,B] is activated for the duration of that frame. There is no need to concurrently activate the reverse path because that path will be activated when frames are received in the reverse direction.

Crossbar Broadcast and Multicast Support. The crossbar switch lends itself to performing broadcast and multicast operations. In this mode, multiple switch points on the crossbar are activated simultaneously, allowing the frame or frames to be delivered to multiple output ports in a single operation.

An illustration of a multicast operation in a crossbar switch is shown in Figure 172. In this example, port B is multicasting frames to ports A, D, E, and F in a single operation by activating the appropriate switch points. The switch points could be controlled by a bit mask with each bit corresponding to one of the switch points associated with a given input port. In this example, the multicast group could be represented as '10011100'b, where a '1' bit represents a member of the multicast group and a '0' bit denotes a non-member.

Broadcast could be viewed as a special case of multicast where all switch points associated with a given input port are activated simultaneously causing frames placed on the bus associated with the input port to be sent to all output ports.

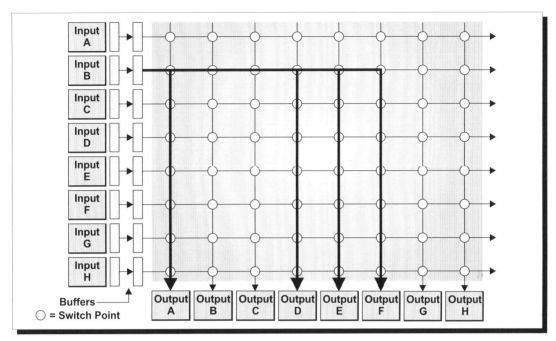

Figure 172. Multicast in a Crossbar Switch

Crossbar Access Control. By disabling selected switch points, access from an input port to one or more output ports can be disabled. This would allow the switch to be configured so a particular input port could only have access to a selected subset of the output ports. An example of this technique is shown in Figure 173 on page 522.

In this example, input port A is enabled to send frames to output ports A, D, E, F, and H. Access to output ports B, C, and G is inhibited because the switch points to those destinations are disabled. Likewise, input port B is enabled to send frames to output ports A, B, C, G, and H with access to output ports D, E, and F disabled.

Limiting access in this manner does not imply that the disabled switch points are not present, simply that they cannot be activated. Inhibiting or allowing a set of output switch points associated with a particular input port could be controlled by a bit map that is set up by a system administrator or through other means. For example, the map for input ports A, D, E, and F in this example would be '10011101'b, the map for ports B, C, and G is '01100011'b and the map for port H is '11111111'b (where a '1' bit represents enabled and a '0' bit indicates disabled).

Crossbar Switch Summary. While the crossbar switch offers many attractive characteristics such as non-blocking connections, and straightforward broadcast and multicast, it does not scale well to larger configurations.

In the eight-ported example switch, the number of switch points is 8^2, or 64. As the size of the switching matrix increases, the number of switch points increases as the square of the number

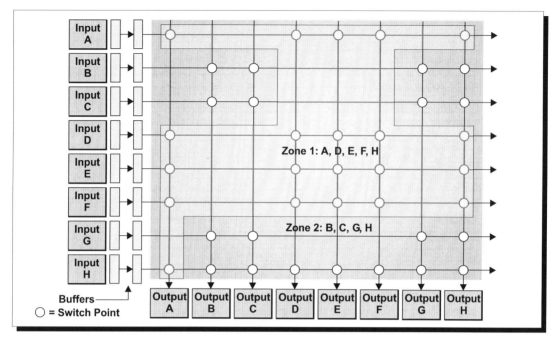

Figure 173. Access Control via Disabled Switch Points

of ports. This means that a 16-port switch will have 16^2, or 256 switch points, and a 256-ported switch would have 256^2, or 65,536 switch points. At some point, the number of switch points becomes unwieldy and a different approach is needed.

36.2.2 Multi-Ported Memory

Another technique for forwarding frames is the multi-ported memory switch shown in Figure 174 on page 523. It represents a dramatically different approach from the crossbar switch shown earlier.

In this switching mechanism, each input port has a queue associated with each output port. When a frame is received by the input port, the frame is stored in the appropriate queue based on the destination address in the frame header. The queues provide the buffering necessary to provide flow control for the associated input ports.

Each output port removes frames from one of the input queues assigned to that output port. When frames exist in multiple input queues, the output port can implement a load-balancing algorithm to ensure that each input queue receives an equal amount of service ensuring that no input port monopolizes an output port.

The input queues can be implemented using a cut-through technique that allows the output port to begin processing a frame from the queue without waiting for the entire frame to be received. It is only necessary to ensure that enough of the frame is present to ensure that the output port does not empty the queue before the end of frame is reached.

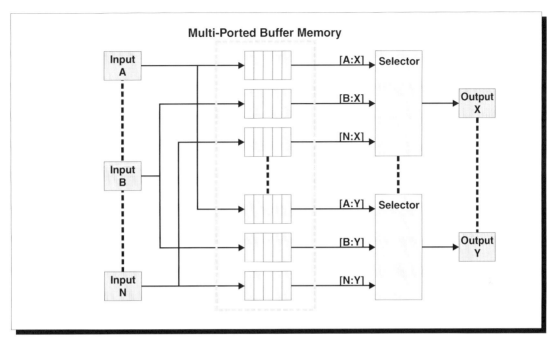

Figure 174. Multi-Port Memory Switch

The memory used for the queues could be implemented with individual memories, one per queue. Other packaging options could be used as well, such as one memory for all the queues associated with a specific output port, one memory containing all the queues for a block of output ports, or even one memory for the entire switch.

The maximum throughput of the switch is determined by the maximum throughput of the memories used to implement the queues. In a 16-port switch with full-speed Fibre Channel links, the bandwidth required to support full throughput on all links is in excess of 1.6 GB per second. Due to the difficulty of achieving this throughput with a single memory, some type of a multiple memory approach would probably be used.

Connection Modes. At first glance, it would appear that this type of switching mechanism does not support Class-1 operation because the path from the input port to the output port cannot be guaranteed. In fact, this may be true if multiple output ports share the same memory and the memory does not have sufficient bandwidth to sustain the full link rate of all associated ports. However, if the memory bandwidth is sufficient and the output selector is locked to one of the input ports, then Class-1 can potentially be supported.

Multicast and Broadcast. Multicast and broadcast can be supported by storing the frame into multiple queues at the same time. To perform a multicast, the frame is stored in all the queues corresponding to output ports in the multicast group. As was discussed earlier for the crossbar switch, the ports contained in the multicast group could be represented by a bit map that is subsequently used to control the gating of frames into the appropriate queues.

For broadcast operation, the frame is simply stored into all the queues and will be subsequently processed by all the output ports.

Unlike the crossbar switch, the frames sent during multicast or broadcast may appear at the different output ports at different times depending upon their position in the respective queues. Normally, this does not represent a problem, but should be kept in mind if the simultaneous delivery of frames is desired.

Access Control (Zoning). The ability of an input port to access the queue associated with an output port can be controlled in the switch allowing for restricted access by a particular input port. Just as the crossbar example used a bit map to indicate the associated switch points, the multi-ported memory can use a bit map to indicate access to the queues associated with the set of output ports.

36.3 Multi-Stage Switching - Cascading Switch Elements

The switching mechanisms examined at the switch level provide the ability to forward frames between a limited number of ports. Typically, individual switches are limited to 16, 32, 64, or sometimes 256 ports.

For some applications, the number of ports provided by a single switch may be sufficient. However, many applications will require routing frames among a larger number of ports than can be implemented in a single switch. Some applications may want to connect physically separate systems or clusters of devices together without the need to run individual links to a common switch point. Finally, if all frames are routed through a single switch and that switch fails, the entire Fibre Channel network is down and no communication is possible.

To address these limitations, the fabric allows multiple switches to be interconnected to create a larger configuration. Fabric is a generic term that is used to indicate "a switch or group of interconnected switches."

This interconnection of individual switches is referred to as cascading and provides considerable flexibility in creating fabrics with many different configurations and capabilities. Figure 175 shown an example of a simple fabric consisting of two connected switches.

In this example, Switch 1 connects to Switch 2 via a pair of Inter-Switch Link (ISL). The ports used to connect the switches together are referred to as expansion ports, or E_Ports for short. Frames from an N_Port on Switch 1 can be delivered to an N_Port on switch S by sending the frames from Switch 1 to Switch 2 via the E_Ports and their associated inter-switch links.

When multiple switches are cascaded in this manner, the switches need to:

- Manage the overall address space so that each attached node port has a unique address. Switches allocate addresses in a manner that facilitates efficient forwarding of frames between switches.

- Build routing tables to facilitate the efficient forwarding of frames from the source port to the destination port.

- Implement a flow control mechanism to manage the flow of frames between switches to ensure that starvation and deadlock conditions are avoided.

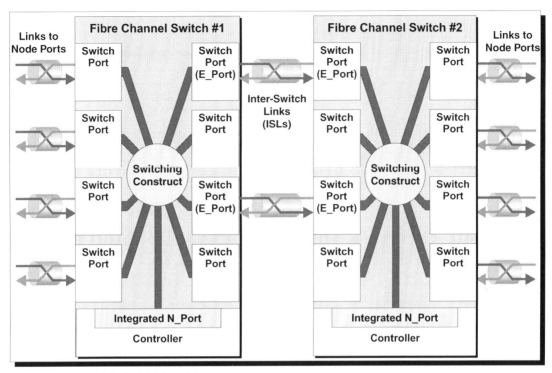

Figure 175. Multi-Switch Fabric Example

Fibre Channel provides an extremely flexible structure for a fabric containing up to 239 switches that can be interconnected in a wide variety of configurations and physical placements. In the simple example shown in Figure 175, the two switches could be in the same room, in different rooms in the same building, in different buildings on a campus, or even in different cities or countries. While a single Fibre Channel link is limited to about 100 km., greater distances can be achieved using repeaters or extenders in the inter-switch link between the switches.

Figure 176 on page 526 shows an example of a more complex fabric consisting of four interconnected switches providing complete redundancy and no single point of failure.

In this example, each node has at least two paths to every other node. The two N_Ports associated with each node are connected to different switches to provided redundancy in case of a link or switch failure. Each switch is connected to every other switch in this configuration to provide redundancy within the fabric configuration (a configuration called a fully-connected mesh). If any one of the inter-switch links fails, frames can be routed via one of the other inter-switch links (passing through one of the other switches) allowing uninterrupted communications while the failed link is repaired.

With this degree of routing flexibility, the switches need to build routing tables used to forward frames to node ports attached to other switches. In this example, the routing tables are relatively simple because the number of available routes is limited and the choices are limited. For

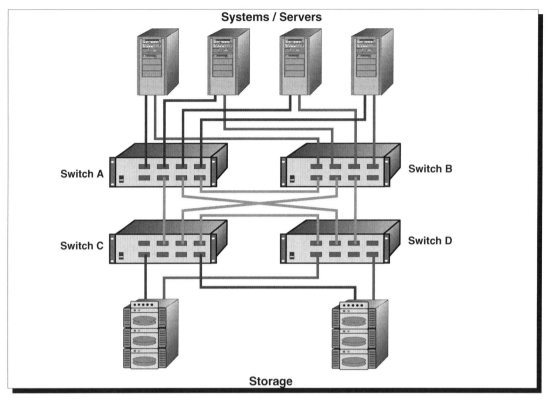

Systems / Servers

Switch A

Switch B

Switch C

Switch D

Storage

Figure 176. Fabric with Redundant Cascaded Switches

example, a frame from Switch A to Switch D could take any of the following routes (other, longer routes exist but are not considered):

- Switch A directly to switch D (1 hop)
- Switch A to switch B, then switch B to switch D (2 hops)
- Switch A to switch C, then switch C to switch D (2 hops)

Because the direct link is the shortest and likely the most efficient, it could be selected as the preferred path. If however, the ISL from Switch A to switch D fails or becomes overly congested, frames could be routed via one of the other available paths.

Routing tables are created automatically by the switches using the Fabric Shortest Path First (FSPF) protocol. Each link is assigned a cost that is inversely proportional to the link speed (faster links have a lower cost). FSPF creates and maintains a replicated topology database in every switch containing information about every ISL in the fabric. Using the information in the topology database, each switch computes its least-cost path to every other switch.

Chapter 36. Fibre Channel Fabric

36.3.1 Frame Delivery Order

When frames are routed through a single switch, it is easy to ensure that frames are delivered to the destination port in the same order as sent by the source port. When multiple switches are interconnected to create a larger fabric, the in-order delivery of frames cannot be assumed if multiple paths are used to deliver a series of frames.

In a connectionless class of service, the fabric may forward the frames using any available path. The selection of a path could occur frame-by-frame, depending on the availability of path resources and bandwidth within the switch. If more than one path exists between a sending and receiving switch, the frames may be routed over different paths and arrive out-of-order at the destination. Figure 177 on page 527 illustrates how out-of-order frame delivery can occur in a fabric environment consisting of multiple switches.

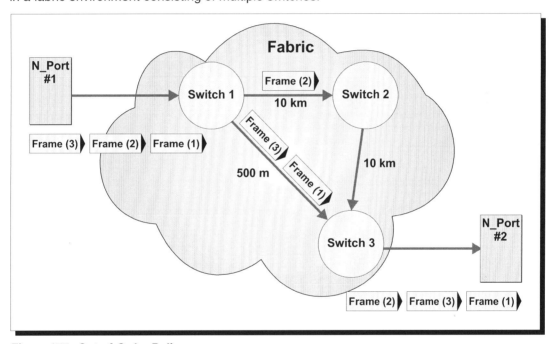

Figure 177. Out-of-Order Delivery

In this example, N_Port 1 sends a series of three frames to N_Port 2. As the frames arrive at Switch 1, frame 1 is forwarded to Switch 3. When frame 2 arrives at the switch, the inter-switch link between Switch 1 and Switch 3 is busy or congested. As a result, Switch 1 forwards frame 2 to Switch 2 for delivery. However, by the time that frame 3 arrives at Switch 1, the congestion has cleared and frame 3 is forwarded directly to Switch 3. Due to the difference in transmission times, frame 3 arrives at the destination before frame 2.

The Fibre Channel architecture allows out-of-order frame delivery and provides mechanisms for the destination node port to reassemble Sequences having frames delivered out of order.

Delivery confirmation (ACK) can be used to ensure that Sequences within an Exchange are delivered in the correct order. This is done by sending the first Sequence and waiting for the final ACK before sending the next Sequence (this doesn't apply to Class-3 operations). However, some applications may wish to prevent out-of-order frame arrival entirely.

One method of preventing out-of-order frame arrival is to use a connection-oriented class of service (Class-1 or Class-6). When this is done, all frames associated with the connection or virtual circuit are routed via the same path preventing out-of-order frame arrival. This also has the additional benefit that the delivery time is predictable.

As an alternative to establishing a connection, the node ports may require the fabric to guarantee in-order frame arrival. The fabric can do this by limiting frame routing between each pair of ports to a single path (unless that path fails). If the frames follow the same path, then the frame arrival order is guaranteed. If the selected path fails, the fabric could begin forwarding frames via an alternate path. This approach is commonly used by Fibre Channel switches to ensure in-order frame delivery in contemporary fabrics.

36.3.2 Inter-Switch Links (ISL)

The Fibre Channel Switched Fabric standard (FC-SW-x) specifies use of a standard Fibre Channel link between E_Ports. As a result, the E_Port function may be provided by a fabric port that supports the switch-to-switch protocols and signaling. A port capable of operating as either an F_Port or E_Port is referred to as a Generic Port, or G_Port (a switch port that can also operate as an FL_Port is called a GL_Port).

Inter-switch links can become bottlenecks and it may be desirable to use higher-speed links (or multiple links) between switches to prevent congestion. Using a higher-speed link allows frames from multiple lower-speed links to node ports to be multiplexed one a single high-speed inter-switch link (ISL).

Switches can also be connected by inter-switch links that are not Fibre Channel links. This type of ISL might be used when a Fibre Channel link cannot provide the necessary capabilities. An example of when a non-Fibre Channel expansion port might be used is when the two switches are located in separate cities. In this case, it may be necessary to lease services from a common carrier that provides the communication services between cities. That communication service may utilize Asynchronous Transfer Mode (ATM), or perhaps Synchronous Optical Network (SONET) to carry the Fibre Channel information.

Because the specifics of the inter-switch link are not visible to the node ports attached to the fabric, the choice of cascading link gives the Fibre Channel fabric a degree of flexibility not available in other topologies.

36.3.3 Cascading Considerations

A configuration with cascaded switch elements emphasizes the network aspects of Fibre Channel. Proper consideration must be given to the nature of the traffic between switches to ensure that the configuration meets the design goals and requirements of the attached nodes. This requires careful planning and foresight to prevent performance bottlenecks or fabric outages due to switch or link failures.

If two fabric switches are connected by a single inter-switch link, that link could become a bottleneck if a significant amount of traffic flows between the switches. This blockage could be severe if Class-1 dedicated connections are established across the inter-switch link. In this case, a single connection would allocate all the available bandwidth on the link and prevent any other traffic until the connection was removed.

In addition to bandwidth considerations, the possibility of a failure of a switch or inter-switch link must also be considered. If all frames are routed through a single switch or inter-switch link and that switch or link fails (or needs to be serviced), all communication between the switches is interrupted.

36.4 Fabric Addressing

The Fibre Channel fabric is an intelligent entity responsible for the management of the address space and assignment of addresses to the attached node ports. The address of a node port is determined by the fabric port to which the node port is attached.

When a fabric consists of a single switch, addressing is straightforward and solely determined by that switch. When multiple switches are interconnected, address assignment is more complex because each switch must be allocated a unique range of addresses. The number of addresses allocated to each switch may vary based on the maximum number of ports the switch has installed or is capable of having installed.

To simplify management of the address space and frame switching, the 24-bit address is divided into three eight-bit fields. The most significant eight bits of the address are referred to as the domain, the middle eight bits are the area, and the low-order eight bits are the port.The relationship of Domain, Area and Port is shown in Figure 178 on page 529.

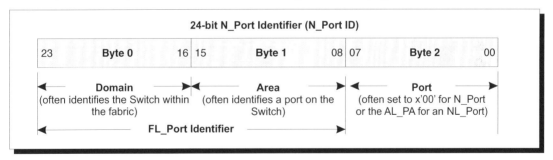

Figure 178. Domain, Area and Port Addressing

Partitioning the address space reduces the size of routing tables by allowing routing decisions to be made first on the domain portion, then the area portion, and finally the port portion of the address. In the example shown by Figure 179 on page 530, each switch is assigned a domain identifier corresponding to the most significant eight bits of the 24-bit address. This allows up to 239 switches to be interconnected in a single fabric (several domain addresses are reserved, as discussed in *Address Space Allocation* on page 531).

When a frame is received by a switch port, the domain portion of the address is examined to determine if the destination is within that switch. If the destination address is located in another domain, the frame is forwarded to the correct domain (switch) based solely on the upper eight bits of the destination address.

Once the frame is in the correct domain (switch), the area identifier (the middle eight bits) are used to forward the frame to the correct area within that domain. The area may represent a port or card position within the switch containing one or more F_Ports or a single FL_Port.

When an area consists of F_Ports, the number of ports is determined by the design of the switch. The low-order eight bits of the address identify which F_Port within that area the frame should be routed to in order to deliver it to the correct node port.

When an area consists of an FL_Port, the number of ports associated with that area is the number of NL_Ports on the attached arbitrated loop. In this case, it is necessary for the FL_Port to open a loop circuit with the destination NL_Port before delivering the frame.

Figure 179 shows one common way in which switches use the area portion of the address to identify the switch port. This scheme is often used by switches having ports that can operate as either F_Ports or FL_Ports.

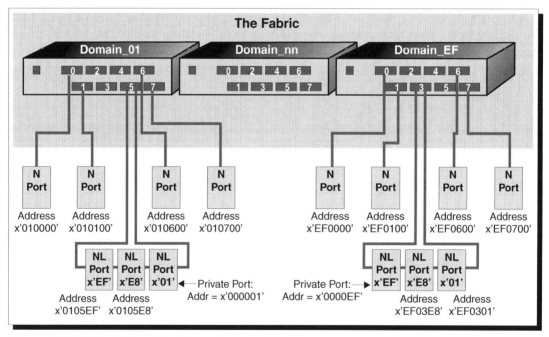

Figure 179. Fabric Addressing Example

While this partitioning of the address space is simple and easy to implement, it may result in inefficient use of addresses space since a large number of addresses may go unused. For example, an eight-ported switch may consume an entire domain's worth of address (65,536 addresses) while only using eight. Even with this inefficiency, the number of usable addresses may be sufficient for many applications. Implementations requiring more addressable ports than this simple scheme provides can manage the domain, area, and port addresses to minimize unused addresses and provide the full address space allowed by the standard.

36.4.1 Address Space Allocation

An initial partitioning of the 24-bit Fibre Channel address space was provided in the Fibre Channel Fabric Generic (FC-FG) standard. The partitioning was subsequently modified in the Fibre Channel Switch Fabric (FC-SW) standard as shown in Table 200 on page 532.

Domain x'00' is reserved and does not have any fabric-assigned addresses associated with it. However, if an arbitrated loop is attached to the fabric via an FL_Port, one or more devices on that loop may choose not to login with the fabric. These devices are designated as private loop devices and occupy addresses in the x'00 00 xx' range as shown in Table 200 on page 532.

There are 239 domains from x'01' through x'EF' for the assignment of domain addresses to switches. Each domain may contain of up to 256 areas (x'00' through x'FF') and each area may containing up to 256 ports (x'00' through x'FF'). This provides a total available address space of 15,663,104 addresses.

Domains x'F0' to x'FE' are reserved and domain x'FF' is used for addresses requiring special handling by the fabric. This includes well-known addresses (x'FF FF Fx'), Domain Controller addresses (x'FF FC xx') and multicast group addresses (x'FF FB xx').

When a switch contains one or more FL_Ports, each FL_Port is assigned an area address. Within this area, port address x'00' is assigned to the FL_Port itself and is used by other ports on the loop to communicate with the FL_Port (this address is referred to as the loop fabric address). Remaining port addresses in the area managed by the FL_Port are used to address NL_Ports on the attached loop. There are only 126 valid arbitrated loop addresses (AL_PAs) in the range of x'01' through x'FF'. The remaining 129 addresses are not valid and are reserved. As a result, while the FL_Port consumes a block of 256 addresses, it can only attach a maximum of 126 NL_Ports, leaving the other addresses unusable by the fabric (they are reserved). In a fabric consisting entirely of FL_Ports, the maximum number of NL_Port addresses would be 239 domains * 256 areas (FL_Ports) * 126 NL_Ports, or a total of 7,709,184 NL_Ports.

36.5 Fabric Flow Control

Managing the flow of frames between an F_Port and its associated N_Port or an FL_Port and the associated NL_Ports is accomplished using buffer-to-buffer flow control. This flow control between the fabric port and node port is needed to prevent frame transmission when no receive buffers are available to hold received frames.

Buffer-to-buffer flow control provides the fabric with a mechanism to prevent congestion within the fabric during heavy traffic. When the fabric detects that the number of frames reaches an undesirable level, the fabric can withhold credit to node ports to limit the transmission of additional frames into the fabric. Congestion control is primarily associated with connectionless classes of service because Class-1 establishes a dedicated connection and reserves the path.

Domain (23-16)	Area (15-08)	Port (07-00)	Port Type	Description
x'00'	x'00'	x'00'		Unidentified (Used by an unidentified N_Port during fabric login)
		x'01-FF'	E_Port	Reserved
			F_Port	Reserved
			FL_Port	If valid AL_PA: Private Loop NL_Port If not valid AL_PA: Reserved
	x'01-FF'	x'00-FF'		Reserved
x'01-EF'	x'00-FF'	x'00'	E_Port	E_Port Identifier
			F_Port	N_Port Identifier
			FL_Port	Loop Fabric Address (used to address the FL_Port)
		x'01-FF'	E_Port	E_Port Identifier
			F_Port	N_Port Identifier
			FL_Port	If valid AL_PA: Public Loop NL_Port If not valid AL_PA: Reserved
x'F0-FE'	x'00-FF'	x'00-FF'		Reserved
x'FF'	x'00-FA'	x'00-FF'		Reserved
	x'FB'	x'00-FF'		Reserved for Multicast Group
	x'FC'	x'00		Reserved
		x'01-EF'		N_Port Identifier for Domain Controller
		x'F0-FF'		Reserved
	x'FD-FE'	x'00-FF'		Reserved
	x'FF'	x'00-EF'		Reserved
		x'F0'		N_Port Controller (used with Virtual Fabrics)
		x'F1-F3'		Well-known Addresses (reserved)
		x'F4'		Event Server
		x'F5'		Multicast Server
		x'F6'		Clock Synchronization Server
		x'F7'		Obsolete (was Key Distribution Server)
		x'F8'		Obsolete (was Alias Server)
		x'F9'		Obsolete (was Quality of Service Facilitator - QoSF)
		x'FA'		Management Server
		x'FB'		Time Server
		x'FC'		Directory Server (Name Server/IP Address Server)
		x'FD'		Fabric Controller
		x'FE'		N_Port Identifier for Fabric F_Port
		x'FF'		Broadcast Address

Table 200. Fabric Address Space Mapping

In cases of severe congestion, the fabric may return F_BSY to Class-2 or Class-F frames that can't be delivered in before R_A_TOV would expire. In Class-3, the fabric may discard frames that can't be delivered in time without notifying the source or destination ports. Busy conditions and discarded frames are undesirable and may result in a failed Sequences or Exchanges and the associated error recovery processing.

Flow control is also required within the fabric. When multiple switches are cascaded, a flow control mechanism is required on each inter-switch link (ISL) to prevent overrunning receive buffers in the E_Ports. To facilitate interoperability between switches, buffer-to-buffer flow control is used on the inter-switch links just as with other Fibre Channel links. Some switches may elect to use vendor-unique flow control mechanisms when connected to another switch from the same manufacturer.

36.6 Priority, Preemption, and Per-Hop Behavior

When connections or circuits are established or frames routed, it may be desirable to assign a priority to that operation. This allows higher-priority operations to take precedence over lower-priority operations.

When the Fibre Channel standard was initially approved, there was no provision for assigning priorities to operations. All operations were essentially considered to have the same priority. When conflicting requests for resources were received simultaneously, the topology decided how to allocate those resources using an implementation-dependent algorithm.

As developers examined using Fibre Channel for real-time applications, it became apparent that the ability to prioritize operations and traffic was needed for those environments. As a result, the Fibre Channel Framing and Signaling (FC-FS) document defines priority and per-hop behavior (PHB) schemes using the CS_CTL field in the frame header.

When priority or per-hop behavior is in enabled, the topology can determine which frames should be delivered first and which should be delayed to accommodate the higher-priority frames. The priority or per-hop behavior value is placed in the CS_CTL field of the frame header. This allows up to 255 levels of priority or behaviors to be assigned (x'00' indicates that no priority has been assigned).

A port indicates it is requesting support of the priority option during Fabric Login (FLOGI). When the fabric sends LS_ACC to the FLOGI, it indicates if priority is operational.

36.6.1 Preemption

Under some circumstances, it may be desirable to preempt an existing connection to establish a new connection associated with a higher-priority process. When a port wishes to preempt an existing connection, it indicates that the requested connection should preempt the existing connection if the priority of the request is greater than that of the existing connection.

If the request is granted, the existing connection is preempted and the two ports notified of the preemption. Preemption may cause Sequences in progress between the two ports to be abnormally terminated, with the attended recovery at a subsequent time.

If the priority of the preemption request is lower than that of the existing connection, the preemption request is rejected and a response sent to the requestor.

36.7 Broadcast and Multicast

In some applications, one port may need to send the same frames to a group of multiple ports, or even all other ports. This type of communication can always be performed by using a series of one-to-one communications from the sender to the group of recipients. However, using a series of one-to-one communications may be inefficient. Instead, a one-to-many communication model may be used to improve the efficiency of the operation. This mode of operation is referred to as multicast.

36.7.1 Multicast

In multicast, frames sent by one port are directed to a defined set of destination ports. This is done by creating a multicast group and assigning a multicast group address to the group. While the exact manner of creating the multicast group may vary from one topology to another, the objective is the same.

Once a multicast group has been created, frames sent to the multicast address are forwarded to every port in the multicast group. Receipt of frames sent to a multicast group may be acknowledged or unacknowledged.

If the originator of the frames does not need delivery confirmation, Class-3 service is used. This is frequently referred to as unreliable multicast, or datagram multicast.

If the originator of the frames wants acknowledgment that the frames were delivered successfully, Class-6 service is used (Class-6 is a variation of Class-1). This is referred to as reliable multicast and requires a server function called the multicast server. The multicast server consolidates the acknowledgments from the members of the multicast group and sends a single acknowledgement to the multicast originator. For more information about the multicast server and an illustration of a reliable multicast operation refer to *Multicast Server* on page 488.

36.7.2 Broadcast

The extreme example of one to many communications is broadcast, where the same frames are sent to every port. Broadcast is used by some networking protocols, such as the Address Resolution Protocol (ARP) to locate other ports when their address is unknown.

Some Fibre Channel switched fabrics may define a special broadcast zone to limit the scope of broadcast frames. When this is done, frames sent to the broadcast address are only forwarded to other members of the broadcast zone.

36.8 Public Arbitrated Loop Topology

The final topology variation is a hybrid configuration rather than a different topology. This is the attachment of one or more arbitrated loops to a switched fabric. This configuration is referred to as a fabric-attached loop, or public arbitrated loop. In order to attach an arbitrated loop to a switched fabric, fabric ports with loop capabilities (FL_Ports) are required. Figure 180 on page 535 shows an example of a fabric with a single public arbitrated loop attached.

When an arbitrated loop is attached to a fabric, the loop becomes part of the fabric's address space. As with all arbitrated loops, the least-significant eight bits of the NL_Port address are

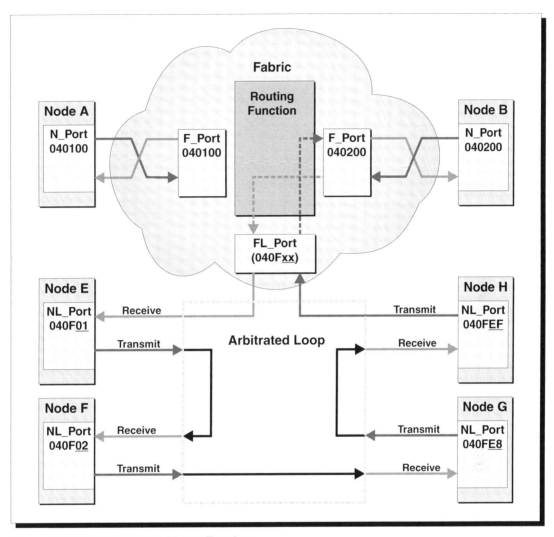

Figure 180. Public Arbitrated Loop Topology

assigned during arbitrated loop initialization and the most-significant 16 bits default to zeros. When the NL_Port performs Fabric Login (FLOGI), the fabric assigns the most-significant sixteen bits of the address.

Because this is a hybrid configuration, it exhibits characteristics of both the switched fabric and arbitrated loop topologies. When an NL_Port wishes to communicate with another NL_Port on the same loop, behavior is identical to normal loop operations.

When an NL_Port wishes to communicate with a node port (N_Port or NL_Port) that is external to the loop, it must arbitrate, win arbitration, and open a loop circuit with the FL_Port. By opening a circuit with the FL_Port, the NL_Port gains access to the fabric and can send or receive frames from other fabric-attached ports (N_Ports or even NL_Ports on other loops). When the NL_Port sends frames into the fabric via the FL_Port, the fabric routes those frames to their final destination using the destination address in the frame header. Following completion of the external communications, the NL_Port closes the loop circuit with the FL_Port allowing other loop ports to win arbitration.

36.9 Virtual Fabrics

Virtual fabrics is a technique that enables a single physical fabric to appear as multiple, independent virtual fabrics to the users. By creating what appear to be independent fabrics, each can be administered independently of the others. An administrator making zoning changes in one virtual fabric is prevented from making changes that might affect a different virtual fabric. Consider the example configuration shown in Figure 181.

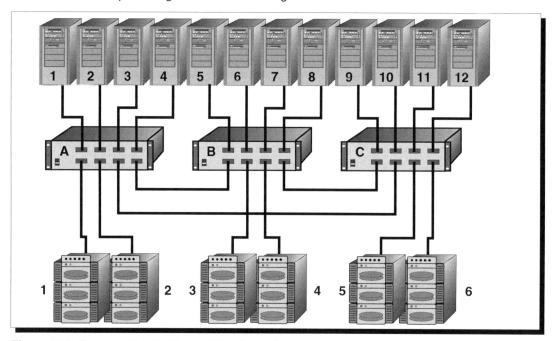

Figure 181. Example Fabric Physical Configuration

In this example, the following devices will be allowed to communicate:

- Servers 1, 5 and 9 and storage devices 1 and 5
- Servers 2 and 10 and storage devices 2 and 6
- Servers 3, 6, 7 and 11 and storage device 3
- Servers 4, 8 and 12 and storage device 4

While zoning could be used to provide the desired access control, this example will use virtual fabrics instead. Each virtual fabric is assigned a 12-bit identifier called the Virtual Fabric ID (VF_ID). In this example, Virtual Fabric ID x'001' is defined to include the switch ports associated with servers 1, 5 and 9, storage devices 1 and 5, and the two interswitch links as shown in Figure 182.

From the perspective of devices in virtual fabric 1, the other devices do not exist. Devices that are not assigned to virtual fabric 1 are not accessible by devices in virtual fabric, 1 nor are there entries in the Name Server or Fabric Configuration Server databases for those devices.

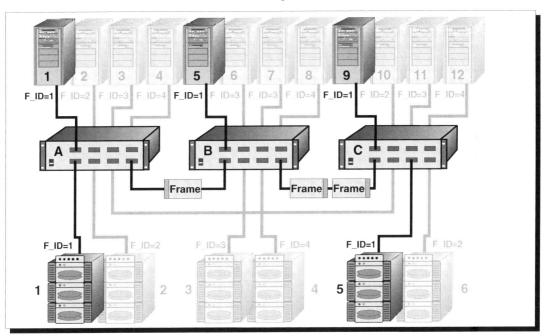

Figure 182. Virtual Fabric 1

In order to provide the next part of the desired access control, Virtual Fabric ID x'002' is defined to include the switch ports associated with servers 2, 6 and 10 and storage devices 2 and 6, and the interswitch link as shown in Figure 183 on page 538.

Switch B is not a part of fabric 2. There are no interswitch links in fabric 2 that go to switch B and there are no entries in the FSPF databases associated with switch B. If switch B fails, is powered off or one or both of the interswitch links disconnected, there is no impact to fabric 2 (of course these events do affect fabric 1).

36.10 Inter-Fabric Routers

Fibre Channel switches forward frames within a single fabric. Fibre Channel routers forward frames between fabrics. Routers provide mechanisms that enable devices in the separate fab-

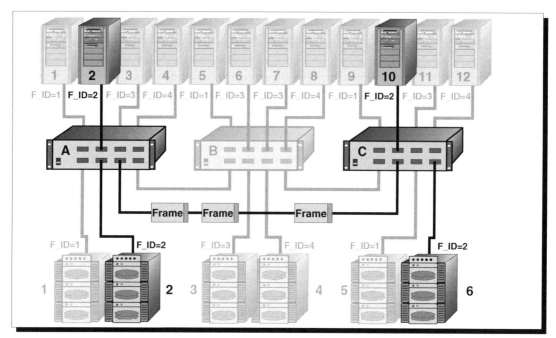

Figure 183. Virtual Fabric 2

rics to communicate without the fabrics themselves being joined. Figure 184 on page 539 shows an example of multiple fabrics connected using a Fibre Channel router.

> NOTE – As of the time of writing, the Fibre Channel Inter-Fabric Routing standard was still in development and the information in this chapter should be considered as preliminary. Functions may change, or new functions added, during the course of standardization.

In Figure 184 on page 539, assume the administrator wants to enable access between the server (in Fabric 1) and storage (in Fabric 3). If there are no addressing conflicts, the router can simply create a proxy for the storage that appears in Fabric 1 and a proxy for the server in that appears in Fabric 3. The proxy entities appear as normal node ports in each fabric's address space and the router makes the appropriate entries in the Name Server databases in each fabric so the devices can be discovered using the normal methods.

When a frame is sent from the server to the address of the storage proxy, the router receives the frame and forwards it to Fabric 3 where it is delivered to the actual storage device. Likewise, when the storage device sends a frame to the address of the server proxy, the router forwards the frame to Fabric 1 where it is delivered to the server.

The method by which the devices are made available may vary from manufacturer to manufacturer; one common approach is to use a variation of the zoning mechanisms (called IFR zoning). By defining an Inter-Fabric Zone at the router containing both the server and storage, the administrator can specify the devices that are allowed to communicate through the router.

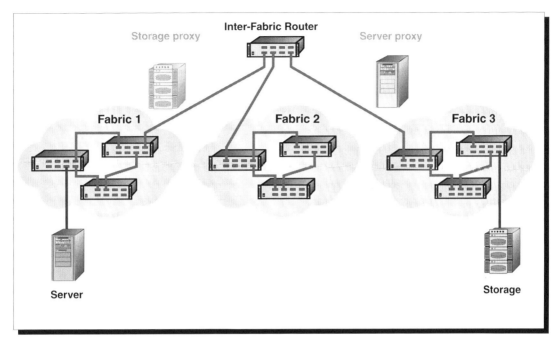

Figure 184. Fibre Channel Router Connecting Multiple Fabrics

Each fabric maintains its own independent FSPF topology and zoning databases. Each contains information about the server and storage devices in this example. By keeping the databases separate, the number of switches affected by routing or zoning changes is minimized.

36.10.1 Fibre Channel Network Address Translation (FC-NAT)

What if an administrator wants to route between fabrics that have conflicting Domain_IDs? In this case, the router can't simply forward frames between the fabrics because duplicate addresses may exist in the different fabrics (the address of the storage device could be the same as that of the server). To accommodate this situation, a router may use Fibre Channel Network Address Translation (FC-NAT) to translate addresses in remote fabrics into unique addresses in the local fabric as shown in Figure 185 on page 540.

In this example, the fabrics containing the server and storage device have overlapping Domain_IDs (both are attached to Domain_ID x'01' in their respective fabrics). In this case, the router can't simply forward frames between the fabrics because of the addressing overlap.

During initialization, the router appears as a switch to each fabric and acquires a Domain_ID in each of the fabrics so that it can provide addresses for proxied devices. In this example, the Router acquires Domain_ID x'3F' in each of the fabrics (although it could acquire a different Domain_ID in each fabric).

The router creates a proxy for the storage device in Fabric 1 and associates it with an address in Fabric 1 (x'3F0101' in this example). The router creates a proxy for the server in Fabric 3

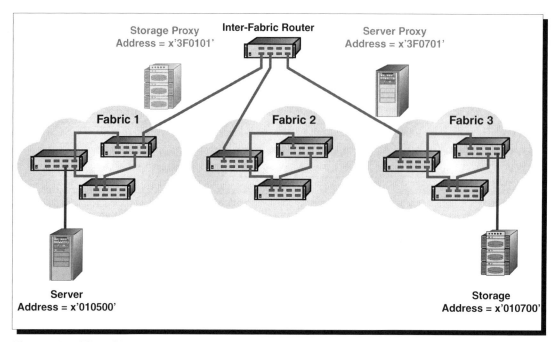

Figure 185. Fibre Channel Network Address Translation (NAT)

and associates it with an address in Fabric 3 (x'3F0701'). Other devices in each of the fabrics can't distinguish the proxy addresses from a normal address.

When the router receives a frame with a destination address of the storage proxy at x'3F0101' it translates the destination address in the frame to x'010700' (the storage device's real address in Fabric 3), translates the source address to x'3F0701' (the server proxy in Fabric 3) and forwards the frame to Fabric 3. When the storage device sends frames to the address of the server's proxy in Fabric 3, the reverse translation takes place and the frames are forwarded into Fabric 1 where they are delivered to the server.

While addresses may be translated by a router, names are never translated. This means that the same name can show up in different fabrics associated with different addresses.

By acquiring a Domain_ID in each fabric and using FC-NAT, the router enables frames to be routed between fabrics, even when there are overlapping addresses in the fabrics. The router creates the appropriate proxy devices, assigns them address from its Domain_ID and maintains a table used to perform the necessary address translation.

36.11 Chapter Summary

Fabric

- Fabric is a term used to describe a generic switched environment
  - Consists of one or more interconnected switches
- Frames are routed based on the destination address in the frame header
- Internal structure and operation of the fabric is not visible to the node ports
  - Path selection
  - Internal flow control
  - Communication between individual switches

Fabric Port (F_Port/FL_Port)

- Each N_Port connects to an F_Port in the fabric
  - NL_Ports connect to an FL_Port
- Fabric ports are interconnected by a switching function allowing frames to flow from one fabric port to another
- Fabric ports are different from node ports. They:
  - Are not the source or destination of frames
  - Do not disassemble or reassemble Sequences
  - Are not concerned with the frame content other than the D_ID, S_ID and maybe the CRC

Fabric Controller

- Fabric Controller is responsible for managing the operation of the fabric
  - Controls the initialization of the fabric
  - Controls the allocation of the fabric addresses
  - Controls the building and maintenance of routing tables
- The Fabric Controller may be a distributed function
  - An instance is present in every switch
- Fabric Controller also performs selected Extended Link Services
  - State Change Notification, registration
  - Alias ID assignment, activation, deactivation

Communication Modes

- In order for two ports to communicate, there must be a physical path between them
  - Point-to-point link
  - Arbitrated loop or fabric
- When the ports wish to communicate, they may reserve resources along the path
  - It so, this Is referred to as a connection-oriented mode
  - If no resources are reserved, it is referred to as connectionless
- Fibre Channel supports both modes through its different classes of service

Connection-Oriented Mode

- Connection-oriented mode establish a connection prior to communications
  - Provided by Class-1 service
- A setup protocol is required to establish the connection
- Reserves exclusive use of the path
  - Referred to as a dedicated connection)
- A removal protocol is used to free path resources when they are no longer needed

Connection-Oriented Mode

- Once a connection has been established, all the frames follow the path that was reserved
  - This provides in-order frame delivery
- Also, the time along the path is deterministic
  - Providing time-reliable delivery
  - Within certain bounds, if a virtual circuit is used rather than an exclusive dedicated connection
- Resources are reserved, whether they are used or not
- The port is busy to other communication

Connectionless Mode

- Rather than establish a connection, a port may simply send frames without one
  - Referred to as connectionless operation or frame switching
  - Called packet switching in the network world
- Each frame is forwarded independently by the topology as resources are available
  - No path is reserved, the topology may use any available path for efficiency
  - No bandwidth is reserved, it is used only as needed to deliver frames
  - Delivery latency is not deterministic because frames may be held up due to congestion

Frame Multiplexing

- When connectionless mode is used, a port can send frames to multiple ports in succession
- The fabric forwards each one independently
- This may provide better link utilization
  - By allowing multiple operations with different ports to be interleaved
- A port may be sending frames to one port while receiving frames from another port
  - Each fibre may be switched separately

Mixed-Mode Operation

- Some designs allow both connection and connectionless at the same time
  - Prevents a port from being inaccessible due to the connection
  - Requires independent capabilities for each type of frame
  - Preference is given to the connection-oriented frames
  - Connectionless frames are handled as bandwidth allows
- Provided by Class-1 Intermix

Frame Forwarding

- Frames are forwarded based on the destination address
- Fabric chooses the path
  - Node port has no control over the path used
  - Node port has no knowledge of path information
  - Relieves the node port of having routing tables
- Path selection may be adaptive
  - Based on current traffic, congestion, or other factors
  - Allows re-routing around failures

Crossbar Switch

- One forwarding mechanism is the crossbar switch
  - Uses an xy matrix allowing any input to be connected to any output
  - A connection between one pair of ports does not block communication between other ports
  - This behavior is referred to as non-blocking
- Allows as many concurrent transfers as there are pairs of ports
  - An eight-port switch with 100 MB/sec per port can provide 800 MB/sec total throughput
- Input buffering is required to hold frames while the path is set up

Crossbar Switch

- Crossbar switch can support both connection and connectionless operation
  - Switch point set for duration of connection
  - Switch point set for duration of frame
- Broadcast and multicast can be supported
  - Activate all switch points for a given input
  - Activate a selected group of switch points
- Access control (zoning) can be provided by disabling selected switch points

Multi-Ported Memory Switch

- Switching can also be done using a multi-ported memory
- Each input port puts received frames in a queue associated with the output port
- Output port selects frames from the queue for delivery
  - Output port can load balance traffic by selecting appropriate queue
- Forwarding begins as soon as possible
  - Cut-through routing, not store and forward

Multi-Ported Memory Switch

- Multi-ported memory can support both connection and connectionless operation
- Lock memory queue for duration of connection
- Dynamically allocate queues for connectionless
- Broadcast can be accomplished by storing frame in every output queue
  - Frames not delivered in unison
- Multicast can be accomplished by storing frame in selected output queues
- Access control (zoning) can be provided by disabling access to selected queues

Cascading Switch Elements

- Cascading multiple switch elements provides configuration flexibility
  - Larger configurations can be created
  - Fabric can be physically distributed
  - Can provide redundancy in the event of a failure
- Cascading requires coordination between switch elements
  - Manage overall address spacc
  - Build routing tables to forward frames to final destination
  - Implement switch-to-switch flow control

Frame Delivery Order

- Connectionless mode may result in out-of-order frame delivery
  - If multiple paths are available between the ports
  - And, the fabric uses them during a series of frames
  - And, if the propagation time is different
  - Then the frames may be received out-of-order
- Out-of-order frames can also result from busy conditions
  - The frame is retransmitted after subsequent frames have been sent

Fabric Addressing

- To facilitate address management a partitioning scheme has been developed
- The 24-bit address is divided into three 8-bit fields
  - The upper 8-bits are the Domain
  - The middle 8-bits are the Area
  - The lower 8-bits are the Port
- The domain usually identifies a switch
  - When a frame is received, it is routed to the correct domain (switch)
- Once it is in the correct domain, it is routed to the correct area
- Finally, the frame is routed to the correct port

Priority and Preemption

- Sometimes it is desirable to give some frames priority over other frames
- Done by assigning priority to frames
- The fabric uses the priority to decide which frames to forward first
- May also want to preempt existing connections to allow higher priority frames through
- Both capabilities added in FC-PH3 to support real-time applications

One-to-Many

- Fibre Channel supports two modes of one-to-many communications
- Used for broadcast and multicast operations
  - Broadcast goes to everybody
  - Multicast goes to a defined group of ports
- The one-to-many communication may not require confirmation of delivery (unreliable)
- Or, may require that all ports in the group confirm delivery (reliable)
  - This is Class-6
- Requires an entity to process all the individual responses and generate a single response to the multicast originator

Hybrid Fabric and Loop

- One or more arbitrated loops may attach to a fabric to create a hybrid topology
  - Communication through the fabric has fabric characteristics
  - Communication on the arbitrated loop has loop characteristics
- This hybrid topology has several benefits:
  - The lower-cost arbitrated loop topology can be used where appropriate
  - Allows multiple NL_Ports to share access to the fabric via a single FL_Port
  - Takes advantage of the fabric's larger address space and connectivity

Virtual Fabrics

- Virtual fabrics enable a single physical fabric to appear as multiple virtual fabrics
- Each virtual fabric has all the characteristics of a separate fabric.
  - Each has its own address space, FSPF routing database, Zoning, Name Server
  - RSCN registration and distribution
- Virtual fabrics are transparent to node ports
  - Each virtual fabric has the appearance of a separate fabric
  - Node ports follow all of the normal behaviors
  - E_Ports may add or remove VFT_Headers, but this is transparent to node ports

Virtual Fabrics vs. Zoning

- Each virtual fabric has its own FSPF, Zoning and Name Server databases
  - May reduce the size of these databases and the amount of associated traffic
  - Change in one database in one fabric does not affect other fabrics' databases
  - May reduce the impact of ISL state changes, zoning changes and Name Server changes
- Each virtual fabric has its own zoning
  - Users can administer their own separate virtual fabrics
  - Changes in one virtual fabric do not affect other virtual fabrics
  - Provides protection against user errors

Inter-Fabric Routers

- Inter-Fabric Routers provide a way to route frames between fabrics
  - Enables selected devices in one fabric to communicate with devices in another fabric
- Router enables frames between selected node ports to pass
- Each fabric maintains its own, independent address space, FSPF database and zoning information
- Provides communication while still maintaining separation of the fabrics

FC Address Translation (FC-NAT)

- If fabrics have non-overlapping addresses, router can simply allow frames to pass
  - Router creates a "proxy" device in the fabric associated with that address
  - Makes appropriate entries in the Name Server database
- If fabrics have overlapping addresses, router must translate addresses
  - Router creates a "proxy" device in the fabric and assigns it a unique address
  - Makes appropriate entries in the Name Server database for the proxy address
- Device appears to be part of the local fabric

37. SCSI-3 FCP Protocol

The Small Computer System Interface (SCSI — pronounced "scuzzy") is probably the most widely used interface for open system storage devices in the server and enterprise markets. With a history of over 20 years of use and development, millions of SCSI systems and devices have been deployed in installations throughout the world.

While the SCSI command set provides a rich set of commands for accessing many different types of peripheral devices, one limitation of SCSI has always been the distance and attachment capabilities of the SCSI bus. While many enhancements have been made to increase the speed and robustness of the SCSI bus, little can be done to increase the distance or number of devices that can attach to the bus.

With the advent of Fibre Channel and other high-speed serial interfaces, the limitations of the SCSI bus have been left behind giving the SCSI command architecture an entrance into a new class of configurations — the storage network.

This chapter describes how the SCSI-3 command protocol is mapped to Fibre Channel. This information is based on the SCSI-3 Fibre Channel Protocol-2 standard and considers not only the differences, but also the similarities with operations on the SCSI bus.

37.1 SCSI-3: A Multi-Level Architecture

Like many current interfaces, SCSI-3 has adopted a layered, multi-level approach to defining the SCSI environment. The SCSI-3 functions and standards documents have been reorganized to reflect the newly defined three-level structure shown in Figure 186 on page 546.

- The top level defines the SCSI-3 architecture and command sets. This level defines SCSI command behavior and command sets for different classes of SCSI devices. Behavior at this level is independent of the physical interface or transport protocols.

- The middle level is the protocol layer specifying SCSI behavior in a manner compatible with the transport services provided by the lower level. This level corresponds to Fibre Channel's FC-4 level and the SCSI-3 Fibre Channel Protocol SCSI-FCP standard.

- The lowest level is the physical interface and associated topology. For Fibre Channel, this is Fibre Channel's FC-2, FC-1, FC-0, and topologies. Other physical interfaces are also supported by the SCSI standards, including the familiar SCSI Parallel Interface (the bus), IEEE-1394 (Firewire), Serial Storage Architecture (SSA), and even the Internet (iSCSI).

Structuring SCSI-3 functions into different levels can also be applied to the programming interface between a SCSI-3 device class driver (implementing the SCSI command architecture for a given class of device, such as disk or tape, and is physical interface independent) and the port driver and associated port (implementing the protocol and physical interface levels). An example of this structuring of functions is shown in Figure 187 on page 547.

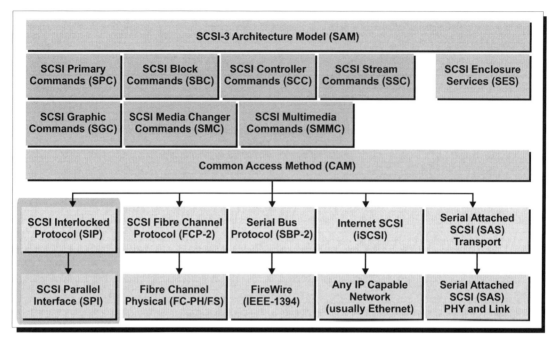

Figure 186. SCSI-3 Layered Structure

37.2 A Brief Overview of SCSI

The SCSI-3 architecture provides a comprehensive set of commands enabling systems to access a wide range of peripheral devices, or even other systems. While SCSI configurations can take on many different forms, all SCSI configurations consist of three key elements:

- one or more SCSI Initiators
- one or more SCSI Targets
- an interconnection interface

A SCSI initiator (server, workstation or other system, storage controller, or other controlling entity) initiates the command process by sending a SCSI command to a SCSI target (disk drive, tape drive, media changer, printer, scanner, or even another computer).

The SCSI command may direct the target to read data, write data, position a magnetic tape to a specific position, move a tape cartridge in a tape library, or print on a printer. Each type of SCSI device has its own set of commands used to access that device class.

The interconnection interface connects the initiator to the target. Each SCSI device requires one or more hardware ports to attach the device to the interconnection interface. In systems, these ports are frequently referred to as host bus adapters, or HBAs (no special term is normally used for targets). A rather abstract, high-level illustration of a SCSI configuration is shown in Figure 188 on page 548.

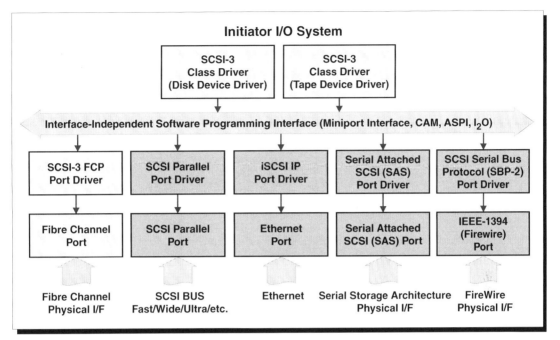

Figure 187. Multiple Physical Interfaces

Historically, the interface used to connect SCSI initiators and targets has been the SCSI bus. However, there is nothing in the SCSI architecture that limits operations to the SCSI bus. In fact, many different types of physical interfaces are currently used to transport SCSI commands including Fibre Channel, the Integrated Device Electronics (IDE) interface, IEEE-1394 (Firewire), the Serial Storage Architecture (SSA), and even the Internet (iSCSI). A key requirement when mapping SCSI commands to other physical interfaces, including Fibre Channel, is separating the logical command protocol from the physical interface characteristics.

37.2.1 Initiator and Target Identification

Because more than one initiator and target may exist in a configuration, it is necessary to provide a means to uniquely identify each initiator and target. This is normally done using an interface address identifier such as the SCSI ID or Fibre Channel N_Port ID. Other means may also be used, for example: Fibre Channel names, IP addresses, or Uniform Resource Locators (URLs). Providing an identifier for each initiator and target enables them to identify the device they wish to communicate with.

37.2.2 SCSI Logical Units

Each SCSI target controls one or more logical units. In many cases, the target and logical unit are one and the same. A disk drive is an example of a SCSI target that normally contains a single logical unit. However, it is possible to have a single target that controls multiple logical units. For example, a RAID controller may control many logical units created from the disk

---

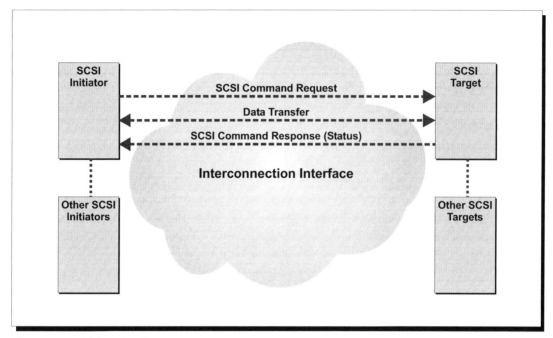

Figure 188. SCSI-3 Configuration

space provided by the attached disk drives or a tape controller may control multiple attached tape drives, each a logical unit.

Each logical unit has an identifier called the logical unit number, or LUN. All targets are required to implement logical unit number zero. This allows an initiator to query logical unit number zero to obtain information about the target and its other logical units, if any.

37.2.3 SCSI Command Queueing

Some initiators and logical units only allow one command at a time to be active between them. While this simplifies operations, it may be inefficient in some cases because the next command can't be sent until the current command completes.

Other initiators and logical units allow more than one command to be active at the same time. In this case, the logical unit places received commands in a command queue (called the task set). When the current command completes or is interrupted, the logical unit can begin processing the next command in the task set. An illustration of the command task set (queue) is shown in Figure 189 on page 549.

When an initiator and logical unit allow more than one command at a time between them, it is necessary to provide a means to identify each command. The identifier is referred to as a 'tag' and the operation of allowing multiple commands at the same time between an initiator and logical unit is referred to as 'tagged command queueing' (in effect the tag is a transaction identifier between the initiator and logical unit).

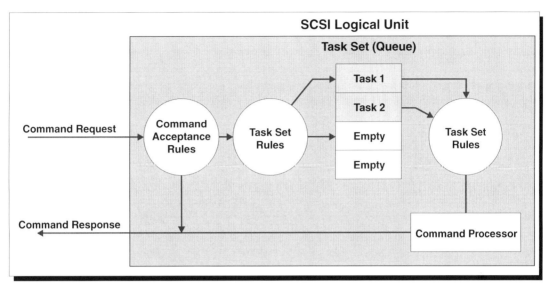

Figure 189. SCSI Task Set (Queue)

The SCSI command architecture goes even further to improve the efficiency of command processing by allowing a logical unit change the order in which it executes commands in the task set. This lets a disk drive, for example, organize commands to minimize the distance it has to move the read-write arm when accessing data.

Sometimes, an initiator may want to prevent the logical unit from changing the order of some commands while still allowing the logical unit to change the order of others. To enable the initiator to control command execution on a per-command basis, a task attribute (queue type) may be associated with each command. The task attributes (queue types) are:

- Untagged: indicates command queueing is not being used. Only one command can be outstanding at a time between the initiator and this logical unit.
- Ordered Queue: directs the logical unit to execute the commands in the order received
- Simple Queue: allows the logical unit to reorder the commands
- Head of Queue: directs the logical unit to place this command at the head of the queue. The command may be executed before commands that have been received previously.
- Auto Contingent Allegiance Queue: used during error recovery to allow the initiator that issued a failed command to perform error recovery.

37.2.4 SCSI Command Multiplexing

Sometimes there are periods of inactivity during execution of a command. When the interconnect interface is shared with other devices, it may improve the utilization of the interface if the initiator and target save the state of the current command and relinquish the interface to allow other communications to occur. When command processing is ready to resume, the interface is re-acquired, the state of the command restored, and the operation continues. On the SCSI bus, this process is performed by the disconnection and reconnection procedures. On a Fibre Channel arbitrated loop, the loop circuit is closed and then re-opened as required.

37.2.5 The SCSI Nexus

Within a given SCSI configuration, it is possible to uniquely identify any command by identifying the initiator that issued the command, the target and logical unit that received the command, and if tagged command queueing is used, the tag associated with that particular command. This relationship is referred to as the ITL (Initiator, Target, LUN) or ITLQ (Initiator, Target LUN, Queue Tag) nexus. When an initiator or logical unit needs to identify a specific command, the ITL or ITLQ nexus is used.

37.2.6 Initiator or Target?

While the roles of initiator and target are usually associated with specific type of devices, they are simply roles. A system may act as an initiator for some operations and a target for others. Likewise, a disk drive may act as a target for some operations and an initiator for others (for example when performing a copy command).

A conceptual model of a SCSI device is shown in Figure 190. Notice that the SCSI device may be an initiator, a target, or both and that the nature of the interconnect interface is not specified at this level.

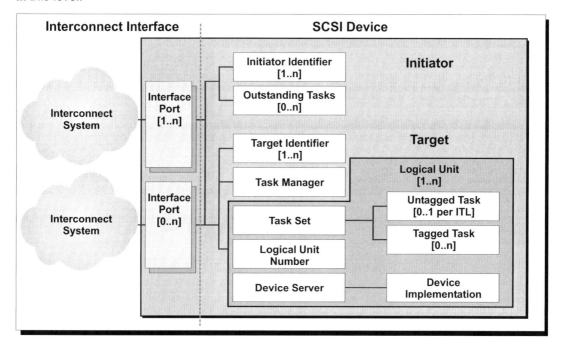

Figure 190. SCSI-3 Device Model

37.2.7 Command Descriptor Block (CDB)

The command descriptor block is a data structure that contains the SCSI command and related parameters. The initiator sends a CDB to tell the logical unit which operation to perform. While different classes of SCSI devices (e.g., disk, tape, media changers) may perform different commands, the general format of the CDB is always the same.

Different commands may transfer different amounts of command-specific parameters and result in different sized CDBs. The first three bits of the first byte (the group code) identify the size of the CDB, while the remaining five bits contain the SCSI command (frequently, the entire first byte is simply referred to as the command). The format of the CDB is shown in Figure 191. Variable-length CDBs (group '011'b') have a slightly different format (not shown).

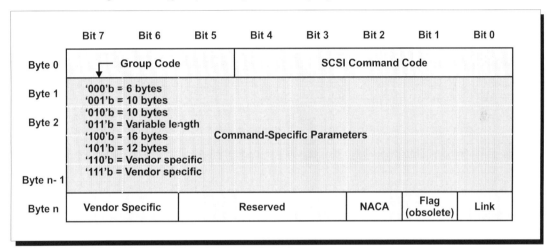

Figure 191. SCSI Command Descriptor Block (CDB)

Bytes 1 through n-1 of the CDB contain command-specific parameters defined by the command contained in the first byte of the CDB. The last byte of the CDB is called the control byte and contains control information applicable to the CDB.

37.2.8 SCSI Command Request

An initiator begins a new command request by sending the command-related information to the desired target and logical unit. Other than the initiator, target, and LUN identifiers, the only other required information is the Command Descriptor Block (CDB).

If tagged command queueing is being used, the initiator must also provide a unique (at that initiator) "tag" to identify the command and the task attribute (queue type); simple-Q, ordered-Q, head-of-queue, or ACA-Queue.

If the command involves a data transfer, the initiator allocates a data buffer to hold the data and may inform the target of the size of that buffer. This allows the target to check that the transfer stays within the bounds of the allocated data buffer.

When command information is received at the target, the target may enter the command into its task set and begin command processing.

37.2.9 SCSI Data Transfer

When an initiator issues a command that transfers data, it allocates a buffer to hold the data. This buffer contains the data-out on a write-type command or will be used to hold the data-in on a read-type command. Each command with a data transfer requires a separate data buffer.

The target accesses the data buffer during the data transfer phase of the operation. On write-type commands, the target requests data from the buffer. On read-type commands, the target stores data into the buffer. Consequently, the target controls the data transfer (not the initiator).

The target is not aware of any memory addresses or locations associated with the data buffer in the initiator. The target can only reference the data buffer by identifying the command, using the ITL or ITLQ nexus, and supplying an "offset" (data pointer) into that buffer.

When the target executes a data transfer command, it may transfer all requested data in a single action, or it may break the transfer into multiple segments (referred to as bursts). The target may segment the transfer because the amount of buffering available in the target is limited and the target is unable to perform the entire data transfer in a single action. An example of a multi-segment data transfer is shown in Figure 192.

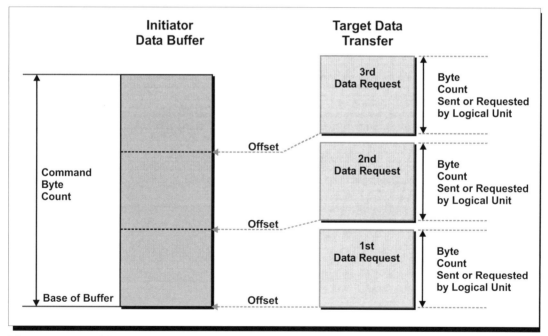

Figure 192. Multi-Segment Data Transfer

In Figure 192 on page 552, the target has broken the data transfer into three segments, or data requests. Each request begins at a specified offset into the data buffer and transfers a specific number of bytes. The manner by which the offset and request byte count are maintained and provided depends on the interconnect interface (in Fibre Channel the target explicitly provides these values).

The target can access the data buffer in a sequential manner, where each data request begins with the first byte following the end of the prior request. This is the access method shown in Figure 192 on page 552 and is the normal method of data transfer.

Although not commonly used, a target can also access the data buffer in a random manner. When random buffer access is used, the target may access the buffer using arbitrary offsets and extents. Random buffer access may be used by a target to improve performance. For example, a target may send data present in its cache first, then send data read from the medium.

37.2.10 SCSI Command Completion

Every SCSI command returns one byte of status, although some error conditions, such as a failure of the target or interconnect interface, may result in no status being returned (in this case, a timeout may be used to detect the error).

Status indicates the associated command has ended at the target when the status is delivered and at the initiator when the status is received. Status byte values are listed in Table 201.

Status Byte	Title	Description
x'00'	Good	The logical unit has successfully completed the command
x'02'	Check Condition	An error or alert has occurred
x'04'	Condition Met	The requested operation is satisfied
x'08'	Busy	The logical unit is busy and unable to accept the command at this time
x'10'	Intermediate	An intermediate command in a series of linked commands is complete
x'14'	Intermediate Condition Met	A combination of Condition Met and Intermediate
x'18'	Reservation Conflict	The logical unit is reserved to another initiator
x'22'	Command Terminated	The logical unit terminated the current task
x'28'	Task Set (Queue) Full	The task set (queue) is full
x'30'	ACA Active	The logical unit is unable to accept the command because an auto contingent condition is active

Table 201. SCSI Status Byte Values

If an error or alert conditions occurs, the logical unit returns status indicating a check condition occurred. A check condition may indicate the command could not be accepted or an error occurred during command processing.

To provide additional information about the error event, the logical unit creates sense information. Sense information provides detailed information about the error event and may be used for error recovery or logging.

Depending on the interconnect interface, sense data may be transferred to the initiator in response to a Request Sense Command (the method used on the SCSI bus), as an Asynchronous Event Report, or automatically with the status byte when a check condition occurs (this method is referred to as autosense and is used when SCSI commands are sent via Fibre Channel). Sense data is reset when it is transferred to the initiator or upon receiving certain new commands from the same initiator.

37.2.11 SCSI-3 Task Management Functions

The SCSI architecture provides several task management functions that can be used to affect the state of the one or more tasks in the target. The initiator sends the task management request to the target and the target returns a response indicating the completion of the request. Because these are not commands, the request is not sent by using a Command Descriptor Block (CDB) and the response is not indicated by SCSI status.

The task management functions are:

Abort Task. Abort the specific task. The task to be aborted is identified by the Initiator identifier, Target identifier, Logical unit, and Queue Tag, if used (ITLQ or ITL).

Abort Task Set. Abort all tasks for the issuing initiator. The tasks to be aborted are identified by the Initiator identifier, Target identifier, Logical unit (ITL).

Clear Task Set. Abort all tasks for all issuing initiators. The tasks to be aborted are identified by the Target identifier and Logical unit (TL).

Target Reset. Reset the specified target. All tasks in all logical units are reset and Unit Attention is set.

Logical Unit Reset. Reset the logical unit. All tasks in the specified logical unit are reset and Unit Attention is set.

Terminate Task (obsolete). This optional function is used to terminate a specific task. Upon completion of this function, the logical unit returns command terminated status to the command. The task to be aborted is identified by the Initiator identifier, Target identifier, Logical unit, and Queue Tag, if used (ITLQ or ITL).

Clear Auto Contingent Allegiance. Clear Auto Contingent Allegiance clears the auto contingent allegiance condition at the specified logical unit. This function is mandatory if the logical unit supports auto contingent allegiance. This function will only be accepted when issued by the initiator associated with the command that caused the auto contingent allegiance condition to be set. The auto contingent allegiance condition is identified by the Initiator identifier, Target identifier, Logical unit (ITL).

37.2.12 Simplified SCSI Command Flow

Putting all of this together, a simplified flow diagram of a SCSI command can be created as shown in Figure 193 on page 555.

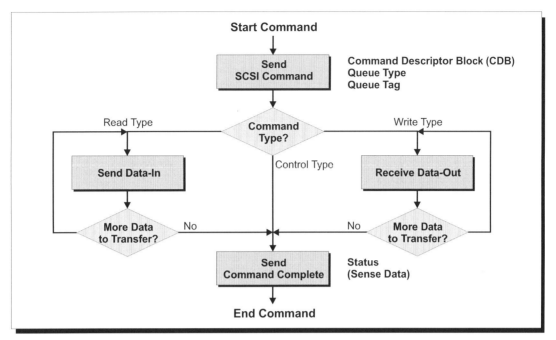

Figure 193. Protocol Services Flowchart

37.3 SCSI-3 Fibre Channel Protocol (SCSI FCP)

The SCSI-FCP protocol mapping specifies how SCSI commands are performed via the Fibre Channel interface. As with all FC-4 protocol mappings, it is necessary to define both the data structures (information sets) transported and use of Fibre Channel facilities.

37.3.1 SCSI FCP Use of the Exchange

Each SCSI-3 task is mapped to a Fibre Channel Exchange. Unless SCSI linking is used, each command corresponds to a Fibre Channel Exchange. When SCSI linking is used, the same Exchange is used for the entire group of linked commands.

The SCSI-3 task is identified by the following Fibre Channel constructs:

* The initiator and target are identified by the Source_ID (S_ID) and Destination_ID (D_ID) address fields in the frame header. The initiator is identified by the S_ID of all frames sent to the target. The target is identified by the S_ID of all frames sent to the initiator.

* Each task between an initiator and target is identified by the Originator Exchange_ID (OX_ID). The FCP protocol mapping requires an initiator to assign a unique OX_ID (between the initiator-target pair) for every open Exchange.

* A target may assign a Responder Exchange_ID (RX_ID). This may assist the target in locating structures associated with the Exchange and simplify task identification.

Different initiators may assign duplicate OX_IDs and a target must use both the initiator's address identifier (S_ID) and the OX_ID to identify a task. If an RX_ID is assigned by the target, the RX_ID can be used as an alias for the initiator identifier and OX_ID. While different targets may assign duplicate RX_IDs, the initiator does not use the RX_ID so this is not a concern.

The Logical Unit Number (LUN) is contained in the FCP_CMND information set. When the FCP_CMND is processed by the target, the LUN is logically bound to the Exchange identifier and is not required in Information Units thereafter.

37.3.2 SCSI FCP Exchange Error Policy

The Exchange error policy is "Abort, discard multiple Sequences". If an error occurs during an Exchange, the Sequence in error is aborted using the Abort Sequence (ABTS) Basic Link Service, and all subsequent Sequences of the Exchange are discarded. This has the effect of aborting the Exchange.

37.3.3 SCSI FCP Classes of Service

SCSI operations may use any class of service supported by both the initiator and target. Most implementations use Class-3.

37.3.4 SCSI-FCP Delivery Order Requirements

Many existing SCSI Fibre Channel implementations require frames be delivered in the same order as sent. When Class-2 or Class-3 is used in a Fibre Channel fabric, the fabric must ensure that frames are delivered in order.

Future SCSI-FCP implementations may remove the requirement for in-order delivery. All information necessary to reorder received commands and Sequences is provided by the existing FCP Information Units and FC-2 mechanisms.

37.4 FCP Information Sets

Five information sets (payloads) are used to transport SCSI commands and task management functions via Fibre Channel.

37.4.1 FCP Command Information Set (FCP_CMND)

The FCP_CMND information set defines the data structure containing the SCSI command-related information. Presence of the FCP_CMND is indicated by setting the R_CTL field of the frame header to x'06' (FC-4 Device Data Frame, Unsolicited Command) and the Type field to x'08' (SCSI FCP).

The format of the FCP_CMND information set is shown in Figure 194 on page 557.

Task Retry Identification. When Task Retry is supported by the initiator and target (see *FCP Error Recovery Examples* on page 576), the initiator may provide a unique task retry identifier in the Parameter field of the frame header of each FCP_CMND. If a retry occurs, the same identifier is also provided in the Parameter field of the Read Exchange Concise (REC) and Sequence Retransmission Request (SRR) link services.

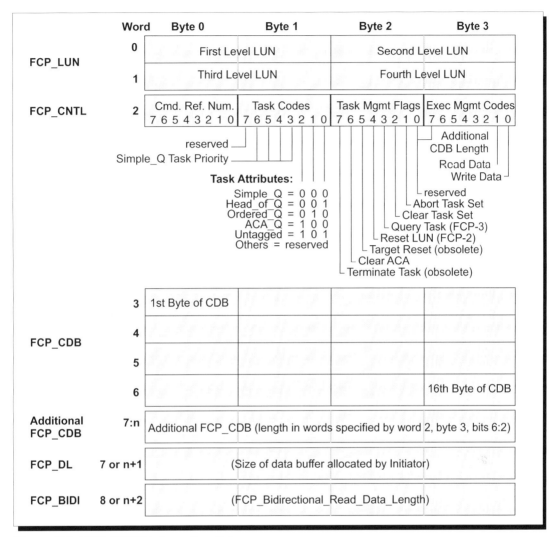

Figure 194. FCP_CMND Information Set

The task retry identifier prevents ambiguity when an Exchange has completed at the initiator but is still open at the target and the initiator reuses the same OX_ID for a new Exchange (if the Exchange is no longer open at the initiator, the OX_ID is available for reuse). If the new Exchange enters into error recovery, the initiator may send REC or SRR. Without the task retry identifier, the target may incorrectly associate the REC or SRR with the old Exchange, not the new one.

FCP_LUN. This field contains the eight-byte Logical Unit Number (LUN) format introduced by SCSI-3. For most devices the LUN in placed in bytes 0 and 1 of the FCP_LUN field shown in Figure 194 on page 557.

Command Reference Number (CRN). This field is used by an initiator to sequentially number commands when the logical unit requires knowledge of the order in which commands were issued. This allows the logical unit to verify commands have been received in the same order as sent and no commands are missing.

Task Codes. This field contains the task attributes (queue type) associated with this command.

Task Management Flags. This byte indicates a task management request is being made. If any bit in this field is set to one, this is a task management request and the command-related fields (e.g., FCP_CDB and FCP_DL) are ignored. If no bits are set, this is a command request and the command-related fields contain valid information.

Additional CDB Length. These bits indicate the number of addition words (beyond 16 bytes) of CDB information contained in the command request.

Execution Management Codes. Bits 1:0 indicate the direction of any data transfer associated with this command.

FCP_CDB. FCP_CDB is a 16-byte fixed-length field containing the SCSI CDB starting in byte 0. When a 6-, 10-, or 12-byte CDB is used, unused bytes in the FCP_CDB field are undefined, but still present. When a long CBD is used, word 2, byte 3, bits 6:2 specify the number of words of additional CDB information.

FCP_DL. For a read or write command, the FCP_DL field specifies the size of the buffer allocated in the initiator for this data transfer. This parameter enables the logical unit to ensure that data transfer does not occur outside the bounds of the allocated buffer. Failure to completely fill the buffer is not necessarily an error and this may be normal behavior for some commands and device types.

For a bidirectional command, this field indicates the size of the buffer allocated in the initiator for the write data transfer portion of the command.

FCP_Bidirectional_Read_DL. For a bidirectional command, this field indicates the size of the buffer allocated in the initiator for the read data transfer portion of the command.

37.4.2 FCP Transfer Ready Information Set (FCP_XFER_RDY)

The FCP_XFER_RDY information set defines the data structure used by a target to request write data from an initiator. FCP_XFER_RDY is indicated by setting the R_CTL field of the frame header to x'05' (FC-4 Device Data Frame, Data Descriptor) and the Type field to x'08'. The format of the FCP_XFER_RDY information set is shown in Figure 195 on page 559.

DATA_RO. The DATA_RO field specifies the offset of the first byte of the FCP_DATA Information Unit that follows. In effect, it specifies the lowest offset value of any byte of

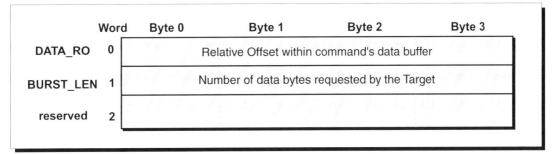

	Word	Byte 0	Byte 1	Byte 2	Byte 3
DATA_RO	0	Relative Offset within command's data buffer			
BURST_LEN	1	Number of data bytes requested by the Target			
reserved	2				

Figure 195. FCP_XFER_RDY Information Set

the FCP_DATA Information Unit. If no relative offset or continuously increasing relative offset is used, the first frame of the FCP_DATA Information Unit carries the data for this relative offset. If random relative offset is used, this is not necessarily the case.

BURST_LEN. The BURST_LEN field specifies the exact length of FCP_DATA being requested by the target. This value cannot exceed the value of the Maximum Burst Size field in the SCSI disconnect-reconnect mode page. If the actual number of bytes transferred by the subsequent FCP_DATA Information Unit does not match this value, the RSP_CODE in the FCP_RSP Information Unit is set to x'01'.

37.4.3 FCP Data Information Set (FCP_DATA)

The FCP_DATA information set is used to transfer data between an initiator and a target. Presence of FCP_DATA is indicated by setting the R_CTL field of the frame header to x'01' (FC-4 Device Data Frame, Solicited Data) and the Type field to x'08' (SCSI FCP).

A SCSI command may transfer one of three different types of data. The Fibre Channel Protocol for SCSI-3 does not distinguish between the types of data. The data types are:

- Command parameter data (e.g., Mode Select data or Format Unit command data)
- Command response data (e.g., Mode Sense data or Inquiry data)
- Logical data (e.g., data associated with a read or write command)

There is no explicit structure to the FCP_DATA information set; it is simply a stream of data bytes associated with the command transferred as a Sequence of one or more frames.

37.4.4 FCP Response Information Set (FCP_RSP)

The FCP_RSP information set defines the data structure containing the SCSI status byte, SCSI autosense, and FCP response code and signals the completion of a SCSI command or task management function (but not necessarily the Fibre Channel Exchange). Presence of the FCP_RSP is indicated by setting the R_CTL field of the frame header to x'07' (FC-4 Device Data Frame, Command Status) and the Type field to x'08' (SCSI FCP).

The format of the FCP_RSP information set is illustrated in Figure 196 on page 560.

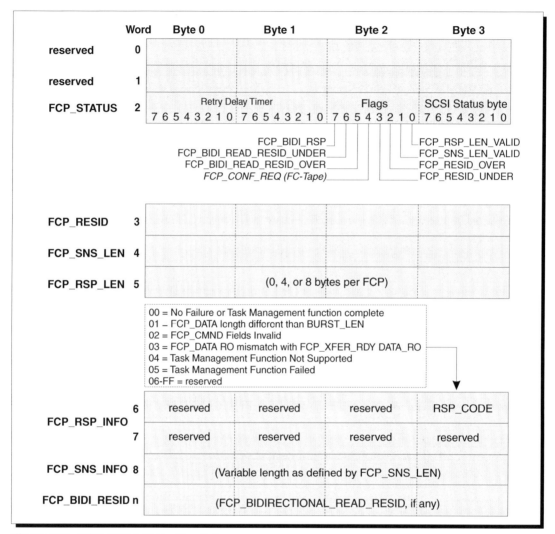

Figure 196. FCP_RSP Information Set

The FCP_RSP is normally the last Sequence of an Exchange (the exceptions occur when command linking or FCP_CONF is used). The FCP_RSP is normally a single-frame Sequence, however, it may require multiple frames if SCSI autosense data causes the size of the FCP_RSP to exceed what can be carried in a single frame.

Retry Delay Timer. If the Status byte is Busy or Task Set Full, this field specifies the number of 100 msec. increments the initiator should wait before sending another command to the logical unit.

Validity Flags. The FCP_STATUS field contains validity bits indicating which of the remaining fields contain valid information and the SCSI status byte.

- **Bit 7: FCP_BIDI_RSP:** This bit indicates that this response is in response to a bidirectional command.

- **Bit 6:** FCP_BIDI_READ_RESID_UNDER indicates that the FCP_BIDI_READ_RESID field is valid and contains the difference between the FCP_DL value and the offset of the highest byte transferred to the initiator buffer during the read portion of a bidirectional command.

- **Bit 5:** FCP_BIDI_READ_RESID_OVER indicates that the FCP_BIDI_READ_RESID field is valid and contains the count of bytes that could not be transferred because the size of the buffer indicated by FCP_DL was not sufficient to contain the entire transfer specified for the read portion of a bidirectional command.

- **Bit 4:** FCP_CONF_REQ indicates that the target is requesting the initiator to send a T12 Information Unit to confirm receipt of the FCP_RSP.

- **Bit 3:** FCP_RESID_UNDER indicates that the FCP_RESID field is valid and contains the difference between the FCP_DL value and the offset of the highest byte transferred to or from the initiator buffer.

- **Bit 2:** FCP_RESID_OVER indicates that the FCP_RESID field is valid and contains the count of bytes that could not be transferred because the size of the buffer indicated by FCP_DL was not sufficient to contain the entire transfer.

- **Bit 1:** FCP_SNS_LEN_VALID indicates that the FCP_SNS_LEN field is valid and contains the count of bytes in the FCP_SNS_INFO field.

- **Bit 0:** FCP_RSP_LEN_VALID indicates that the FCP_RSP_LEN field is valid and contains the count of bytes in the FCP_RSP_INFO field.

SCSI Status. This byte contains the SCSI status byte as described in *SCSI Command Completion* on page 553.

FCP_RESID. If either the FCP_RESID_UNDER or the FCP_RESID_OVER bit is set to one, the FCP_RESID field contains the number of residual data bytes that were not transferred in the FCP_DATA Information Units for this command. Upon successful completion of a command, the residual value is normally zero and the FCP_RESID value is not valid. Devices having indeterminate data lengths may have a nonzero residual byte count after completing valid operations. Targets are not required to verify the data length implied by the contents of the CDB and may create an overrun or underrun after beginning execution of the command.

FCP_SNS_LEN. If the FCP_SNS_LEN_VALID bit is set to one, this field specifies the number of bytes of sense information present in the FCP_SNS_INFO field.

FCP_RSP_LEN. If the FCP_RSP_LEN_VALID bit is set to one, this field specifies the number of bytes of response information present in the FCP_RSP_INFO field.

FCP_RSP_INFO. The FCP_RSP_INFO field provides task or task management response information that cannot be communicated using the SCSI status byte or sense information. It is used to provide information about FCP Information Unit errors, data transfer consistency, or response to a Task Management request. The Fibre Channel Protocol for SCSI-3 standard defines this as a variable length field of zero, four, or eight bytes with other values reserved for possible future standardization. The convention being adopted by the disk drive community is that this field will be either zero or eight bytes in length with the one-byte response code in byte 3 (byte 0 is the most significant byte of the word). The actual length of the response information is indicated in the FCP_RSP_LEN field.

FCP_SNS_INFO. The FCP_SNS_INFO field contains the SCSI sense information. The length of the sense information field is indicated in the FCP_SNS_LEN field and is less than or equal to 255 bytes. Some profiles may restrict the number of sense bytes to ensure that the entire FCP_RSP fits within a single 128-byte frame. As an example, the Private Loop Direct Attach Technical Report restricts the sense data to 78 bytes or less to allow the entire response frame to fit within a single 128-byte frame.

FCP_BIDI_READ RESID. If either the FCP_BIDI_READ_RESID_UNDER or the FCP_BIDI_READ_RESID_OVER bit is set to one, the FCP_BIDI_READ_RESID field contains the number of residual data bytes that were not transferred during the read portion of a bidirectional command. Upon successful completion of a command, the residual value is normally zero and the FCP_BIDI_READ_RESID value is not valid. Devices having indeterminate data lengths may have a nonzero residual byte count after completing valid operations. Targets are not required to verify the data length implied by the contents of the CDB and may create an overrun or underrun after beginning execution of the command.

37.4.5 FCP Confirm Information Set (FCP_CONF)

FCP confirm is used by an initiator to confirm receipt of an FCP_RSP with the FCP confirm request (FCP_CONF_REQ) bit set to one. FCP_CONF is indicated by setting the R_CTL field in the frame header to x'03' (Solicited Control) and the Type field to x'08' (SCSI FCP).

There is no payload associated with FCP_CONF, all necessary information is contained in the frame header.

37.5 FCP Information Units

Figure 202 summarizes the FCP Information Units. In addition to specifying the information set contained in each Information Unit, control information is associated with the Information Unit. This control information corresponds to bits in the frame header and is used to define when an Exchange begins and ends and Sequence Initiative is transferred. Other information in this table is provided for the convenience of the user and is not transported via the interface.

IU Name	Command or Operation Phase	R_CTL	Information Set (Payload) Content	F/M/L	SI	M/O
Information Units Sent by an Initiator						
T1	Command or Task Management Request	06	FCP_CMND	F	T	M
T2	Command Request	06	FCP_CMND	F	H	O
T3	Command Request (linked)	06	FCP_CMND	M	T	O
T4	Command Request (linked)	06	FCP_CMND	M	H	O
T6	Data Out	01	FCP_DATA	M	T	M
T7	Data Out	01	FCP_DATA	M	H	O
T12	FCP Confirm	03	(no payload)	L	T	O
Information Units Sent by a Target						
I1	Data Delivery Request (Write)	05	FCP_XFER_RDY	M	T	M
I3	Data In	01	FCP_DATA	M	H	M
I4	Command/Task Management Response	07	FCP_RSP	L	T	M
I5	Command Response (linked or confirm)	07	FCP_RSP	M	T	O

1. Cat. is the information category value in the R_CTL field of the frame header
2. Content in the payload of the sequence
3. F/M/L is First, Middle, Last sequence of the exchange (see F_CTL bits 21, 20)
4. SI is Sequence Initiative Transferred or Held (see F_CTL bit 16)
5. M/O is Mandatory or Optional
6. T5, T8, T9, T10, and T11 were obsoleted by FCP-2
7. I2, I6, and I7 were obsoleted by FCP-2

Table 202. SCSI FCP Information Units

37.6 FCP Information Unit Flow

Figure 197 on page 564 shows how the FCP Information Units are used to perform SCSI commands. The Exchange begins on entry to the outer box and ends on exit from the outer box. Each rectangle corresponds to an Information Unit (and therefore a Sequence of frames within the Exchange). Upon entry to each rectangle, a new Sequence is initiated (SOFix) and terminated (EOFt) upon exit. When going from an "I" Information Unit to a "T" Information Unit or vice-versa, Sequence Initiative (SI) for the Exchange is transferred.

When linking is used, two optional Information Units are used; the I5 Information Unit to send status without ending the Exchange and the T3 Information Unit to send the linked command.

If a target wants confirmation that an FCP_RSP was received by the initiator, it may send an I5 Information Unit with the FCP_CONF_REQ bit in word 2, byte 2 set. This requests the initiator to confirm reception of the I5 by sending a T12 Information Unit in response.

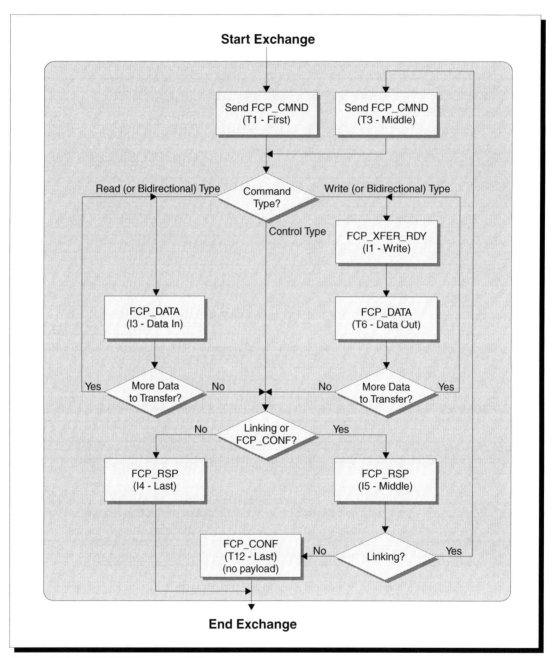

Figure 197. SCSI FCP Command Flow

37.7 Exchange (Target) Authentication

Some Fibre Channel technical reports require that after completion of arbitrated loop initialization command execution is not resumed until the integrity of existing login sessions is verified. Authentication is required because loop initialization indicates a potential configuration change and validity of the existing login sessions cannot be guaranteed.

37.7.1 Private Loop Port Authentication

Consider the configuration shown in Figure 198. The two identical loops are operating independently. Each has an initiator at address x'00 00 01' logged in with a target at address x'00 00 EF'. Because these are separate loops, there is no interaction between them.

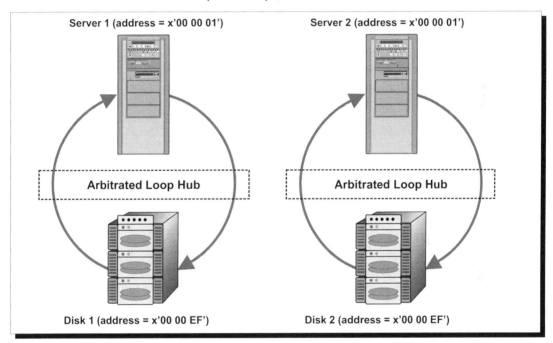

Figure 198. Exchange Authentication, Part 1

Now, assume a cable is connected between the two arbitrated loop hubs and a loop initialization occurs. During loop initialization, one of the ports becomes the Loop Initialization Master (LIM) and begins the process of address assignment.

For this example, assume that server 1 becomes the LIM and reclaims its existing address (x'00 00 01'). Server 2 can acquire a new address but is unable to reclaim its former address because it was already taken by server 1. Disk 2 reclaims its former address (x'00 00 EF'). Disk 1 can acquire a new address but is unable to reclaim its former address because it was already taken by disk 2. This results in the configuration shown in Figure 199.

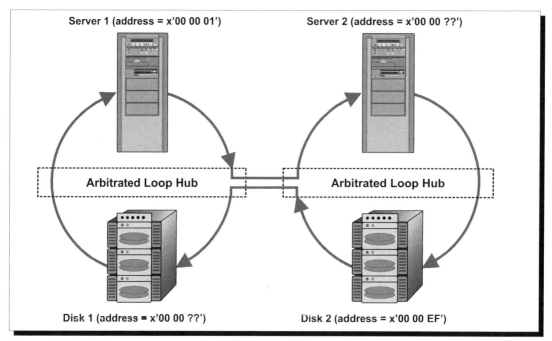

Server 1 (address = x'00 00 01')   **Server 2 (address = x'00 00 ??')**

Arbitrated Loop Hub   **Arbitrated Loop Hub**

Disk 1 (address = x'00 00 ??')   **Disk 2 (address = x'00 00 EF')**

Figure 199. Exchange Authentication, Part 2

Because loop initialization does not affect existing login sessions for ports able to reacquire their same addresses, server 1 is still logged in with address x'00 00 EF (however, it is not the same device at that address as prior to the initialization). Likewise, disk 2 is still logged in with address x'00 00 01' (again, not the same device as prior to the initialization).

If server 1 issues a command to address x'00 00 EF', it will go to the wrong disk and potentially corrupt the data. To prevent this from happening, Exchange authentication is required before command execution is allowed to resume.

SCSI initiators perform Exchange authentication by sending the Discover Address (ADISC) Extended Link Service to each logged-in target (Discover N_Port Service Parameters (PDISC) may be used by some legacy implementations, but ADISC is recommended). The ADISC request and response both contain the port name and address of the sending port.

Upon receipt of the ADISC (or PDISC) request, the target authenticates its login session by verifying that the port name and address of the initiator match its current logged-in values. If the values match, LS_ACC is sent and command execution between that initiator and target can resume. If the values do not match, the authentication fails and the target sends either LS_RJT or LOGO depending on the class of service used for the request.

If a target does not receive ADISC (or PDISC) within RR_TOV (see *Resource Recovery Timeout Value (RR_TOV)* on page 567), it may logout the initiator and release resources currently dedicated to that initiator. Failure to receive ADISC or PDISC from an initiator can occur when the initiator is removed from the configuration or is unable to reacquire its prior address.

37.7.2 Public Loop Port Authentication

Public ports on an arbitrated loop perform a different authentication following loop initialization. This authentication uses the Fabric Address Notification (FAN) Extended Link Service (see *Fabric Address Notification (FAN)* on page 341).

Following loop initialization, the FL_Port will send FAN to all NL_Ports in the loop that have completed fabric login. The FAN contains the Port_Name, Fabric_Name, and address of the FL_Port. This enables the public NL_Port to verify it is still attached to the same FL_Port and fabric and that the address of the FL_Port hasn't changed. Until the FAN is received, public NL_Ports do not resume command execution.

If the public NL_Port is an initiator logged in with private targets in the loop, it initiates private NL_Port authentication after completion of FAN processing. This enables the initiator to verify that its address and login sessions are valid before performing authentication with the targets.

37.8 SCSI-FCP Timers

In addition to the E_D_TOV and R_A_TOV timers specified by Fibre Channel's FC-2 level, the FCP protocol mapping adds three timers unique to SCSI-FCP operations:

- Resource Recovery timeout value (RR_TOV)
- Read Exchange Concise (REC) timeout value (REC_TOV)
- ULP timeout value (ULP_TOV)

Table 203 on page 568 lists the default values for each timer and indicates support requirements for both SCSI initiators and targets for each timer.

37.8.1 Resource Recovery Timeout Value (RR_TOV)

The Resource Recovery timeout value (RR_TOV) specifies the minimum time a target must wait after arbitrated loop initialization or transfer of Sequence Initiative before it is permitted to free resources associated with an initiator. This can occur due to the following conditions:

- Following completion of arbitrated loop initialization (receipt of a CLS while in the OPEN-INIT state), some technical reports require Exchange authentication before resuming command execution (see *Exchange (Target) Authentication* on page 565).
- Following transfer of Sequence Initiative, a target fails to receive an expected initiator response.

If either of these conditions occurs and the expected action does not happen within RR_TOV, the target may implicitly or explicitly logout the initiator and reclaim any resources associated with the logged-out initiator.

The value of RR_TOV may be set using the Fibre Channel Port Control mode page (mode page x'19').

Timer	Description	Default Value		Mandatory or Optional	
		Priv. Loop	Pub. Loop	Initiator	Target
E_D_TOV	Error Detect timeout value	2 sec.	2 sec.	M	O (note 1)
R_A_TOV (note 2)	Resource Allocation timeout value				
	for timing reuse of Sequence qualifiers	0 sec.	10 sec.	M	O (note 1)
	for timing ELS responses	2 sec.	10 sec.	M	M
RR_TOV	Resource Recovery timeout value				
	Process Login (PRLI) RETRY bit set to 0	2 sec.	2 sec.	n/a	M
	Process Login (PRLI) RETRY bit set to 1	$\geq$ 3 times REC_TOV		n/a	M
REC_TOV	REC timeout value	$\geq$ E_D_TOV plus 1 sec.		M	M (note 3)
ULP_TOV	Upper-Level Protocol timeout value	$\geq$ operation-specific timer plus 4 times REC_TOV		M	n/a

1. Targets that support Class-2 service must support this timer.
2. R_A_TOV is defined by FC-FS. The values listed are default values for SCSI initiator and target devices. If ELSs are used to set R_A_TOV, the same value is used for both functions.
3. REC_TOV is required by the target for FCP_CONF error detection.

Table 203. SCSI-FCP Timers

37.8.2 Read Exchange Concise Timeout Value (REC_TOV)

There may be times when the state of an Exchange becomes ambiguous at an initiator or target. The Read Exchange Concise (REC) link service (see *Read Exchange Concise (REC)* on page 369) provides a mechanism to aid in determining the state of an Exchange.

Querying the state of an Exchange too frequently using REC may create unacceptable processing overhead in the other port and may result in Exchange timeouts. REC_TOV specifies a minimum interval that must elapse between transmission of a command and the first use of REC to query the state of the corresponding Exchange.

An initiator starts or restarts REC_TOV for an Exchange when any of the following events occur for that Exchange:

- The FCP_CMND Information Unit is sent to the target
- An FCP_DATA Information Unit is sent to the target
- Read Exchange Concise (REC) was sent and an LS_ACC response is received indicating that the Exchange is still in progress

The REC_TOV for the Exchange is stopped when FCP_RSP is received for the Exchange or the Exchange is aborted.

A target starts REC_TOV for an Exchange when it transmits an FCP_RSP with the FCP_CONF_REQ bit set to one. A target stops REC_TOV when it receives the FCP_CONF or the Exchange is aborted. If REC_TOV expires, the target may transmit an REC to determine if the FCP_RSP was received by the initiator.

37.8.3 Upper-Level Protocol Timeout Value (ULP_TOV)

The ULP_TOV is an operation-specific timer maintained by the upper-level protocol used to time completion of Exchanges associated with upper-level protocol operations (commands). Because the time required for a specific command is dependent on both the command and target device, FCP simply establishes a minimum time to ensure that the error recovery procedures can function correctly. This time is a minimum of four times REC_TOV plus the operation-specific time.

37.9 SCSI Mode Pages for Fibre Channel

SCSI mode pages provide a mechanism for an initiator to configure operational modes or parameters at target devices. The SCSI-FCP standard defines two new Fibre Channel-specific mode pages (x'18' and x'19') and modifies the interpretation of selected fields in the Disconnect-Reconnect mode page (x'02').

37.9.1 Disconnect-Reconnect Mode Page (x'02')

Table 204 on page 570 shows the format of the Disconnect-Reconnect mode page. Fibre Channel-specific fields are described following the table. If a field is not mentioned, the function is not affected by the Fibre Channel environment.

Bus Inactivity Limit. This field specifies the maximum time (measured in transmission words) a target is permitted to maintain an arbitrated loop circuit or Class-1 connection without transferring information.

Disconnect Time Limit. This field specifies the minimum delay (measured in increments of 128 transmission words) between arbitrated loop circuits or Class-1 connections.

Connect Time Limit. This field specifies the maximum duration (measured in increments of 128 transmission words) of an arbitrated loop circuit or Class-1 connection.

Maximum Burst Size. This field specifies the maximum size (expressed in increments of 512 bytes) of an FCP_DATA Information Unit. If this field is zero there is no limit on the size of an FCP_DATA Information Unit.

Enable Modify Data Pointers (EMDP). If this bit is set to zero, the target is required to generate continuously increasing relative offset for each FCP_DATA Information Unit in a single command. If this bit is set to zero, data overlay is prohibited, even if the 'Data Overlay Allowed' bit is set to one during Process Login (PRLI).

If the EMDP bit is set to one, the target may transfer FCP_DATA Information Units for a command in any order.

FAA, FAB, FAC. The fairness access bits specify whether a target in an arbitrated loop configuration is required to observe access fairness. When one of these bits is set to one, the target is required to observe access fairness for the corresponding frames. When set to zero, the target may choose to not observe access fairness for the corresponding frames.

Bit --> Byte	7	6	5	4	3	2	1	0
0	PS	reserved	Page Code (x'02')					
1	Page Length (x'0E')							
2	Buffer Full Ratio							
3	Buffer Empty Ratio							
4	(msb)	Bus Inactivity Limit						
5								(lsb)
6	(msb)	Disconnect Time Limit						
7								(lsb)
8	(msb)	Connect Time Limit						
9								(lsb)
10	(msb)	Maximum Burst Size						
11								(lsb)
12	EDMP	FAA	FAB	FAC	restricted	restricted		
13	reserved							
14	(msb)	First Burst Size						
14								(lsb)

Table 204. Disconnect-Reconnect Mode Page (x'02)

- **FAA** controls arbitration when the target wishes to send one or more FCP_DATA frames to an initiator.

- **FAB** controls arbitration when the target wishes to send one or more FCP_XFER_RDY frames to an initiator.

- **FAC** controls arbitration when the target wishes to send one or more FCP_RSP frames to an initiator.

If a target intends to send more than one type of frame during the subsequent loop circuit, it may choose not to observe access fairness if any of the applicable bits are zero.

First Burst Size. When FCP_XFER_RDY is disabled on write commands, this field specifies the maximum size (expressed in increments of 512 bytes) of the first FCP_DATA Information Unit. If this field is zero, there is no limit on the size of the first FCP_DATA Information Unit.

If all data associated with a command is transferred by the first FCP_DATA Information Unit, no FCP_XFER_RDY is transmitted by the target. If additional data remains to be transmitted, the target requests that data using one or more FCP_XFER_RDYs.

37.9.2 Fibre Channel Logical Unit Control Mode Page (x'18')

Table 205 shows the format of the Logical Unit Control mode page. All FCP devices are required to implement this page.

Bit --> Byte	7	6	5	4	3	2	1	0
0	PS	reserved	Page Code (x'18')					
1	Page Length (x'06')							
2	reserved				Protocol Identifier (FCP=b'0000')			
3	reserved							EPDC
4	reserved							
5	reserved							
6	reserved							
7	reserved							

Table 205. Fibre Channel Logical Unit Control Mode Page (x'18)

Enable Precise Delivery Checking (EPDC). When set to one, this bit indicates that the logical unit shall use the command reference number (CRN) to verify the delivery order of commands (see *Command Reference Number (CRN)* on page 558). When set to zero, the command reference number is ignored.

If this mode page is supported by the target and the command reference number is not supported, by the target this bit is masked as not changeable. If this mode page is not supported by a target, the initiator shall assume the command reference number (CRN) is not supported.

37.9.3 Fibre Channel Port Control Mode Page (x'19')

Table 206 on page 572 shows the format of the Fibre Channel Port Control mode page. This mode page is only implemented by LUN zero. Support for any bit and its associated function is optional.

Some bits in this mode page enable behaviors that violate the Fibre Channel arbitrated loop standard. These non-standard behaviors were deemed desirable in some environments.

Disable Target Originated Loop Initialization (DTOLI). When set to one, this bit specifies that an arbitrated loop attached target shall not generate a LIP following insertion into the loop. When set to zero, LIP is generated following insertion into the loop. In either case, the target must respond to received LIPs as specified in the arbitrated loop standard.

Disable Target Initiated Port Enable (DTIPE). When set to one, this bit specifies that an arbitrated loop attached target shall wait for an initiator to send Loop Port Enable (LPE) before inserting itself into the loop. If the target has a hard address available, it shall use that in recog-

Bit --> Byte	7	6	5	4	3	2	1	0
0	PS	reserved	Page Code (x'19')					
1	Page Length (x'06')							
2	reserved				Protocol Identifier (FCP=b'0000')			
3	DTFD	PLPB	DDIS	DLM	RHA	ALWI	DTIPE	DTOLI
4	reserved							
5	reserved							
6	reserved				RR_TOV Units			
7	Resource Recovery Timeout Value (RR_TOV)							

Table 206. Fibre Channel Port Control Mode Page (x'19)

nizing the LPE. If the target recognizes an LPE addressed to the broadcast address, it shall also recognize that.

When the DTIPE bit is set to zero, the target follows the rules specified in the arbitrated loop standard (FC-AL-2).

Allow Login Without Loop Initialization (ALWLI). When set to one, this bit specifies that an arbitrated loop attached target shall use the hard address provided, enter the monitoring state in a participating mode, and accept logins without using the loop initialization procedures.

When the ALWLI bit is set to zero, the target follows the rules specified in the arbitrated loop standard (FC-AL-2).

Require Hard Address (RHA). When set to one, this bit specifies that an arbitrated loop attached target shall only attempt to acquire the hard address provided. If the hard address cannot be obtained during loop initialization, the port shall be non-participating and not attempt to acquire a soft address.

When the RHA bit is set to zero, the target follows the rules specified in the arbitrated loop standard (FC-AL-2).

Disable Loop Master (DLM). When set to one, this bit specifies that an arbitrated loop attached target shall not attempt to become loop initialization master (LIM). When the DLM bit is set to zero, the target follows the rules specified in the arbitrated loop standard (FC-AL-2).

Disable Discovery (DDIS). When set to one, this bit specifies that an arbitrated loop attached target shall not wait for Exchange authentication (see *Exchange (Target) Authentication* on page 565) following arbitrated loop initialization and may resume command processing once initialization completes.

When the DDIS bit is set to one, the target waits for Exchange authentication before resuming command execution.

Prevent Loop Port Bypass (PLPB). When set to one, this bit specifies that an arbitrated loop attached target shall ignore all Loop Port Bypass (LPB) and Loop Port Enable (LPE) Primitive Sequences. When this bit is set to zero, the target follows the rules specified in the arbitrated loop standard (FC-AL-2).

DTIPE and PLPB can't both be set to one as this would prevent the port from ever entering the loop.

Disable Target Fabric Discovery (DTFD). When set to one, this bit specifies that an arbitrated loop attached target shall not recognize the presence of an FL_Port in the loop or perform Fabric Login (FLOGI). When this bit is set to zero, the target follows the rules specified in the arbitrated loop standard (FC-AL-2).

RR_TOV Units. This field specifies the time unit for the RR_TOV field as shown in Table 207.

Byte 6			Unit of Measure for RR_TOV
bit 2	bit 1	bit 0	
0	0	0	No timer is specified
0	0	1	0.001 seconds
0	1	1	0.1 seconds
1	0	1	10 seconds
All other values			Reserved

Table 207. RR_TOV Units

37.10 SCSI FCP Process Login

Much as SCSI mode pages allow an initiator to configure target behavior and parameters, process login allows an initiator and target to establish a session and configure their FCP behavior. Process login is performed when the initiator transmits a Process Login (PRLI) Extended Link Service request (see *Process Login (PRLI)* on page 360) to the target and is required before SCSI operations are accepted.

Process login is protocol specific. Each protocol using process login defines protocol-specific service parameters communicated during the PRLI request and response. The format of the SCSI-FCP information is shown in Figure 200 on page 574.

The process login session can be ended by a Process Logout (see *Process Logout (PRLO)* on page 364) or Third Party Process Logout (see *Third-Party Process Logout (TPRLO)* on page 398) Extended Link Service request or any action that causes a port logout to occur.

37.11 SCSI-FCP FC-4 Link Services

The SCSI-FCP FC-4 link services provide a set of SCSI FCP protocol-specific functions that can be used by an initiator to perform a specified function or service at a target.

Each FC-4 link service operation is performed using a separate Exchange. An FC-4 link service operation consists of a request Sequence with a transfer of Sequence Initiative and a re-

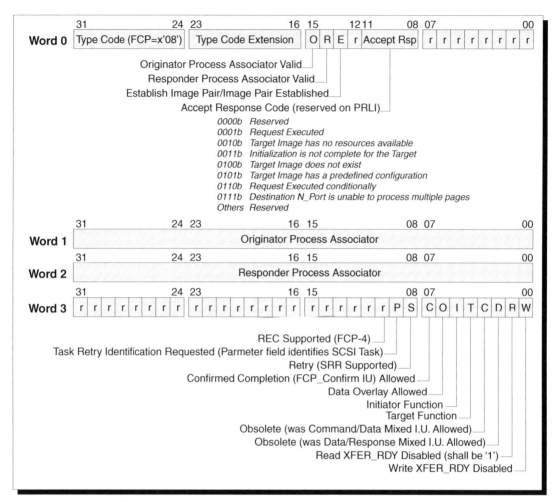

Figure 200. SCSI-FCP Process Login Payload

ply Sequence that ends the Exchange. Each Sequence consists of one or more frames and observes normal Sequence identification and management rules. An illustration of the FC-4 link service protocol operation is shown in Figure 201 on page 575.

- FC-4 link services may use any class of service that is available between the two ports and follow all the normal class of service and flow control rules defined for that class of service. The type field in the frame header is set to x'08' for both the FC-4 link service request and reply Sequences to specify the SCSI-FCP protocol.

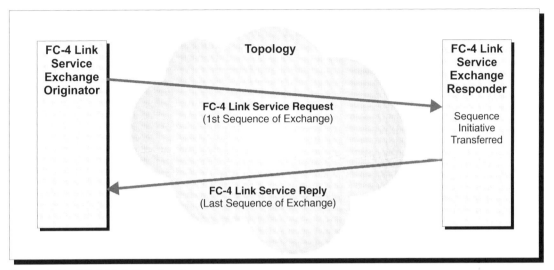

Figure 201. FC-4 Link Service Operation

37.11.1 FC-4 Link Service Request

- The R_CTL field in the frame header of the request Sequence is set to x'32' (FC-4 Link Data Frame, Unsolicited Control) to indicate a request Sequence.

- The First_Sequence of Exchange bit (F_CTL bit 21) is set to one, the Exchange Error Policy (F_CTL bits 5:4) are set to Abort, Discard Multiple (b'00'). Both FC-4 link services have expected reply Sequences and set the Last_Sequence of Exchange bit (F_CTL bit 20) to zero and transfer Sequence Initiative (F_CTL bit 16 is set to a one).

- The parameter field of the frame header may be set to the task retry identifier supplied in the FCP command for the associated Exchange.

- The first byte of the FC-4 link service request Sequence payload contains the FC-4 link service command. The remaining three bytes of the first word contain command-specific parameters as defined by the specific FC-4 link service request.

37.11.2 FC-4 Link Service Reply

FC-4 link service Accept (FC-4_ACC) indicates completion of the FC-4 link service request and provides any applicable information associated with the FC-4 link service command request. FC-4 link service reject (FC-4_RJT) indicates the request was not accepted and provides a reason code and explanation.

- The R_CTL field in the frame header of the reply Sequence is set to x'33' (FC-4 Link Data Frame, Solicited Control) to indicate a reply Sequence.

- The Last_Sequence of Exchange bit in the F_CTL field (bit 20) is set to one. The setting of the Sequence Initiative bit is not defined.

- The first word of the FC-4 link service reply payload indicates whether the request was accepted (FC-4_ACC) or rejected (FC-4_RJT). The remaining three bytes of this word contain command-specific parameters defined by the specific FC-4 link service request.

37.11.3 Sequence Retransmission Request (SRR)

Sequence Retransmission Request (SRR) requests retransmission of all Sequences for the designated Exchange beginning with the specified Information Unit and relative offset.

The Exchange is specified by the OX_ID and RX_ID values supplied in the request. The first Sequence to be retransmitted is indicated by specifying the R_CTL value corresponding to that Sequence (word 3, bits 31:24 of the payload). The relative offset, if any, of the retransmission request is specified in the Relative Offset field (word 2, bits 31:0).

The SRR recipient begins retransmission with the indicated Sequence at the relative offset specified or a relative offset of lesser value chosen by the SRR recipient. The SRR recipient may back up further than requested, if necessary. SRR implicitly transfers Sequence Initiative for the designated Exchange.

Sequence Retransmission Request (SRR) Request. The format of the SRR FC-4 link service request is shown in Table 208,

Word	Bits 31-24	Bits 23-16	Bits 15-8	Bits 7-0
0	Command = x'14'	x'00'	x'00'	x'00'
1	OX_ID of Exchange for which retransmission is being requested))		RX_ID (of Exchange for which retransmission is being requested)	
2	Relative Offset (requested starting offset of retransmission)			
3	R_CTL (for I.U. to be retransmitted)	Reserved		

Table 208. Sequence Retransmission Request (SRR) Request

Sequence Retransmission Request (SRR) Reply. The SRR accept is shown in Table 209. If the SRR recipient is unable to accept the request, it may return FC-4_RJT with a reason code of x'05' (Logical Busy) and an explanation of x'2A' (Unable to Supply Requested Data).

Word	Bits 31-24	Bits 23-16	Bits 15-8	Bits 7-0
0	FC-4 Accept = x'02'	x'00'	x'00'	x'00'

Table 209. Sequence Retransmission Request (SRR) Accept Reply

37.12 FCP Error Recovery Examples

The SCSI-FCP protocol mapping specifies use of the "Abort, discard multiple Sequences" Exchange error policy. If an error occurs, the initiator aborts the failed Sequence using the ABTS Basic Link Service (see *Abort Sequence (ABTS)* on page 311). Following transmission of ABTS, the initiator discards any frames or ACKs received for that Exchange.

The target responds to ABTS with BA_ACC with Last_Sequence set in the F_CTL field of the frame header (ABTS-LS). After transmitting BA_ACC, the target also discards any frames or ACKs received for the Exchange.

After waiting R_A_TOV for frames in transit to be delivered and discarded, the initiator transmits Reinstate Recovery Qualifier (RRQ) to end frame discarding for the aborted Exchange.

Figure 202 shows an example of basic error recovery during a write command. If any Sequence of the Exchange has an error, subsequent Sequences are not sent and the SCSI command timer expires while awaiting command completion.

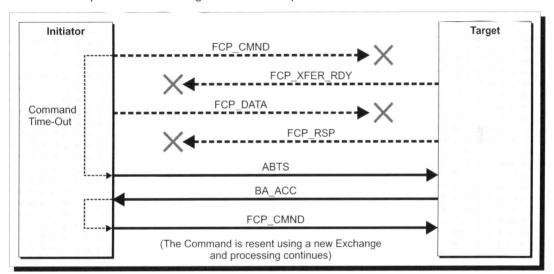

Figure 202. FCP Basic Error Recovery — Any Information Unit Lost

Aborting failed Exchanges may result in undesirable side effects for devices such as tape because aborting an Exchange usually causes the drive to stop tape movement. Before retrying a failed operation, the position of the media must be determined and any necessary repositioning performed.

Enhanced error recovery techniques may allow an initiator and target to recover from a Sequence error without aborting the entire Exchange. Enhanced error recovery uses the Read Exchange Concise (REC) extended link service and Sequence Retransmission Request (SRR) FC-4 link services described earlier. Some examples of enhanced error recovery are shown in the following sections.

37.12.1 FCP Command Lost

In the example shown in Figure 203 on page 578, the FCP_CMND is lost due to an error. After waiting REC_TOV, the initiator may poll the status of the command using the Read Exchange Concise (REC) extended link service. In this case, the LS_RJT response indicates the Exchange is unknown at the target.

The initiator performs recovery from the lost command by retransmitting the FCP_CMND in a new Exchange using the same command reference number and class of service.

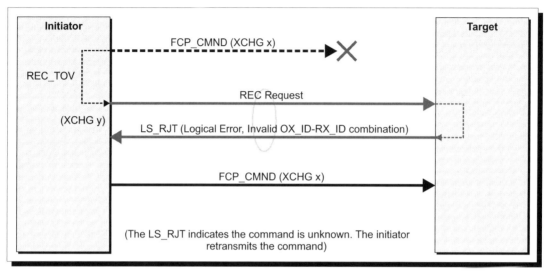

Figure 203. Enhanced Error Recovery — FCP_CMND Lost

37.12.2 FCP Response Lost

In the example shown in Figure 204, the FCP_RSP is lost due to an error. After a minimum interval of REC_TOV, the initiator may poll the status of the command using the Read Exchange Concise (REC) extended link service. In this case, the LS_ACC response indicates the Exchange is complete and the initiator holds the Sequence Initiative.

The initiator performs recovery by transmitting a Sequence Retransmission Request (SRR) FC-4 Link Service asking for retransmission of the FCP_RSP Information Unit (IC=x'07'). If the target is capable of retransmitting the FCP_RSP, the SRR request is accepted and the target retransmits the FCP_RSP completing the recovery.

If the target is unable to retransmit the FCP_RSP, the SRR is rejected and the initiator aborts the Exchange. Recovery is performed by reissuing the command in a new Exchange following any necessary clean-up activity.

37.12.3 FCP Read Data Lost

In the example shown in Figure 205, the last frame of a read FCP_DATA is lost due to an error. Because this example assumes Class-3 service, the target is unaware of the error and transmits FCP_RSP containing the SCSI status (even in an acknowledged class of service, the target may send the FCP_RSP without waiting for ACK to the data frames).

When the initiator receives FCP_RSP, it knows the data Sequence is incomplete. If the topology or class of service guarantees in-order delivery of frames, the initiator knows an error has occurred. If in-order delivery is not guaranteed, the data frame may simply be delayed.

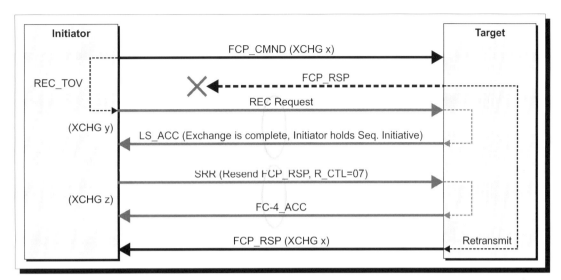

Figure 204. Enhanced Error Recovery — FCP_RSP Lost

After waiting REC_TOV, the initiator may poll the status of the command using the Read Exchange Concise (REC) extended link service. In this case, the LS_ACC response indicates the Exchange is complete and the initiator holds the Sequence Initiative. However, the initiator knows the data Sequence is incomplete and an error has occurred.

The initiator performs recovery by transmitting a Sequence Retransmission Request (SRR) FC-4 link service asking for retransmission of the FCP_DATA Information Unit (IC=x'01'). The SRR request is accepted and the target retransmits the FCP_DATA and FCP_RSP using new Sequences completing the error recovery.

37.12.4 FCP Transfer Ready Lost

In the example shown in Figure 206, the FCP_XFER_RDY is lost due to an error. After a minimum interval of REC_TOV, the initiator may poll the status of the command using the Read Exchange Concise (REC) extended link service. In this case, the LS_ACC response indicates the Exchange is open and the initiator holds the Sequence Initiative.

The initiator performs recovery by transmitting a Sequence Retransmission Request (SRR) asking for retransmission of the FCP_XFER_RDY Information Unit (IC=x'05'). The SRR request is accepted and the target retransmits the FCP_XFER_RDY in a new Sequence (new SEQ_ID) and command execution continues.

37.12.5 FCP Write Data Lost

In Figure 207 on page 581, a write FCP_DATA frame is lost due to an error (in this example, it is the last frame of the Sequence). After a minimum interval of REC_TOV, the initiator may poll the status of the command using the Read Exchange Concise (REC) extended link service. In

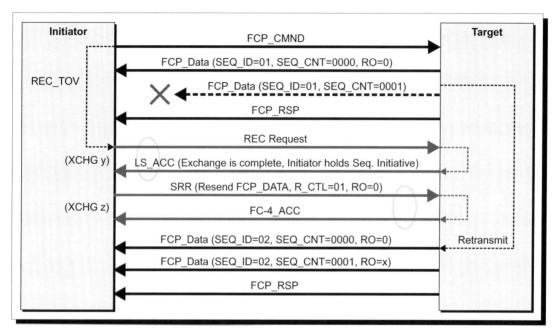

Figure 205. Enhanced Error Recovery — Read FCP_Data Frame Lost

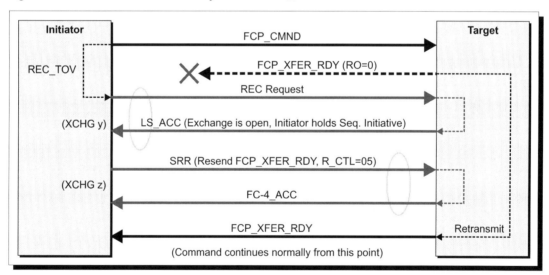

Figure 206. Enhanced Error Recovery — FCP_XFER_RDY Lost

this case, the LS_ACC response indicates the Exchange is open and the initiator holds the Sequence Initiative.

The initiator performs recovery by sending a Sequence Retransmission Request (SRR) asking for retransmission of the FCP_XFER_RDY Information Unit (IC=05) beginning with the relative offset associated with the failed data Sequence. The SRR request is accepted and the target retransmits the FCP_XFER_RDY in a new Sequence (new SEQ_ID), the initiator retransmits the failed FCP_DATA Sequence in a new Sequence and command execution continues.

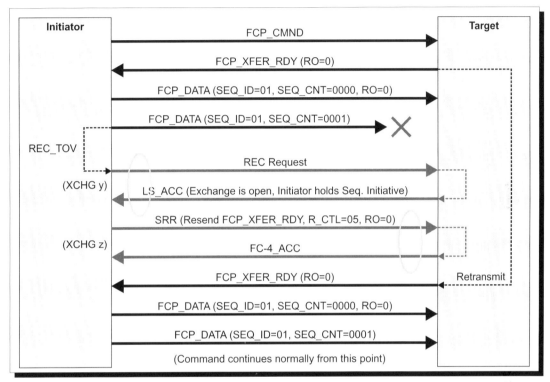

Figure 207. Enhanced Error Recovery — Write FCP_DATA Frame Lost

37.13 SCSI-FCP Read Command Trace

Figure 208 shows a trace of the beginning of a SCSI-FCP read operation.

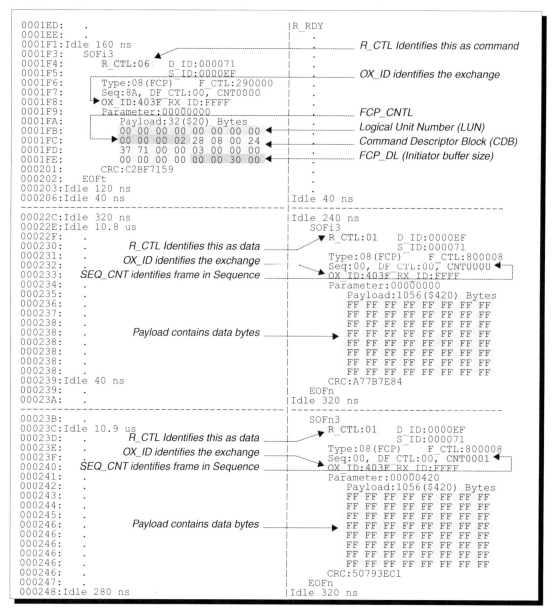

Figure 208. SCSI FCP Read Command Trace (part 1)

Figure 209 shows the completion of the SCSI-FCP read operation beginning with the eleventh frame of the read data transfer. *(Note: this trace should be used for informational purposes only and not as the basis of an implementation).*

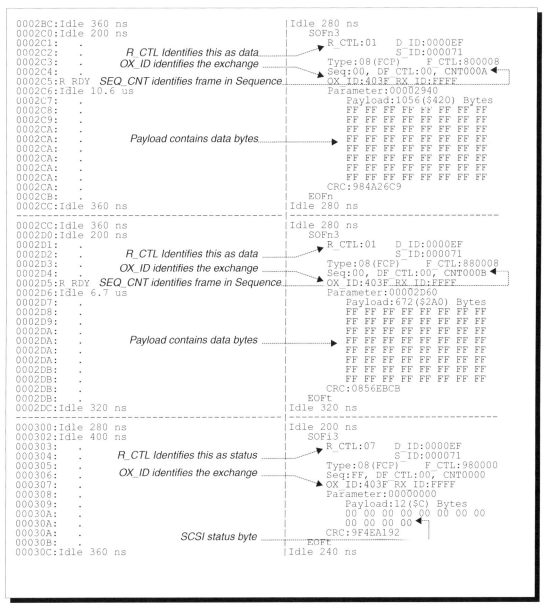

Figure 209. SCSI FCP Read Command Trace (part 2)

37.14 SCSI-FCP Write Command Trace

Figure 210 shows a trace of the beginning of a SCSI-FCP write operation.

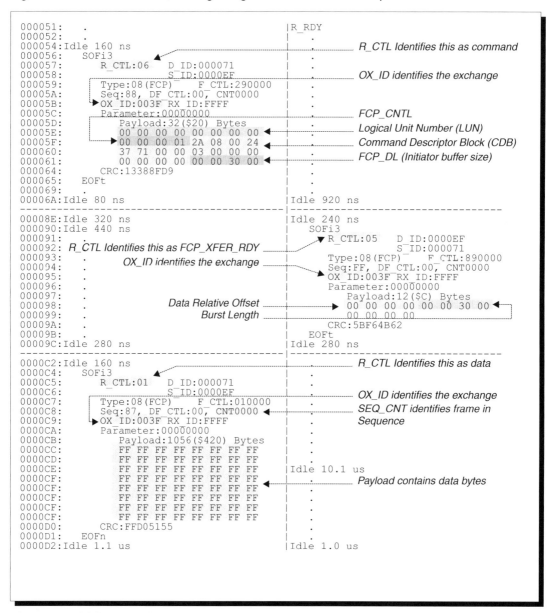

Figure 210. SCSI FCP Write Command Trace (part 1)

Figure 211 shows the completion of the SCSI-FCP write operation beginning with the eleventh frame of the data transfer. *(Note: this trace should be used for informational purposes only and not as the basis of an implementation).*

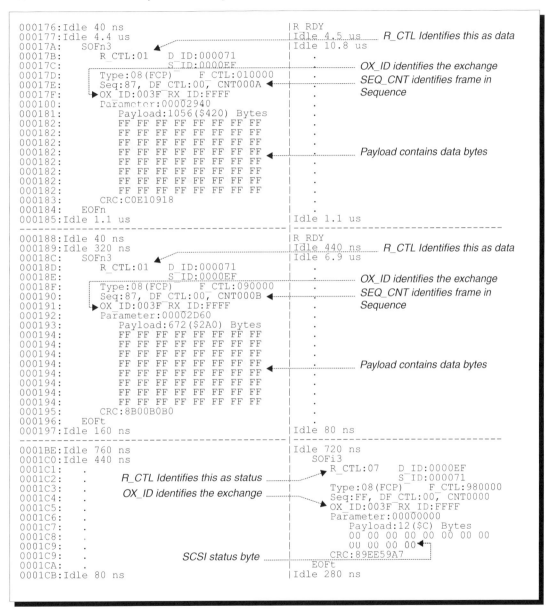

Figure 211. SCSI FCP Write Command Trace (part 2)

37.15 Chapter Summary

SCSI-3 Introduction

- SCSI-3 is widely used open-system peripheral device interface
  - Provides a rich set of commands for many types of peripheral devices
  - Can use the SCSI bus or serial interfaces such as Fibre Channel
- The SCSI bus provides a high-speed interface for modest size configurations
  - Ultra-2 wide (80 MB/sec.)
  - Ultra-3 wide (160 MB/sec.)
  - Ultra-320 wide (320 MB/sec.)
- However, distances and connectivity are limited
  - 12 meters maximum distance (LVD)
  - 16 devices maximum per bus

SCSI-3 Architecture

- SCSI-3 is a multi-level architecture
  - Upper level defines the command architecture and command sets
  - Middle level defines the protocol used to send SCSI commands across the lower level
  - Lower level defines the physical interface
- Many different physical interfaces and associated transport protocols are supported
  - SCSI bus and the SCSI Interlocked Protocol
  - Fibre Channel and the SCSI Fibre Channel Protocol (FCP)
  - Internet and iSCSI

Layered Architecture Benefits

- Multi-level approach allows SCSI commands to be sent over a variety of interfaces
  - Each with its own unique characteristics; speed, distance, number of devices
- Command sets and command behavior remains the same
  - Same device class driver (tape and disk), regardless of interface
  - This helps preserve the existing investment in software

SCSI Configuration

- Many different configurations are possible, but all consist of three key elements
- One or more initiators that originate commands to targets:
  - Server, workstation, RAID controller, etc.
- One or more targets that respond to commands from initiators:
  - Disk drive, tape drive, printer, etc.
- An interconnection interface that connects the devices:
  - SCSI bus, Fibre Channel, the Internet, etc.

Identification and Addressing

- More that one initiator and target may exist in a configuration
- Must have a way to identify each
  - May use an interface-specific identifier such as the SCSI_ID or Fibre Channel N_Port ID
  - May use other identifiers such as Fibre Channel names or Internet Uniform Resource Locators (URLs)
- Each target controls one or more logical units
  - May be physically part of the target or may be attached to the target
  - Logical unit has a Logical Unit Number (LUN)
  - LUN zero is required of all targets

Command Queueing

- Some initiators and targets only allow one command active at a time
- Others allow multiple commands to be in progress between the initiator and target
  - Target places the commands in a queue called the task set
  - Executes commands from the task set as conditions allow
  - Must provide a way to identify ("tag") each command

Task Attribute (Queue Type)

- A task attribute (queue type) is associated with each queued command
- Defines how the target should handle the command
  - Ordered Queue: preserve the command execution order
  - Simple Queue: target may reorder the commands for efficiency
  - Head of Queue: place this command at the head of the queue
  - ACA Queue: Used during error recovery
- Give the initiator control on a per-command basis

Command Multiplexing

- Many commands have periods of inactivity
  - Disk drive is seeking, reading, or writing data to the disk
- When the interface is shared with other devices, relinquishing the interface may improve efficiency
  - Must save the state of the current operation, then relinquish the interface
  - When ready to resume, must re-acquire the interface and restore the state of the operation before continuing

The SCSI Nexus

- Any SCSI command in the configuration can be uniquely identified by:
  - The Initiator that originated the command
  - The Target and Logical Unit that received the command
  - The Queue tag assigned to the command, if command queueing is used
- This is referred to as the **ITL** or **ITLQ** nexus
- The nexus is used when it is necessary to identify a specific operation
  - For example, when resuming an interrupted operation

Command Descriptor Block (CDB)

- The CDB contains the SCSI command and related parameters to tell the target which operation to perform
- Different groups of commands transfer different amounts of command-specific parameters
  - CDBs come in different sizes (6, 10, 12, 16 bytes, and new variable length CDBs)
  - First three bits of the of the first byte of the (the group code) identify the size of the CDB
- Middle bytes of the CDB contain command-specific parameters
- Last byte of the CDB (the control byte) contains control information

SCSI Data Transfer

- When an initiator issues a command that transfers data it allocates a buffer to hold the data
- The target accesses the data buffer during data transfer
  - Requests data from the buffer (data-out)
  - Sends data to the buffer (data-in)
- Target is not aware of memory addresses or locations
  - It identifies the command using the ITL or ITLQ nexus
  - Supplies an "offset" (data pointer) into the buffer

Multi-Segment Transfers

- The target is not required to transfer all the data in a single action
  - It may break the data transfer into multiple segments (data requests)
  - This may be necessary due to the amount of buffering available in the target
  - Each data request begins at a provided offset and transfers a specific amount of data
- Normally, each segment begins with the byte following the end of the prior segment
  - Referred to as sequential data transfer
  - Although not common, it could begin with a non-sequential byte

SCSI Status Byte

- Every SCSI command returns one byte of status
  - Status indicates the type of command completion
  - x'00' = Good
  - x'02' = Check Condition
  - x'08' = Busy, etc.
- If an error or alert occurs, status indicates a check condition occurred
  - May indicate the command could not be accepted
  - May indicate an error occurred during command execution

Sense Information

- When a check condition occurs, the target creates sense information
  - Provides detailed information about the error event
  - May be used for error recovery or logging
- Sense data may be transferred to the initiator
  - In response to a Request Sense command (normal behavior on the SCSI bus)
  - Automatically, when the status is sent (this is the normal behavior in Fibre Channel and is referred to as autosense)
  - As an Asynchronous Event Report (not common)

Task Management Functions

- SCSI provides several task management functions
  - Used to manage tasks in the task set
  - Abort or terminate task(s)
- Scope of action depends on the function
  - May affect a single task
  - May affect all tasks in the LUN for a single initiator
  - May affect all tasks in the LUN for all initiators
- Task management functions are not commands
  - Request is not made using a CDB
  - The response is not status

SCSI-3 Task Management

- Abort Task
  - Abort the specified task (ITL or ITLQ)
  - Abort Tag message of the parallel bus
  - Mandatory
- Abort Task Set
  - Abort all tasks for the issuing initiator (ITL)
  - Abort Queue message on the parallel bus
  - Mandatory
- Clear Task Set
  - Abort all tasks for all initiators (TL)
  - Clear Queue message on the parallel bus
  - Mandatory if Tagged tasks supported

SCSI-3 Task Management

- Target Reset (Target ID)
  - Reset the target, set Unit Attention
  - Mandatory function
- Reset LUN (TL)
  - New addition to SCSI-3 Architecture
- Terminate Task (obsolete)
  - Terminates the specified task (ITL or ITLQ)
  - Command Terminated status is returned
  - Optional function, being obsoleted
- Clear Auto Contingent Allegiance condition for the LUN
  - Mandatory if LUN supports ACA, optional otherwise

SCSI FCP Basics

- The SCSI Fibre Channel protocol mapping was done by the NCITS SCSI committee (T10)
  - Part of the work to extend SCSI commands to other physical interfaces
- 1st generation mapping (FCP) approved in 1996
  - Provided basic functionality for implementing SCSI commands over Fibre Channel
- 2nd generation mapping (FCP) is in the final stages of approval
  - Enhances the functionality provided in FCP
  - Provides enhanced error recovery capabilities
  - Removes unnecessary features that had not been implemented

FCP Use of the Exchange

- Each SCSI-3 task maps to an Exchange
  - The task is a single command or a group of linked commands
- Initiator must assign an Originator Exchange_ID
  - Must be a unique value at that initiator other than x'FFFF'
  - The OX_ID replaces the Queue tag used on the SCSI parallel bus
- Target may assign a Responder Exchange_ID
  - An RX_ID may help the target manage open Exchanges
  - Eliminates the need to index on the initiator's S_ID and OX_ID
  - Target uses x'FFFF' if no RX_ID is assigned

Classes of Service

- Class-1 and Class-2 are supported in all topologies
- Class-3
  - Initially supported on Private Arbitrated Loops
  - Allowed in fabrics that guarantee in-order delivery of frames
  - Now the most common class used for SCSI operations over Fibre Channel

Information Sets

- Four different information sets (payloads) are defined
- FCP_CMND (R_CTL=06)
  - Transports a command or task management function
- FCP_XFER_RDY (R_CTL=05)
  - Used by the target to request data from an initiator on write-type commands
- FCP_DATA (R_CTL=01)
  - Transports data (all types) between the initiator and target
- FCP_RSP (R_CTL=07)
  - Transports the SCSI status, Autosense (when present) and FC-4 Response codes

FCP Information Unit Tables

- FCP defines both mandatory and optional Information Units (IUs)
  - Mandatory Information Units implement basic functionality with one information set per IU
  - Optional Information Units support advanced features
- Linking is supported via optional Information Units
- Multiple information sets per IU were supported via optional IUs (obsoleted by FCP)
  - Combined command and data-out
  - Combined data-in and response (status)

SCSI-FCP With Linking

- When linking is supported, additional Information Units are required
  - There is now a command that is not First in the Exchange
  - And a status that is not Last
- The T3 Information Unit allows a command to be issued within an existing Exchange
  - T3 would also be used if the Terminate Task function is supported
- The I5 Information Unit allows the target to send status without ending the Exchange

Task Management Functions

- Task management functions use the same Information Units as commands
  - A task management operation looks like a control-type command
- T1 and T3 are used to send the request to the target
  - T1 to send all except Abort Task and Terminate Task
  - T3 to send a Terminate Task request
  - When any Task Management bit is set in T1 or T3, the command-related fields are ignored
- I4 is used to send the Task Management response in the FCP_RSP_CODE field

Precise Delivery Order

- Some devices must ensure the order of command execution is maintained
  - Tape, media changers, other "stateful" devices
- Fibre Channel does not inherently guarantee the delivery order of commands
  - Commands may be lost due to errors
  - Switched fabric topology may deliver commands out of order in Classes 2 and 3
- Could ensure the correct order operationally
  - Issue one command, wait for status, then issue the next command
- Or, use the FCP Command Reference Number (CRN)

Command Reference Number (CRN)

- The command reference number provides a way to detect lost or mis-ordered commands
  - Uses a formerly unused byte (word 2, byte 0) in the FCP CMND information set
- Command reference number values:
  - Zero indicates command reference numbering is not being used
  - 1 to 255 indicates the order of commands from a given initiator to a logical unit (ITL)
  - Count can wrap back to one if delivery of previous usage has been confirmed
- Task management requests use a value of zero

Confirmed Completion

- Sometimes, the logical unit requires delivery confirmation of the FCP_RSP
  - Typically occurs when the FCP_RSP contains sense information
  - Logical unit needs to know the sense information was delivered before resetting it
  - When using Class-3, there is no acknowledge
- FCP_CONF provides the confirmation
  - Logical unit requests FCP_CONF when it sends the FCP_RSP
  - Sets FCP_CON_REQ bit in the response
  - Initiator sends FCP_CONF upon receipt of the FCP_RSP

Data Retransmission

- If the initiator detects an error during data transmission, it may request retransmission
  - Function must be supported by both the initiator and logical unit
  - Discovered during Process Login (PRLI)
- Initiator requests retransmission with Sequence Retransmission Request (SRR)
  - SRR is an FC-4 Link Service
  - Contains the IU information category and offset
- Logical unit begins retransmission with the specified IU and offset
  - If the logical unit is unable to retransmit the data, it may reply with FCP_RJT

Task Retry Identification

- During error recovery, task identification may become ambiguous
  - Logical unit is holding FCP_RSP for possible retransmission
  - Initiator received the FCP_RSP and sent FCP_CONF (but has not yet been received)
  - Original Exchange is complete at the initiator but still open at the logical unit
- Initiator now originates a new Exchange with the same OX_ID as one still open at the logical unit
  - If the new command fails, ambiguity exists during recovery because of duplicate OX_IDs

Task Retry Identification

- Devices that support task retry should support Task Retry Identification to prevent ambiguity
  - The parameter field of FCP_CMND contains a 32-bit value that is unique to this task
- Used by recovery FC-4 Link Services to identify the task (also in the Parameter field)
  - Read Exchange Concise (REC)
  - Sequence Retransmission Request (SRR)
- Ensures that the REC and SRR are associated with the correct Exchange

38. IP Over Fibre Channel (IPFC)

Like most networks, Fibre Channel uses a layered structure. While the Fibre Channel levels do not correspond directly to the layers defined by other protocols, it may be helpful to review the OSI seven-layer reference model and compare it to Fibre Channel's levels.

38.1 OSI Reference Model

The Open Systems Interconnection (OSI) Reference Model provides a basis for understanding layered network architectures. This model defines a seven-layer structure that provides a basis for the architecture and implementation of open systems networks as shown in Figure 212.

Examining existing I/O interfaces in light of this layered model may prove to be enlightening and aid in understanding networked storage. Most existing I/O interfaces provide only the lower three layers of this structure.

Each layer in this structure logically communicates with the corresponding layer in the other device. The application layer in one device logically communicates with the application layer in another device, the data link layer in one device communicates with the data link layer in the other device, etc. While this structure provides a basis for the logical functions communications associated with each layer, all physical communications takes place only at the lowest layer, the physical interface.

OSI Layer 1: Physical. The physical layer manages transmission and reception of bits between two entities. It specifies the signaling rates, transmitter and receiver characteristics, distance capabilities, transmission error rates, and cable and connector characteristics.

OSI Layer 2: Datalink. The data link layer defines the transmission coding schemes, frames and link protocols used to send information between entities and verify the validity of received frames. This layer also defines link-level addresses used to determine the intended recipient of transmitted frames.

When multiple nodes are attached to a shared medium, the data link layer specifies the mechanism used to provide media access control. Some common approaches include Carrier Sense Multiple Access/Collision Detect (CSMA/CD), token passing, or arbitration.

The IEEE family of networks divides layer-2 into two separate sub-layers; the media access control (MAC) layer and the Logical Link Control (LLC) layer.

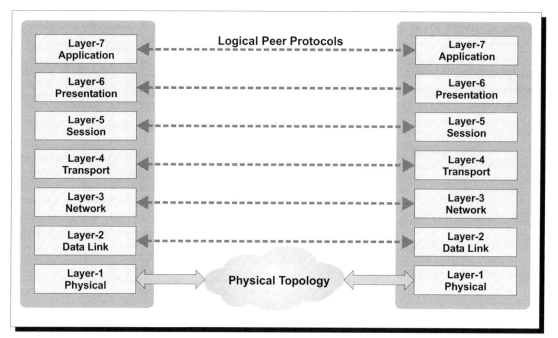

Figure 212. OSI Reference Model

OSI Layer 3: Network. The primary function of the network layer is to allow multiple data links to be aggregated into a network for transferring frames between end points. Probably the prime example of a network protocol is the Internet Protocol, IP.

The network layer may provide its own network-wide addressing scheme in addition to the addressing provided by the data link in layer 2. This allows information to be routed among networks using different data link addressing schemes.

The network layer may also provide segmentation and reassembly services, making the unit of information transfer at the network layer independent of the data link frame size.

OSI Layer 4: Transport. The purpose of the transport layer is to enable reliable data transport by providing flow control, acknowledgment, multiplexing different application data streams to the same data link, and error detection and control.

The Transmission Control Protocol (TCP) is an example of a transport protocol. It implements flow control through a sliding window process, provides acknowledgements, supports the multiplexing of different application data streams to the same data link, and performs retransmissions when necessary.

The User Datagram Protocol (UDP) is another example of a transport protocol. UDP provides multiplexing of different application data streams to the same data link but does not provide flow control or error recovery. UDP is typically used when applications can live with frame loss, or provide their own flow control and error handling.

OSI Layer 5: Session. The session layer is responsible for establishing and terminating sessions between entities.

OSI Layer 6: Presentation. The presentation layer deals with the data being transferred within the network by hiding data representation issues such as bit-ordering, bit-endian vs. little endian, and code sets such as ASCII.

OSI Layer 7: Application. The application layer represents the application using the network services. Some examples of network applications are file transfer using the File Transfer Protocol (FTP), email using the Simple Mail Transfer Protocol (SMTP), network management using the Simple Network Management Protocol (SNMP).

38.1.1 Encapsulation

In the OSI model, as data is passed from a higher layer to a lower layer for processing, the lower layer adds its own layer-specific header to the data passed to it, encapsulating information from the next higher level. When a data unit is passed from a lower layer to a higher layer, the layer-specific header is removed. An illustration of this successive encapsulation and decapsulation is shown in Figure 213.

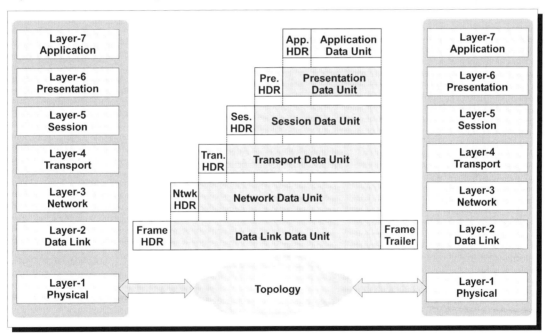

Figure 213. Data Unit Encapsulation

Each layer is only aware of its layer-specific header and has no visibility to the lower-layer headers that are added when the data unit is processed by the lower layer or removed before the data unit is passed up to this layer. A layer does not interpret the higher-layer's data unit. All information needed by each layer in its layer-specific header.

38.2 Fibre Channel Levels vs. OSI Layers

In the OSI reference model, Fibre Channel corresponds primarily into the data link (layer 2) and physical layers (layer 1). This relationship is shown in Figure 214.

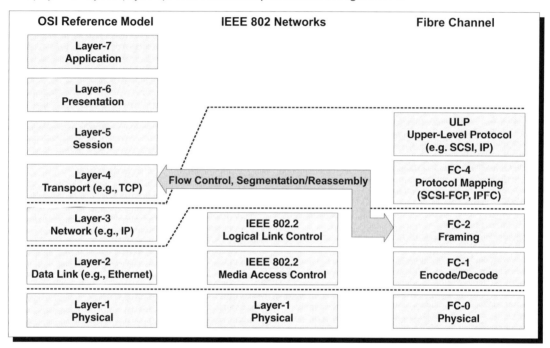

Figure 214. Fibre Channel Levels vs. OSI Layers

From this figure, it can be seen that there is a direct correspondence between Fibre Channel's FC-0 and Layer 1 as both define physical interface characteristics.

Fibre Channel's FC-1 and FC-2 correspond to layer 2 to and provide all the functions associated with layer 2 data links. In addition, Fibre Channel's FC-2 provides functions more commonly associated with layer 4 such as flow control and segmentation and reassembly.

Within a single Fibre Channel network, frames can be routed from one node port to any other node port in the network using the addresses in the frame header. Therefore, Fibre Channel is a routable network and does not require the network addressing provided by OSI layer 3. If inter-networking between Fibre Channel networks and non-Fibre Channel networks is desired, then layer 3 addressing is required to provide inter-network addressing. This would typically be accomplished by using the Internet Protocol (IP over Fibre Channel) as the network protocol.

Fibre Channel's FC-4 maps various upper-level protocols (ULPs) to the Fibre Channel interface, among them the SCSI command protocol and the Internet Protocol (IP). In the OSI reference model, the Internet Protocol is a layer 3 protocol. Therefore, Fibre Channel's FC-4 and associated ULPs correspond to layer 3 in the OSI model.

38.3 Internet Protocol (IP)

The Internet Protocol (IP) was developed to provide a common inter-networking protocol for communicating between computing systems across different types of physical networks. The original goal was to provide a network-independent protocol that could be implemented on a wide variety of platforms.

The Internet suite initially defined four applications, and their associated protocols for file transfer (FTP), electronic mail (Simple Mail Transfer Protocol, SMTP), terminal emulation (TELNET), and network management (Simple Network Management Protocol, SNMP). More recently, the graphics-based HyperText Transfer Protocol (HTTP) has been added to support Worldwide Web applications.

The Transmission Control Protocol (TCP) provides a reliable data delivery service by providing delivery confirmation and flow control of the higher-layer data units. The User Datagram Protocol (UDP) provides a best-effort delivery datagram service.

The combination of user applications and a network independent protocol have made the Internet suite the most widely used inter-networking protocol ever developed. A diagram of the Internet Protocol suite is shown in Figure 215.

In the Internet model, the network layer data units (IP datagrams, ARP and Reverse ARP requests, and ICMP messages) can be transported over a wide variety of data link types (e.g. Ethernet, Token Ring, Fibre Channel). The network layer data units are encapsulated in the data link frame for transmission.

The maximum size of the IP datagram (including the IP header) is 65,535 octets. This is due to the use of a 16-bit length field in the IP header. However, in most networks, the size of the IP datagram is limited to correspond to the size of the network data length frame. In an Ethernet environment, this is on the order of 1536 bytes, in an FDDI network 4500 bytes. As a result, a maximum-sized IP datagram may have to be fragmented into multiple data link frames based on the network capability. This fragmentation is normally done by the software driver associated with the port and can impose a significant processing overhead at both the sending and receiving ports.

The Internet Protocol was designed to use a 32-bit IP address that is unique within the domain of the Internet. Due to the rapid growth of the Internet, the 32-bit address space is rapidly being exhausted and may not be sufficient to accommodate future growth. To address this, the Internet Engineering Task Force (the steering body for the Internet) has recently adopted a 128-bit address for use in IP version 6 (IPv6).

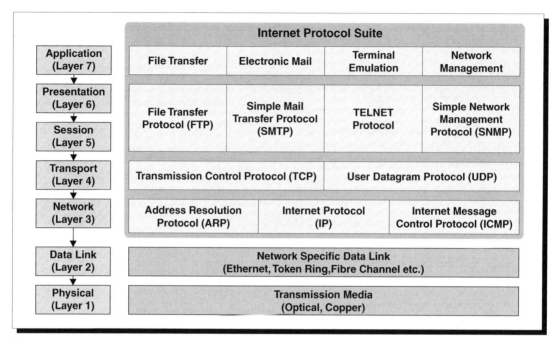

Figure 215. Internet Protocol Suite

38.4 IP Over Fibre Channel Concepts

Mapping the Internet Protocol (IP) to Fibre Channel was done by the Internet Engineering Task Force (IETF) in RFC 4338. IETF is the standards body responsible for Internet related protocols and functions.

RFC-2625 defines a method to encapsulate Internet Protocol datagrams (with IEEE 802.2 Logical Link control and SNAP headers) in Fibre Channel Information Units (that are then delivered using Sequences of frames). In this mapping, Fibre Channel is viewed as just another data link (layer 2) for transporting the IP datagrams.

38.4.1 IP over FC Information Unit

Only one Information Unit is used for transporting IP-related protocols over Fibre Channel. It consists of an IP or ARP datagram or ICMP message preceded by IEEE 802.2 Logical Link Control (LLC) and SNAP headers (set to fixed values). The format of a Fibre Channel frame containing an IP datagram is shown in Table 210 on page 597.

- R_CTL is set to x'04': FC-4 device data frame, information category of unsolicited data.

- The Type field is set to x'05' to indicate IEEE 802.2 LLS/SNAP Encapsulation (Unordered).

	Word	Bits 31-24	Bits 23-16	Bits 15-8	Bits 7-0
Frame Header	0	R_CTL = x'04'	Destination_ID (D_ID)		
	1	CS_CTL = x'00'	Source_ID (S_ID)		
	2	Type = x'05'	Frame_Control (F_CTL)		
	3	SEQ_ID	DF_CTL = x'20'	SEQ_CNT	
	4	OX_ID		RX_ID	
	5	Parameter			
Network Header	0	NΛΛ = x'1'	x'000' (12 bits)	Destination MAC (2 most significant bytes)	
	1	Destination MAC (4 least significant bytes)			
	2	NAA = x'1'	x'000' (12 bits)	Source MAC (2 most significant bytes)	
	3	Source (4 least significant bytes)			
LLC Header	4	DSAP = x'AA'	SSAP = x'AA'	Control = x'03'	Org Code = x'00'
	5	Org Code (continued) = x'00 00'		Ethertype = x'08 00' (IP) or x'08 06' (ARP)	
IP Datagram	6	Remaining IP Data			
	n				

Table 210. Encapsulated IP Datagram

- The DF_CTL field is set to indicate the Network optional header is present (first frame of the Sequence only). Use of the network optional header is required by this mapping.
- The Parameter field may contain the relative offset of the portion of the IP datagram contained in this frame.

The Network optional header is present in the first frame of the Sequence and contains the Fibre Channel names of the destination node port (words 0 and 1 of the payload) and source node port (words 2 and 3 of the payload).

Following the Network optional header are the IEEE 802.2 LLC and SNAP headers (set to fixed values and used to identify the protocol, IP, ARP, or ICMP).

Finally, following the LLC and SNAP headers is the IP or ARP datagram or ICMP message. The IP datagram may be segmented across multiple frames within the same Sequence.

38.4.2 Use of the Fibre Channel Exchange

The Fibre Channel Exchange provides a mechanism to identify a set of related Sequences between two ports. Within an Exchange, only one Sequence can be active at a time (see the Exchange state flowchart in Figure 88 on page 175). Because of this, the Exchange is a half-duplex construct.

To support full-duplex protocols that may have Sequences active in both directions simultaneously, two separate Exchanges are used and Sequence Initiative is never transferred. Each Exchange is a logical connection between the Exchange originator and responder for unidirectional information flow. An example of full-duplex operation using two Exchanges is shown in Figure 216 on page 598.

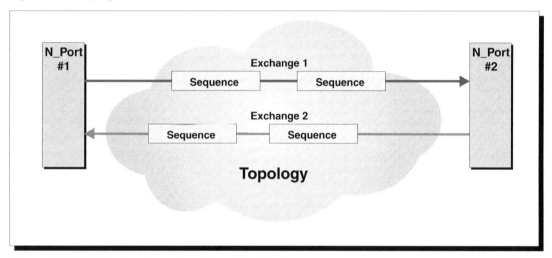

Figure 216. Full-Duplex Operation Using Two Exchanges

An IP Information Unit can be the first, middle, or last Sequence of the Exchange (F_CTL bits 21 and 20).

38.4.3 Classes of Service

Most networks provide frame delivery characteristics similar to Fibre Channel's Class-3 service. Consequently, many applications will use Class-3 for transporting IP via Fibre Channel networks.

However, the characteristics provided by one of the other classes of service may be advantageous for some applications. For example, for high-throughput bulk data transfers, Class-1 may provide significant benefits. IP over Fibre Channel allows the use of any class of service available between the two node ports.

38.4.4 Exchange Error Policy

IP over Fibre Channel uses the Discard error policy. Under this error policy, Sequences in error are discarded (i.e., not used by the Sequence recipient). If the Discard a Single Sequence policy is used, subsequent Sequences may be used if they are complete and deliverable. If the Discard Multiple Sequences policy is used, then subsequent Sequences are not used by the Sequence recipient.

38.4.5 Maximum Transmission Unit

From a functional standpoint, the maximum size of the Information Unit is not limited by Fibre Channel's FC-2 transport level. However, to limit the size of buffers associated with the transmission and reception of these Information Units, the maximum transmission unit size of the encapsulated 802.2 LLC data unit to 65,280 bytes. This restriction on the maximum transmission unit size ensures that the encapsulated IP data unit along with the 802.2 LLC and SNAP headers fit within a 64k byte buffer.

The ability to use a large transmission unit size provides a significant performance benefit when compared with other transport layers that require the protocol data unit to be restricted in size to accommodate the network frame or packet size (or fragmented by the software).

When the Information Unit is larger than the Fibre Channel frame size, FC-2 segments the Information Unit into a Sequence of frames. Conceptually, this is no different from the fragmentation performed by the software on other networks. However, in Fibre Channel, it occurs within the port, usually at hardware speeds and completely transparent to the higher-level process.

38.5 IP Over Fibre Channel Addressing

Addressing becomes somewhat convoluted when transporting IP over Fibre Channel. This is due to the different addresses involved.

The Internet Protocol (IP) provides its own addressing based on 32-bit (IPv4) or 128-bit (IPv6) addresses. These addresses are associated with the IP protocol and are not related to lower-level addresses (such as IEEE 802 MAC addresses or 24-bit Fibre Channel addresses).

The existing network protocol stacks in current operating systems are written to facilitate communications between IEEE 802 compliant networks such as Ethernet and Token Ring. They assume that each network interface card (NIC) has 48-bit MAC address.

When the Internet Protocol (IP) is enabled, the existing protocol stack attempts to resolve the IP address to a 48-bit MAC address to facilitate communication with the other port. This process is called address resolution. When Fibre Channel is introduced into the picture, another address is added — the 24-bit Fibre Channel N_Port identifier.

In order to accommodate Fibre Channel networks in the existing IP protocol stack structure, there must still be a way to map an IP address to a 48-bit value that looks like an IEEE 802 MAC address. Without this capability, existing protocol stack implementations will not work.

The 48-bit value used in place of the MAC address is obtained from the least significant 48 bits of a format-1 Fibre Channel name (see *IEEE Name (Format 1)* on page 408). These bits have the same format as a 48-bit MAC address on an IEEE 802 compliant network interface card (NIC). Because of this use of the Fibre Channel name, Fibre Channel ports intending to support the Internet Protocol over Fibre Channel must use format-1 Port_Names. Furthermore, if a vendor also builds network interface cards (NICs), the least-significant 48 bits of the Fibre Channel name must not duplicate the MAC address used on a network interface card.

The IP address is now mapped to the least-significant 48 bits of the Fibre Channel name, then the Fibre Channel name is mapped to the 24-bit address of the other port. This allows existing protocol stack implementations to continue to function without change while still allowing frames to be routed using Fibre Channel addresses.

To facilitate bridging and routing functions, the Fibre Channel name is provided in every Information Unit. This is provided by the Network optional header which is mandatory in the IP over Fibre Channel protocol mapping. This allows bridges, routers, and ports to map between the 48-bit MAC address space and Fibre Channel names and addresses.

38.6 Address Resolution

When the Internet Protocol is used there are three addresses involved:

- the IP address,
- a 48-bit MAC address used by the protocol stack,
- the Fibre Channel N_Port address.

Some means is needed to associate these different identifiers — that mechanism is called address resolution.

38.6.1 Address Resolution Protocol (ARP) Broadcast

The Internet protocol suite provides a mechanism for address resolution through the Address Resolution Protocol, or ARP. When a system needs to resolve an IP address to a network (MAC) address, it can broadcast an ARP request containing the IP address (or MAC address) of the target. Figure 217 shows the format of the ARP request.

This method of address resolution requires that the topology support a broadcast mechanism and that all potential destinations recognize the broadcast address (x'FF FF FF') as an alias. Furthermore, a Fibre Channel destination must accept the broadcast frame even though no PLOGI is in effect with the originator of the ARP broadcast frame.

38.6.2 ARP Information Unit

One Information Unit is used by ARP over Fibre Channel. It consists of the ARP datagram preceded by an IEEE 802.2 Logical Link Control (LLC) and SNAP headers (set to fixed values). The format of a Fibre Channel frame containing an ARP datagram is shown in Table 211 on page 601.

When the ARP target recognizes the ARP request and recognizes its IP or MAC address, the Fibre Channel S_ID and MAC address (Port_Name) of the sending port are saved and an

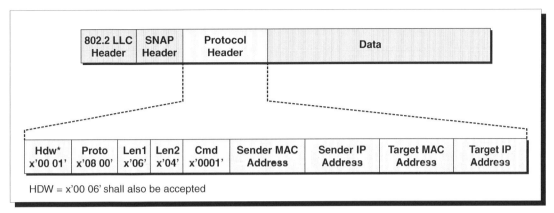

Figure 217. Encapsulated ARP Packet

	Word	Bits 31-24	Bits 23-16	Bits 15-8	Bits 7-0
Frame Header	0	R_CTL = x'04'	Destination_ID (D_ID)		
	1	CS_CTL = x'00'	Source_ID (S_ID)		
	2	Type = x'05'	Frame_Control (F_CTL)		
	3	SEQ_ID	DF_CTL = x'20'	SEQ_CNT	
	4	OX_ID		RX_ID	
	5	Parameter			
Network Header	0	NAA = x'1'	x'000' (12-bits)	Destination MAC (2 most significant bytes)	
	1	Destination MAC (4 least significant bytes)			
	2	NAA = x'1'	x'000' (12-bits)	Source MAC (2 most significant bytes)	
	3	Source (4 least significant bytes)			
LLC Header	4	DSAP = x'AA'	SSAP = x'AA'	Control = x'03'	Org Code = x'00'
	5	Org Code (continued) = x'00 00'		Ethertype = x'08 06' (ARP)	
ARP Datagram	6	Hardware Type = x'00 01'		Protocol Type = x'08 00'	
	7	Hardware Address Length = x'06'	Protocol Address Length = x'04'	Operation Code Request = x'00 01' / Reply = x'00 02'	
	8	Hardware Address of Sender			
	9	Hardware Address of Sender (continued)		IP Address of Sender	
	10	IP Address of Sender (continued)		Hardware Address of Target	

Table 211. Encapsulated ARP Datagram

N_Port Login is sent to establish a login session with the ARP originator. When the N_Port Login is complete, an ARP reply is transmitted to complete the process. An example of the ARP process is shown in Figure 218 on page 602.

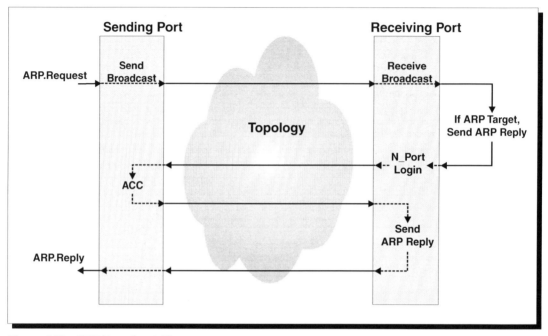

Figure 218. ARP Broadcast Flow

While the example shown waits for the ARP reply before logging in with the other port, it is also possible for the N_Port Login (PLOGI) to be initiated upon receipt and recognition of the ARP request without waiting for the ARP reply to be generated.

38.6.3 Address Resolution Using the Directory Server

One final method of address resolution is to send a query to the directory server (see *Directory Server* on page 484). This method is preferred when a directory server is present because it reduces the amount of network traffic compared to the use of broadcasting.

The request could be directed to the Name Server sub-function or IP Address Server sub-function, depending on which sub-function is available.

The directory server database provides entries for N_Port address, Port_Name (that can be related to a MAC address), and IP address.

38.7 IP Over Fibre Channel Traces

A trace of an ARP operation over Fibre Channel is shown in Figure 219 on page 603.

Chapter 38. IP Over Fibre Channel (IPFC)

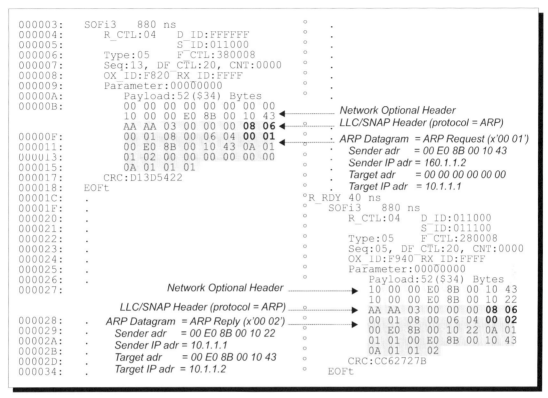

```
000003:    SOFi3    880 ns
000004:      R_CTL:04    D_ID:FFFFFF                    o    .
000005:                  S_ID:011000                    o    .
000006:      Type:05    F_CTL:380008                    o    .
000007:      Seq:13, DF_CTL:20, CNT:0000                o    .
000008:      OX_ID:F820 RX_ID:FFFF                      o    .
000009:      Parameter:00000000                         o    .
00000A:        Payload:52($34) Bytes                    o    .
00000B:          00 00 00 00 00 00 00 00
                 10 00 00 E0 8B 00 10 43  ◄·········· Network Optional Header
                 AA AA 03 00 00 00 08 06  ◄·····o···· LLC/SNAP Header (protocol = ARP)
00000F:          00 01 08 00 06 04 00 01  ◄·····o···· ARP Datagram = ARP Request (x'00 01')
000011:          00 E0 8B 00 10 43 0A 01        o   ·  Sender adr   = 00 E0 8B 00 10 43
000013:          01 02 00 00 00 00 00 00        o   .  Sender IP adr = 160.1.1.2
000015:          0A 01 01 01                    o   .  Target adr    = 00 00 00 00 00 00
000017:      CRC:D13D5422                        o   .  Target IP adr = 10.1.1.1
000018:      EOFt                                o   .
00001C:      .                                 oR_RDY 40 ns
00001F:      .                                  o    SOFi3    880 ns
000020:      .                                  o      R_CTL:04    D_ID:011000
000021:      .                                  o                  S_ID:011100
000022:      .                                  o      Type:05    F_CTL:280008
000023:      .                                  o      Seq:05, DF_CTL:20, CNT:0000
000024:      .                                  o      OX_ID:F940 RX_ID:FFFF
000025:      .                                  o      Parameter:00000000
000026:      .                                  o        Payload:52($34) Bytes
000027:                  Network Optional Header ··········►  10 00 00 E0 8B 00 10 43
                                                             10 00 00 E0 8B 00 10 22
                    LLC/SNAP Header (protocol = ARP) ·o·····►  AA AA 03 00 00 00 08 06
000028:      .   ARP Datagram  = ARP Reply (x'00 02') ·o·····►  00 01 08 00 06 04 00 02
000029:      .   Sender adr    = 00 E0 8B 00 10 22        o      00 E0 8B 00 10 22 0A 01
00002A:      .   Sender IP adr = 10.1.1.1                 o      01 01 00 E0 8B 00 10 43
00002B:      .   Target adr    = 00 E0 8B 00 10 43        o      0A 01 01 02
00002D:      .   Target IP adr = 10.1.1.2                 o    CRC:CC62727B
000034:      .                                           o    EOFt
```

Figure 219. ARP Broadcast and Reply Trace

A trace of an IP operation over Fibre Channel is shown in Figure 220 on page 604. In this trace, a "ping" operation is being performed using the ICMP protocol.

A second sample IP trace is shown in Figure 221 on page 605. In this trace, a Transmission Control Protocol (TCP) operation is shown.

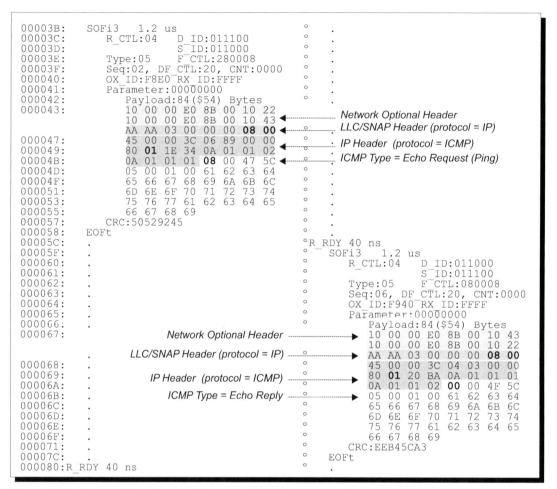

```
00003B:    SOFi3   1.2 us                        o   .
00003C:      R_CTL:04    D_ID:011100             o   .
00003D:                  S_ID:011000             o   .
00003E:      Type:05     F_CTL:280008            o   .
00003F:      Seq:02, DF_CTL:20, CNT:0000         o   .
000040:      OX_ID:F8E0 RX_ID:FFFF               o   .
000041:      Parameter:00000000                  o   .
000042:        Payload:84($54) Bytes             o   .
000043:          10 00 00 E0 8B 00 10 22              Network Optional Header
                 10 00 00 E0 8B 00 10 43              LLC/SNAP Header (protocol = IP)
                 AA AA 03 00 00 00 08 00          o
000047:          45 00 00 3C 06 89 00 00          o   IP Header (protocol = ICMP)
000049:          80 01 1E 34 0A 01 01 02          o   ICMP Type = Echo Request (Ping)
00004B:          0A 01 01 01 08 00 47 5C          o
00004D:          05 00 01 00 61 62 63 64          o   .
00004F:          65 66 67 68 69 6A 6B 6C          o   .
000051:          6D 6E 6F 70 71 72 73 74          o   .
000053:          75 76 77 61 62 63 64 65          o   .
000055:          66 67 68 69                      o   .
000057:      CRC:50529245                         o   .
000058:    EOFt                                   o   .
00005C:    .                                      o R_RDY 40 ns
00005F:    .                                      o   SOFi3   1.2 us
000060:    .                                      o     R_CTL:04    D_ID:011000
000061:    .                                      o                 S_ID:011100
000062:    .                                      o     Type:05     F_CTL:080008
000063:    .                                      o     Seq:06, DF_CTL:20, CNT:0000
000064:    .                                      o     OX_ID:F940 RX_ID:FFFF
000065:    .                                      o     Parameter:00000000
000066:    .                                      o       Payload:84($54) Bytes
000067:         Network Optional Header              10 00 00 E0 8B 00 10 43
                                                       10 00 00 E0 8B 00 10 22
           .     LLC/SNAP Header (protocol = IP)  o     AA AA 03 00 00 00 08 00
000068:    .                                      o     45 00 00 3C 04 03 00 00
000069:    .     IP Header (protocol = ICMP)      o     80 01 20 BA 0A 01 01 01
00006A:    .     ICMP Type = Echo Reply           o     0A 01 01 02 00 00 4F 5C
00006B:    .                                      o     05 00 01 00 61 62 63 64
00006C:    .                                      o     65 66 67 68 69 6A 6B 6C
00006D:    .                                      o     6D 6E 6F 70 71 72 73 74
00006E:    .                                      o     75 76 77 61 62 63 64 65
00006F:    .                                      o     66 67 68 69
000071:    .                                      o     CRC:EEB45CA3
00007C:    .                                      o   EOFt
000080:R_RDY 40 ns                                o   .
```

Figure 220. IP over Fibre Channel Trace — ICMP Ping Operation

Chapter 38. IP Over Fibre Channel (IPFC)

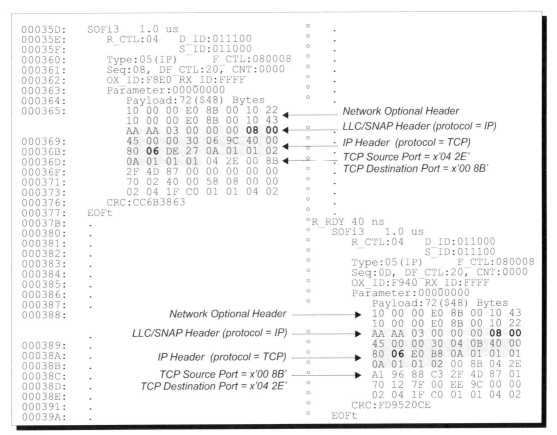

```
00035D:    SOFi3   1.0 us              o   .
00035E:      R_CTL:04    D_ID:011100   o   .
00035F:                  S_ID:011000   o   .
000360:    Type:05(IP)    F_CTL:080008 o   .
000361:    Seq:08, DF_CTL:20, CNT:0000 o   .
000362:    OX_ID:F8E0 RX_ID:FFFF        o   .
000363:    Parameter:00000000           o   .
000364:      Payload:72($48) Bytes     o   .
000365:       10 00 00 E0 8B 00 10 22  ←————————— Network Optional Header
               10 00 00 E0 8B 00 10 43  ←—————— LLC/SNAP Header (protocol = IP)
               AA AA 03 00 00 00 08 00  ←—— IP Header  (protocol = TCP)
000369:        45 00 00 30 06 9C 40 00  ←——————— IP Header  (protocol = TCP)
00036B:        80 06 DE 27 0A 01 01 02  ←—— TCP Source Port = x'04 2E'
00036D:        0A 01 01 01 04 2E 00 8B  ←—— TCP Destination Port = x'00 8B'
00036F:        2F 4D 87 00 00 00 00 00   o   .
000371:        70 02 40 00 58 08 00 00   o   .
000373:        02 04 1F C0 01 01 04 02   o   .
000376:    CRC:CC6B3863                  o   .
000377:    EOFt                          o   .
00037B:    .                            o R_RDY 40 ns
000380:    .                            o   SOFi3   1.0 us
000381:    .                            o     R_CTL:04    D_ID:011000
000382:    .                            o                 S_ID:011100
000383:    .                            o   Type:05(IP)    F_CTL:080008
000384:    .                            o   Seq:0D, DF_CTL:20, CNT:0000
000385:    .                            o   OX_ID:F940 RX_ID:FFFF
000386:    .                            o   Parameter:00000000
000387:    .                            o     Payload:72($48) Bytes
000388:             Network Optional Header ———————►  10 00 00 E0 8B 00 10 43
                                                       10 00 00 E0 8B 00 10 22
000389:    .      LLC/SNAP Header (protocol = IP) ——►  AA AA 03 00 00 00 08 00
00038A:    .                                           45 00 00 30 04 0B 40 00
00038B:    .         IP Header  (protocol = TCP) ———►  80 06 E0 B8 0A 01 01 01
00038C:    .        TCP Source Port = x'00 8B' ——————►  0A 01 01 02 00 8B 04 2E
00038D:    .        TCP Destination Port = x'04 2E'      A1 96 88 C3 2F 4D 87 01
00038E:    .                                            70 12 7F 00 EE 9C 00 00
000391:    .                                            02 04 1F C0 01 01 04 02
00039A:    .                            o   CRC:FD9520CE
                                        o   EOFt
```

Figure 221. IP over Fibre Channel Trace — TCP Operation

38.8 Chapter Summary

IP Over Fibre Channel (IPFC)

- IP over Fibre Channel defined by the Internet Engineering Task Force (IETF) in RFC 4338
  - Uses IEEE 802.2 Logical Link Control (LLC) and SNAP headers
- Uses SNAP header to define type of encapsulated protocol data unit
  - Ethertype x'0800' = Internet Protocol (IP)
  - Ethertype x'0806' = Address Resolution Protocol (ARP)
- Maximum Transmission Unit (MTU) limited to 65,280 octets
  - MTU and LLC/SNAP header fits in 64k buffer

Assignment of Port Name

- Port_Name is restricted to Format-1 (IEEE)
  - Allows use of Port_Name as MAC address outside of the Fibre Channel environment
  - Facilitates bridging between Fibre Channel and non-Fibre Channel networks
- Network optional header is required
  - Present in the first frame of the Sequence only
  - Carries Fibre Channel Name (used as a MAC address by existing protocol stacks)

Use of Exchange

- IP on Fibre Channel uses two separate unidirectional Exchanges
  - One Exchange in each direction
  - No transfer of Sequence Initiative
- Exchange is simply a construct to support the transmission of Sequences
- Any class of service may be used, including Class-3
- The error policy is Discard a Single Sequence
  - Each Sequence represents an IP datagram
  - Error recovery occurs by resending the failed datagram

Internet Protocol (IP)

- Internet protocol results in a three-level addressing structure
  - IP address contained in the IP datagram
  - 48-bit MAC address used by IEEE 802.2 networks
  - Fibre Channel's 24-bit N_Port address
- The network protocol stack normally maps the IP address to a 48-bit MAC address
- Still need to map the 48-bit address to a Fibre Channel N_Port address

Address Resolution

- Must be able to resolve IP addresses to FC addresses
- Existing protocol stacks map IP to MAC address
  - MAC address corresponds to Fibre Channel Name
  - Need to discover N_Port address
- Use standard Address Resolution Protocol (ARP)
  - Broadcast an ARP request containing destination's IP address
  - Destination initiates N_Port Login
  - Then sends ARP reply

Glossary

Active   The state of a Sequence at a Sequence initiator between transmission of the first and last frames of a Sequence. The state of a Sequence at a Sequence recipient between receipt of the first and last frames of a Sequence.

Address identifier   A 24-bit value used to identify the source (S_ID) or destination (D_ID) of a frame.

AL_PA   *See Arbitrated Loop Physical Address.*

Alias address identifier   An address identifier recognized by a port in addition to its Native Address Identifier. An alias address identifier may be shared by multiple node ports.

Alias AL_PA   An AL_PA value recognized by an arbitrated loop port in addition to its assigned AL_PA.

Arbitrated loop topology   A Fibre Channel topology structured as a loop and requiring a port to successfully arbitrate prior to establishing a circuit to send and/or receive frames.

Arbitrated Loop Physical Address (AL_PA)   A one-byte value used to identify a port in an arbitrated loop topology. The value of the AL_PA corresponds to bits 7:0 of the 24-bit Native Address Identifier.

Attenuation   A reduction in signal strength or power through a transmission medium or connectors, usually expressed in units of dB.

Available BB_Credit   A value used by a transmitter to determine permission to transmit frames, and if so, how many. The transmitter may transmit a frame when available BB_Credit is greater than zero.

Available receive buffers   The number of buffers in a receiving port that are currently available for receiving frames at link rate.

Average power   The optical power measured by an average reading power meter when a specified code sequence is being transmitted.

Arbitration wait timeout value (AW_TOV)   The minimum time that an L_Port waits while arbitrating before originating a loop initialization.

AW_TOV   *See Arbitration Wait Timeout Value.*

B_Port   The port within a bridge device used to extend a Fibre Channel inter-switch link. A B_Port connects only to an E_Port on a switch.

Bandwidth   The maximum information carrying capacity of a system.

Baud   The encoded bit rate per second.

BB_Credit   *See Buffer-to-Buffer Credit.*

Beginning running disparity   The disparity present at the transmitter when the special character associated with an Ordered Set is encoded. The disparity present at the receiver when the special character associated with an Ordered Set is decoded.

Bit-error rate (BER)   The probability that a transmitted bit will be received in error. The bit-error rate is expressed as the ratio of error bits to total number of bits.

Bit synchronization   The state when the receiver is delivering correctly clocked bits at the required bit-error rate.

BNC   Bayonet Neil Councilman. A coaxial connector specified by EIA/TIA 403-A and MIL-C-39012.

Block   Upper-level application data assigned a single information category and transferred within a single Sequence.

Byte   A group of eight data bits with the most significant bit denoted 7 and least significant bit denoted 0. The most significant bit is shown on the left side unless specifically stated otherwise.

Buffer-to-Buffer Credit (BB_Credit)   A link-level flow control mechanism.

Cable plant   The passive interconnection between a transmitter and receiver consisting of cables, connectors, patch panels, splices, etc.

Circuit   1. An arbitrated loop circuit as described in *Loop Circuit*.

Cladding   The part of an optical fiber that surrounds the core and keeps the light confined to the core.

Class of service   A frame delivery scheme exhibiting a specified set of delivery characteristics and attributes.

Class-1   A class of service providing a dedicated connection between two ports with confirmed delivery or notification of non-deliverability.

Class-2   A class of service providing a frame switching service between two ports with confirmed delivery or notification of non-deliverability.

Class-3   A class of service providing a frame switching datagram service between two ports or a multicast service between a multicast originator and one or more multicast recipients.

Class-4   (Obsolete) A class of service providing a fractional bandwidth virtual circuit between two ports with confirmed delivery or notification of non-deliverability.

Class-6   A variation of Class-1 service providing a multicast connection between a multicast originator and one or more multicast recipients with confirmed delivery or notification of non-deliverability.

Class-F   A class of service providing a frame switching service on the inter-switch link between two switch ports with confirmed delivery or notification of non-deliverability.

Code balance   The ratio of "one" bits to the total number of bits in a transmitted bit stream.

Code violation   An error that occurs when a received transmission character does not conform to the 8b/10b coding rules.

Comma   The seven-bit sequence b'0011111' or b'1100000' in the encoded data stream.

Comma character   A special character containing the comma pattern.

Connection initiator   The node port that initiates a Class-1 dedicated connection and receives a valid response.

Connection recipient   The node port that receives a Class-1 dedicated connection request and transmits a valid response.

Connector   A mechanical device mounted at a signal source, receiver, or end of a cable.

Core   The part of an optical fiber that carries the light.

Credit   Permission given by a receiving port to a sending port to send a specified number of frames.

CT_HDR   Common Transport Header. An Information Unit header defined by the Fibre Channel Common Transport (FC-CT) protocol.

CT_IU   Common Transport Information Unit. An Information Unit defined by the Fibre Channel Common Transport (FC-CT) protocol.

Current Fill Word (CFW)   The fill word that the LPSM uses when a fill word is required.

DAS   *See Direct Attached Storage.*

dBm   Decibels below 1 mw.

Direct Attach Storage (DAS)   Storage devices that are directly attached to a system.

DMA   Direct Memory Access. A hardware function providing direct access to memory for reading or writing data.

Error detect timeout value (E_D_TOV)   A general purpose timeout value used to detect missing events at the FC-2 level.

E_D_TOV   *See Error Detect Timeout Value.*

E_Port   The port within a Fibre Channel switch that connects to another Fibre Channel switch or bridge device via an inter-switch link.

Exchange   A mechanism for identifying and managing a transaction between two ports.

Exchange_ID   A 16-bit identifier assigned to a specific transaction between two node ports.

F_Port   The port within a fabric that provides an attachment for one N_Port.

Fabric_Name   A 64-bit unique identifier assigned to each Fibre Channel fabric. The Fabric_Name is communicated during the fabric login and fabric discovery processes.

Fabric Port (Fx_Port)   A generic term for the port within a fabric that provides an attachment for node ports.

FC_Port   A generic term for a Fibre Channel port (B_Port, E_Port, F_Port, FL_Port, N_Port, or NL_Port).

FC-AL   The Fibre Channel Arbitrated Loop standard.

FC-AL-2   The second generation Fibre Channel Arbitrated Loop standard.

FC-PH   The Fibre Channel Physical and Signaling standard ANSI X3.230.

FCP   The mapping of SCSI-3 operations to Fibre Channel.

FIFO   A First-In, First-Out data buffer.

Fill word   A transmission word that is either an IDLE or ARB Ordered Set.

FL_Port   A fabric port with arbitrated loop capabilities that allows attachment of one or more NL_Ports.

Frame   A data structure used to transport information from one Fibre Channel port to another.

FS   Fibre Channel Service. A service, such as the Name Server, defined by the Fibre Channel standards and existing at a well-known address.

FS_IU   Fibre Channel Services Information Unit. An Information Unit defined by a Fibre Channel Service.

FS_ACC   Fibre Channel Services Accept. An Information Unit indicating acceptance of a Fibre Channel Services request.

FS_RJT   Fibre Channel Services Reject. An Information Unit indicating a Fibre Channel Services request could not be processed.

FS_REQ   Fibre Channel Services Request. An Information Unit requesting a specific Fibre Channel Services function be performed, or providing notification of a specific event or condition.

Full-duplex   A mode of communications allowing simultaneous frame transmission and reception.

Fx_Port   A generic term for either an F_Port or FL_Port.

G_Port   A port than can operate as either an E_Port or F_Port.

GL_Port   A port than can operate as either an E_Port, F_Port, or FL_Port.

Half-duplex   A mode of communications allowing either frame transmission or reception at any point in time, but not both (other than link control frames which are always permitted).

Hard address   The AL_PA that an NL_Port attempts to acquire in the LIHA Loop Initialization Sequence.

HBA   *See Host Bus Adapter.*

Host Bus Adapter (HBA)   A hardware facility in a node that provides an interface attachment.

HSSDC High-Speed Serial Data Connector. An electrical connector used by some Fibre Channel links. Referred to as a style-2 connector by the standards.

IDE *See Integrated Device Electronics (IDE).*

IN_ID Initial Identifier. A field in the FC-CT preamble used to indicate the N_Port ID of the client originating a Fibre Channel Services request.

Information Unit An information structure defined by an upper-level protocol mapping or higher level process protocol definition.

Integrated Device Electronics An interface where the controller electronics are integrated into the device.

IP Internet Protocol.

IPA Initial Process_Associator. An identifier associated with a process at a node port.

IU *See Information Unit.*

JBOD Acronym for 'just a bunch of disks" referring to multiple disks connected to one or more controllers.

LAN *See Local Area Network.*

Link A connection between two Fibre Channel ports consisting of a transmit fibre and a receive fibre.

Link Services A Fibre Channel protocol for performing link-related actions such as establishing login sessions or retrieving Fibre Channel error or status information.

LIS_HOLD_TIME The maximum time allowed for each node on an arbitrated loop to forward a loop initialization Sequence.

LM_TOV *See Loop Master Timeout Value.*

Login BB_Credit On an arbitrated loop, a value equal to the number of receive buffers that a receiving NL_Port guarantees to have available when a loop circuit is established. Login BB_Credit is communicated in the FLOGI, PLOGI, or PDISC link services.

Local Area Network A network connecting devices within a single building or campus.

Loop circuit A temporary point-to-point like path that allows bidirectional communications between two loop-capable ports. The loop circuit begins when the arbitration winner port enters the OPEN state and ends when that port receives a CLS while in the transfer or transmitted close states, or sends a CLS while in the received close state.

Loop_ID Loop_IDs are seven-bit values numbered contiguously from zero to 126 decimal and represent the 127 legal AL_PA values on a loop (not all 256 hex values are allowed as AL_PA values per FC-AL).

Loop failure Loss-of-Synchronization for greater than R_T_TOV or Loss-of-Signal.

Loop Master Timeout Value (LMTOV) The minimum time that the loop master waits for a loop initialization Sequence to return.

Loop Port State Machine (LPSM) A logical entity that performs the arbitrated loop specific protocols.

Loop Tenancy The period between when a port wins arbitration and when it returns to the monitoring state.

LPSM *See Loop Port State Machine.*

L_Port A node or fabric port capable of performing arbitrated loop functions and protocols. NL_Ports and FL_Ports are examples of loop-capable ports.

Loop Port A node or fabric port capable of performing arbitrated loop functions and protocols. NL_Ports and FL_Ports are examples of loop-capable ports.

MAN *See Metropolitan Area Network.*

Metropolitan Area Network (MAN)   A network connecting devices within a metropolitan area.

N_Port   The port within a node that provides Fibre Channel attachment.

NAA   Network Address Authority. An identifier indicating the format of a network address, especially when used as a Fibre Channel name.

NAS   *See Network Attached Storage.*

Network Attached Storage   Storage attached to a network and accessed using network protocols.

Network Operating System   An operating system designed to support network communications between nodes.

NL_Port   A node port with arbitrated loop capabilities.

Node   An entity with one or more N_Ports or NL_Ports.

Node_Name   A 64-bit unique identifier assigned to each Fibre Channel node. The Node_Name is communicated during the login and port discovery processes.

Node Port   A generic term for the port within a node that provides Fibre Channel attachment.

Non-L_Port   A node port or fabric port that is not capable of performing the arbitrated loop functions and protocols. N_Ports and F_Ports are examples of ports that are not loop-capable.

Non-participating mode   A mode within an L_Port that inhibits that port from participating in loop activities. L_Ports in this mode continue to retransmit received transmission words but are not permitted to arbitrate or originate frames. An L_Port in the non-participating mode may or may not have an AL_PA.

NOS   *See Not Operational Primitive Sequence (NOS).*

NPIV   N_Port ID Virtualization. A protocol that enables an N_Port to acquire multiple N_Port IDs by using the FDISC extended link service.

Nx_Port   A generic term for either an N_Port or NL_Port.

Open   An arbitrated loop protocol used to establish a loop circuit.

Open originator   The L_Port on an arbitrated loop that won arbitration, sent an OPN Ordered Set, and entered the OPEN state.

Open recipient   The L_Port on an arbitrated loop that received an OPNy Ordered Set and entered the OPENED state.

Originator Exchange_ID   A 16-bit identifier assigned by the Exchange originator to identify a specific Exchange.

OX_ID   *See Originator Exchange_ID.*

Participating mode   A mode within an L_Port that allows the port to participate in loop activities. A port must have a valid AL_PA to be in participating mode.

PDU   Protocol Data Unit. A unit of information defined by an upper-level protocol, such as the Internet Protocol (IP).

PLDA   *See Private Loop Direct Attach.*

Port   A hardware facility in a node or fabric that provides the Fibre Channel interface attachment.

Port_Name   A 64-bit unique identifier assigned to each Fibre Channel port. The Port_Name is communicated during the login and port discovery processes.

Preferred address   The AL_PA that an NL_Port attempts to acquire first during loop initialization.

Previously acquired address   During loop initialization, the AL_PA that was in use prior to receipt of LIP. A port that was just powered on does not have a previously acquired address.

Private Loop Direct Attach (FC-PLDA)   A technical report that defines a subset of the relevant standards suitable for the operation of SCSI-3 block-type devices on a private arbitrated loop.

Private NL_Port   An NL_Port that does not attempt login with the fabric and only communicates with other NL_Ports on the same loop.

Protocol   A defined convention defining communication between two entities.

Public NL_Port   An NL_Port that attempts login with the fabric and can observe the rules of either public or private loop behavior. A public NL_Port may communicate with both private and public NL_Ports.

RAID   Redundant Array of Independent Disks. A collection of disk drives containing redundant data.

Resource Allocation Timeout Value (R_A_TOV)   Minimum time that a node port waits before reinstating the Recovery Qualifier.

R_A_TOV   *See Resource Allocation Timeout Value.*

Resource Recovery Timeout Value (RR_TOV)   Minimum time that the Private Loop Direct Attach technical report requires a Target to wait for an ADISC or PDISC Extended Link Service Request following loop initialization before it is allowed to implicitly log out a SCSI Initiator.

Responder Exchange_ID   A 16-bit identifier assigned by the Exchange responder to a specific operation.

RR_TOV   *See Resource Recovery Timeout Value.*

RX_ID   *See Responder Exchange_ID.*

SAN   *See Storage Area Network.*

SCSI   *See Small Computer System Interface.*

Service rate   The rate at which an entity is able to service requests (e.g., the rate at which an arbitrated loop is able to service arbitration requests).

SI   Sequence Initiative.

Small Computer System Interface   An interface designed for attaching peripheral devices to small computer systems.

SNMP   Simple Network Management Protocol. A protocol defined for providing network management and monitoring functions.

Storage Area Network (SAN)   A configuration allowing one or more systems and storage devices to be interconnected and accessed using storage command-level protocols.

Topology   An interconnection scheme that allows multiple Fibre Channel ports to communicate. Point-to-point, arbitrated loop, and switched fabric are all Fibre Channel topologies.

TNC   Threaded Neil Councilman. A coaxial connector specified by MIL-C-39012 and MIL-C-23329.

Transfer   An optional procedure that may be used by an L_Port in the OPEN state to establish a series of sequential circuits with other L_Ports without re-arbitrating for each circuit.

Transmission character   A 10-bit character encoded according to the rules of the 8B/10B algorithm.

Transmission word   A 40-bit group consisting of four 10-bit transmission characters.

UDP   User Datagram Protocol. A protocol defined as a part of the Internet Protocol (IP) suite.

ULP process   A function executing within an FC node that conforms to Upper Layer Protocol (ULP) defined requirements when interacting with other ULP processes.

Upper-Level Timeout Value   The minimum time that a SCSI upper-level process (ULP) waits for SCSI Status before initiating ULP recovery.

ULP_TOV   *See Upper-Level Timeout Value.*

WAN   *See Wide Area Network.*

Wide Area Network   A network connecting devices beyond a single metropolitan area.

Worldwide Name   A 64-bit worldwide unique identifier assigned to Fibre Channel entities.

Index

Numerics

10 Gigabit Fibre Channel (10GFC) 33
8b/10b Encoding/Decoding 23, 91, 95
    3b/4b Subblock 100
    5b/6b Subblock 99
    code balance 23, 47, 92, 96
    code violations 108
    comma pattern **106**, 128, 149, 608
    disparity errors 108
    error detection 107
    maximum run length 47
    special character encoding 106

A

Abort Exchange (ABTX) 319
Abort Sequence (ABTS) 183, 184, 185, 195, 197, 199,
      207, 214, 243, 249, 299, 301, 302, 303, 304, 308,
      309, 310, **311–314**, 345, 346, 358, 359, 373, 556,
      576, 577
    frame delimiters used for 311
    Last_Sequence bit set 314
    No Sequences Aborted 312
    One or More Sequences Aborted 313
    received while holding Sequence Initiative 312
    Sequence Count in 312
    using to abort an exchange 311
Abort Sequence Condition 183, 214, **216**, 300, 301,
      302, 303, 304
    Abort, discard a single Sequence 214, 217
    Abort, discard multiple Sequences 214, 217
    Discard multiple Sequences with immediate retrans-
        mission 214, 217
    in ACK 252
    Process policy with infinite buffers 214, 217
Abort Task 554
Abort Task Set 554
Abort, discard a single Sequence **184**, 197, 198, 214,
      217, 303
Abort, discard multiple Sequences **184**, 185, 197, 198,
      214, 217, 302, 482, 556, 576
ABTS *see Abort Sequence (ABTS)*
Access control
    security 447
    virtual fabrics 537
ACK_0 240, **242–243**
    ACK precedence 243

Capable in service parameters 420, **423**
    end-to-end flow control 268
    Parameter field setting 240
    process error policy 185, 304
    R_CTL field value 207
    required by F_CTL ACK_Form bits 213
    response to Class-1 connect request 243
    Sequence Count (SEQ_CNT) setting 194
    Supported, in service parameters 423
    X_ID interlock 243
ACK_1 240, **241–242**
    default service parameters 425, 426
    end-to-end credit 268
    end-to-end credit recovery 269
    Parameter field setting 240
    R_CTL field setting 207
    required by F_CTL ACK_Form bits 213
    response to Fabric Login (FLOGI) 344, 345
    response to N_Port Login (PLOGI) 357, 358
    Sequence Count (SEQ_CNT) setting 194
ACK_Form 213, **215**, 423
Acknowledge (ACK) 202, 239
    ACK generation assistance 243, 420, 423
    ACK_Form 213, 215, 423
    Class-1 connection confirmation 275
    Class-1 unidirectional connection 282
    connect request 281
    final ACK in Class-1 277
    generation 244
    history bit 240, 244, 268, 269
    no retransmission after F_BSY 240
    parameter field usage 240
    precedence 243
    SEQ_ID and SEQ_CNT in 222
    unexpected 251
Active (AC) state 49, 129, **130**, 130, 131, 133, 135, 137,
      297
Address Resolution Protocol (ARP) 482, 534, **600**
Addresses
    alias address identifier 208, 607
    Alias Server 9
    allocation of 9
    area 529
    assignment 497
    Broadcast 9, 482
    Clock Synchronization Server 9

Index

Login Control List Management (LCLM) 319
LOGO *see Logout (LOGO)*
Logout 14
  explicit N_Port 435
  implicit
    by new login 435
    during FAN 341
    F_Port 443
  implicit N_Port 435
  N_Port (LOGO) 14, 318, 319, 435, 566
Logout (LOGO) 14, 299, 318, 319, **352**, 430, 435, 566
Loop
  Port 610
Loop Fabric Address 341, 353, 354
Loop Initialization
  timeout 378
Loop Initialization Master (LIM) 503, 565, 572
Loop Initialization Primitive Sequence (LIP) 120, **121**,
    147, 333, 465, 503, 611
  in LINIT 353
  inhibited by DTOLI 571
  LIP(AL_PD,AL_PS) 120, **122**, 147
  LIP(F7,AL_PS) 120, **121**, 147
  LIP(F7,F7) 120, **121**, 147
  LIP(F8) 378
  LIP(F8,AL_PS) 120, **121**, 147
  LIP(F8,F7) 120, **121**, 147
  LIP(fx) 120, 147
Loop Initialize (LINIT) 320, **353**
Loop Master Timeout Value (LM_TOV) 610
Loop Port Bypass (LPB) 120, 573
  LPB(fx) 120, **122**, 147
  LPB(yx) 120, **122**, 147
Loop Port Control (LPC) 320
Loop Port Enable (LPE) 120, 571, 573
  LPE(fx) 120, **122**, 147
  LPE(yx) 120, **122**, 147
Loop Port State Machine (LPSM) 23, 122, 142, 502,
    503, 511, 608, 610
Loop State 354
Loop State in LSTS reply 354
Loop Status (LSTS) 320, **354**
Loop Switches 510
Loop_ID 610
Loopback mode 129
Loss budget 57
Loss-of-Signal 79, 131, 132, 134, 135, 137, 138, 295,
    296, 370, 378, 443, 610
Loss-of-Synchronization 49, 131, 132, 137, 138, 295,
    296, 378, 610
  in loopback mode 129
Lowest Version Supported 415, 416
LPB, *see Loop Port Bypass (LPB)*

LPE, *see Loop Port Enable (LPE)*
LR Receive substate (LR2) 129, 131, 132, 133, **134**,
    134, 135, 137
LR Transmit substate (LR1) 129, 131, 133, **133**, 134,
    135
LRR Receive substate (LR3) 129, 131, 132, 133, **135**,
    135
LS_ACC *see Extended Link Services Accept*
LS_RJT *see Extended Link Services Reject*
LSS 147
LSTS *see Loop Status (LSTS)*
LUN 474
  SCSI Report LUNs command 474
LUN, *see Logical Unit Number (LUN)*

M

MAC address 599, 600
MAN, *see Metropolitan Area Network (MAN)*
Management Server 481, 486, 532
  address 9
Management server
  address 479
Maximum Burst Size 559
Maximum Burst Size *see SCSI-3 mode pages*
Maximum Size
  in RNFT 381
Maximum Transmission Unit 599
Media Interface Adapter (MIA) 43
Metropolitan Area Network (MAN) 611
MIL-STD-1553 36
Modal dispersion 55
MRK(tx) 115, 147
Multicast 534
  Class-3 (unreliable) 288
  Class-6 (reliable) 288
  Link Reset (LR) 290
Multicast Group 347, 532
  Initial Process_Associator (IPA) 348
Multicast Group IPA (MG_IPA) 348
Multicast Groups 10
Multicast Server 289, **488**, 532, 534
  address 9, 479
Multi-drop connections 493
Multimode
  optical fiber 53
  optical links 54, 55
Multiple N_Port IDs Assignment 417
Multiple N_Port IDs Supported 415
Multi-Stage Switching 524

N

N_Port **7**, 7, 12, 13, 31, 77, 376, 511, 611
N_Port Activate Alias_ID (NACT) 319, 349, **355**
N_Port Busy *see P_BSY*
N_Port Controller 479

OPN(yy) 115, **119**, 147, 505
Optical
  extinction ratio 56
  modal dispersion 55
  relative intensity noise 56
Optical fiber 10, 51, 52
  cladding 51
  core 51
  modal dispersion 55
  multimode 39, 55
  RMS Spectral Width 56
  single-mode 39, 54
  spectral center 55
  splices 57
  total internal reflection 51
Optical Power 56
Optical switches 46
Optical test equipment
  cleaning kit 59
  optical test source 58
  power meter 58
  time domain reflectometer (OTDR) 58
Optional Headers **223**
  Association header 220, 226
  Device header 220, 228
  Encapsulating Security Payload 224, 450, 451, 453, 456
  Expiration_Security 220
  Network 220, 225, 597, 600, 601
  Operation_Associator 227
Ordered Sets 23, 92, 96
  Fill Word separation 116
Originator Exchange_ID (OX_ID) 18, **176**, 177, 178, 180, 182, 186, 196, 222, 422, 611
  and SCSI task retry identifier 557
  FCP requires assignment of 555
  in ABTS 311
  in ACK 240
  in BA_ACC 312
  in BA_RJT 309
  in Link Credit Reset (LCR) 253
  in Reinstate Recovery Qualifier (RRQ) 373
  in Request Sequence Initiative (RSI) 389
  in response frames 193
  in Sequence Status Block (SSB) 199
Originator Process_Associator 360
  in PRLO 364
  in TPLRO 398
  in TPLS 396
  validity in PRLI 361
  validity in PRLO 365
OSI Reference Model 591
Overshoot 47

OX_ID *see Originator Exchange_ID (OX_ID)*

P

P_BSY **247–248**, 253, 268, 358, 359
  action code 247
  class-1 247
    in response to connection request 276, 282
  class-2 247
  class-3, not allowed in 247
  class-6
    partial multicast busy 289
  link control frame, not allowed in response to 247
  reason codes 247
  Sequence Count (SEQ_CNT) setting 194
P_RJT **248–249**, 302, 358, 359
  action codes 249
  class-6
    multicast server 289
  end-of-frame delimiter usage 253
  end-to-end credit handling 268
  in response to class-1 connection request 276, 282
  P_RJT transmitted bit in S_STAT 199
  R_CTL field setting 207
  Reason Codes 249
    class of service not supported 250, 254
    class of service not supported by x'FF FF FE' 251
    dedicated simplex not supported 251
    delimiter usage error 250
    excessive Sequences attempted 251
    exchange error 182, 251
    incorrect length 251
    insufficient resources for VC 251
    invalid class of service 251
    invalid CS_CTL 251
    invalid D_ID 250, 254
    invalid DF_CTL 250
    invalid F_CTL field 250
    invalid link control 250
    invalid OX_ID 250
    invalid parameter field 251
    invalid R_CTL field 250
    invalid RX_ID 250
    invalid S_ID 250
    invalid SEQ_CNT 251
    invalid SEQ_ID 250
    invalid VC_ID 251
    login required 251
    multicast error 289
    multicast error terminate 290
    protocol error 251
    TYPE not supported 250
    unable to establish exchange 251